Introduction to QUICKBOOKS® PRO 2002

SLEETER

Mc Graw Hill **Glencoe McGraw-Hill**

New York, New York   Columbus, Ohio   Woodland Hills, California   Peoria, Illinois

Glencoe/McGraw-Hill

A Division of The McGraw·Hill Companies

Copyright © 2003 by Glencoe/McGraw-Hill, a division of the McGraw-Hill Companies. All rights reserved. Except as permitted under the United States Copyright Act, no part of this publication may be reproduced or distributed in any form or by any means, or stored in a database or retrieval system, without prior written permission from the publisher, Glencoe/McGraw-Hill.

Printed in the United States of America.

Send all inquiries to:
Glencoe/McGraw-Hill
21600 Oxnard Street, Suite 500
Woodland Hills, California 91367

ISBN 0-07-829680-3 (Student Edition)
ISBN 0-07-829681-1 (Instructor Manual)

1 2 3 4 5 6 7 8 9   009   07 06 05 04 03 02

Preface

FROM THE PUBLISHER

For individuals and small businesses, QuickBooks® is very popular because it is one of the easiest accounting software programs available. Learning how to use QuickBooks is even easier with this textbook, which includes hands-on practices and a CD-ROM with tutorial and problem templates for each chapter.

Using this text, you will gain confidence in every aspect of QuickBooks by trying out each feature as you complete problems and simulations of a "real" business. The well-illustrated text includes step-by-step instructions in the hands-on computer tutorials, which provide you with the practical experience needed to achieve operating skill. You will want to keep this text for reference, and will come back to consult its comprehensive appendix, valuable index, and helpful glossary of terms again and again.

The package was developed by Douglas Sleeter, a leading educator on QuickBooks, along with a consulting team of accounting teachers, business computer specialists, and prominent industry systems managers. In short, this textbook provides you with the tips of the trade by those who know how a business works.

FROM THE AUTHOR

On behalf of our whole team at The Sleeter Group, I would like to thank you for purchasing this text.

We work very hard each year to make *Introduction to QuickBooks® Pro 2002* as understandable, complete, and relevant as possible, and we believe that after completing your study in this book you will be prepared to apply your QuickBooks skills as a bookkeeper or as the owner of a small business.

Throughout the text, we've tried to include as many real-world transactions and situations as possible, so you'll have a chance to work through problems before you confront them out there in the business world. Also, we've included many unique and innovative data entry methods to help you streamline your bookkeeping and to ensure the most accurate financial information possible. We hope to save you valuable time in your business by giving you the advantage of our many years of experience with QuickBooks.

I would also like to extend my thanks to the following people for their contributions to this book:

Joe Woodard really made the 2002 edition possible. He dedicated countless hours to rewriting sections of the text, contributing ideas, and testing the material in actual classroom situations. I can't express how grateful I am to him.

Joe Reed contributed significantly to the end-of-chapter exercises and case studies. Donna Sobzak proofed much of the early text and provided support throughout the project. Sherrill, my wife, kept our business running with little help from me, and Thomas, my son, put up with my frequent, though reluctant, absences from our family life.

I would also like to thank the reviewers: L.T. Herrman devised the real world simulation. Cindy Calvin and Doug Buhrer created the glossary. Victoria Pavlik (Ohio State University) developed many of the end-of chapter questions.

Also, I have to thank the editor, Vi Brunson at Glencoe/McGraw-Hill. She kept us all on schedule and made countless suggestions for improving the quality of the book. She is a joy to work with and she provided valuable assistance and support throughout the project. I could not have done this without great support from her.

PROGRAM RESOURCES

Student Textbook

The textbook consists of 10 chapters that address several accounting and QuickBooks topics. Each chapter is designed to aid understanding, by providing a list of objectives, numerous hands-on tutorial practices, key terms, a chapter summary, and many sidebar features. The end-of-chapter applications include review questions, problems, workplace applications, and a case study, all of which focus on the way QuickBooks functions in the business environment. Additional practice can be found in the Millennium Simulation. At the end of each chapter, you will find information about helpful Web sites in the Internet Connection feature.

The textbook includes a CD-ROM with tutorial and problem templates for every chapter and the simulation. By performing the tutorial and problem steps, students gain hands-on experience with the topics discussed in the chapter.

Academy Glass, Inc. is the model company used throughout the chapters. Students will perform computer practices and solve problems based on the day-to-day operations of this small corporation.

Chapter 1 provides an overview of accounting basics and of the QuickBooks software. Chapters 2 through 9 introduce the QuickBooks approach to fundamental accounting concepts, procedures, and functions, such as Accounts Receivable, Accounts Payable, Cash Receipts, Inventory, Reconciliations, Job Costing, financial reports, Payroll and others. Chapter 10 guides the student through setting up a company.

Following the tutorial chapters, there is a Business Simulation exercise called the *Millennium Financial Planning Business Scenario*, which provides additional "real business" practice through a much broader range of accounting transactions. The Appendix contains information helpful to the student, such as the QuickBooks accounts and menus, and keyboard shortcuts, and also provides the student with detailed instructions on how to back up QuickBooks data files. The Glossary provides a list of definitions for several accounting and QuickBooks-specific terms, and the Index provides comprehensive coverage of terms and topics.

Instructor Manual

This manual contains preparation guidelines to teach the course, teaching strategies, answers to Comprehension Questions, Multiple-Choice Questions, Completion Statements, Workplace Applications and Case Study questions. It also provides printouts of the solutions to the problems and a CD-ROM that includes the solution templates for all problems in the textbook. The Instructor Manual also provides a test bank of multiple-choice questions with answers.

PowerPoint Presentations

The PowerPoint Presentations are available in a separate CD-ROM package. These 10 concise, full-color presentations (one for each chapter) in full color list chapter objectives, important topics with figures, key terms, and comprehension questions.

The PageOut® Distance Learning Tool

PageOut® is McGraw-Hill's custom course website management tool. It allows you to build online courses, add your own content, integrate this textbook content, post announcements, upload files, create quizzes, build a syllabus, hold discussions and maintain a gradebook. You can learn more about PageOut® at www.pageout.net.

The *Introduction to QuickBooks® Pro 2002* PageOut® template and its course material, syllabus, test bank and chapter readings is available for customization to meet the individual teaching needs of each instructor from the McGraw-Hill PageOut® Library at the PageOut® Web site.

Contents

1 Introducing QuickBooks

OBJECTIVES

After completing this chapter, you should be able to:

1. Describe the features in QuickBooks.
2. Understand how the menus and Navigation System work.
3. Describe the process of entering transactions.
4. Understand the function of Items.

QuickBooks is one of the most powerful tools you'll use in managing your business. It is much more than a bookkeeping system. It's a management tool. When set up and used properly, QuickBooks provides you with detailed information that is essential to making good business decisions. Throughout this book, you will find tips from the experts on how to set up and use QuickBooks to properly provide managers with the information needed to make informed business decisions.

This chapter teaches the basic functions of QuickBooks Pro 2002. You'll be introduced to a sample business called Academy Glass, which is used throughout the book to teach the examples.

ACCOUNTING 101

Before you begin learning about how QuickBooks can help you manage your business better, let's look at two questions that will prepare you for managing in this way. After all, you probably would not do anything else in your business without understanding why you are doing it, what the benefits are, and what it entails.

The two questions are:

"On what does accounting focus?" and

"Why do I need to do it?"

The answers are not, as you might suppose:

"Money" and

"Because the IRS makes us do it."

Accounting's Focus

Accounting is primarily concerned with accurately counting wealth or net worth. Put another way, accounting's focus is on whether your organization is succeeding and how well it is succeeding.

Your organization's purpose includes a lot of different goals, but among them is producing a net worth, or equity in excess of the cost of operations. This goal is true whether your organization is for-profit or not-for-profit. The difference is that the former has a primary goal of producing profit; the latter needs a profit to continue operations.

Both kinds of organizations need to replace or upgrade equipment, provide income and raises for staff, or invest money to safeguard against shortfalls in income. The examples in this book are about a for-profit company called Academy Glass, but the same need for information and tracking would exist in a not-for-profit organization.

Accounting allows all kinds of organizations to assess their position relative to both current and future obligations (liabilities), current capabilities to meet those obligations and continue operations (assets), and the difference between them (net worth or equity). The fundamental equation, called the *accounting equation*, that governs all accounting is

$$\text{Assets} = \text{Liabilities} + \text{Equity}$$
$$\text{or Equity} = \text{Assets} - \text{Liabilities}.$$

Seems pretty simple, so why do we need a software package to handle it?

Accounts, Accounts, Everywhere Accounts

Many factors go into making an organization work. Money and value are attached to everything that is associated with operating a company—equipment, rent, utilities, salaries and wages, raw materials, merchandise, and so on. For an organization to understand its equity, the money needed has to be counted, summed, and balanced according to the rules of accounting.

Different categories of value are usually tracked separately in different records or ledgers, called *accounts*. The summary of all ledgers in a company is the *General Ledger*, which is the record of everything that happens to money and valuable items in the company. Another term associated with the General Ledger is the "Chart of Accounts." This chart lists all the accounts in the company. The list is sorted by type: assets first, followed by liabilities, equity, income, and expenses.

Each account represents something that increases or decreases the equity in your organization. (That's the accounting equation again.) So a picture of your accounts is a picture of your organization.

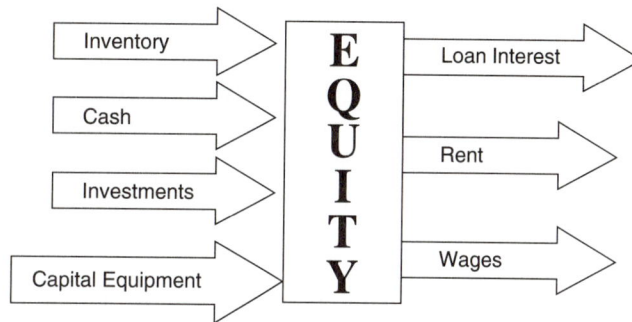

Tracking all the accounts in your organization can be time-consuming unless you have help. That is where QuickBooks comes in. QuickBooks allows you to manage a much larger number of accounts than you could manage manually in the same amount of time. This means you can get timely information with enough detail to allow you to manage your organization and know what you can and cannot do in the future.

You still need to be careful to set up only those accounts that are really informative to the managers of the company. So, you may track major income categories individually, and you may group less significant ones into one account.

Back to the accounting equation. Every account is either an asset account, a liability account, an income account, an expense account, or an equity account. (Income and expense accounts are tracked throughout the year and are used at the year-end to calculate net income, which increases equity.) Adding up the values of all the accounts in each category lets you know what the overall value is in each category and the overall value of your organization.

Adding up the values of all the accounts also lets you know whether you entered all the information correctly. That is because the accounting equation for your organization will not work if there are errors in an account. If you enter $1,000 too much in an asset account and do not also show a $1,000 increase (or decrease) in another account, the accounting equation will be $1,000 out of balance.

The good news is that QuickBooks will not allow you to make a mistake like this. If you try to enter a transaction that doesn't balance, QuickBooks won't let you store it.

Double-Entry Accounting

Sooner or later, someone will ask if you are using double-entry accounting. The short answer is yes, as long as you are using QuickBooks.

Double-entry accounting is a technique that looks at each account as having two sides—one side is a record of transactions that increase the account, and the other side lists all transactions that decrease the account. One side is for debits, and the other is for credits. Depending on the type of account, a debit might increase the account or decrease it. The same is true of credits. So debits are not always bad and credits are not always good. They are just part of a method of accounting.

In double-entry accounting, every transaction creates a debit in one or more accounts and a credit in one or more accounts. That is why it is called *double*-entry accounting. If the debits and credits for any transaction are not equal, an error has been made. The goal is to be sure that transactions are recorded accurately with respect to the accounting equation.

Fortunately, QuickBooks handles this for you. Every transaction you enter in the program automatically becomes a debit to one or more accounts and a credit to one or more other accounts. Thus you can focus on entering transactions by filling out forms like invoices and checks, and the program takes care of the rest. It also means you can create reports that show the transactions in the full double-entry accounting format.

Accounting for the Future: Cash or Accrual?

Another critical aspect of accounting is managing for the future. Many times, your organization will have assets and liabilities that you know about but are not due yet. For example, you may have sold something to a customer and sent an invoice, but the invoice is not yet paid. Also, you may have a bill for electricity that has been received but is not yet due.

A good accounting system tracks these and uses them in evaluating a company's equity. This is called *accrual accounting* because the liabilities and assets are entered when you know about them, and they are used to identify what you need on hand to meet future obligations, both current and known.

Although certain types of organizations can use a cash accounting method instead (many are not allowed to do so under IRS regulations), the accrual method provides the most accurate picture for your organization.

In the cash method, you do not log transactions until cash changes hands. So a sale is not recorded until the customer pays the bill, and a utility bill is not recorded until you write the check. You have to use a system outside your accounting program to track transactions such as open invoices and unpaid bills. Also you cannot generate a complete picture of your organization's status without going to several places to find information.

In contrast, the accrual method provides the most complete picture of the business operation.

QuickBooks can provide reports for either method, so everything you learn about the program will work for you regardless of the method you use for taxes. You should check with your tax accountant to determine which method is best for you.

Your Focus

Letting QuickBooks handle the "accounting behind the scenes" means that you can focus on your organization and identify the important factors that will help you succeed. Once these factors are identified, use QuickBooks to monitor them and provide information that will guide you in managing your operations.

As you think through the examples with Academy Glass, ask yourself what parallels you see to your own organization. Certainly, areas such as salaries, utilities, equipment, and others will be part of your setup; but the names and specifics of the accounts, items, lists, and forms will be different.

WHAT IS QUICKBOOKS?

1. A full-featured accounting program that's very powerful and easy to use
2. A double-entry accounting system
3. An estimating, invoicing, and accounts receivable system
4. A bill paying, check printing, and accounts payable system
5. A purchase order and inventory management system
6. A job-costing system
7. A sales tax tracking system
8. A time tracking and billing system
9. A payroll system

With all of these features, QuickBooks provides nearly everything required by most small businesses. It is so easy to use, it has become the most popular accounting package on the market. While it may not be perfect for every business, it is by far the most widely used.

Updating QuickBooks Releases

Occasionally, errors are found in the QuickBooks software after the product is released for sale. As errors are discovered, Intuit fixes the problem and provides program "patches" via the Internet. Each patch increases the **Release Level** of the QuickBooks application. To see what release level of the software you have, press <Ctrl+1> (or <F2>) while QuickBooks is running.

This textbook is based on QuickBooks Pro version 2002, release 2 and higher. To patch your software with the latest maintenance release, download the latest release by selecting the *File* menu and then choosing **Upgrade QuickBooks**. Follow the instructions on these screens to download and install maintenance releases in QuickBooks via the Internet. This task requires Internet access. Ensure that your **Internet Connection Setup** settings from the *Help* menu are configured correctly to enable you Internet access from within QuickBooks.

If you do not have access to the Internet to update QuickBooks with release 2 or higher, you may see some minor differences between the screens displayed in the textbook and on your screen. All of the functions of QuickBooks will be the same, except for the bank reconciliation reports and the payroll tax calculations.

About QuickBooks Files

QuickBooks has two primary types of files: Data files and Backup files. A QuickBooks data file name always ends with ".QBW" and a QuickBooks backup file name always ends with ".QBB." For example, if you name your company file ABC, QuickBooks will store the data file on disk as "ABC.QBW". When you backup your company file using the QuickBooks Backup function, QuickBooks will store your backup file with the name "ABC.QBB." The letters after the dot (.) are referred to as the file extension. This extension (e.g. QBB, QBW, DOC, etc.) is used by Microsoft Windows to associate files with the appropriate application program.

With QuickBooks, you can only enter data or create reports in a data file with the ".QBW" extension. From inside the QuickBooks program, you can "Open" data files (QBW files), but you must "Restore" backup files (QBB files) and convert them into data files (QBW files) before you can use them.

WORKING WITH THE TUTORIAL AND PROBLEM TEMPLATES

Copying the Template Files from the CD-ROM

QuickBooks tutorial and problem templates are located on the CD-ROM in the back of this book. These files are used for the computer tutorial practices and the end-of-chapter problems.

To easily access these files while working with the textbook, you can create a folder on the server called "QuickBooks Class Files" and copy all of the files from the CD-ROM into this directory.

Tutorial Template Files

In the beginning of each chapter, the Restore This File box instructs you to restore the tutorial template for that chapter (for example, Chapter 1.QBB) to use for the computer tutorial practices. These practices are identified in the textbook with the words "COMPUTER TUTORIAL" and a computer icon. You will use the same tutorial template to complete all computer tutorials throughout the chapter. You restore the template files by following the steps in the *Restoring Backup Files* section on page 7. The tutorial templates are QuickBooks backup files, which you can ONLY RESTORE but you cannot open. Once the file is restored, then you can open it.

Problem Templates

Before you start working on a problem at the end of each chapter, you will be instructed to restore the template file for that problem. You will use these templates to do the problems at the end of every chapter. Each problem usually has its own template (for example, Problem 2-1.QBB). The problem templates are backup files, which you can ONLY RESTORE, but you cannot open. Once the file is restored, then you can open it.

Restoring Backup Files

To restore QuickBooks backup files, follow these steps.

1 Insert the CD-ROM into your disk drive.

2 Launch the QuickBooks program. If you see the Welcome to QuickBooks Pro screen, click **Cancel**.

3 Select the *File* menu, and then choose **Restore** (see Figure 1-1).

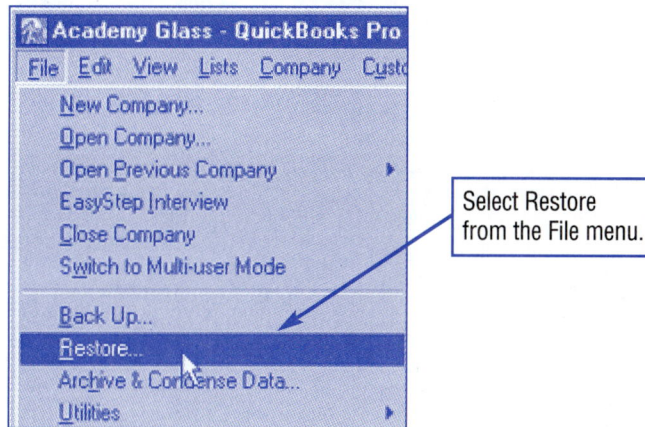

Figure 1-1 The File menu.

4 Set the name and location of your backup disk by setting the *Filename* and *Location* fields in the Get Company Backup From section (see Figure 1-2).

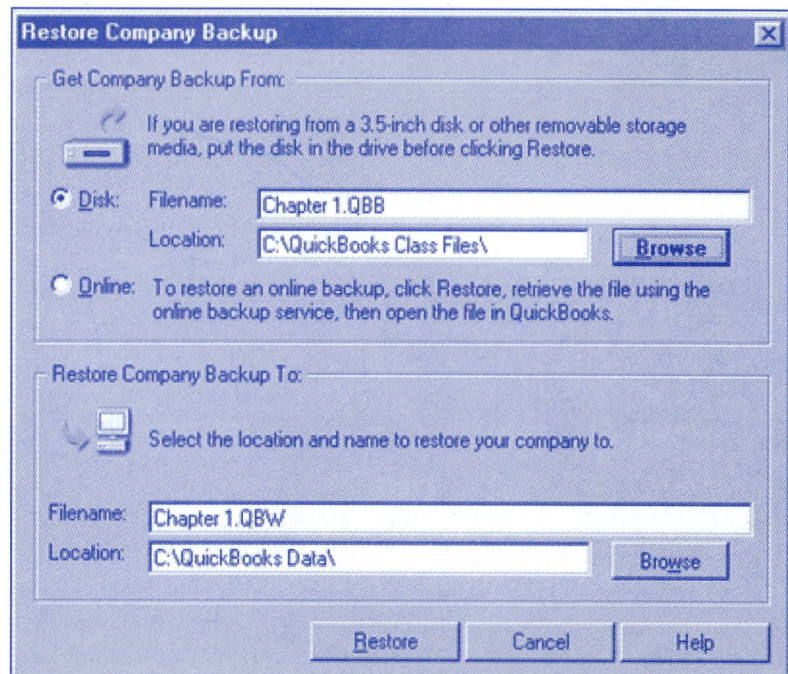

Figure 1-2 Restore Company Backup screen.

If you're not sure of the exact location and name of your backup file, click the **Browse** button in the top half of the screen in Figure 1-2. The Restore From screen opens (see Figure 1-3).

To select the disk drive and folder, click the down-arrow and choose the drive from the list.

Figure 1-3 Select the file to restore.

5   Select the drive and folder location from the *Look in* field. Click to select the file and click **Open**. This sets the fields on the top half of the Restore Company Backup screen to point to the exact file that you want restored.

NOTE

If you're not using your own computer, you should choose a folder on the hard disk specified by your instructor.

6   Set the *Filename* and *Location* fields at the bottom of the Restore Company Backup screen where you want to store your file (see Figure 1-4). If you're not sure of the drive and directory name where you want your file, click the **Browse** button on the bottom half of the Restore Company Backup screen. The Restore To screen opens (see Figure 1-5).

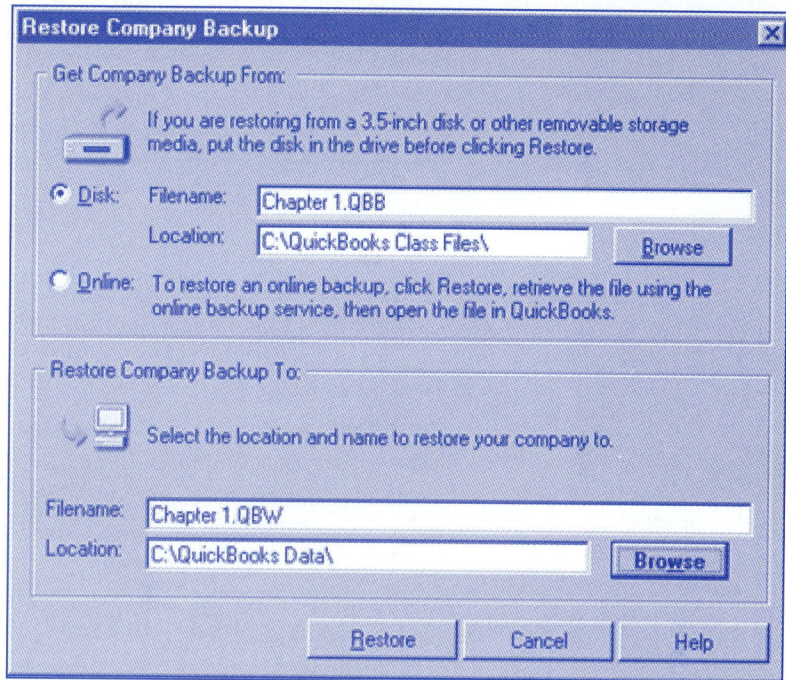

Figure 1-4 Restore Company Backup screen.

7 Select the drive and folder location from the *Save in* field. Click to select the file and click **Save**. This sets the fields on the bottom half of the Restore Company Backup screen to point to the exact location of your restored file.

8 Click **Restore** on the Restore Company Backup screen (Figure 1-4).

QuickBooks will then copy your backup file into the folder you specified on your hard disk.

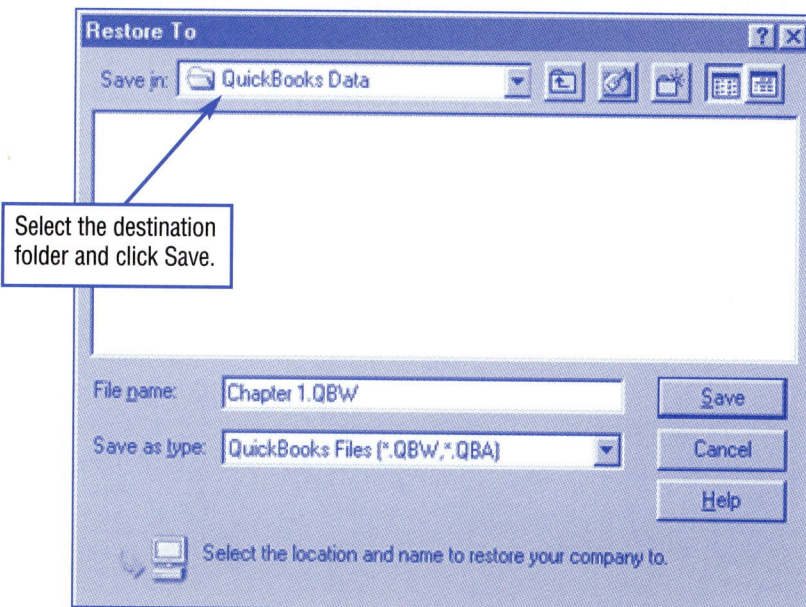

Figure 1-5 Select the destination folder in the Save in field.

> ### RESTORE THIS FILE
>
> This chapter uses Chapter 1.QBB. To open this file, restore the tutorial template called **Chapter 1.QBW** to your hard disk.

WORKING WITH THE ACADEMY GLASS VIRTUAL COMPANY

Throughout this textbook, you will see references to a fictitious company called Academy Glass. Academy Glass is a home improvement contracting corporation. Since the company provides window replacement services in addition to selling windows, doors, and skylights, it is both a service and a merchandising company. This company uses QuickBooks for its accounting and business management. Academy Glass might not be exactly like your business but it will guide you on how to use QuickBooks through its daily activities.

Academy Glass has two stores, one located in San Jose and another located in Walnut Creek. In order for management to separately track sales and expenses for each store, Academy Glass uses classes in QuickBooks. As you proceed through the book, you'll see how each transaction (bills, checks, invoices, etc.) is tagged with what "class" it belongs to, so that later you can get reports like Profit & Loss by Class. Classes can be used to separately track departments, profit-centers, store locations, or funds in any business.

Academy Glass also needs to separately track revenues and expenses for each customer or job it has. When a customer orders windows, Academy Glass needs to track all of the revenue and expenses specifically related to that job so it can look back and see how profitable the job was. This concept is called *job-costing*, and many different businesses need to track jobs in similar ways.

QUICKBOOKS FEATURES

When you first launch QuickBooks, take a moment to familiarize yourself with its key tools.

QuickBooks provides a number of shortcuts and aids that assist the user in entering information and data. There are five methods of accessing the data entry screens: the menus, the icon bar, the shortcut bar, the navigators, and the shortcut keys.

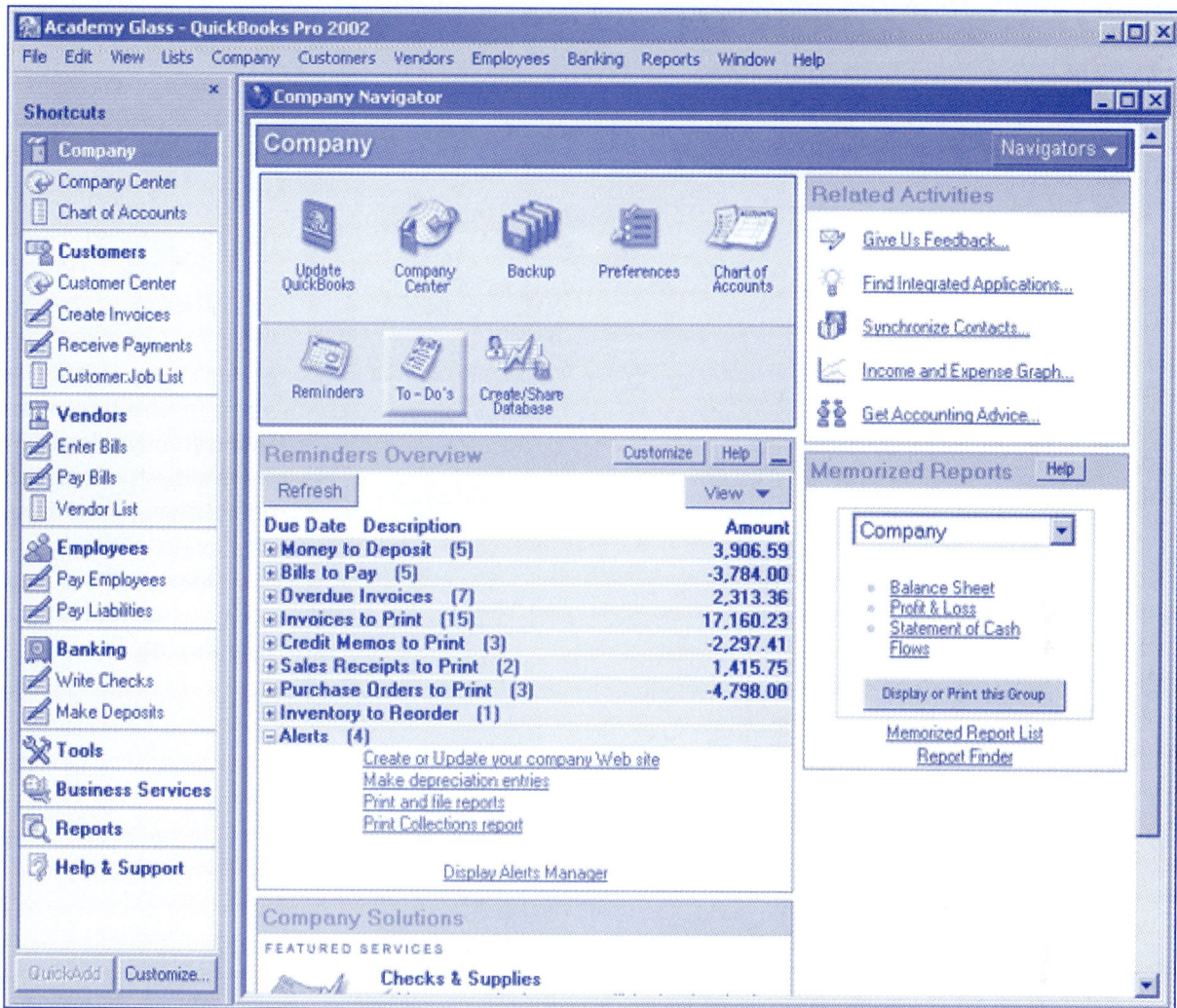

Figure 1-6 QuickBooks Pro 2002.

Menus

Menus run along the top of the screen. To open a menu, such as the File or Edit menus, select the menu name and then choose the option desired (see Figure 1-7).

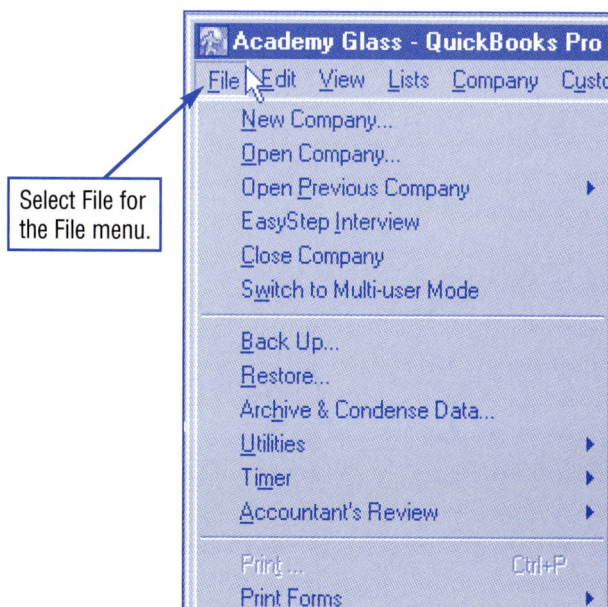

Select File for the File menu.

Figure 1-7 The File menu in QuickBooks Pro 2002.

Icon Bar

Figure 1-8 The Icon Bar

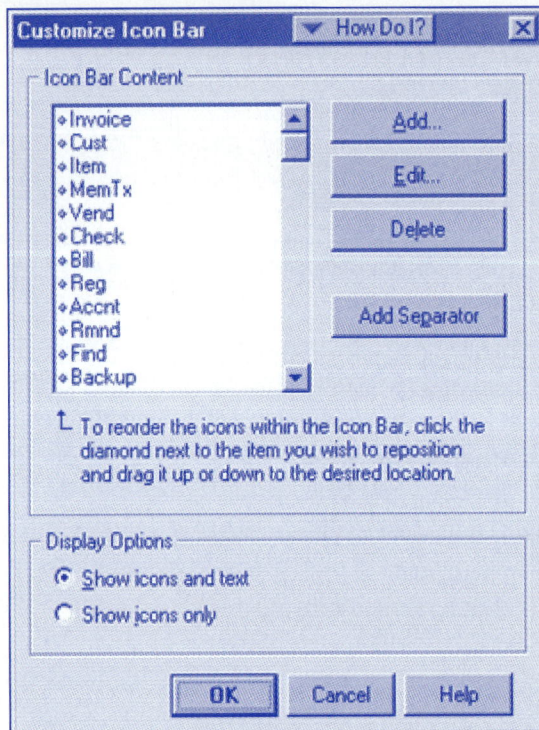

Figure 1-9 The Customize Icon Bar screen

The QuickBooks Icon Bar (see Figure 1-8) allows you to select activities and lists by clicking icons on the bar. For example, you can display a new invoice by clicking **Invoice** on the Icon Bar. To modify the contents or position of the icons on the Icon Bar, select the *View* menu, and then choose **Customize Icon Bar** (see Figure 1-9).

Shortcut List

The QuickBooks Shortcut List (see Figure 1-10) allows you to select activities and lists by picking them from items on a bar located at the right or left of the screen. Click **Customize** at the bottom of the Shortcut List to modify the contents or position of the list.

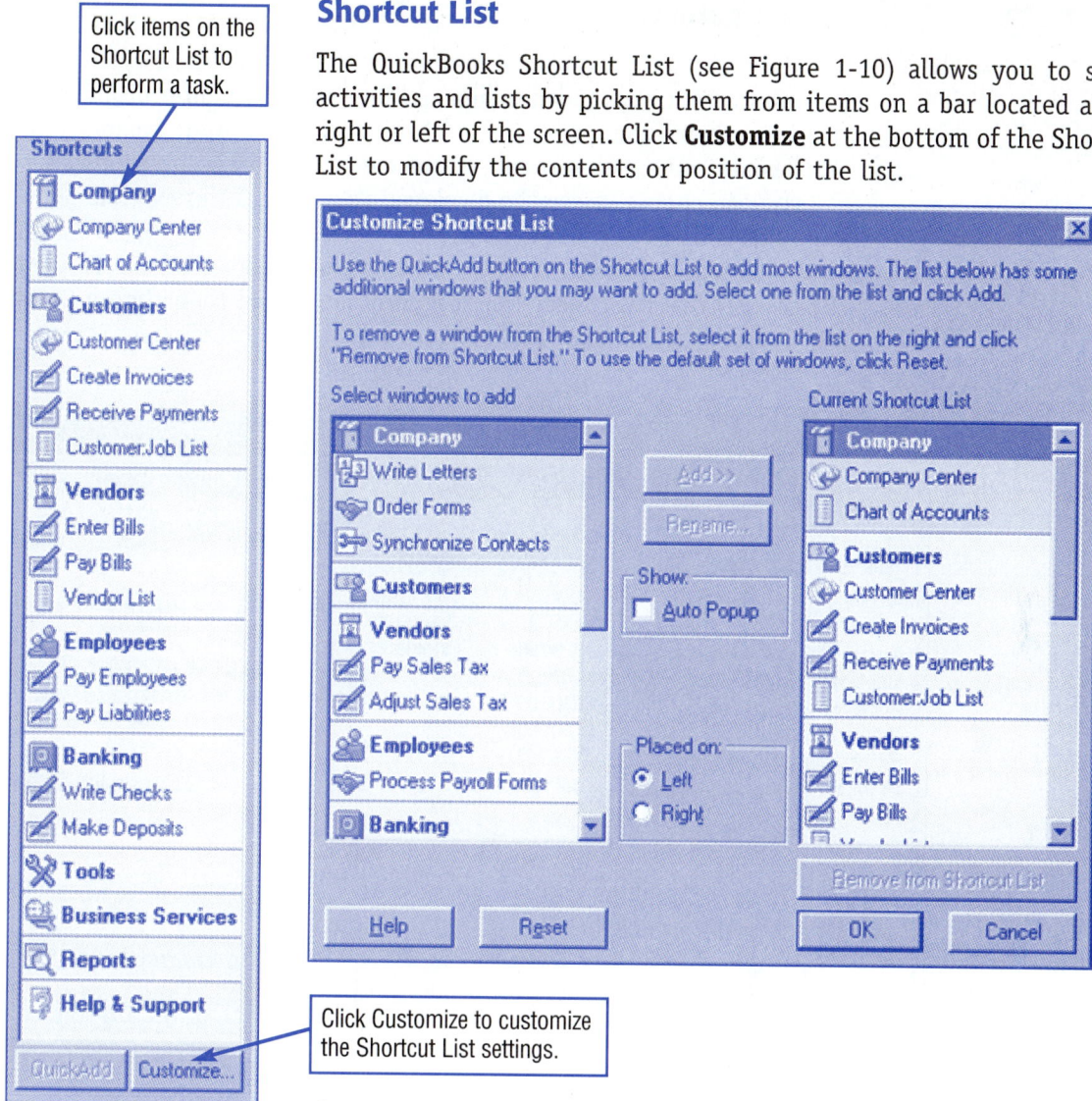

Click items on the Shortcut List to perform a task.

Shortcuts

Company
- Company Center
- Chart of Accounts

Customers
- Customer Center
- Create Invoices
- Receive Payments
- Customer:Job List

Vendors
- Enter Bills
- Pay Bills
- Vendor List

Employees
- Pay Employees
- Pay Liabilities

Banking
- Write Checks
- Make Deposits

Tools

Business Services

Reports

Help & Support

QuickAdd Customize...

Click Customize to customize the Shortcut List settings.

Customize Shortcut List

Use the QuickAdd button on the Shortcut List to add most windows. The list below has some additional windows that you may want to add. Select one from the list and click Add.

To remove a window from the Shortcut List, select it from the list on the right and click "Remove from Shortcut List." To use the default set of windows, click Reset.

Select windows to add

Company
- Write Letters
- Order Forms
- Synchronize Contacts

Customers

Vendors
- Pay Sales Tax
- Adjust Sales Tax

Employees
- Process Payroll Forms

Banking

Add >>
Rename...

Show:
☐ Auto Popup

Placed on:
⦿ Left
○ Right

Current Shortcut List

Company
- Company Center
- Chart of Accounts

Customers
- Customer Center
- Create Invoices
- Receive Payments
- Customer:Job List

Vendors
- Enter Bills
- Pay Bills

Remove from Shortcut List

Help   Reset   OK   Cancel

Figure 1-10 The Shortcut List and the Customize Shortcut List screen

NOTE

QuickBooks calculates some of the amounts in the Company Center screen based on the current Windows system date. There may be discrepancies between the amounts that show in Figure 1-11 and those that show in your QuickBooks file (Chapter 1.QBW).

Navigators

There are several different navigators that allow you to view snapshot information about your company. The Company Center displays various facts about your business, such as current account balances and an income and expense graph. There are several drop-down lists on which you can choose to see the displayed item for a different time period for what is displayed.

There are also "centers" for customers and vendors. To view the company center, select the **Company** menu and then choose **Company Center**. The customer and vendor centers are located under their respective menus.

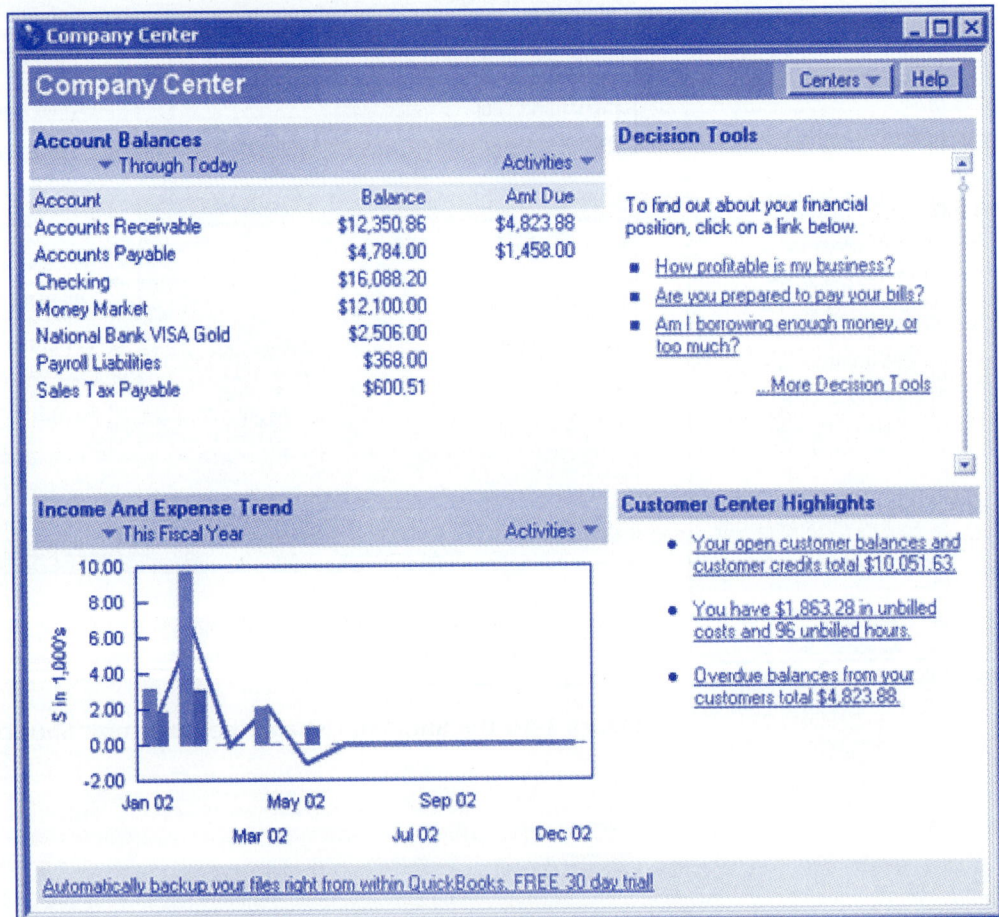

Figure 1-11 The Company Center

Shortcut Keys

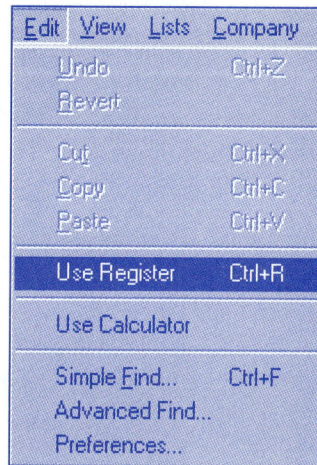

You may use your mouse or the keyboard shortcut keys to select the menu options. To use the keyboard, press <ALT + the underlined letter on the menu>. This displays the menu. Then press the underlined letter of the desired menu item.

Sometimes, menu items have control-key shortcuts that are indicated on the right side of the menu. For example, to open a register, you can press <Ctrl + R>, as indicated on the *Edit* menu (see Figure 1-12).

Figure 1-12 Menu showing shortcut keys

Open Previous Company

You can open a previous company file by selecting it from the **Open Previous** Company submenu of the *File* menu. QuickBooks lists the last few companies you have most recently used allowing you to open any one of them without going to **Open Company** and navigating through your directory structure (see Figure 1-13). You can set the number of previous companies that show on the list (from 1 to 20).

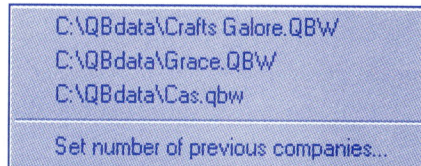

Figure 1-13 Open Previous Companies list

> **NOTE**
>
> When you access the Open Previous Companies list in your QuickBooks file (Chapter 1.QBB), the previous companies you see will be different from those shown in Figure 1-13.

Entering Data in Forms

Figure 1-14 shows a QuickBooks "Enter Bills" form. Most data entry forms in QuickBooks have some or all of the elements shown in Figure 1-14. Drop-down lists are very helpful in that you don't have to remember the spelling of a customer or account. You can just select it from the list. The Pop-up calendar allows you to pick a date on the calendar rather than entering the whole date.

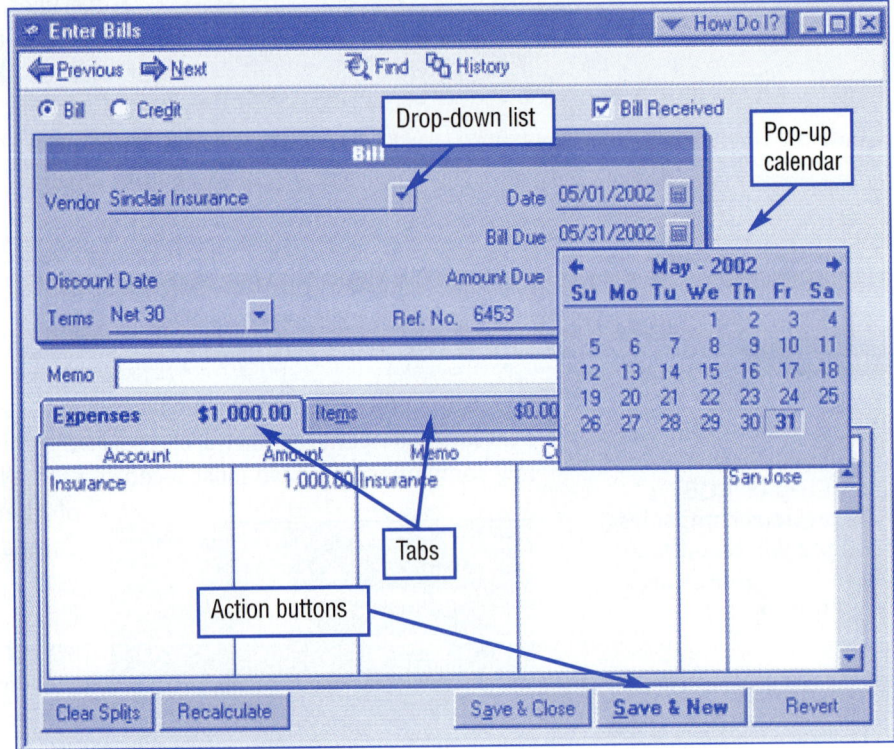

Figure 1-14 The Enter Bills screen

Support Resources

There are a wide variety of support resources available in QuickBooks. Some of these resources are on the Internet so that they can be updated frequently. To access the support resources, select the *Help* menu and then choose **Help & Support** (see Figure 1-15).

Figure 1-15 The Information and Support Window

Context-Sensitive Help

QuickBooks provides a comprehensive on-line manual (see Figure 1-16) that is accessible from anywhere in the software. QuickBooks onscreen Help guides you through the completion of tasks with step-by-step instructions. You can access onscreen Help by clicking the **How Do I** button on any screen, or by pressing the <F1> key. Depending on what you are doing at the time, you'll get advice from the Help system that is relevant to what you're doing. This is known as Context-Sensitive Help.

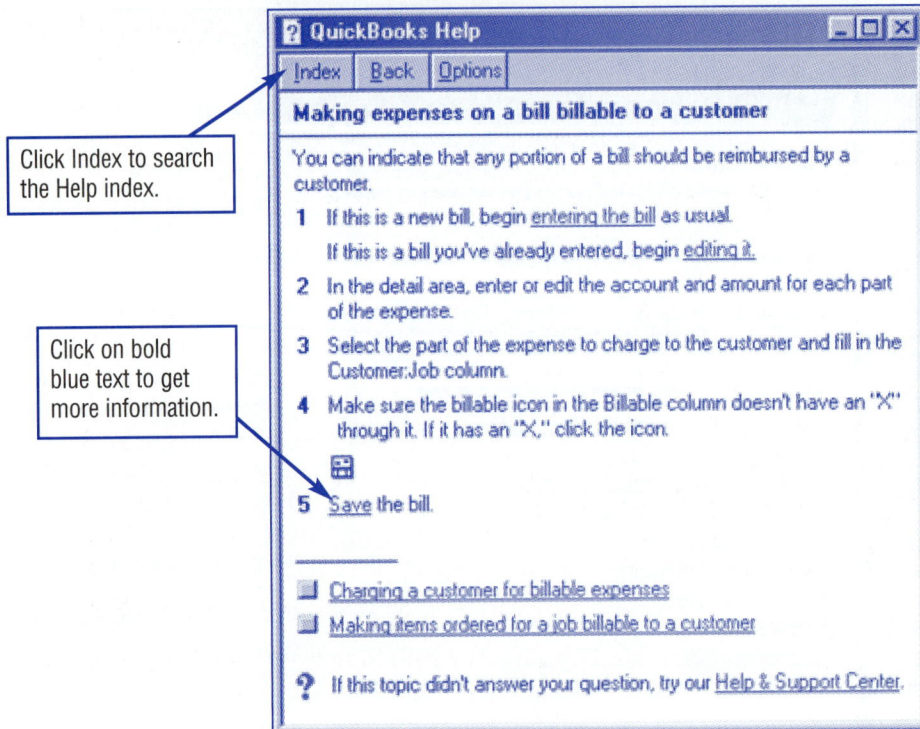

Click Index to search the Help index.

Click on bold blue text to get more information.

QuickBooks Help

Index   Back   Options

Making expenses on a bill billable to a customer

You can indicate that any portion of a bill should be reimbursed by a customer.

1 If this is a new bill, begin entering the bill as usual.

   If this is a bill you've already entered, begin editing it.

2 In the detail area, enter or edit the account and amount for each part of the expense.

3 Select the part of the expense to charge to the customer and fill in the Customer:Job column.

4 Make sure the billable icon in the Billable column doesn't have an "X" through it. If it has an "X," click the icon.

5 Save the bill.

   Charging a customer for billable expenses

   Making items ordered for a job billable to a customer

   If this topic didn't answer your question, try our Help & Support Center.

Figure 1-16 The help system

To print any help topic, choose **Print Topic** from the *Options* menu inside the Help window (see Figure 1-17).

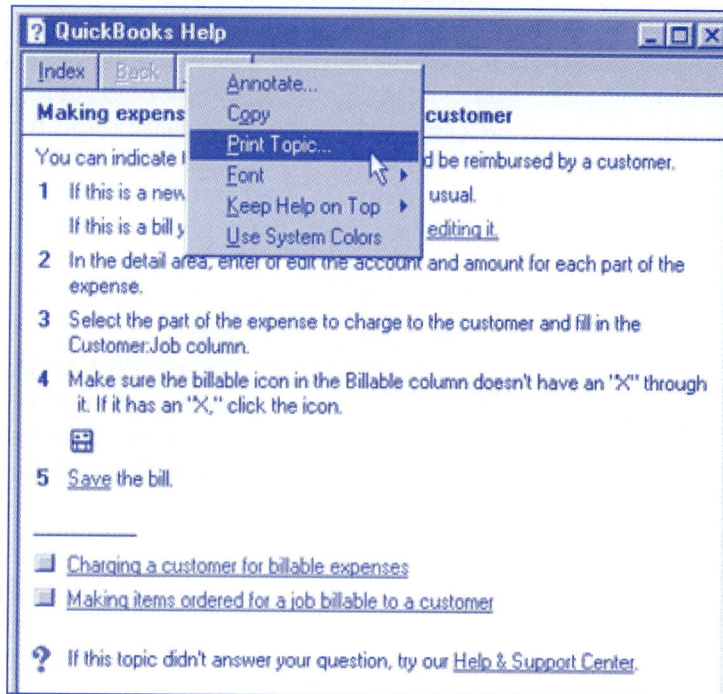

Figure 1-17 Print a Help topic.

COMPUTER TUTORIAL

① Select the *Help* menu and choose **Help Index**.

② Click **OK** on the Help & Support Help Search screen.

③ Enter "Balance Sheet" in field 1.

④ Click Balance Sheet in the list of topics.

⑤ Click the **Display** button.

⑥ From the Topics Found window, select Balance sheet accounts (glossary definition), and click the **Display** button.

⑦ Select the *Options* menu and choose **Print Topic**.

⑧ Select the printer and then click **Print**.

⑨ Close the QuickBooks Help screen.

ENTERING TRANSACTIONS IN QUICKBOOKS

Whenever you buy or sell products or services, pay a bill, make a deposit at the bank, or transfer money, you enter a **transaction** into QuickBooks. These transactions record what happens each day in your business and they are summarized on reports such as the Profit & Loss, Balance Sheet, and Trial Balance.

Transactions are created by filling out familiar-looking **forms** such as invoices, bills, and checks. As you fill out forms, you choose names from **lists** such as the customer list, the Item list, and the account list. When you finish filling out a form, QuickBooks creates a transaction in one or more of its **registers**.

Each transaction has a Form view and a Register view. So you can look at a check as a line in your register, or you can look at that same check in the Write Checks (Form) view. Keep this concept in mind as you learn about entering transactions into QuickBooks. Please note that the figures in the following sections that display how to enter transactions are for reference only. Later chapters of this textbook provide instructions on accessing each of these screens.

Forms

Figure 1-18 shows an invoice form. To create an on-account sales transaction for one of your customers, you'll fill out this form.

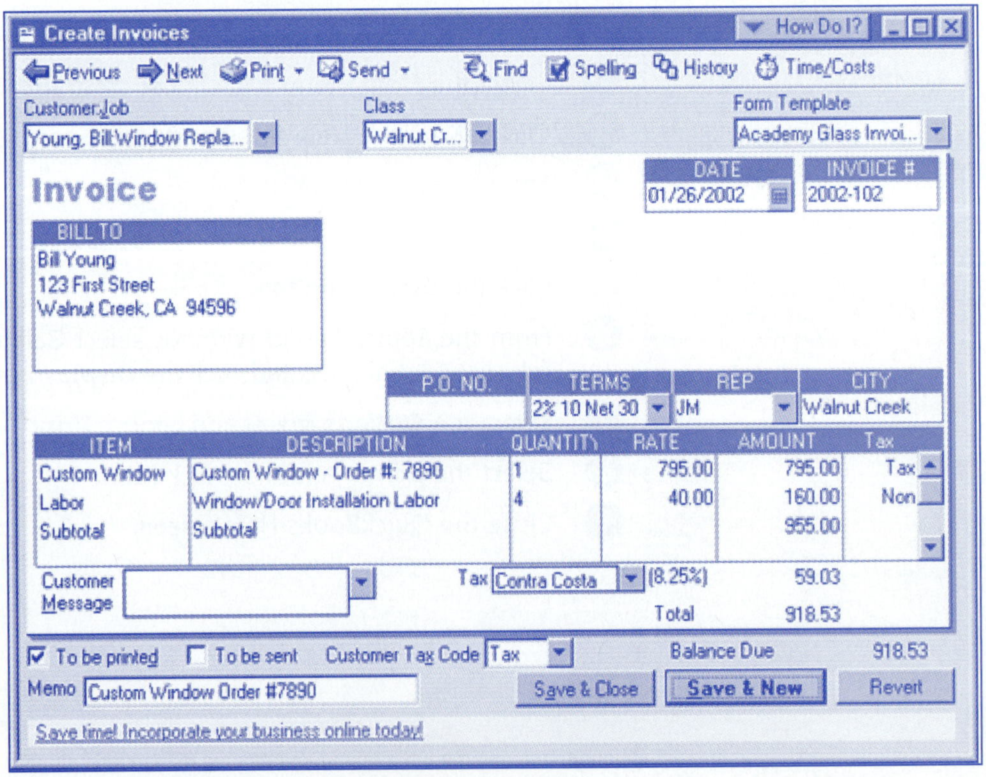

Figure 1-18 A QuickBooks Invoice

Registers

When you record transactions, they show in account registers. An account register shows the chronological listing of all of the transactions in that account. Every asset, liability, and equity account (except Retained Earnings) has a register, so that you can easily see transactions posted to those accounts. Income and expense accounts don't have registers. For information on how to set up your accounts, see the section on Setting Up the Chart of Accounts – Step 3 beginning page 509.

Registers are designed to look like checkbook registers (see Figure 1-19) to make them easier to learn and use.

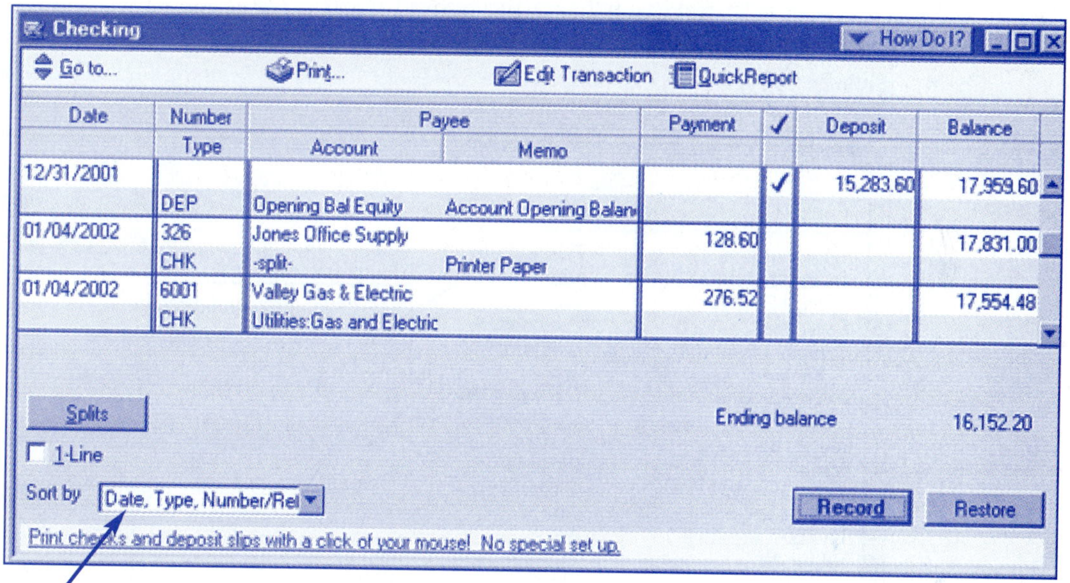

You can sort your registers by date, check number, or otherwise. Choose your preference from this menu. Tip: it's best to keep it set to "Date, Type, Number/Ref."

Figure 1-19 The Checking register

Lists

As you fill out each form, you'll choose from lists (see Figure 1-20). For example, to enter the customer name on an invoice, you'll choose a customer from the Customer:Job list. This is easier than typing the whole name of the customer, and it prevents errors by making sure your spelling is consistent.

Later you'll see that you can set up your lists in advance, or you add new list entries as needed. Lists are the key to customizing QuickBooks to fit almost any business. Several of the fields on each form have lists behind them. Any field that has the down-arrow to the right of it is a field that has a list behind it.

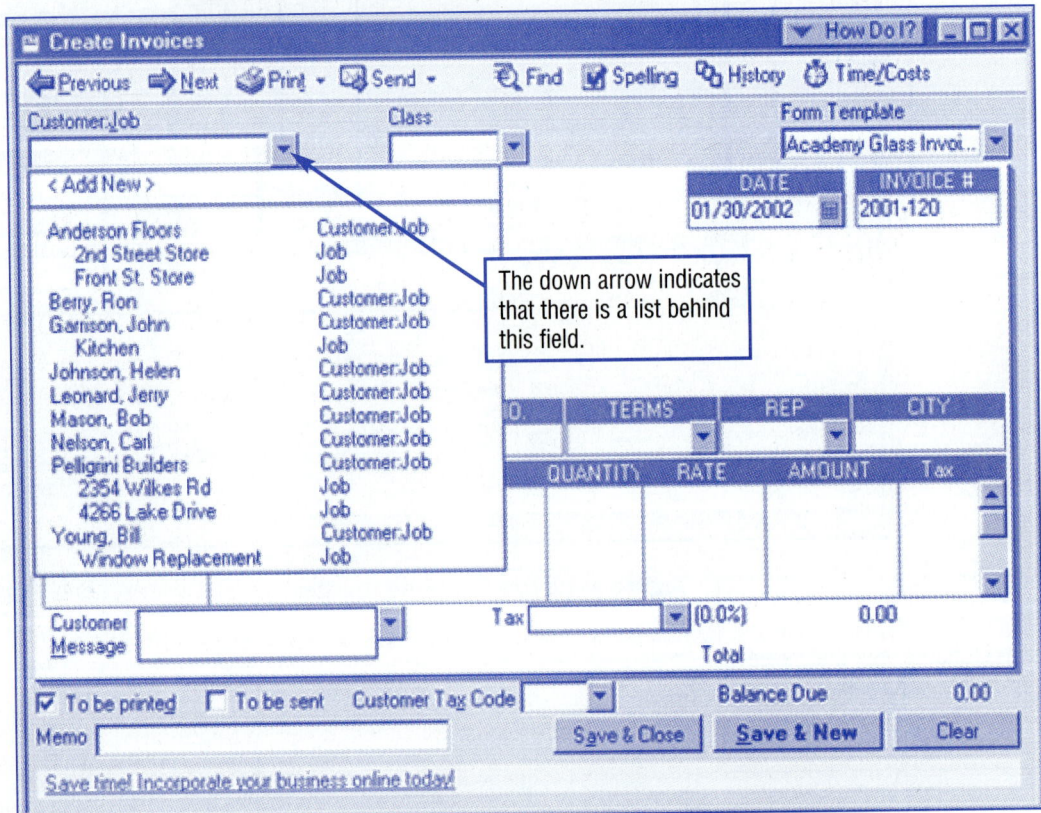

Figure 1-20 Lists are available to help in filling out forms.

QUICKBOOKS ITEMS

The **Item list** is a very special list. It is used to identify the products and services your business purchases and/or sells. You can also create Items to identify discounts, subtotals on Invoices, and sales tax rates. Since every business has its own unique set of products and services, QuickBooks can be customized to your business by creating Items for each service or product.

When you define Items, you associate Item names with Accounts in your Chart of Accounts. This association between Item names and Accounts is the magic that allows QuickBooks to automatically track the accounting details behind each of your transactions.

Items help the management of a company see detailed information about what is happening in the business. For example, Item reports can show managers which product or service sells the most, the average price of each sale, or how much inventory is on hand. At the same time, when an Item is used on a transaction such as an Invoice, QuickBooks uses the definition of the Item to record the transaction in the General Ledger. Using Items is optional on all forms except Invoices, Estimates, and Purchase Orders. Some businesses will choose to use Items only where they are required.

QuickBooks provides ten different types of Items. Some, such as Service Items or Inventory Items, record the services and products your business buys and sells. Others, such as subtotals or discount Items, are used to perform calculations on sales forms.

How Items Are Used

Items are used on forms throughout QuickBooks. For example, when you fill out an invoice, you use an Item to indicate what is being sold. Since Items are associated with accounts, the accounting is handled automatically by QuickBooks. On the invoice in Figure 1-21, 4 hours of design services and 12 hours of labor are being sold. Since the labor *Item* is associated with the Services Income *account*, the transaction increases the number of labor hours (the Item) as well as the balance in Services Income (the Account).

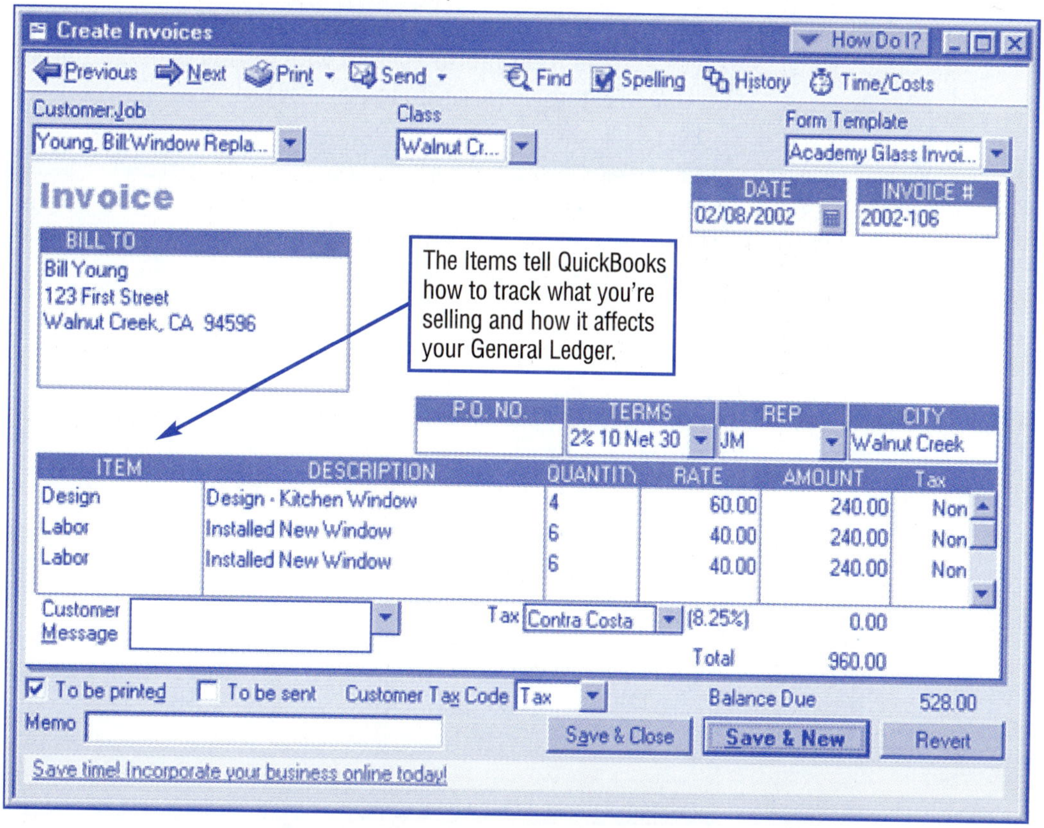

Figure 1-21 On invoices, items indicate what is being sold.

Similarly, when you fill out a Purchase Order, the Item column indicates which Item you are purchasing (see Figure 1-22).

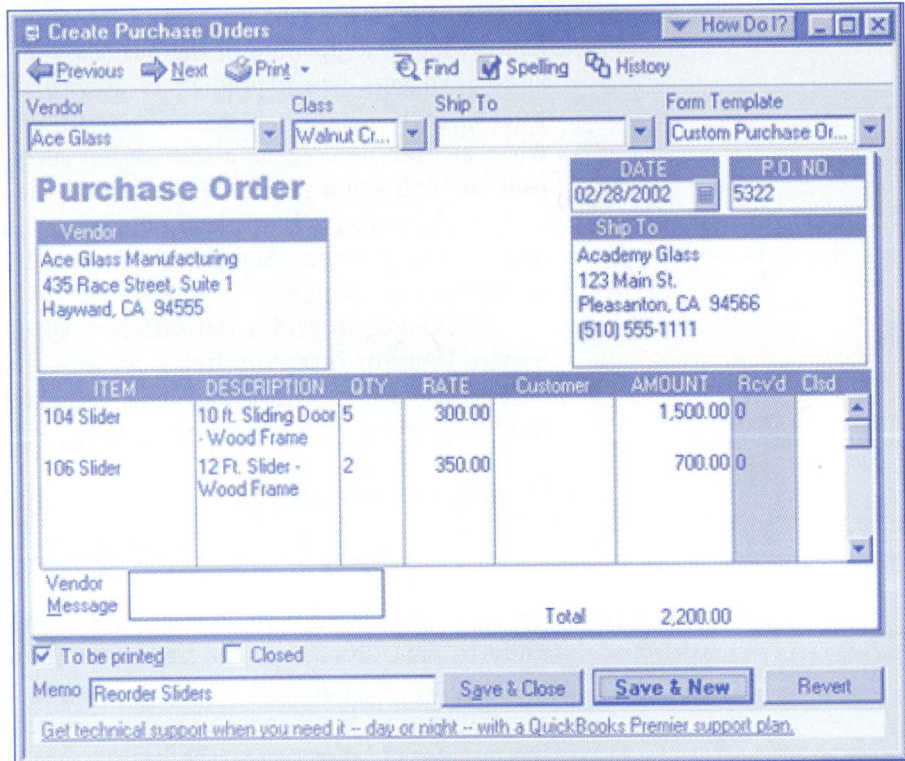

Figure 1-22 Items appear on Purchase Orders.

On bills, checks, and credit card charge forms, you'll sometimes select the Item tab to specify which Item is being purchased (see Figure 1-23, Figure 1-24, and Figure 1-25).

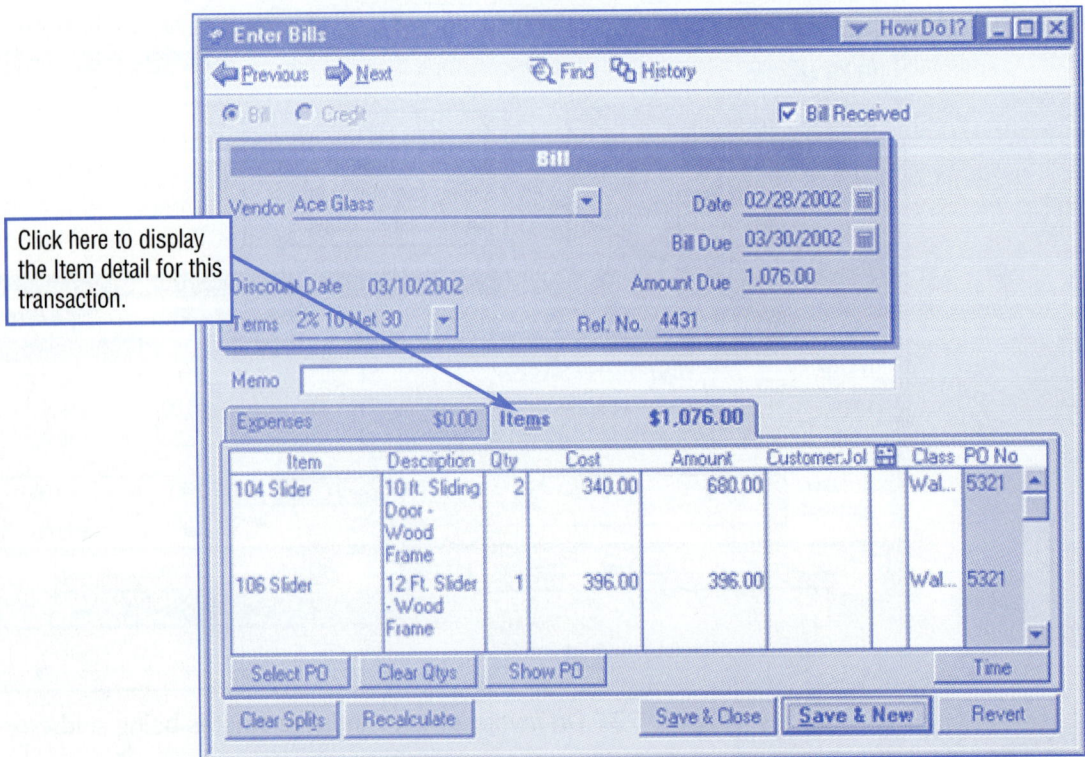

Click here to display the Item detail for this transaction.

Figure 1-23 Items on a bill

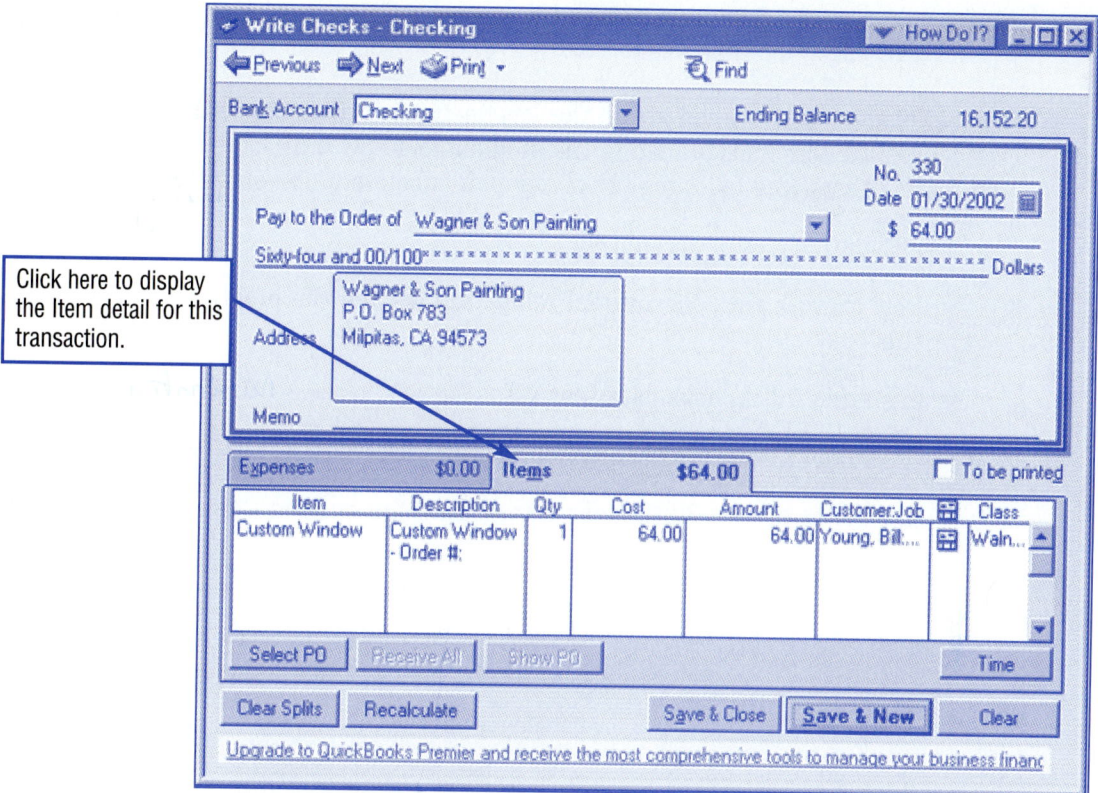

Figure 1-24 An Item on a check

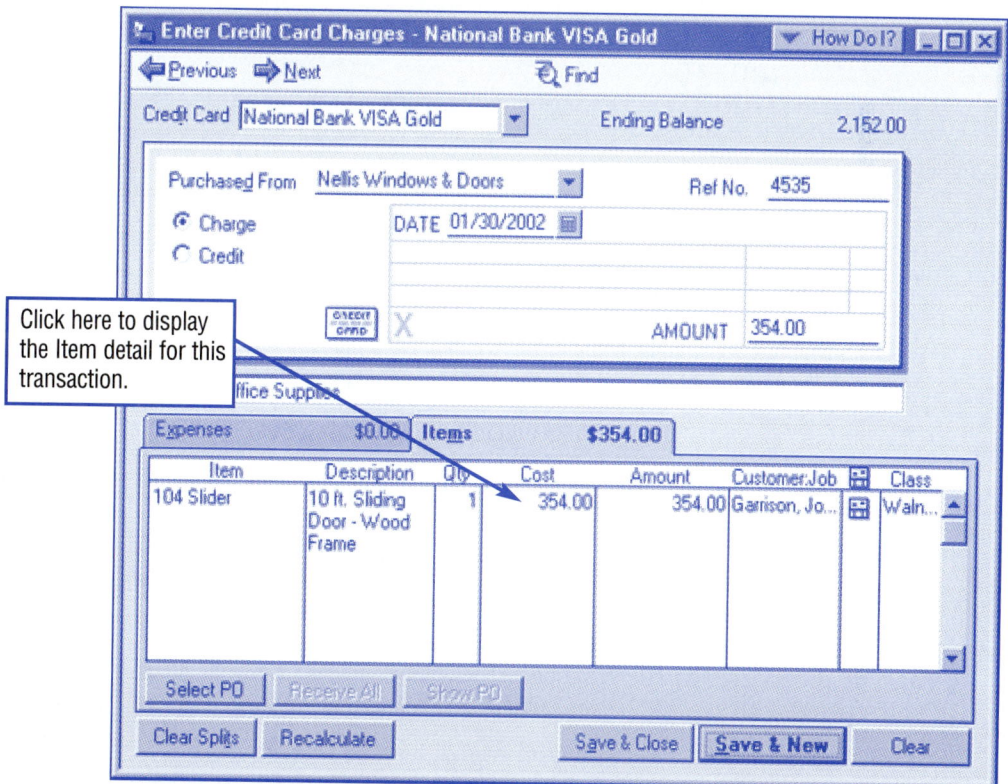

Figure 1-25 An Item on a credit card charge

In Chapter 2, you'll learn more about using items on sales forms and setting up item lists.

SUMMARY OF KEY POINTS

In this chapter you learned about the key features in QuickBooks Pro 2002. The section introduced the terminology used in the program and how transactions are entered by filling out forms. Review the following list of key points before proceeding to the applications.

◆ Basic principles of accounting (Page 2)

◆ How to work with the tutorial template files and the problem template files in this book (Page 6)

◆ Restoring QuickBooks data files (Page 7)

◆ QuickBooks Menus, Icons, Navigators, and Shortcuts (Page 10)

◆ The basics of how QuickBooks transactions are entered (Page 20)

Name _____ **Date** _____

Workplace *Applications*

DISCUSSION QUESTIONS

These questions are designed to help you apply what you are learning about QuickBooks to your own organization. Use your notebook to record your answers and your thoughts.

1. Is your organization for-profit or not-for-profit?

2. How do you know (or find out) what the equity is in your company now?

3. How many divisions or locations do you need to track separately for your organization?

ACTIVITY

Identify some of the transactions that occur in your organization. Create a list with ways in which you think QuickBooks can benefit your organization.

*inter*NET CONNECTION

The American Institute of Certified Public Accountants has approximately 330,000 members and has been existence since 1887. The group offers news, products, and technical information about the accounting profession. The AICPA has a website (with a page especially for students) and has offices in New York and Washington, D.C.: **www.aicpa.org**

Managing Revenue

OBJECTIVES

After completing this chapter, you should be able to:

1 Set up customer records and enter sales transactions.

2 Record Sales Receipts and track cash receipts.

3 Record Invoices and Payments from customers.

4 Record bank deposits of cash, check, and credit card receipts.

5 Record customer returns and credits.

6 Write off bad debts.

7 Create and print customer statements and assess finance charges.

8 Set up lists for terms, price levels and custom fields.

9 Modify Form Templates.

10 Create Sales Reports.

RESTORE THIS FILE

This chapter uses Chapter 2.QBB. To open this file, restore the tutorial template called **Chapter 2.QBW** to your hard disk. (See page 7 for instructions on restoring files.)

In this chapter, you'll learn how QuickBooks can help you record and track your sales.

Each time you sell products or services, you'll record the transaction using one of QuickBooks' forms. When you fill out a QuickBooks **Invoice** or **Sales Receipt**, QuickBooks tracks the detail of each sale, allowing you to create reports about your sales. You can get reports of your sales that show details of each sale, or you can see summaries of sales by customer, job, rep, or class.

TRACKING COMPANY SALES

Depending on your business, you might choose to track each sale separately as we'll show here, or you might combine your total sales for the day into one transaction. For example, if you have a cash register that tracks each sale, use the register tape (z-total) each day and create one Sales Receipt or Invoice for the total sales for the day. On the other hand, if you need to track detailed information about each sale, or if you extend credit to your customers, you'll enter the detail of each sale on a QuickBooks form such as an Invoice.

Academy Glass tracks each sale individually on either an **Invoice** form (for sales to credit customers) or a **Sales Receipt** form (for customers that pay cash).

The QuickBooks Sales Process

To record sales, you, follow a few basic steps. Table 2-1 shows each step in the sales process.

Business Transaction	Cash Customers		Credit Customers	
	QuickBooks Transaction	**Accounting Entry**	**QuickBooks Transaction**	**Accounting Entry**
Recording a Sale	*Enter Sales Receipt*	Increase (debit) **Undeposited Funds**, increase (credit) **income** account.	*Create Invoice*	Increase (debit) **Accounts Receivable**, increase (credit) **income** account.
Receiving Money in Payment of an Invoice			*Receive Payments*	Decrease (credit) **Accounts Receivable**, increase (debit) **Undeposited Funds**.
Depositing Money in the Bank	*Make Deposit*	Decrease (credit) **Undeposited Funds**, increase (debit) **bank** account.	*Make Deposit*	Decrease (credit) **Undeposited Funds**, increase (debit) **bank** account.

Table 2-1 Steps in the sales process

For cash customers, use the **Sales Receipt** form to record your sale. The Sales Receipt form records the details of what you've sold and to whom you sold it. The accounting entry behind the scenes, performed automatically by QuickBooks, increases (with a debit) **Undeposited Funds**, and increases (with a credit) the appropriate **income** account.

For credit customers create an **Invoice** for each sale. The Invoice form records the details of what you've sold and to whom you sold it. The accounting entry behind the scenes performed automatically by QuickBooks, increases (with a debit) **Accounts Receivable** and increases (with a credit) the appropriate **income** account.

As shown in Table 2-1, when you receive money from your credit customers, use the **Receive Payments** function to record the receipt. The accounting entry behind the scenes increases (with a debit) **Undeposited Funds** and decreases (with a credit) **Accounts Receivable**.

The last step in the process is to make a deposit to your bank account. This step is the same for both cash and credit customers. Use the **Make Deposits** function to record the deposit to your bank account.

Recording the deposit is the last step in the sales tracking process. After you complete this step, QuickBooks has increased both the income account and the balance in your bank account. The increase in both of these accounts is the end result of the sales process. In the following sections, you'll learn about each step in detail.

Setting Up Customers

For each of your customers, create a record in the Customer:Job list. Academy Glass has a new credit customer – Dr. Carl Nelson. To add this new customer, follow these steps:

COMPUTER TUTORIAL

① Select the *Lists* menu and choose **Customer:Job List** or press <Ctrl+J> (see Figure 2-1).

② To add a new customer, select the *Customer:Job* menu at the bottom of the Customer:Job List and choose **New** (Figure 2-2).

③ Enter "Nelson, Carl" in the *Customer Name* field and press <TAB>.

If you want to sort your customers alphabetically, enter the last name first.

TIP

There are four name lists in QuickBooks: Vendor, Customer:Job, Employee, and Other Names. After you enter a customer's name in the *Customer* field of the New Customer record, you cannot use that name in any of the other three lists in QuickBooks, and vice versa.

Customer:Job List			How Do I?	
Name	Balance	Notes	Job Status	Estimate Total
◆ Anderson Floors	160.00			0.00
◆ 2nd Street Store	160.00			0.00
◆ Front St. Store	0.00	📄	Pending	0.00
◆ Berry, Ron	0.00			0.00
◆ Garrison, John	0.00			1,651.88
◆ Kitchen	0.00		Pending	1,651.88
◆ Leonard, Jerry	0.00			0.00
◆ Mason, Bob	2,746.08		In progress	0.00
◆ Pelligrini Builders	0.00			0.00
◆ 2354 Wilkes Rd	0.00			0.00
◆ 4266 Lake Drive	0.00		Closed	0.00
◆ Young, Bill	2,586.40			0.00
◆ Window Replacement	2,586.40	📄	Awarded	

Customer:Job ▼   Activities ▼   Reports ▼   ☐ Show All

Figure 2-1 The Customer:Job List

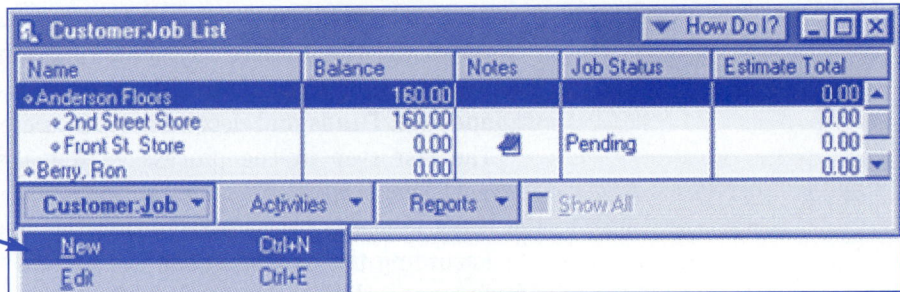

To create a new customer record, choose New from this menu.

Figure 2-2 Add new Customer records by selecting **New**.

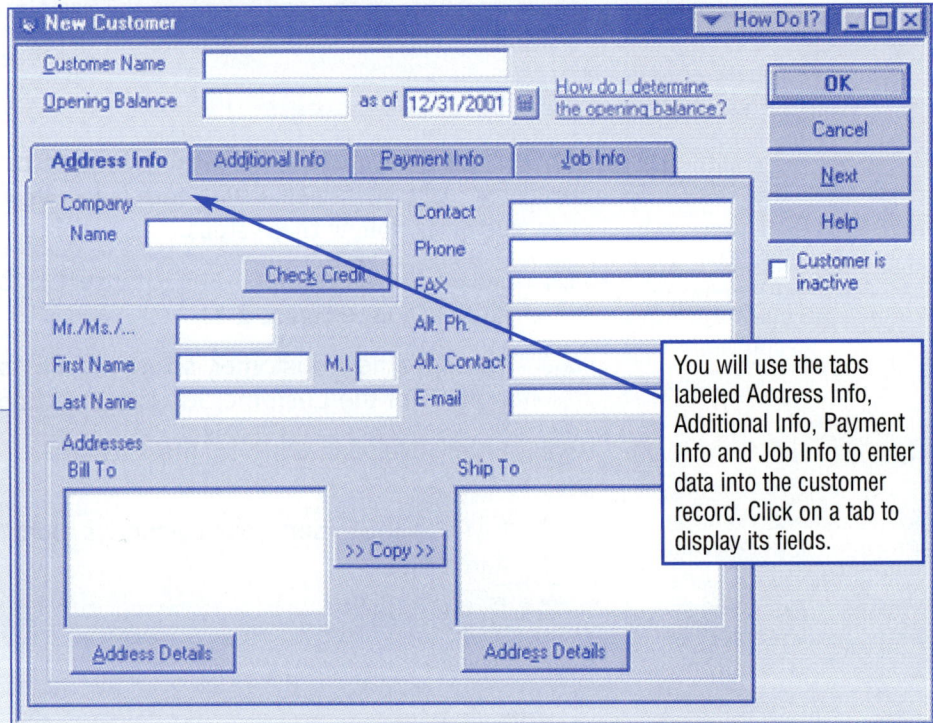

You will use the tabs labeled Address Info, Additional Info, Payment Info and Job Info to enter data into the customer record. Click on a tab to display its fields.

Tip

When Customers are Vendors
When you sell to and purchase from the same company, you'll need to create two records, one in the Vendor List and one in the Customer:Job List. Make the two names slightly different. For example, you could enter "Nelson, Carl – C" in the New Customer screen and "Nelson, Carl – V" in the New Vendor screen. The vendor and customer records for Carl Nelson can contain the same contact information.

Figure 2-3 New Customer screen

④ Press <TAB> twice to skip the *Opening Balance* and *as of* fields (see Figure 2-4).

The date in the *as of* field defaults to the current date. Since you will not enter an amount in the O*pening Balance* field, there is no need to change this date. The *Opening Balance* field shows on customer records only when you first create the record. Later, when you edit this customer record, this field will not show.

> **IMPORTANT**
>
> It is best NOT to use the *Opening Balance* field in the customer record. When you enter an opening balance for a customer in the *Opening Balance* field, QuickBooks creates an Invoice that increases (debits) Accounts Receivable, and increases (credits) Uncategorized Income. You or your accountant will then need to adjust the balance in Uncategorized Income before you can use QuickBooks reports to prepare your tax return. (For additional problems created by using this field see page 501.) Instead, enter each unpaid Invoice separately after you create the customer record.

5 Because this customer is not a company, skip the *Company Name* field by clicking <TAB>.

6 Press <TAB> to skip the **Check Credit** button.

QuickBooks 2002 provides Dun & Bradstreet credit information for your customers for a fee per credit report or by subscription. To activate the QuickBooks Credit Check Service, you would select the **Company** menu, choose **Business Services Navigator**, and then choose **Get a D&B Credit Report**.

7 Continue entering the rest of the fields using the data in Table 2-2. Press <TAB> after each entry.

Field	Data
Mr./Ms./…	Dr.
First Name	Carl
M.I.	S.
Last Name	Nelson
Bill To Address	Carl Nelson 300 Main St, Suite 3 Danville, CA 95111
Contact	Carl Nelson
Phone	925-555-8900
FAX	925-555-8901
Alt. Ph.	925-555-6711
Alt. Contact	Don Woodard
E-Mail	carl@bignetwork.com
Ship To	Press the >> **Copy** >> button. This copies the Bill To address information into the Ship To address field, saving you the hassle of reentering it.

Table 2-2 Data to complete the Address Info Tab

Figure 2-4 shows the finished Address Info section of the customer record. Verify that your screen matches Figure 2-4.

8 Click the Additional Info tab to continue entering information about this customer.

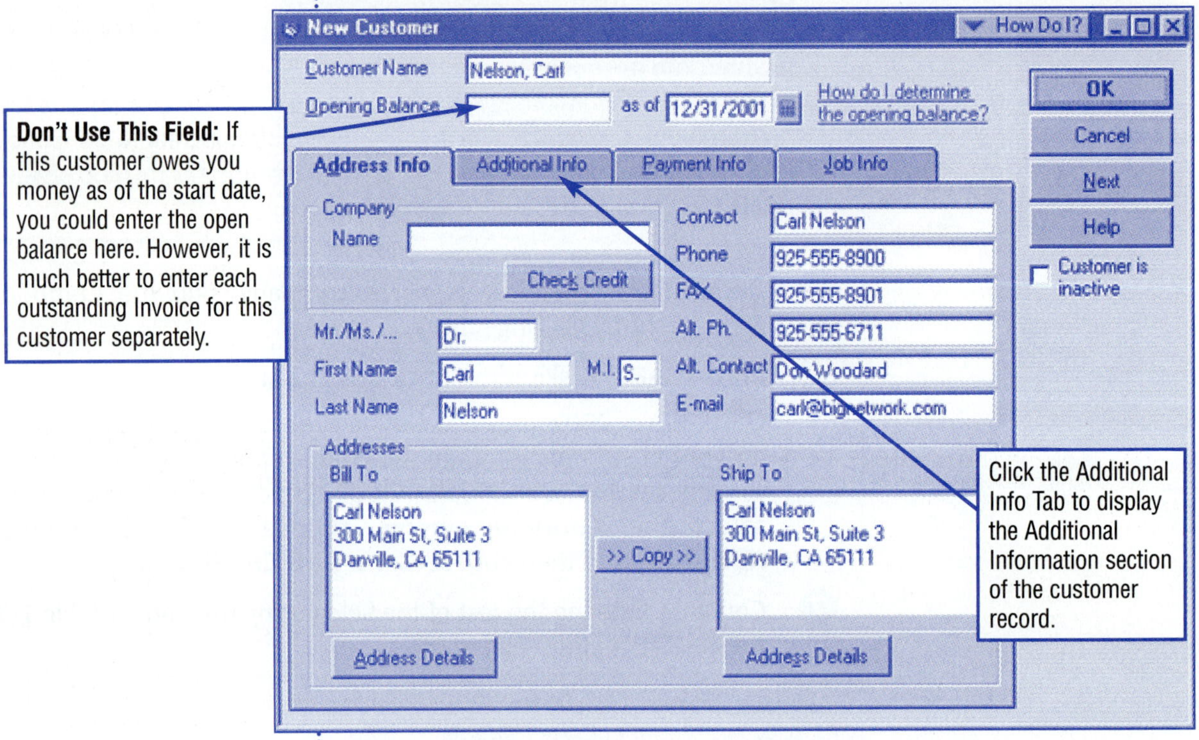

Don't Use This Field: If this customer owes you money as of the start date, you could enter the open balance here. However, it is much better to enter each outstanding Invoice for this customer separately.

Click the Additional Info Tab to display the Additional Information section of the customer record.

Figure 2-4 Completed Address Info Tab

9 Select "Business" from the *Type* field drop-down menu and press <TAB>.

QuickBooks allows you to group your customers into common types. By grouping your customers into types, you'll be able to create reports that focus on one or more types. For example, if you create two types of customers, Residential and Business, and you tag each customer with a type, you can later create mailing labels for all residential customers.

10 Select "Net 30" from the *Terms* drop-down menu as the terms for this customer and press <TAB>.

QuickBooks is *terms smart*. For example, if you enter terms of 2% 10 Net 30 and a customer pays within 10 days QuickBooks will automatically calculate a 2% discount. For more information about setting up your Terms list, see page 96.

11 Select "JM" in the *Rep* drop-down menu and press <TAB>.

The *Rep* field can contain the initials of one of your employees. Use this field to assign a sales rep to this customer. If you use the *Rep* field, you can create reports (e.g., Sales by Rep report) that provide the sales information you need to pay commissions. Each sales form (Invoice or Sales Receipt) can have a different name in the *Rep* field.

⑫ Press <TAB> to accept the default setting of "None" in the *Preferred Send Method* field.

You would use the *Preferred Send Method* field if you planned to fax or email Invoices to a customer on a regular basis.

⑬ Press <TAB> to accept the "Tax" default sales code Tax in the *Tax Code* field.

Sales Tax Codes serve two purposes. First, they determine the default taxable status of a customer and sale. Since the Sales Tax Code called "Tax" indicates that an item is taxable, each Sales Receipt or Invoice for Carl Nelson will also be treated as taxable. You can override the Sales Tax Code on each individual Sales Receipt or Invoice entered for the customer. Secondly, Sales Tax Codes can be used to identify the type of tax exemption and track it separately, such as "GOV" for a Government Sale, "RSR" for Resale and others (see Figure 2-5).

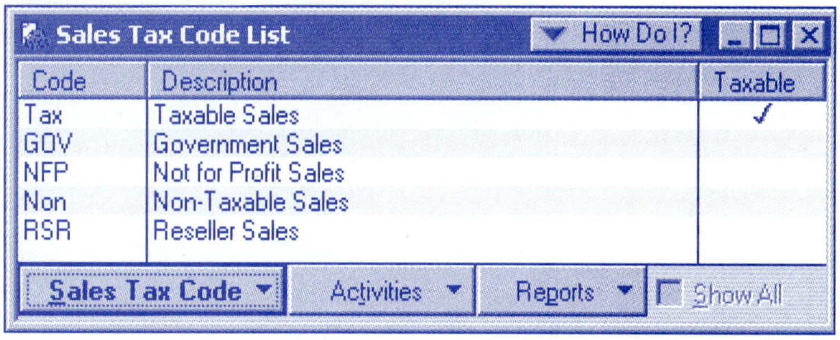

Figure 2-5 The Sales Tax Code List

⑭ The preselected "Contra Costa" *Tax Item* indicates which sales tax rate to charge and which agency collects the tax (see Figure 2-6). Press <TAB>.

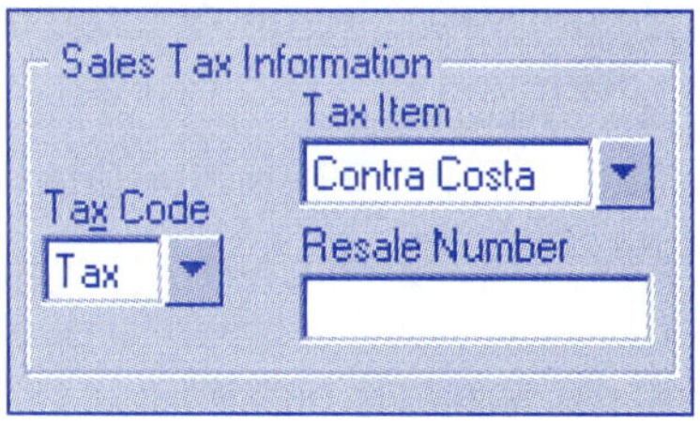

Figure 2-6 Sales Tax Information in the customer record.

⑮ Press <TAB> to leave the *Resale Number* field blank.

If the customer is a reseller, you would enter his or her reseller number.

⑯ Select "Commercial" from the *Price Level* field drop-down menu. See page 98 for information on setting up and using price levels.

⑰ Enter "Danville" in the *City* field and "Contra Costa" in the *County* field.

TIP

In most states, you charge sales tax based on the delivery point of the shipment. So the Sales Tax Item should be consistent with the Ship To address on the Address Info Tab.

The **Define Fields** button on the New Customer Additional Information screen allows you to define custom fields to track more information for your customers. For more information on setting up and using custom fields, see page 101.

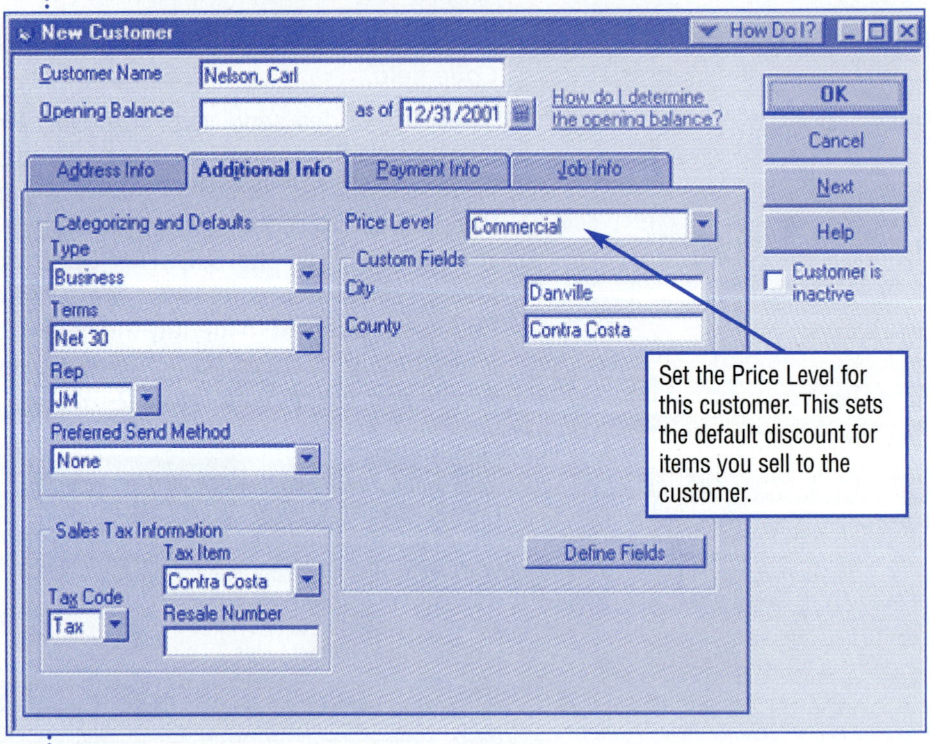

Figure 2-7 Completed Additional Info Tab.

⑱ Verify that your screen matches Figure 2-7. Then click the Payment Info tab to continue entering information about this customer.

⑲ Enter "3543" in the *Account* field to assign a customer number by which you can sort or filter reports. Press <TAB>.

⑳ Enter "3,000.00" in the *Credit Limit* field and press <TAB>.

QuickBooks will warn you if you record an Invoice to this customer when the balance due (plus the current sale) exceeds the credit limit. Even though QuickBooks warns you, you'll still be able to record the Invoice.

㉑ Select "VISA" from the *Preferred Payment Method* drop down menu.

Once having set the fields on this screen, you won't have to enter the credit card information each time you receive money from the customer.

NOTE

If you want to assign your customer a unique number, you can use the *Account* field. QuickBooks allows you to sort and filter reports by customer number. If you use online banking and you want to send an online payment to this customer, you would need to fill in this field. If you don't use customer numbers, you can leave this field blank.

TIP

If more than one person accesses your QuickBooks file, set up a separate user name and password for the additional user and restrict them from accessing "sensitive accounting activities." This will prevent the additional user from seeing the customer's credit card number. See Chapter 10 for more information about setting up user names and passwords.

NOTE

It is best NOT to enter job information on the Job Info tab of the customer record. If you want to track jobs for this customer, you can create separate job records in the Customer:Job List. See Chapter 10 for more information about setting up Jobs in QuickBooks.

22 Enter the data in Figure 2-8 in the Preferred Payment Method section. Click **OK** to save the customer record.

23 If you were adding several customers at a time, you would now click **Next** to begin adding another customer. In this case, though, click **OK** and close the Customer:Job List screen.

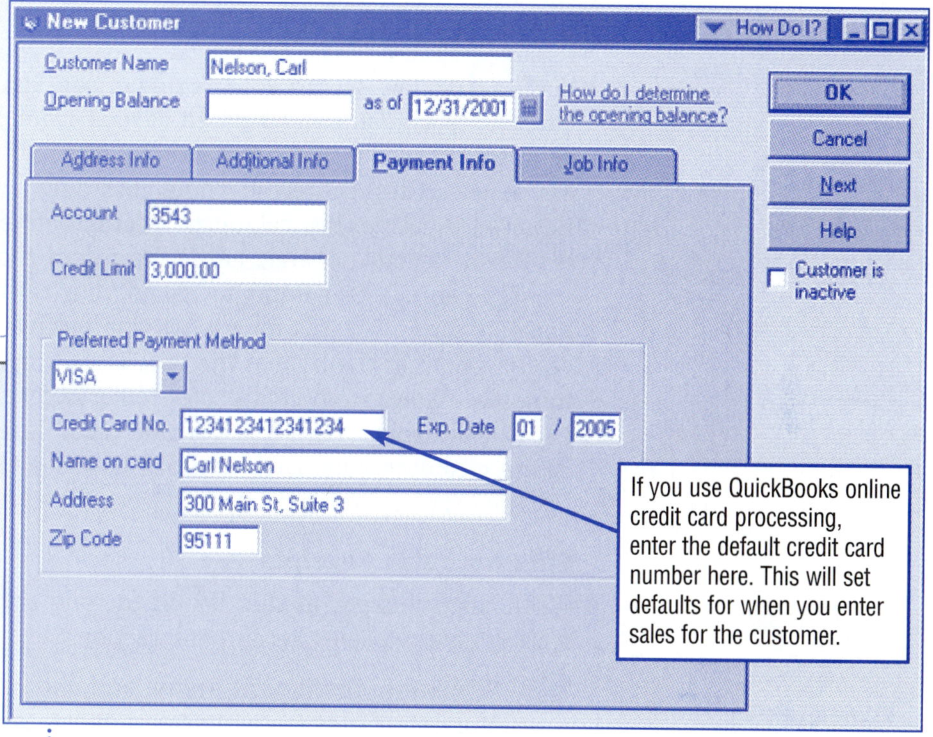

If you use QuickBooks online credit card processing, enter the default credit card number here. This will set defaults for when you enter sales for the customer.

Figure 2-8 Completed Payment Info Tab.

Job Costing

KEY TERM

Tracking income and expenses separately for each job is known as **Job Costing**. If your company needs to track job costs, make sure you enter the job name on each income and expense transaction as you enter them.

QuickBooks tracks jobs in addition to customers. For each customer in the Customer:Job List, you can create one or more jobs. This helps you track income and expenses on each Job, so that you can create reports showing detailed or summarized information about each Job.

The *Customer:Job* field shows the Customer name first, followed by a colon (:) and then the Job name, as shown in Figure 2-9.

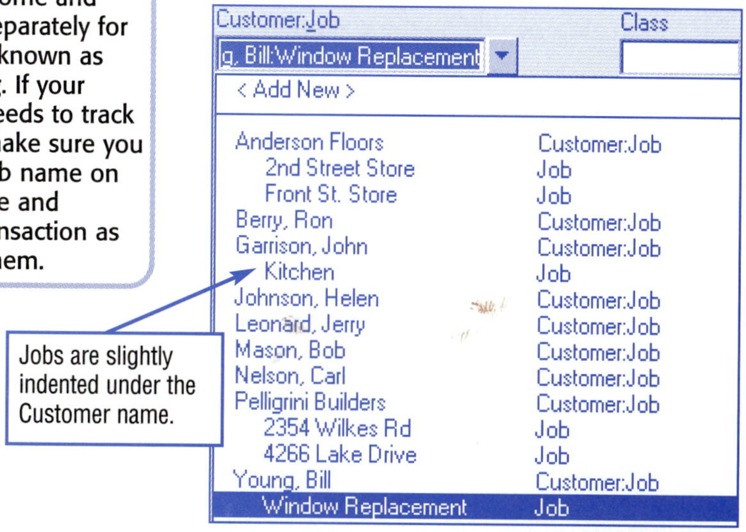

Jobs are slightly indented under the Customer name.

Figure 2-9 The Customer:Job drop-down list

To Quick Add a Job for a Customer, enter the Customer's name followed by a colon. After the colon, enter the name of the job. QuickBooks will then prompt you to either Quick Add or Set Up the Job. (If the *Customer record* includes job information, you won't be able to use Quick Add to create a Job for the customer. In this case, you will need to create the Job in the Customer:Job List before you begin entering the sales form.)

Recording Sales

Now that you've set up your Customer:Job List, you're ready to begin entering sales. You don't have to have all your customers set up before you begin entering sales transactions. As you'll see, it's possible to create a new customer record while recording a sale to that customer. However, creating the customer records beforehand will significantly reduce the amount of time needed to record each sale.

You can use two forms to record your sales. The first is the **Sales Receipts** form. Use this form when you receive a cash, check, or credit card payment at the time of the sale. The second is the **Invoice**. Use this form when you record credit sales to customers.

If you collect sales tax, turn on Sales Tax tracking in Preferences before recording your sales. To learn how, see the section called *Setting Up Sales Tax* beginning on page 92.

Entering Sales Receipts

When customers pay at the time of the sale either by check or by credit card, create a Sales Receipt transaction.

COMPUTER TUTORIAL

➤ ANOTHER ➤
◄ WAY ◄

You can also click **Sales Receipt** on the Icon bar to open the Sales Receipts form.

NOTE

Quick Add works on all your lists. Whenever you type a new name into any field on any form, QuickBooks prompts you to Quick Add the name.

❶ Select the **Customers** menu, and choose **Enter Sales Receipts**. The Enter Sales Receipt screen opens (see Figure 2-10).

❷ Enter "Johnson, Helen" in the *Customer:Job* field and press <TAB>.

❸ When the Customer:Job not found warning window appears, click **Quick Add** to add this new customer to the Customer:Job List, without adding all of the address information (see Figure 2-11). You can always go back later and add the address and other information by editing the customer record.

❹ Enter "San Jose" in the *Class* field and press <TAB>.

QuickBooks uses classes to separately track income and expenses for departments, functions, activities, locations, or profit centers.

TIP

It's a good idea to enter your customers with the last name first. This makes your Customer:Job List sort by last name so it will be easier to find names in the list.

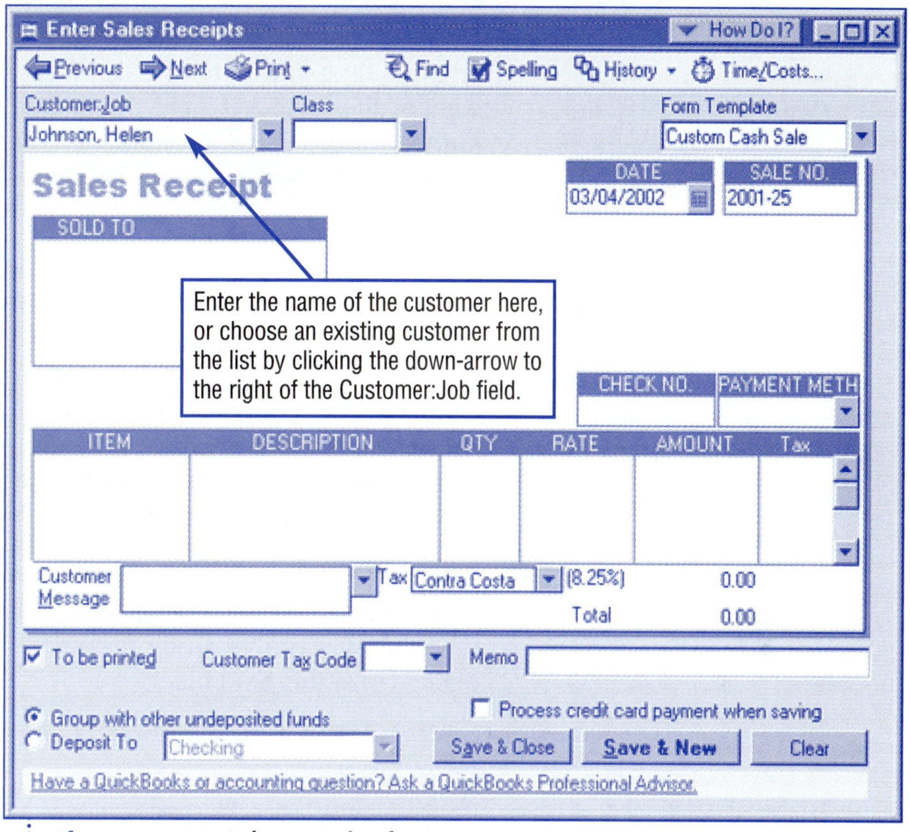

Figure 2-10 A Sales Receipt form

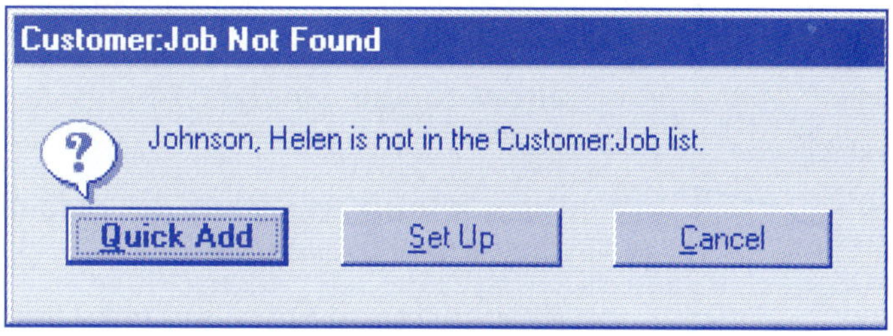

Figure 2-11 Use Quick Add to add new customers.

5. In the *Form Template* field, "Custom Cash Sale" is preselected. Press <TAB>.

   The tutorial file has just one Sales Receipt template, but you can create your own custom forms, as you'll learn in the section called *Modifying Sales Form Templates* beginning on page 103.

6. Enter "01/25/2002" in the *Date* field, and then press <TAB> (see Figure 2-12).

   QuickBooks defaults to using today's date when you enter a sale, but you can override the date if you wish.

Whenever you enter a date in QuickBooks, you can use any of several shortcut keys to quickly change the date. For example, if you want to change the date to the beginning of the year, press <y>. "Y" is the first letter of the word "year," so it's easy to remember this shortcut. The same works for the end of the year: press <r> since that's the last letter of the word "year." The same works for "month" (<m> and <h>) and "week" (<w> and <k>). You can also use the <+> and <-> keys to move the date one day forward or back. Finally, press <t> for "today." See page 564 for a list of shortcut keys that help you quickly enter dates.

7 Enter "2002-101" in the *SALE NO.* field and press <TAB>.

The first time you enter a Sales Receipt, enter any number you want in the *SALE NO.* field. Then, QuickBooks will automatically number future Sales Receipts incrementally. You can change or reset the numbering at any time by overriding the number on a Sales Receipt.

8 Press <TAB> to bypass the *SOLD TO* field.

QuickBooks automatically fills in this field, using the information in the *Bill To* field of the customer record. Since you used Quick Add to add this customer, there is no address information. You could enter an address in the *SOLD TO* field by typing it in directly on the sales form. When you record the Sales Receipt, QuickBooks will give you the option of adding the address to the *Bill To* field of the customer record.

9 Enter "3612" in the *CHECK NO.* field and press <TAB>.

The number you enter here shows up on your printed deposit slips. If you were receiving a cash or credit card payment, you would leave this field blank.

10 Select "Check" from the *PAYMENT METH* drop down menu and press <TAB>.

If you wanted to add a new payment method, you would type the new method in this field. QuickBooks would prompt you to either Quick Add or Set Up the new Payment Method.

11 Select "Skylight" from the *ITEM* drop-down menu (the down-arrow to the far right of this section of the form) and press <TAB>.

12 Press <TAB> to accept the default description "Skylight" in the DESCRIPTION column.

As soon as you enter an Item, QuickBooks enters the description, rate and sales tax code, using information from the Item's setup screen.

13 Enter "1" in the QTY (quantity) column and press <TAB>.

⑭ Enter "485.00" in the RATE column and press <TAB>.

Usually, when you enter an Item, the RATE column fills in automatically. However, the skylight Item setup does not include a default rate because Academy Glass uses the Skylight Item to track several different models and sizes of skylights, each with a different sales price. For more information about setting up and using Items see page 87.

⑮ Press <TAB> to accept the calculated amount in the AMOUNT column.

After you enter the rate and press <TAB>, QuickBooks calculates the amount by multiplying the quantity and rate. If you override the *AMOUNT* field, QuickBooks calculates a new rate by dividing the amount by the quantity.

⑯ In the Tax column, the "Tax" sales tax code is preselected. Press <TAB>.

⑰ Select "Design" from the ITEM drop-down menu and press <TAB> twice.

⑱ Enter "2" in the QTY (quantity) column and press <TAB>.

⑲ Press <TAB> to accept the default rate of "60.00".

You can override this amount directly on the Sales Receipt if necessary. As with the line above, QuickBooks calculates the total in the AMOUNT column and QuickBooks uses the default sales tax code "Non" which is set up for the "Design" Item. For more information on setting up Items, see page 87.

⑳ Select "Thank you for your business." from the *Customer Message* drop-down menu.

You can enter a message in the *Customer Message* field that shows on the printed Sales Receipt. This is typically a thank you message, but it can be whatever you want. If you type in a new message, Quick Add will prompt you to add your new message to the Customer Messages list.

㉑ Press <TAB> to accept "Contra Costa" in the *Tax* field.

The "Contra Costa" Sales Tax Item is preselected because it is the "Most common sales tax item" selected in the Sales Tax Company Preferences. Refer to *Setting Up Sales Tax* beginning on page 92. The Sales Tax Item shown in the *Tax* field determines the rate of tax to be charged on all Taxable Items shown on the form. Each line in the body of the Invoice is marked with a Sales Tax Code that determines the taxability or non-taxability of the Item on that line (see Figure 2-12).

Important: This should nearly always be set to "Group with Other Undeposited Funds" as shown here.

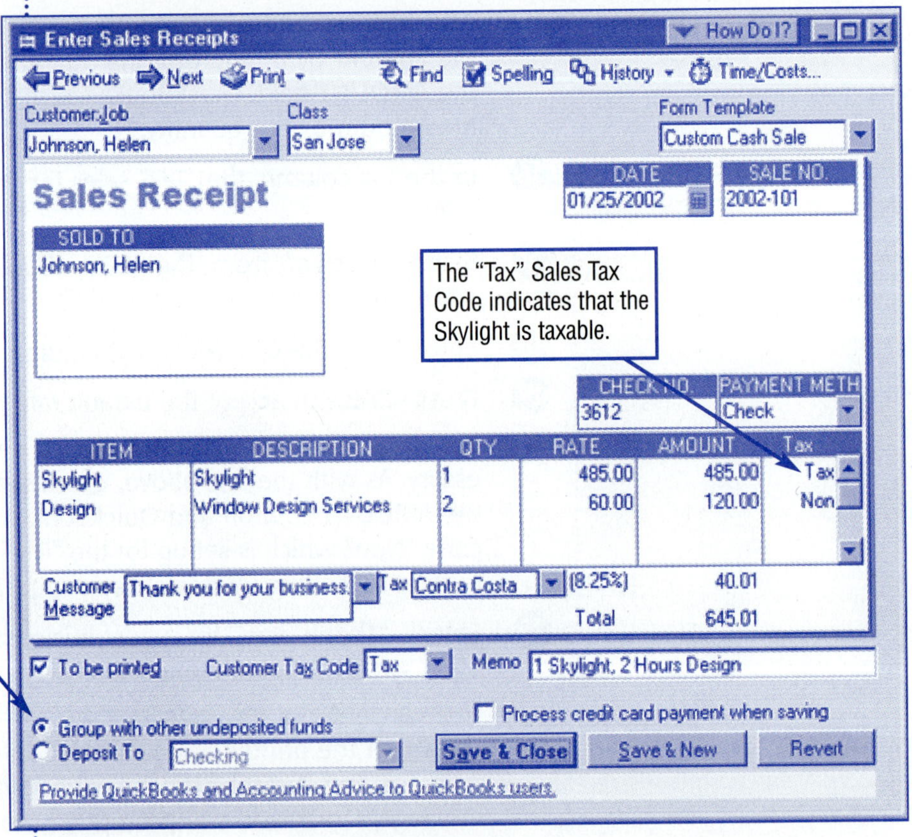

Figure 2-12 Completed Sales Receipt

㉒ Enter "1 Skylight, 2 Hours Design" in the *Memo* field.

㉓ At the bottom of the form, "Group with other undeposited funds" is preselected. You will usually choose this option. See *Recording Undeposited Funds* on page 47 for more details.

24 To print the sale on blank paper or on a preprinted form, click **Print** on the Icon bar.

You could choose to print all your sales in one batch. To do this, you would save each Sales Receipt without printing. Since QuickBooks checks the "To be printed" box by default, you would print all of the forms together after you have finished entering your Sales Receipts by selecting **Print Forms** from the *File* menu, and then choosing **Sales Receipts**.

25 Click **Save & Close** to record the sale.

QuickBooks does not record any of the information on any form until you save the transaction by clicking **Save & Close**, **Save & New**, or **Next**.

Recording Undeposited Funds

When you record Sales Receipts, QuickBooks gives you a choice of grouping all of the cash together into one account called **Undeposited Funds** or immediately depositing the funds to one of your bank accounts. Unless you only make one sale each day and your deposit includes funds from only that single sale, you'll want to **group** the funds from this sale with the other cash receipts for the day. Later, you'll gather all of the receipts for the day into one **deposit** that you'll take to the bank.

On Sales Receipts, the setting at the bottom of the form determines where the funds from the sale go. Setting the option to "Group with other undeposited funds" (see Figure 2-13) causes the funds from your sale to increase the balance in Undeposited Funds. Later, when you make your deposits, you'll group all of the funds from several sales into one deposit in the bank.

Figure 2-13 Setting to group a Sales Receipt with other undeposited funds

You'll *almost never* choose this option on Sales Receipts.

Figure 2-14 Choose this option when you enter only one sale per day.

You'll *rarely* choose the option shown in Figure 2-14. Using the "Deposit to checking" option causes the funds from your sale to increase the balance in the QuickBooks Checking account. If you have several sales each day, then this setting causes a separate deposit transaction to show in the QuickBooks Checking account for each sales receipt. This is a problem when you reconcile the bank account at the end of the month. If you make a single bank deposit each day but each sales receipt appears separately in the QuickBooks checking account register, the bank statement will show one deposit while QuickBooks will show separate deposits for each sale.

Think of the Undeposited Funds account as your cash drawer. It increases each time you enter Sales Receipts or when you receive payments from your accounts receivable customers. When you make deposits to your bank account, Undeposited Funds decreases.

Creating Invoices

Invoices are very similar to the Sales Receipt form. The only difference is that Invoices increase Accounts Receivable while Sales Receipts increase Undeposited Funds (or the QuickBooks bank account specified). You will use Invoices only for your credit customers.

COMPUTER TUTORIAL

① Select the **Customers** menu, and then choose **Create Invoices**.

② Select "Mason, Bob" from the *Customer:Job* drop-down menu and press <TAB> (see Figure 2-15).

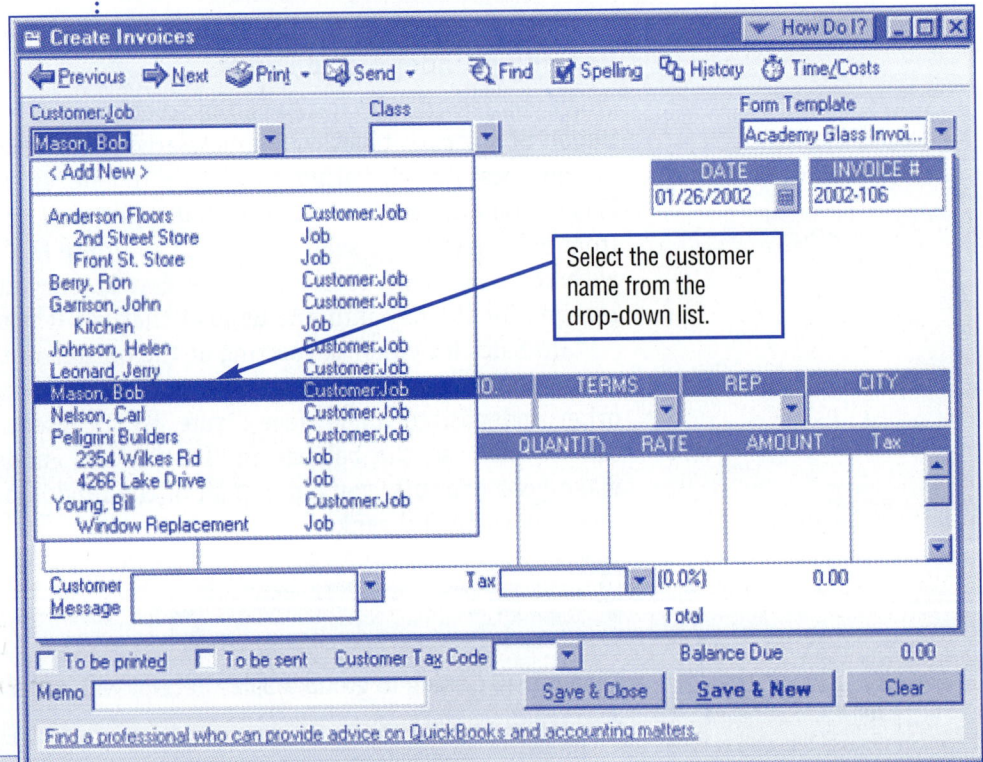

Figure 2-15 Select a customer name.

③ Enter "San Jose" in the *Class* field and press <TAB>.

④ In the *Form Template* field, "Academy Glass Invoice" is preselected. Press <TAB>.

⑤ Enter "1/26/2002" in the *DATE* field and press <TAB>.

⑥ Leave "2002-106" in the *INVOICE* # field and press <TAB>.

The first time you enter an Invoice, enter any number you want in the *INVOICE* # field. Then, QuickBooks will automatically number future Invoices incrementally. You can change or reset the numbering at any time by overriding the number on a future Invoice.

DID YOU KNOW When you type the first few characters of any field that has a list behind it, QuickBooks completes the field using a feature called **QuickFill**. QuickFill uses the first few characters you type to "guess" which entry in the list you want. If it guesses wrong, keep typing until it guesses right.

7 Press <TAB> to accept the default information in the *BILL TO* field.

QuickBooks automatically enters the address in this field, using the information in the *Bill To* field of the customer record. If necessary, change the Bill To address by typing over the existing data.

8 Leave the *P.O. NO* field blank and press <TAB>.

The P.O. (purchase order) number helps the customer identify your Invoice. When your customers use purchase orders, make sure you enter the P.O. numbers on their Invoices.

9 In the *TERMS* field, "2%10 Net 30" is preselected. Press <TAB> to skip to the next field.

The *TERMS* field on the Invoice indicates when the Invoice is due and how long your customer can take to pay you. The entry in this field determines how this Invoice is reported on A/R reports such as A/R Aging Summary and the Collections Report.

10 In the *REP* field, "JM" is preselected. Press <TAB> to move to the next field.

11 In the *CITY* field, "Morgan Hill" is preselected. Press <TAB> to skip to the next field.

The *CITY* field is a Custom Field. For more information on setting up custom fields, see *Custom Fields* on page 101.

12 Enter the sale of 2 Skylights and 4̷5̶ hours of Design services into the body of the Invoice as shown in Figure 2-16.

13 Choose "Thank you for your business" from the *Customer Message* drop-down menu.

14 "Santa Clara" in the *Tax* field is preselected.

As with Sales Receipts, QuickBooks preselects the Sales Tax Item based on the defaults in the Sales Tax Preferences or the Customer record. See page 93 for more information.

15 Enter "2 Skylights, 5 Hours Design" in the *Memo* field at the bottom of the form.

TIP

Many of your customers may reject Invoices that do not reference a P.O. number.

DID YOU KNOW If you intend to send statements to your customers, the memo field is extremely important. Only the information in the *INVOICE #*, *DATE*, and *Memo* fields will show on customer statements, along with a three letter code (INV), representing the Invoice transaction. Therefore, it is best to include information about the products or services you sold to the client when in the *Memo* field.

16 Compare your screen with the Invoice shown in Figure 2-16. If you see any errors, correct them. Otherwise, click **Save & Close** to record the Invoice.

Figure 2-16 Completed Invoice

QuickBooks automatically tracks all of the accounting details behind this transaction so that all your reports will immediately reflect the sale. For example, the Open Invoices report, the Profit & Loss Standard report, and the Balance Sheet Standard report will all change when you record this invoice.

Adding Calculating Items to an Invoice

On the next Invoice you'll learn how to add discounts and subtotals to an Invoice. Discounts and subtotals are called *calculating Items*.

COMPUTER TUTORIAL

1 Select the **Customers** menu, and choose **Create Invoice**, or press <Ctrl+I>).

2 Select the "Window Replacement" Job for Bill Young from the *Customer:Job* drop-down menu. Then press <TAB>.

3 Enter "Walnut Creek" in the *Class* field and press <TAB>.

Calculating Items use the amount of the preceding line to calculate their amount. For example, if you enter 10% in the Discount Item setup screen and then enter the Discount Item on an Invoice, QuickBooks will multiply the line just above the Discount Item by 10% and enter that number, as a negative, in the AMOUNT column for the discount line.

④ The Academy Glass Invoice template in the *Form Template* drop-down menu is preselected. Press <TAB>.

⑤ Enter 1/26/2002 in the *DATE* field, and press <TAB>.

⑥ Notice the INVOICE # is automatically entered for you with the next Invoice number (i.e. 2002-107). Press <TAB> to skip to the next field.

⑦ Press <TAB> to skip the *BILL TO* field.

⑧ Leave the data that's automatically filled into the *P.O. NO.*, *TERMS*, *REP*, and *CITY* fields. Press <TAB> four times to skip past these fields.

⑨ Enter the two items shown in Table 2-3 in the body of the Invoice.

Item	Description	Qty	Rate	Amount
Custom Window	Custom Window—Order # 7890	1	795.00	795.00
Labor	Window/Door Installation Labor	4	40.00	160.00

Table 2-3 Data for use in the Invoice

DID YOU KNOW You can insert or delete lines on an Invoice (or any other form). To insert a line between two existing lines, click on the line that you want to move down and press <Ctrl+Insert> (or select the **Edit** menu and choose **Insert Line**). To delete a line, click on the line you want to delete and press <Ctrl+Delete> (or select the **Edit** menu and choose **Delete Line**).

⑩ On the third line of the body of the Invoice, in the ITEM column, enter "Subtotal" to sum the previous two item lines, and press <TAB> twice.

Notice that QuickBooks automatically calculates the sum of the first two lines on the Invoice.

⑪ Enter "Disc 10%" in the ITEM column and press <TAB>.

The "Disc 10%" Item is a special Calculating Item that calculates a percentage of the preceding line on sales forms. Since it's a discount Item, QuickBooks performs the calculation and enters a negative amount for your discount. This subtracts the discount from the total of the Invoice and adjusts sales tax accordingly.

⑫ Leave the *Customer Message* field blank.

⑬ Leave "Contra Costa" in the *Tax* field. Also leave "Tax" in the *Customer Tax Code* field.

⑭ Enter "Custom Window Order # 7890" in the *Memo* field.

⑮ Verify that your screen matches Figure 2-17. If you have errors correct them before recording your Invoice. To save the Invoice, click **Save & Close**.

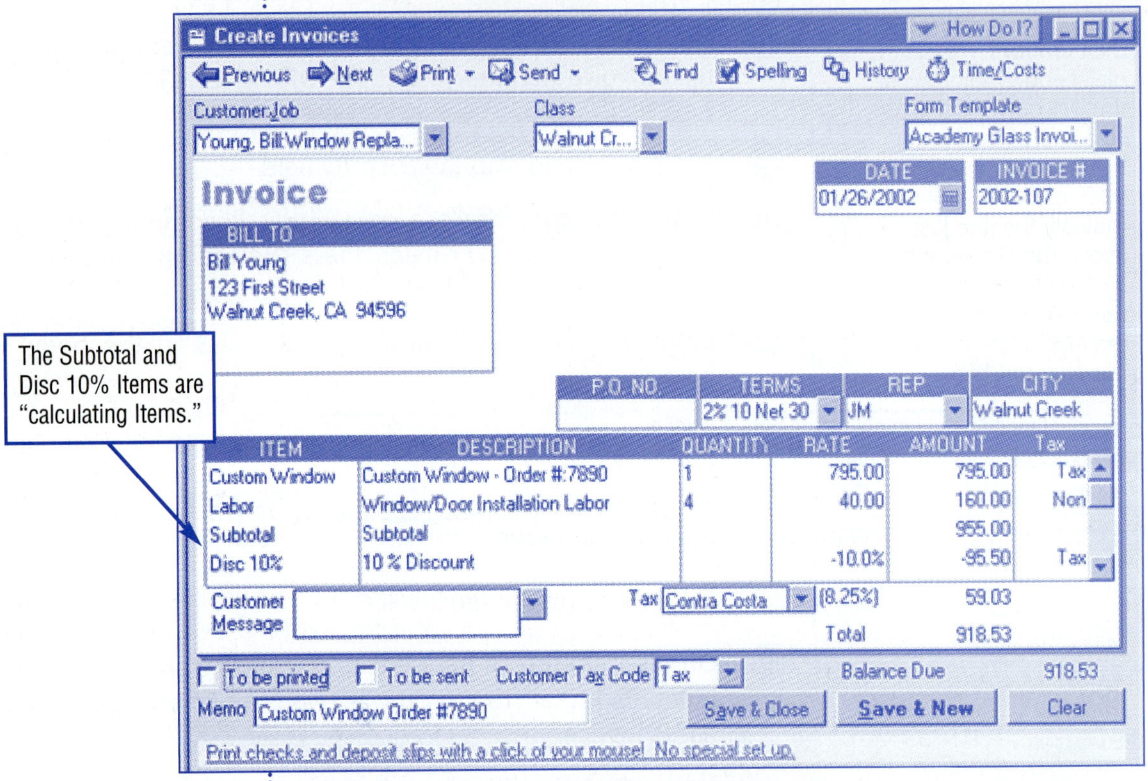

The Subtotal and Disc 10% Items are "calculating Items."

Figure 2-17 Completed Invoice with discount.

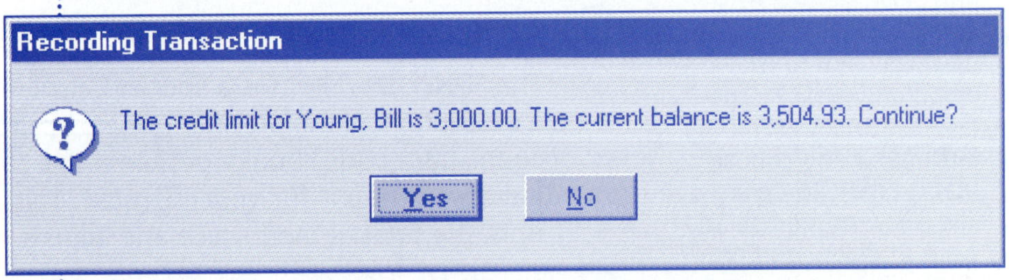

Figure 2-18 The Recording Transaction screen, warning about the customer's credit limit

⑯ When you see the Recording Transaction warning about the customer exceeding his/her credit limit (Figure 2-18), click **Yes**.

Open Invoices Report

Now that you've entered Invoices for your customers, QuickBooks' reports reflect the Invoices that are "open" and the "age" of each Invoice. The Open Invoices report is shown in Figure 2-19.

COMPUTER TUTORIAL

① Select the *Reports* menu, choose **Customers & Receivables**, and then choose **Open Invoices**.

② Set the *Dates* field at the top of the screen to "01/31/2002" and press <TAB>.

③ Verify that your Open Invoices report matches Figure 2-19.

④ Print this report by clicking **Print** at the top of the report screen.

The columns in this report show the *Type* of transaction (mostly Invoices, but there could be some Credit Memos), the *Date* of the transaction, *Number*, *P.O. #*, *Terms*, *Due Date* (calculated by adding the terms to the transaction date), the *Class*, *Aging*, and the *Open Balance* (the amount owed on each Invoice).

⑤ Close the report by clicking the (**X**) in the upper right corner of the screen.

If you see the Memorize Report screen, asking if you want to memorize the report, click **No**. See Chapter 5 for more information about memorized reports.

> **DID YOU KNOW** You can adjust the report columns by dragging the small diamond at the right of the column title to the left (narrowing the columns) or to the right (widening the columns).

Figure 2-19 Open Invoices report

Receiving Payments from Customers

Receiving Payments by Check

To record payments received from your customers and apply the payments to specific Invoices, follow these steps:

1 Select the **Customers** menu, and choose **Receive Payments** (see Figure 2-20).

Figure 2-20 The Receive Payments screen

2 Select "Mason, Bob" from the *Customer:Job* drop-down menu. Then press <TAB>.

After you select the customer name, notice the Applied To: section shows the open Invoices for the customer. Figure 2-21 shows that Bob Mason has three open Invoices. You can see the dates of the Invoices, along with the Invoice number and amount due.

✓	Date	Number	Orig. Amt.	Amt. Due	Payment
	12/18/2001	3947	415.68	415.68	0.00
	01/09/2002	2002-104	2,330.40	2,330.40	0.00
	01/26/2002	2002-106	1,057.75	1,057.75	0.00
		Totals	3,803.83	3,803.83	0.00

Figure 2-21 The unpaid Invoices appear for a selected customer.

3 Enter "1/27/2002" in the *Date* field and press <TAB> (see Figure 2-22).

4 Enter "415.68" in the *Amount* field and press <TAB>.

5 Enter "5256" in the *Check No.* field and press <TAB>.

6 Select "Check" from the *Pmt. Method* drop-down menu, and press <TAB>.

7 Enter "Payment Received - Invoice #3947" in the *Memo* field, and press <TAB>.

When entering a memo, type "Payment Received" followed by the Invoice number. Memos do not affect the application of payments to specific Invoices, but they are helpful in two very important ways. First, if you send your customers statements, only the information in the *Ref./Check No.*, *Date*, and *Memo* fields will show on statements, along with a three letter code (PMT), representing the Payment transaction. Also, if you ever have to go back to the transaction and verify that you've applied the payment to the correct Invoice(s), you'll be able to look at the *Memo* field to see the Invoice(s) to which you *should* have applied the payments.

8 "Group with other undeposited funds" is preselected.

9 In the Applied To: section, Invoice #3947 is preselected.

The checkmark to the left of the Date column indicates the Invoice to which QuickBooks will apply the payment. QuickBooks automatically selected this Invoice because the amount of the customer's check is the same as the unpaid amount of the Invoice. (See *Preferences for Applying Payments* on page 58.) You can deselect the Invoice by clicking on the checkmark. You can then select another Invoice from the list.

NOTE

When One Payment Applies to More than One Invoice
You can apply one check from a customer to multiple Invoices. When you receive payments, you can override the amounts in the Payment column (in the Applied To: section) to apply the payment to Invoices in whatever combination is necessary.

NOTE

If you don't want to apply the entire amount of the customer's check to the pre-selected Invoice, reduce the amount in the Payment column. You can apply the remaining balance of the customer's check to additional Invoices. If you do not, QuickBooks will hold the remaining balance as a credit for the customer.

10 Verify that your screen matches Figure 2-22. If you see errors, correct them.

11 Click **Save & Close** to record the Payment transaction.

Enter the date you received the payment from the customer.

You can manually override any amount in the Payment column.

Figure 2-22 Completed Receive Payments screen

NOTE

Handling Partial Payments If a customer pays only a portion of an Invoice, record the payment as shown in Figure 2-22. Apply the payment to the appropriate Invoice. The Invoice will remain open for the unpaid amount. The next time you use the Receive Payments function for that customer, the Invoice will show, with the remaining amount due. You can record additional payments to the Invoice in the same way as before.

In the last example, Bob Mason paid Invoice #3947 in full on 1/27/2002.

Receiving Payments by Credit Card

The next example shows that Anderson Floors paid off the amount owing on its 2nd Street Job from last year. Anderson Floors used a credit card to pay their Invoice, so this example shows how to receive credit card payments.

1 Select **Customers**, and choose **Receive Payments**.

2 Fill the *Received From*, *Date* and *Amount* fields as shown in Figure 2-23.

3 Leave the *Ref./Check No.* field blank.

4 Enter "American Express" in the *Pmt. Method* field and press <TAB>.

COMPUTER TUTORIAL

(5) Enter "1234-123456-12345" in the *Card No.* field and enter "05/2005" in the *Exp. Date* field.

QuickBooks shows the credit card number with x's in the middle for security purposes.

(6) Enter "Payment Received – Invoice #4003" in the *Memo* field.

(7) The "Group with other undeposited funds" box is preselected.

You select "Group with other undeposited funds" when you process all of the credit cards at the end of the day in a single batch, so you can group all of your credit card receipts onto a single Make Deposit form. If you processed credit card charges individually, you would select "Deposit To" and choose the bank account into which your merchant account service deposits credit card funds.

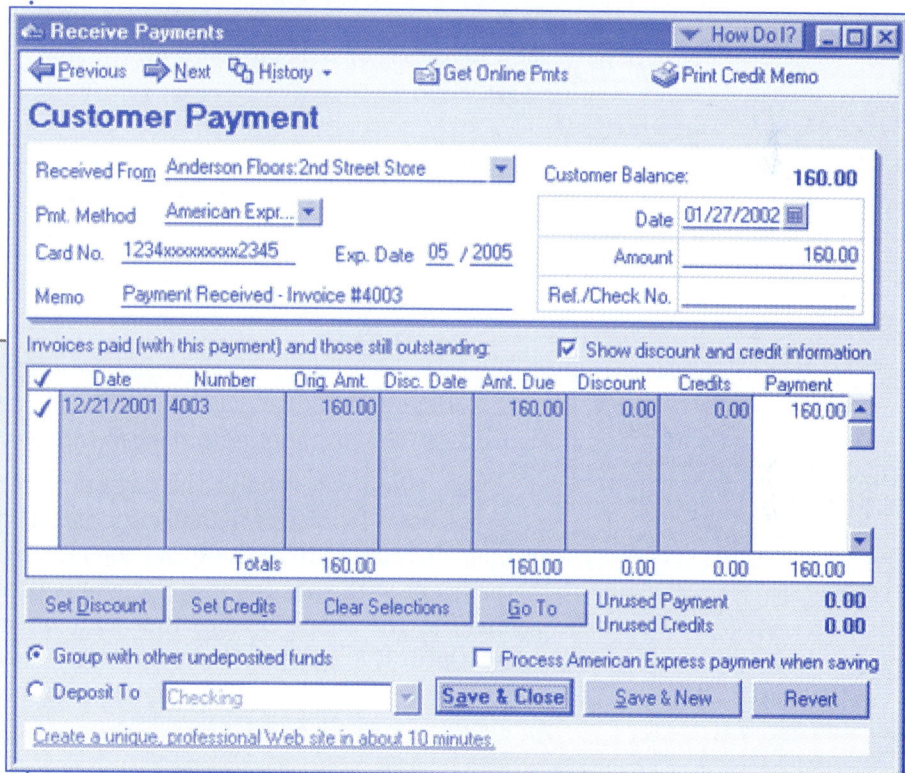

Figure 2-23 Customer Payment by American Express

If you want to keep a record of the customer's credit card information, including card number, expiration date, billing address and billing zip code, enter credit card information into the Payment Info Tab of the Customer or Job record before you process the payment through the Receive Payment screen. When you enter the customer or job name, QuickBooks will enter the credit card information automatically.

(8) Verify that your screen matches Figure 2-23 and click **Save & Close**.

Where Do the Payments Go?

Unless you specifically deselect the "Group with other undeposited funds" in the Receive Payments screen (something that is not recommended), QuickBooks does not increase your bank balance when you receive payments. If it's not clear why this is so, see the section on *Undeposited Funds* on page 47.

Receiving payments reduces the balance in Accounts Receivable (credit) and increases the balance in Undeposited Funds (debit). In order to have your received payments show up in your bank account (and reduce Undeposited Funds), you must choose **Make Deposits** from the *Banking* menu.

Preferences for Applying Payments

As soon as you type in the customer name at the top of the Receive Payments screen and press <TAB>, QuickBooks displays all of the open Invoices for that customer in the lower section of the screen. See Figure 2-24.

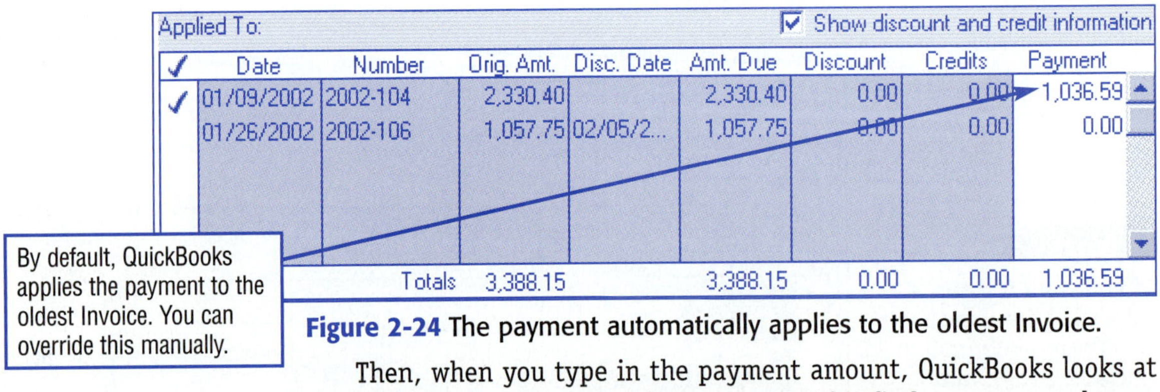

	Date	Number	Orig. Amt.	Disc. Date	Amt. Due	Discount	Credits	Payment
✓	01/09/2002	2002-104	2,330.40		2,330.40	0.00	0.00	1,036.59
	01/26/2002	2002-106	1,057.75	02/05/2...	1,057.75	0.00	0.00	0.00
	Totals		3,388.15		3,388.15	0.00	0.00	1,036.59

Applied To: ☑ Show discount and credit information

By default, QuickBooks applies the payment to the oldest Invoice. You can override this manually.

Figure 2-24 The payment automatically applies to the oldest Invoice.

Then, when you type in the payment amount, QuickBooks looks at all of the open Invoices for that customer. If it finds an amount due on an open Invoice that is the exact amount of the payment, it matches the payment with that Invoice. If there is no such match, it applies the payment to the oldest Invoice first and continues applying to the next oldest until the payment is completely applied. Any partially paid Invoice is held open for the unpaid amount. This is a feature called *Automatically Apply Payments*.

COMPUTER TUTORIAL

To modify QuickBooks so that it DOES NOT automatically apply your payments, you'll need to change the Sales & Customers Company preferences as follows:

① Select the *Edit* menu, and choose **Preferences** (see Figure 2-25).

② Scroll down and click the **Sales & Customers** icon and click the Company Preferences Tab.

③ Uncheck the "Automatically apply payments" box.

With this feature disabled, you'll have to click **Auto Apply** on the Receive Payment screen for each payment you process or specifically apply payments to Invoices by clicking in the column to the left of the Invoice and modifying the amount in the Payment column as necessary.

In most situations, it is faster to use the *Automatically apply payments* feature when receiving payments. However, if your customers regularly pay only part of their open balance, or if they pay more than one Invoice with a single check, the *Automatically apply payments* feature could slow data entry and increase the potential for data entry errors. You will need to decide which option is best for you and set the preference accordingly.

④ Click **Cancel** to discard your changes.

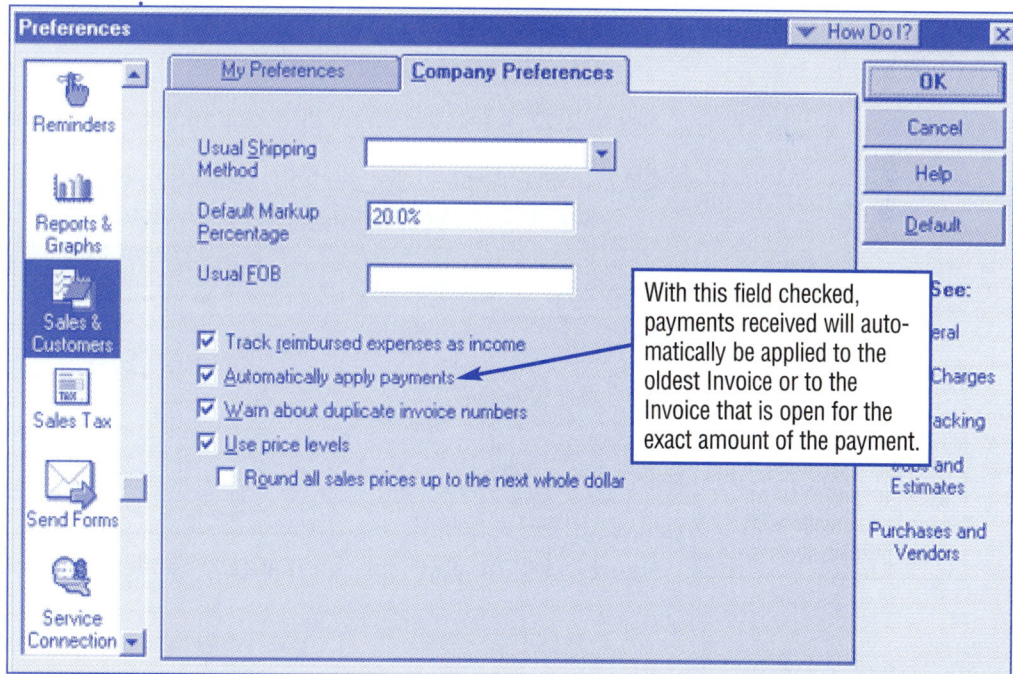

Figure 2-25 Choose a preference to automatically apply payments.

Recording Customer Discounts

What if your customer takes advantage of the discount you offer on your Invoice? In the next example, the payment you receive is less than the face amount of the Invoice because the customer took advantage of the 2% 10 Net 30 discount terms that Academy Glass offers.

COMPUTER TUTORIAL

1   Select the *Customers* menu, and choose **Receive Payments**.

2   Enter all the customer payment information as shown in Figure 2-26.

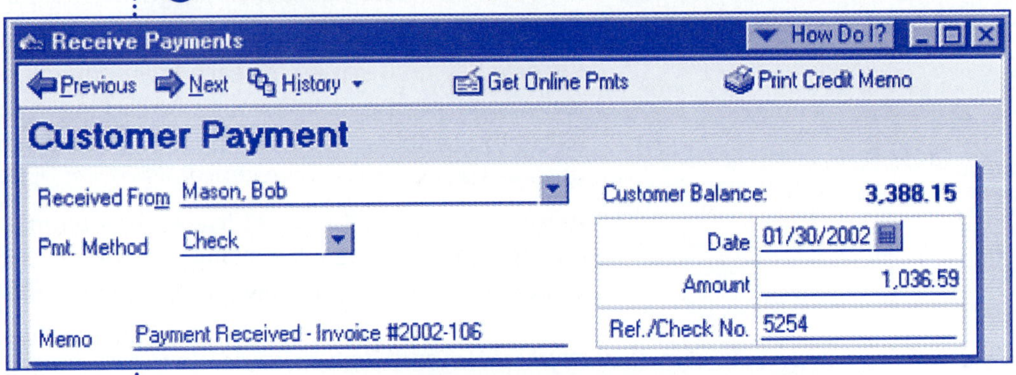

Figure 2-26 Use this data in the Receive Payments screen.

3   Check the "Show discount and credit information" box as shown in Figure 2-27.

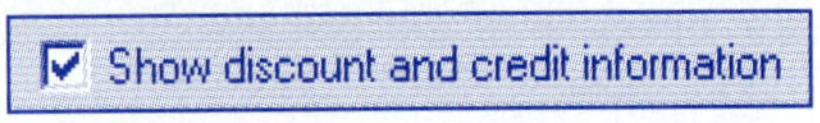

Figure 2-27 Select the Show discount and credit information field.

4   In the Applied To: section, QuickBooks will automatically select the first Invoice listed. Click on Invoice #2002-104 to uncheck it.

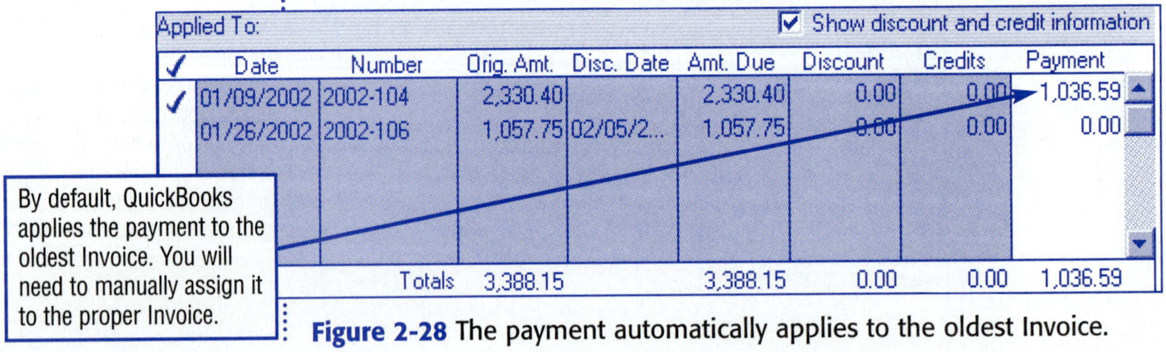

By default, QuickBooks applies the payment to the oldest Invoice. You will need to manually assign it to the proper Invoice.

Figure 2-28 The payment automatically applies to the oldest Invoice.

5 Click to check Invoice #2002-106 (see Figure 2-29) to apply payments correctly. You have now applied the payment to Invoice #2002-106.

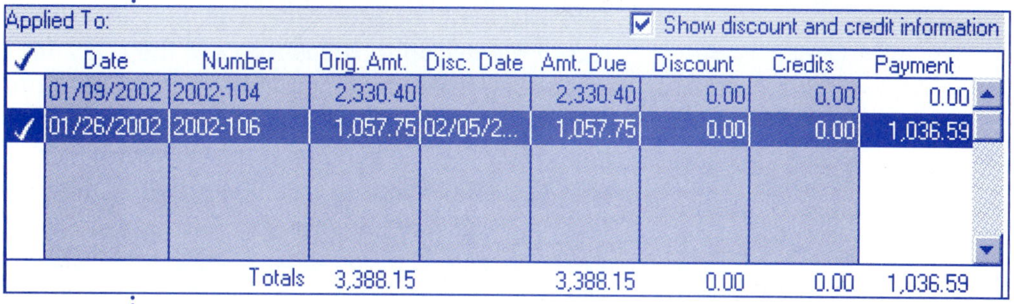

✓	Date	Number	Orig. Amt.	Disc. Date	Amt. Due	Discount	Credits	Payment
	01/09/2002	2002-104	2,330.40		2,330.40	0.00	0.00	0.00
✓	01/26/2002	2002-106	1,057.75	02/05/2...	1,057.75	0.00	0.00	1,036.59
		Totals	3,388.15		3,388.15	0.00	0.00	1,036.59

Applied To: ☑ Show discount and credit information

Figure 2-29 The payment is now applied to the correct Invoice.

6 Since the customer took advantage of the 2%10 Net 30 terms that Academy Glass offered him, you'll need to reduce the amount due by 2%. To apply the discount to this Invoice, click **Set Discount** on the left side of the Receive Payments screen.

QuickBooks automatically calculates a suggested discount based on the terms on the customer's Invoice as shown in Figure 2-30. You can override this amount if necessary.

7 "Sales Discounts" is preselected in the *Discount Account* field. Click **Done**.

The *Discount Account* field is where you assign an income account that tracks the discounts you give to your customers.

After recording the discount, your Receive Payments screen reflects the discounted amount due on the Invoice.

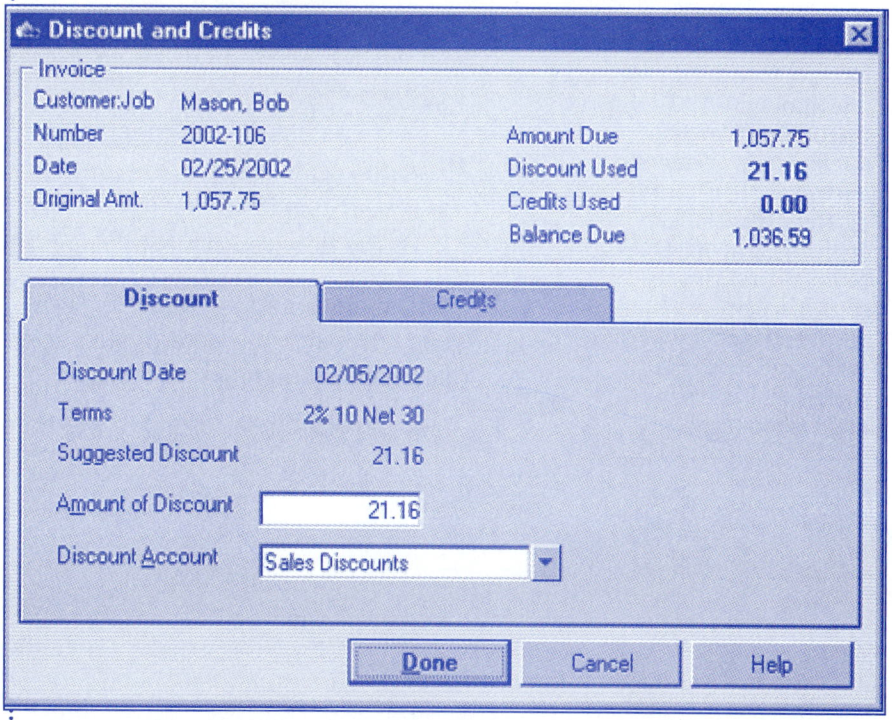

Discount and Credits

Invoice
Customer:Job   Mason, Bob
Number   2002-106   Amount Due   1,057.75
Date   02/25/2002   Discount Used   **21.16**
Original Amt.   1,057.75   Credits Used   **0.00**
                                 Balance Due   1,036.59

Discount | Credits

Discount Date   02/05/2002
Terms   2% 10 Net 30
Suggested Discount   21.16
Amount of Discount   21.16
Discount Account   Sales Discounts

Done   Cancel   Help

Figure 2-30 QuickBooks automatically calculates discounts.

If you use class tracking, you won't be able to assign a class to your discount. In that case, consider using a Credit Memo to record the discount. You can record the class on the Credit Memo just as you do on Invoices. This creates a credit for the customer. Then use the Receive Payments screen and click **Set Credits** to apply your Credit Memo to an open Invoice. For more information about Credit Memos, see *Recording Customer Returns and Credits*, beginning on page 71.

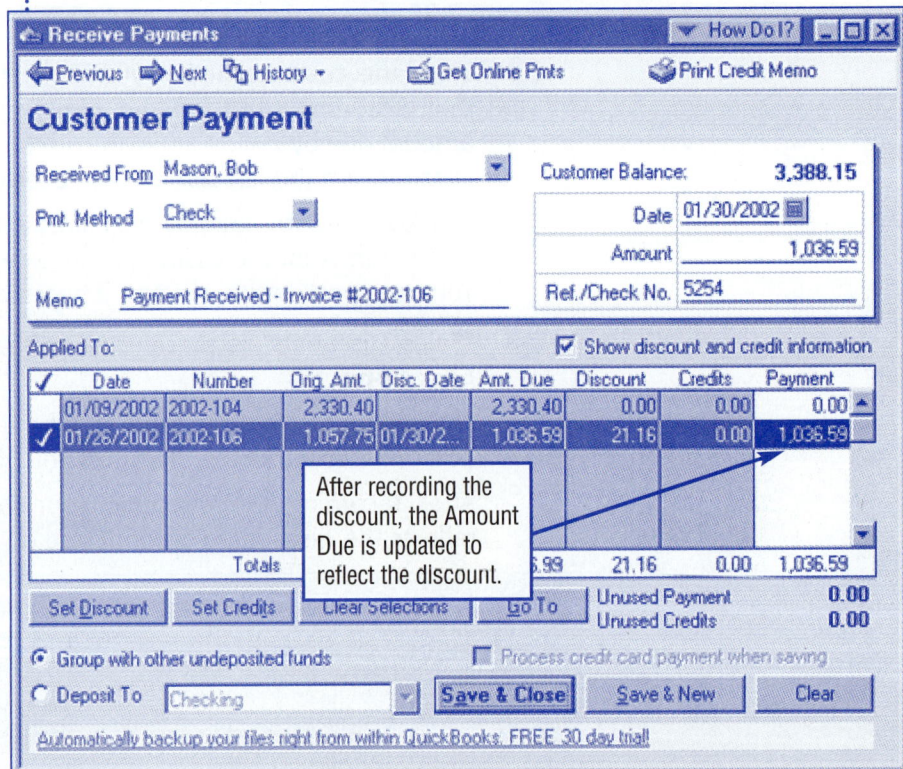

Figure 2-31 The Receive Payments screen after recording the discount.

TIP

If the payment amount doesn't add up exactly to the discounted amount, you'll need to make a choice. If the payment is too high, you could reduce the amount of the discount by lowering the amount in the Discount Info screen. If the payment is too low, you could raise the amount in the Discount Information screen. If the payment amount is significantly different, you can just apply the amount of the payment and either send a statement (if the payment is too low) or send a refund to the customer (if the payment is too high).

8 Verify that your screen matches Figure 2-31. The *Disc. Date* column may not match the date of your screen; instead, it may show the date when you entered the discount.

9 Click **Save & Close** to record the transaction.

Making Bank Deposits

As you receive payments from customers using the Sales Receipts and Receive Payments screens, you will probably post these payments to a special QuickBooks account called Undeposited Funds. When you are ready to deposit these payments into your bank, you will transfer the money from the Undeposited Funds account to the appropriate bank account. As you will see in this section, QuickBooks provides a special screen (the Payments to Deposit screen) to assist you with this transfer.

As you will probably receive payments from your customers in several different ways (checks, cash, and credit cards), you'll want to transfer these different kinds of receipts from Undeposited Funds to your bank accounts separately. Doing so will make your deposits in QuickBooks match what actually takes place at your bank. You will therefore group the checks and cash together and the MasterCard and VISA credit card receipts together. Then you will enter the American Express, Discover, and other credit card receipts separately.

Depositing Checks and Cash

COMPUTER TUTORIAL

1 Select the *Banking* menu, and choose **Make Deposits**.

Since you have funds stored in the Undeposited Funds account, QuickBooks displays the Payments to Deposit screen.

TIP

Deposit all of the checks and cash separately from your credit card receipts. This makes it easier to reconcile your bank statement.

2 Click on the last three lines (all of the checks) as shown in Figure 2-32.

A checkmark in the column on the left indicates that QuickBooks will include the payment (check, cash, or credit card) on the deposit.

3 Click **OK**. The Make Deposits screen opens.

✓	Date	Type	No.	Pmt Meth	Name	Amount
	01/27/2002	PMT		American E	Anderson Floors:2	160.00
✓	01/25/2002	RCPT	2002-1(	Check	Johnson, Helen	645.01
✓	01/27/2002	PMT	5256	Check	Mason, Bob	415.68
✓	01/30/2002	PMT	5254	Check	Mason, Bob	1,036.59

Select the payments you want to deposit, and then click OK.

OK | Cancel | Help | Select All | Select None

Select each check that is to be deposited. Notice the American Express charge is **not** selected here. We'll create a separate deposit for the credit card receipts.

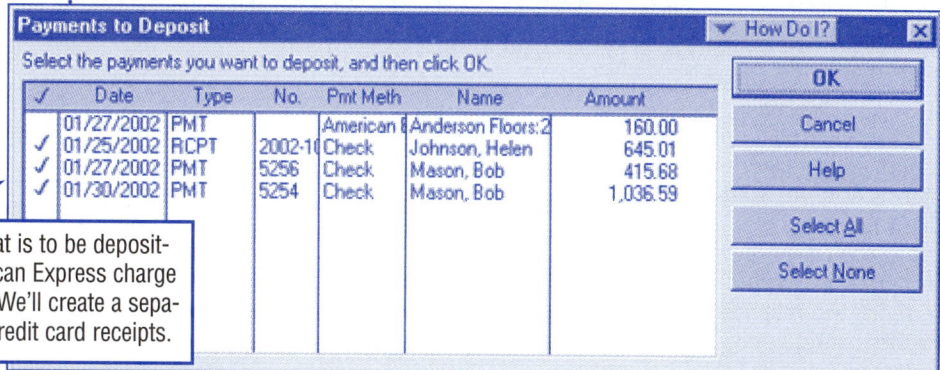

Figure 2-32 Select the payments to deposit.

④ The "Checking" account is preselected in the *Deposit To* field. This is the bank account into which you need to deposit these funds (see Figure 2-33).

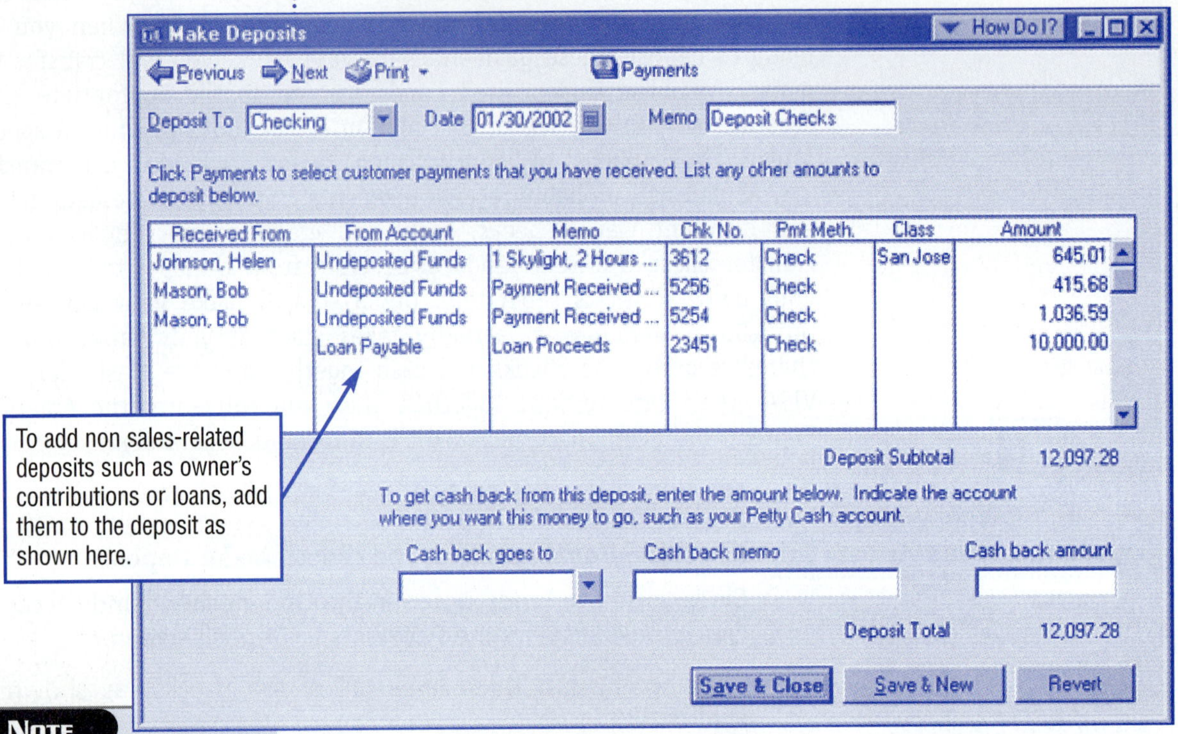

To add non sales-related deposits such as owner's contributions or loans, add them to the deposit as shown here.

The From Account column on the Make Deposits screen shows the account that the deposit is coming "from." In the deposit transaction in Figure 2-33, the checking account will increase (with a debit) by the total of the deposit ($12,097.28). All of the customer checks are coming from the Undeposited Funds account, and the loan proceeds are coming from the Loan Payable account. This will decrease (credit) the balance in Undeposited Funds and increase (credit) the balance in the Loan Payable account.

Figure 2-33 The Make Deposits screen

⑤ Enter "1/30/2002" in the *Date* field and press <TAB>.

⑥ Enter "Deposit Checks" in the *Memo* field and press <TAB>.

⑦ Here we will add another non sales-related items to the deposit, as follows:

On the first blank line of the From Account column, enter "Loan Payable" and press <TAB>.

Enter "Loan Proceeds" in the Memo column and press <TAB>.

Enter "23451" in the Chk No. column and press <TAB>.

Enter "Check" in the Pmt Meth. column and press <TAB>.

Press <TAB> to skip the Class column.

Enter "10,000.00" in the Amount column.

⑧ Click **Save & Close** to record the deposit.

Holding Cash Back from Deposits

If you hold cash back when you make your deposits to the bank, fill in the bottom part of the deposit slip indicating the account to which you want QuickBooks to post the transaction (see Figure 2-34).

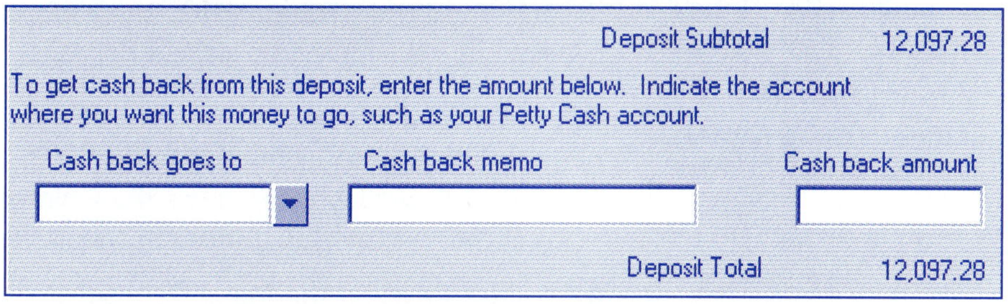

	Deposit Subtotal	12,097.28

To get cash back from this deposit, enter the amount below. Indicate the account where you want this money to go, such as your Petty Cash account.

Cash back goes to	Cash back memo	Cash back amount
▼		

	Deposit Total	12,097.28

Figure 2-34 The bottom of the deposit slip deals with cash back.

There are two ways of tracking cash back from deposits. If you're holding back $20.00 from the deposit so that you can buy some office supplies, you could enter "Office Supplies Expense" in the Cash back goes to field. QuickBooks will increase (debit) Office Supplies Expense. Then enter a memo that describes what you plan to purchase, and enter $20.00 in the *Cash back amount* field.

On the other hand, if you routinely hold back large amounts from your deposits that you use for several different purchases, you should set up a new QuickBooks bank account called Petty Cash and enter that account in the *Cash back goes to* field. QuickBooks will increase (debit) the balance in the Petty Cash account. The Petty Cash account is not really a bank account, but it's an account where you can track all your cash expenditures. For more information on tracking your Petty Cash, see *Tracking Petty Cash* starting on page 164.

COMPUTER TUTORIAL

Printing Deposit Slips

QuickBooks can print deposit slips on MICR-encoded deposit slips. ("MICR" refers to the special ink that banks use for checks and deposit slips.)

To make this feature work for you, you'll need to order preprinted deposit slips from Intuit. With these deposit slips, you can print a deposit slip each time you make a deposit.

① Display the last deposit transaction by selecting the *Banking* menu and choosing **Make Deposits**.

Click **Cancel** when you see the Payments to Deposit screen. Then click the **Previous** button on the Make Deposits screen.

② Click **Print** on the Make Deposits screen (see Figure 2-35).

③ Select "Deposit slip and deposit summary" on the screen shown in Figure 2-36 and click **OK**.

Normally, you would load the preprinted deposit slips into the printer before printing. However, since you won't have deposit slips in class, you'll print on blank paper.

TIP

Even if you don't have any pre-printed deposit slips, it's still a good idea to keep a printed record of your deposits. In that case, you would select "Deposit summary only" on the Print Deposit screen shown in Figure 2-36. Then you would continue with the rest of the steps.

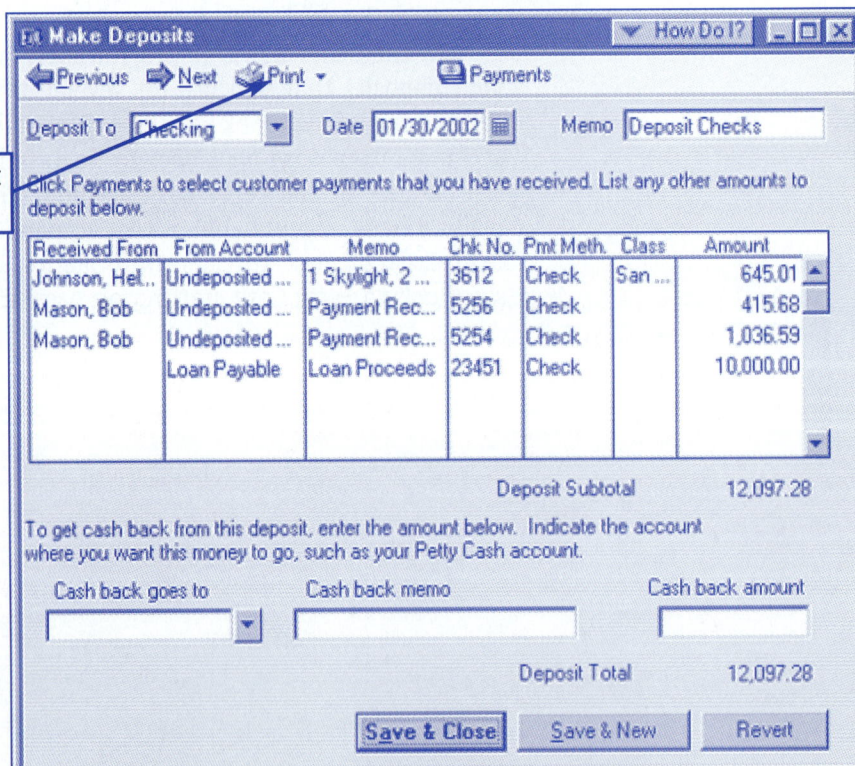

To print the deposit slip, click Print.

Figure 2-35 From the Make Deposits screen, click Print.

Print Deposit [x]

What would you like to print?

○ Deposit slip and deposit summary

○ Deposit summary only

[OK]

[Cancel]

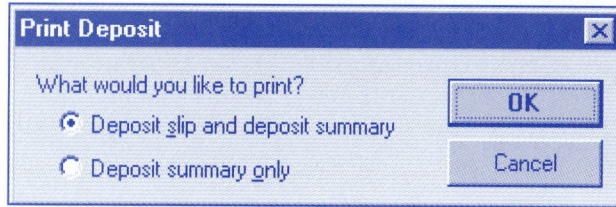

Figure 2-36 The Print Deposit screen for deposit slips

4   Check the settings on the Print Deposits Slips screen shown in Figure 2-37.

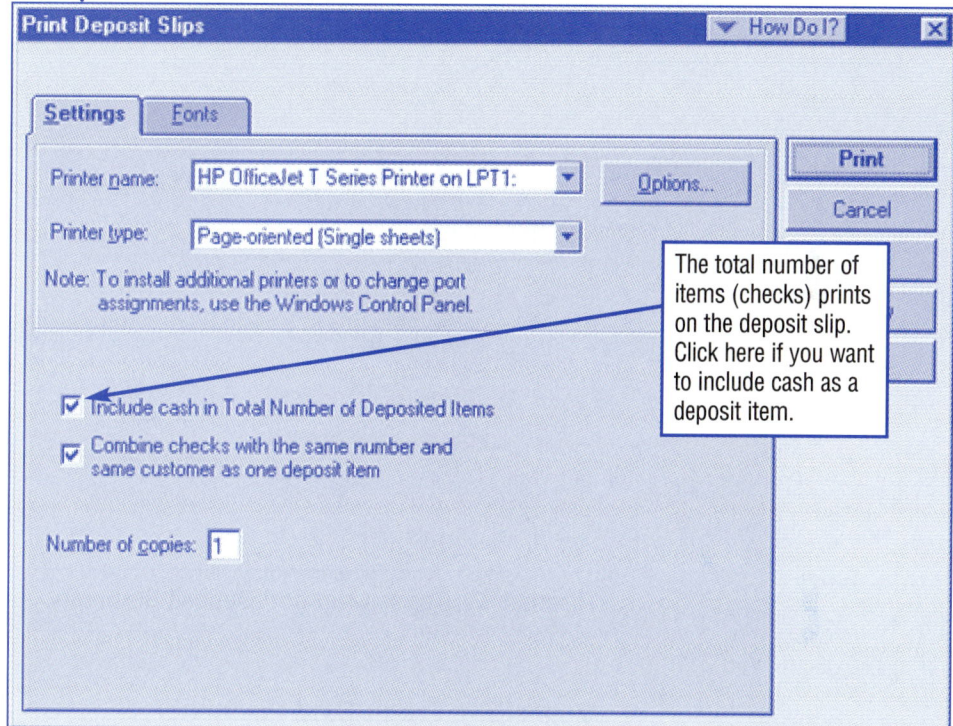

Print Deposit Slips   ▼ How Do I?   [x]

| Settings | Fonts |

Printer name: HP OfficeJet T Series Printer on LPT1:   ▼   [Options...]

[Print]

[Cancel]

Printer type: Page-oriented (Single sheets)   ▼

Note: To install additional printers or to change port assignments, use the Windows Control Panel.

The total number of items (checks) prints on the deposit slip. Click here if you want to include cash as a deposit item.

☑ Include cash in Total Number of Deposited Items

☑ Combine checks with the same number and same customer as one deposit item

Number of copies: [1]

Figure 2-37 Check the settings on the Print Deposit Slips screen.

Select your printer in the *Printer name* field. There is no need to change the *Printer type* field. The "Include cash in Total Number of Deposited Items" checkbox causes QuickBooks to include the cash you deposit (if any) as a separate Item on the deposit slip.

⑤ Click **Print** to print the deposit slip (see Figure 2-38).

645.01

415.68

1,036.59

10,000.00

1/30/2002   12,097.28

> Deposit slips are perforated to help you separate the top part (for the bank) from the part you keep.

04                              $12,097.28

Deposit Summary   3/12/2002

Summary of Deposits to Checking on 01/30/2002

Chk No.	PmtMethod	Rcd From	Memo	Amount
3612	Check	Johnson, Helen	1 Skylight, 2 Hours Design	645.01
5256	Check	Mason, Bob	Payment Received - Invoice #3947	415.68
5254	Check	Mason, Bob	Payment Received - Invoice #2002-...	1,036.59
23451	Check		Loan Proceeds	10,000.00
			Deposit Subtotal:	12,097.28
			Less Cash Back:	
			Deposit Total:	12,097.28

Figure 2-38 Deposit slip and Deposit Summary

Depositing Credit Card Payments

To ensure that your bank reconciliations go smoothly, you should always deposit your checks and cash separately from your credit cards payments. That way, the total of each type of deposit (Checks & Cash, VISA and MasterCard, and American Express, Discover and other credit cards) will match with the actual deposit on your bank statement. Deposit Visa and MasterCard together and deposit American Express, Discover and any others separately.

COMPUTER TUTORIAL

① Select the *Banking* menu, and choose **Make Deposits**. The Payments to Deposit screen opens.

② Click in the left column on the line to select the American Express receipt (see Figure 2-39) for the next deposit. Then click **OK**. The Make Deposits screen opens.

③ The "Checking" account is preselected in the *Deposit to* field. Press <TAB>.

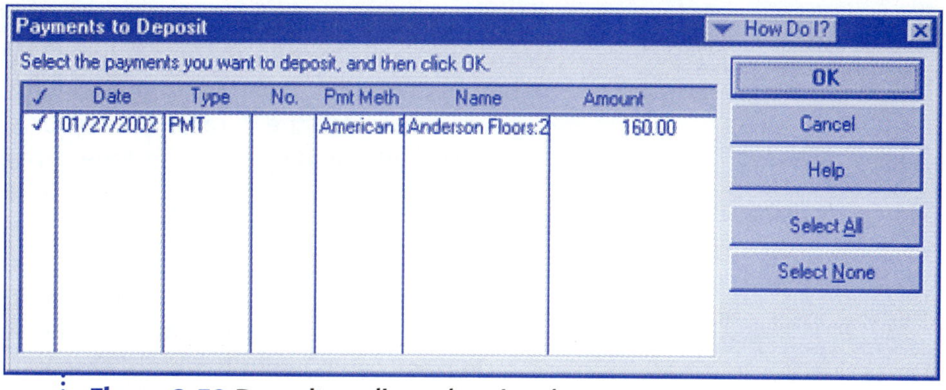

Payments to Deposit

Select the payments you want to deposit, and then click OK.

✓	Date	Type	No.	Pmt Meth	Name	Amount
✓	01/27/2002	PMT		American E	Anderson Floors:2	160.00

OK
Cancel
Help
Select All
Select None

Figure 2-39 Deposit credit cards using the Payments to Deposit screen.

④ Enter "01/30/2002" in the *Date* field, and press <TAB>.

⑤ Enter "Deposit American Exp" in the *Memo* field. Do not record the deposit at this time. You will use this deposit in the next section.

As stated earlier, make sure you group together receipts in a way that agrees to the actual deposits made to your bank. This is a critical step in making your bank reconciliation process go smoothly.

⑥ On the first blank line on the deposit slip, enter "Bankcard Fees" in the From Account column, and then press <TAB>.

You will enter this line if your credit card processing company (or your bank) charges a discount fee on each credit card deposit rather than monthly.

⑦ Enter "Discount Fee" in the Memo column and press <TAB>.

⑧ Press <TAB> to skip the Chk NO column.

⑨ Enter "American Express" in the Pmt Meth. column and press <TAB>.

⑩ Enter "Walnut Creek" in the Class column and press <TAB>.

⑪ Enter "160.00 * -.02" in the Amount column and press <ENTER>. You can use the QuickMath feature to enter the discount fee directly on the Make Deposit screen.

QuickMath is a feature that helps you add, subtract, multiply, or divide in any QuickBooks *Amount* field. When you enter the first number (160.00), it shows normally in the Amount column. Then when you enter the * (asterisk key or <Shift+8>), QuickMath shows a little adding machine tape on your screen (see Figure 2-40). Continue typing your formula for recording the discount fee. If the discount is 2%, enter "-.02" (minus point zero two) and press <ENTER>. The result of the calculation (-3.20) shows in the Amount column. **The minus sign makes the result a negative number and reduces the amount of your deposit.** This also increases (debits) your Bankcard Discounts Expense account.

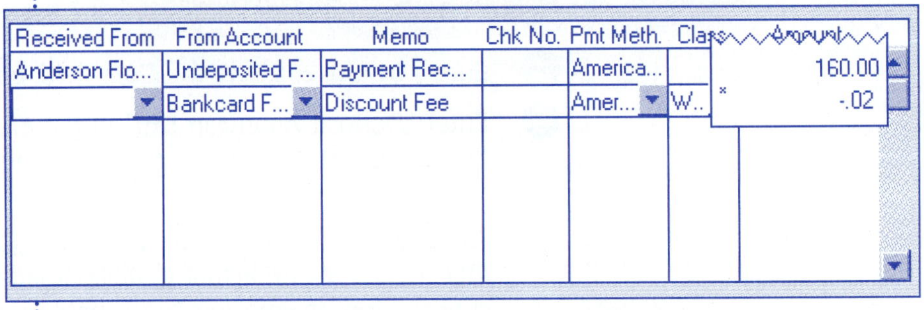

Received From	From Account	Memo	Chk No.	Pmt Meth.	Class	Amount
Anderson Flo...	Undeposited F...	Payment Rec...		America...		160.00
	Bankcard F...	Discount Fee		Amer...	W...	-.02

Figure 2-40 An adding machine tape appears when you do QuickMath.

⑫ Verify that your screen matches Figure 2-41. Click **Save & Close** to record the deposit.

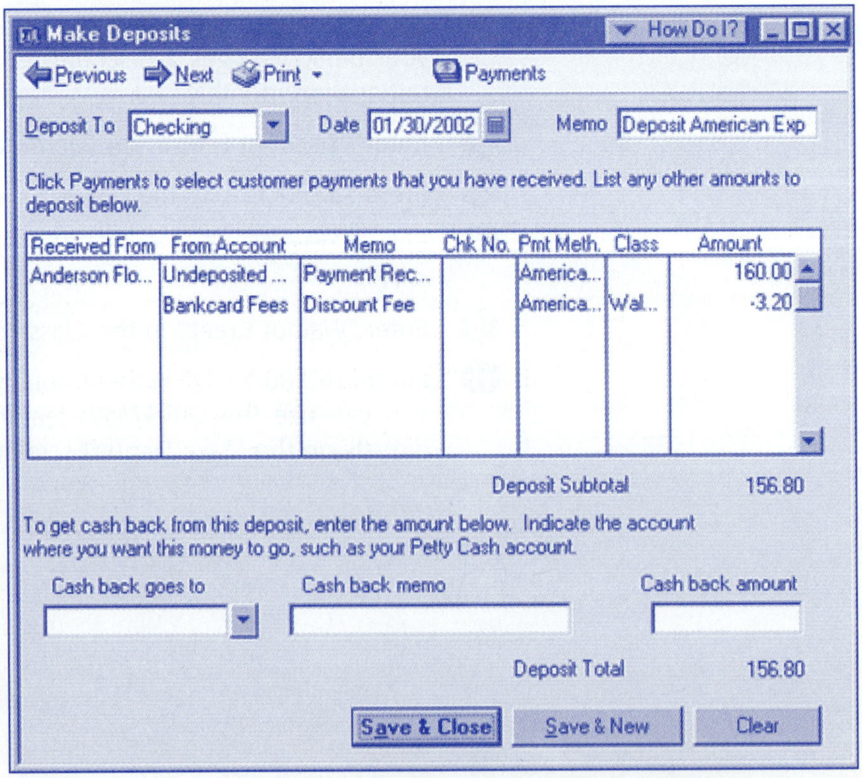

Figure 2-41 The Make Deposits screen after a credit card deposit

Now that you've entered your deposits, the checking account register shows each deposit. In Figure 2-42, you can see the two deposit transactions at the bottom of the register. The "-split-" on each of the deposits means that there is more than one account (or line) in the deposits. To see the detail of a deposit, select the transaction in the register and click the **Edit Transaction** icon at the top of the register.

To display the Checking register, select the *Company* menu and choose **Chart of Accounts** (or press <Ctrl+A>) and then double-click on the Checking account.

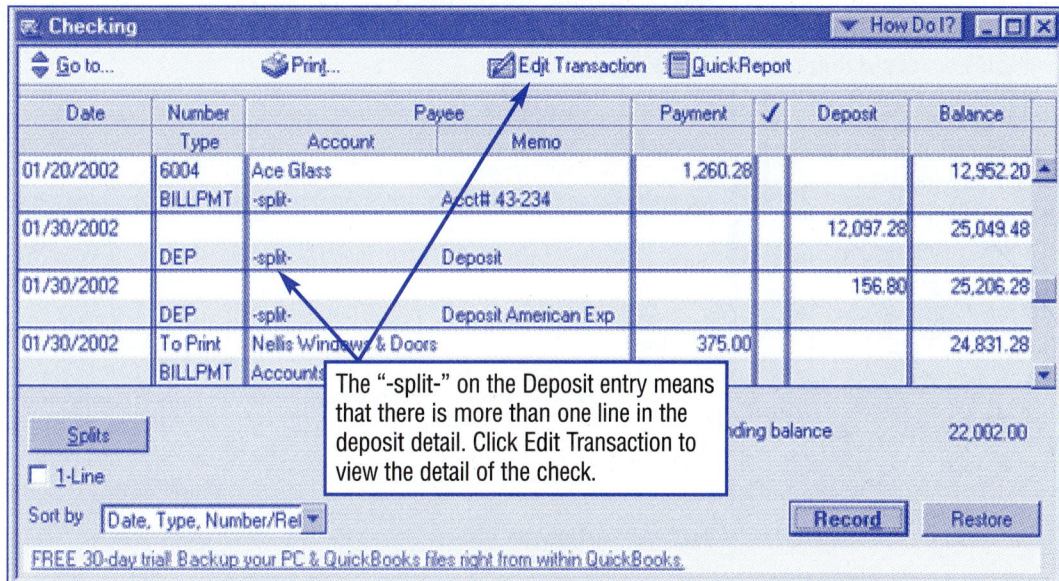

Figure 2-42 The Checking register after entering deposits

RECORDING CUSTOMER RETURNS AND CREDITS

To record customer returns or credits, use QuickBooks Credit Memos. Credit Memos are used for the following situations:

◆ To record a return of merchandise from a customer.

◆ To record a credit-on-account for a customer.

◆ To issue a refund check to a customer.

In this example, Bill Young canceled an order that Academy Glass recorded on Invoice 2002-107. Since that Invoice shows in your books as unpaid, you could just void or delete the Invoice, but accounting conventions dictate that instead of deleting the Invoice, you should add a new transaction (a Credit Memo) to your books to record the cancellation. Then you'll need to apply the credit to the open Invoice.

COMPUTER TUTORIAL

❶ Select the *Customers* menu, and choose **Create Credit Memos/Refunds**.

Credit Memos look similar to Invoices, but they perform the opposite function. That is, a Credit Memo reduces (credits) Accounts Receivable and reduces (debits) Sales. See Figure 2-43.

KEY TERM

Credit Memos are sales forms that reduce the amount that a customer owes the company. They work exactly opposite to an Invoice in that they reduce (credit) Accounts Receivable and reduce (debit) income and sales tax. Use Credit Memos to record returns of merchandise, or courtesy discounts being applied to previously recorded Invoices.

2 Select "Young, Bill:Window Replacement" from the *Customer:Job* drop-down list and press <TAB>.

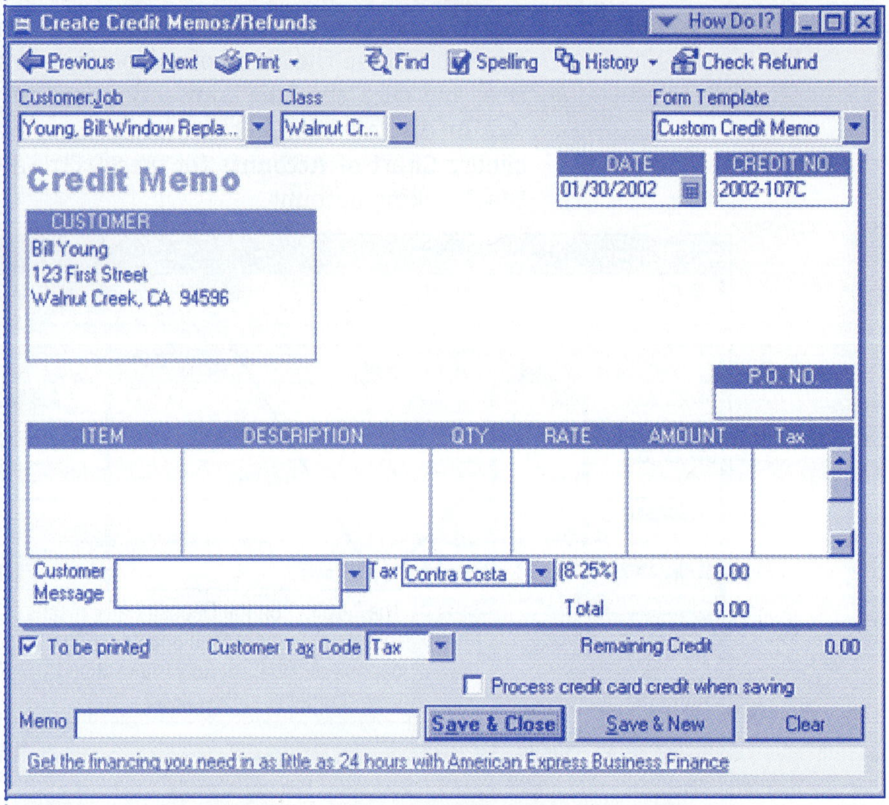

Figure 2-43 The Create Credit Memos/Refunds screen

3 Enter "Walnut Creek" in the *Class* field and press <TAB>.

4 "Custom Credit Memo" is preselected in the *Form Template* field. Press <TAB>.

5 Enter "1/30/2002" in the *DATE* field and press <TAB>.

6 Enter "2002-107C" in the *CREDIT NO.* field and press <TAB>.

This credit transaction is included on statements and customer reports, so using the Invoice number followed by a "C" in the *CREDIT NO.* field helps your customers to connect this credit memo to the Invoice.

7 Enter the data shown in Figure 2-44 into the body of the Credit Memo.

ITEM	DESCRIPTION	QTY	RATE	AMOUNT	Tax
Custom Window	Custom Window - Order #:7890	1	795.00	795.00	Tax
Labor	Window/Door Installation Labor	4	40.00	160.00	Non
Subtotal	Subtotal			955.00	
Disc 10%	10 % Discount		-10.0%	-95.50	Tax

Customer Message | Tax Contra Costa (8.25%) 59.03

Total 918.53

☑ To be printed Customer Tax Code Tax Remaining Credit 918.53

Figure 2-44 Enter this data in the body of the Credit Memo.

8 Enter "Refund - Custom Window Order #7890" in the *Memo* field.

9 Verify that all of the data on your screen matches Figure 2-43 and Figure 2-44. Click **Save & Close** to record the Credit Memo.

Customer Open Balance Report

Now, create a Customer Open Balance report to ensure that the Credit Memo shows for this customer.

1 Select the *Lists* menu, and choose **Customer:Job List** (or press <Ctrl+J>).

2 Select the "Window Replacement" job in the Customer:Job List as shown in Figure 2-45.

Name	Balance	Notes	Job Status	Estimate Total
◇Johnson, Helen	0.00			
◇Leonard, Jerry	0.00			0.00
◇Mason, Bob	2,330.40		In progress	0.00
◇Nelson, Carl	0.00			
◇Pelligrini Builders	0.00			0.00
◇2354 Wilkes Rd	0.00			0.00
◇4266 Lake Drive	0.00		Closed	0.00
◇Young, Bill	2,586.40			0.00
◇Window Replacement	2,586.40		Awarded	

Customer:Job | Activities | Reports | ☐ Show All

QuickReport: Window Replacement Ctrl+Q
Open Balance: Window Replacement
Show Estimates: Window Replacement

Figure 2-45 Selected job and report in Customer:Job List.

3 At the bottom of the Customer:Job List screen, click *Reports* and choose **Open Balance:Window Replacement** (see Figure 2-45).

4 Notice that the Credit Memo shows with a negative balance of 918.53 and the Invoice shows with an offsetting positive balance of 918.53. Click the (**X**) at the top right of the screen to close the report.

Figure 2-46 Customer Open Balance report.

Applying a Credit Memo to an Invoice

COMPUTER TUTORIAL

1. Select the **Customers** menu, and choose **Receive Payments**.

2. Enter "Young,Bill:Window Replacement" in the *Customer:Job* field, and press <TAB>.

3. Enter "01/31/2002" in the *Date* field.

4. DO NOT enter an amount in the *Amount* field.

5. Verify that the "Show discount and credit information" box is preselected.

6. Select Invoice #2002-107 by clicking on the Invoice's row, in any column *except* the Check column to the left of the Invoice date. QuickBooks will highlight the Invoice after you have selected it (see Figure 2-47).

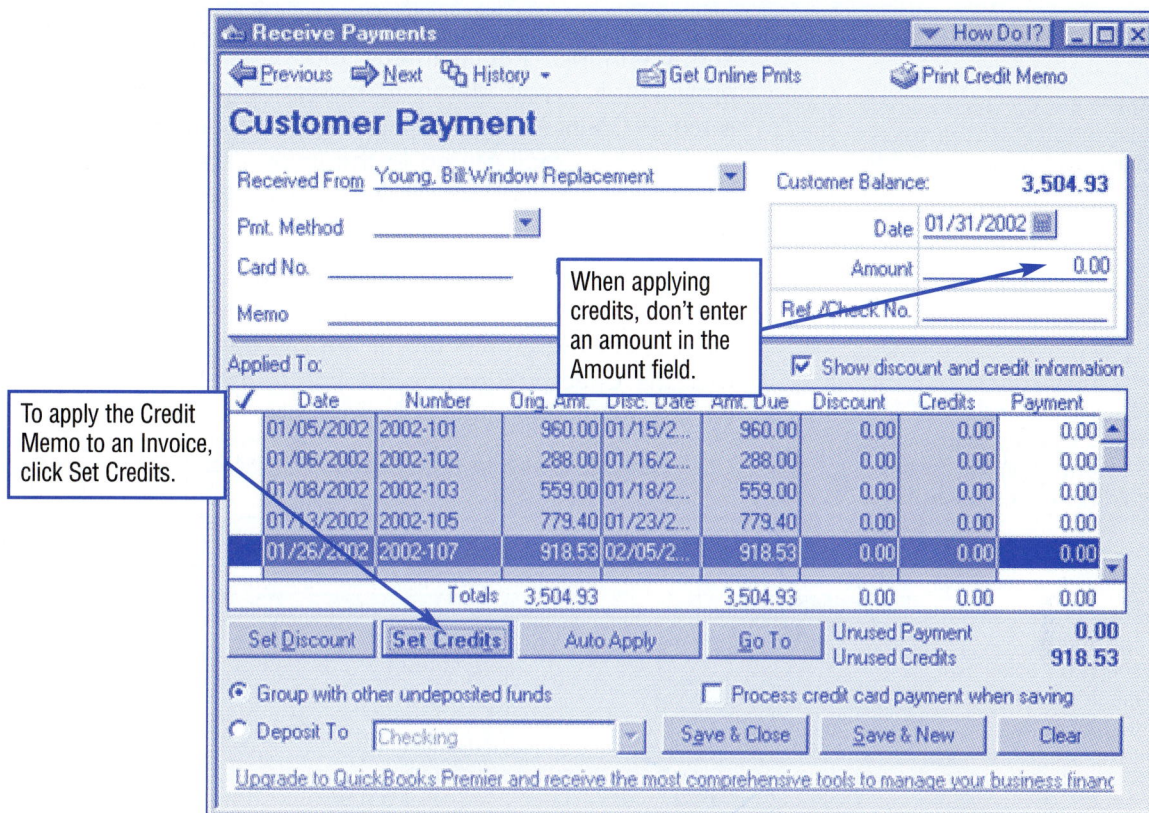

Figure 2-47 Receive Payments screen with Invoice selected

7 Click **Set Credits** and verify that QuickBooks applied Credit Memo #2002-107C to Invoice #2002-107 (see Figure 2-48). Click **Done**.

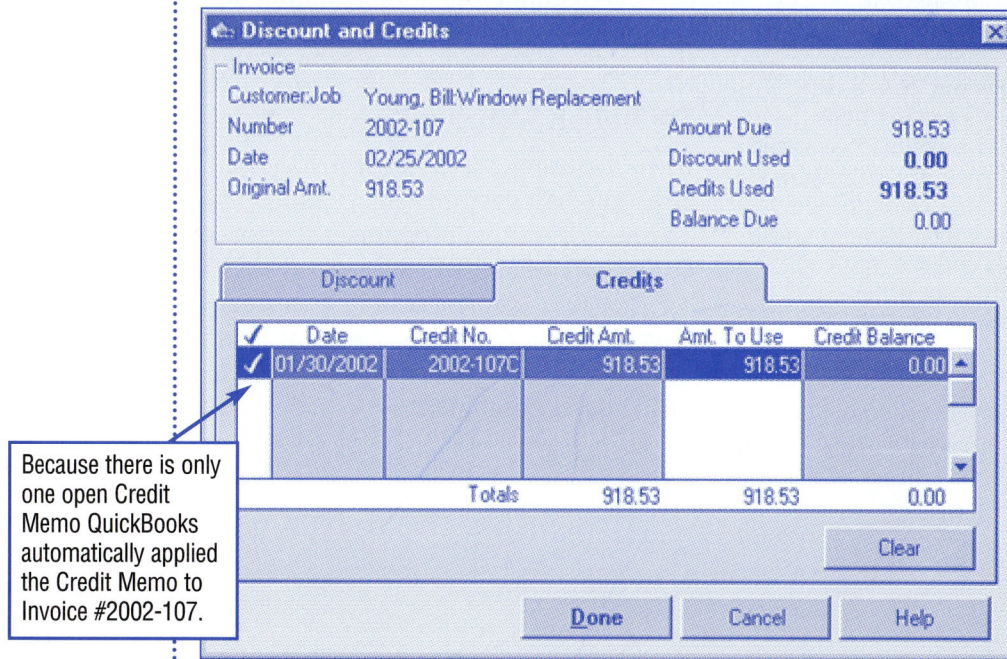

Figure 2-48 The Credits Tab of the Discounts and Credits screen

Since there is only one open (unapplied) Credit Memo for Bill Young:Window Replacement job, QuickBooks automatically applied the Credit Memo to Invoice #2002-107. If there were multiple Credit Memos for this job, QuickBooks would have auto-applied this Credit Memo to the Invoice using the same criteria as explained in *Preferences for Applying Payments* on page 58.

If the amount of the Credit Memo does not match the amount of the Invoice, or if the auto-apply feature is turned off, you may need to manually apply the Credit Memo to the appropriate Invoice. On the Credits tab of the Discounts and Credits screen, click the Check column on the line of the Invoice to which you wish to apply the credit.

8 Click **Save & Close** to apply the Credit Memo to the Invoice.

QuickBooks now shows the amount of the Credit Memo in the Credits column.

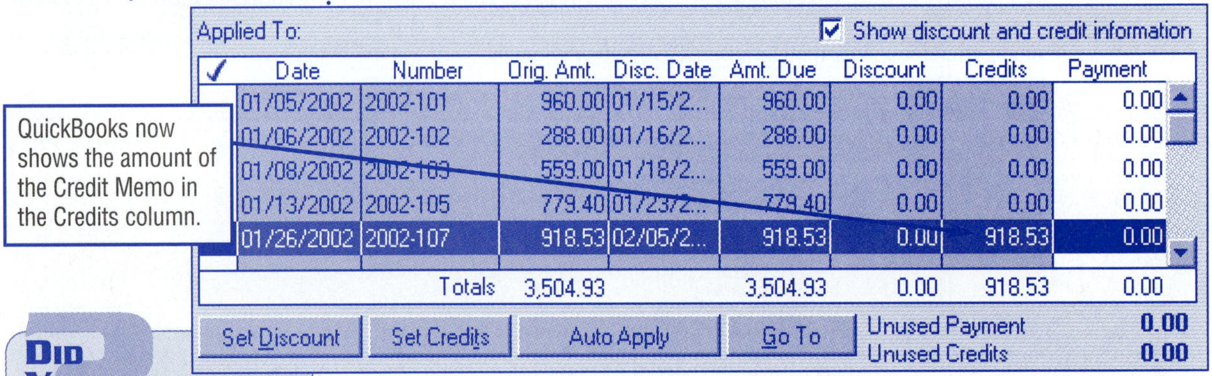

✓	Date	Number	Orig. Amt.	Disc. Date	Amt. Due	Discount	Credits	Payment
	01/05/2002	2002-101	960.00	01/15/2...	960.00	0.00	0.00	0.00
	01/06/2002	2002-102	288.00	01/16/2...	288.00	0.00	0.00	0.00
	01/08/2002	2002-103	559.00	01/18/2...	559.00	0.00	0.00	0.00
	01/13/2002	2002-105	779.40	01/23/2...	779.40	0.00	0.00	0.00
	01/26/2002	2002-107	918.53	02/05/2...	918.53	0.00	918.53	0.00
	Totals		3,504.93		3,504.93	0.00	918.53	0.00

Applied To: ☑ Show discount and credit information

Set Discount   Set Credits   Auto Apply   Go To   Unused Payment   0.00
Unused Credits   0.00

Figure 2-49 Applied To: section of Receive Payments screen with Credit Memo applied

Refunding Customers

When a customer pays for merchandise and then returns the merchandise, you may need to send a refund check to your customer. You may also need to refund a customer if they request a discount on merchandise or services for which they have already paid.

The first step in issuing a customer refund is to create a Credit Memo showing the detail of what is being refunded. Typically, the detail will include the products and/or services returned or discounted, in exchange for a refund.

If the customer paid with cash or check, you will need to issue a refund check. If the customer paid with a credit card, you will need to credit the customer's credit card account.

Refunding by Check

COMPUTER TUTORIAL

1 Select the *Customers* menu, and choose **Create Credit Memos/Refunds**.

2 Fill in the top portion of the Credit Memo to match Figure 2-50.

Figure 2-50 Fill in the top portion of the Credit Memo.

3 In the body of the Credit Memo, enter each Item shown in Figure 2-51.

Use the "Restocking" Item to reduce the amount of the refund. The "Restocking" Item is an Other Charge Item with a price of "-10%". To learn more about setting up *Other Charge Items, see Other Charge Items* beginning on page 92.

> **IMPORTANT**
>
> You may also need to issue a refund to a customer if his/her payment exceeds the total amount of his/her Accounts Receivable balance. In this case, do not enter anything in the body of the Credit Memo as shown in Figure 2-51. Instead, you would create a Credit Memo with the top portion filled in as shown in Figure 2-50, then skip directly to Step 4 of this Tutorial.

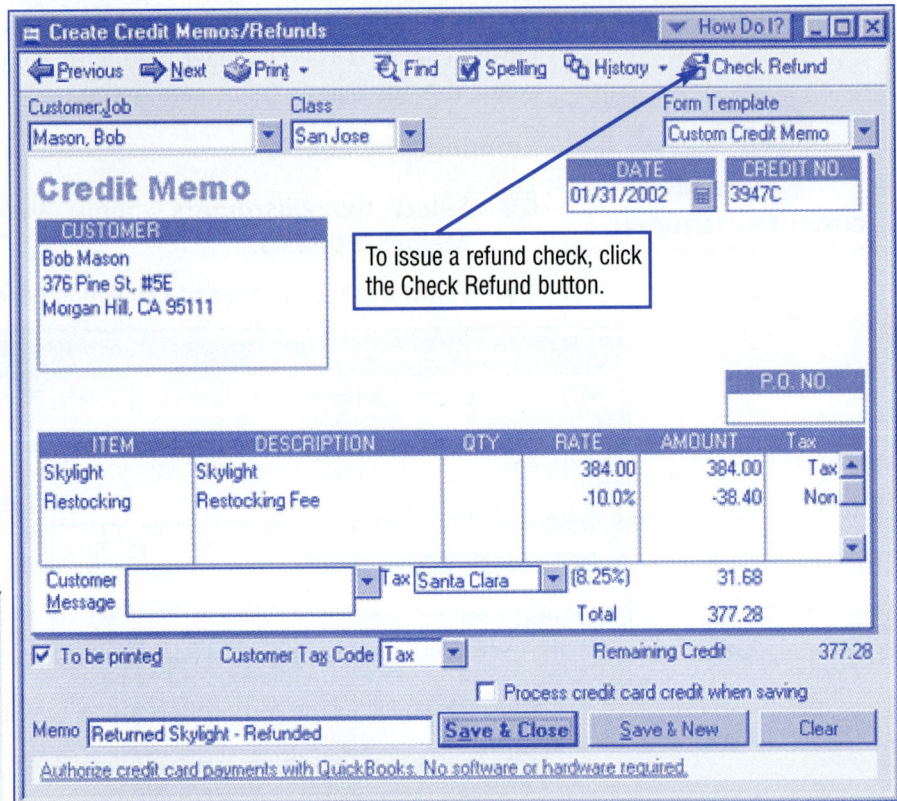

Figure 2-51 Use this data for the Credit Memo.

NOTE

If you're refunding a customer who previously overpaid, the check amount won't be filled in automatically. You'll need to enter the amount of the refund manually. Leave everything else on the check as it is.

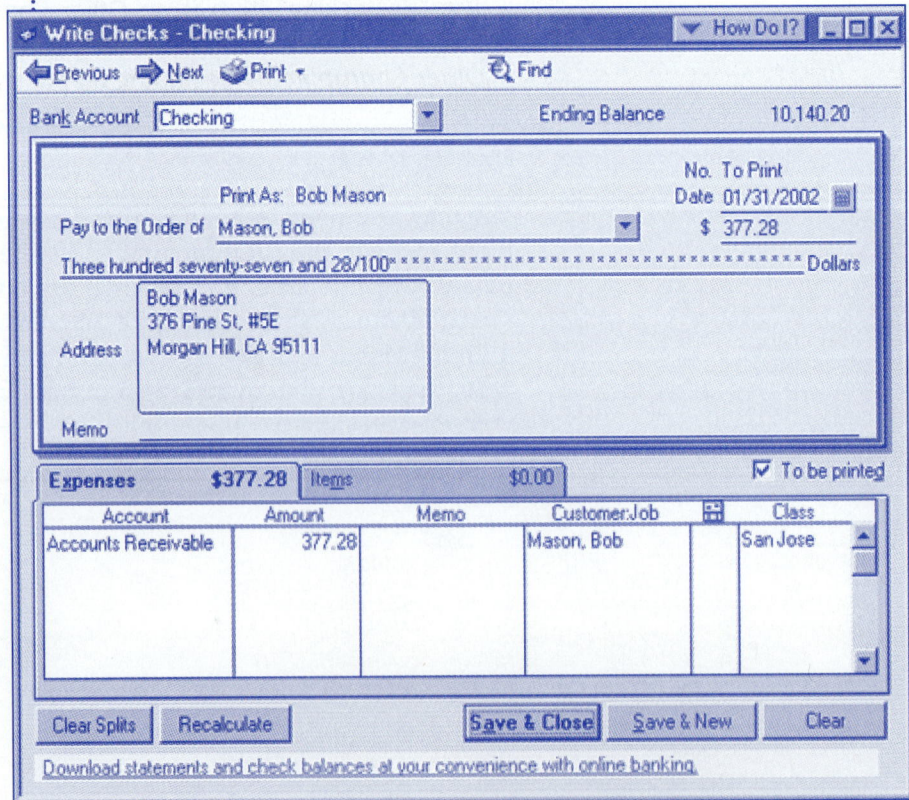

Figure 2-52 A Refund check is always coded to Accounts Receivable.

④ To create the refund check, click the **Check Refund** icon.

QuickBooks automatically opens the Write Checks screen and creates a refund check as shown in Figure 2-52. Notice the check is completely filled out.

⑤ Although you won't do it now, this is the point at which you would print the check by clicking the **Print** icon.

If you had preprinted checks, you would load a check in your printer and click **Print**. See Chapter 3 for more information on printing checks in QuickBooks.

To skip the check printing step, click here to clear the "To be printed" box.	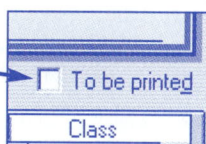

To skip the check-printing step and assign a check number to the check, clear the "To be printed" box as shown in Figure 2-53.

Figure 2-53 Clear the "To Be Printed" box to skip printing.

⑥ Click **Save & Close** to record the check.

⑦ Press <ESC> to close the Credit Memo screen. QuickBooks recorded the Credit Memo when you recorded the check.

Refunding Credit Cards

If you need to issue a refund to a customer's credit card, do the following when you create the refund check as shown in Figure 2-52.

(Don't perform these steps now. They are for reference only.)

1. Clear the "To be Printed" box as shown in Figure 2-53, and enter "CC-VISA" (or other card name) in the *No.* field in the top right of the check. If your credit card deposits go to a bank account different from the default account, change the account in the *Bank Account* field at the top of the check.
2. Click **Save & Close**.
3. Then process the credit card credit through the credit card machine.

WRITING OFF A BAD DEBT

If an Invoice becomes uncollectible, you'll need to write off the debt using a Credit Memo.

Use the Bad Debt Item on a Credit Memo for each uncollectible Invoice. Credit Memos that use the Bad Debt Item (shown in Figure 2-54) reduce Accounts Receivable for the customer shown on the Credit Memo and increase Bad Debts Expense.

COMPUTER TUTORIAL

1 Select the **Customers** menu, and choose **Create Credit Memos/Refunds**.

Figure 2-54 Write off a bad debt with a Credit Memo.

> **NOTE**
>
> You can use the Bad Debt Item on the Credit Memo, or you could use the original Items that were on the original Invoice that you're writing off.
>
> If you use the Bad Debt item approach, set up your Bad Debt Item so that it points to an expense account called Bad Debt Expense. For more information about setting up Items in QuickBooks see *QuickBooks Items and Other Lists* beginning on page 87.

> **NOTE**
>
> If you do use the Bad Debt Item and the sale you're writing off was for taxable items, select the Tax column drop down menu and change the Sales Tax Code from "Non" to "Tax." Doing so will reduce your sales tax liability by calculating the tax on the Bad Debt Item.

2 Fill out the Credit Memo as shown in Figure 2-54.

3 You will then see then a warning (Figure 2-55) because Invoices and Credit Memos are primarily designed to respectively increase or decrease Income accounts, rather than Expense accounts. Click **OK**.

4 Click **Save & Close** to record the Credit Memo.

5 To associate this Credit Memo to the open Invoice, select the **Customers** menu, and choose **Receive Payments**.

Figure 2-55 Warning about the Bad Debt Item pointing to an expense account.

6 Enter "Young, Bill:Window Replacement" in the *Received From* field.

7 In the Applied To section, select Invoice #2002-102 by clicking on the Invoice's row, in any column *except* the Check column to the left of the Invoice date. QuickBooks will highlight the Invoice after you select it.

8 Click **Set Credits** and make sure the credit is applied to the Invoice you're writing off (see Figure 2-56). Click **Done**.

9 Click **Save & Close**.

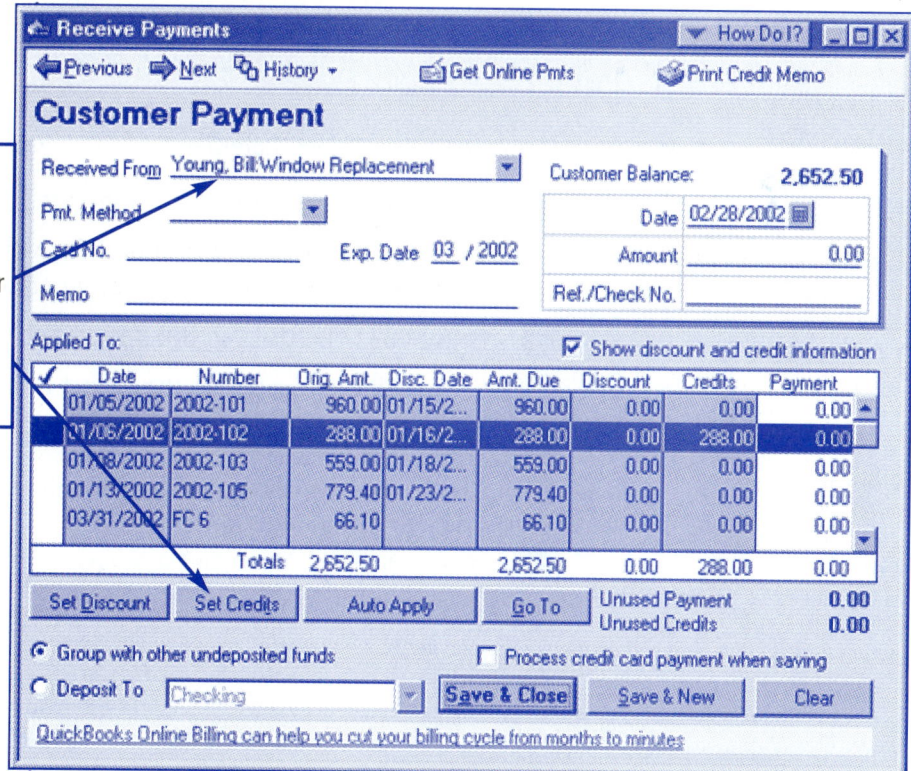

Figure 2-56 Receive Payments screen after writing off bad debt

CREATING CUSTOMER STATEMENTS

COMPUTER TUTORIAL

QuickBooks customer statements provide a summary of all of the activity for an accounts receivable customer during the period you specify.

① Select the *Customers* menu, and choose **Create Statements** (see Figure 2-57).

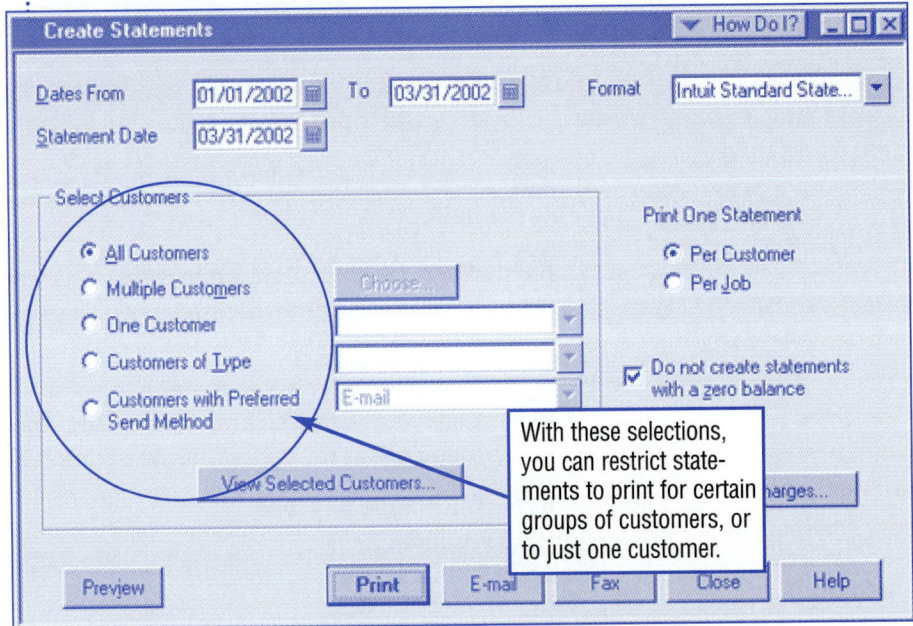

Figure 2-57 The Select Statements to Print screen.

② Set the *Dates* fields to "01/01/2002" and "03/31/2002".

These dates include the period for which Accounts Receivable transactions show on the customer statement.

③ Leave "03/31/2002" in the *Statement Date* field.

④ Leave "All Customers" in the Select Customers section.

⑤ Leave "Per Customer" in the Print One Statement section.

⑥ Check the "Do not create statements with a zero balance" box.

⑦ Click **Preview**.

8 After reviewing your statements in the Print Preview screen (see Figure 2-58), click **Close**. You'll see the Create Statements screen again. Leave this screen open. You will use it in the next tutorial.

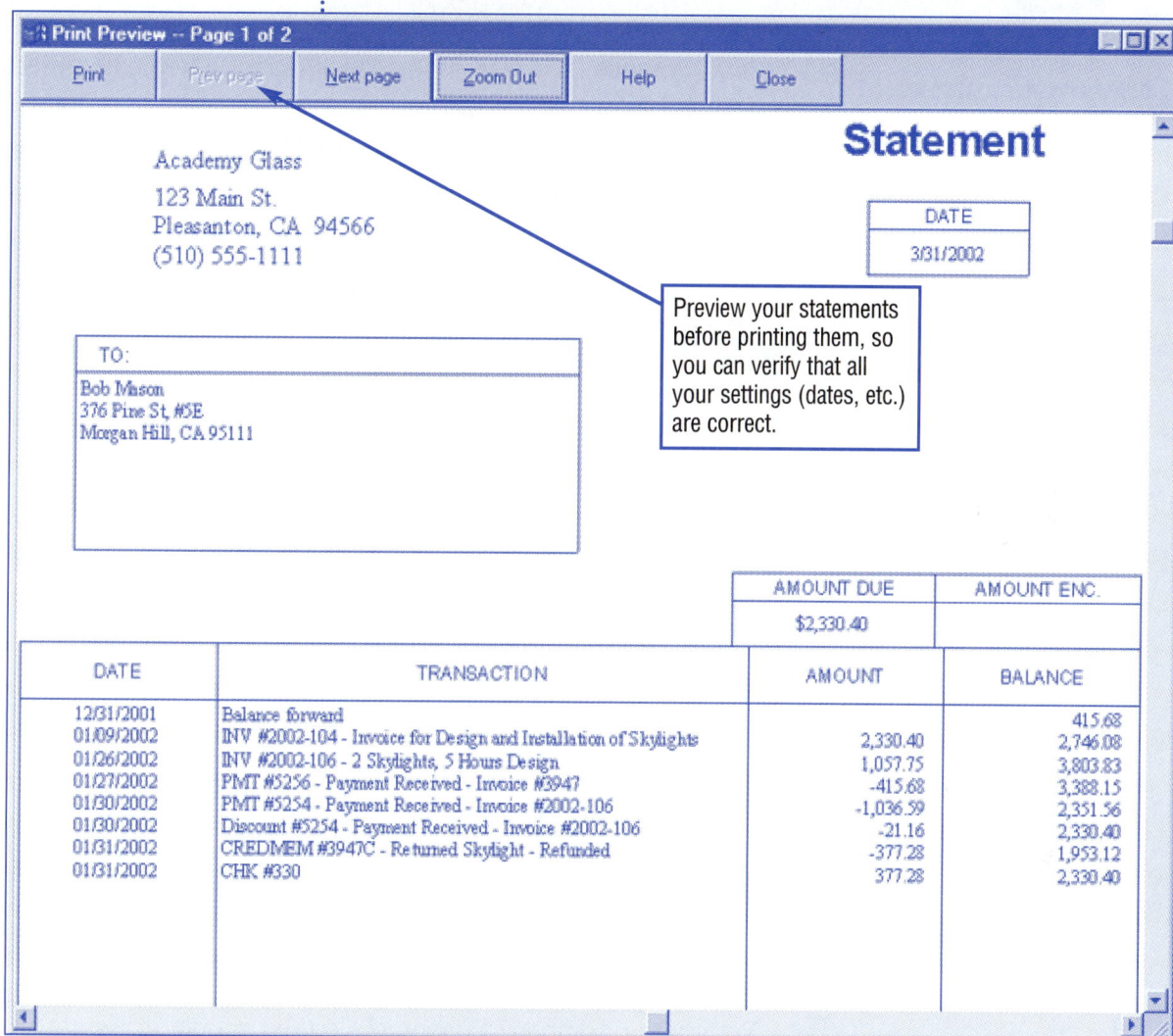

Figure 2-58 Preview your statements before printing.

ASSESSING FINANCE CHARGES

COMPUTER TUTORIAL

When a customer is late in paying an invoice, you can assess finance charges. To set up your finance charge settings, follow these steps:

1 Click **Finance Charges** from the Create Statements screen (Figure 2-57).

2 Click **Settings** on the Assess Finance Charges screen to display your finance charge settings (see Figure 2-59).

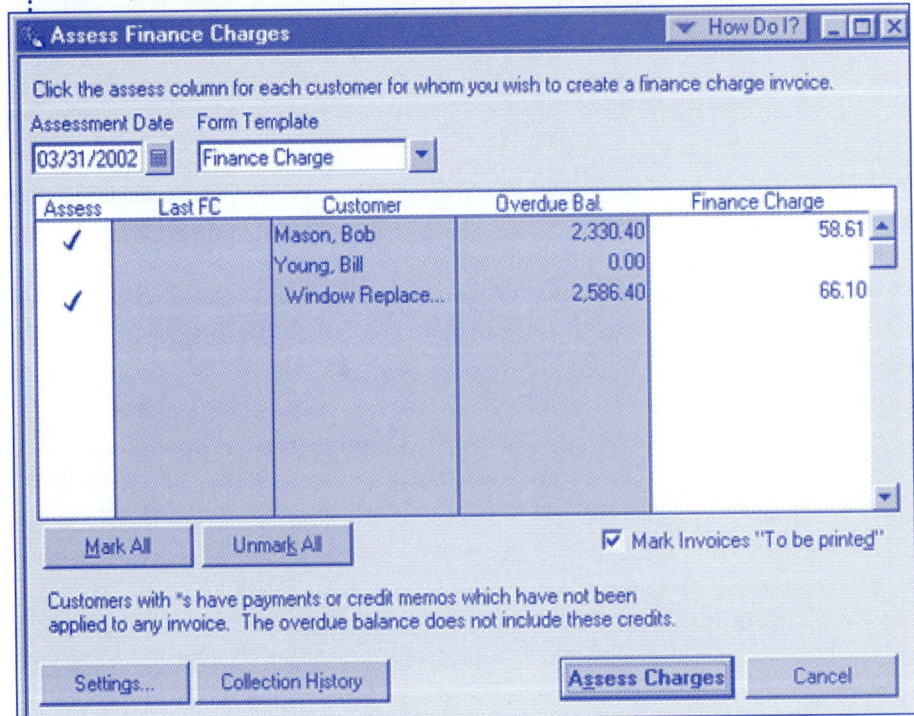

Figure 2-59 Set up your finance charge preferences from by clicking Settings.

3 Review the Company Preferences screen shown in Figure 2-60 and click **OK**.

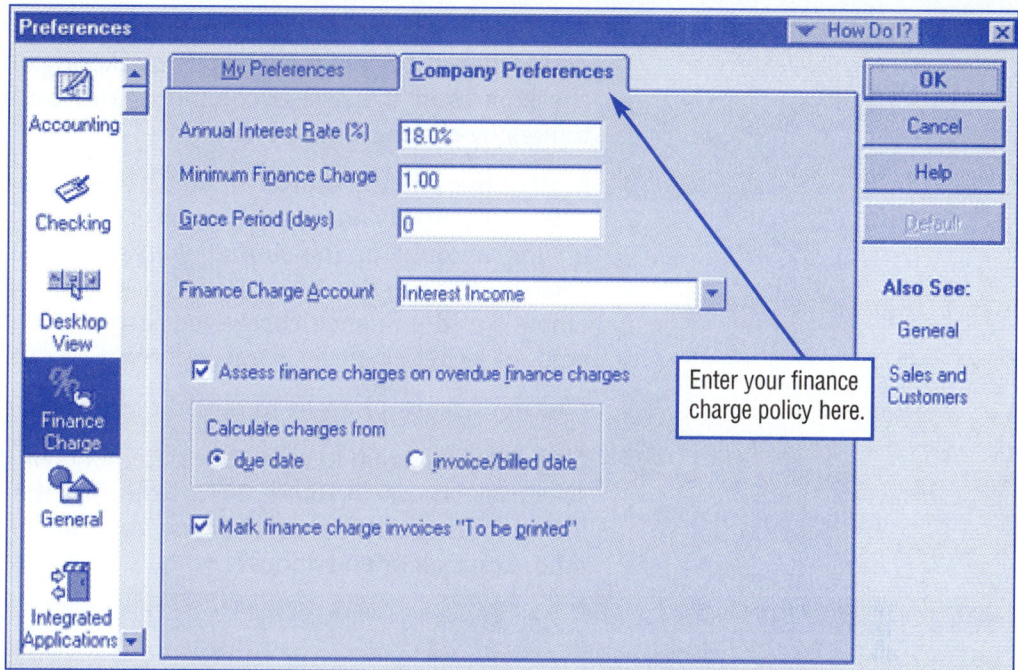

Figure 2-60 Click Settings to set up your finance charge preferences.

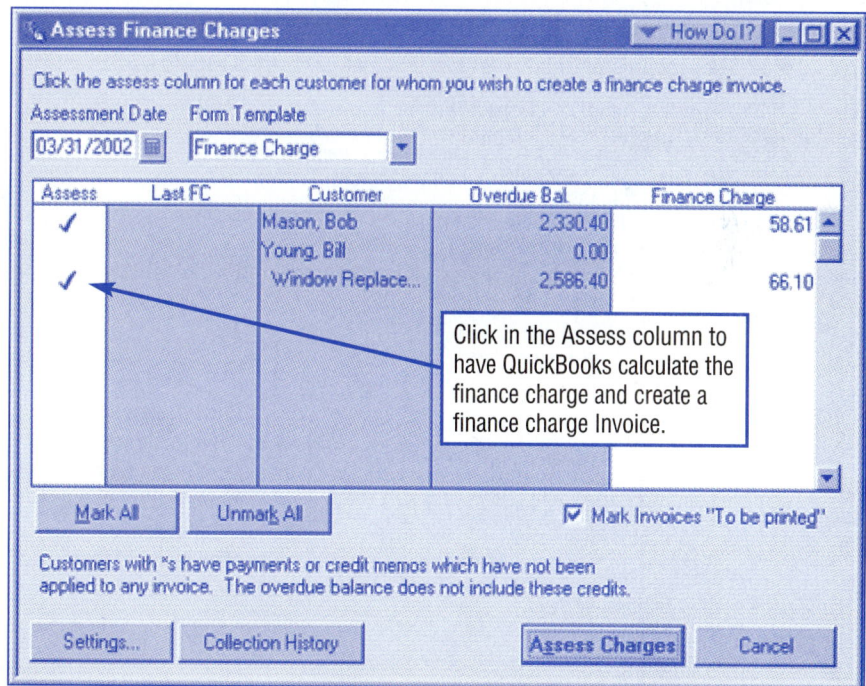

Figure 2-61 Customers with an overdue balance are indicated.

Each customer with an overdue balance shows in the Assess Finance Charges screen as shown in Figure 2-61.

4 Enter "03/31/2002" in the *Assessment Date* field and press <TAB>.

5 The Assess column for each customer is preselected. You can deselect each customer separately by clicking on the appropriate checkmarks in the Assess column or you can deselect all customers by clicking **Unmark All**.

6 Review the finance charge amounts in the Finance Charge column. QuickBooks automatically calculated these amounts based on the amount in the *Annual Interest Rate (%)* field of the Finance Charge Company Preferences. You can override the amount of the finance charge for each customer by editing the amount in the Finance Charge column.

7 Click on **Assess Charges** to record the finance charges.

8 Click **Preview** again to view your statements on the Print Preview screen as shown in Figure 2-62. Note that the statements now include assessed finance charges. You can print these at any time. Close all open windows.

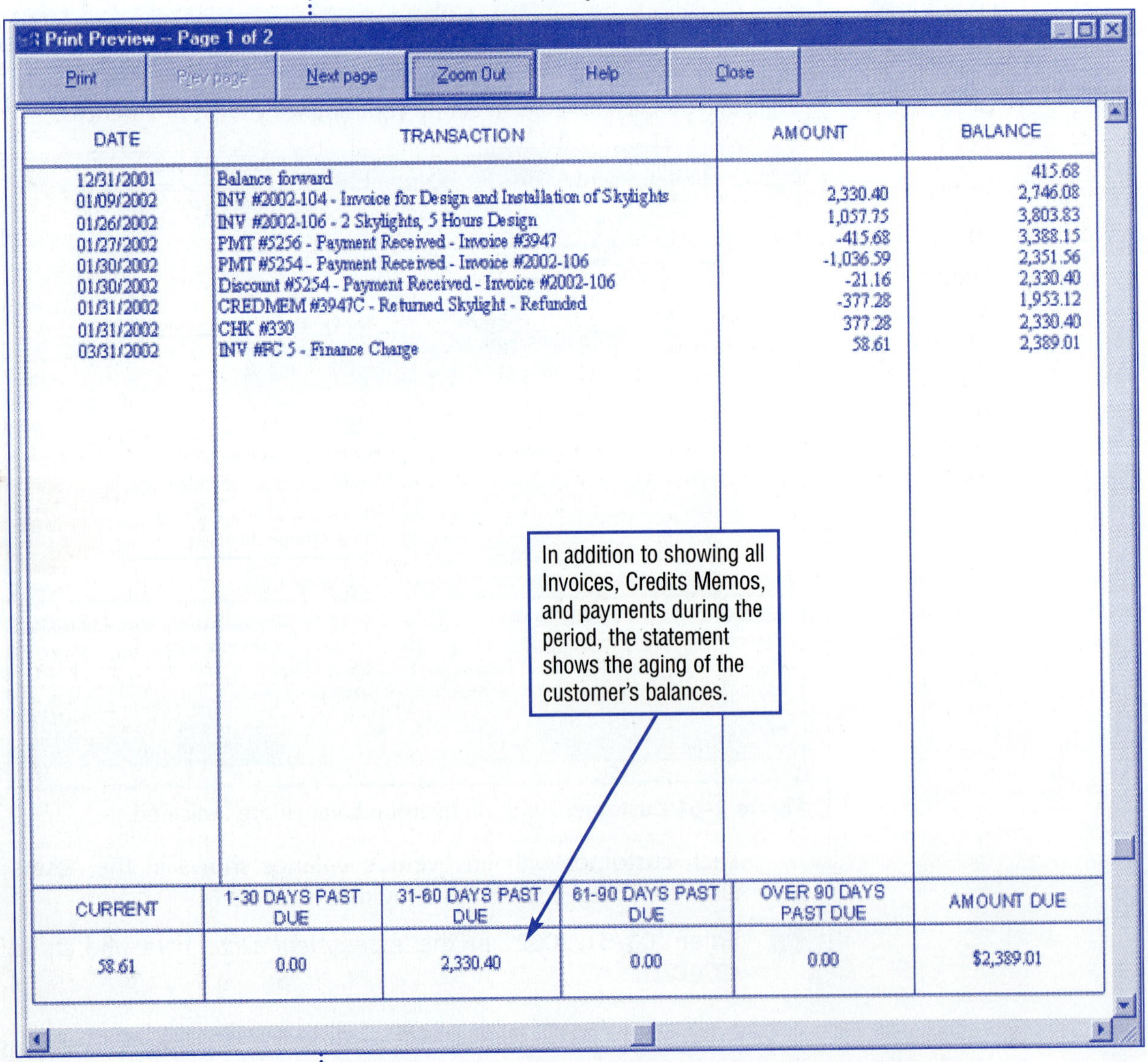

DATE	TRANSACTION	AMOUNT	BALANCE
12/31/2001	Balance forward		415.68
01/09/2002	INV #2002-104 - Invoice for Design and Installation of Skylights	2,330.40	2,746.08
01/26/2002	INV #2002-106 - 2 Skylights, 5 Hours Design	1,057.75	3,803.83
01/27/2002	PMT #5256 - Payment Received - Invoice #3947	-415.68	3,388.15
01/30/2002	PMT #5254 - Payment Received - Invoice #2002-106	-1,036.59	2,351.56
01/30/2002	Discount #5254 - Payment Received - Invoice #2002-106	-21.16	2,330.40
01/31/2002	CREDMEM #3947C - Returned Skylight - Refunded	-377.28	1,953.12
01/31/2002	CHK #330	377.28	2,330.40
03/31/2002	INV #FC 5 - Finance Charge	58.61	2,389.01

In addition to showing all Invoices, Credits Memos, and payments during the period, the statement shows the aging of the customer's balances.

CURRENT	1-30 DAYS PAST DUE	31-60 DAYS PAST DUE	61-90 DAYS PAST DUE	OVER 90 DAYS PAST DUE	AMOUNT DUE
58.61	0.00	2,330.40	0.00	0.00	$2,389.01

Figure 2-62 View statements after adding finance charge.

QUICKBOOKS ITEMS AND OTHER LISTS

To help you track more details about your sales, QuickBooks provides several lists that allow you to add more information to each transaction. In this section, you'll learn how to create items in the Item list, the Terms list, the Price Level list, and the Templates list. You'll also learn how Custom fields can be used to add more detail to several of your lists in QuickBooks.

QuickBooks Items

In Chapter 1, you learned that the **Item list** is a very special list. It is used to identify the products and services your business purchases and/or sells. Throughout this chapter, you've been using Items to indicate which products and services were sold on invoices and sales receipt forms. In this section, you'll learn more about QuickBooks items, and how they impact the "accounting behind the scenes" as you create transactions.

The Item list is a list of all products and services that you purchase and/or sell. The Item list (see Figure 2-63) shows all of the items you've defined along with details about each Item.

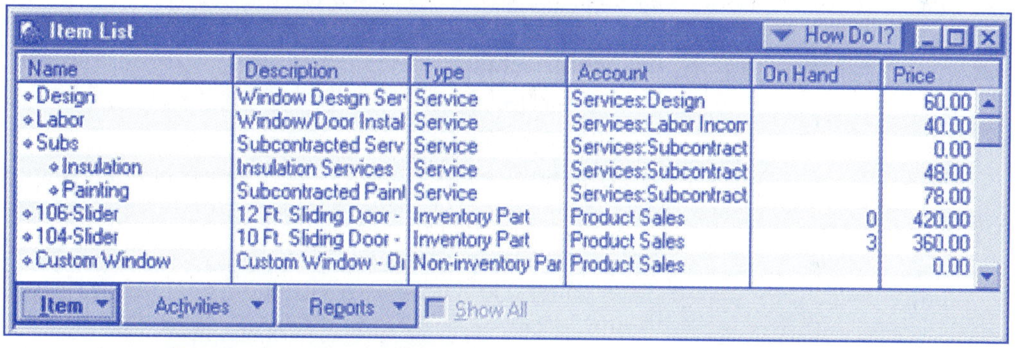

Figure 2-63 The Item list

Item Types

There are several different types of items in QuickBooks (see Figure 2-64). When you create an Item, you indicate the Item type along with the name of the Item and the account with which the Item is associated.

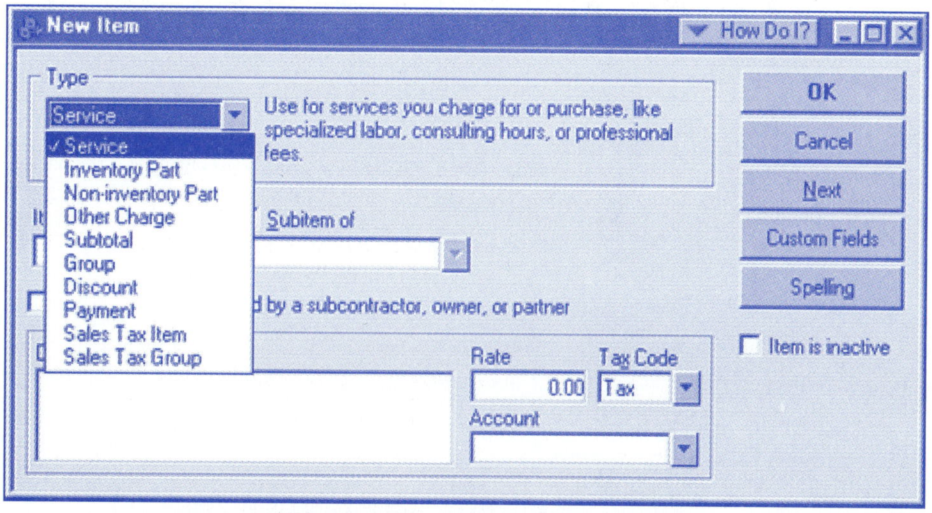

Figure 2-64 The Type menu in the New Item screen

Service Items
Used to track services you buy and/or sell.

Inventory Parts Items
Used to track your purchases and sales of inventory.

Non-inventory Parts Items
Used to track products you buy and/or sell but don't keep in inventory.

Other Charge Items
Used to track miscellaneous charges such as shipping and finance charges.

Subtotal Items
Used to display subtotals on sales forms.

Group Items
Allows you to use one item to "bundle" several items together. For example, if you always sell three products together in a "kit," you could track each item separately but use a Group item that combines them together as a kit or assembly.

Discount Items
Used to calculate and display discounts on sales forms.

Payment Items
Used to show payments collected on the face of an Invoice.

Sales Tax Items
Used to track sales taxes in each location where you sell taxable goods and services.

Sales Tax Group Items
Used when you pay sales tax to more than one tax agency. The Sales Tax Group allows you to group several Sales Tax items together into one total. The total tax from each Sales Tax item in the group is the amount of tax charged when you use the group on sales forms; but QuickBooks tracks each Sales Tax item in the group separately. In most states, you don't need to use Sales Tax Groups. Use these Group items only if you pay sales tax to more than one agency.

Service Items

Academy Glass sells design services by the hour. To track the sales of a **Service** Item create an Item called *Design*, and associate the item with the Design Services income account.

(Don't perform these steps now. They are for reference only.)

1. Select the *Lists* menu and choose **Item List**.
2. Select the *Item* menu and choose **New**.
3. Select "Service" from the Type drop-down list shown in Figure 2-64, and fill in the detail of the Item as shown in Figure 2-65.
4. Click **OK** to save the Item.

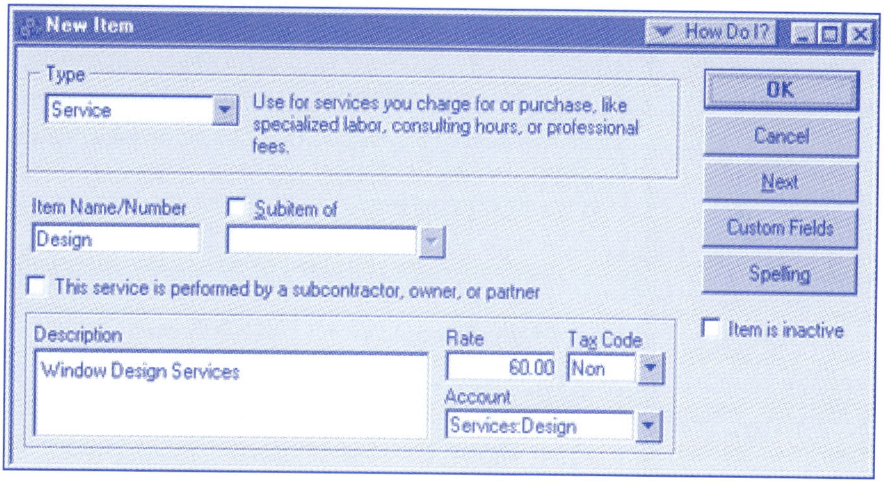

Figure 2-65 Selecting items

   If the rate you charge for this service changes, you can override this amount when you use it on a sales form, so when you set up the Item enter the rate you normally charge.

Subcontracted Services

To help track your subcontracted services you can set up a special Item to track both the income and the expense of the subcontractors. By using a single Item to track both the income and expense for this sub-contracted service, you can automatically track the profitability of your subcontractors. You might want to have a separate Item for each vendor that is a subcontractor.

(Don't perform these steps now. They are for reference only.)

1. With the Item List displayed, press <Ctrl+N>.
2. Select "Service" from the Type drop-down list, and press <TAB>.
3. Enter "Insulation" in the *Item Name/Number* field and check the "Subitem of" box.
4. Select "Subs" from the "Subitem of" drop-down list.
5. Check the box next to "This service is performed by a subcontractor, owner, or partner."
   This box allows you to use the same Item on purchase transactions and sales transactions, but have the Item affect different accounts depending on the transaction.

6. Enter the *Description on Purchase Transactions, Cost* (purchase price), *Expense Account*, and *Preferred Vendor* for this Item as shown in Figure 2-66.
7. Select "Non" in the *Tax Code* field.
8. Enter the *Description on Sales Transactions, Sales Price*, and *Income Account* for this Item as shown in Figure 2-66.
9. Click **OK** to save the Item.

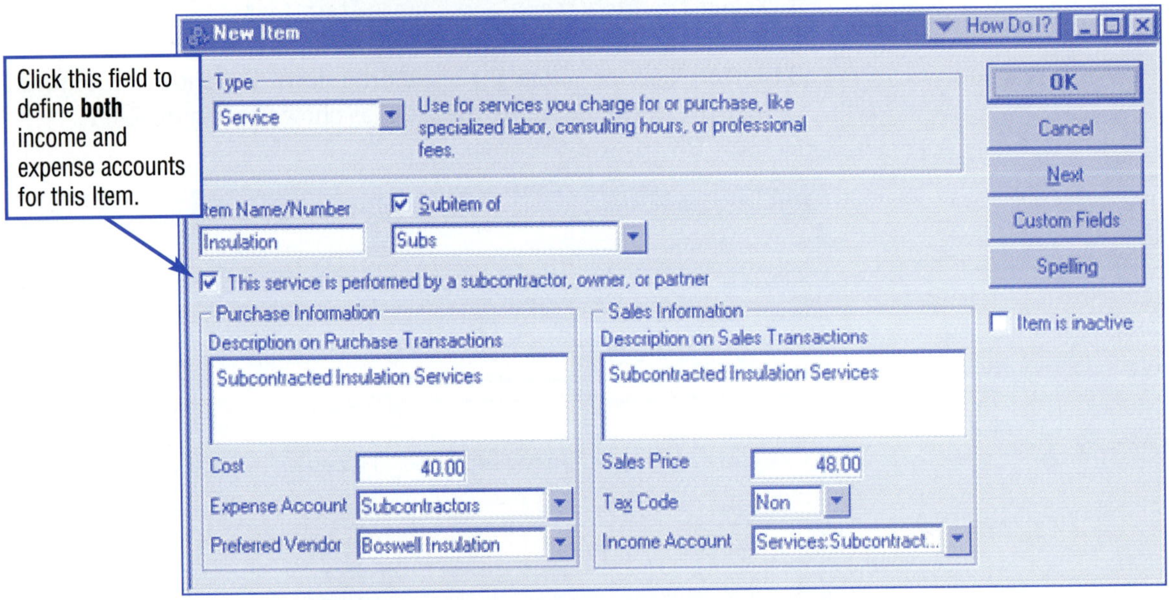

Click this field to define **both** income and expense accounts for this Item.

Figure 2-66 Subcontracted Service Item

Non-Inventory Parts

To track products that you sell, but don't keep in inventory, set up **Non-Inventory Part Items.**

Academy Glass doesn't carry skylights in inventory, and they don't differentiate between the different types of skylights, so they use one generic Item called Skylight. You can be more specific by creating separate Items for each different skylight after you are more familiar with QuickBooks. For now, to keep things simple, just use one generic skylight Item.

> **Don't perform these steps now. They are for reference only.**

1. With the Item List displayed, press <Ctrl+N>. Select "Non-Inventory Part" from the Type drop-down list and fill in the detail of the Item as shown in Figure 2-67.
2. Click **OK** to save the item.

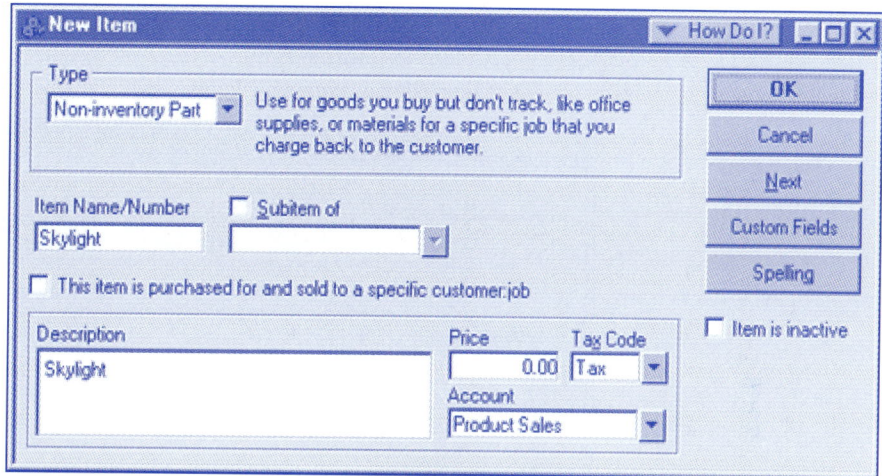

Figure 2-67 Non-inventory Part Item

Non-Inventory Parts – Passed Through

You can also specifically track the income and expenses for each Non-Inventory Part. This is particularly useful when you pass the costs on to your customers for special-ordered parts. For example, Academy Glass tracks Custom Window orders with one Non-Inventory Part Item.

> **Don't perform these steps now. They are for reference only.**

1. With the Item List displayed, press <Ctrl+N>. Select "Non-Inventory Part" from the Type drop-down list. Fill in the detail of the Item as shown in Figure 2-68.
2. Click **OK** to save the item.

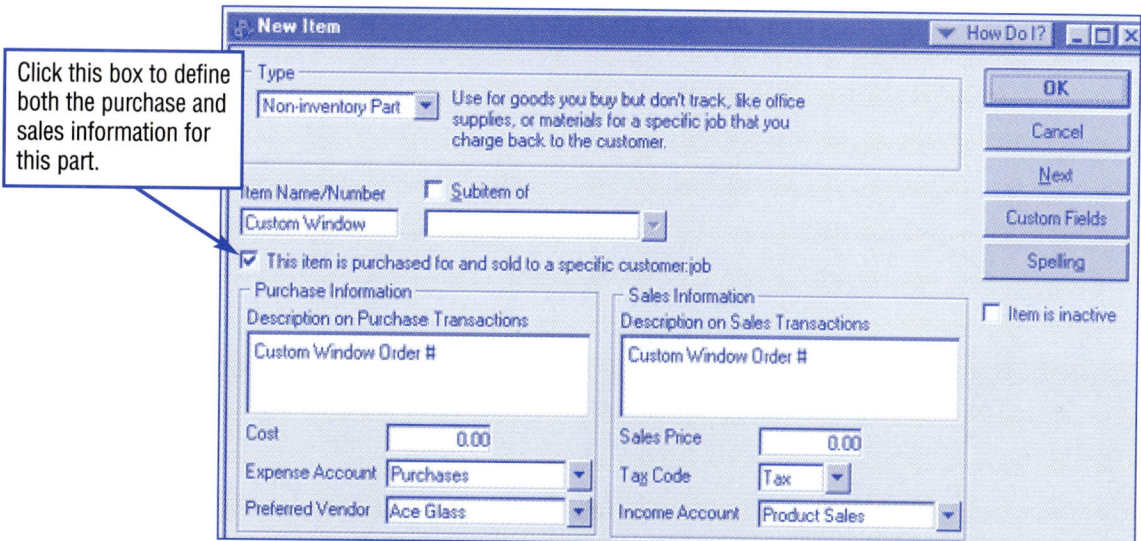

Figure 2-68 Non-inventory Part Item - passed through

Other Charge Items

To track charges like freight, finance charges, or expense reimbursements on your Invoices, use Other Charge Items.

Don't perform these steps now. They are for reference only.

1. With the Item List displayed, press <Ctrl+N>. Select "Other Charge" from the Type drop-down list and fill in the detail of the Item as shown in Figure 2-69.
2. Click **OK** to save the Item.

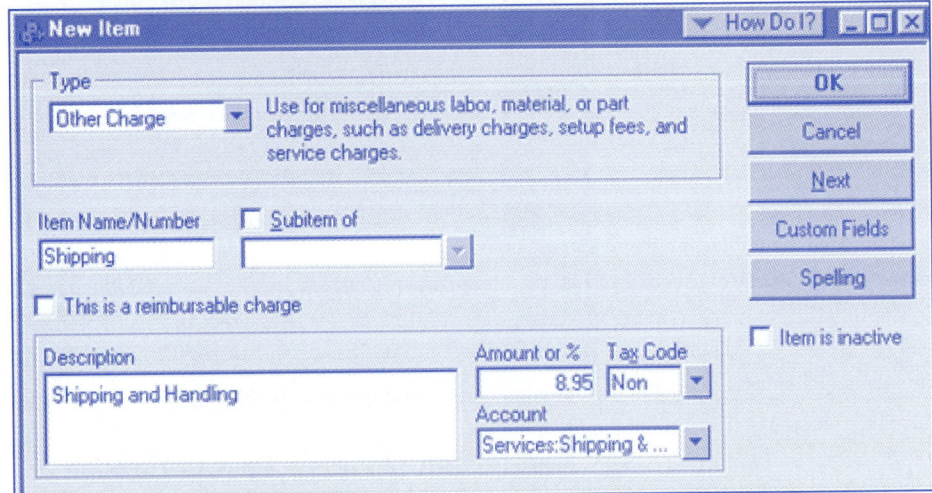

Figure 2-69 Track shipping charges with an Other Charge Item

Setting Up Sales Tax

If you sell products, chances are you'll need to collect **sales tax**. In most states, each county has a different tax rate, and your sales tax agency requires you to track and report all your sales by county. After you set up your company file to track sales tax, QuickBooks automates almost every part of the sales tax process.

Sales Tax Preferences

The sales tax preferences have already been set up in the tutorial template file, but when you create your own company file, follow the steps below to set up your preferences.

> **Don't perform these steps now. They are for reference only.**

1. Select the *Edit* menu and choose **Preferences**.
2. Scroll down and click on **Sales Tax**, and then click on **Company Preferences**.
3. Select "Yes" under Do you charge Sales Tax? to turn on sales tax tracking.
4. Set the *Most common sales tax* field to "Contra Costa."

   The *Most common sales tax* field stores the sales tax item you use on most of your sales. When you set up a new customer, QuickBooks uses this as the default sales tax to be charged for that customer. Also, when you enter a new sale (Invoice or Sales Receipt), this will be the default sales tax item unless it is overridden by the information from a customer record.
5. "Monthly" in the Pay Sales Tax section is preselected.

   You set this field to match how often you pay your sales tax.
6. The "Mark taxable amounts with "T" when printing" box should be checked.

   Checking this field causes QuickBooks to print a "T" by a taxable item on sales forms. Invoices and Sales Receipts show the Sales Tax Code on the screen, but the printed forms will show a "T" for taxable and a blank for non-taxable items.

   Your screen should look like Figure 2-70. Click **OK** to save your preferences.

> **NOTE**
>
> If you charge sales tax, make sure you *always* use sales forms (Invoices or Sales Receipts) to record sales. If you directly deposit money into your bank account (and omit the sales forms), QuickBooks won't have the information it needs to accurately show your sales tax liabilities.

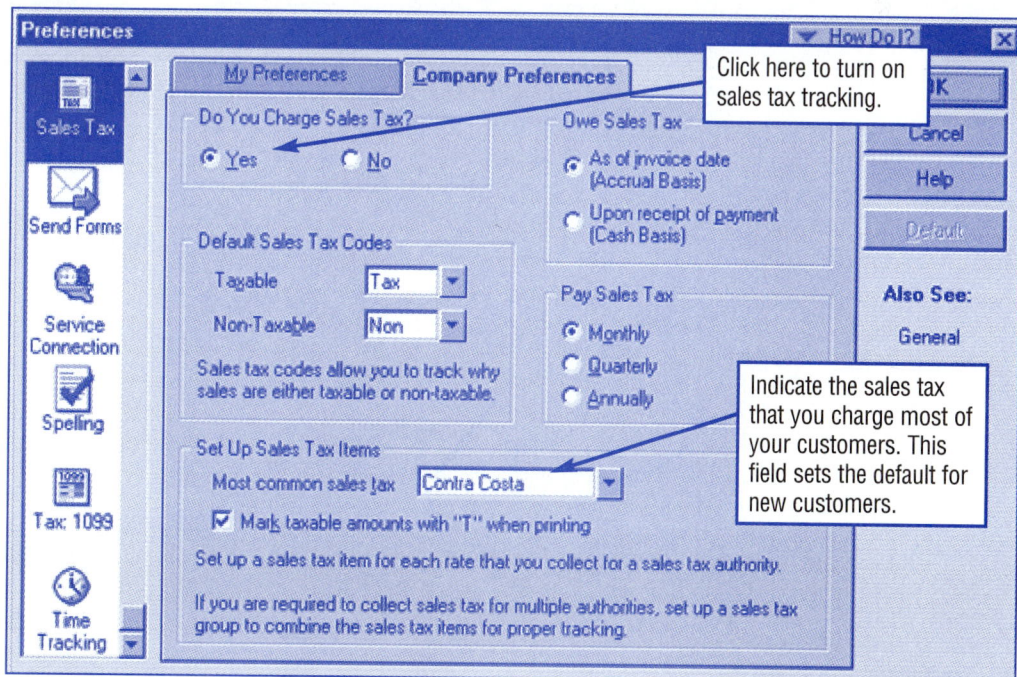

Figure 2-70 Set sales tax preferences in the Company Preferences Tab

Sales Tax Items

The sales tax items in this section have already been set up in the tutorial template file, but when you create your own company file, follow the steps below to create the appropriate items for your company.

> **Don't perform these steps now. They are for reference only.**

1. With the Item List displayed, press <Ctrl+N>. Select "Sales Tax Items" from the Type drop-down list and fill in the detail of the Item as shown in Figure 2-71.

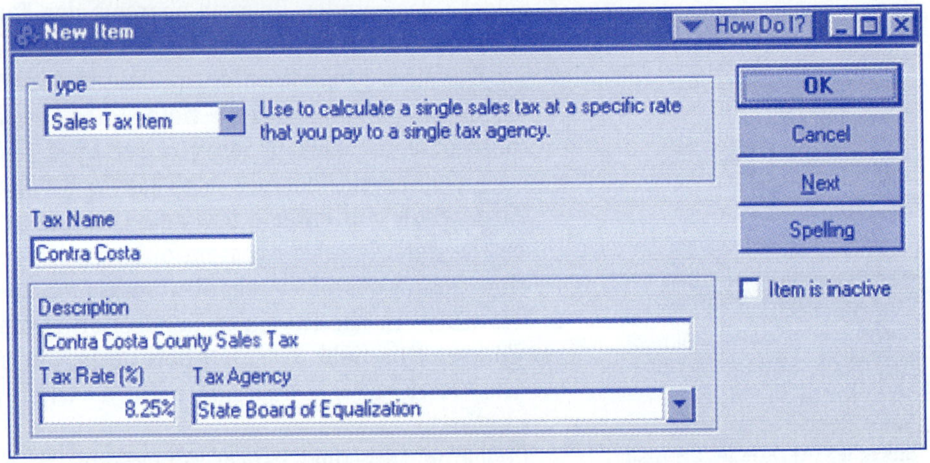

Figure 2-71 Track sales tax with the Sales Tax item.

Make sure you enter the name of your tax collector in the *Tax Agency* field. QuickBooks needs this name for sales tax reports and sales tax payments.

2. Click **OK**.

Use this Sales Tax Item for all sales in Contra Costa County. When you do, the sales tax reports will show all sales (taxable and nontaxable) in that county.

Printing the Item List

COMPUTER TUTORIAL

To print the Item List, follow these steps:

1 Select the *Reports* menu, choose **List**, and then choose **Item Listing** (see Figure 2-72).

Item Listing				How Do I?
Modify Report...	Memorize...	Print...	Excel...	Hide Header	Refresh	Sort By	Default

5:19 PM

Academy Glass
Item Listing

Item	Description	Type	Cost	Price	Sales Ta
Design	Window Design Services	Service	0	60.00	Non
Labor	Window/Door Installation Labor	Service	0.00	40.00	Non
Subs	Subcontracted Services	Service	0.00	0.00	Non
Subs:Insulation	Insulation Services	Service	40.00	48.00	Non
Subs:Painting	Subcontracted Painting Services	Service	65.00	78.00	Non
106-Slider	12 Ft. Sliding Door - Wood Frame	Inventory Part	350.00	420.00	Tax
104-Slider	10 Ft. Sliding Door - Wood Frame	Inventory Part	300.00	360.00	Tax
Custom Window	Custom Window - Order #:	Non-inventory P...	0.00	0.00	Tax
Skylight	Skylight	Non-inventory P...	0	0.00	Tax
Doors	Doors	Non-inventory P...	0.00	34.00	Tax
Window	Window	Non-inventory P...	0.00	0.00	Tax
Shipping	Shipping and Handling	Other Charge	0	8.95	Non
Restocking	Restocking Fee	Other Charge	0	-10.0%	Non
Deposit	Customer Prepayments & Deposits	Other Charge	0	0.00	Non
Bad Debt	Bad Debt - Write off	Other Charge	0	0.00	Non
Fin Chg	Finance Charges on Overdue Balan...	Other Charge	0	18.0%	Non
Reimb Exp	Reimbursable Expenses	Other Charge	0.00	0.00	Non
Reimb Subt	Reimbursable Expenses Subtotal	Subtotal	0		
Subtotal	Subtotal	Subtotal	0		
Reimb Group	Total Reimbursable Expenses	Group	0		
104 Replace	Remove and Replace 104 Slider	Group	0		
Disc 10%	10 % Discount	Discount	0	-10.0%	Tax
Santa Clara	Santa Clara County Sales Tax	Sales Tax Item	0	8.25%	
Contra Costa	Contra Costa County Sales Tax	Sales Tax Item	0	8.25%	
Out of State		Sales Tax Item	0.00	0.00	

Figure 2-72 The Item Listing report

2 Click **Print** at the top of the report (or select **Print Report** from the *File* menu).

In addition to the Item list, there are several additional lists in QuickBooks that you will use when setting up customers and recording sales transactions. An understanding of how to set up and use these lists is essential to operating QuickBooks for your company.

The Terms List

The **Terms list** is where you define the payment terms for your Invoices and Bills. QuickBooks uses the terms to calculate when the Invoice or Bill is due. If the terms specified on the transaction include a discount for early payment, QuickBooks also calculates the date on which the discount expires.

QuickBooks allows you to define two types of terms:

◆ **Standard terms** are based on how many days from the Invoice or Bill date the payment is due or a discount is earned.

◆ **Date-Driven terms** are based on the day of the month that an Invoice or Bill is due or a discount is earned.

You can override the default terms on each sale as necessary. When you create reports for Accounts Receivable (A/R), or Accounts Payable (A/P). QuickBooks takes into account the terms on each Invoice or Bill.

COMPUTER TUTORIAL

① Select the *Lists* menu, choose **Customers & Vendor Profile Lists**, and then choose **Terms List** (see Figure 2-73).

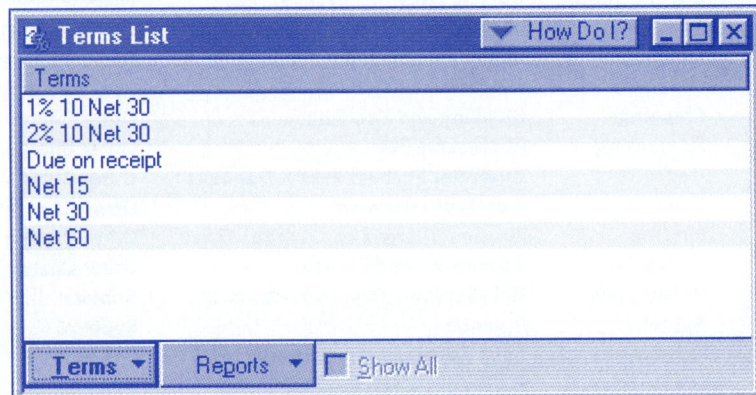

Figure 2-73 The Terms list screen

② The tutorial template file already includes several terms items (see Figure 2-73). To set up additional terms items, select the *Terms* menu from the Terms List screen, and then choose **New**, or press <Ctrl+N>.

③ To setup a standard term, complete the New Terms screen as shown in Figure 2-74, and click **OK**.

The screen in Figure 2-74 shows how the 2% 7 Net 30 item is defined. It is a standard terms item that indicates full payment is due in 30 days. If the customers pay within 7 days of the Invoice date, they are eligible for a 2% discount.

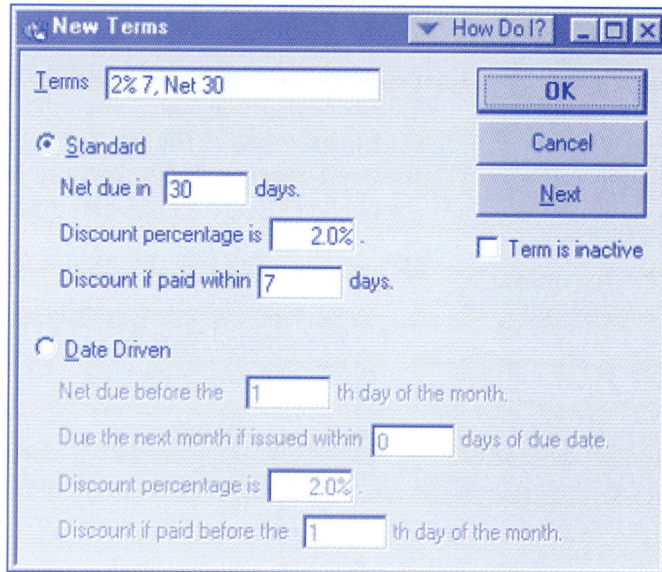

Figure 2-74 The New Terms screen with standard terms

④ To set up a date-driven terms item, press <Ctrl+N>.

⑤ Select the "Date Driven" radio button.

⑥ Fill in the fields as shown in Figure 2-75. Then click **OK**.

The terms in Figure 2-75 are an example of date-driven terms, where payment is due on the 10th of the month. If the Invoice is dated less than 10 days before the due date, the Invoice (or Bill) is due on the 10th of the following month.

⑦ Close the Terms list by clicking (**X**) in the upper right corner.

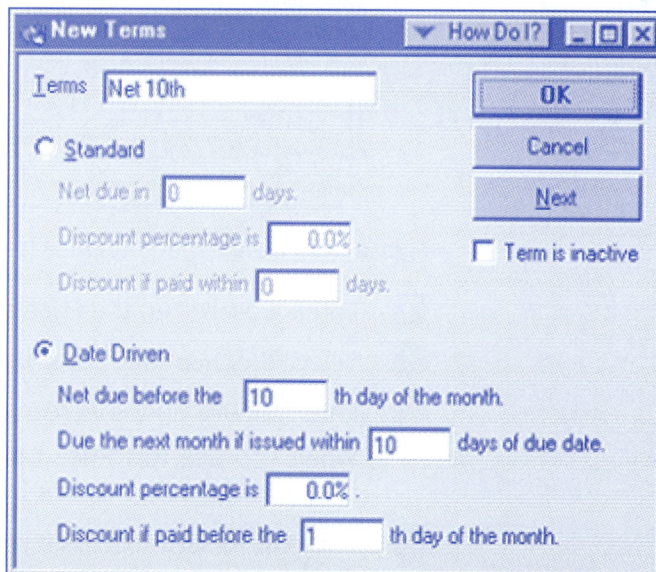

Figure 2-75 The New Terms screen with date driven terms

Price Levels

In QuickBooks Pro, you can create Price Levels. Use Price Levels on Invoices or Sales Receipts to adjust the sales amount of a particular Item.

For example, if the base rate for Labor is $40/hour and commercial customers receive a 10% discount on all labor, you could set up a Price Level called "Commercial" and define it as a 10% discount.

COMPUTER TUTORIAL

1 Select the *Lists* menu and choose **Price Level List**.

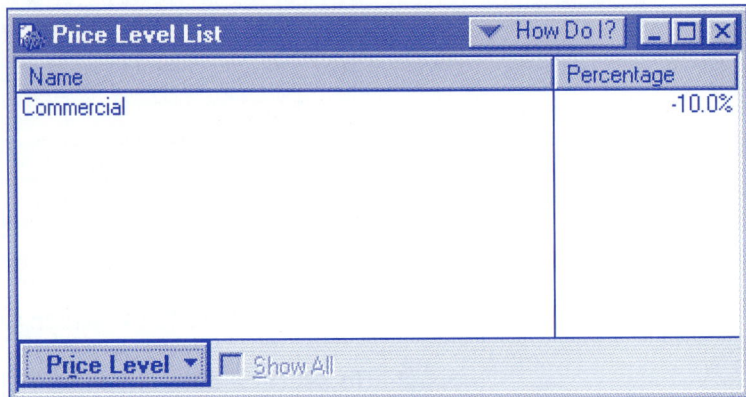

Figure 2-76 The Price Level List

2 Select the *Price Level* menu and choose **New** or press <Ctrl+N>.

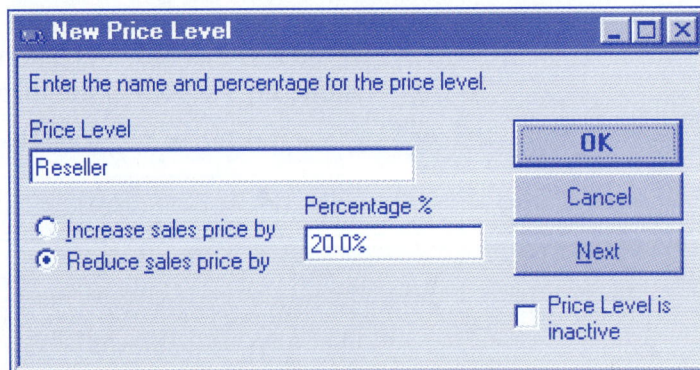

Figure 2-77 Defining a new price level

3 Enter "Reseller" in the *Price Level* field.

4 Select "Reduce sales price by" and press <TAB>.

5 Enter "20.0%" in the *Percentage %* field.

When you use this Price Level on sales forms, QuickBooks will reduce the amount of sale by 20%.

6 Click **OK** to save this Price Level.

Adding Price Level Defaults to Customer Records

You can also add default Price Levels to each customer record. This sets the default price increase or decrease on all Items sold to the customer.

COMPUTER TUTORIAL

1 Display the Customer:Job List and then double-click on the customer record for Pelligrini Builders. Then click the Additional Info tab (see Figure 2-78).

2 Select "Commercial" from the Price Level drop-down list.

3 Click **OK** to save your change.

Figure 2-78 Setting a Price Level on a Customer's Record

When you create an Invoice for Pelligrini Builders, QuickBooks automatically applies the 10% Commercial discount (see Figure 2-79).

Do not save the Invoice shown in Figure 2-79 in your tutorial file.

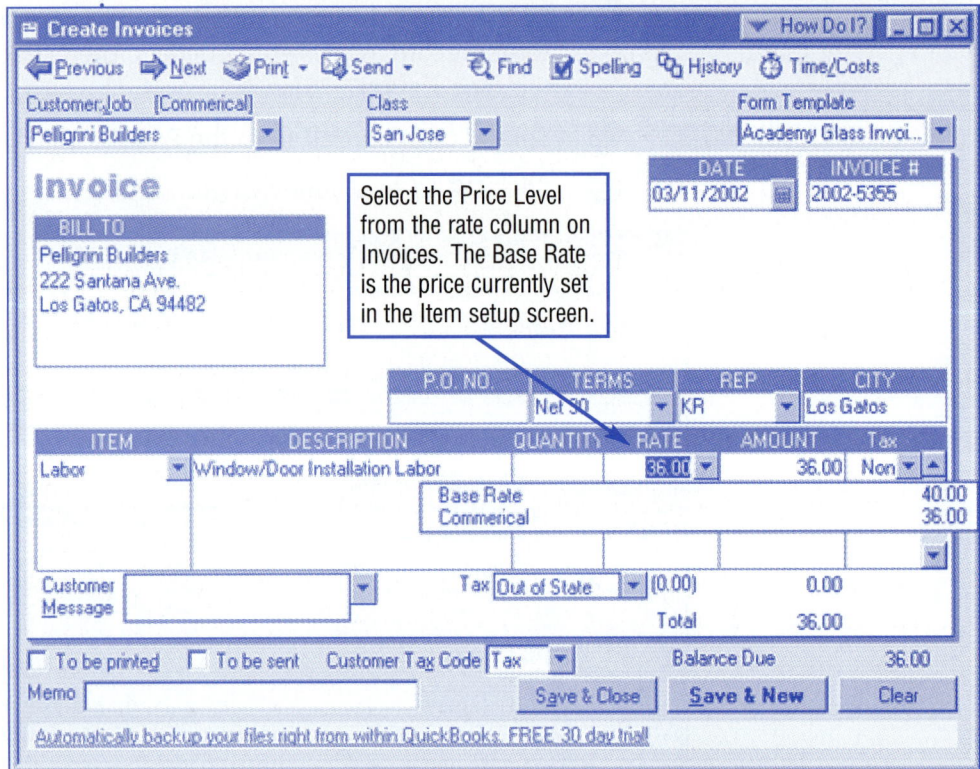

Figure 2-79 Selecting a Price Level on an Invoice

You can manually choose a Price Level by selecting it from the drop-down list next to the Rate column.

CUSTOM FIELDS

When you set up a new Customer record, you can define custom fields for tracking additional information specific to your customers, vendors, and employees.

Academy Glass tracks each customer and vendor by city and county in order to create reports of total purchases and sales in a city or county. This information allows them to determine the best area to expand business operations.

To define custom fields, you would follow these steps:

Don't perform these steps now. They are for reference only.

1. Click the **Define Fields** button on the Additional Info tab of a Customer or Vendor record (see Figure 2-80).
2. In the screen shown in Figure 2-81, you can define up to fifteen custom fields for tracking your customers, vendors, and employees.

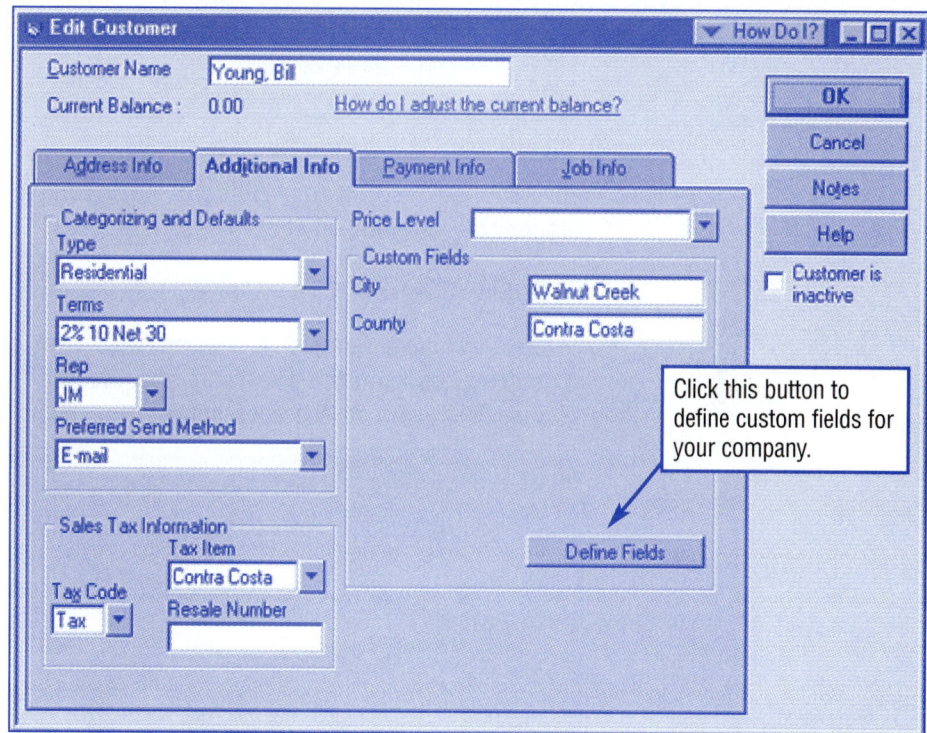

Figure 2-80 Click Define Fields in the Additional Info Tab.

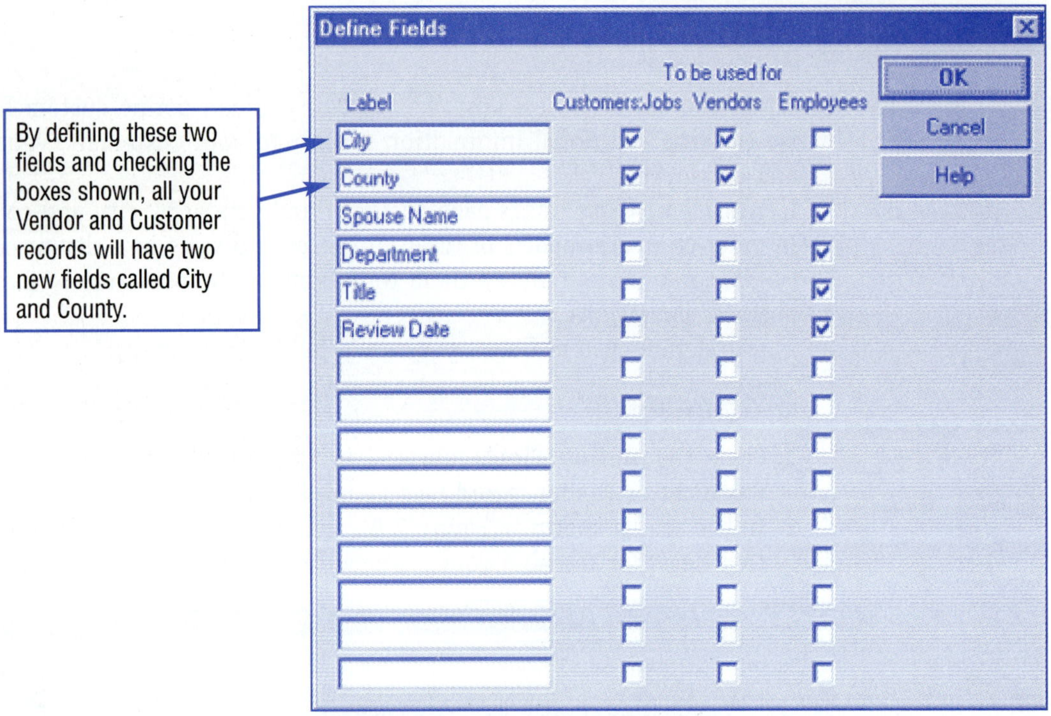

By defining these two fields and checking the boxes shown, all your Vendor and Customer records will have two new fields called City and County.

Figure 2-81 The Define Fields screen

You can use Custom Fields in your company in a variety of ways, depending on your business needs.

Adding Custom Field Data to Customer Records

After you have defined a custom field and checked the box in the Customer:Job column, the field appears on the Customer record (see Figure 2-82). Fill in the data just as you did for the other fields.

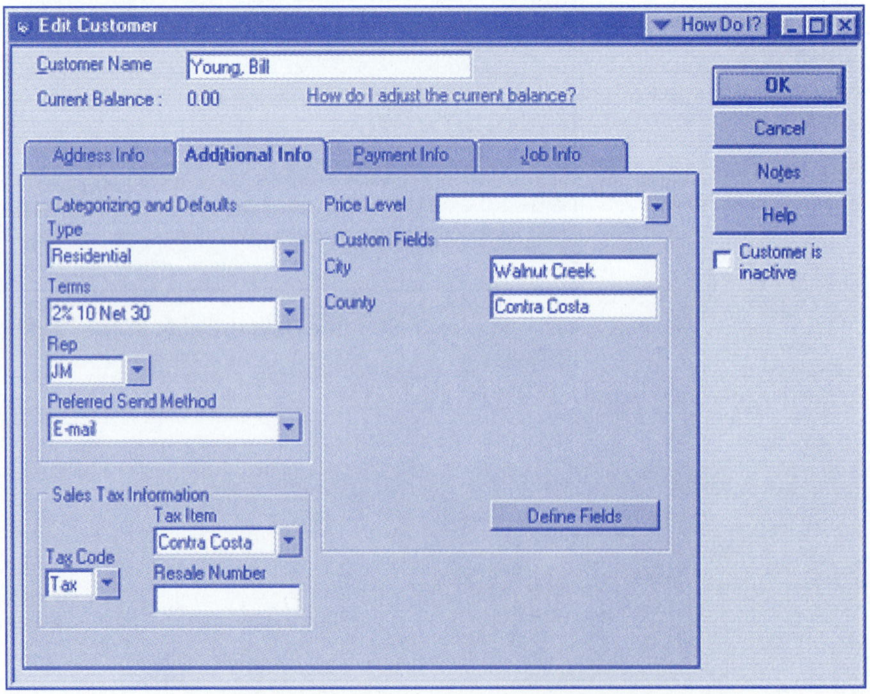

Figure 2-82 Fill in the Custom Fields for each customer.

MODIFYING SALES FORM TEMPLATES

QuickBooks provides templates so that you can customize your sales forms. You can choose from the standard forms that QuickBooks provides or you can customize the way your forms appear on both the screen and the printed page. The first step in modifying your forms is to create a template for the form you want. The templates for all forms are in the Templates list.

COMPUTER TUTORIAL

1 Select the *Lists* menu, and choose **Templates** (see Figure 2-83).

This list shows the standard templates that come with QuickBooks, as well as any form templates the user may have created.

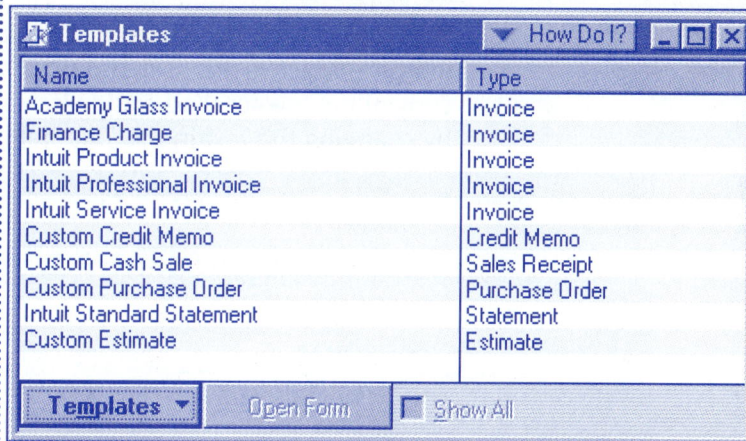

Name	Type
Academy Glass Invoice	Invoice
Finance Charge	Invoice
Intuit Product Invoice	Invoice
Intuit Professional Invoice	Invoice
Intuit Service Invoice	Invoice
Custom Credit Memo	Credit Memo
Custom Cash Sale	Sales Receipt
Custom Purchase Order	Purchase Order
Intuit Standard Statement	Statement
Custom Estimate	Estimate

Figure 2-83 The Templates list

2 Select "Intuit Service Invoice." Then select the *Templates* menu and choose **Duplicate**. The Intuit Service Invoice is the template you are using as the basis to create your custom template.

3 Select "Invoice" on the Select Template Type window, and click **OK** (see Figure 2-84).

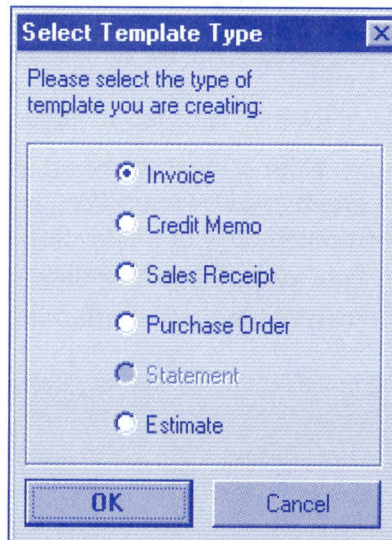

Select Template Type

Please select the type of template you are creating:

- ⦿ Invoice
- ○ Credit Memo
- ○ Sales Receipt
- ○ Purchase Order
- ○ Statement
- ○ Estimate

OK   Cancel

Figure 2-84 Select Template Type window

④ Select "DUP: Intuit Service Invoice." Choose the **Templates** menu and choose **Edit**.

⑤ Enter "My Invoice Template" in the *Template Name* field (see Figure 2-85).

You must enter a unique template name. If the name you choose is already on the list, you will not be able to save the template. You must give your template a descriptive name, so that you'll easily recognize it when selecting the template on QuickBooks sales forms.

⑥ Review the fields in the Header tab. Do not edit any of the fields on this screen.

You would click the boxes in the Screen and Print columns to indicate which fields will show on the screen and the printed copy of the Invoice. You could also modify the titles for each field by changing the text in the *Title* fields (see Figure 2-85).

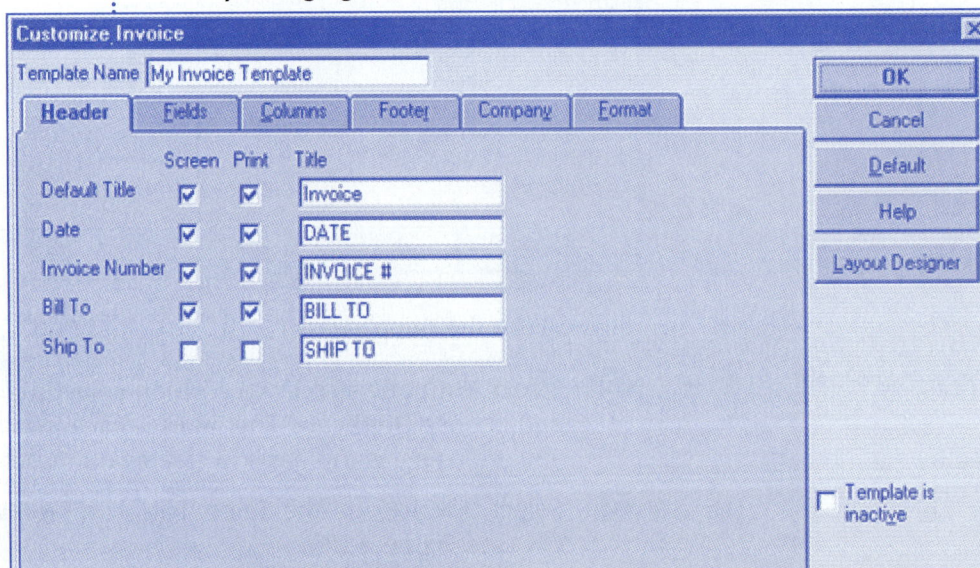

Figure 2-85 Rename the template in the Customize Invoice screen.

⑦ Click the Fields tab to continue modifying the template.

⑧ Set the screen as shown in Figure 2-86 to show the *P.O. No.*, *Terms*, *REP*, *Project/Job*, and *City* on both the screen and the printed copy of the Invoice.

The *Project/Job* field always shows on the screen because it's part of the *Customer:Job* field at the top of each Invoice.

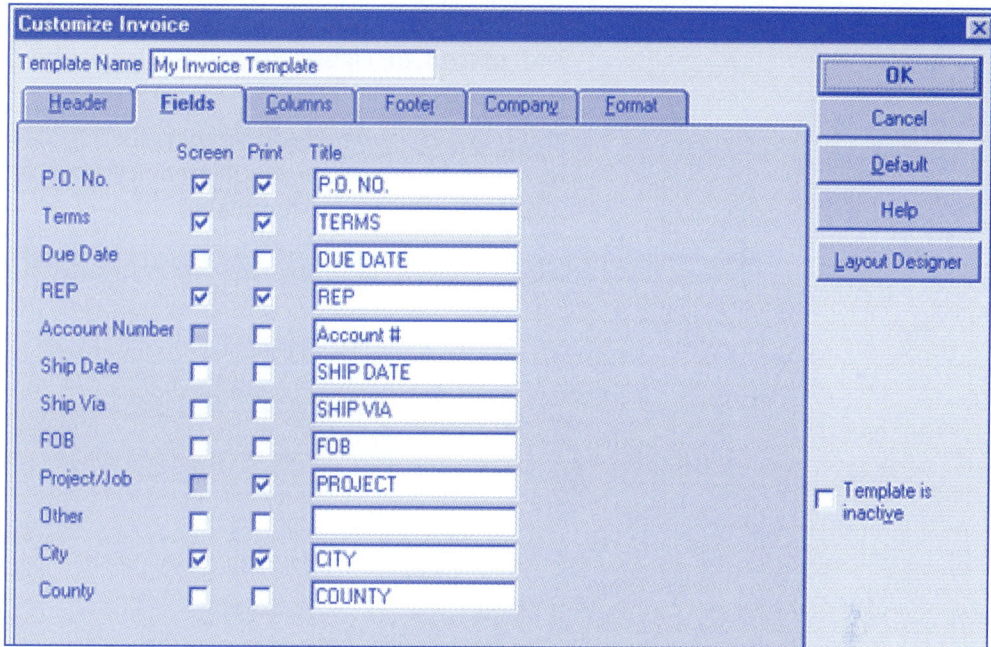

Figure 2-86 The Fields tab of the Customize Invoice screen

9 Click the Columns tab to modify how the columns display on the Invoice.

10 Modify the order of the columns by entering the numbers in the Order column as shown in Figure 2-87.

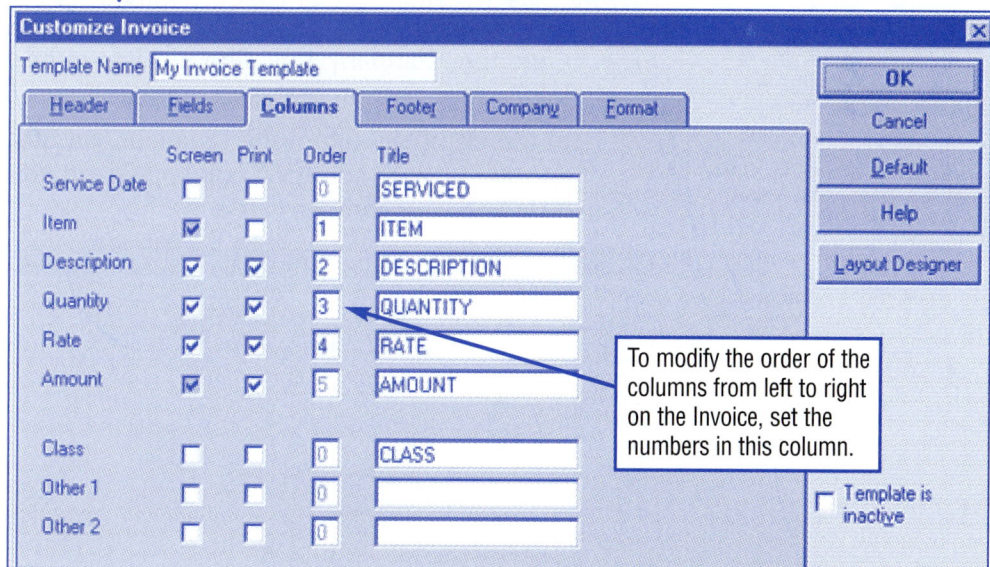

To modify the order of the columns from left to right on the Invoice, set the numbers in this column.

Figure 2-87 The Columns tab of the Customize Invoice screen

⑪ Click the Footer tab. In the *Long text (disclaimer)* field, enter the text shown in Figure 2-88. Also, click the "Print" box on the Balance Due line.

You use the *Long text (disclaimer)* field to describe your payment terms or to provide a disclaimer. This text will appear on every Invoice that uses this template.

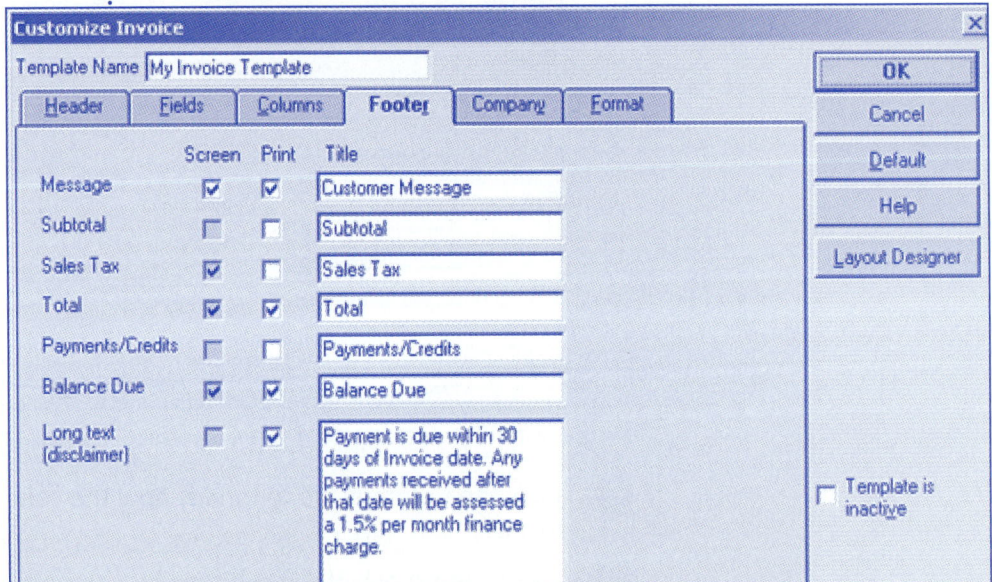

Figure 2-88 The Footer tab of the Customize Invoice screen

⑫ Click the Company tab. Check all four boxes in the Contact Information section of the screen (see Figure 2-89).

In the Company tab of the template, you decide what information about your company will appear on your printed Invoices, including your company logo.

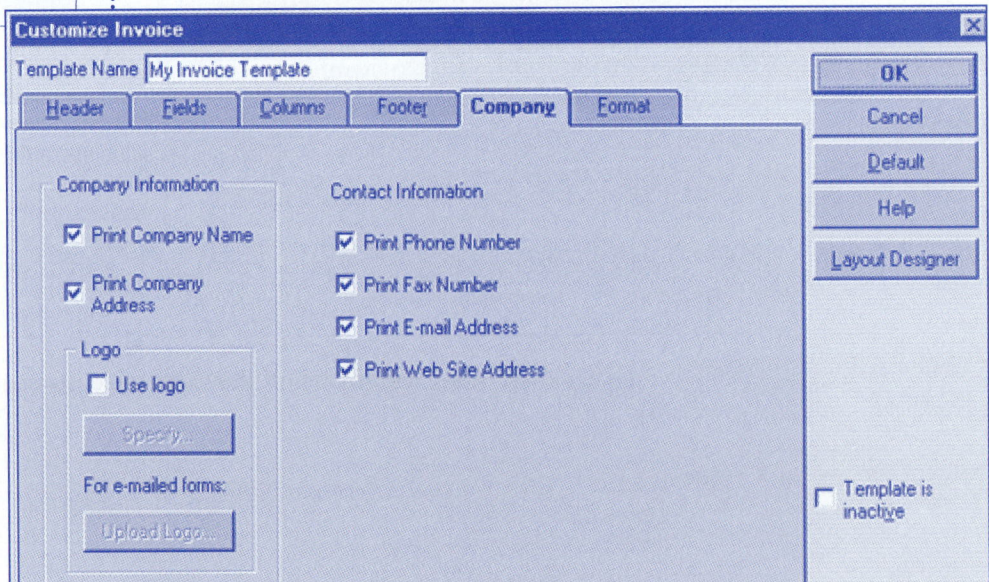

Figure 2-89 The Company tab of the Customize Invoice screen

⓭ Click the Format tab (see Figure 2-90). Do not edit any of the fields or screens on this tab.

The Format tab allows you to edit the default fonts of each section in the sales form.

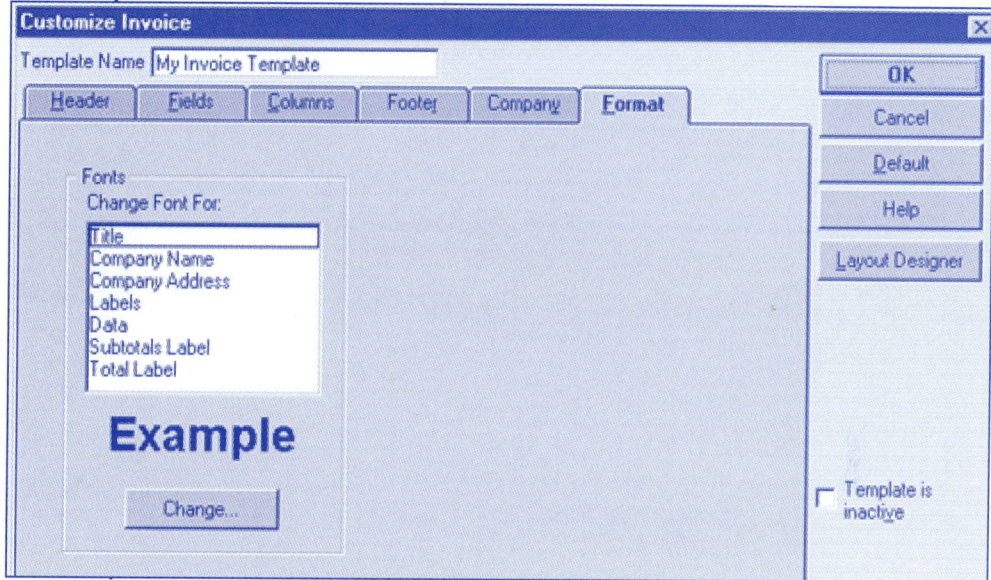

Figure 2-90 The Format tab of the Customize Invoice screen

⓮ To manually design the layout of the form, click **Layout Designer**.

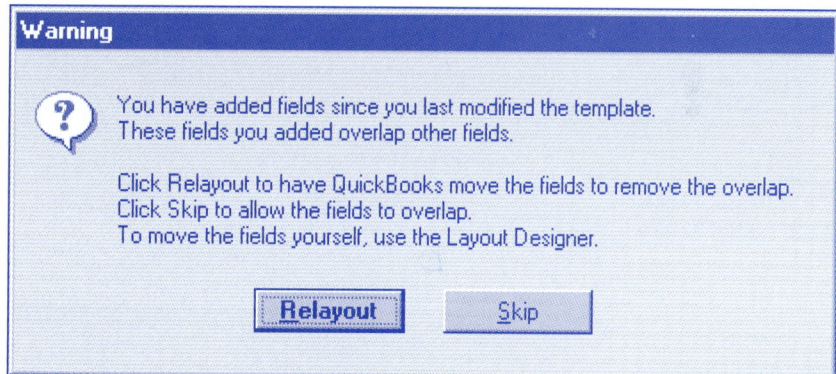

Figure 2-91 Click Relayout to modify the template.

When you add new fields to the Invoice, QuickBooks may need to completely reformat the form. QuickBooks will do this automatically when you click **Relayout** when the Warning message appears (see Figure 2-91). With the Layout Designer, you have complete control of where fields and information appear on your forms.

⑮ Click and drag columns to stretch them or shrink them. Drag fields to place them where you want them on the form (see Figure 2-92).

⑯ When you're finished designing the form, click **OK** on both the Layout Designer screen and the Custom Invoice template to save your template.

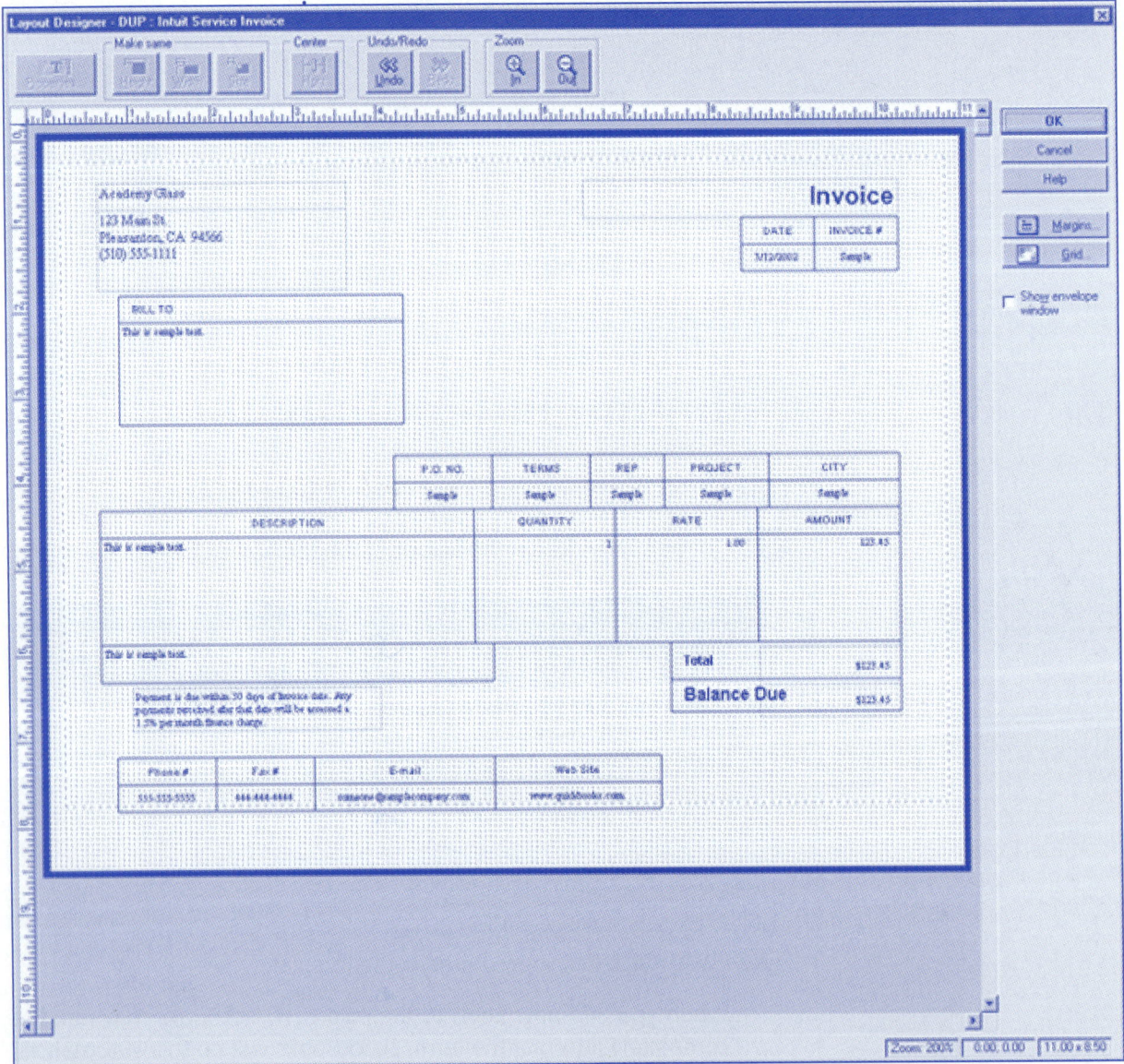

Figure 2-92 Move the fields around using Layout Designer.

CREATING SALES REPORTS

QuickBooks can create reports on just about anything you want by creating customized reports, but many of the common management reports are pre-configured in the program.

Sales by Customer Report

The Sales by Customer report shows how much you've sold to each of your customers over a given date range. To create this report, follow these steps:

① Select the *Reports* menu, choose **Sales**, and then choose **Sales by Customer Summary**.

② Enter "01/01/2002" (or press <y>) in the *From* date field and press <TAB>.

③ Enter "02/28/2002" (or press <yhh> for the beginning of the year and then the end of the second month) in the *To* date field and press <TAB>.

The date shortcuts are really helpful for entering dates quickly. Try to memorize them.

Figure 2-93 shows the Sales by Customer Summary for the first two months of 2002. Verify that your screen matches this Figure.

④ To print the report, click **Print** at the top of the report.

COMPUTER TUTORIAL

Academy Glass
Sales by Customer Summary
January through February 2002

	Jan - Feb 02
Johnson, Helen	605.00
Mason, Bob	2,814.40
Young, Bill	
Window Replacement	2,157.60
Total Young, Bill	2,157.60
TOTAL	5,577.00

Figure 2-93 Your Sales by Customer Summary report should look like this.

⑤ Close the Sales by Customer Summary report. You can opt to memorize this report by clicking **Yes** in the Memorize Report window.

COMPUTER TUTORIAL

Sales by Item Report

The Sales by Item report shows how much you've sold of each Item over a given date range. To create this report, follow these steps:

1 Select the *Reports* menu, choose **Sales**, and then choose **Sales by Item Summary**.

2 Enter "01/01/2002" (or press <y>) in the *From* date field and press <TAB>.

3 Enter "02/28/2002" (or press <yhh> for the beginning of the year and then the end of the second month) in the *To* date field and press <TAB>.

Figure 2-94 shows the Sales by Item Summary for the first two months of 2002. Verify that your screen matches this Figure.

	Qty	Amount	% of Sa...	Avg Pri...	COGS	Avg CO...	Gross M..	Gross M...
Inventory								
104-Slider	2	720.00	12.9%	360.00	600.00	300.00	120.00	16.7%
Total Inventory		720.00	12.9%		600.00		120.00	16.7%
Parts								
Custom Window	1	477.60	8.6%	477.60				
Skylight	2	801.00	14.4%	400.50				
Total Parts		1,278.60	22.9%					
Service								
Design	31	1,860.00	33.4%	60.00				
Labor	24	960.00	17.2%	40.00				
Subs								
Insulation	21	1,008.00	18.1%	48.00				
Total Subs		1,008.00	18.1%					
Total Service		3,828.00	68.6%					
Other Charges								
Restocking	0	38.40	0.7%					
Bad Debt	-1	-288.00	-5.2%	288.00				
Total Other Charges		-249.60	-4.5%					
Discounts								
Disc 10%		0.00	0.0%					
Total Discounts		0.00	0.0%					
TOTAL		5,577.00	100.0%					

Academy Glass
Sales by Item Summary
January through February 2002
Jan - Feb 02
Accrual Basis

Figure 2-94 Your Sales by Item Summary report should look like this.

4 To print the report, click **Print** at the top of the report.

5 Close the Sales by Item Summary report. You can opt to memorize this report by clicking **Yes** on the Memorize Report screen.

Name _Michele Nall_   **Date** _____

3.   Enter an Invoice using the data in the table below. Print the Invoice on blank paper.

Done

Field	Data
Customer:Job	Anderson Floors:2nd Street Store
Class	San Jose
Custom Template	Academy Glass Invoice
Date	01/31/2002
Sale #	2002-106
Sold To	Anderson Floors 5647 Cirrus Rd. San Jose, CA 95199
PO Number	6543
Terms	Net 30
Rep	JM
City	San Jose
Item	Window, Qty 2, $497 each
Item	Labor, Qty 5 (hrs), $40/hour
Sales Tax	Santa Clara (8.25%) – Auto Calculates
Total Sale	$1,276.01
Memo	2 Windows and Installation Labor

Table 2-5 Use this data for an Invoice in Step 3.

4.   Enter a second Invoice using the data in the table below. Print the Invoice on blank paper.

Field	Data
Customer:Job	Woodard, Ed
Class	San Jose
Custom Template	Academy Glass Invoice
Date	01/31/2002
Sale #	2002-107
Sold To	Ed Woodard 2500 Johnson Parkway Santa Clara, CA 95111
PO Number	3773
Terms	2% 10 Net 30
Rep	JM
City	Santa Clara
Item	Skylight, Qty 5, $834.00 each
Sales Tax	Santa Clara (8.25%) – Auto Calculates
Total Sale	$4,514.03
Memo	5 Skylights

Table 2-6 Use this data for an Invoice in Step 4.

Done

5. Create and print an Open Invoices report for 1/31/2002.

6. Record a payment dated 2/5/2002 in the amount of $4,423.75 from Ed Woodard (check #5343) and apply it to Invoice 2002-107. On the payment transaction, record a discount for 2% of the Invoice amount and code the discount to Sales Discounts account. Group the payment with other undeposited funds.

7. Record a Credit Memo (#2002-106C dated 2/5/2002) for Anderson Floors' 2nd street job in the San Jose Class. The customer returned one window that cost $497.00. Charge a restocking fee of 10%. Apply the credit to Invoice #2002-106.

8. Print a Customer Open Balance report for Anderson Floors 2nd street job.

9. Print a Customer Statement dated 3/31/2002 for Anderson Floors' 2nd street job for the period of 12/1/2001 through 3/31/2002. Print on blank paper.

10. On 2/5/2002, record a payment from Anderson Floors 2nd street job. The payment, in the amount of $947.71 was by American Express #4444-3333-2222-1111, expiring in 5/2005. Apply the payment to both open Invoices and group the payment with other undeposited funds.

11. On 2/5/2002, deposit everything from the Undeposited Funds account. Separate credit card deposits and checks onto separate deposits. Record a 2% bankcard discount fee (use QuickMath to calculate) on the credit card deposit. Print each deposit (Deposit summary only) onto blank paper.

12. Create and print a Sales by Customer Summary report for January and February 2002.

13. Create and print a Sales by Item Summary report for January and February 2002.

Name _Michelle Nall_   **Date** _____

EXTEND YOUR KNOWLEDGE

PROBLEM 2-2

> Restore the Problem 2-2.QBB file from the CD-ROM and store it on your hard disk according to your instructor's directions.

1. Add Douglas Moore to the Customer:Job. List using the data in the table below. Any unspecified fields should be left blank or with the default values.

Address	200 Main Street, Danville, CA 95111
Phone number	925-555-8700
Type	Business
Terms	2%10, Net 20
Sales Rep	JM
Preferred Send Method	None
Sales Tax Item	Contra Costa
Tax Code	Tax
Price Level	Commercial
City	Danville
County	Contra Costa
Account	#3701
Credit limit	$5,000
Preferred payment method	Check

2. Edit Bob Mason's customer record and add a fax number, 925-555-9812.

3. Record each of the transactions listed below.

Transactions

Feb 2, 2002	Sales Receipt #2002-125 to David Weiss. (QuickAdd the customer) Class: San Jose. Paid by check (#473). Total: $829.50. The customer purchased 2 Skylights ($300 each), 3 hrs Design ($60 per hour). Taxable in Santa Clara County. **Note:** Override the default sales tax item.
Feb 5	Received Check #1744 for $1500 from Bill Young for the window replacement job. Apply to the oldest Invoices.
Feb 8	Sent invoice #2002-106 to Ron Berry for the window and design. Class: Walnut Creek. Terms 2%10, Net 30. Rep: JM. Items: 2 windows ($250.00 each). Labor (for installation) 6 hrs ($40 per hour). Design: 4 hrs ($60 per hour). Contra Costa Sales Tax. Invoice total is $1,021.25. **Note:** Special terms apply to this Invoice only.

Transactions *(continued)*

Feb 10	Invoiced Pelligrini Builders for job on 2354 Wilkes Rd. Invoice #2002-107. Class: San Jose. Sales Rep: JM. Items: 2 skylights ($400 each), Design: 4 hours ($60 per hour). Santa Clara County Sales Tax. Invoice total is $1,106.00.
Feb 16	Received $1,000.82, Check #1810 from Ron Berry in full payment of Invoice #2002-106. He took a 2% discount.
Feb 18	Sent invoice #2002-109 to Bob Mason for new skylight and design services. Class: San Jose. 2 Skylights ($400.00), Design: 2 hrs ($60 per hour). Invoice total was $986.00.
Feb 19	Sales Receipt #2002-126 to Janet Green. Class: San Jose. Paid by VISA. Items: 2 doors ($34.00 each). Santa Clara County Sales Tax. Total sale was $73.61.
Feb 24	Bill Young called and gave his VISA credit card number to pay off the remaining balance on all open invoices for the window replacement job. Amount of payment was $1,086.40. Visa #4444-3333-2222-1111, Exp 05/2005.
Feb 26	Invoiced Jerry Leonard. Inv #2002-110. Class: Walnut Creek. Sales Rep: JM. Items: Custom Window – Order #8015, $897.50; Labor 5 hrs ($40 per hour), gave 10% discount on all items. Contra Costa County Sales Tax. The invoice total was $1,054.39.
Feb 28	Received Check #5254 for $1,106.00 from Pelligrini Builders for the 2354 Wilkes Rd. job in payment of Invoice #2002-107.
Feb 28	Issued refund to Bill Young (window replacement job) for Invoice #2002-105. Two 104-sliders ($360.00 each). A 10% restocking fee applies. Credit memo #2002-105C, Class: Walnut Creek. Contra Costa County Sales tax. Refunded his VISA card. Total refund: $707.40.

(handwritten margin notes: "?" ; "10% Discount Forced 117.15 Should be 89.75")

4. Deposit all checks to the bank account on February 28, 2002. Print the deposit summary.

5. Deposit all VISA receipts on February 28, 2002. VISA charges a 2% bankcard fee. Print the deposit summary.

6. Print a Sales by Customer Summary for January 1 through February 28, 2002.

7. Print a Sales by Item Summary for February 1 through February 28, 2002.

8. Create customer statements for the period of February 1 through February 28, 2002. Assess finance charges of 18%, with a minimum $5 charge. The assessment date should be February 28, 2002. Then print statements for all customers who have a balance due.

Name _____ **Date** _____

Workplace *Applications*

DISCUSSION QUESTIONS

These questions are designed to help you apply what you are learning about QuickBooks to your own organization. Take some time to begin a notebook for your answers and your thoughts about how your company could use QuickBooks to organize information and track performance.

Some of your answers may lead to more questions you would like to ask about your organization. Make note of these, too, and perhaps also think of the person who could best answer them.

1. What products or services does your organization provide? Are sales of these services or products taxable?

2. List some of your customers or clients. Which products and/or services do each of your customers buy or use most frequently?

3. How does each of the clients you listed pay for your products and services? Does each pay at the time of the sale or do you send Invoices later? What is the credit limit offered to each of your customers?

4. What is your organization's return policy? Do you have many client returns? If you don't have returnable products or services, how does your organization handle dissatisfied clients?

5. Does your organization use its own Invoice layout or Cash Sale form layout? How do they differ from the forms in QuickBooks? Will your organization continue to use these forms? If not, how will they change? Will you purchase preprinted forms, or will you use blank paper to print your sales from QuickBooks?

6. Do any of your clients pay for more than one sale or Invoice at a time? What is your organization's policy regarding how to apply payments to open Invoices? Oldest first? Specific matching? What is the policy regarding overpayments and underpayments? Are overpayments refunded?

ACTIVITY

Evaluate your organization's Invoice layout or Sales Receipt forms compared to the QuickBooks predesigned forms. Using the Chapter 2 tutorial template file, create a new invoice template that would best suit your company's needs. Print one of your newly designed invoices.

CASE STUDY

SOFTWARE SUPPORT, INC.

Software Support, Inc. is a company that provides computer consulting services for clients throughout the Chicago metropolitan area. The company provides computer setup, training, and troubleshooting services for small business clients. They charge a flat fee of $200 for computer setup, and they charge $50 per hour for training and $75 per hour for troubleshooting.

Questions

These questions are designed to help you apply what you are learning about QuickBooks to this case study. Use your notebook to record your answers and your thoughts.

1. How would you set up the Item list in QuickBooks to track each service that Software Support, Inc. sells?

2. What transactions would you use to record sales to customers who are allowed to pay within 30 days of service?

3. What report would you use to view the details of which customers owe you money?

interNET CONNECTION

To learn more about QuickBooks software, visit the QuickBooks site at **www.quickbooks.com.**

3

Managing Expenses

OBJECTIVES

After completing this chapter, you should be able to:

1. Set up vendors in the Vendor list.

2. Understand how Classes are used in QuickBooks.

3. Use QuickBooks for job costing.

4. Enter expense transactions in several different ways.

5. Manage Accounts Payable transactions.

6. Print checks.

7. Create and apply vendor credits.

8. Manage vendor prepayments (deposits) and refunds.

9. Track petty cash.

10. Track credit card charges and payments.

RESTORE THIS FILE

This chapter uses Chapter 3.QBW. To open this file, restore the file called **Chapter 3.QBB** to your hard disk. (See page 7 for instructions on restoring files.)

In this chapter, we'll discuss several ways to track your company's expenditures and vendors. We'll start by adding vendors to your file, and then we'll discuss several methods for paying them. In addition, this chapter shows you how to track expenses by job.

ENTERING EXPENSES IN QUICKBOOKS

When you record your expenses in QuickBooks, you'll follow a few basic steps. Table 3-1 shows each step in the process.

Consider the business transactions that occur every day in your business. When bills come in the mail, you'll use the **Enter Bill** function in QuickBooks to record what you purchased and the amount you owe to the vendor. Then, when it's time to pay your bills, you'll use the **Pay Bills** function in QuickBooks to select the ones you want to pay. Sometimes you'll need to write a check that is not for the payment of a bill. In that case you'll use the **Write Checks** function. The next step in the process is to print the checks, one check at a time, or in a batch.

In Table 3-1 you can see each of these steps and the accounting entries that occur as a result of your actions.

For some of your vendors, you'll decide to use Accounts Payable to track bills and bill payments. We will refer to these as your **Credit** vendors.

With other Vendors you'll skip the Accounts Payable account and just write checks, coding the checks to the appropriate expense accounts. We will refer to these as your **Cash** vendors. Although you might not pay these vendors with cash, we'll use the term Cash vendor to distinguish them from vendors that you track in Accounts Payable.

You'll want to treat vendors as **Credit** vendors if they send you bills or if you pay only part of vendor's bill each month. This is also best if you combine more than one bill from a vendor onto an individual bill payment to the vendor.

	Cash Vendors		Credit Vendors	
Business Transaction	**QuickBooks Transaction**	**Accounting Entry**	**QuickBooks Transaction**	**Accounting Entry**
Recording a Bill from a Vendor			*Enter Bill*	Increase (debit) **Expenses**, increase (credit) **Accounts Payable**.
Paying Bills	*Write Checks*	Decrease (credit) **Checking**, increase (debit) **Expense**.	*Pay Bills*	Decrease (debit) **Accounts Payable**, decrease (credit) **Checking account**.
Printing One Check at a Time	*Click Print on Check*	QuickBooks assigns a check number to the printed check.	*Click Print on Check*	QuickBooks assigns a check number to the printed check.
Printing Checks in Batches	*Print Checks from File Menu*	QuickBooks assigns check numbers to all printed checks.	*Print Checks from File Menu*	QuickBooks assigns check numbers to all printed checks.

Table 3-1 Steps for entering expenses

On the other hand, you may treat vendors as Cash vendors if they don't send bills, or if you always pay the exact amount of the bills they send without delaying payment until the due date.

There is a trade-off between Cash and Credit vendors. With Cash vendors, you have fewer data to enter (because you skip the Enter Bills step), but with Credit vendors, you get more detailed Accounts Payable reports. A store where you write checks for retail purchases is a good example of a Cash vendor. Your supplier who always sends bills for each of your purchases is a good example of a Credit vendor.

Note that QuickBooks doesn't distinguish between these two types of vendors, so you don't set up records for your Cash vendors any differently from your Credit vendors, except that you don't need to fill in all of the details (such as credit limit and Terms) for Cash vendors.

SETTING UP VENDORS

Vendors include everyone from whom you purchase products or services, including trade vendors, service vendors, and 1099 contract workers. You cannot write a check in QuickBooks without recording the name of the payee on one of QuickBooks' four name lists: Customer, Vendor, Employee, or Other.

When your vendor is also your customer, you will need to set up two separate records: a vendor record in the Vendor List, and a customer record in the Customer:Job List. The customer name must be slightly different than the vendor name. For example, you could enter Boswell Insulation as "Boswell Insulation-V" as the vendor name in the New Vendor screen, and "Boswell Insulation-C" as the customer name in the New Customer:Job screen. The contact information for both customer and vendor record can be identical.

To set up a vendor, follow these steps:

COMPUTER TUTORIAL

1 Select the *Lists* menu, and choose **Vendor List** (see Figure 3-1).

Figure 3-1 Add new vendors to the Vendor list.

2 To add a new vendor, select the ***Vendor*** menu at the bottom of the Vendor list, and choose **New** (see Figure 3-2). The New Vendor screen displays (see Figure 3-3). Notice there are two tabs labeled Address Info and Additional Info.

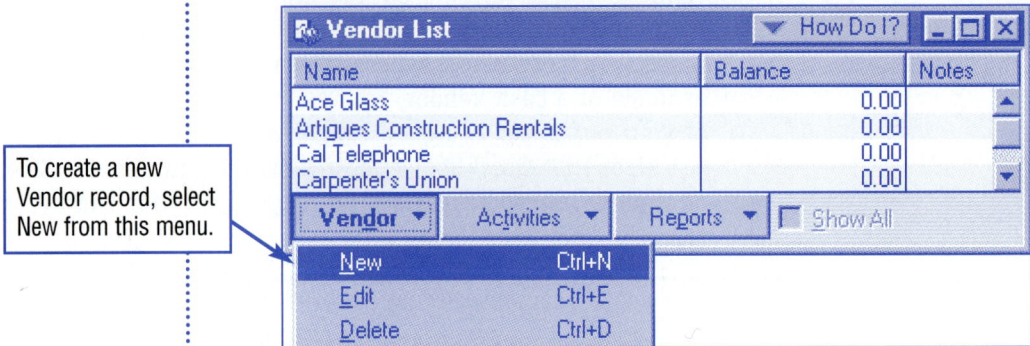

To create a new Vendor record, select New from this menu.

Figure 3-2 Select New to add a vendor.

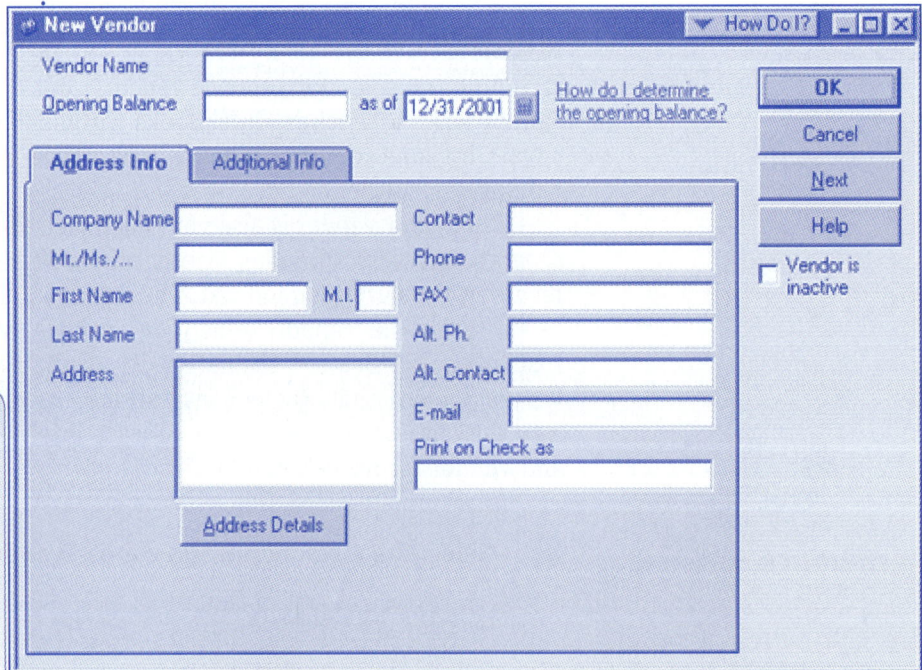

> **TIP**
> The **Vendor** list sorts alphabetically, just like the **Customer** list. Therefore, if your vendor is an individual person, enter the last name first, followed by the first name.

> **TIP**
> There are four name lists in QuickBooks: Vendor, Customer:Job, Employee, and Other Names. After you enter a customer's name in the *Vendor* field of the New Vendor record, you cannot use that name in any of the other three lists in QuickBooks, and vice versa.

Figure 3-3 The Vendor Information screen with the Address Info tab selected

3 Enter "Boswell Insulation" in the *Vendor Name* field and press <TAB>.

4 Press <TAB> twice to skip the *Opening Balance* and *as of* fields (see Figure 3-4).

The *Opening Balance* field shows only on New Vendor screens. You will not see this field on Edit Vendor screens. The date in the *as of* field defaults to the current date. Since you will not be entering an amount in the *Opening Balance* field, there is no need to change this date.

> **IMPORTANT**
>
> It is best **not** to use the *Opening Balance* Field in the vendor record. When you enter an opening balance for a vendor in the *Opening Balance* field, QuickBooks creates a Bill that increases (credits) Accounts Payable, and increases (debits) Uncategorized Expense. You or your accountant will then need to adjust the balance in Uncategorized Expense before you can use QuickBooks reports to prepare your tax return. Instead, enter each unpaid bill separately after you create the vendor record.

5 Enter "dba Boswell Insulation" in the *Company Name* field of the Address Info tab, and press <TAB>.

The "dba" stands for "doing business as" and is a common way of describing sole proprietorships on legal documents. The text you enter in the *Company Name* field shows on the IRS Form 1099 for that vendor. If the vendor is a corporation, enter the corporate name in this field (e.g., Boswell Insulation, Inc.).

6 Continue entering the rest of the fields on the Vendor record, as shown in Figure 3-4. Press <TAB> after each entry.

Note that QuickBooks automatically inserts the text from the *Company Name* field into both the *Address* and *Print on Check as* fields. You will need to delete the abbreviation "dba" from each of these fields. Verify that your screen matches Figure 3-4 before proceding to the next step.

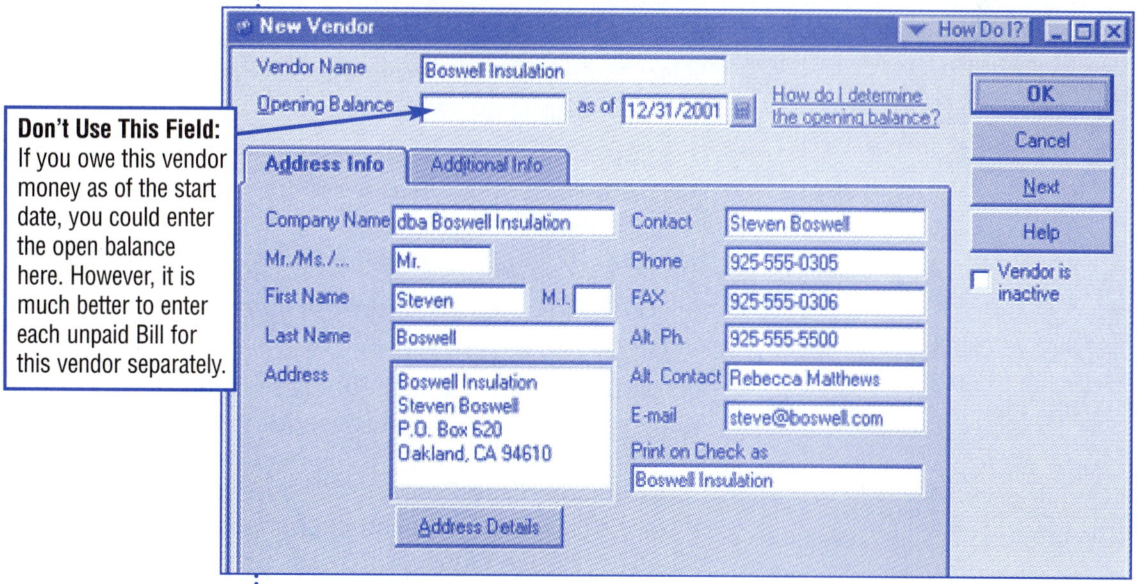

Don't Use This Field: If you owe this vendor money as of the start date, you could enter the open balance here. However, it is much better to enter each unpaid Bill for this vendor separately.

Figure 3-4 Your screen should look like this after completing the Address Info section.

7 Click the Additional Info tab (see Figure 3-5) to continue entering information about this vendor.

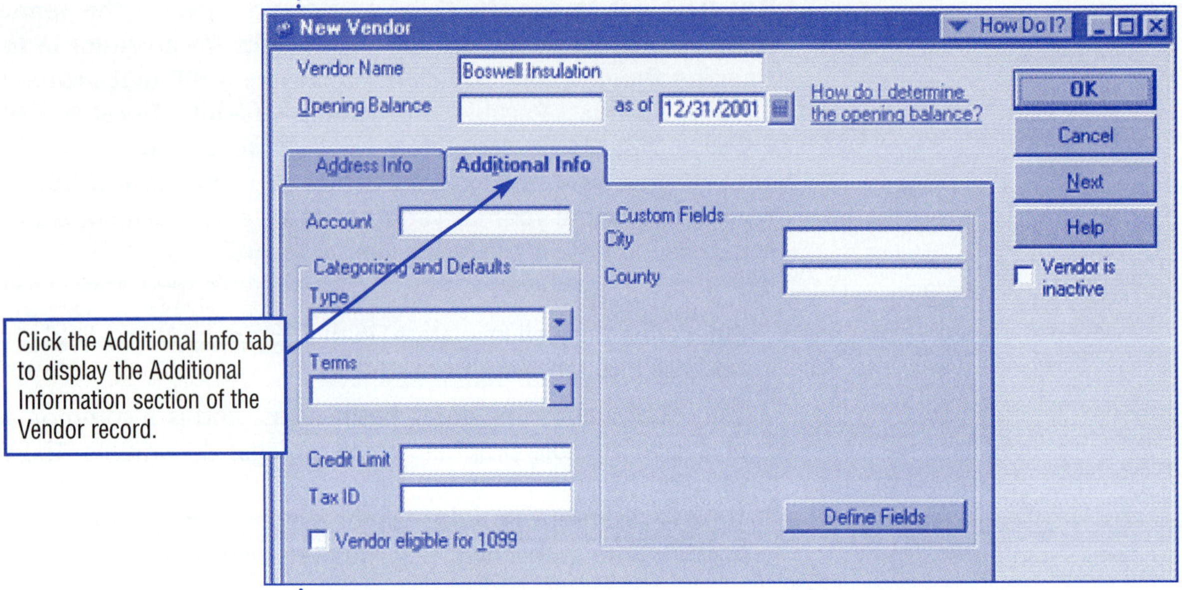

Click the Additional Info tab to display the Additional Information section of the Vendor record.

Figure 3-5 The Additional Info tab of the New Vendor screen

8 Enter "Acct #66-112" in the *Account* field and press <TAB>.

In this field, you enter the number that your vendor uses to track you as a customer. If your vendor requires that you enter your account number on the checks you send, enter it here and QuickBooks will automatically print the number when you pay this vendor's bill.

9 Select "Subcontractors" from the *Type* field drop-down menu and press <TAB>.

QickBooks allows you to group your vendors into common types. For example, if you create a Vendor type called Subcontractors and you tag each of your subcontractors' Vendor records with this type, you could later create a report specific to this Vendor Type.

10 Select "2% 10 Net 30" from the *Terms* field drop-down menu and press <TAB>.

QuickBooks is *terms smart*. For example, the terms of 2% 10 Net 30 means that if you pay this vendor within 10 days, you are eligible for a 2% discount. In this field, you can set the payment terms default. QuickBooks uses these default terms on all new bills for this vendor. You can override the default terms on each bill as necessary. When you create reports for Accounts Payable (A/P), QuickBooks takes into account the terms on each bill.

11 Press <TAB> to leave the *Credit Limit* field blank.

⑫ Enter "123-12-1234" in the *Tax ID* field.

The *Tax ID* field is where you enter the social security or taxpayer identification number of your 1099 subcontractors. QuickBooks prints this number on the 1099 at the end of the year.

⑬ Click the box next to "Vendor eligible for 1099."

Select this box for all vendors for whom you expect to file 1099s. See the QuickBooks Help index for more information about tracking and printing 1099s.

⑭ Enter "Oakland" in the *City* field and press <TAB>.

The *City* field is a Custom Field. The **Define Fields** button on the New Vendor Additional Information screen allows you to define Custom Fields to track more information about your vendors. In the *City* field, you'll tag each vendor with the city in which it is headquartered. This allows you to create reports later that include geographic information about purchases from vendors.

⑮ Enter "Alameda" in the *County* field and press <TAB>.

The *County* field is another Custom Field. In this field, you'll tag each vendor with the county in which it is headquartered. This allows you to create reports later that include geographic information about purchases from vendors.

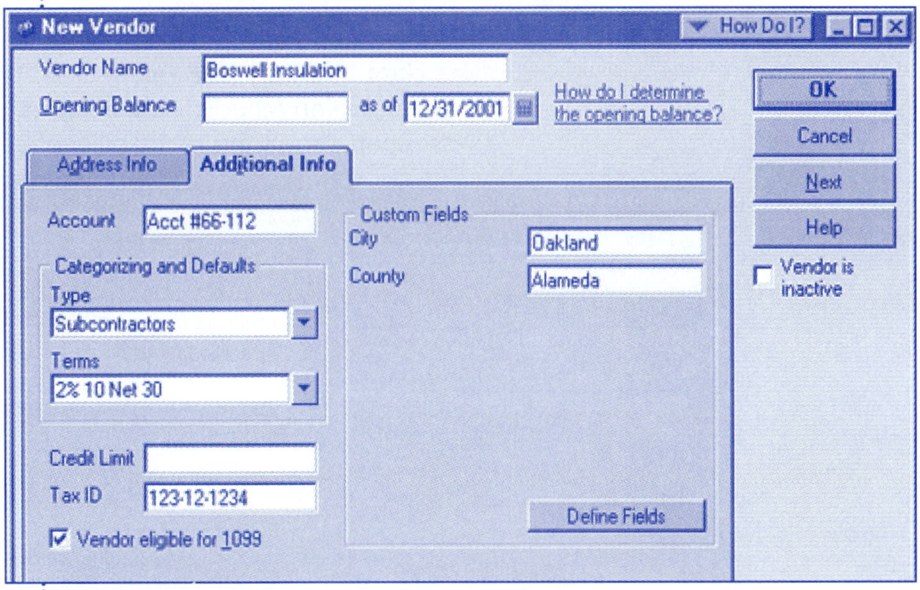

Figure 3-6 The completed Boswell Insulation Vendor record

⑯ Verify that your screen matches Figure 3-6, and then click **OK**.

If you were adding several vendors at a time, you would click **Next** instead, and begin adding another vendor. Close all open windows.

ACTIVATING CLASS TRACKING

In QuickBooks, classes give you a way to *classify* your transactions. You can use QuickBooks classes to classify your income and expenses by department, location, profit centers, or any other meaningful breakdown of your business.

For example, a dentist might classify all income and expenses as relating to either the dentistry or hygiene department. A law firm formed as a partnership might classify all income and expenses according to which partner generated the business. If you use classes, you'll be able to create separate reports for each *class* of the business. So the dentist could create separate Profit and Loss reports for the dentistry and hygiene departments, and the law firm could create separate reports for each partner.

In our sample company, Academy Glass uses classes to track income and expenses for each of its two stores located in San Jose and Walnut Creek. You might use classes to separate *departments* or *profit centers* within your company. Or if your business is a not-for-profit organization, you could use classes to separately track transactions for each *Fund* or *Program* within the organization.

COMPUTER TUTORIAL

1. Select the *Edit* menu, and choose **Preferences**.

2. Then scroll to the top and click **Accounting**.

3. Select the Company Preferences tab, and check the box next to "Use class tracking" (see Figure 3-7). When you use classes on each transaction (checks, bills, invoices, etc.), the Profit & Loss by Class report shows the profitability of each Class.

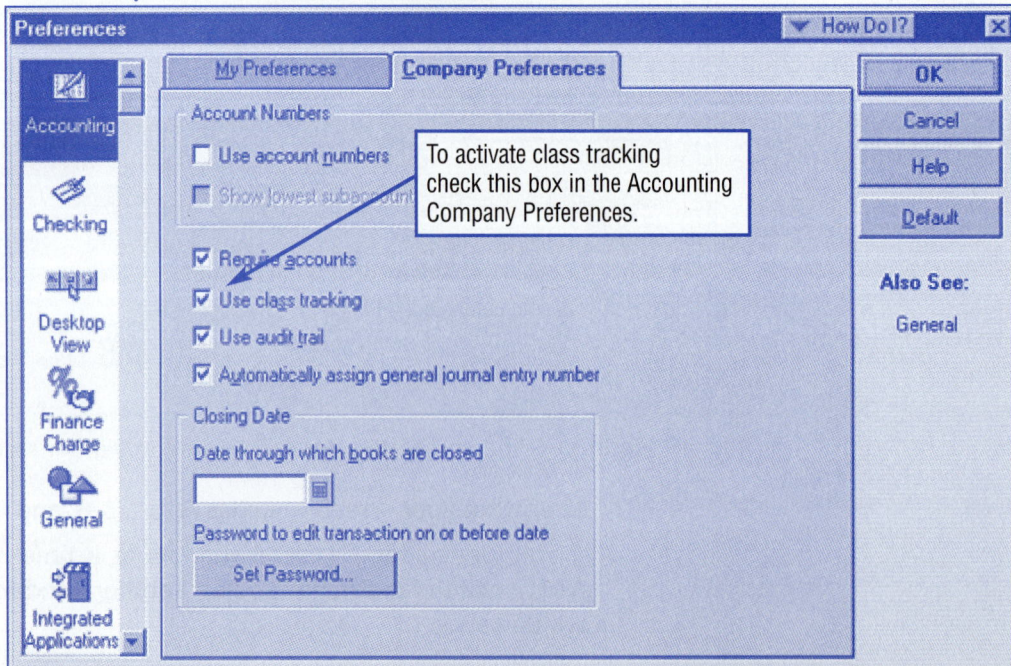

Figure 3-7 Use class tracking to track separate departments or locations.

4. Click **OK**.

In Figure 3-8, the Class column is tagged with "San Jose." This feeds this expense to the San Jose Class (the San Jose store) so that the Profit & Loss by Class report shows the expense under the column for the San Jose Class (see Figure 3-9).

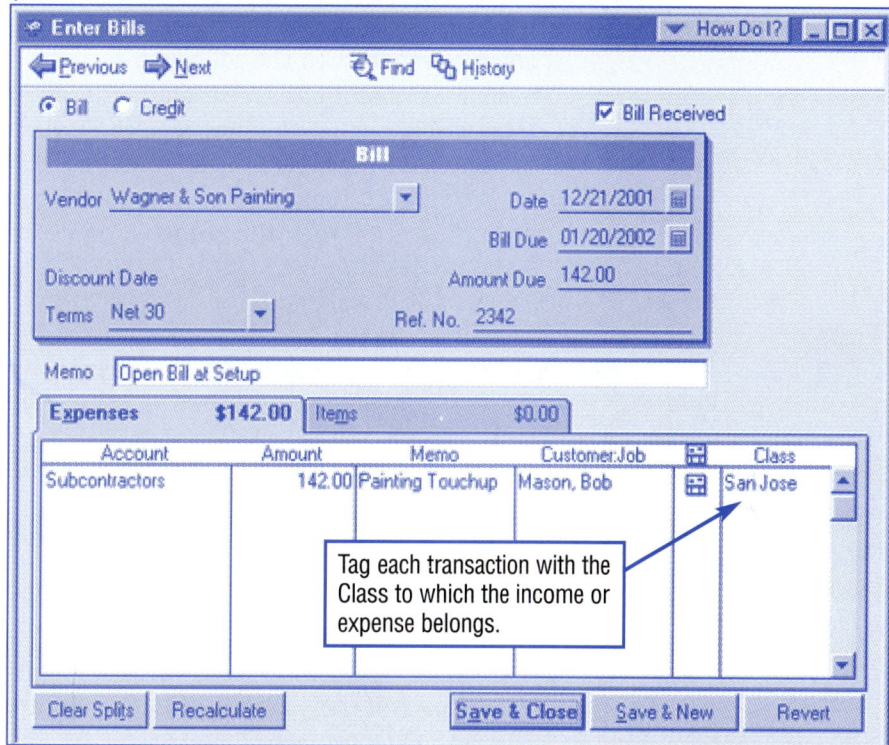

Tag each transaction with the Class to which the income or expense belongs.

Figure 3-8 The Class field shows on many screens in QuickBooks, including Enter Bills.

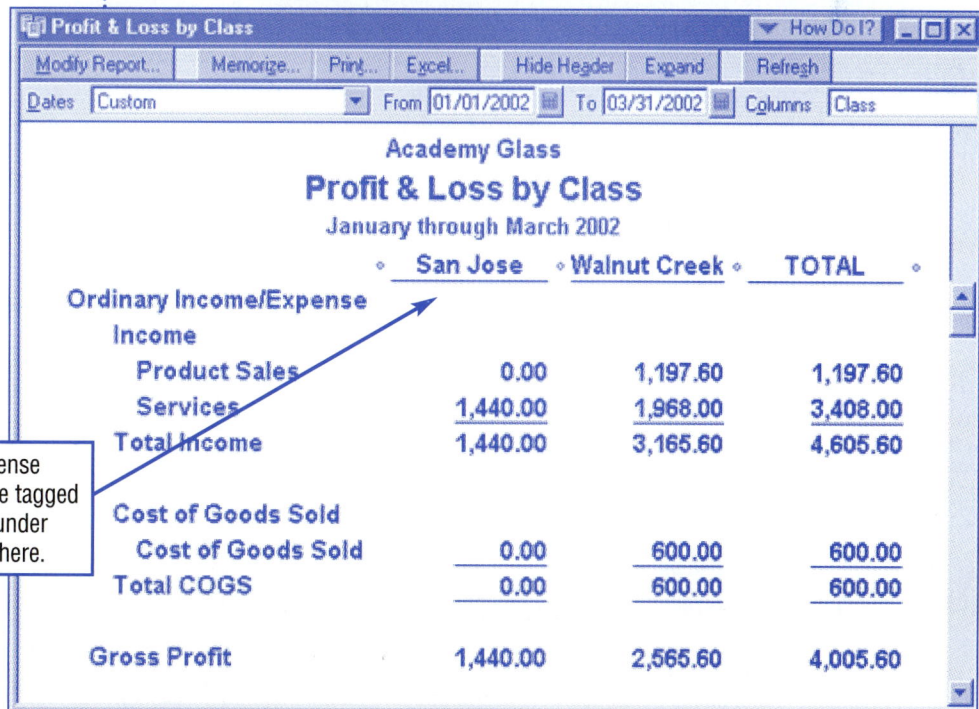

All income and expense transactions that are tagged with a Class show under their Class column here.

Academy Glass

Profit & Loss by Class

January through March 2002

	San Jose	Walnut Creek	TOTAL
Ordinary Income/Expense			
Income			
Product Sales	0.00	1,197.60	1,197.60
Services	1,440.00	1,968.00	3,408.00
Total Income	1,440.00	3,165.60	4,605.60
Cost of Goods Sold			
Cost of Goods Sold	0.00	600.00	600.00
Total COGS	0.00	600.00	600.00
Gross Profit	1,440.00	2,565.60	4,005.60

Figure 3-9 Class tracking groups expenses on reports.

TRACKING JOB COSTS

If you want to track the expenses for each customer or job (i.e., track job costs), you'll need to tag each expense transaction with the customer or job to which the expense should apply. You tag expenses when you pay vendors. In the following sections, you'll learn about recording expense transactions in several different situations. In some of the transactions, you'll see how to record job costs, but in others you will not enter any customer or job information.

Use the Customer:Job column (see Figure 3-10) to tag each expense account or Item with the customer or job to which it applies.

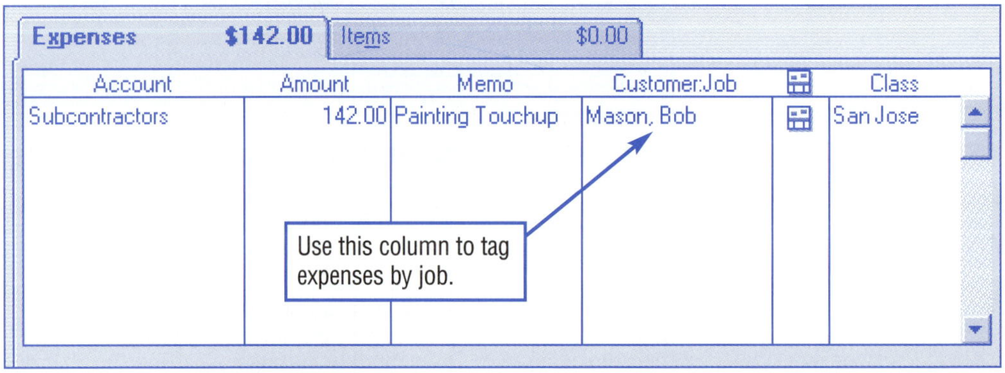

Figure 3-10 The Customer:Job column is used to tag expenses to jobs.

When you track job costs, you can create reports such as the Profit & Loss by Job report (see Figure 3-11) that shows income and expenses separately for each job. See Chapter 5 for more information about this report.

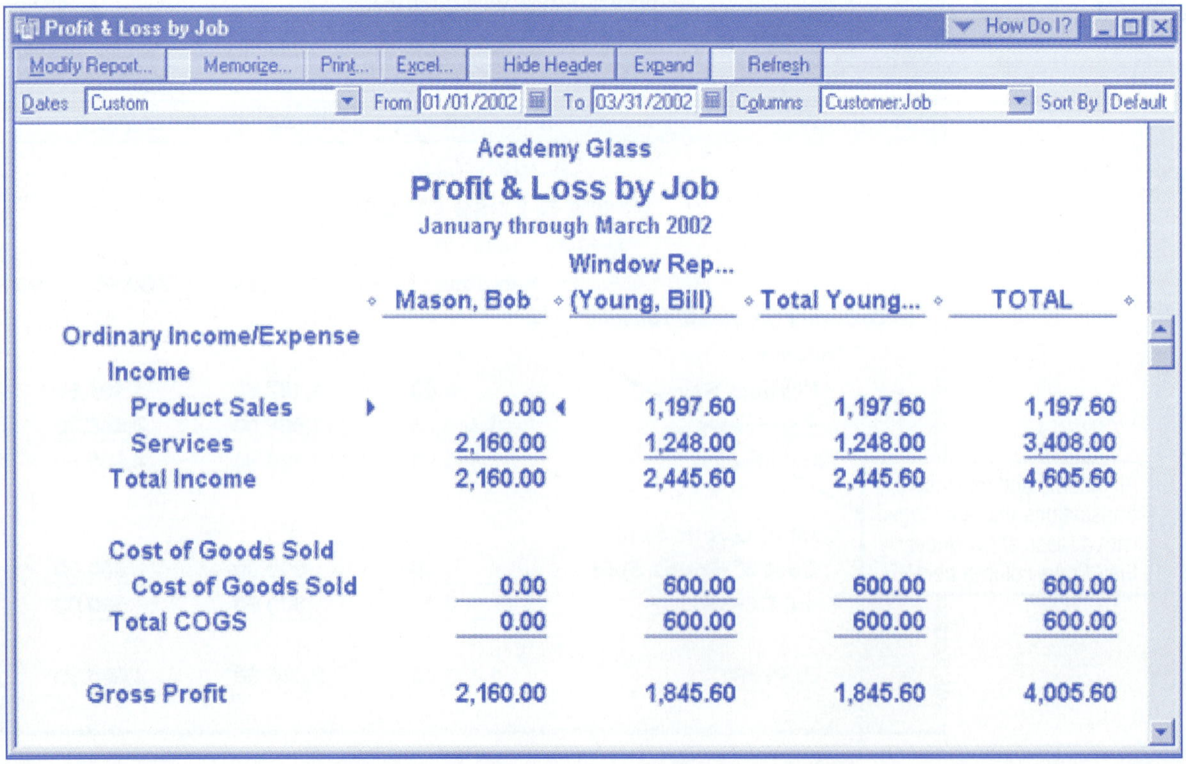

Figure 3-11 The Profit and Loss by Job report

The Customer:Job List (see Figure 3-12) includes the totals as well as information about the individual jobs for each customer. You can see that Anderson Floors has two jobs listed, the 2ⁿᵈ Street Store, and the Front St. Store.

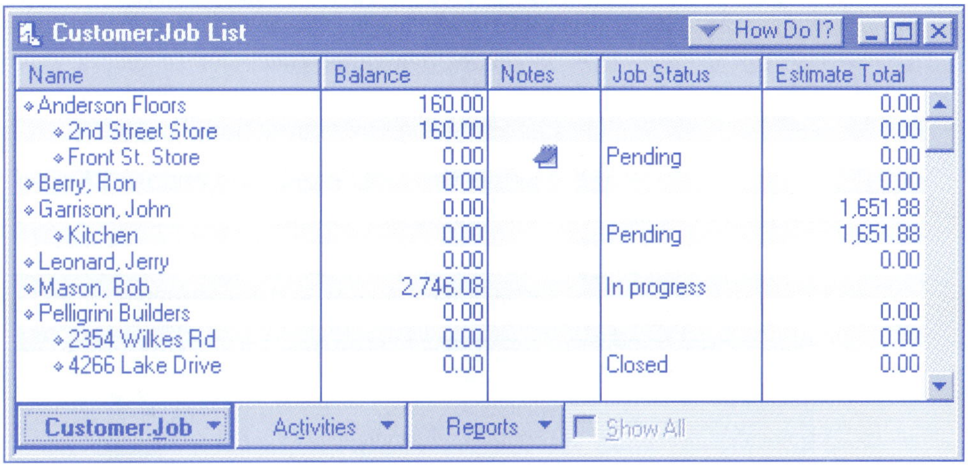

Name	Balance	Notes	Job Status	Estimate Total
◆ Anderson Floors	160.00			0.00
◆ 2nd Street Store	160.00			0.00
◆ Front St. Store	0.00		Pending	0.00
◆ Berry, Ron	0.00			0.00
◆ Garrison, John	0.00			1,651.88
◆ Kitchen	0.00		Pending	1,651.88
◆ Leonard, Jerry	0.00			0.00
◆ Mason, Bob	2,746.08		In progress	
◆ Pelligrini Builders	0.00			0.00
◆ 2354 Wilkes Rd	0.00			0.00
◆ 4266 Lake Drive	0.00		Closed	0.00

Figure 3-12 The Customer:Job List

PAYING VENDORS

With QuickBooks, just as in real life, you can pay your vendors in several ways. You can pay by check, credit card, electronic funds transfer, or in cash (although cash is not recommended).

Most of the time, you'll use checks to pay your vendors, so this section covers three different situations for paying by check. The three situations are:

1. Using the Register to record manual checks and Electronic Funds Transfers after they occur.

2. Using the Write Checks function to write and print checks without using Accounts Payable.

3. Using the Enter Bills function to record Accounts Payable and then using the Pay Bills function to pay all of the outstanding bills.

Using Registers

When paying vendors you can use QuickBooks to write and print a check. In this example, you won't pay a bill (i.e., a payable); you'll just use QuickBooks to prepare and print a check for one of your vendors. This section covers the direct register entry method.

To record a manual check, or to record a payment made by electronic funds transfer, you can go directly to the Checking account register and enter the transaction.

COMPUTER TUTORIAL

① Select the *Lists* menu and choose **Chart of Accounts** to display the Charts of Accounts.

② Double-click the **Checking** account in the Chart of Accounts. The Checking account register displays (see Figure 3-13).

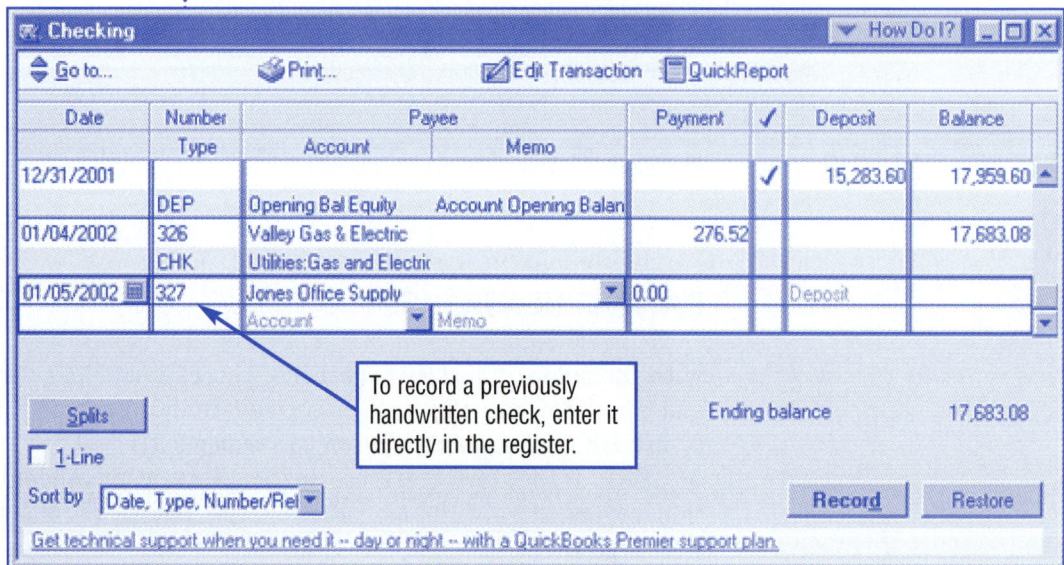

Date	Number	Payee		Payment	✓	Deposit	Balance
	Type	Account	Memo				
12/31/2001					✓	15,283.60	17,959.60
	DEP	Opening Bal Equity	Account Opening Balan				
01/04/2002	326	Valley Gas & Electric		276.52			17,683.08
	CHK	Utilities:Gas and Electric					
01/05/2002	327	Jones Office Supply		0.00		Deposit	
		Account	Memo				

To record a previously handwritten check, enter it directly in the register.

Ending balance 17,683.08

Figure 3-13 Checking account register

ANOTHER WAY

To display the Chart of Accounts, press <Ctrl+A>.

③ Enter "01/05/2002" in the first empty line of Date column to begin entering the check. Press <TAB>.

④ Enter "327" in the Number column, if it does not automatically display, and press <TAB>.

Since you're entering a previously handwritten check, make sure this number matches the number on the physical check.

⑤ Enter "Jones Office Supply" in the Payee column and press <TAB>.

Since "Jones Office Supply" is not in the Vendor List, QuickBooks prompts you to **Quick Add** or **Set Up** the Vendor. Click **Quick Add** on the Name Not Found message window (see Figure 3-14).

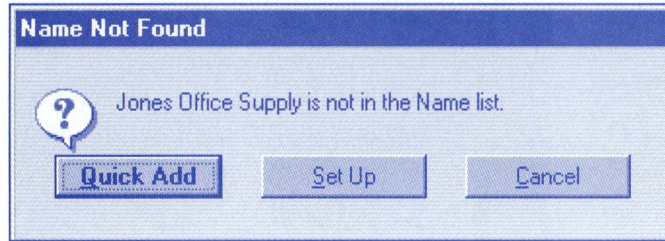

Figure 3-14 Quick Add will add the vendor to the Vendor List.

6 Clicking **Quick Add** will add this Vendor to the Vendor List without entering all of the address information. You can always go back later and add the address and other information by editing the Vendor record. Click **OK** on the Select Name Type window to add Jones Office Supply to the Vendor List (see Figure 3-15).

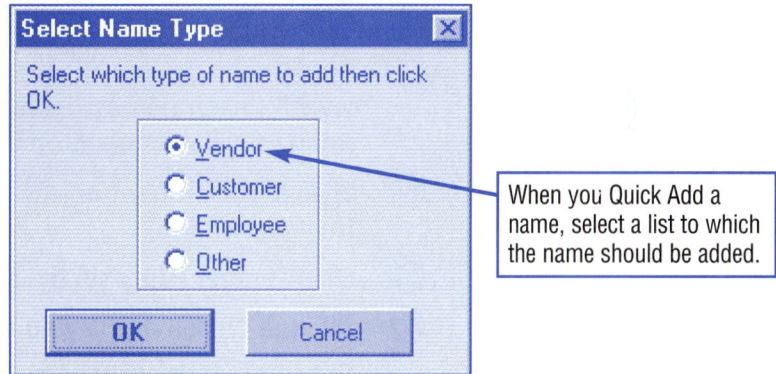

When you Quick Add a name, select a list to which the name should be added.

Figure 3-15 Quick Add asks you to choose a list.

7 Enter "128.60" in the Payment column and press <TAB>.

8 Using QuickFill, enter "Of" (the first two letters of "Office Supplies") in the Account column and press <TAB>.

After you enter the first few characters of the word "Office" in the Account column, notice that QuickBooks automatically fills in the rest of the field with "Office Supplies." This is the **QuickFill** feature helping you to enter data faster (see Figure 3-16).

Enter the first few characters of the Account name and notice that QuickFill helps you finish.

| 01/05/2002 | 327 | Jones Office Supply | 128.60 | Deposit | |
| | CHK | Office Supplies | Memo | | |

Figure 3-16 QuickFill will supply account names.

9 Enter "Printer Paper" in the Memo column.

10 Verify that you've entered all of the fields in the transaction correctly, and click **Record** to save the transaction.

Notice that QuickBooks automatically updates your account balance when you record the transaction.

Splitting Transactions

Sometimes you will need to apply your purchase to more than one account. Let's say that the check you just wrote to Jones Office Supply was actually for the following expenses:

◆ $100.00 for printer paper, to be used in the San Jose store (Class).

◆ $28.60 for 500 copies of the newsletter for the Walnut Creek store (Class).

In order to track your printing costs separately from your office supplies, you will need to split this check up and assign each expense to separate accounts.

COMPUTER TUTORIAL

1. With the Checking register open, click Check #327 to select it.

2. Click **Splits** at the bottom left of the register.

   QuickBooks displays an area below the check where you can add several lines, memos, and amounts for *splitting* the expenses among several different accounts.

3. Change the amount on the first line from "128.60" to "100.00." Then press <TAB>.

4. Enter "Printer Paper" in the Memo column and press <TAB>.

5. Skip the Customer:Job column by pressing <TAB>.

   This is the column where you can enter the customer or job name to which this expense should apply.

6. Enter "San Jose" in the Class column, and press <TAB>.

7. On the second line, enter "Printing and Reproduction" in the Account column, and press <TAB>.

8. QuickBooks calculates the amount "28.60" in the Amount column, and press <TAB>.

9. Enter "500 copies of newsletter" in the Memo column, and press <TAB>.

10. Skip to the Class column, and enter "Walnut Creek."

⑪ When you've finished entering the information, verify that your screen matches Figure 3-17, and press **Record** to save the transaction.

⑫ Close all open screens.

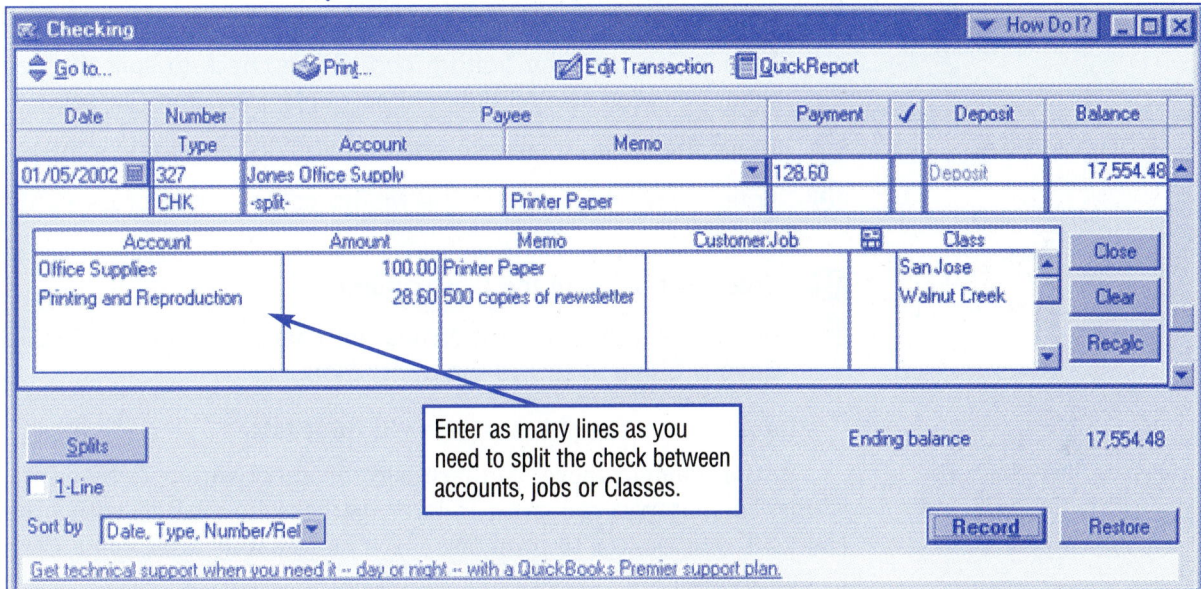

Figure 3-17 You can split the transaction for different accounts, jobs, or Classes.

Using Write Checks Without Using A/P

If you're tracking job costs or classes, it's best to use the Write Checks function. If you use Items to track purchases, you must use the Write Checks screen.

COMPUTER TUTORIAL

→ ANOTHER →
← WAY ←

To access the Write Checks screen, press <Ctrl+W>.

❶ To display the Write Checks screen, select the *Banking* menu and choose **Write Checks** (see Figure 3-18).

❷ "Checking" in the *Bank Account* field is preselected. Press <TAB>.

❸ To indicate that you want QuickBooks to print this check on your printer, click the "To be printed" box to the right of the Items tab or enter "To Print" in the *No.* field.

When you actually print the check later, QuickBooks will assign the next check number sequentially.

❹ Enter "01/05/2002" in the *Date* field and press <TAB>.

❺ Select "Orlando Properties" from the *Pay to the Order of* field drop-down menu, and press <TAB>.

Notice that QuickBooks enters the name and address from the Vendor record as soon as you choose the Vendor name from the menu.

6. Enter "3,200.00" in the *$* field and press <TAB>.

7. Press <TAB> three times to skip the *Address* and *Memo* fields, and the "To be printed" box.

8. Enter "Rent" in the Account column of the Expenses tab, and press <TAB>.

   If necessary, use the bottom part of the check to split the payment between several different accounts, jobs, and Classes.

9. Leave the Amount column set to "3,200.00" and press <TAB>.

10. Enter "San Jose Rent" in the Memo column, and press <TAB> twice.

11. Enter "San Jose" in the Class column.

12. Verify that your screen matches the check in Figure 3-18. Click **Save & Close** to record the transaction.

   Do not print the check now; we'll do it later.

   In the example above, you recorded the check with a To be printed status, so that you can print it later, perhaps in a batch with other checks. If you wanted to print the check immediately after you entered it, you would have clicked Print at the top of the Write Checks screen. QuickBooks would ask you for the appropriate check number.

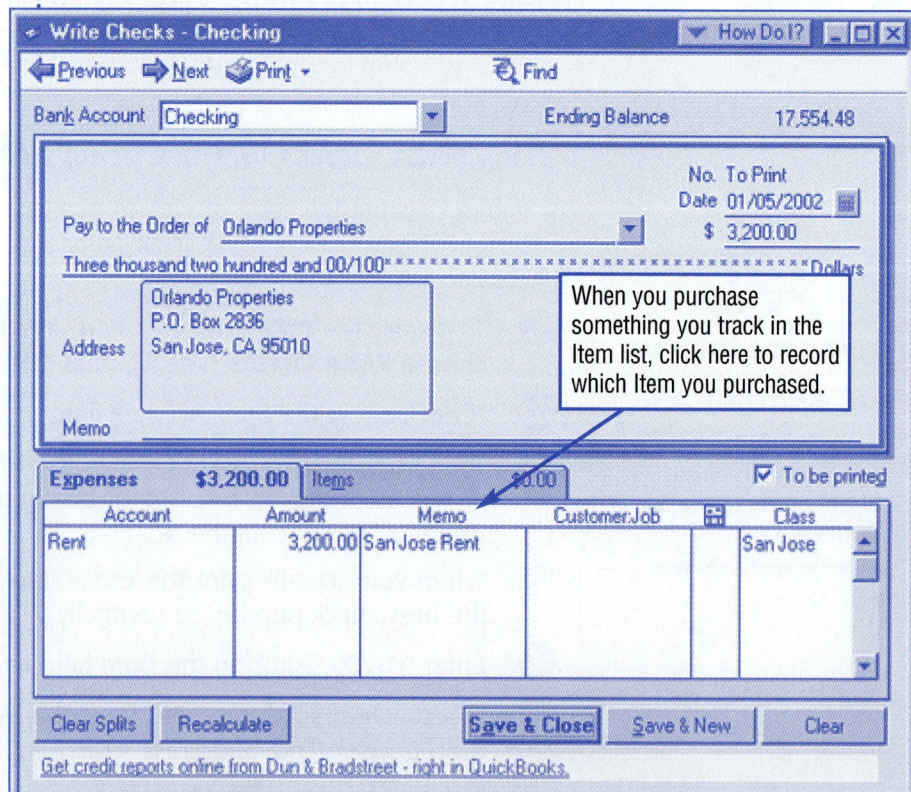

Figure 3-18 Use this information to complete the check.

Using QuickBooks Bills for Accounts Payable

You can also pay your vendors by paying bills that you have previously recorded in Accounts Payable.

When you receive a bill from a vendor, enter it into QuickBooks using the Enter Bills screen. Recording a bill allows QuickBooks to track the amount you owe to the vendor along with the detail of what you purchased. For a bill to be considered paid by QuickBooks, you must pay it using the Pay Bills function, as discussed here.

Entering Bills

When a bill arrives from your vendor, enter it into QuickBooks using the Enter Bills screen.

COMPUTER TUTORIAL

❶ Select the *Vendors* menu and choose **Enter Bills**. The Enter Bills screen displays (see Figure 3-19).

Figure 3-19 Blank Enter Bills screen

❷ Enter "Ace Glass" in the *Vendor* field and press <TAB>.

❸ Enter "01/18/2002" in the *Date* field and press <TAB>.

Notice that QuickBooks completes the *Discount Date*, *Terms*, and *Bill Due* fields automatically when you enter the Vendor name. QuickBooks used information from the Vendor record to complete these fields. You can override this information as necessary. QuickBooks calculates the *Discount Date* and the *Bill Due* fields by adding the terms information to the date entered in the *Date* field. If the terms do not include a discount, the Discount Date will not appear (as on Figure 3-19).

④ Press <TAB> to skip the *Bill Due* field and to accept the due date that QuickBooks has calculated.

⑤ Enter "1,286.00" in the *Amount Due* field and press <TAB>.

⑥ "2% 10 Net 30" in the *Terms* field is preselected. Press <TAB>.

⑦ Enter "2084" in the *Ref. No.* field and press <TAB>.

You should always enter a Ref. No. that matches the number on the bill from the vendor. The *Ref. No.* field is important for two reasons. First, it's the number you'll use to identify this bill later when you use the Pay Bills function, and second, it's the number that shows on the voucher of the Bill Payment check.

⑧ Enter "Window Purchase for Young Job" in the *Memo* field and press <TAB>.

⑨ Enter "Purchases" in the Account column of the Expenses tab, and press <TAB>.

⑩ "1,286.00" in the Amount column is preselected. Press <TAB>.

⑪ Enter "Windows" in the Memo column, and press <TAB>.

⑫ To job cost this purchase, enter "Young Bill:Window Replacement" in the Customer:Job column, and press <TAB>.

⑬ Enter "Walnut Creek" in the Class column.

⑭ Verify that your screen matches that shown in Figure 3-20. Click **Save & Close** to record the bill.

> **TIP**
>
> We call A/P transactions "bills," but our vendors call them "invoices." So the *Ref. No.* field should match the number on the invoice your vendor sends.

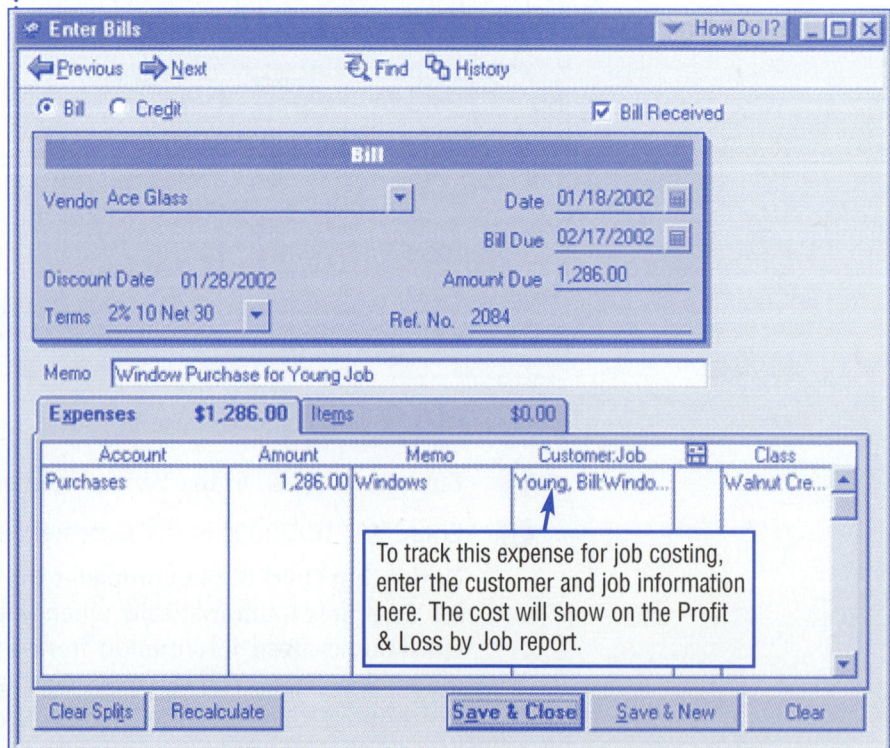

Figure 3-20 Completed Bill

Confirming the Accuracy of Your Bill Entries

After you have entered your bills into QuickBooks, open an Unpaid Bills Detail report and check the date, bill numbers, due date, and amount in QuickBooks against your actual bills from the vendor.

COMPUTER TUTORIAL

① Select the *Reports* menu, choose **Vendors & Payables**, and then choose **Unpaid Bills Detail**.

② Enter "01/18/2002" in the *Date* field and press <TAB> (see Figure 3-21).

③ Verify that your screen matches Figure 3-21, and close all open windows. Click **No** if the Memorize Report message appears.

Figure 3-21 Use the Unpaid Bills Detail report to confirm your entries.

COMPUTER TUTORIAL

Paying Bills

QuickBooks keeps track of all your bills in the Accounts Payable account. When you pay your bills, you'll reduce the balance in Accounts Payable by creating checks (actually Bill Payment checks) or credit card charges.

1 Select the *Vendors* menu and choose **Pay Bills**.

The Pay Bills screen (see Figure 3-22) shows all of the bills that are currently unpaid as of the date shown in the *Due on or before* field.

Figure 3-22 The Pay Bills screen

2 Enter "02/19/2002" in the *Due on or before* field.

3 You can filter the Pay Bills screen so that only the bills due on or before a given date are shown (see Figure 3-23). That way, you can focus on the bills that need immediate attention.

Select "Due Date" from the *Sort Bills By* field drop-down menu.

If you have several bills from the same vendor, it's sometimes easier to see all of the bills sorted by "Vendor." You can also sort the bills by "Discount Date" or "Amount Due."

NOTE

The *Due on or before* field applies only to the bill due date. There is no way to have this show only the bills whose *discounts* expire on or before a certain date.

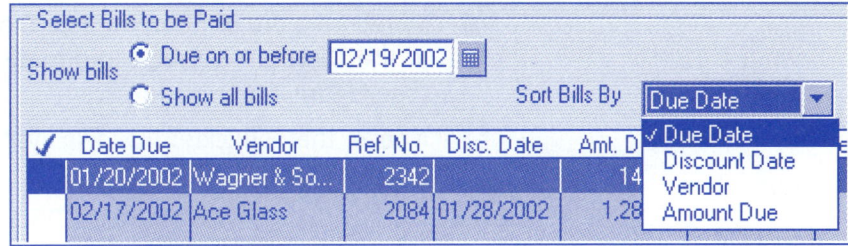

Figure 3-23 The Sort Bills By field allows you to sort bills as needed.

④ Leave "Checking" in the *Payment Account* field and "Check" in the *Payment Method* field. Ensure that the "To be printed" radio button is selected (see Figure 3-24).

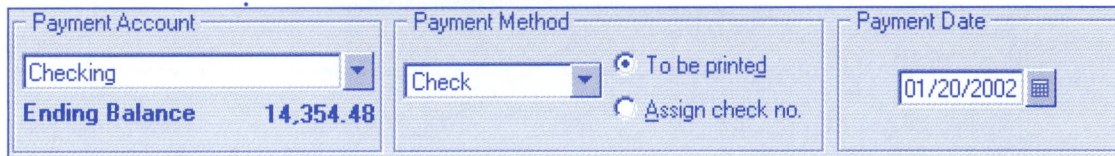

Figure 3-24 Set the Account, Payment Method and Date of your payment.

The *Payment Method* field allows you to choose to pay the bills by check or credit card. If you pay by check, QuickBooks automatically creates a check in your Checking account for each bill you select for payment. If you plan to pay by credit card, select "Credit Card" and choose the name of the credit card account representing the Credit Card you want to charge. QuickBooks will create a separate credit card charge transaction for each bill payment.

⑤ Enter "01/20/2002" in the *Payment Date* field.

⑥ Select the two bills to be paid by clicking in the far left column of each bill (see Figure 3-25).

Figure 3-25 Select which bills to pay in the Pay Bills screen.

TIP

If you want to display the original bill, select the bill on the Pay Bills screen and click Go to Bill. This displays the original bill so you can edit it if necessary.

If you ever wanted to make a partial payment on a bill, you would enter only the amount you wanted to pay in the Amt. To Pay column. If you paid less than the full amount due, QuickBooks would track the remaining amount due for that bill in Accounts Payable. The next time you go to the Pay Bills screen, the partially paid bills would show with the remaining amount due.

7 To record a discount on the Ace Glass bill, select the bill and look at the Discount & Credit Information for Highlighted Bill section (see Figure 3-26).

Notice that QuickBooks displays the terms and a suggested discount for the bill.

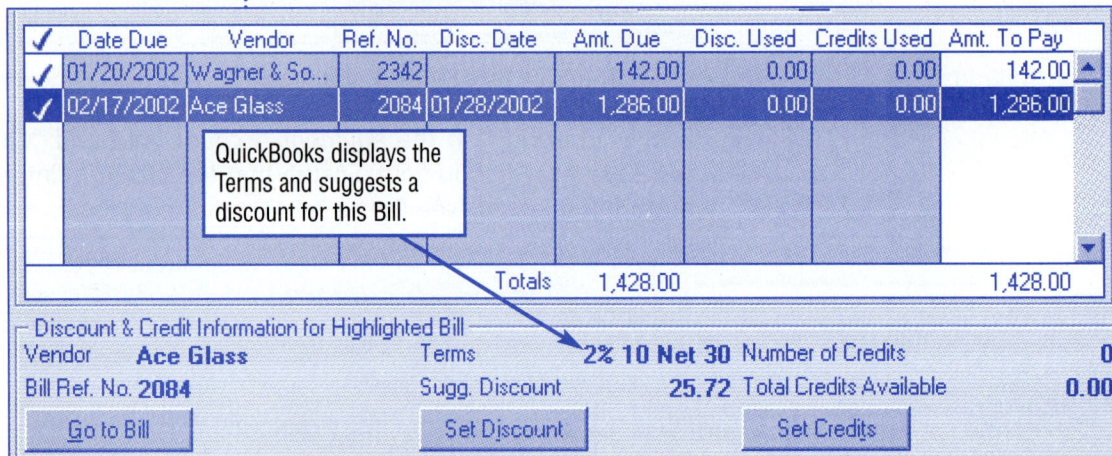

✓	Date Due	Vendor	Ref. No.	Disc. Date	Amt. Due	Disc. Used	Credits Used	Amt. To Pay
✓	01/20/2002	Wagner & So...	2342		142.00	0.00	0.00	142.00
✓	02/17/2002	Ace Glass	2084	01/28/2002	1,286.00	0.00	0.00	1,286.00

> QuickBooks displays the Terms and suggests a discount for this Bill.

| | | Totals | 1,428.00 | | 1,428.00 |

Discount & Credit Information for Highlighted Bill

Vendor	**Ace Glass**	Terms	**2% 10 Net 30**	Number of Credits	**0**
Bill Ref. No. **2084**		Sugg. Discount	25.72	Total Credits Available	**0.00**

Go to Bill   Set Discount   Set Credits

Figure 3-26 Select the bill to be discounted.

8 Click **Set Discount**.

In the Discounts and Credits screen, notice that QuickBooks automatically calculated the discount according to the 2% 10 Net 30 Terms.

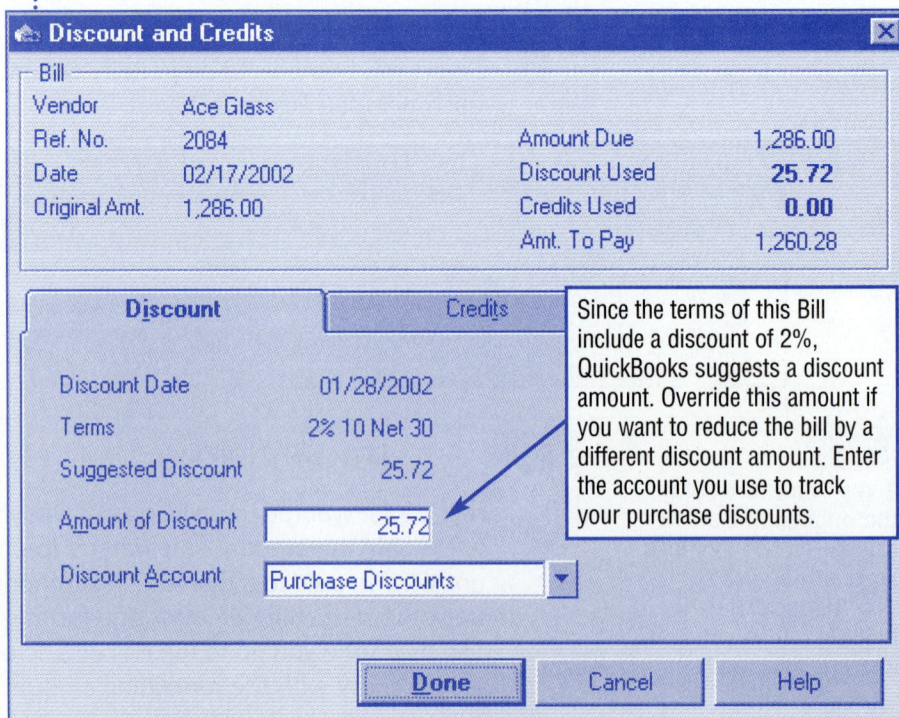

Discount and Credits

Bill

Vendor	Ace Glass		
Ref. No.	2084	Amount Due	1,286.00
Date	02/17/2002	Discount Used	**25.72**
Original Amt.	1,286.00	Credits Used	**0.00**
		Amt. To Pay	1,260.28

Discount | Credits

Discount Date	01/28/2002
Terms	2% 10 Net 30
Suggested Discount	25.72
Amount of Discount	25.72
Discount Account	Purchase Discounts

> Since the terms of this Bill include a discount of 2%, QuickBooks suggests a discount amount. Override this amount if you want to reduce the bill by a different discount amount. Enter the account you use to track your purchase discounts.

Done   Cancel   Help

Figure 3-27 The Discount and Credits screen

NOTE

If you select more than one bill for the same vendor, QuickBooks combines all of the amounts onto a single Bill Payment.

9. Select "Purchase Discounts" in the *Discount Account* field to assign this discount to the proper income account.

   If you use Class tracking or job costing, you won't be able to assign a class or a job to your discount. In that case, consider using a Bill Credit to record your discount before paying the bill. You can record the Class and job information on the Bill Credit just as you do on bills. Then, in the Pay Bills screen, click **Set Credits** to apply the Bill Credit to the bill. For more information, see the section entitled *Applying Vendor Credits* beginning on page 152.

10. Click **Done**. You will return to the Pay Bills screen.

11. Verify that your Pay Bills screen matches that shown in Figure 3-28. Click **Pay & Close** to record the Bill Payments.

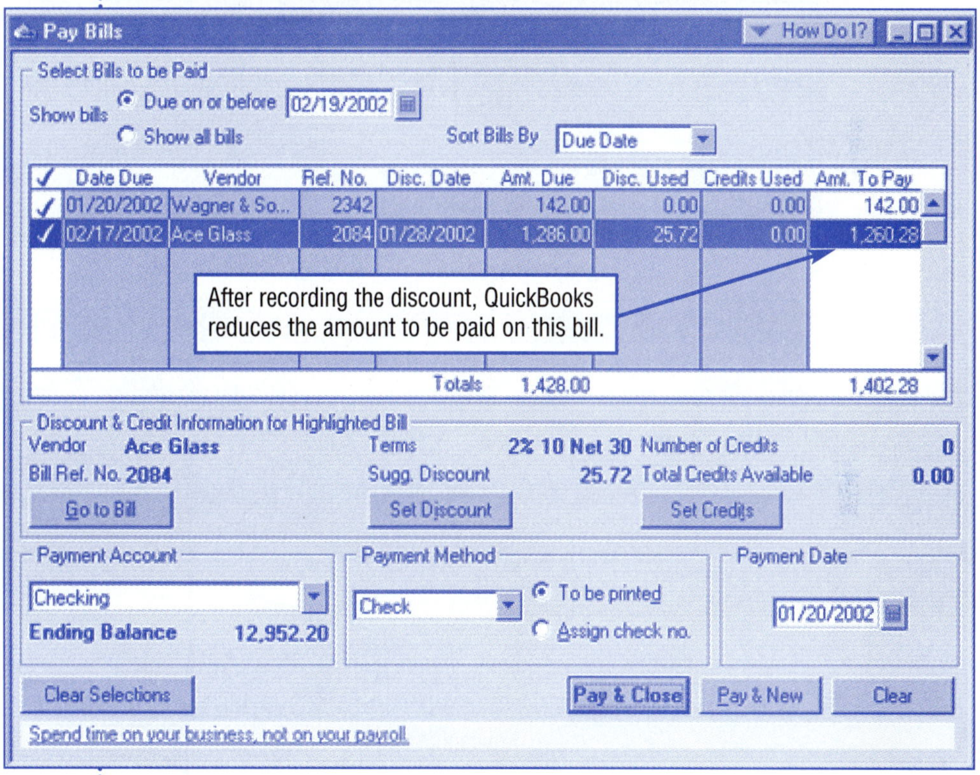

Figure 3-28 The completed Pay Bills screen after recording a discount

When you use a check to pay bills, QuickBooks records each Bill Payment in the Checking account register and in the Accounts Payable account register (see Figure 3-29 and Figure 3-30). Bill Payments *reduce* the balance in both the Checking account and the Accounts Payable account.

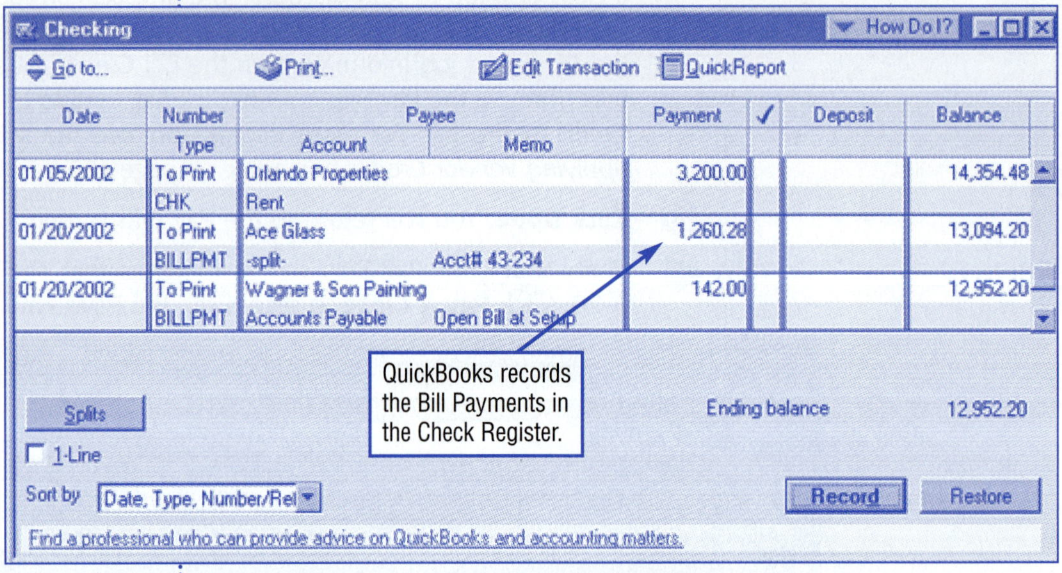

Figure 3-29 The Checking account register

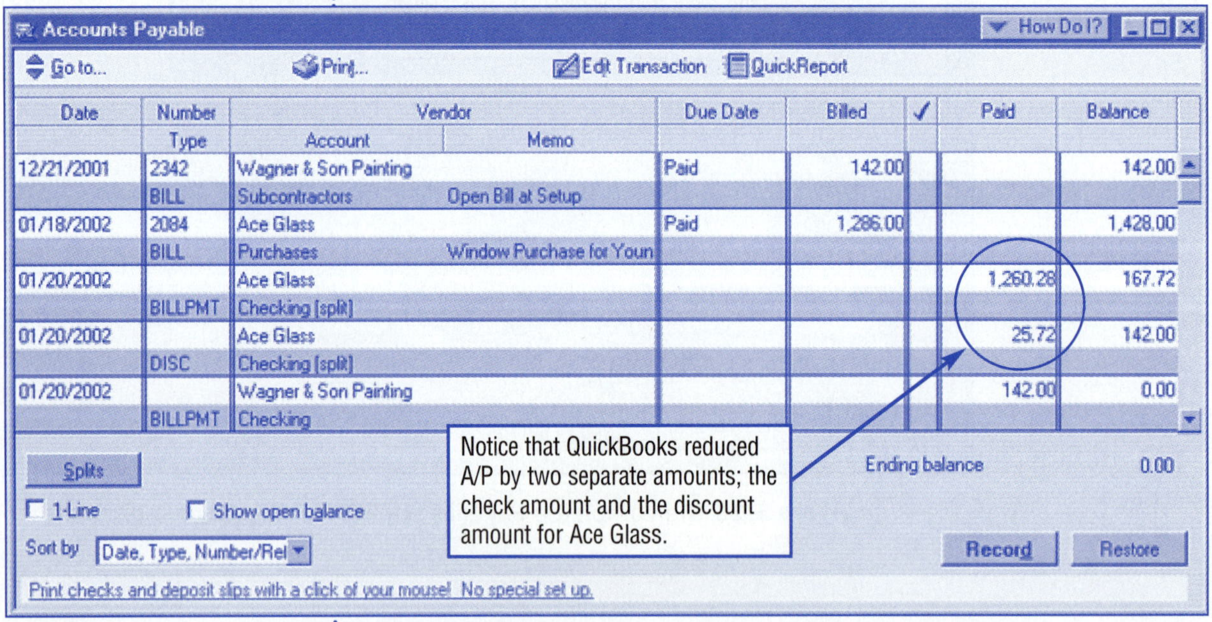

Figure 3-30 The Accounts Payable account register

PRINTER SETUP

COMPUTER TUTORIAL

Before printing checks for the first time, you'll need to set your printer settings.

1 Select the *File* menu and choose **Printer Setup**. The Printer setup screen displays.

2 Choose "Check/PayCheck" from the *Form Name* field drop-down menu.

3 In the Printer Setup screen you will indicate the type of printer and checks you have. Most businesses should use voucher checks. You will need to order preprinted checks from Intuit or from another vendor that supplies QuickBooks-compatible checks.

The appearance of the screen in Figure 3-31 will vary depending on your printer. Select the settings you want for your checks and then click **OK**.

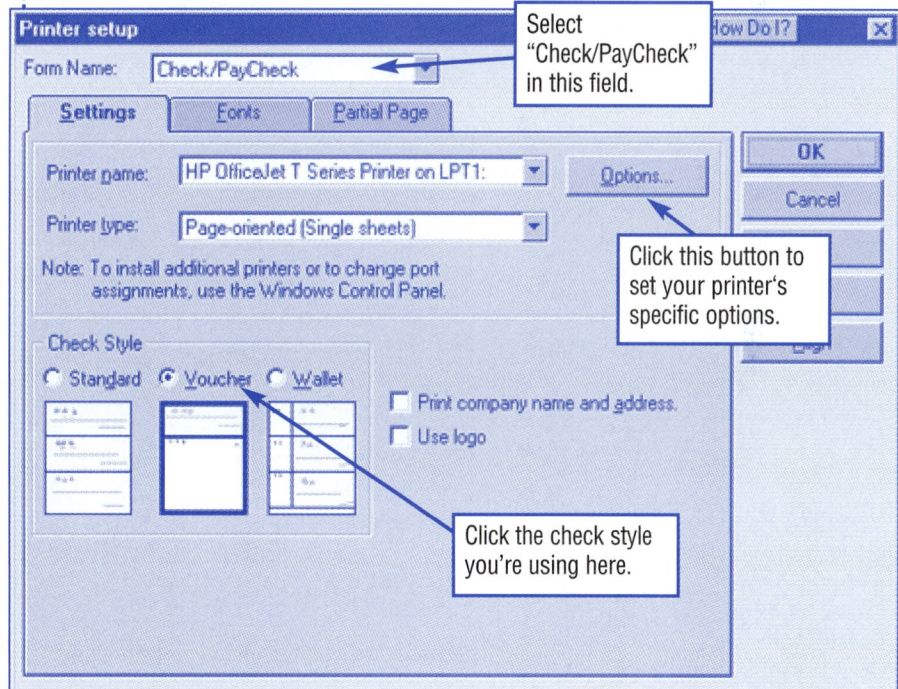

Figure 3-31 The Printer setup screen

PRINTING CHECKS

You do not need to print each check or bill payment separately in QuickBooks. As you write checks and pay bills, you have the option to record each check with a To be Printed status. Follow these steps to print checks and bill payments that you have previously recorded with a To be Printed status:

COMPUTER TUTORIAL

1 Select the *File* menu, choose **Print Forms**, and then choose **Checks** (see Figure 3-32).

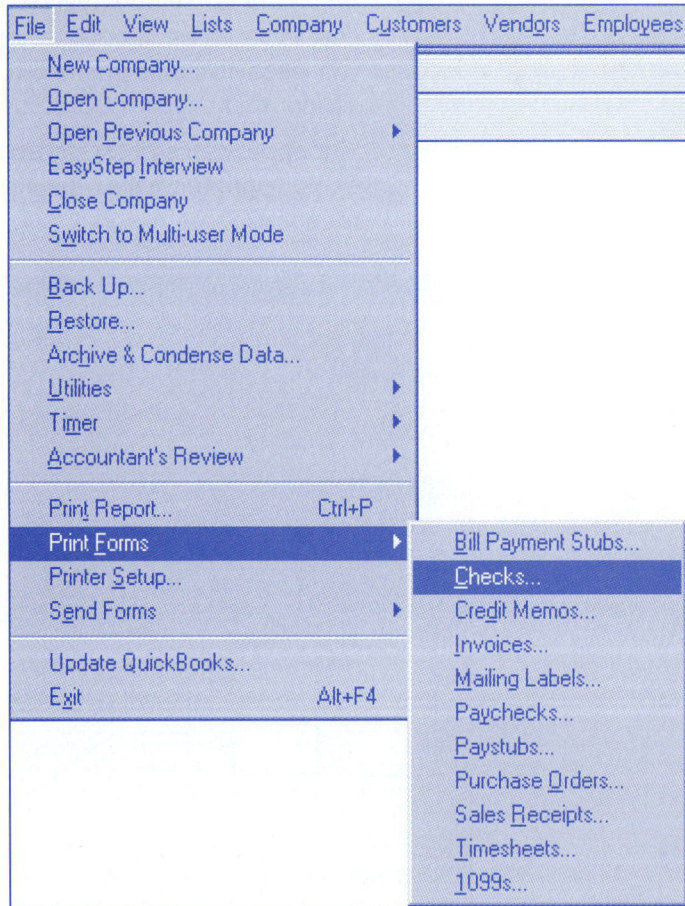

| File | Edit | View | Lists | Company | Customers | Vendors | Employees |

New Company...
Open Company...
Open Previous Company ▶
EasyStep Interview
Close Company
Switch to Multi-user Mode

Back Up...
Restore...
Archive & Condense Data...
Utilities ▶
Timer ▶
Accountant's Review ▶

Print Report...   Ctrl+P
Print Forms ▶   Bill Payment Stubs...
Printer Setup...   Checks...
Send Forms ▶   Credit Memos...
                         Invoices...
Update QuickBooks...   Mailing Labels...
Exit   Alt+F4   Paychecks...
                         Paystubs...
                         Purchase Orders...
                         Sales Receipts...
                         Timesheets...
                         1099s...

Figure 3-32 Choose Print Forms and Checks from the File menu.

2 "Checking" in the *Bank Account* field is preselected (see Figure 3-33). This is the bank account on which the checks are written. Press <TAB>.

3 Enter "6001" in the *First Check Number* field.

The *First Check Number* field is where you set the number of the first check you put in the printer.

NOTE

Check Numbers in QuickBooks
QuickBooks assigns check numbers when it prints checks. You have the opportunity to set the check number just before you print the checks and after you assign a check number. QuickBooks keeps track of each check it prints and keeps the check number up to date.

④ QuickBooks automatically selects all of the checks for printing. Click **OK**.

You can unclick in the left column next to each check that you do not want to print.

Since we didn't print the rent check, it shows in Figure 3-33 along with the two Bill Payments. We'll include it here so we can "batch print" all of the checks together.

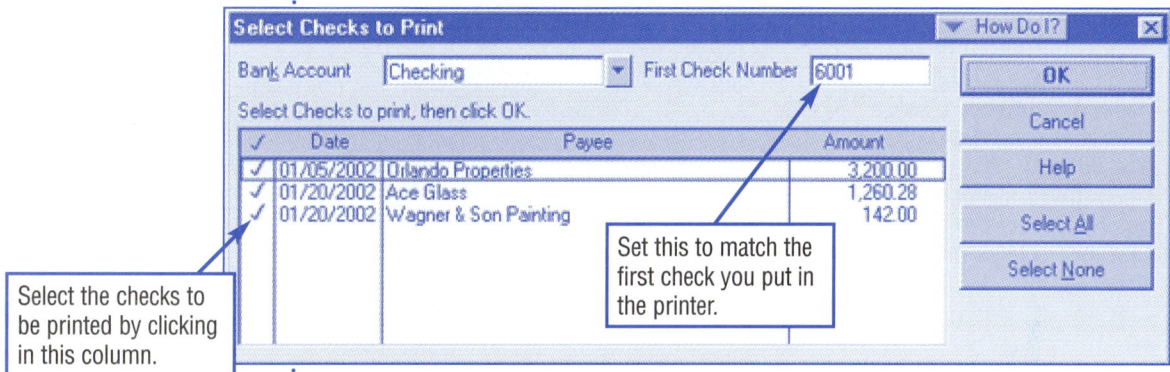

Select the checks to be printed by clicking in this column.

Set this to match the first check you put in the printer.

Figure 3-33 Select the checks to print by clicking in the left column.

⑤ Confirm your printer settings on the Print Checks screen (see Figure 3-34), and click **Print** when you're ready to print.

TIP

Make sure your checks are oriented correctly in the printer. With some printers, you feed the top of the page in first, and some you feed in bottom first. With some printers, you need to put the check face up and with others, face down.

NOTE

If your printer damages your checks and you use the Did check(s) print OK? screen to reprint them, you will need to re-enter and void each damaged check in the bank account register or on the Write Checks screen.

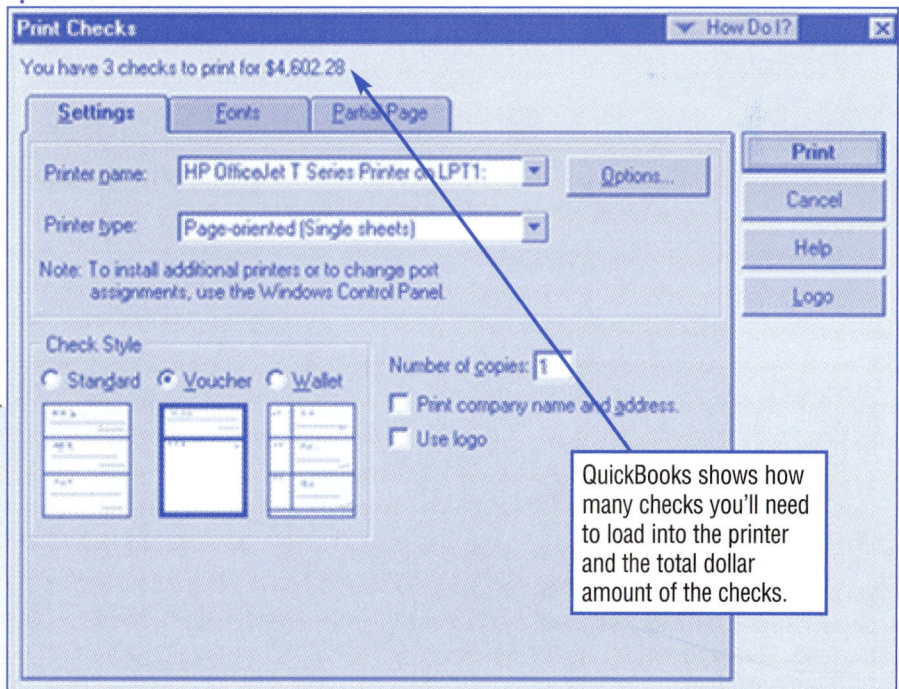

QuickBooks shows how many checks you'll need to load into the printer and the total dollar amount of the checks.

Figure 3-34 The Print Checks screen

6 When QuickBooks has finished printing the checks, you'll see the message in Figure 3-35.

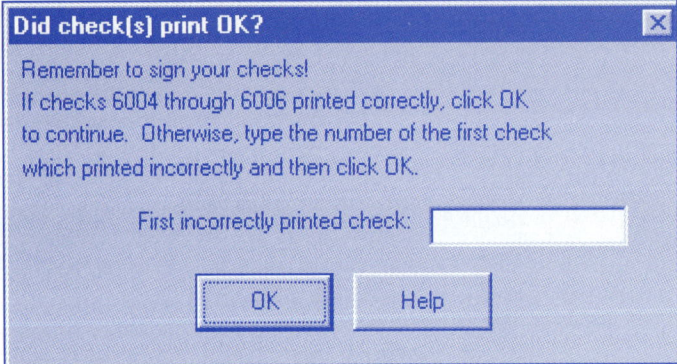

Did check(s) print OK?

Remember to sign your checks!
If checks 6004 through 6006 printed correctly, click OK to continue. Otherwise, type the number of the first check which printed incorrectly and then click OK.

First incorrectly printed check:

OK   Help

Figure 3-35 This message prompts you to verify correctness of your checks.

7 Click **OK**.

VOIDING CHECKS

QuickBooks allows you to keep the information about voided checks, so that you retain a record of these checks. It's important to enter each check into your register even if the check is voided. Doing so will prevent gaps in your check number sequence.

COMPUTER TUTORIAL

1 Open the Checking account register and select check "6002."

2 Select the *Edit* menu and choose **Void Bill Pmt-Check** (see Figure 3-36).

| Edit | View | Lists | Company | Customers | Vendors | Employees | Banking | Reports | Window | Help |

| Undo Typing | Ctrl+Z |
| Revert | |

Cut	Ctrl+X
Copy	Ctrl+C
Paste	Ctrl+V

Edit Bill Pmt -Check	Ctrl+E
New Bill Pmt -Check	Ctrl+N
Delete Bill Pmt -Check	Ctrl+D
Void Bill Pmt -Check	
Go To Transfer	Ctrl+G
Transaction History...	Ctrl+H
Use Register	Ctrl+R
Notepad	
Change Account Color...	

R. Checking

Go to...   Print...   Edit Trans-

Date	Number	Payee	
	Type	Account	Memo
01/05/2002	327	Jones Office Supply	
	CHK	-split-	Printer Paper
01/05/2002	6001	Orlando Properties	
	CHK	Rent	
01/20/2002	6002	Ace Glass	
	BILLPMT	-split-	Acct# 43-234
01/20/2002	6003	Wagner & Son Painting	
	BILLPMT	Accounts Payable	Open Bill at Setup

Figure 3-36 Select the check and use the Edit menu to void a check.

> **IMPORTANT**
>
> Don't void checks from a prior year if you've already filed your tax return for that year. Instead, enter a deposit in the current period using the amount, account(s), classes, and job costing information for the check you wish to void. See *Correcting or Voiding Transactions in Closed Accounting Periods* on page 189. This is necessary so that your net income and the balance in the Retained Earnings (or Owner's Equity) account will agree with your company's tax return and the financial statements prepared by your accountant.

3 When you void a check, QuickBooks changes the amount to zero and it marks the check "cleared." Click **Record** to save your change.

Since you're voiding a Bill Payment, QuickBooks warns you that this change will affect the application of this check to the bills (see Figure 3-37). In other words, voiding a Bill Payment will make the bill payable again.

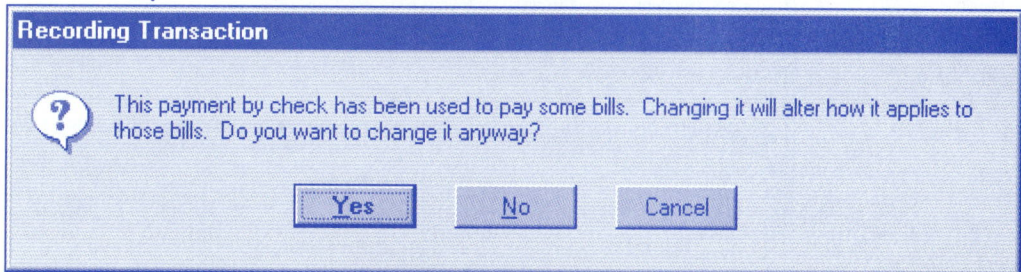

Figure 3-37 QuickBooks warns that voiding a check makes a bill payable again.

4 Click **Yes**.

Notice that the transaction shows as cleared in the register, and that QuickBooks resets the amount to zero (see Figure 3-38).

5 Close all open windows.

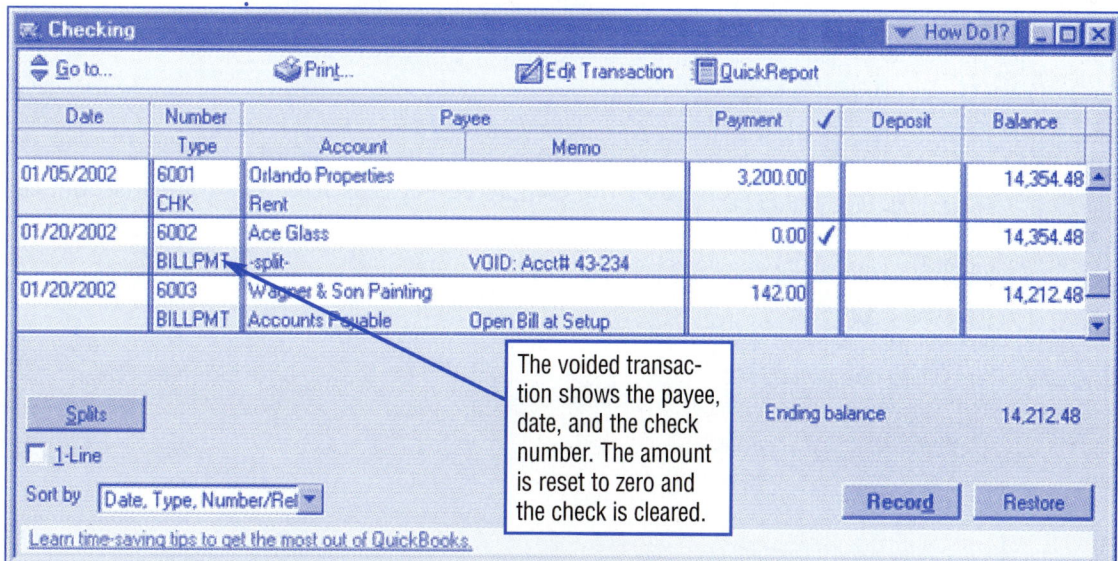

Figure 3-38 Voided transactions are marked cleared in the register.

COMPUTER TUTORIAL

To repay the bill, repeat the bill paying and printing process by following the steps below.

1 Select the *Vendors* menu and choose **Pay Bills**.

2 Enter "02/19/2002 in the *Due on or before* field (see Figure 3-39).

3 Leave "Checking" in the *Payment Account* field, "Check" in the *Payment Method* field, and enter "01/20/2002" in the *Payment Date* field.

4 Select the Ace Glass bill.

5 Click **Set Discount** and apply the discount as you did in the previous Tutorial.

6 Click **Done** on the Discounts & Credits screen.

TIP

Since the voided check was a Bill Payment, QuickBooks "unpays" the bill and adds it back to your Accounts Payable account. Therefore, to pay the bill again, you must repeat the bill paying process.

Figure 3-39 The completed Pay Bills screen with the discount taken

7 Verify that your screen matches that shown in Figure 3-39. Click **Pay & Close** on the Pay Bills screen to record the bill payment.

8 Next, print the new Bill Payment check. Select the *File* menu, choose **Print Forms**, and then choose **Checks**.

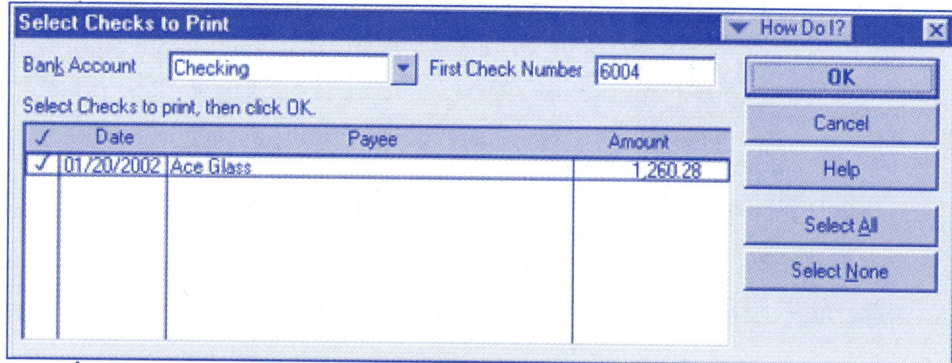

Select Checks to Print			▼ How Do I?	✕
Bank Account	Checking ▼	First Check Number 6004	**OK**	
Select Checks to print, then click OK.			Cancel	
✓ Date	Payee	Amount	Help	
✓ 01/20/2002 Ace Glass		1,260.28		
			Select All	
			Select None	

Figure 3-40 The Select Checks to Print screen

9 Click **OK** on the Select Checks to Print screen (see Figure 3-40).

10 Then click **Print** to print the check, and then click **OK** on the Did check(s) print OK? screen.

APPLYING VENDOR CREDITS

When a vendor credits your account, you'll need to record that transaction in the Enter Bills form as a Credit and apply it to one of your unpaid bills.

In many situations, it is best to use a Bill Credit instead of the Discount screen to record vendor credits, because the Discount screen does not allow you to record any of the following information:

- ◆ Classes – There is no way to tag a discount by class.
- ◆ Reference numbers or memos – These may be important for reference later.
- ◆ Allocation of the credit to multiple accounts or jobs – This may be critical in many situations.

COMPUTER TUTORIAL

① Select the *Vendors* menu and choose **Enter Bills**.

② Enter the bill shown in Figure 3-41.

Figure 3-41 Enter a bill from Nellis Windows & Doors.

③ When you're finished entering the data in Figure 3-41, click **Save & New**.

④ On the next (blank) bill form, select "Credit" radio button at the top right of the screen.

5 Fill in the bill credit information as shown in Figure 3-42. Click **Save & Close** to record the credit.

When you record a Vendor Credit as shown in Figure 3-42, QuickBooks reduces (debits) Accounts Payable and reduces (credits) Expenses.

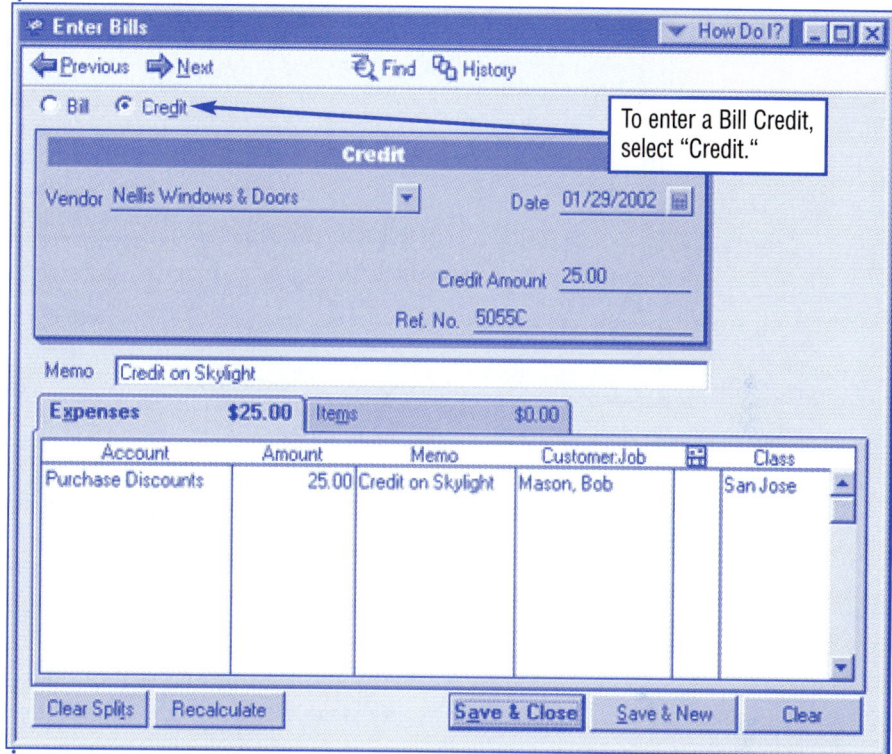

Figure 3-42 The Enter Bills – Credit screen

6 To Apply the Vendor Credit to a bill for that vendor, select the **Vendors** menu and choose **Pay Bills**.

7 Enter "02/28/2002" in the *Due on or before* field.

8 Leave "Checking" in the *Payment Account* field, "Check" in the *Payment Method* field, and enter "01/30/2002" in the *Payment Date* field.

IMPORTANT

In order to apply a Bill Credit, the vendor name must be the same on both the bill and the Bill Credit.

9 Select the open bill for Nellis Windows & Doors as shown in Figure 3-43.

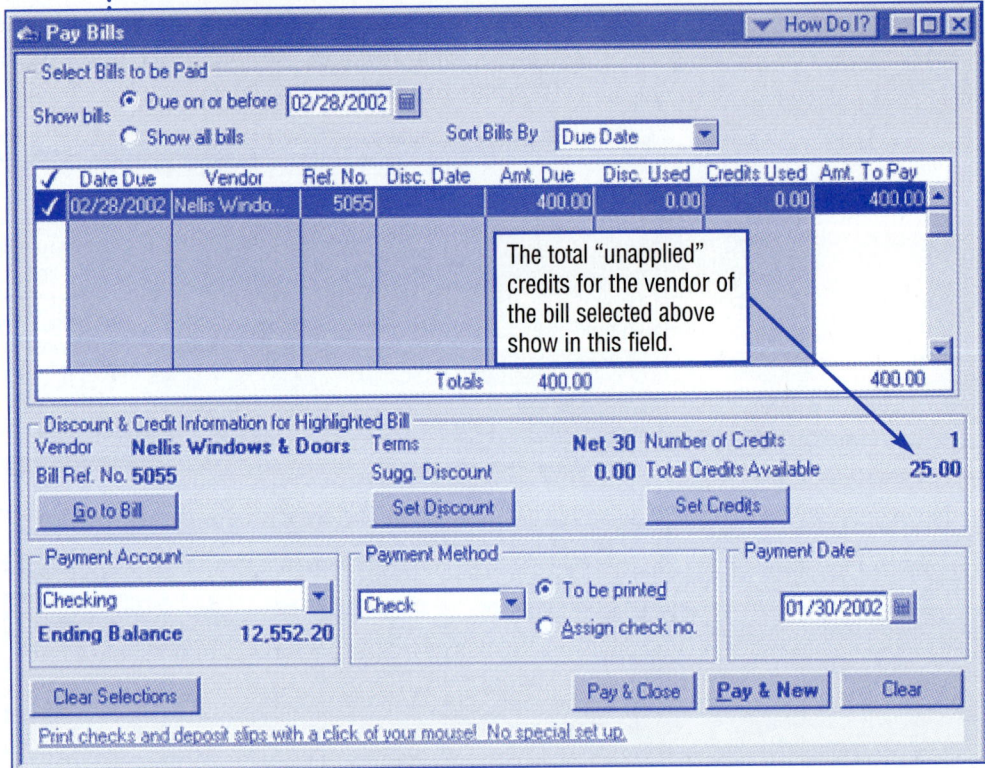

Figure 3-43 The Pay Bills screen with a bill selected for a vendor with an existing credit

When you select a bill from a vendor for whom unapplied credits exist, QuickBooks displays the total amount of all credits for the vendor in the *Total Credits Available* field. Notice in Figure 3-43 that credits for Nellis Windows & Doors total $25.00.

10 Click in the checkmark column to the far left of the bill from Nellis Windows & Doors. Notice that the **Set Credits** button activates when you select the bill (see Figure 3-44).

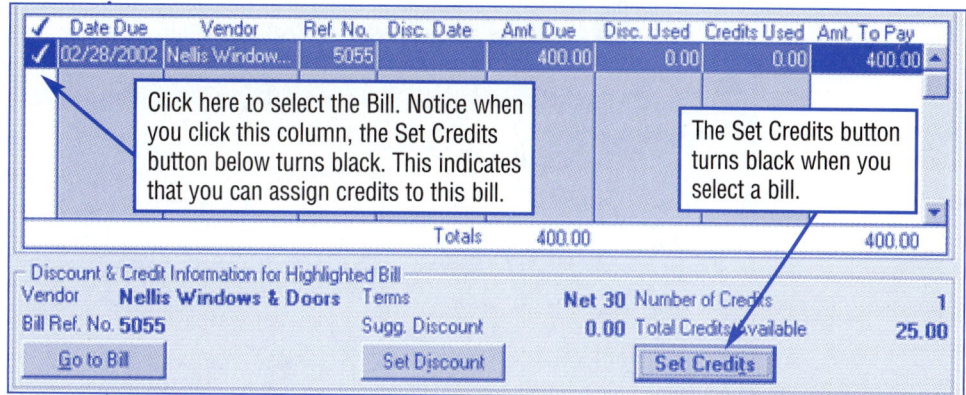

Figure 3-44 To apply the credit, click in the checkmark column to the left of the bill, and then click **Set Credits**.

⑪ Click **Set Credits**.

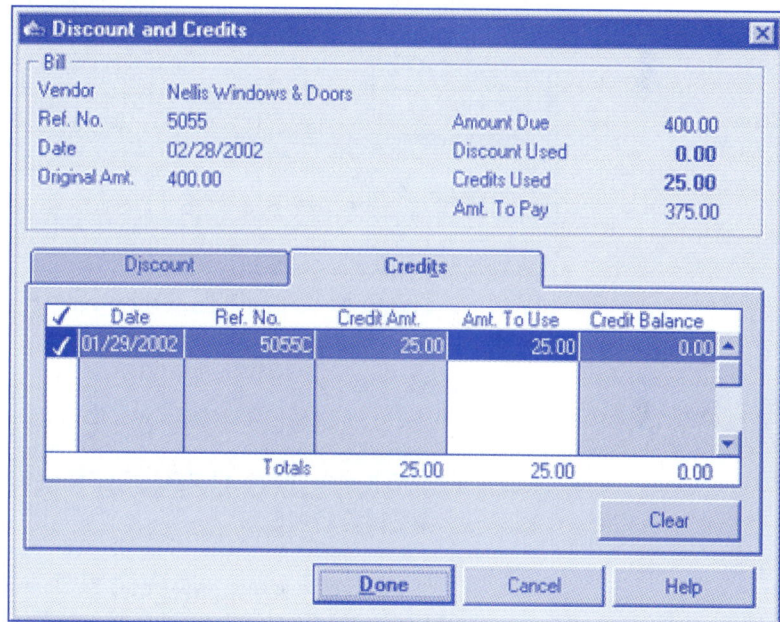

Figure 3-45 The Discounts and Credits screen

On the Discounts and Credits screen, notice that QuickBooks selected the credits to be applied to the bill. You can override what's shown by deselecting the credit (removing the checkmark), or by entering a different amount in the Amt. To Use column.

⑫ Leave the credit selected as shown in Figure 3-45 and click **Done**.

In Figure 3-46, you can see that QuickBooks applied the $25.00 credit to Bill #5055 and reduced the amount in the Amt. To Pay column to $375.00.

NOTE

If you want to apply the credit without paying the bill, reduce the Amt. To Pay column to zero.

13   Click **Pay & Close** to pay the bill.

Figure 3-46 Pay Bills screen with credit applied

HANDLING DEPOSITS AND REFUNDS FROM VENDORS

This section covers how to handle more complicated transactions between you and your vendors. These transactions include deposits paid to vendors in advance of receiving the bill, refunds received from vendors for overpayment of a bill, and refunds received from vendors when Accounts Payable is not involved.

Vendor Deposits — When You Use Accounts Payable

Sometimes vendors require you to give them a deposit before they will provide you with services or products. To do this, create a check for the vendor and code it to Accounts Payable. This creates a credit in QuickBooks for the vendor that you can apply to the bill when it arrives.

COMPUTER TUTORIAL

1   Select the **Banking** menu and choose **Write Checks**.

2   Enter the data as shown in Figure 3-47. Notice that this check is coded to Accounts Payable. You only code checks to A/P when you are sending deposits to a vendor prior to receiving the bill.

3 Deselect the "To be printed" box. Notice that QuickBooks automatically generates the check number. Then click **Save & Close**.

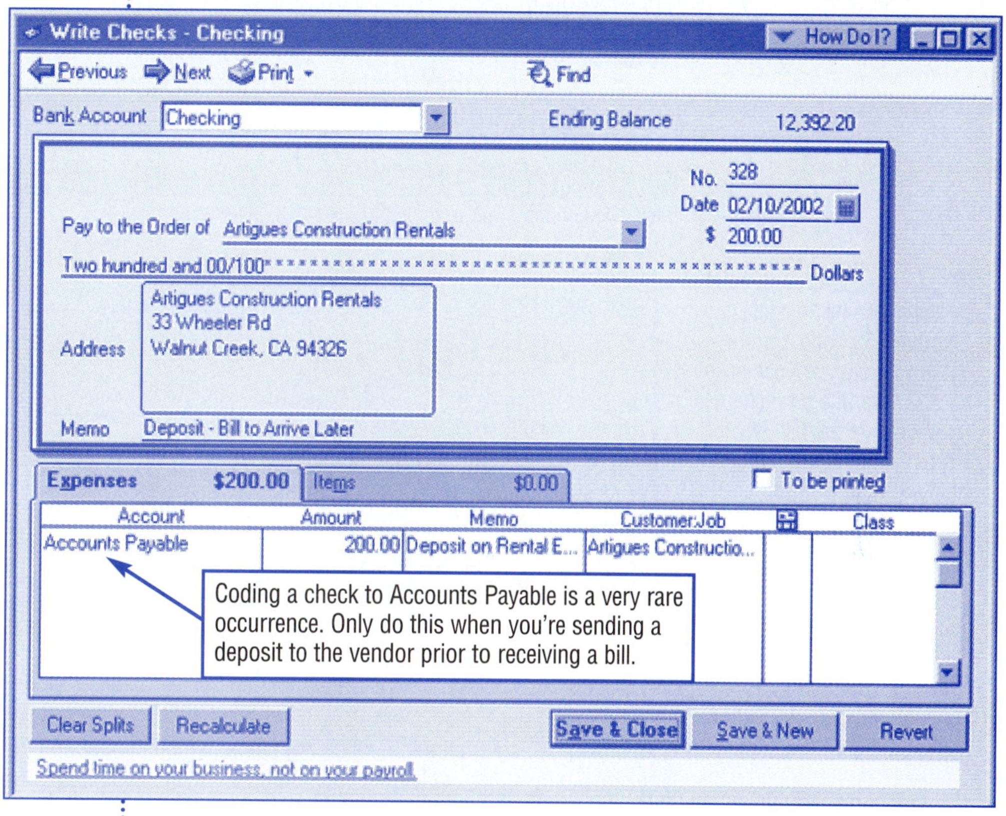

Figure 3-47 A check written to a vendor as a "deposit" prior to receiving a bill

Vendor Refunds — When You Use Accounts Payable

When you receive a refund from a vendor, the kind of transaction you enter in QuickBooks will depend on how you originally paid the vendor.

If you prepaid the vendor using the method above and the amount of your prepayment was more than the bill, your Accounts Payable account will have a negative (debit) balance for that vendor. In this case, you will apply the refund check from the vendor to this credit balance in A/P.

On the other hand, if you simply wrote a check to the vendor and coded the check to an expense account, you'll need to reduce the expense by the amount of the refund. The following tutorials address each of these situations.

To record a refund from a vendor that you prepaid using the deposit transaction in Figure 3-47, follow the steps below. In this example, you paid Artigues Construction Rentals $200.00 in advance of receiving the bill. On a later date, Artigues Construction Rentals sent a bill for $185.00. Since your deposit was more than the bill, the vendor also sent you a refund check for $15.00.

COMPUTER TUTORIAL

Start by entering the bill from the vendor just like any other bill. Then you will use the Make Deposits screen to record your refund from the vendor.

1 Open the Enter Bills screen and enter the bill from Artigues Construction Rentals as shown in Figure 3-48. Click **Save & Close** to record the bill.

> Enter this bill just like any other bill. Code it to the appropriate expense account and enter the total charges shown on the bill. Do not apply the deposit (prepayment) at this time.

Figure 3-48 A bill from Artigues Construction Rentals

2 Select the *Banking* menu and choose **Make Deposits**.

3 "Checking" in the *Deposit To* field is preselected (see Figure 3-49). Press <TAB>.

4 Enter "02/15/2002" in the *Date* field and press <TAB>.

5 Enter "Refund from Artigues Construction" in the *Memo* field and press <TAB>.

6 Enter "Artigues Construction Rentals" in the Received From column and press <TAB>.

7 Enter "Accounts Payable" in the From Account column and press <TAB>.

8 Enter the rest of the data as shown in Figure 3-49.

Make Deposits							How Do I?

Previous Next Print ▼   Payments

Deposit To [Checking ▼]   Date [02/15/2002 📅]   Memo [Refund from Artigue ...]

Click Payments to select customer payments that you have received. List any other amounts to deposit below.

Received From	From Account	Memo	Chk No.	Pmt Meth.	Class	Amount
Artigues Construc...	Accounts Payable	Refund from Artigu...	423	Check	Walnu...	15.00

> Enter the vendor's name in the Received From column so that QuickBooks will apply this refund check to Artigues Construction Rentals in A/P reports.

Deposit Subtotal   15.00

To get cash back from this deposit, enter the amount below. Indicate the account where you want this money to go, such as your Petty Cash account.

Cash back goes to   Cash back memo   Cash back amount
[▼]   [   ]   [   ]

Deposit Total   15.00

[Save & Close]   [Save & New]   [Revert]

Figure 3-49 Record the refund from the vendor on the Make Deposits screen.

9 Click **Save & Close**.

COMPUTER TUTORIAL

After you have recorded the deposit shown in Figure 3-49, you'll need to apply the prepayment check for $200.00 to the bill and the refund check you just received. Your A/P reports will not be correct until you make this application.

1 Select the *Vendors* menu and choose **Pay Bills**.

2 Enter "03/07/2002 in the *Due on or before date* field and press <TAB>.

3 Leave "Checking" in the Payment Account "column and "Check" in the *Payment Method* field, and enter "02/25/2002" in the *Payment Date* field.

④ Select the first line in the Pay Bills screen (Ref. No. 423) and then click **Set Credits** as shown in Figure 3-50.

Though this line looks like one of two bills for Artigues Construction Rentals, it is actually the refund check you recorded using the Make Deposits screen as shown in Figure 3-49.

⑤ In the Discounts and Credits screen, QuickBooks automatically applies $15.00 of the $200.00 credit to refund check #423 (see Figure 3-51). Click **Done.**

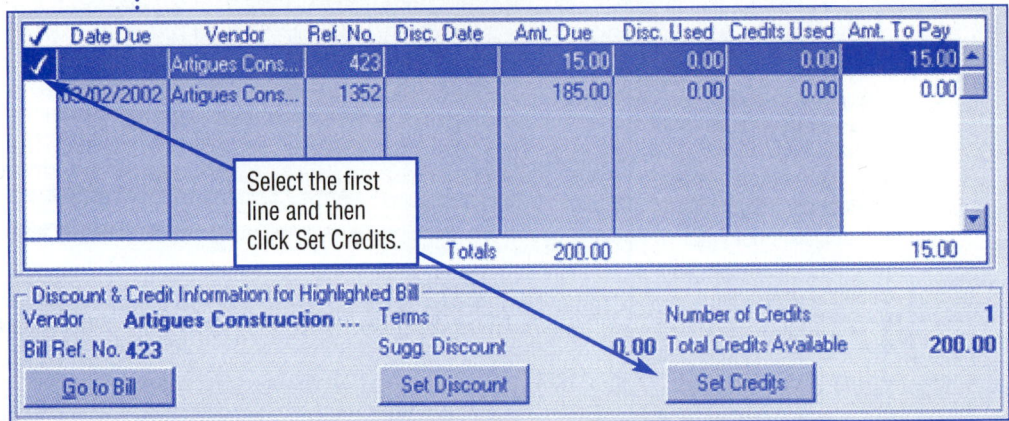

✓	Date Due	Vendor	Ref. No.	Disc. Date	Amt. Due	Disc. Used	Credits Used	Amt. To Pay
✓		Artigues Cons...	423		15.00	0.00	0.00	15.00
	03/02/2002	Artigues Cons...	1352		185.00	0.00	0.00	0.00

Select the first line and then click Set Credits.

Totals   200.00   15.00

Discount & Credit Information for Highlighted Bill
Vendor   **Artigues Construction ...**   Terms   Number of Credits   1
Bill Ref. No. **423**   Sugg. Discount   **0.00** Total Credits Available   **200.00**
[Go to Bill]   [Set Discount]   [Set Credits]

Figure 3-50 Selecting the applicable credits before clicking Set Credits

⑥ The second line in the Pay Bills screen is the actual bill from Artigues Construction Rentals. Select this bill and click **Set Credits** (Figure 3-52).

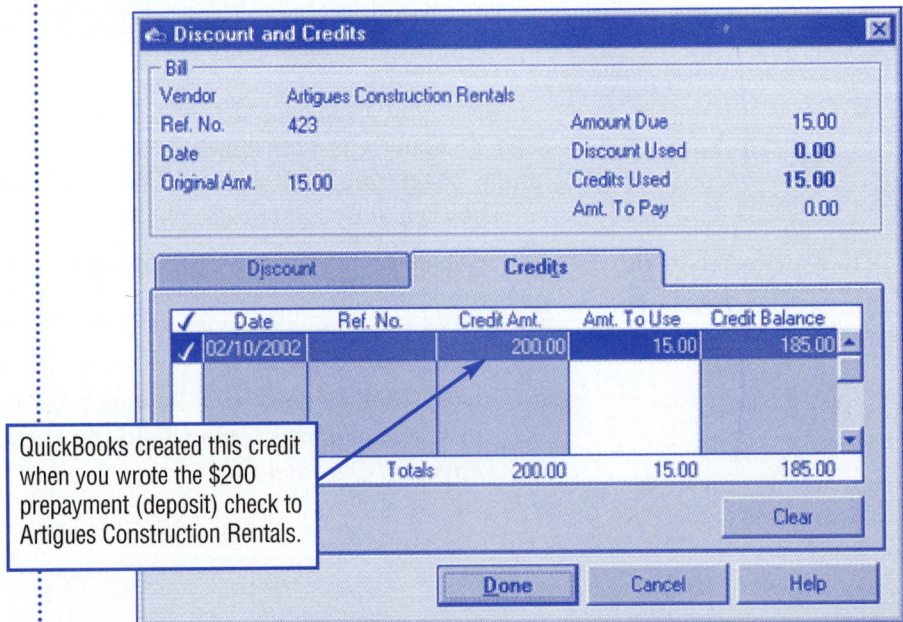

Discount and Credits

Bill
Vendor   Artigues Construction Rentals
Ref. No.   423   Amount Due   15.00
Date   Discount Used   **0.00**
Original Amt. 15.00   Credits Used   **15.00**
                                           Amt. To Pay   0.00

[Discount]   [Credits]

✓	Date	Ref. No.	Credit Amt.	Amt. To Use	Credit Balance
✓	02/10/2002		200.00	15.00	185.00

QuickBooks created this credit when you wrote the $200 prepayment (deposit) check to Artigues Construction Rentals.

Totals   200.00   15.00   185.00

[Clear]

[Done]   [Cancel]   [Help]

Figure 3-51 QuickBooks applies $15.00 of the prepayment check (Credit) to check #423

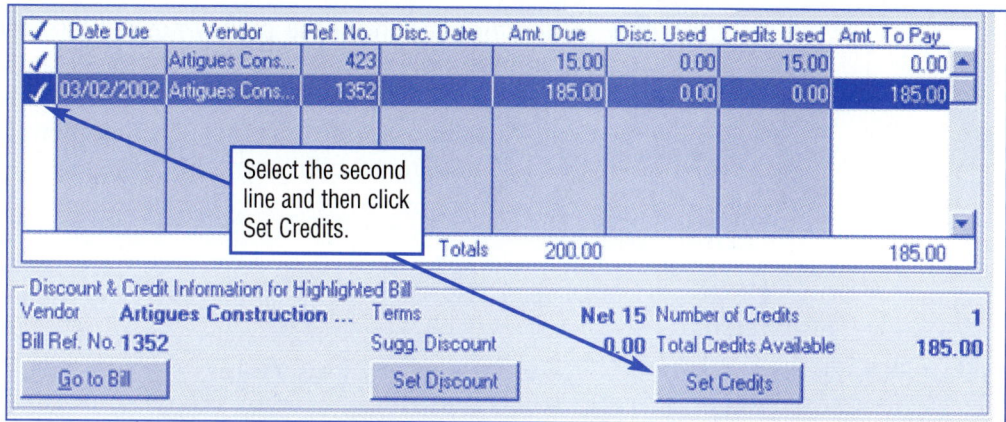

Figure 3-52 Selecting the second credit.

7 In the Discounts and Credits screen, QuickBooks automatically applies $185.00 of the $200.00 credit to Bill #1352 (see Figure 3-53). Click **Done**.

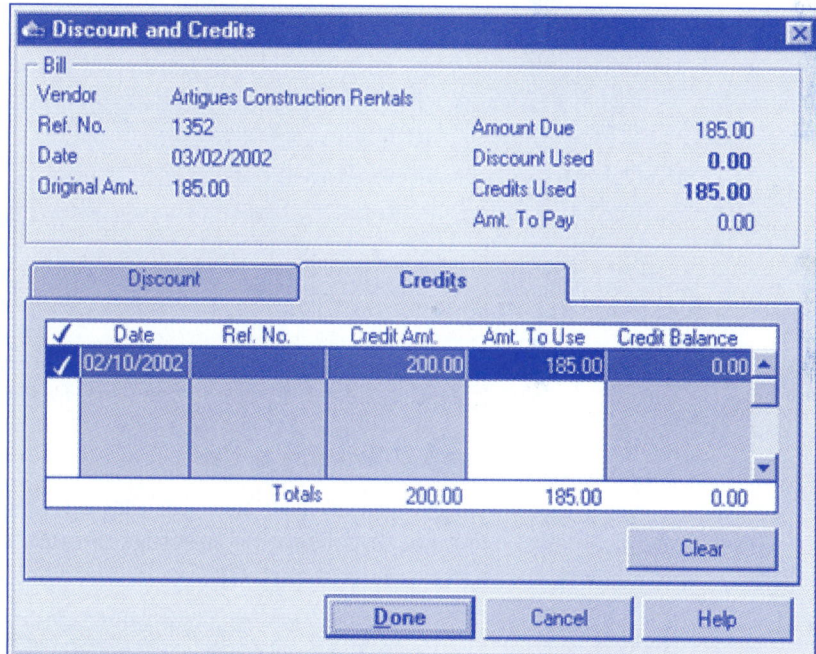

Figure 3-53 QuickBooks applies $185.00 of the prepayment check (credit) to check #1352

8️⃣ Since the amount of the prepayment ($200) is the same as the total of the bill ($185) plus the refund check ($15.00), the total in the *Amt. To Pay* field is zero (see Figure 3-54). QuickBooks will link these transactions together, clearing them from A/P reports, but will not create a Bill Payment.

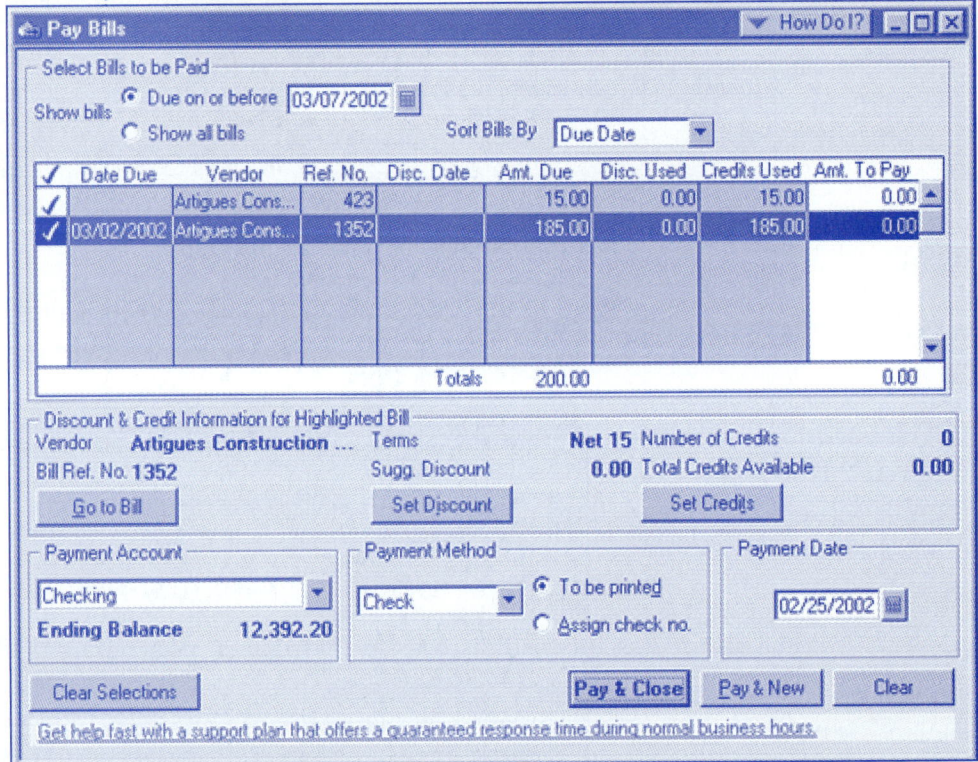

Figure 3-54 The total in the Amt. To Pay column is now zero.

9️⃣ Click **Pay & Close**.

🔟 When you use the Pay Bills screen to connect credits to bills, you'll see the message shown below. Read the message carefully and click **OK**.

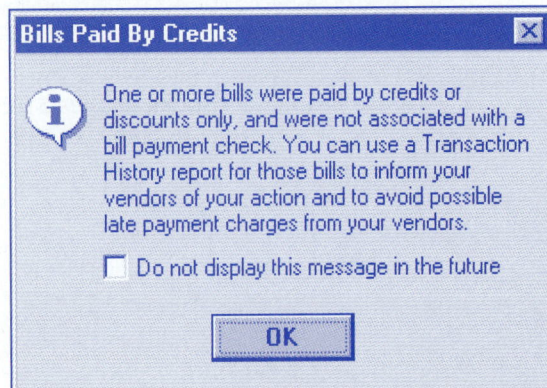

Figure 3-55 Important message about bills being paid by credits only – read this carefully.

Vendor Refunds — When You Directly Expensed Payment

If you did not use the Accounts Payable features but instead wrote a check to the vendor and coded the check to an expense account, enter the expense account that should be reduced due to the vendor's refund in the Make Deposits screen (see Figure 3-56).

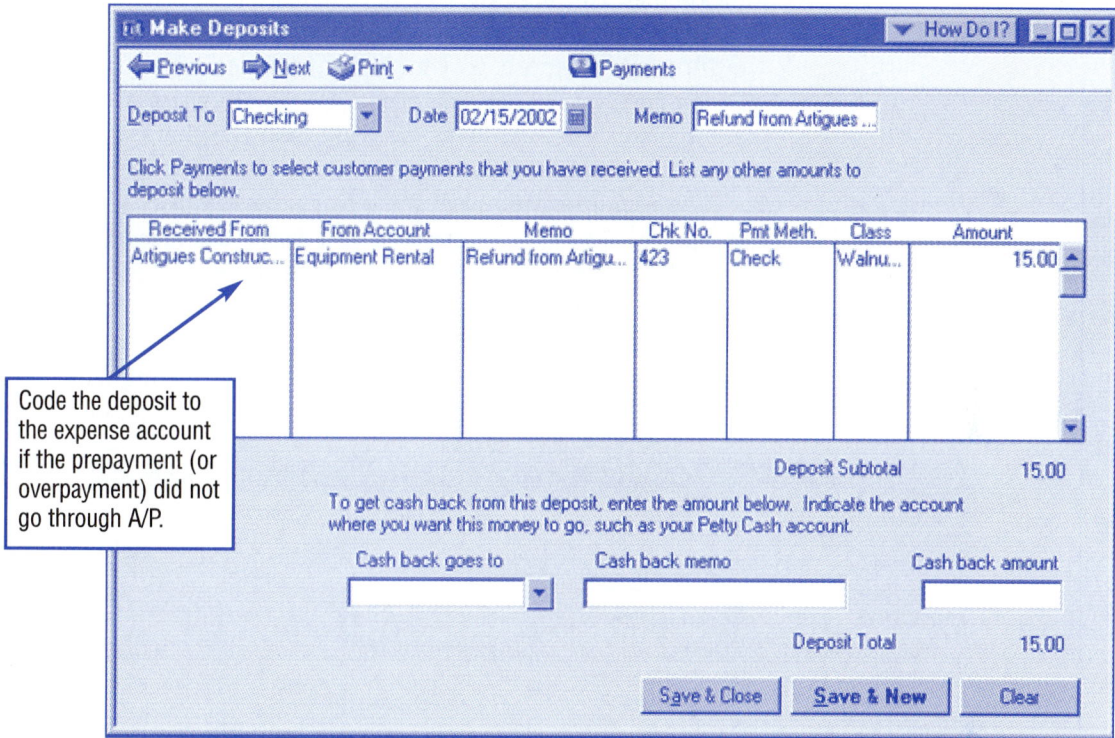

Code the deposit to the expense account if the prepayment (or overpayment) did not go through A/P.

Figure 3-56 Reduce the expense account in the Make Deposits screen.

TRACKING PETTY CASH

It is sometimes necessary to use cash for minor expenditures, such as office supplies, postage, parking, or other small Items. In order to track these expenditures, you can set up a separate bank account in QuickBooks. This account can be called Petty Cash (see page 512 on how to set up a new account in QuickBooks).

To track a deposit to your petty cash account (and the withdrawal of cash from your Checking account), simply write a check to a designated person, the *custodian*, who will cash the check at a local bank and replenish petty cash. Code the check to the Petty Cash account.

When you use the cash for a company expense, enter the expenditure in the Payment column of the Petty Cash account register (see Figure 3-57). This reduces the balance in the Petty Cash account, so that it always agrees with the actual amount of cash you have on hand. Code each cash expenditure to the appropriate payee, account, Class and job. Click the **Splits** button to split the expenditure among multiple accounts or to assign customer names or classes to the transaction.

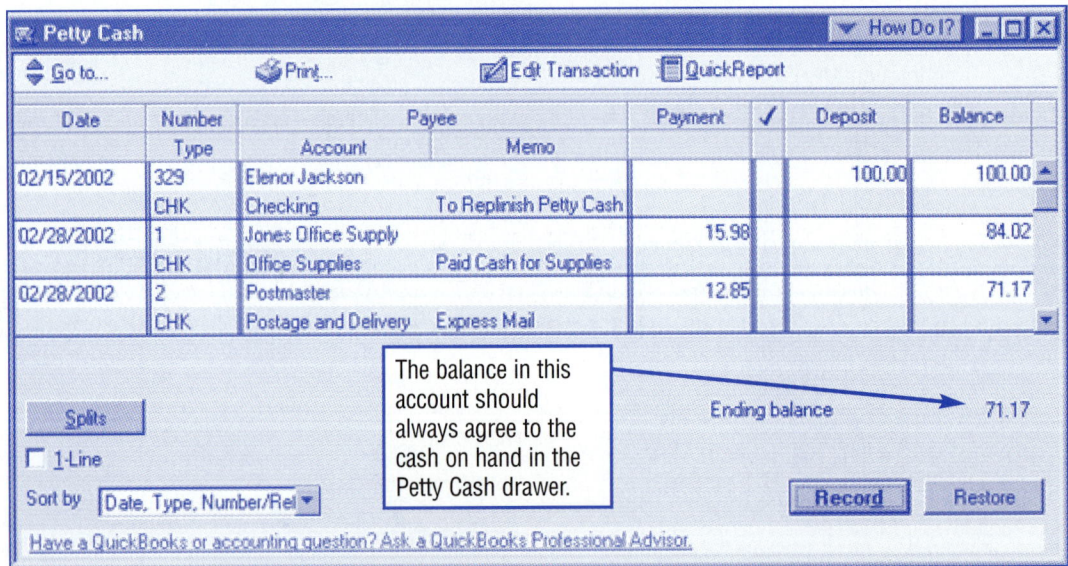

Figure 3-57 Enter cash used for company expenses in the Petty Cash register.

TRACKING COMPANY CREDIT CARDS

To track your charges and payments on your company credit card, set up a separate credit card account in QuickBooks for each card (see page 512 on how to set up a new account). Then enter each charge individually using the Enter Credit Card Charges screen. To pay the credit card bill, use **Write Checks** and code the check to the credit card account.

Entering Credit Card Charges

Each time you use a company credit card, use the Enter Credit Card Charges screen to record the transaction. When you record credit card charges, QuickBooks increases (credits) your Credit Card Payable liability account and increases (debits) the expense account shown at the bottom of the screen.

COMPUTER TUTORIAL

① Select the *Banking* menu and choose **Enter Credit Card Charges**.

② "National Bank VISA Gold" is preselected in the *Credit Card* field. Press <TAB>.

③ Enter "Jones Office Supply" in the *Purchased From* field and press <TAB>.

④ Enter "65432" in the *Ref No.* field and press <TAB>.

The *Ref No.* field is optional. Its purpose is to tag each charge with the number on the charge slip.

Figure 3-58 Completed Credit Card screen

5 "Charge" is preselected. Press <TAB> twice.

If you used your card when receiving a refund or credit from a vendor, you would select "Credit" instead of "Charge" on this step. QuickBooks will then reduce the balance on your credit card when you record this transaction.

6 Verify that "2/15/2002" displays in the *Date* field and press <TAB>.

7 Enter "86.48" in the *Amount* field and press <TAB>.

8 Enter "Office Supplies" in *Memo* field and press <TAB>.

9 Enter "Office Supplies" in the Account column and press <TAB>.

10 Skip the Amount and Memo columns by pressing <TAB> twice.

11 Skip the Customer:Job column by pressing <TAB>.

You can "job cost" this expense by entering the customer and job information in this column just as you do for bills and checks.

12 Enter "San Jose" in the Class column.

13 Verify that your screen matches Figure 3-58. Click **Save & New** to record the credit card charge.

14 Enter another credit card charge that matches Figure 3-59. Click **Save & Close** when you are done entering both credit card charges.

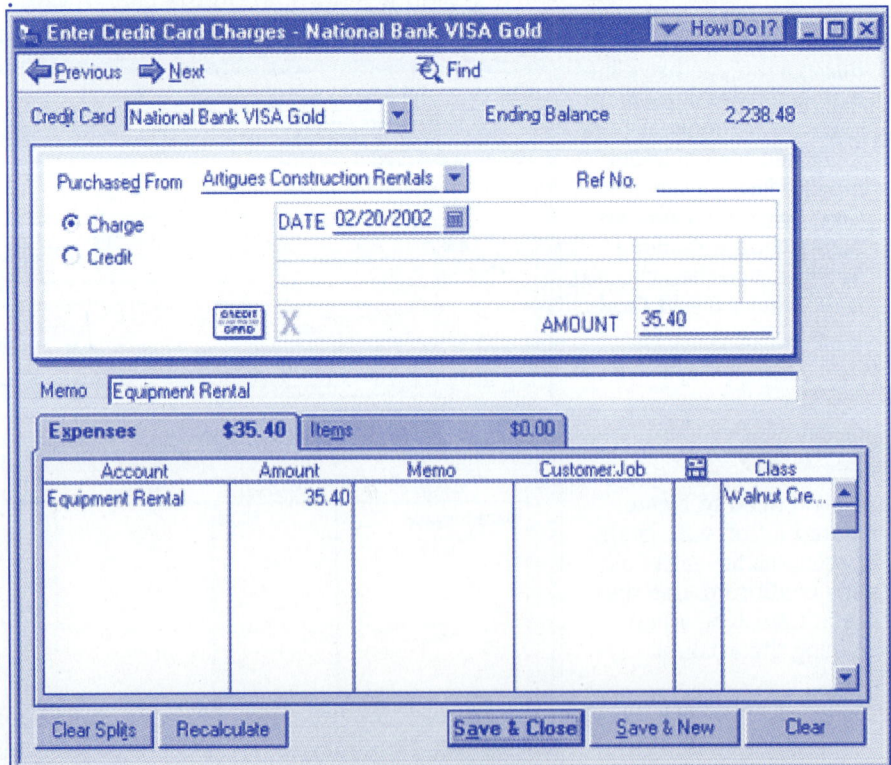

Figure 3-59 Use this data for the second practive credit card charge.

Paying the Credit Card Bill

COMPUTER TUTORIAL

Follow the steps below to write a check to pay your credit card bill. When you record a credit card payment, QuickBooks reduces (credits) the Checking account and reduces (debits) the Credit Card liability account.

① Select the *Banking* menu and choose **Write Checks**.

② Enter the check as shown in Figure 3-60. Notice that you will enter the credit card account name in the Account column of the Expenses tab.

③ Click **Save & Close** to record the transaction.

Figure 3-60 Use Write Checks to pay your credit card bill.

To see the detail of your credit card charges and payments, look in the National Bank VISA Gold account register (see Figure 3-61). There are two ways to quickly get to this register. Display a charge form (shown in Figure 3-59), right-click the mouse and choose **Use Register**. You can also display the register by double-clicking the credit card account on the Chart of Accounts list.

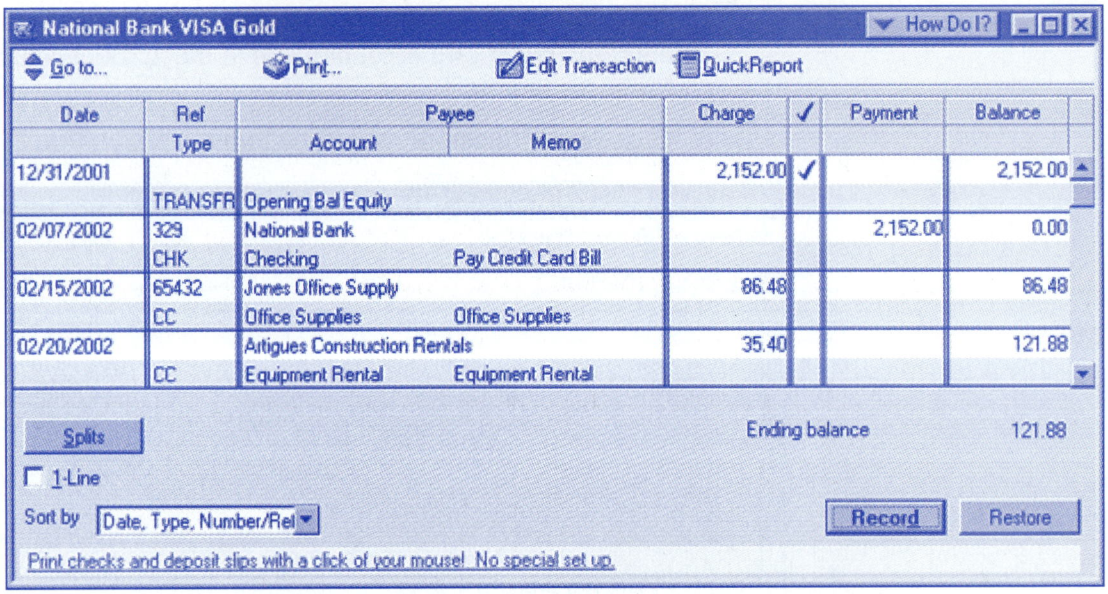

National Bank VISA Gold ▼ How Do I? _ □ X

♦ Go to...   🖨 Print...   📝 Edit Transaction   📋 QuickReport

Date	Ref	Payee		Charge	✓	Payment	Balance
	Type	Account	Memo				
12/31/2001				2,152.00	✓		2,152.00
	TRANSFR	Opening Bal Equity					
02/07/2002	329	National Bank				2,152.00	0.00
	CHK	Checking	Pay Credit Card Bill				
02/15/2002	65432	Jones Office Supply		86.48			86.48
	CC	Office Supplies	Office Supplies				
02/20/2002		Artigues Construction Rentals		35.40			121.88
	CC	Equipment Rental	Equipment Rental				

Splits

☐ 1-Line

Sort by [Date, Type, Number/Ref ▼]

Ending balance   121.88

Record   Restore

Print checks and deposit slips with a click of your mouse! No special set up.

Figure 3-61 National Bank VISA Gold account register

A/P REPORTS

QuickBooks has several reports that you can use to analyze and track your purchases and vendors. Following are two example reports for you to create, and you can explore the other A/P reports on your own. Also see Chapter 5 for more information about QuickBooks reports.

Vendor Balance Detail

The Vendor Balance Detail report shows the detail of each bill from, and payment to, each vendor. However, this report includes only transactions that "go through" Accounts Payable. That is, it shows only transactions such as bills and Bill Payments. If you just write checks to your vendors directly (without using Bills), those transactions won't show in this report.

COMPUTER TUTORIAL

1 Select the *Reports* menu, choose **Vendors & Payables**, and then choose **Vendor Balance Detail** (see Figure 3-62).

2 To print the report, click **Print** at the top of the report. Close all open windows. Click **No**, if the Memorize Report message appears.

Type	Date	Num	Account	Amount	Balance
Ace Glass					
Bill	01/18/2002	2084	Accounts Payable	1,286.00	1,286.00
Bill Pmt -Check	01/20/2002	6002	Accounts Payable	0.00	1,286.00
Discount	01/20/2002	6002	Accounts Payable	0.00	1,286.00
Bill Pmt -Check	01/20/2002	6004	Accounts Payable	-1,260.28	25.72
Discount	01/20/2002	6004	Accounts Payable	-25.72	0.00
Total Ace Glass				0.00	0.00
Artigues Construction Rentals					
Check	02/10/2002	328	Accounts Payable	-200.00	-200.00
Bill	02/15/2002	1352	Accounts Payable	185.00	-15.00
Deposit	02/15/2002	423	Accounts Payable	15.00	0.00
Total Artigues Construction Rentals				0.00	0.00
Nellis Windows & Doors					
Bill	01/29/2002	5055	Accounts Payable	400.00	400.00
Credit	01/29/2002	5055C	Accounts Payable	-25.00	375.00
Bill Pmt -Check	03/21/2002		Accounts Payable	-375.00	0.00
Total Nellis Windows & Doors				0.00	0.00
Wagner & Son Painting					
Bill	12/21/2001	2342	Accounts Payable	142.00	142.00
Bill Pmt -Check	01/20/2002	6003	Accounts Payable	-142.00	0.00
Total Wagner & Son Painting				0.00	0.00
TOTAL				0.00	0.00

Figure 3-62 The Vendor Balance Detail report

Transaction List by Vendor

The Transaction List by Vendor report shows all transactions associated with your vendors, even if the transactions did not "go through" Accounts Payable (e.g., checks and credit card charges).

1 Select the *Reports* menu, choose **Vendors & Payables**, and then choose **Transaction List by Vendor**.

2 Set the date fields on the report to "01/01/2002" through "03/31/2002."

3 Close all open windows. Click **No**, if the Memorize Report message appears.

COMPUTER TUTORIAL

Transaction List by Vendor

Modify Report | Memorize | Print | Excel | Hide Header | Refresh

Dates Custom   From 01/01/2002 To 03/31/2002   Sort By Default

Academy Glass
Transaction List by Vendor
January through March 2002

Type	Date	Num	Memo	Account	Clr	Split	Amount
Ace Glass							
Bill	01/18/2002	2084	Window Pur...	Accounts Payable		Purchases	-1,286.00
Bill Pmt -Check	01/20/2002	6002	VOID: Acct#...	Checking	✓	-SPLIT-	0.00
Bill Pmt -Check	01/20/2002	6004	Acct# 43-234	Checking		-SPLIT-	-1,260.28
Artigues Construction Rentals							
Check	02/10/2002	328	Deposit - Bi...	Checking		Accounts Pa...	-200.00
Bill	02/15/2002	1352	Saw Rental	Accounts Payable		Equipment R...	-185.00
Credit Card Cha...	02/20/2002		Equipment ...	National Bank VIS...		Equipment R...	-35.40
Jones Office Supply							
Check	01/05/2002	327	Printer Paper	Checking		-SPLIT-	-128.60
Credit Card Cha...	02/15/2002	65432	Office Supp...	National Bank VIS...		Office Suppl...	-86.48
National Bank							
Check	02/07/2002	329	Acct#1234-1...	Checking		National Ban...	-2,152.00
Nellis Windows & Doors							
Bill	01/29/2002	5055	Skylight for...	Accounts Payable		Purchases	-400.00
Credit	01/29/2002	5055C	Credit on S...	Accounts Payable		Purchase Dis...	25.00
Bill Pmt -Check	01/30/2002		Skylight for...	Checking		Accounts Pa...	-375.00
Orlando Properties							
Check	01/05/2002	6001		Checking		Rent	-3,200.00
Valley Gas & Electric							
Check	01/04/2002	326		Checking		Gas and Elec...	-276.52
Wagner & Son Painting							
Bill Pmt -Check	01/20/2002	6003	Open Bill at...	Checking		Accounts Pa...	-142.00

Figure 3-63 The Transaction List by Vendor report

Name _____ Date _____

   4. Using Write Checks, enter a check (To be printed) to Orlando Properties, dated 1/15/2002 and in the amount of $1,500.00, for Rent in the San Jose store. Make the check printable, but don't print it.

   5. Enter a bill from Nellis Windows & Doors on 1/18/2002. The bill (#1500) is in the amount of $643.00 with terms of Net 30. It is for Purchases of Windows on the Bob Mason job, so code it to Cost of Goods Sold. Bob Mason is a customer in the San Jose store, so tag the expense with the appropriate job and Class.

   6. Enter a bill from Sinclair Insurance on 1/19/2002. It is Bill #3453 for $1,250.00 for Liability insurance for the San Jose store. Terms: Net 15. Expense the whole bill to Insurance:Liability Insurance and allocate 100% of the cost to the San Jose store. Note: the default terms for Sinclair Insurance should remain Net 30.

   7. Create and print an Unpaid Bills Detail report dated 1/20/2002.

   8. Pay all of the bills due on or before 2/28/2002. Pay the bills from the Checking account on 1/19/2002. Make the Bill Payments "printable" checks.

   9. Print all of the checks in the Checking account. Print them on blank paper and start the check number sequence at 6001.

  10. Enter a credit card charge on the National Bank VISA card from Jones Office Supply (Use Quick Add to add the vendor), reference #1234, dated 1/25/2002. The purchase was in the amount of $152.53 for office supplies in the Walnut Creek store.

  11. Enter a bill from Ace Glass on 1/25/2002. The bill (#4635) was for $1,500.00 with terms of 2% 10, Net 30. Code the bill to Cost of Goods Sold. It was for supplies on the Ron Berry job in the San Jose class.

  12. Enter a Bill Credit from Ace Glass on 1/30/2002 for $500.00. Use reference number 4635C on the credit. Code the credit to Cost of Goods Sold and tag the credit with the Ron Berry job and the San Jose class.

  13. Apply the credit to Bill #4635 and pay the remainder of the bill on 1/30/2002 using a printable check. On this bill payment, take the appropriate discount and code it to Purchase Discounts.

  14. Print the check (#6005) on blank paper.

  15. Print a Vendor Balance Detail report for January and February 2002.

  16. Print a Balance Sheet for 2/28/2002. Select **Reports**, then **Company & Financial**, and then **Balance Sheet Standard**. Set the date at the top of the report to 2/28/2002.

EXTEND YOUR KNOWLEDGE

PROBLEM 3-2

> **Restore the Problem 3-2.QBB file from the CD-ROM and store it on your hard disk according to your instructor's directions.**

1. Add Ingalls Woodworks to the Vendor list.

   Contact: Charles Ingalls. Address: P.O. Box 820, Oakland, CA 94610. Phone number (510) 555-0405. Email charles@ingalls.net. Print on check as: Ingalls Woodworks.

   Acct # 94871. Type: Subcontractor. Terms 2%10, Net 30. Credit Limit: $10,000. Tax ID 124-13-1324. He will receive a 1099. He is headquartered in Oakland in Alameda County.

2. Add Hendrickson Windows and Doors to the vendor list.

   Contact: Paul Hendrickson. Address: 217 Broad Street, San Jose, CA 94326. Phone number (408) 555-3207. Email paul@hendrickson.biz. Print on check as: Hendrickson Windows and Doors.

   Acct #73821. Type: Construc Materials. Terms: Net 15. Credit Limit: $50,000. Tax ID 987-43-6521. He will receive a 1099. He is headquartered in San Jose in Santa Clara County.

3. Record the transactions below.

Transactions

February 1, 2002	Record manual check #327 to Postmaster $200, dated February 1, 2002, for postage. Class: San Jose
February 1	Issue check for rent on the San Jose location to Orlando Properties, $1750.00. Set the check to be printed, but do not print it yet. Class: San Jose
February 2	Record the January cell phone bill (# 643-4411) to Cal Telephone of $147.55. Terms: Net 30 (Terms for Cal Telephone should always default to Net 30.) Account: Cellular Phone Class: Overhead
February 5	Record Bill #951 from Sinclair Insurance, $1,250.00 for liability insurance. Terms: Net 30 Account: Liability Insurance Class: San Jose

continued on next page

Name _____ **Date** _____

Transactions *(continued)*

✓	February 5	Record Bill #64-44, for $500 to Artigues Construction Rentals for rental equipment. Terms: Net 15 Account: Equipment Rental Job: Mason, Bob Class: San Jose
✓	February 5	Record Bill #223 from Ingalls Woodworks for the Bill Young, Window Replacement job. $175.00. Terms: 2%10 net 30 Account: Subcontractors Expense Job: Bill Young, Window Replacement Class: Walnut Creek
✓	February 5	Pay bills due on or before 1/31/2002. Print the two checks in the checking register. Starting check number is #6001.
✓	February 8	Purchased window on credit from Nellis Windows & Doors for Bill Young's window replacement $200. Invoice: #6072 Terms: Net 30 Account: Cost of Goods Sold Class: Walnut Creek
✓	February 12	Issued manual check #328 to Express Delivery Service, $37.50 for package delivery. Account: Postage & Delivery Class: San Jose
✓	February 15	Select bills for payment. Pay bills due on or before 2/28/2002. You should already have printed check #6003.
✓	February 17	Check #6003 was accidentally destroyed and must be voided. After voiding the check, issue a new bill payment check for this Bill. Print check #6004. (**Hint:** Use Pay Bills to repay the bill.)
✓	February 22	Received a credit for $15.00 from Nellis Windows and Doors. This credit should be applied to Invoice #6072. Account: Cost of Goods Sold Job: Young, Bill:Window Replacement Job Class: Walnut Creek
✓	February 22	Record bill from Valley Gas and Electric in the amount of $288 for gas and electric. Invoice: # 64666 Terms: Due on Receipt Class: Overhead
✓	February 25	Charged meals for client luncheon at Academy Grille for $97.54 to National Bank Visa Gold Card. Use Quick Add to add Academy Grille to vendor list. Account: Meals & Entertainment Class: Walnut Creek
✓	February 28	Select bills for payment. Pay bills due on or before 3/14/2002. Print the checks.

4. Print check #6005 through 6009 on blank paper.

5. Print a Vendor Balance Detail Report for all transactions.

6. Print a Check Detail report for February 2002. Select the Reports menu, choose Banking, then choose Check Detail. Set the dates to February 1, 2002 through February 28, 2002 and print the report.

DISCUSSION QUESTIONS

These questions are designed to help you apply what you are learning about QuickBooks to your own organization. Take some time to begin a notebook for your answers and your thoughts about how your company could use QuickBooks to organize information and track performance.

1. How many locations does your organization have? Does your organization track purchases or costs by each location?

2. Does your organization keep track of the costs of specific jobs or projects completed for a customer? If so, how does your organization use that information? Does it affect the estimates or prices for future jobs or projects? If yes, what is the process you follow?

3. Which of your vendors send you invoices (bills)? Do they offer you discount terms? If so, list some of the different discount terms you receive.

4. What is your organization's cash management policy that determines when you will pay your bills?

5. Does your organization have vendor returns or disputes that result in vendor credits? How did you receive them? Were they separate pieces of paper? Were they listed on your next customer statement, or did you receive refunds?

6. Does your organization have company credit cards? How many? Are they issued in an individual's name or only in the organization's name? How is their use controlled currently? In what ways will QuickBooks' credit card-tracking function improve your ability to manage credit card expense?

ACTIVITY

1. List some of the products and/or services your organization purchases and the method(s) you use to pay for each of them.

2. List the vendors from whom you purchase products or services. Determine which vendors should be treated as Cash vendors and which should be Credit vendors. Explain why you would classify them in each category.

Workplace Applications

Name _____ **Date** _____

MUSIC CENTRAL

Music Central sells and services musical instruments and teaches music lessons. One of the store's piano students, Peter Cornish, a long-time customer, has just mentioned to you that he can sell you guitar strings for repairing and restringing your guitars. He has said that he will sell you 100 strings for only $500. However, if you can pay the bill in 10 days, he will give you a discount of $50. He has asked you to let him know later today and would like to be paid by check.

Questions

These questions are designed to help you apply what you are learning about QuickBooks to this case study. Use your notebook to record your answers and your thoughts.

1. If you chose Peter Cornish as a vendor, do you have to enter him as a vendor since he is already in QuickBooks as a customer? Do you enter his name the same or differently?

2. How would you enter the terms that Cornish specified for payment?

3. Since Cornish wants a check, do you need to enter this as an account payable or just write a check from the check register?

4. If you had a petty cash account and one of your assistants paid Cornish from Petty cash, what steps would you take to record the transaction?

*inter*NET
CONNECTION

Do you have questions about accounting issues? Try posting them to a discussion group. Find such groups at **http://www.electronicaccountant.com/#search**

Bank Reconciliation

OBJECTIVES

After completing this chapter, you should be able to:

1 Reconcile your bank account.

2 Find bank reconciliation errors.

3 Correct several different types of errors in your bank accounts.

4 Deal with corrections to transactions in closed accounting periods.

5 Handle bounced checks.

6 Reconcile your credit card accounts and record a bill for later payment.

7 Set the Beginning Balance amount on the Bank Reconciliation screen the first time you reconcile an account.

RESTORE THIS FILE

This chapter uses Chapter 4.QBW. To open this file, restore the file called **Chapter 4.QBB** to your hard disk. (See page 7 for instructions on restoring files.)

In this chapter, you'll learn how to reconcile your bank account and correct errors that are discovered during the bank reconciliation. The two examples used in this chapter are for a checking account and a credit card account, but you can use the same process presented here to reconcile nearly all of your balance sheet accounts.

RECONCILING BANK ACCOUNTS

Each month, you need to reconcile your QuickBooks bank account with the bank statement you receive from the bank. In doing so you can identify and correct any discrepancies between your records and the bank's. Before reconciling any account in QuickBooks, make sure you've entered all of the transactions for that account. For example, if you make automatic payments from your checking account (EFTs) or have automatic charges on your credit card, you will need to enter those transactions before you start the reconciliation.

Reconciling Your Checking Account

Each month, when you receive your bank statement, follow these steps to reconcile your QuickBooks account with the bank statement. Use the sample bank statement shown in Figure 4-2 for this Tutorial.

COMPUTER TUTORIAL

1 Display the account register for the Checking account.

2 Review the register and verify that you have entered all of the transactions for the month (e.g., automatic drafts from your checking account, NSF charges, bounced checks, etc.).

3 With the Checking account register still open, select the **Banking** menu and choose **Reconcile**.

4 Look for the beginning balance on the bank statement. Compare the beginning balance with the *Beginning Balance* field on the Begin Reconciliation screen (see Figure 4-1). Notice that they are the same.

QuickBooks automatically enters the amount in the *Beginning Balance* field by calculating the total of all previously cleared transactions.

NOTE

If the beginning balance doesn't match the bank statement, you have probably made changes to transactions cleared during a previous bank reconciliation. See *Finding Bank Reconciliation Errors* on page 187 for more information.

Begin Reconciliation

Select an account to reconcile, and then enter the ending balance from your account statement.

Account Checking   ▼ last reconciled on 12/31/2001.

Statement Date   01/31/2002

Beginning Balance   15,283.60   What if my beginning balance doesn't match my statement?

Ending Balance   15,104.90

Enter any service charge or interest earned.

Service Charge 10.00   Date 01/31/2002   Account Bank Service Charges ▼
Interest Earned 8.62   Date 01/31/2002   Account Interest Income ▼

[Continue]   [Cancel]   [Help]

Figure 4-1 The Begin Reconciliation screen

5 Enter "15,104.90" in the *Ending Balance* field. This amount is the ending balance shown on the bank statement in Figure 4-2.

Account:		Academy Glass–Main Checking	

| Last Statement Date | 12/31/2001 |
| This Statement Date | 1/31/2002 |

Beginning Balance	$15,283.60
Less: Checks & Withdrawals	$15,441.40
Plus: Total Deposits	$15,262.70
Ending Balance	$15,104.90

Checks	Date	Amount
325	2-Jan	$324.00
326	7-Jan	$276.52
327	10-Jan	$128.60
6001**	10-Jan	$3,200.00
6003**	25-Jan	$142.00
6004	26-Jan	$1,260.28
Total Checks:		$5,331.40

Deposits	Date	Amount
Customer Deposit	2-Jan	$3,000.00
Customer Deposit	30-Jan	$12,097.28
Customer Deposit	30-Jan	$156.80
Interest Earned	31-Jan	$8.62
Total Deposits:		$15,262.70

Other Debits

ATM Withdrawal	30-Jan	$100.00
Transfer	31-Jan	$10,000.00
Service Charge	31-Jan	$10.00
Total Other Debits	$10,110.00	

Figure 4-2 Sample bank statement

6 Enter "10.00" in the *Service Charge* field and press <TAB>.

7 Leave "01/31/2002" in the *Date* field and press <TAB>.

QuickBooks automatically enters the last day of the month after the last bank reconciliation. Since this account was last reconciled on 12/31/01, QuickBooks entered "01/31/02." Confirm that this is the date on your bank statement before proceeding to the next field.

8 Leave "Bank Service Charges" in the *Account* field and press <TAB>.

QuickBooks automatically enters the expense account you used on the last bank reconciliation for this account. Confirm that this is the correct expense account before proceeding to the next field.

9 Enter "8.62" in the *Interest Earned* field and press <TAB>.

NOTE

If you use class tracking or job costing in QuickBooks, you should enter monthly service charges and interest earned directly in the account register using the Splits function, or in the Write Checks window. QuickBooks does not allow you to assign a class or job when recording these transactions on the Begin Reconciliation screen.

⑩ Leave "01/31/2002" in the *Date* field and press <TAB>.

⑪ Leave "Interest Income" in the *Account* field and click **Continue**.

If you had any bank service charges or interest earned in the bank account, you would enter those amounts in the appropriate fields on the Begin Reconciliation screen. When you enter these amounts, QuickBooks adds new transactions to your bank account.

⑫ On the Reconcile – Checking screen, match the deposits on the bank statement with the deposits shown in the Deposits, Interest and Other Credits section. Click in the far left-hand column of each line, to mark it as a cleared deposit (see Figure 4-3).

Notice that QuickBooks calculates the sum of your marked items at the bottom of the screen in the Items you have marked cleared section. Compare the figures to your bank statement. If you find a discrepancy with these totals, you will know you have an error. Search for an item that you forgot to mark or marked in error.

⑬ Match the checks and other debits on the bank statement with the ones listed in the Checks, Payments and Service Charges section. Click in the far left-hand column of each line to mark it as a cleared check (see Figure 4-3).

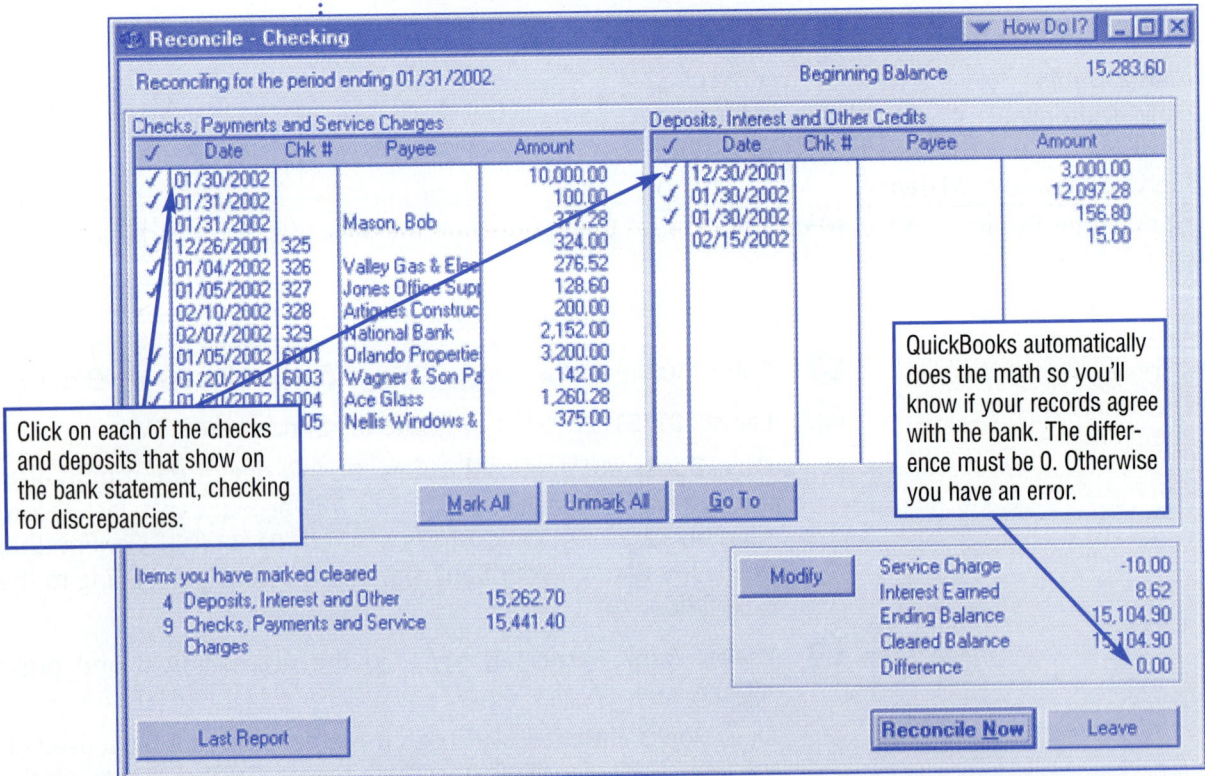

Figure 4-3 The Reconcile – Checking screen

⑭ After you've clicked off each check and deposit, look at the *Difference* field. It should be "0.00," indicating that your bank account is reconciled.

If the *Difference* field is not zero, check for errors. See *Finding Bank Reconciliation Errors* on page 187 for help in troubleshooting your bank reconciliation.

⑮ If the *Difference* field is zero, you've successfully reconciled; click **Reconcile Now**.

⑯ Select "Detail" from the Select Reconciliation Report screen and click **Display** (see Figure 4-4).

When you finish performing the bank reconciliation, always print a Reconciliation Detail report for your files.

Select Reconciliation Report   ☒

Congratulations! Your account is balanced. All marked items have been cleared in the account register.

Select what type of reconciliation report you'd like to run.

○ **Detail**
○ **Summary**

| Display | Print... | Cancel | Help |

Figure 4-4 Select Detail in the Select Reconciliation Report screen.

⑰ Click **OK** on the information message that says this report shows current data.

The Reconciliation Detail report is shown in Figure 4-5. The length of the report will depend on how many transactions you cleared on this reconciliation and how many uncleared transactions remain in the account.

⑱ To print the report, click **Print** at the top of the report.

19 Close all open windows.

🗐 Reconciliation Detail					▼ How Do I?	_ □ ×

Modify Report...	Memorize...	Print...	Excel...	Hide Header	Refresh	

Academy Glass

Reconciliation Detail

Checking, Period Ending 01/31/2002

Type	Date	Num	Name	Clr	Amount	Balance
Beginning Balance						15,283.60
Cleared Transactions						
Checks and Payments - 9 items						
▶ Check	12/26/2001	325		✓	-324.00	-324.00 ◀
Check	01/04/2002	326	Valley Gas & Electric	✓	-276.52	-600.52
Check	01/05/2002	327	Jones Office Supply	✓	-128.60	-729.12
Check	01/05/2002	6001	Orlando Properties	✓	-3,200.00	-3,929.12
Bill Pmt -Check	01/20/2002	6004	Ace Glass	✓	-1,260.28	-5,189.40
Bill Pmt -Check	01/20/2002	6003	Wagner & Son Painting	✓	-142.00	-5,331.40
Transfer	01/30/2002			✓	-10,000.00	-15,331.40
Transfer	01/31/2002			✓	-100.00	-15,431.40
Check	01/31/2002			✓	-10.00	-15,441.40
Total Checks and Payments					-15,441.40	-15,441.40
Deposits and Credits - 4 items						
Transfer	12/30/2001			✓	3,000.00	3,000.00
Deposit	01/30/2002			✓	156.80	3,156.80
Deposit	01/30/2002			✓	12,097.28	15,254.08
Deposit	01/31/2002			✓	8.62	15,262.70
Total Deposits and Credits					15,262.70	15,262.70
Total Cleared Transactions					-178.70	-178.70
Cleared Balance					-178.70	15,104.90
Uncleared Transactions						
Checks and Payments - 2 items						
Bill Pmt -Check	01/30/2002	6005	Nellis Windows & Doors		-375.00	-375.00
Check	01/31/2002		Mason, Bob		-377.28	-752.28
Total Checks and Payments					-752.28	-752.28
Total Uncleared Transactions					-752.28	-752.28
Register Balance as of 01/31/2002					-930.98	14,352.62

Figure 4-5 The Reconciliation Detail report

NOTE

The update (patch) of QuickBooks 2002 released in March 2002 affected the format of this report. If you have not updated QuickBooks 2002 on your computer, your report may differ slightly from the report shown in Figure 4-5.

Bank Reconciliation Reports

As discussed above, each time you complete a bank reconciliation, QuickBooks walks you through creating a bank reconciliation report for that reconciliation. However, you can create bank reconciliation reports at any time by following the steps below.

Note however, that you can only print the report for the most recent reconciliation, not for any earlier reconciliations. Many accountants have a special edition of QuickBooks that allows them to print bank reconciliation reports for every reconciliation performed, not just for the most recent reconciliation. Contact your accountant for more information.

COMPUTER TUTORIAL

1 Select the *Reports* menu, choose **Banking**, and then choose **Reconciliation Detail**.

You could also choose the Reconciliation Summary report, but this example shows the detail report.

2 Then select the appropriate bank account in the *Account* field of the Select Reconciliation Report window and click **Display** (see Figure 4-6).

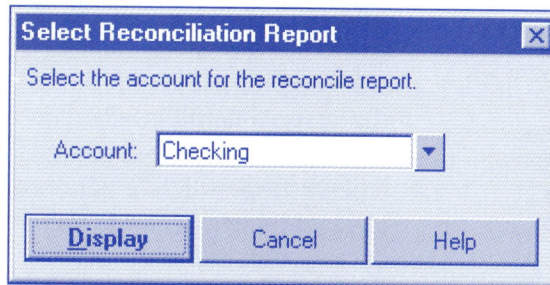

Figure 4-6 The Select Reconciliation Report window

3 With the report displayed, you can click **Print** to print the report. Close the bank reconciliation report.

BANK RECONCILIATION ERRORS

Finding Bank Reconciliation Errors

If you've finished checking off all of the deposits and checks but the *Difference* field at the bottom of the screen is not zero, there must be an error somewhere in your records. Don't worry, you *can* find the error.

To find errors in your bank reconciliation, try the following steps:

> **Don't perform these steps now. They are for reference only.**

1. Verify that the amount in the *Beginning Balance* field matches the beginning balance on your bank statement. If it doesn't, you are not ready to reconcile. You need to find the error in last month's reconciliation. Did you delete a reconciled transaction? Did you remove a checkmark from a transaction in the register? Did you modify the amount of a reconciled transaction? Any of these actions will cause

your opening balance to disagree with the bank's. Perform the following steps to identify the problem:

2. Click **Cancel** on the Begin Reconciliation screen (or **Leave** on the Reconcile – Checking screen) to exit the Bank Reconciliation feature.

3. Print a Bank Reconciliation Detail report. This report will show the transactions you cleared while performing your last bank reconciliation.

4. Review the Checking register to confirm that all of the transactions marked "cleared" on the Bank Reconciliation Detail report are still cleared in the register. Cleared transactions show a checkmark between the Payment and Deposit columns. If you find an uncleared (unreconciled) transaction that should be cleared, click the field between the Payment and Deposit columns to add a checkmark. Then click **Record** to save your change.

5. Review the Checking register to confirm that the amounts of all cleared transactions in the register agree to the amounts shown on the Bank Reconciliation Detail report. If any amount is different, change the amount so that it agrees to the report.

6. Create a Missing Checks report. Select the **Reports** menu, choose **Banking**, and then choose **Missing Checks**. Review the report for breaks in the check number sequence. If there is a break in the sequence you may have deleted a previously cleared check. If this is the case, you will need to re-enter the transaction and mark the check cleared in the account register. The amount in the *Beginning Balance* field will still not agree to the beginning balance on your bank statement, but you will be able to perform the bank reconciliation nonetheless. When you perform your next bank reconciliation, QuickBooks will update the amount in the *Beginning Balance* field.

7. Verify that you've entered the correct amount in the *Ending Balance* field. The amount you enter must match the ending balance on the bank statement.

8. Verify that the total of the debits on the bank statement matches the Total Checks, Payments and Service Charges shown on the Reconcile screen (see Figure 4-3). If the totals don't match, you will know you have a discrepancy on one of your checks, payments, or service charges.

9. Verify that the total of the credits on the bank statement matches the total Deposits, Interest and Other Credits shown on the Reconcile screen (see Figure 4-3). If they don't match, you will know you have a discrepancy on one of your deposits, in the amount of your interest or with some other credit.

10. Look for a figure that matches the difference exactly. Did you mark one accidentally? Did you forget to mark one?

11. Divide the difference by 9. If the result is a whole number, check for transpositions. A *transposition* is when you reverse the digits in a number (e.g., typing "78" instead of "87").

NOTE

If you have the Audit Trail turned on, QuickBooks keeps a record of all voids, changes and deletions by date and user name. The Audit Trail report may help you to identify changes to reconciled transactions. Also, many accountants have special editions of QuickBooks that allow them to track changes made to cleared bank transactions. Contact your accountant for more information.

TIP

To "lock" your transactions so you cannot change or delete them, set the **Closing Date** to the date of the bank statement each time you reconcile. That way, once your bank reconciliation is complete, you will not be able to modify transactions dated on or before the statement date. See page 475 for more information about setting the Closing Date in QuickBooks.

Correcting Errors Found During Reconciliation

When you find a discrepancy between an amount in QuickBooks and an amount on the bank statement, you will need to correct it. You'll use a different method to correct the error depending on the date of the transaction.

Correcting or Voiding Transactions in the Current Accounting Period

If you find that you need to correct a transaction in QuickBooks and the transaction is dated in the current accounting period (a period for which financial statements haven't been issued, and/or tax returns have not yet been filed), correct the error as described in the following paragraphs.

When You Made the Error

If you made an error in your records, you must make the change in QuickBooks, so that your records will agree with the bank's. For example, if you wrote a check for $400 but recorded it in QuickBooks as $40, you'll need to change the check in QuickBooks. Double-click the transaction in the Reconcile screen, make the correction, and click **Save & Close**. This will return you to the Reconcile screen and you'll see the updated amount.

When the Bank Made the Error

If the bank made an error, make a General Journal Entry to adjust for the error (see *Recording Adjustments and General Journal Entries* on page 458) and continue reconciling the account. Then call or write the bank to arrange for a credit to your account. When you receive the bank statement showing the correction, enter a subsequent General Journal Entry to record the bank's adjustment. This General Journal Entry will show on your next bank reconciliation, where you can clear it like the other transactions.

Voiding Checks and Stop Payments

When you find a check, dated in the current accounting period, that you know will not clear the bank (e.g., if you stop payment on a check), you will need to void the check. Double-click the check from the Reconcile screen. Then select the *Edit* menu and choose **Void Check**. Then click **Save & Close** to return to the Reconcile screen.

Correcting or Voiding Transactions in Closed Accounting Periods

You don't want to change transactions dated in a closed accounting period because doing so would change net income in a period for which you have already issued financial statements and/or filed the tax returns.

To correct or void a check or deposit that is dated in a closed accounting period, follow the procedure described below.

When You Made the Error

If you entered the wrong amount on a bank transaction (e.g., check or deposit) and the transaction is dated in a closed accounting period, enter a reversing entry in QuickBooks. A reversing entry is a deposit (if the error transaction is a check) or a check (if the error transaction is a deposit). Date the transaction in the current accounting period (i.e., the current date) and use the same account that you used for the original transaction so that the two transactions cancel each other out. Both the original transaction and the reversing transaction will show on the Reconcile screen. Clear both transactions.

Next, enter the correct amount in a new transaction dated in the current accounting period. This new transaction should be checked in the reconciliation screen.

The net effect on the Profit & Loss report in the current period is the difference between the reversing entry and the new transaction.

When the Bank Made the Error

If the bank made the error to a transaction in a closed accounting period, enter the adjustments as you would if the transaction were in a current period. Record both General Journal Entries in the current account period (i.e., the current date) See *When the Bank Made the Error* on page 189.

Voiding Checks and Stop Payments

To properly account for voiding a check or stopping payments on checks in a closed accounting period, follow the steps below.

Don't perform these steps now. They are for reference only.

1. Find the check in the register and note the account or accounts to which in the check is posted. The check in Figure 4-7 is posted to the "Postage and Delivery" expense account.

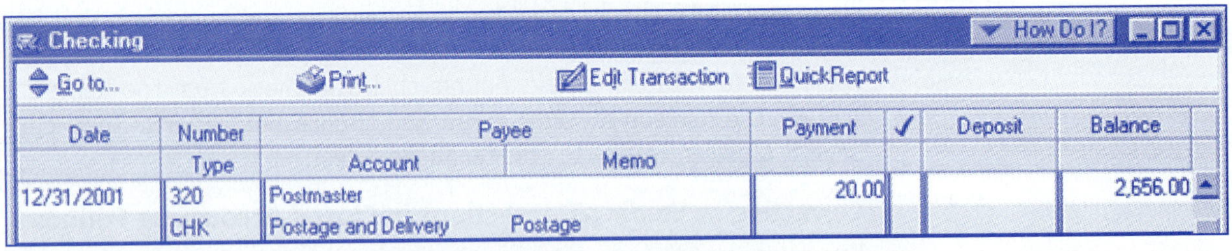

Figure 4-7 Display the check you need to void.

2. Add a Deposit transaction in the current accounting period that "reverses" the check that will never clear (see Figure 4-8).

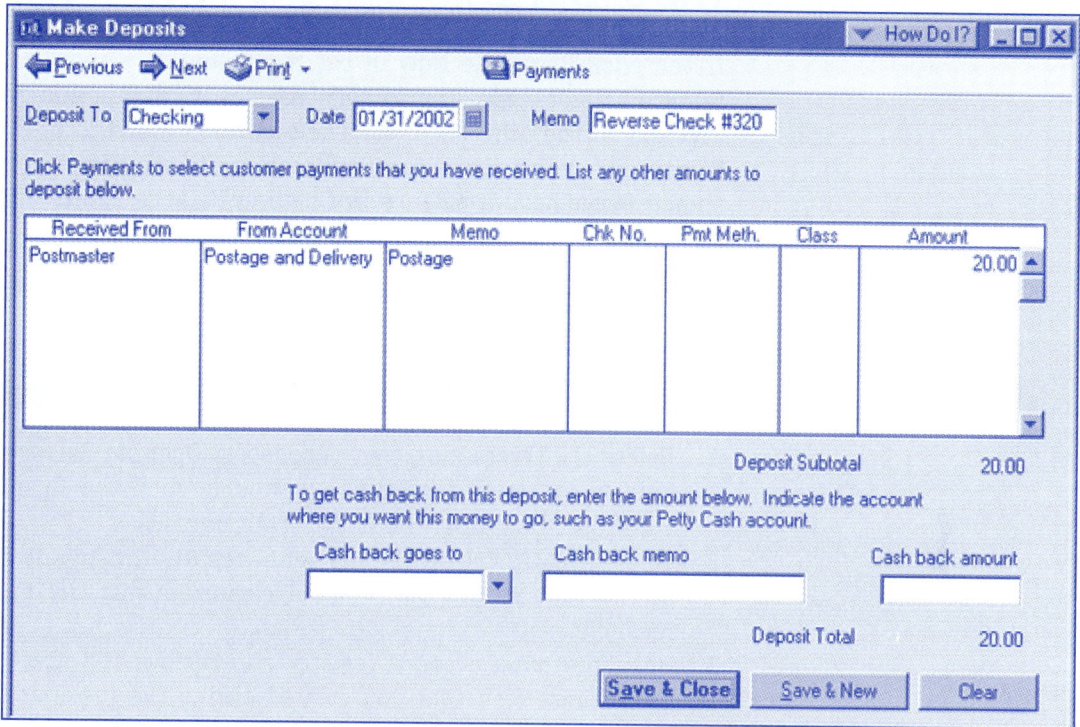

Figure 4-8 Add a Deposit transaction to reverse the check.

3. On the next reconciliation for this account, clear both the check and the deposit (reversal). These two transactions effectively cancel each other out.

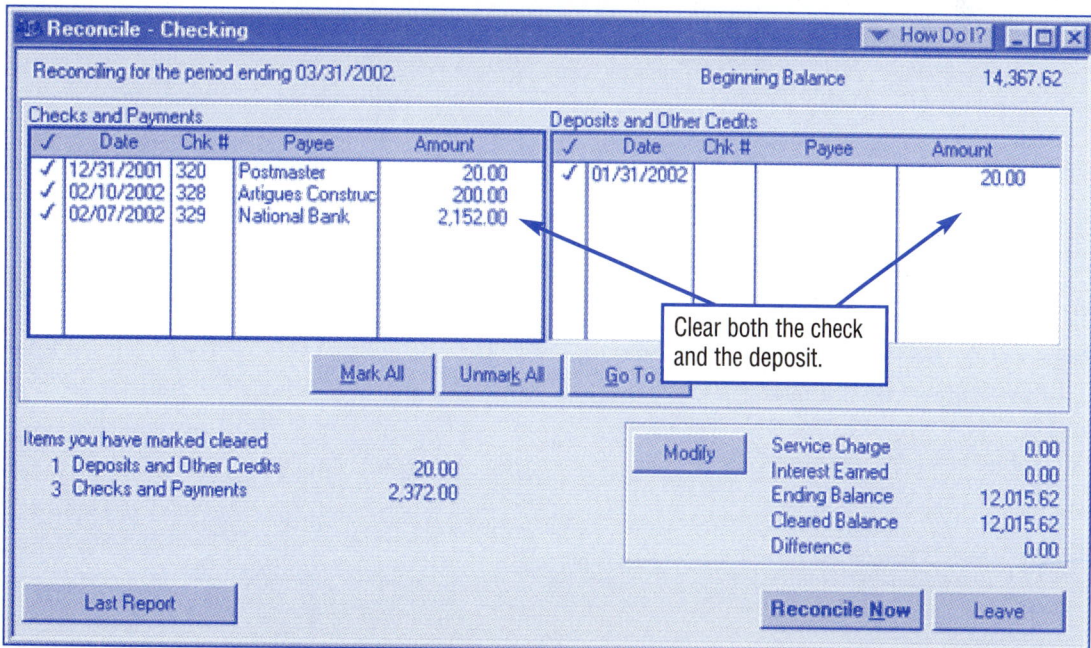

Figure 4-9 Clear both the check and the deposit on the Reconcile – Checking screen

WHEN QUICKBOOKS AUTOMATICALLY ADJUSTS THE BALANCE IN YOUR CHECKING ACCOUNT

If you click **Reconcile Now** in the reconciliation screen, when the difference is not zero, QuickBooks creates a transaction in the bank account for the difference. The transaction is coded to Opening Balance Equity. You can't leave this transaction in the register because you should never have a balance in Opening Balance Equity after setup. A balance in Opening Balance Equity usually indicates an over- or understatement of net income. (See Chapter 10 for more information about the proper use of the Opening Balance Equity account.)

Perform the following steps to correct the problem.

Don't perform these steps now. They are for reference only.

1. Delete the transaction that is coded to Opening Balance Equity. (To quickly locate this transaction, double-click the Opening Balance Equity account from the Chart of Accounts.)
2. Create a Bank Reconciliation Detail report. This report will show all of the transactions you marked cleared during the previous bank reconciliation.
3. Open the bank account register and remove the check mark from each transaction that you cleared during the previous bank reconciliation. This will "unclear" the transactions and, in effect, undo the bank reconciliation.
4. Re-perform the bank reconciliation correctly, ensuring that the *Difference* field shows "0.00" before clicking **Reconcile Now**.

HANDLING BOUNCED CHECKS

Banks and accountants often refer to bounced checks as NSF (non-sufficient funds) transactions. This means there are insufficient funds in the account to cover the check.

When Your Customer's Check Bounces

COMPUTER TUTORIAL

If your bank returns a check from one of your customers, enter an NSF transaction in the banking account register.

① Add two new transactions to your bank account register, one for the amount of the check that bounced and one for the fee charged by the bank.

In this example, Bob Mason bounced a check for $415.68 and the bank charged our account $10.00. Enter the two transactions shown in Figure 4-10. Notice that the bounced check is coded to Accounts Receivable. This transaction creates a receivable from the customer that will show in your A/R reports and customer statements until the customer repays you.

Date	Number	Payee		Payment	✓	Deposit	Balance
	Type	Account	Memo				
02/01/2002	Bounce	Mason, Bob		415.68			13,936.94
	CHK	Accounts Receivable	Bounced Check				
02/01/2002	Bounce	Mason, Bob		10.00			13,926.94
	CHK	Bank Service Charges	Bounced Check Charge				

Figure 4-10 Add two transactions to your checking register.

Assuming that you charge your customers a service fee for processing their NSF checks, enter an Invoice to the customer as follows:

② Create an Other Charge Item called "NSF Charges" as shown in Figure 4-11.

NOTE

The check that you entered in the register increases (debits) Accounts Receivable and reduces (credits) the Checking account for the amount of the original check. The Invoice increases (debits) Accounts Receivable and decreases (credits) Bank Service Charges.

New Item

Type: Other Charge — Use for miscellaneous labor, material, or part charges, such as delivery charges, setup fees, and service charges.

Item Name/Number: NSF Charge
☐ Subitem of

☐ This is a reimbursable charge

Description: NSF Service Charge for Bounced Check #
Amount or %: 20.00   Tax Code: Non
Account: Other Income

OK / Cancel / Next / Custom Fields / Spelling
☐ Item is inactive

Figure 4-11 Use an "Other Charge" Item to charge your customers an NSF fee.

③ Create an Invoice for the amount of the NSF charge as shown in Figure 4-12. Use the NSF Charge "Other Charge" Item.

④ When you add the NSF Charge item to the invoice, QuickBooks displays a warning that says the item is associated with an expense account. Click **OK**.

⑤ Fill out the rest of the fields on the invoice to match Figure 4-12.

⑥ Click **Save & Close** to record the Invoice.

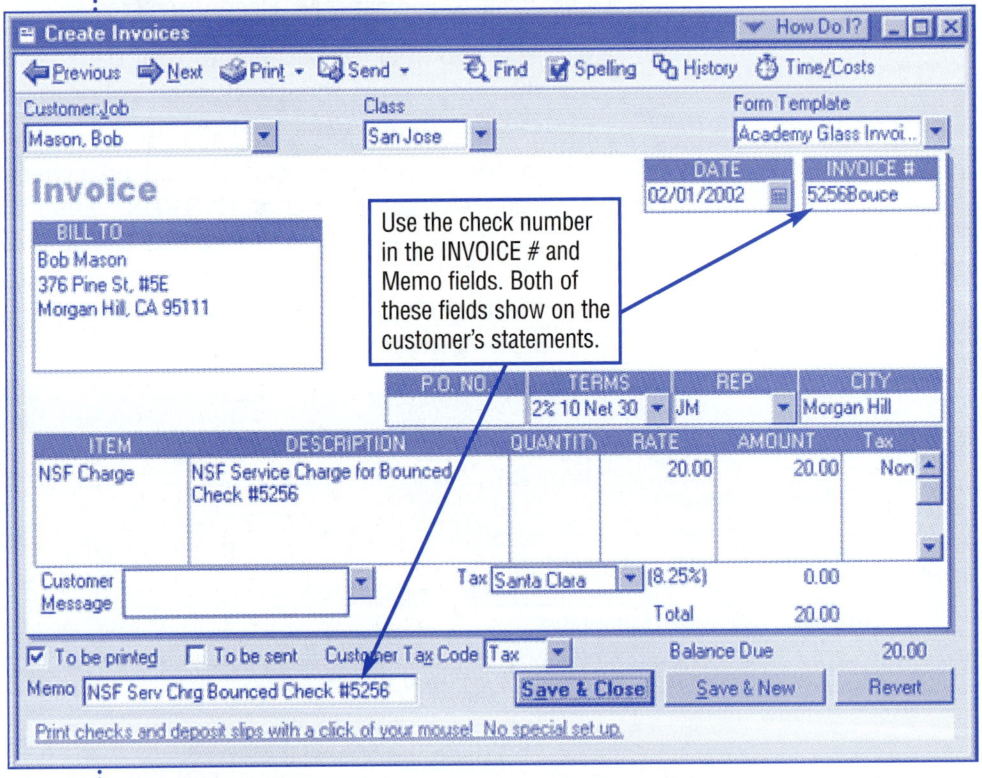

Figure 4-12 Invoice to charge the customer an NSF service charge

Receiving and Depositing the Replacement Check

To record the transactions for receiving and depositing a replacement check, follow these steps:

1 Select the **Customers** menu, and choose **Receive Payments**.

2 In this example, Bob Mason sent a replacement check that includes the amount of the check plus the NSF service charge of $20.00. Fill in the customer payment information as shown on the screen in Figure 4-13.

Make sure you apply the payment against both the bounced check and the service charge Invoice. Click **Save & Close**.

If you're just re-depositing the same check, this amount will only be $415.68. In that case, the customer would still owe $20.00.

Figure 4-13 The Receive Payments window showing the replacement check

③ Then add the check to your next deposit just as you would any other check. Select the **Banking** menu and choose **Make Deposits** (see Figure 4-14).

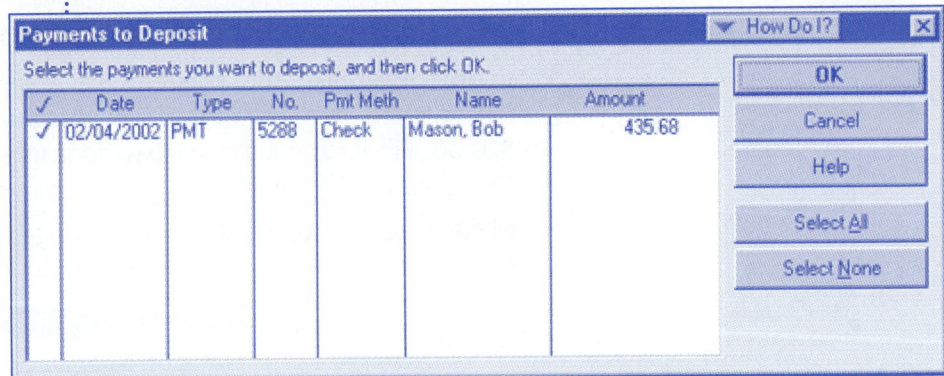

Figure 4-14 Add the replacement check to your deposit.

④ Click **OK** on the Payments to Deposit window and then click **Save & Close** on the Make Deposits screen to record the deposit.

When Your Check Bounces

If you write a check that overdraws your account and your bank returns the check, follow these steps:

◆ Call your vendor and apologize. Decide with your vendor how to handle the NSF Check (i.e., send a new check, redeposit same check, or pay by credit card).

◆ When the bank sends you a notice that your check was returned, there will be a charge from your bank. Enter a transaction in the Check register. Code the transaction to Bank Service Charges and use the actual date that the bank charged your account.

◆ If your balance is now sufficient for the check to clear, tell the vendor to redeposit the check.

◆ If your balance is not sufficient, consider other ways of settling with the vendor, such as paying with a credit card. Alternatively, negotiate delayed payment terms with your vendor.

◆ If your vendor charges you an extra fee for bouncing a check, enter a Bill (or use Write Checks) and code the charge to the Bank Service Charge account.

◆ If you bounce a payroll check, use the same process as described. Offer to reimburse your employee for any bank fees incurred as a result of your mistake.

RECONCILING CREDIT CARD ACCOUNTS AND PAYING THE BILL

If you use a credit card liability account to track all of your credit card charges and payments, you should reconcile the account every month just as you do with your bank account. The credit card reconciliation process is very similar to the bank account reconciliation, except that when you finish the reconciliation, QuickBooks asks you if you want to pay the credit card immediately or if you want to enter a bill for the balance of the credit card.

COMPUTER TUTORIAL

① Select the *Banking* menu and choose **Reconcile**.

② On the Begin Reconciliation screen, enter "National Bank VISA Gold" in the *Account* field and press <TAB>.

③ Verify that "02/28/2002" displays in the *Statement Date* field and press <TAB>.

④ Verify that the *Beginning Balance* field shows "2,152.00."

⑤ Enter "139.81" in the *Ending Balance* field and press <TAB>.

The *Ending Balance* field is where you enter the ending balance shown on your credit card statement.

⑥ Enter "17.93" in the *Finance Charge* field and press <TAB>.

⑦ Enter "02/28/2002" in the *Date* field and press <TAB>.

⑧ Enter "Interest Expense" in the *Account* field and press <TAB>.

⑨ Verify that your screen matches Figure 4-15 and click **Continue**.

Begin Reconciliation

Select an account to reconcile, and then enter the ending balance from your account statement.

Account: National Bank VISA Gold — last reconciled on 01/31/2002.

Statement Date: 02/28/2002

Beginning Balance: 2,152.00 — What if my beginning balance doesn't match my statement?

Ending Balance: 139.81

Enter any finance charge.

Finance Charge: 17.93 — Date: 02/28/2002 — Account: Interest Expense

[Continue] [Cancel] [Help]

Figure 4-15 Enter your credit card statement information on the Begin Reconciliation screen.

⑩ Click the **Mark All** button to clear all charges and payments.

Normally, you would click on each transaction individually as you match it with the statement. However, for our example, we're assuming that everything has cleared.

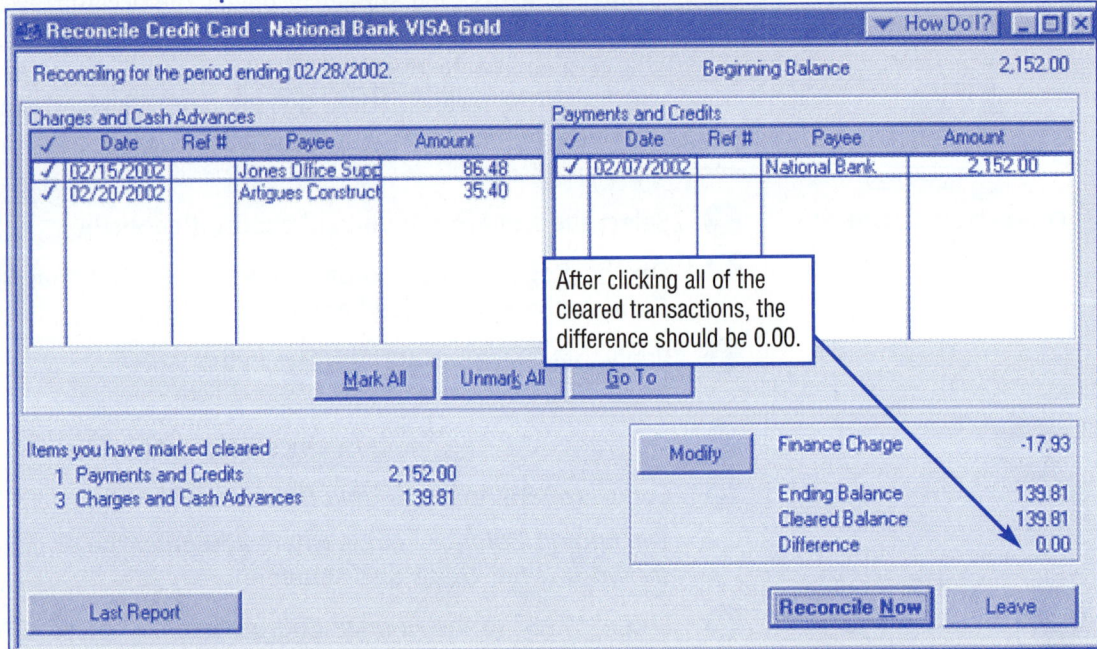

Figure 4-16 The Difference field should show a difference of 0.00 after reconciling.

⑪ Verify that the *Difference* field shows "0.00" (see Figure 4-16). If it doesn't, you should look for discrepancies between your records and the credit card statement.

⑫ Verify that your screen looks like Figure 4-16 and click **Reconcile Now**.

⑬ On the Select Reconciliation Report screen click **Cancel**.

Normally you would select "Detail" and click **Print**. In this Tutorial, however, you will skip this step. See page 187 for more information about Bank Reconciliation reports.

⑭ On the Make Payment screen (see Figure 4-17), click **Enter a bill for payment later**, and click **OK**.

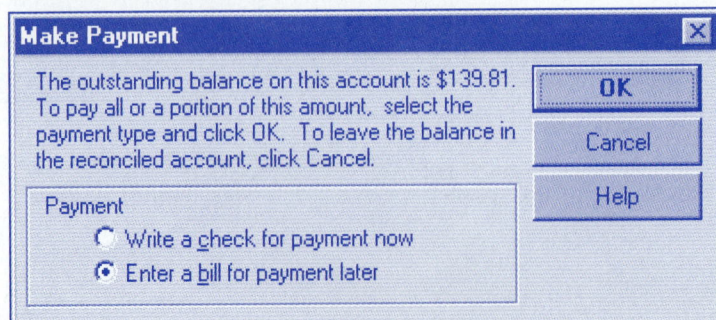

Figure 4-17 The Make Payment screen

⑮   Fill out the bill for the VISA payment, as shown in Figure 4-18.

Important:
If you intend to leave a balance on the credit card, enter only the amount that you intend to pay.

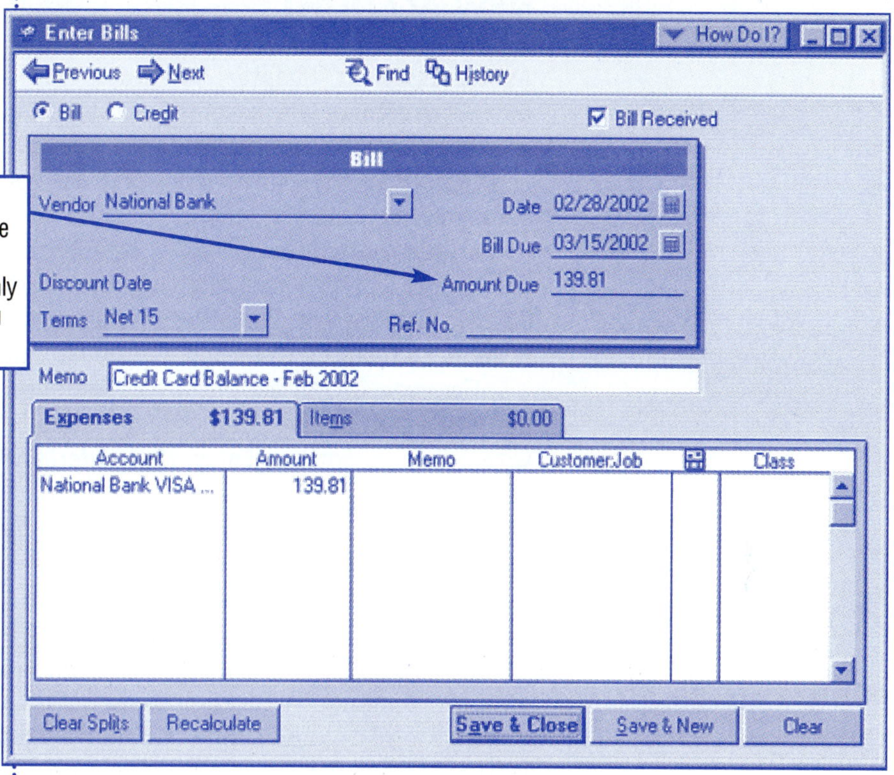

NOTE

QuickBooks pre-selects the National Bank VISA Gold account on the Expenses Tab. This reduces the Credit Card liability account (debit) and increases Accounts Payable (credit).

Figure 4-18 Use this data to pay the VISA bill.

If you don't want to pay the whole amount due on a credit card, don't just change the amount in the Pay Bills screen. Instead, edit the original bill to match the amount you actually intend to pay. By changing the bill, you reduce the amount that is transferred out of the Credit Card account (and into A/P) to the exact amount that is paid. That way, the amount you don't pay remains in the balance of the Credit Card liability account. Unless you do this, your Credit Card liability account balance won't match the balance on the next credit card statement.

⑯   Click **Save & Close** to record the bill.

The next time you access Pay Bills, your credit card bill will show up in the list of bills to pay.

SETTING THE BEGINNING BALANCE FIELD ON A NEW ACCOUNT

As discussed in Chapter 10, when you set up a new account in QuickBooks there are several ways to enter the opening balance. For your first bank reconciliation to work properly in QuickBooks, you must use the *statement ending balance* from your most recently reconciled bank statement as the opening balance for the account.

If you enter the opening balance in the New Account screen, QuickBooks will automatically copy the opening balance to the *Beginning Balance* field in the Bank Reconciliation screen. (See *Entering Opening Balances* in Chapter 10 for more information about setting up accounts.)

However, if transactions are already posted to the account, you will need to enter the opening balance directly in the account register or with a General Journal Entry. (See *Entering Opening Balances* in Chapter 10 for more information.) When you do so, QuickBooks will not automatically copy the opening balance to the *Beginning Balance* field in the Bank Reconciliation screen.

For example, if the opening balance on your last bank statement for the savings account was $12,000, and the bank statement date is 4/30/2002, you would make the register entry shown in Figure 4-19 to enter the opening balance for the account. At this point, extra steps are required to reset the *Beginning Balance* field in the Bank Reconciliation feature so that it reflects this opening balance.

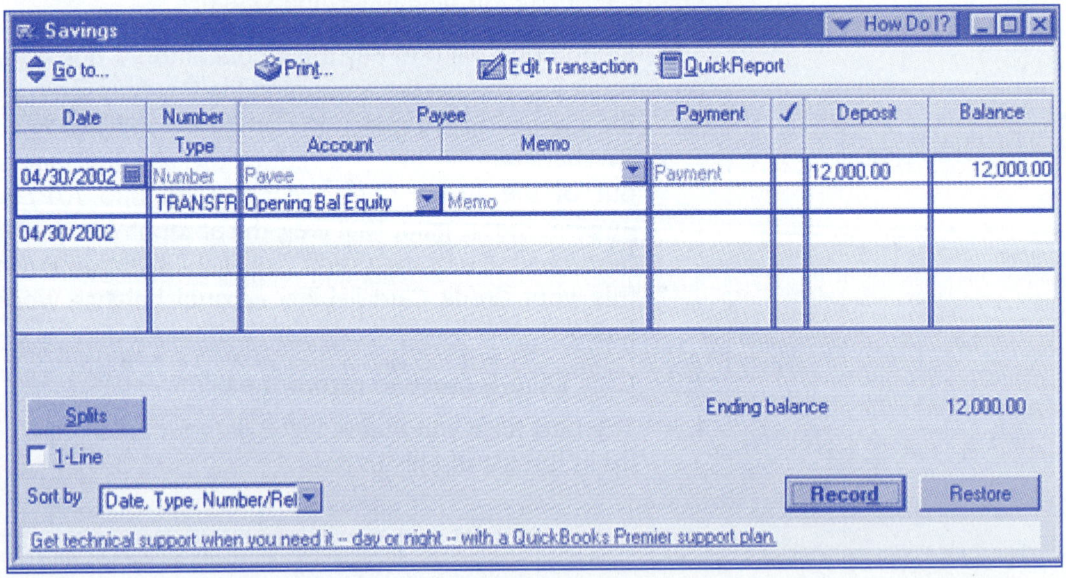

Figure 4-19 Enter the Opening Balance in the Savings account register.

COMPUTER TUTORIAL

1 Select the *Banking* menu and choose **Reconcile**.

2 Select "Savings" from the *Account* field drop-down menu (see Figure 4-20). Then note that the *Beginning Balance* field shows "0.00."

3 Enter "04/30/2002" in the *Statement Date* field and press <TAB>.

4 Enter "12,000.00" in the *Ending Balance* field and click **Continue**.

Begin Reconciliation

Select an account to reconcile, and then enter the ending balance from your account statement.

Account   Savings

Statement Date   04/30/2002

Beginning Balance   0.00   What if my beginning balance doesn't match my statement?

Ending Balance   12,000.00

Enter any service charge or interest earned.

Service Charge   0.00   Date 03/31/2002   Account
Interest Earned   0.00   Date 03/31/2002   Account

Continue   Cancel   Help

Figure 4-20 The Begin Reconciliation screen

5 Select the opening balance transaction in the Deposits and Other Credits section of the Reconcile – Savings screen, as shown in Figure 4-21.

Reconcile - Savings   How Do I?

Reconciling for the period ending 04/30/2002.   Beginning Balance   0.00

Checks and Payments

✓	Date	Chk #	Payee	Amount

Deposits and Other Credits

✓	Date	Chk #	Payee	Amount
✓	04/30/2002			12,000.00

Mark All   Unmark All   Go To

Items you have marked cleared
1 Deposits and Other Credits   12,000.00
0 Checks and Payments   0.00

Modify
Service Charge   0.00
Interest Earned   0.00
Ending Balance   12,000.00
Cleared Balance   12,000.00
Difference   0.00

Last Report   Reconcile Now   Leave

Figure 4-21 Select the opening balance on the Reconcile – Savings screen.

6 Confirm that the *Difference* field shows "0.00" and click **Reconcile Now**.

7 Click **Cancel** on the Select Reconciliation Report screen.

Normally you will print a Reconciliation Detail Report after you reconcile an account, but since you are just setting the Beginning Balance amount at this time, click **Cancel**.

8 Select the *Banking* menu and choose **Reconcile**. Select "Savings" from the *Account* field drop-down menu. Then note that the opening balance "12,000.00" shows in the *Beginning Balance* field.

9 Click **Cancel**. You have successfully set the beginning balance for this account.

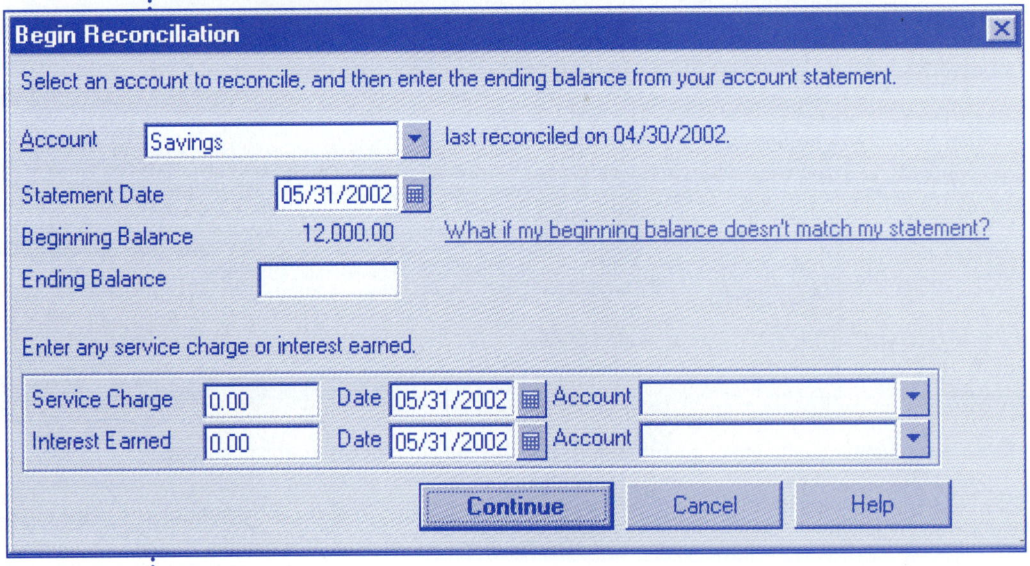

Begin Reconciliation	☒

Select an account to reconcile, and then enter the ending balance from your account statement.

Account	Savings ▼	last reconciled on 04/30/2002.

Statement Date   05/31/2002 ▦

Beginning Balance   12,000.00   <u>What if my beginning balance doesn't match my statement?</u>

Ending Balance   ☐

Enter any service charge or interest earned.

Service Charge	0.00	Date	05/31/2002 ▦	Account	▼
Interest Earned	0.00	Date	05/31/2002 ▦	Account	▼

[**Continue**]   [Cancel]   [Help]

Figure 4-22 The Beginning Balance field now shows "12,000."

Name _____ **Date** _____

Use the additional information below for Helen Johnson's invoice:

Invoice number	2002-101B
Address	432 Johnson Drive, San Ramon, CA 94666
Terms	Due on Receipt
Class	San Jose

4. Enter the transactions necessary to record the redeposit of Helen Johnson's original check (not including the bounce charge). Date the redeposit on 2/6/2002.

5. Using the sample bank statement shown below, reconcile the checking account for 2/28/02.

Account: **Academy Glass–Main Checking**

Last Statement Date	1/31/2002	
This Statement Date	2/28/2002	

Beginning Balance	$20,947.76
Less: Checks & Withdrawals	$4,418.29
Plus: Total Deposits	$4,653.77
Ending Balance	**$21,183.24**

Checks	Date	Amount
328	8-Feb	$200.00
329	10-Feb	$2,152.00
330	15-Feb	$377.28
331	4-Feb	$375.00
332	7-Feb	$654.00
Total Checks:		**$3,758.28**

Deposits	Date	Amount
Customer Deposit	3-Feb	$156.80
Customer Deposit	4-Feb	$2,330.40
Customer Deposit	7-Feb	$645.01
Customer Deposit	10-Feb	$960.00
Customer Deposit	11-Feb	$559.00
Interest Earned	31-Jan	$2.56
Total Deposits:		**$4,653.77**

Other Debits		
NSF Check	1-Feb	$645.01
NSF Charge	1-Jan	$10.00
Service Charge	28-Feb	$5.00
Total Other Debits		**$660.01**

Figure 4-24 Sample bank statement

6. Print a reconciliation detail report dated 2/28/02.

7. Print a customer statement for Helen Johnson for the period 1/1/2002 through 2/28/2002.

Workplace *Applications*

DISCUSSION QUESTIONS

These questions are designed to help you apply what you are learning about QuickBooks to your own organization. Use your notebook to record your answers and your thoughts about how your company could use QuickBooks to organize information and track performance.

1. How many bank accounts does your organization have? With how many banks? List all the banks your organization uses and what types of accounts are held at each.

2. How many bank statements does your organization receive? Are they monthly or quarterly statements? What is your organization's policy for how quickly statements should be reconciled?

3. What service charges do the banks charge your company for maintaining the accounts? Are there charges per transaction (check, deposit, etc.)?

ACTIVITY

1. Research your company's policy with regard to outstanding transactions. Identify payers with records of transactions outstanding for more than three months.

2. Research your company's policy with regard to non-sufficient funds. Identify the payers with records of NSF checks.

Name _____ **Date** _____

SOFTWARE SUPPORT, INC.

Software Support, Inc., is a company that provides computer consulting services for clients throughout the Chicago metropolitan area. The company provides computer setup, training, and troubleshooting services for small business clients.

On February 23, 2002, a customer, Lenny Blake, paid invoice #2002-202 for 800.00 with check #2433. This check was deposited that day to the company's checking account. On the next day, the bank returned the check with a note explaining that the account on which the check was drawn did not have sufficient funds to pay the check. The bank charged the account a $10 returned check fee.

On 2/27/2002, you received a replacement check (#2438) from Lenny for $820.00 to cover the check plus the service charge.

Questions

These questions are designed to help you apply what you are learning about QuickBooks to this case study. Use your notebook to record your answers and your thoughts.

1. What transactions would you record in Software Support's QuickBooks file to record the bounced check, and to pass on a $20 fee to Lenny Blake?

2. How would you record the receipt of the replacement check?

*inter***NET**
CONNECTION

Are you suited to accounting? Take a quiz at
http://www.tscpa.org/studentlounge/pupils/add_up.html and
http://www.advisorteam.com/user/ktsintro.asp

These web sites allow you to explore the field of accounting and take a simple test to find out if you are well suited to the accounting field.

Reports and Graphs

OBJECTIVES

After completing this chapter, you should be able to:

1. Create several types of reports.

2. Understand the differences between cash and accrual reports.

3. Create graphs.

4. Customize the look of reports and filter the data on reports.

5. Memorize reports.

6. Group reports for batch printing.

7. Print reports.

8. Use various methods to find transactions.

9. Export reports to spreadsheets for further analysis and modification.

RESTORE THIS FILE

This chapter uses Chapter 5.QBW. To open this file, restore the file called **Chapter 5.QBB** to your hard disk. (See page 7 for instructions on restoring files.)

QuickBooks reports allow you to get the information you need to make critical business decisions. In this chapter, you'll learn how to create a variety of reports to help you manage your business. Every report in QuickBooks gives you immediate, up-to-date information about your company's performance.

There are literally hundreds of reports available in QuickBooks that allow you to manipulate the numbers so that you can look at your data in any way you wish. In addition to the built-in reports, you can modify reports to include or exclude whatever data you want. To control the look of your reports, you can customize the formatting of headers, footers, fonts, or columns.

When you get a report looking just the way you want, you can memorize it so that you can quickly create it again later.

TYPES OF REPORTS

There are four basic categories of reports in QuickBooks: List, Register, Summary, and Transaction reports. **List** reports show the contents of one of your lists. For example, the Chart of Accounts List shows the list of accounts, such as the Checking account. **Register** reports show the transactions in any of your account registers. For example, the Check Register shows all the individual Checking account transactions. **Summary** reports summarize a group of transactions. For example, the Profit & Loss report summarizes the total of all transactions relating to revenue and expenses. **Transaction** reports show individual transactions, such as the Open Invoices report, which shows details of all outstanding invoices. Table 5-1 summarizes the types of reports that are available to you in QuickBooks.

Before you create a report, first think about whether you want the report to include names in *lists*; transactions in a single *register* (e.g., Checking), *transactions* in several registers, but related in some other way; or a *summary* of several transactions.

Report Type	Example Reports
List Reports	Chart of Accounts, Vendor List, Employee List, Customer:Job List
Register Reports	Checking Account Register, A/P Register
Summary Reports	Profit & Loss, Balance Sheet, Trial Balance, A/R Aging Summary
Transaction Reports	Transaction Detail by Account, Open Invoices, Unpaid Bills Detail

Table 5-1 Types of QuickBooks reports

CASH VERSUS ACCRUAL REPORTS

> **NOTE**
>
> QuickBooks only refers to Accounts Receivable and Accounts Payable transactions when converting reports from the accrual basis to the cash basis.

> **TIP**
>
> If you pay tax on the cash basis, use a cash-basis Balance Sheet and Profit & Loss report when you prepare the information for your tax return. Use accrual-basis reports the rest of the time so you can have a more accurate picture of your business.

QuickBooks can automatically convert reports from the accrual basis to the cash basis, depending on how you set your preferences or on how you customize reports. See Chapter 1 for more information about cash basis and accrual basis reports.

To summarize, if you use **Cash Basis** accounting, you regard income or expenses as occurring at the time you actually receive a payment from a customer or pay a bill from a vendor. If you use **Accrual Basis** accounting, you regard income or expenses as occurring at the time you ship a product, render a service, or receive a bill from your vendors. Under this method, the date that you enter a transaction and the date that you actually pay or receive cash may be two separate dates.

In QuickBooks, an accrual-basis report shows income regardless of whether your customers have paid, and shows expenses regardless of whether you have paid your bills. However, a cash-basis report shows income only if you have received it and expenses only if you have paid them.

You can set the default for all QuickBooks summary reports to the cash basis by selecting "Cash" in the **Summary Reports Basis** section of the Reports & Graphs Preferences screen.

For most situations, it is recommended that you leave QuickBooks preferences set to the accrual basis. Then, if you want to create a cash-basis report, you will choose **Modify** in the Report screen and select "Cash" in the Report Basis section (see Figure 5-1).

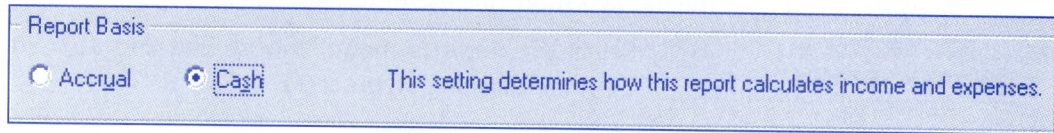

Report Basis

○ Accrual ● Cash   This setting determines how this report calculates income and expenses.

Figure 5-1 Select the report basis in the Modify Report screen.

LIST REPORTS

Use List reports to print a Customer list, a Price list, or mailing labels for one or more of your lists (Customers, Items, Vendors, Employees, Accounts, etc.).

In the following tutorials, you will create a few sample list reports. To find more list reports, select the **Reports** menu and choose **List**.

Customer Phone List

The phone list shown in Figure 5-2 is a listing of each of your customers and their phone numbers. You can customize this report to include other columns, such as an address or contact name.

Customer	Phone
Anderson Floors	555-6579
Anderson Floors:2nd Street Store	555-6579
Anderson Floors:Front St. Store	555-6579
Berry, Ron	555-2248
Garrison, John	(408) 555-6687
Garrison, John:Kitchen	(408) 555-6687
Johnson, Helen	
Leonard, Jerry	555-4411
Mason, Bob	555-9811
Nelson, Carl	555-8900
Pelligrini Builders	555-2222
Pelligrini Builders:2354 Wilkes Rd	555-2222
Pelligrini Builders:4266 Lake Drive	555-2222
Young, Bill	(510) 555-1111
Young, Bill:Window Replacement	(510) 555-1111

Academy Glass — Customer Phone List — April 4, 2002

Figure 5-2 Customer Phone List report

COMPUTER TUTORIAL

❶ Select the **Reports** menu, choose **List**, and then choose **Customer Phone List**.

Vendor Contact List

COMPUTER TUTORIAL

The **Vendor Contact List** shown in Figure 5-3 is a listing of your vendors along with each vendor's address and telephone information. You can customize and filter this list to include only a selected subset of vendors.

1 Select the **Reports** menu, choose **List** and then choose **Vendor Contact List** (see Figure 5-3).

Academy Glass
Vendor Contact List
April 4, 2002

Vendor	Account No.	Address	Contact
Ace Glass	Acct# 43-234	Ace Glass Manufacturing 435 Race Street, Suite 1 Hayward, CA 94555	Arlene
Artigues Construction Rentals		Artigues Construction Rentals 33 Wheeler Rd Walnut Creek, CA 94326	Ron Artigues
Boswell Insulation	Acct# 66-112	Boswell Insulation Steven Boswell PO Box 620 Oakland, CA 94610	Steven Boswell
Cal Telephone	415-555-5484-0053	Cal Telephone P.O. Box 1100 San Francisco, CA 94482	
Carpenter's Union			
City of San Jose		City of San Jose 100 Main St San Jose, CA 94326	
City of Walnut Creek		City of Walnut Creek City Hall P.O. Box 1 Walnut Creek, CA 94482	
Employment Development Department		Employment Development Department P.O. Box 123456 Sacramento...	
Express Delivery Service		Express Delivery Service	
Internal Revenue Service			
Jones Office Supply		Jones Office Supply	
Merrill Lynch		Merrill Lynch	
National Bank		National Bank P.O. Box 522 San Jose, CA 94326	
Nellis Windows & Doors		Nellis Windows & Doors P.O. Box 5033 Concord, CA 94511	Susan Nellis
Orlando Properties		Orlando Properties P.O. Box 2836 San Jose, CA 95010	Leslie J Orlando
Pease, William S., CPA		William S. Pease, CPA 200 Royal Rd Pleasanton, CA 94326	William S. Pease
Postmaster		Postmaster	
Sinclair Insurance	786-35	Sinclair Insurance P.O. Box 6666 Santa Cruz, CA 95063	David
State Board of Equalization	ABCD 11-234567	State Board of Equalization P.O. Box 3456 Sacramento CA 94280	
Valley Gas & Electric	Acct# 123656	Valley Gas & Electric 123 A Street San Francisco, CA 90001	
Wagner & Son Painting		Wagner & Son Painting P.O. Box 783 Milpitas, CA 94573	Mike Wagner

Figure 5-3 The Vendor Contact List report

Item Price List

COMPUTER TUTORIAL

1 Select the **Reports** menu, choose **List**, and then choose **Item Price List** (see Figure 5-4).

After reviewing the Item Price List, close all open windows.

```
Item Price List                                                          ▼ How Do I?  _ □ ×
Modify Report...  Memorize  Print  Excel  Hide Header  Refresh  Sort By Default  ▼
```

Academy Glass
Item Price List
April 4, 2002

Item	Description	Preferred Vendor	Price
Design	Window Design Services		60.00
Labor	Window/Door Installation Labor		40.00
Subs	Subcontracted Services		0.00
Subs:Insulation	Insulation Services	Johnson, Helen	48.00
Subs:Painting	Subcontracted Painting Services		78.00
106-Slider	12 Ft. Sliding Door - Wood Frame	Ace Glass	420.00
104-Slider	10 Ft. Sliding Door - Wood Frame	Ace Glass	360.00
Custom Window	Custom Window - Order #:	Ace Glass	0.00
Skylight	Skylight		0.00
Doors	Doors		34.00
Window	Window		0.00
BounceChg	Returned Check Fee		10.00
Restocking	Restocking Fee		-10.0%
Deposit	Customer Prepayments & Deposits		0.00
Bad Debt	Bad Debt - Write off		0.00
Fin Chg	Finance Charges on Overdue Balance		18.0%
Reimb Exp	Reimbursable Expenses		0.00
Disc 10%	10 % Discount		-10.0%

Figure 5-4 The Item Price List report

COMPUTER TUTORIAL

Mailing Labels

① Select the *File* menu, choose **Print Forms**, and then choose **Mailing Labels**.

② In the Select Mailing Labels to Print screen (see Figure 5-5), select the names and addresses you want to print on your mailing labels or Rolodex cards.

```
Select Mailing Labels to Print                                    ×

Print mailing labels for                              OK
Names from
    ⦿ Name       All names              ▼           Cancel

    ○ Customer Type  All Customer Types  ▼           Help

    ○ Vendor Type    All Vendor Types    ▼

    ☐ with Zip Codes that start with  [        ]

Sort mailing labels by   Name              ▼

☐ Print Ship To addresses where available.
```

Figure 5-5 The Select Mailing Labels to Print screen

You can target your mailing list by selecting specific names and Zip Codes and then sorting the labels. For specific geographic areas, check the "with Zip Codes that start with" box and enter a specific Zip Code or part of a Zip Code. The more of the Zip Code you enter, the further you restrict the range of labels that QuickBooks will print. For example, if you enter "94", you'll get the names in all Zip Codes that start with 94 (94001, 94002, 94500, 94601, etc.). If you enter an entire Zip Code "94025-2413," you'll get just the labels for addresses in that Zip code.

To print shipping addresses instead of Billing addresses, check the "Print Ship To addresses where available" box. (If a customer does not have a separate ship-to address, QuickBooks will print the bill-to address.)

3 For this tutorial, you will print all names. Leave all fields unselected except the *Name* field. Confirm that "All names" shows in that field and click **OK** to print the list.

4 On the Print Labels screen, select the type of labels you want in the *Label Format* field (see Figure 5-6).

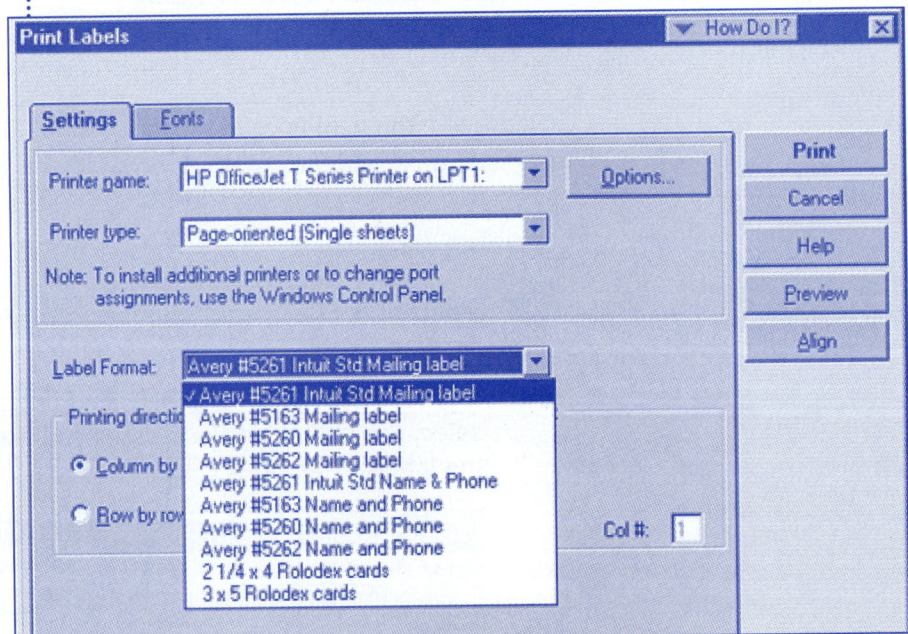

Figure 5-6 Select the type of label you are using.

5 Set the options for the printing direction and the label range.

The Printing direction section (see Figure 5-7) allows you to specify whether the labels should print in order across each of the rows or down each of the columns. If you select "Column by Column", names will print in order from top to bottom in column 1 first, then column 2, and so on. If you select "Row by Row", names will print in order from left to right in row 1 first, then row 2, and so on. You can also select the print range for your labels (see Figure 5-8).

6 Load your labels or Rolodex cards into your printer and click **Print**.

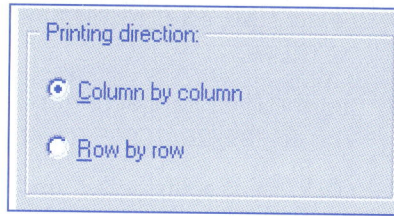

Figure 5-7 The Printing direction section

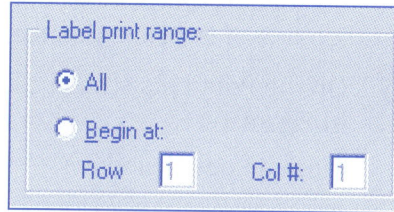

Figure 5-8 The Label print range section

REGISTER REPORTS

COMPUTER TUTORIAL

Every asset, liability, and equity account (except Retained Earnings) has a register that you can print. You can see each account type in the Chart of Accounts list under the Type column.

1 Display the Chart of Accounts screen (see Figure 5-9).

All Balance Sheet accounts (except Retained Earnings) have registers that you can print. Double-click the account name to display its register, and choose Print Register from the File menu.

Figure 5-9 The Chart of Accounts

② Double-click the Checking account to display its register.

③ Select the *File* menu and choose **Print Register** or press <CTRL+P>.

④ Set the Date Range for the Register report to *From* "01/01/2002" and *To* "02/28/2002" (see Figure 5-10).

⑤ Click "Print splits detail" and click **OK**.

When you select this option, QuickBooks prints all of the accounts to which you coded your checks. If you do not choose this option, QuickBooks only prints the expense account on the top line of the Expenses tab of each check.

⑥ On the Print Lists screen, click **Print**. The printed report is shown in Figure 5-11.

Close all open windows.

Check this box to print the detailed split transactions.

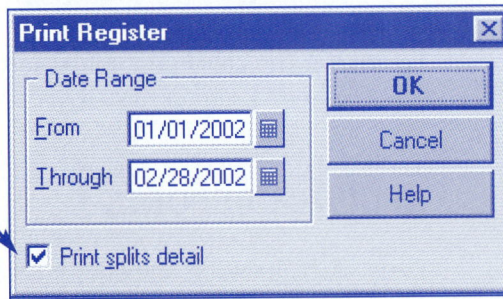

Print Register

Date Range

From 01/01/2002

Through 02/28/2002

OK

Cancel

Help

☑ Print splits detail

Figure 5-10 Set the correct Date Range for the report.

The Register report shows each transaction in the account.

Academy Glass   4/4/2002

Register: Checking
From 01/01/2002 through 02/28/2002
Sorted by: Date, Type, Number/Ref

Date	Number	Payee	Account	Memo	Payment	C	Deposit	Balance
01/04/2002	326	Valley Gas & Electric	Utilities:Gas and Elect...		276.52	X		17,663.08
01/05/2002	327	Jones Office Supply	-split-	Printer Paper	128.60	X		17,534.48
			Office Supplies	Printer Paper	-100.00			
			Printing and Reproduc...	500 Copies of ...	-28.60			
01/05/2002	6001	Orlando Properties	Rent		3,200.00	X		14,334.48
01/20/2002	6002	Ace Glass	Accounts Payable	VOID: Acct# 4...		X		14,334.48
01/20/2002	6003	Wagner & Son Paint...	Accounts Payable	Open Bill at Se...	142.00	X		14,192.48
01/20/2002	6004	Ace Glass	-split-	Acct# 43-234	1,260.28	X		12,932.20
			Accounts Payable		-1,260.28			
			Accounts Payable		-25.72			
			Purchase Discounts		25.72			

Figure 5-11 The Checking Register report

SUMMARY REPORTS

There are several built-in reports that summarize a group of transactions. These reports help you analyze the performance of your business.

Profit & Loss

The **Profit & Loss** report (sometimes called the *Income Statement*) shows all your income and expenses for a given period.

As discussed in the *Accounting 101* section in Chapter 1, the goal of accounting is to provide the financial information you need to measure the success (or failure) of your organization. The Profit & Loss report is one of the most valuable sources of this financial information.

COMPUTER TUTORIAL

① Select the *Reports* menu, choose **Company & Financial**, and then choose **Profit & Loss Standard**.

② Set the *Dates* fields to *From* "01/01/2002" and *To* "03/31/2002." Press <TAB>.

The Profit & Loss report (see Figure 5-12) summarizes the totals of all your income accounts, followed by Cost of Goods Sold accounts, and then expenses. At the bottom of the report you see your Net Income for the period you specified in the *Dates* fields.

Note that the screen as shown in Figure 5-12 is not the complete report. You have to scroll down to see the rest of it.

The Profit & Loss standard report shows income account totals, followed by Cost of Goods Sold accounts and then expense accounts.

Academy Glass		
Profit & Loss		
January through March 2002		
		Jan - Mar 02
Ordinary Income/Expense		
Income		
Product Sales		2,037.00
Services		
Design	1,860.00	
Labor Income	960.00	
Subcontracted Labor	1,008.00	
Total Services		3,828.00
Sales Discounts		-21.16
Purchase Discounts		50.72
Total Income		5,894.56
Cost of Goods Sold		
Cost of Goods Sold		600.00
Purchases		1,686.00
Total COGS		2,286.00
Gross Profit		3,608.56

Figure 5-12 The upper portion of the Profit & Loss report (scroll down to see the remainder)

Analyzing the Profit & Loss Report

The first section of the Profit & Loss report shows the total of each of your income accounts for the period specified on the report. If you have subaccounts (see, for example, under the Services subhead), QuickBooks indents those accounts on the report and subtotals them. To hide subaccounts on this report (or any summary report), click **Collapse** at the top of the report.

The next section of the report shows your Cost of Goods Sold accounts. You use these accounts to record the costs of the products you sell in your business (e.g., your inventory).

Below the Cost of Goods Sold section, QuickBooks calculates the *Gross Profit* for the period. For companies that sell products, this is a very important number because it represents the amount of revenue you have left after paying your suppliers. You can then use this money to pay expenses such as rent, office supplies, employee salaries, etc. You can see the detail of these payments in the Expenses section of the Profit & Loss report.

At the bottom of the report, QuickBooks calculates your *Net Income* – the amount of your revenue less your Cost of Goods Sold (e.g., inventory) and your expenses. Needless to say, you want this number to be as high as possible.

You may want to view your expenses as a percentage of total income to help you spot trouble in your business.

COMPUTER TUTORIAL

① Click the **Modify Report** button at the top of the Profit & Loss report.

② Click the "% of Income" box (see Figure 5-13).

Click here to see expenses as a percentage of total income on your Profit & Loss report.

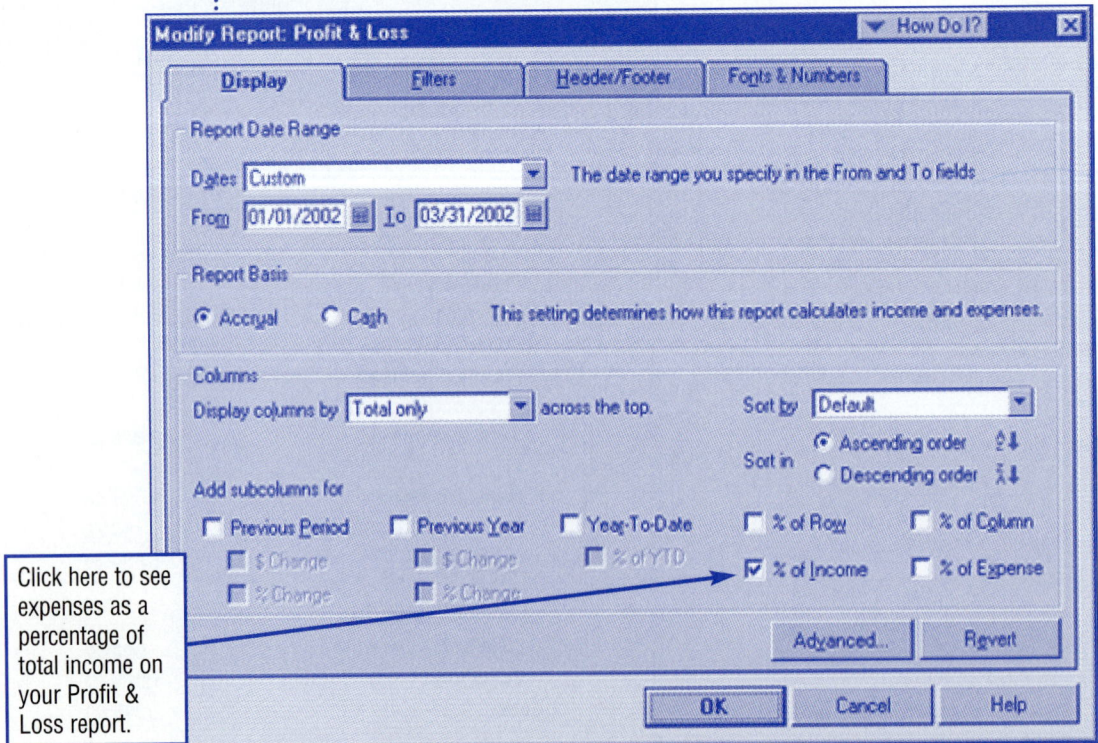

Figure 5-13 The Customize Report screen

3 Click **OK**.

Your Profit & Loss report now has a % of Income column (see Figure 5-14) where you can quickly pick out numbers that diverge from the norm. Familiarize yourself with the percentages of expenses in your business and review this report periodically to make sure you stay in control of expenses.

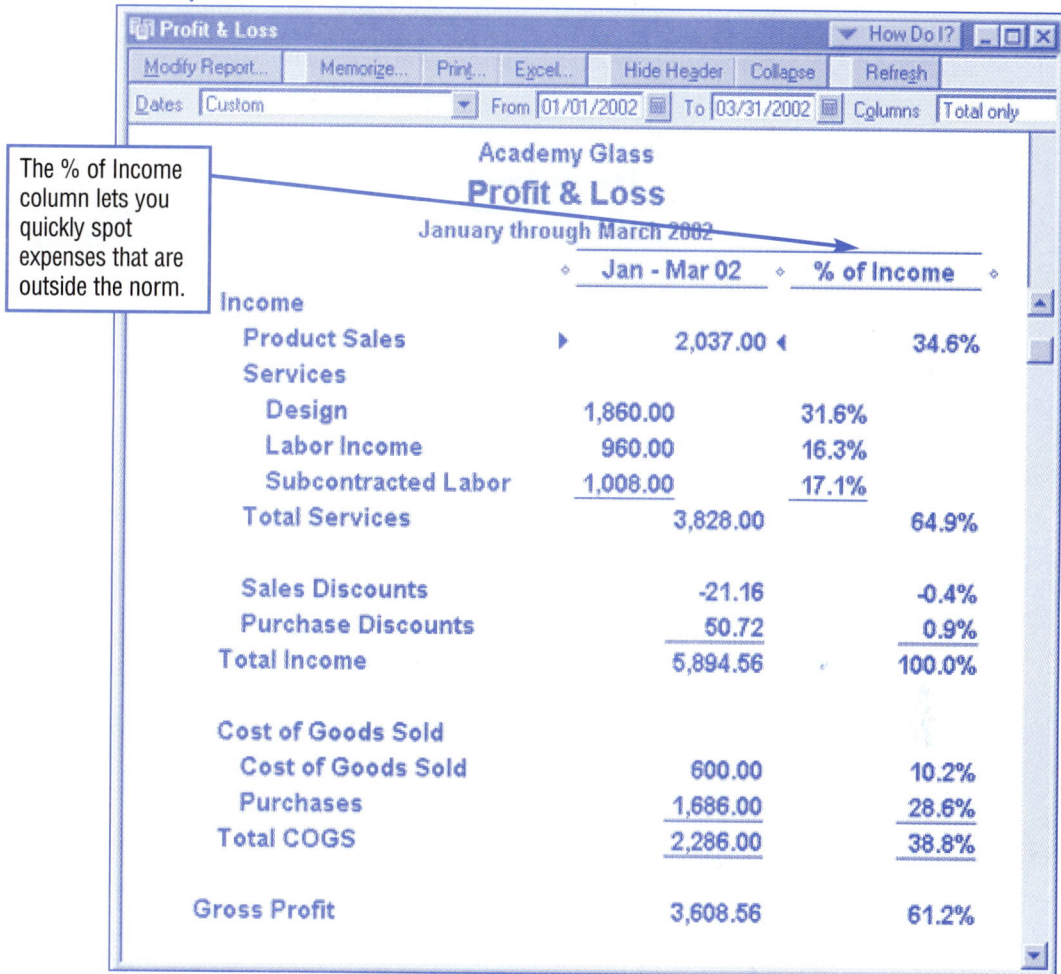

The % of Income column lets you quickly spot expenses that are outside the norm.

Profit & Loss	How Do I?

| Modify Report... | Memorize... | Print... | Excel... | Hide Header | Collapse | Refresh |

Dates | Custom | From 01/01/2002 To 03/31/2002 | Columns | Total only

Academy Glass
Profit & Loss
January through March 2002

	Jan - Mar 02	% of Income
Income		
Product Sales	2,037.00	34.6%
Services		
Design	1,860.00	31.6%
Labor Income	960.00	16.3%
Subcontracted Labor	1,008.00	17.1%
Total Services	3,828.00	64.9%
Sales Discounts	-21.16	-0.4%
Purchase Discounts	50.72	0.9%
Total Income	5,894.56	100.0%
Cost of Goods Sold		
Cost of Goods Sold	600.00	10.2%
Purchases	1,686.00	28.6%
Total COGS	2,286.00	38.8%
Gross Profit	3,608.56	61.2%

Figure 5-14 Customized Profit & Loss report

④ To find the details behind any of these numbers, you will use QuickZoom (explained on page 230). At this time, you will examine the detail of your purchases. To do this, double-click on the number next to the Purchases account.

The screen shown in Figure 5-15 shows each transaction that you coded to the Purchases account. Double-click on any of these numbers to see the actual transaction.

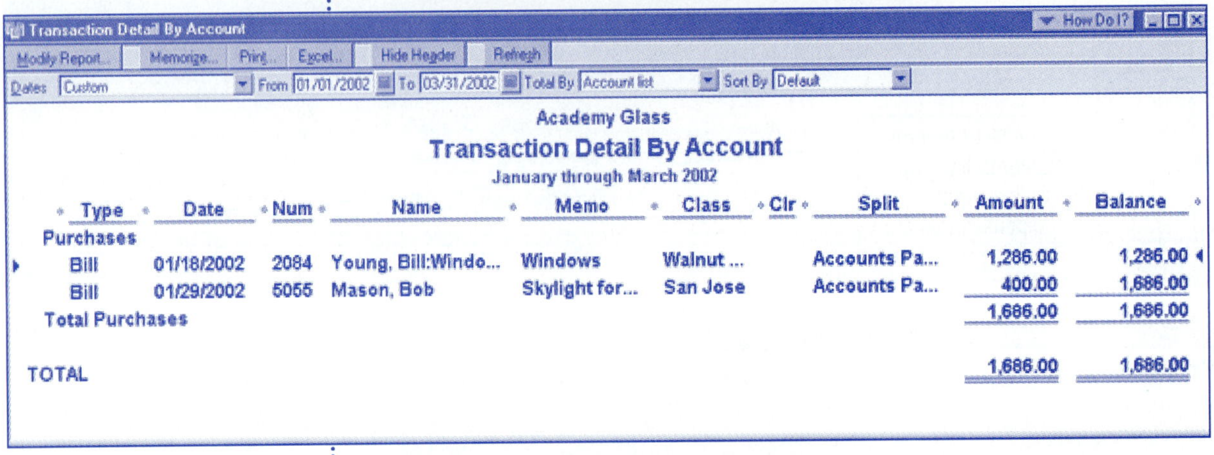

	Transaction Detail By Account							How Do I? □ ×
Modify Report	Memorize...	Print	Excel...	Hide Header	Refresh			
Dates	Custom	▼ From	01/01/2002	To	03/31/2002	Total By	Account list ▼	Sort By Default ▼

Academy Glass
Transaction Detail By Account
January through March 2002

◈ Type ◈	Date ◈	Num ◈	Name ◈	Memo ◈	Class ◈	Clr ◈	Split ◈	Amount ◈	Balance ◈
Purchases									
▸ Bill	01/18/2002	2084	Young, Bill:Windo...	Windows	Walnut ...		Accounts Pa...	1,286.00	1,286.00 ◀
Bill	01/29/2002	5055	Mason, Bob	Skylight for...	San Jose		Accounts Pa...	400.00	1,686.00
Total Purchases								1,686.00	1,686.00
TOTAL								1,686.00	1,686.00

Figure 5-15 The Transaction Detail by Account report for the Purchases account

Profit & Loss by Class Report

To divide your Profit & Loss report into departments (or classes), use the Profit & Loss by Class report.

To create this report, follow these steps:

1 Select the *Reports* menu, choose **Company & Financial**, and then choose **Profit & Loss by Class**.

2 Set the *Dates* fields to *From* "01/01/2002" and *To* "03/31/2002." Press <TAB>.

Compare your screen to the report shown in Figure 5-16. Notice that each class is presented in a separate column.

COMPUTER TUTORIAL

Profit & Loss by Class · How Do I?

Modify Report... | Memorize... | Print... | Excel... | Hide Header | Collapse | Refresh

Dates Custom ▾ From 01/01/2002 To 03/31/2002 Columns Class ▾ Sort By Default ▾

Academy Glass
Profit & Loss by Class
January through March 2002

	Overhead	San Jose	Walnut Cre...	Unclassified	TOTAL
Ordinary Income/Expen...					
Income					
Product Sales	0.00	839.40	1,197.60	0.00	2,037.00
Services					
Design	0.00	1,620.00	240.00	0.00	1,860.00
Labor Income	0.00	240.00	720.00	0.00	960.00
Subcontracted ...	0.00	0.00	1,008.00	0.00	1,008.00
Total Services	0.00	1,860.00	1,968.00	0.00	3,828.00
Sales Discounts	0.00	0.00	0.00	-21.16	-21.16
Purchase Discou...	0.00	25.00	0.00	25.72	50.72
Total Income	0.00	2,724.40	3,165.60	4.56	5,894.56
Cost of Goods Sold					
Cost of Goods Sold	0.00	0.00	600.00	0.00	600.00
Purchases	0.00	400.00	1,286.00	0.00	1,686.00
Total COGS	0.00	400.00	1,886.00	0.00	2,286.00
Gross Profit	0.00	2,324.40	1,279.60	4.56	3,608.56

Figure 5-16 The Profit & Loss by Class report

Classifying and Reclassifying Transactions

The Unclassified column appears whenever you have transactions that you did not assign to a class. To remove the Unclassified column, you must *classify* all the transactions. There are two ways to classify transactions: double-click on the numbers in the report, and edit each transaction; or use a General Journal Entry to classify all the figures at once. For more information about General Journal Entries, see page 458.

The General Journal Entry approach is usually the most efficient way to classify unclassified transactions, but, when possible, it is best instead to edit the original transaction to include a class (or classes).

Notice that the Unclassified column shows Purchase Discounts amounting to 25.72 (see Figure 5-16). Since it is impossible to add a class to this transaction, you will need to use a General Journal Entry to assign the class.

COMPUTER TUTORIAL

1. Select the *Banking* menu and choose **Make Journal Entry**.

2. Enter "01/31/2002" in the *Date* field and press <TAB>.

3. "2002-2" in the *Entry No.* field is preselected. (QuickBooks automatically assigns numbers to General Journal Entries as it does with Checks and Invoices.) Press <TAB>.

4. Enter "Journal Entries" on the first line of the Account column.

   To track all your General Journal Entries in one place, you should create a *Bank* account called **Journal Entries**. Then, on each General Journal Entry, always use this account on the first line, with no amounts in the debit or credit column. By creating this account, you can always go to one place (the Journal Entries account register) to quickly locate all your General Journal Entries. This account is already setup for you in the template file.

5. On the next line, enter "Purchase Discounts" in the Account column and press <TAB>.

   This is the name of the account that appears in the Unclassified column of the Profit & Loss by Class report.

6. Enter "25.72" in the Debit column and press <TAB> twice.

   We want to zero out the balance of Purchase Discounts because it has not been classified. Since Purchase Discounts is an income account, positive balances are credits. Therefore, to zero out the account, you need to debit the account for its current balance and leave the *Class* field blank.

7. Enter "To reclassify Purchase Discounts" in the *Memo* field.

8 On the next line, enter the same account as the first line, "Purchase Discounts," and enter "25.72" in the Credit column. Skip to the Class column and enter "Walnut Creek."

The second line of the General Journal Entry restores the balance of the account, but since there is a class on that line, it attributes the balance to the Walnut Creek class.

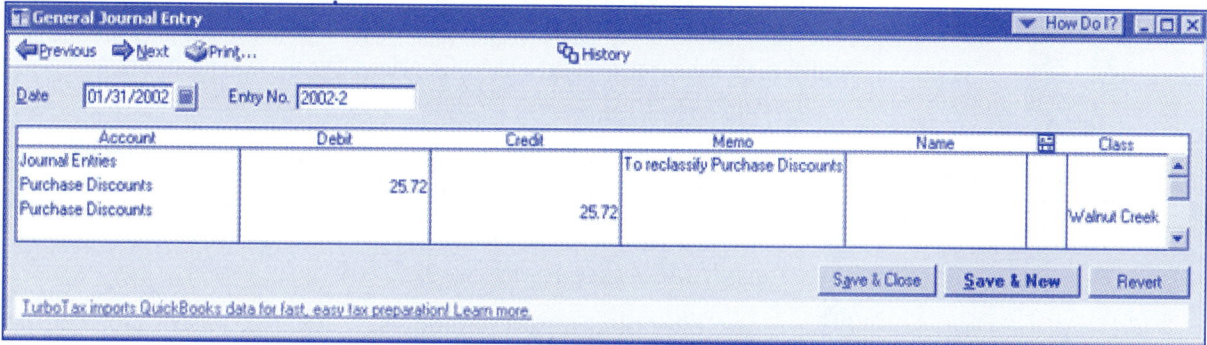

Figure 5-17 The General Journal Entry screen

9 Click **Save & Close** to record the General Journal Entry.

Now your Profit & Loss by Class report will show the Purchase Discounts income under the Walnut Creek class (see Figure 5-17).

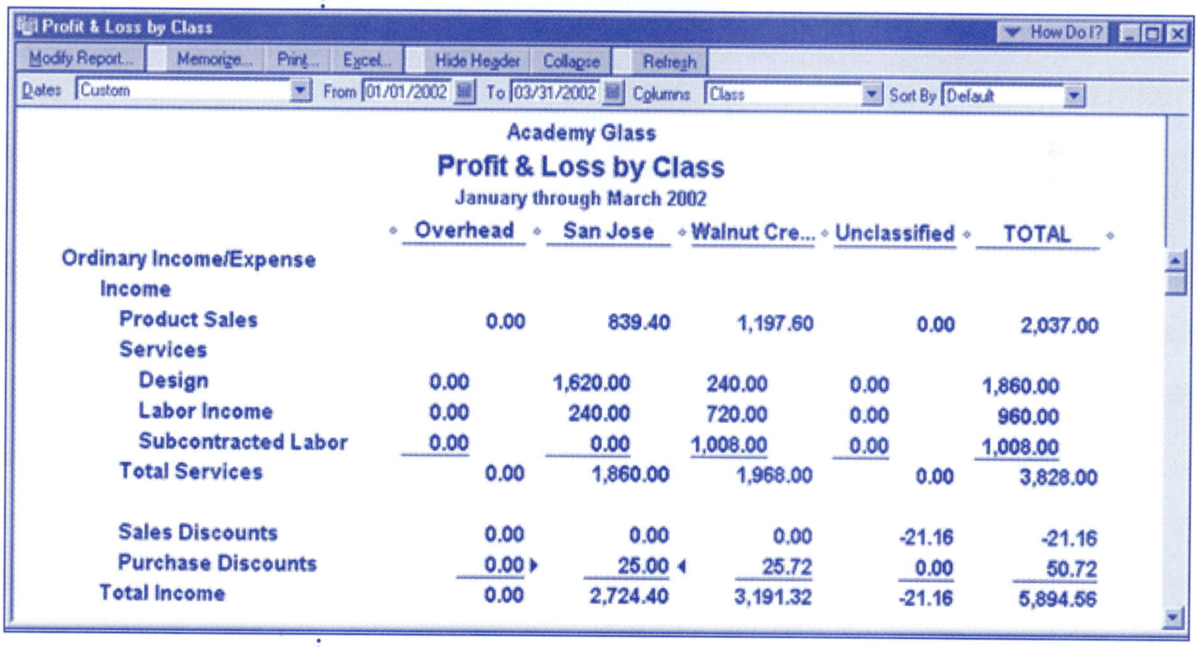

Figure 5-18 Profit & Loss by Class with Purchase Discounts in the Walnut Creek column

Profit & Loss by Job Report

To divide your Profit & Loss report into **Customers** or **Jobs**, use the **Profit & Loss by Job report**. This allows you to view the income and expenses for each of your jobs. This report is sometimes called the Job Cost report and it can be used to quickly see your profitability on each customer or job. This information can be used to help you price your products and services in the future. For example, if this report showed that you lost money on all the jobs where you installed a door, you would probably want to adjust your prices for installing doors.

To create a Profit & Loss by Job report, follow these steps:

COMPUTER TUTORIAL

1 Select the *Reports* menu, choose **Company & Financial**, and then choose **Profit & Loss by Job**.

2 Set the *Dates* fields to *From* "01/01/2002" and *To* "02/28/2002." Press <TAB> (see Figure 5-19).

3 Close all open report windows. Click **No** when QuickBooks prompts you to memorize the reports.

	Johnson, Helen	Mason, Bob	Window Replace... (Young, Bill)	Total Young, Bill	TOTAL
Ordinary Income/Expense					
Income					
Product Sales	485.00	354.40	1,197.60	1,197.60	2,037.00
Services					
Design	120.00	1,500.00	240.00	240.00	1,860.00
Labor Income	0.00	240.00	720.00	720.00	960.00
Subcontracted Labor	0.00	720.00	288.00	288.00	1,008.00
Total Services	120.00	2,460.00	1,248.00	1,248.00	3,828.00
Sales Discounts	0.00	-21.16	0.00	0.00	-21.16
Purchase Discounts	0.00	25.00	0.00	0.00	25.00
Total Income	605.00	2,818.24	2,445.60	2,445.60	5,868.84
Cost of Goods Sold					
Cost of Goods Sold	0.00	0.00	600.00	600.00	600.00
Purchases	0.00	400.00	1,286.00	1,286.00	1,686.00
Total COGS	0.00	400.00	1,886.00	1,886.00	2,286.00
Gross Profit	605.00	2,418.24	559.60	559.60	3,582.84

Academy Glass
Profit & Loss by Job
January through February 2002

This report shows the income and expenses for each customer and job.

Figure 5-19 Profit & Loss by Job report

Balance Sheet

Another important report for analyzing your business is the **Balance Sheet**. The Balance Sheet is a report that shows your financial position, as defined by the balances in each of your asset, liabilities, and equity accounts on a given date.

1 Select the *Reports* menu, choose **Company & Financial**, and then choose **Balance Sheet Standard**.

2 Set the *As Of* field to 01/31/2002 and press <TAB>.

In Figure 5-20, you can see a partial Balance Sheet for Academy Glass on 1/31/2002. Familiarize yourself with how your Balance Sheet changes throughout the year. Banks examine this report very closely before approving loans. Often, the bank will calculate the ratio of your current assets divided by your current liabilities. This ratio, known as the *current ratio*, tells the bank a lot about your ability to satisfy your debts.

COMPUTER TUTORIAL

Figure 5-20 The Balance Sheet for Academy Glass on 1/31/2002

Statement of Cash Flows

The **Statement of Cash Flows** provides information about the cash receipts and cash payments of your business during a given period. In addition, it provides information about investing and financing activities, such as purchasing equipment or borrowing.

COMPUTER TUTORIAL

1 Select the **Reports** menu, choose **Company & Financial**, and then choose **Statement of Cash Flows**.

2 Set the *Dates* fields to *From* "01/01/2002" and *To* "02/28/2002." Press <TAB>.

On the report shown in Figure 5-21, you can see that although there was a net loss of $1,027.55, there was a net increase in cash in the business over the first two months of the year. Bankers look closely at this report to determine if your business is able to generate a positive cash flow, or if your business requires additional capital to satisfy its cash needs.

3 Close all open report windows. Click **No** when QuickBooks prompts you to memorize the reports.

Figure 5-21 Statement of Cash Flows for Academy Glass for 1/1/2002 – 2/28/2002

TRANSACTION DETAIL REPORTS

QuickReports

A **QuickReport** can quickly give you information about a customer, vendor, or Item. You can generate QuickReports from account registers, forms, or lists. Table 5-2 shows different types of QuickReports.

When you're in a	The QuickReport shows you
Register (with a transaction selected)	All transactions in that register for the same name.
Form (Invoice, Bill, or Check)	All transactions for that particular customer, vendor, or payee within the same account as the current transaction. For example, if you display an Invoice and run a QuickReport, you'll get all Accounts Receivable transactions for that customer. The report would show Invoices, payments, and credit memos for the customer whose name appears on the displayed Invoice.
List (with an Item or Name selected)	All transactions for that Item or Name.

Table 5-2 Types of QuickReports

COMPUTER TUTORIAL

1 Open the Checking register, click on 6004 and click **QuickReport** at the top of the register (see Figure 5-22).

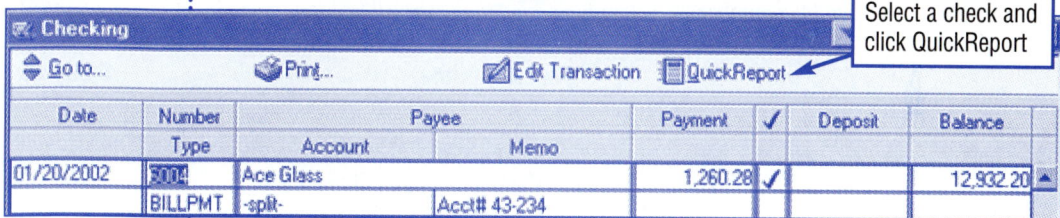

Select a check and click QuickReport

Figure 5-22 Select the Check and click QuickReport.

This creates a report of all transactions using the same name as the selected transaction (see Figure 5-23).

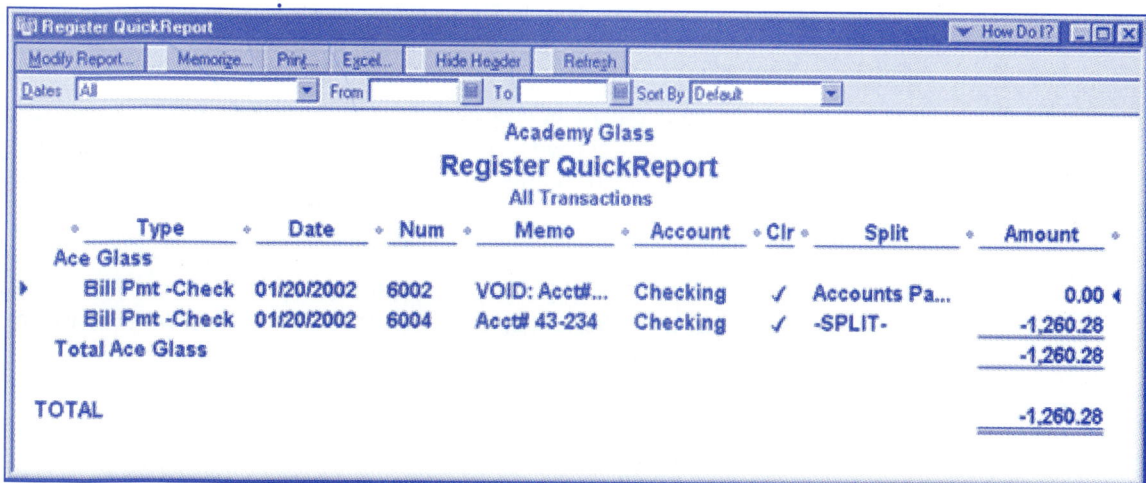

Figure 5-23 A QuickReport

Using QuickZoom

QuickBooks provides a convenient feature called **QuickZoom**, which allows you to see the detail behind numbers on reports.

For example, the Profit & Loss report in Figure 5-24 shows $2,037 of Product Sales income. To see the detail of this amount, double-click on the amount in the report.

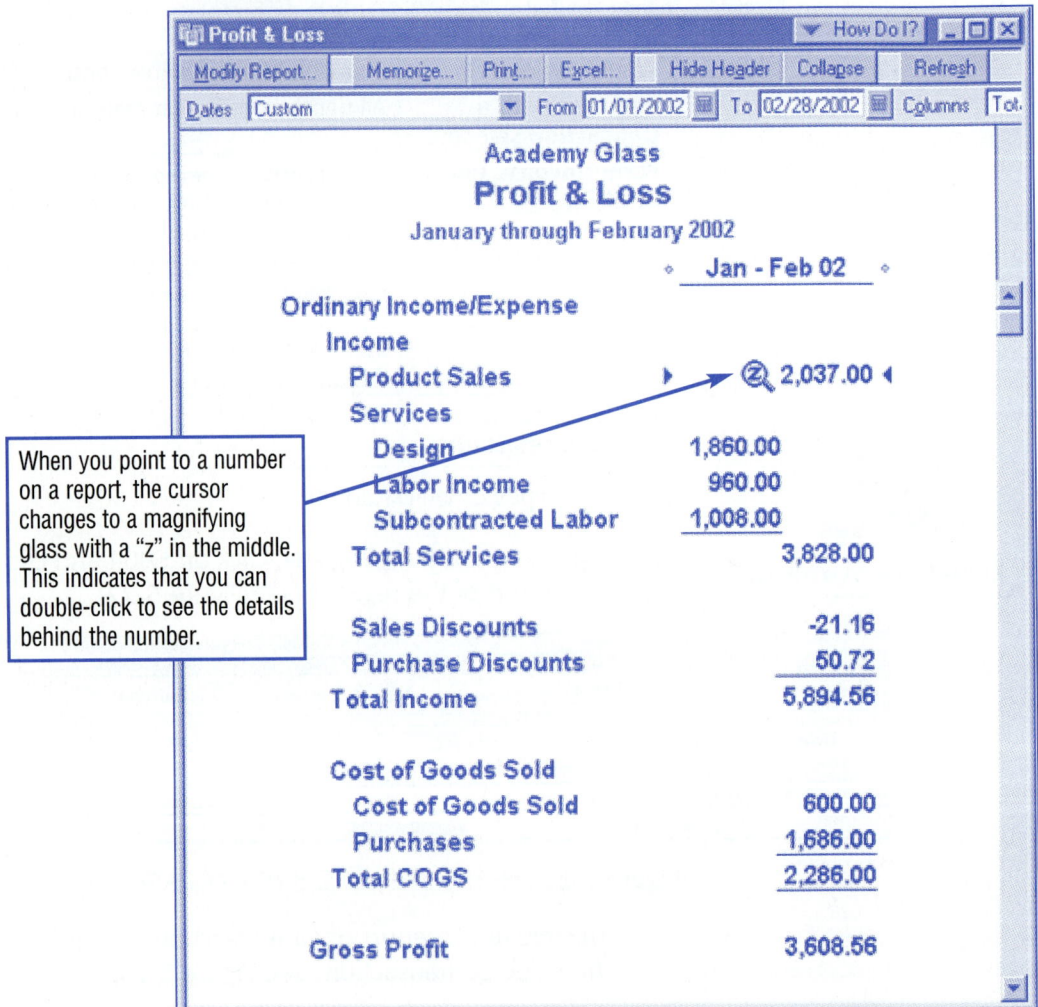

When you point to a number on a report, the cursor changes to a magnifying glass with a "z" in the middle. This indicates that you can double-click to see the details behind the number.

Figure 5-24 QuickZoom allows you to see the details behind a number.

As your cursor moves over numbers on the report, it will turn into a magnifying glass with a "z" in the middle. The magnifying icon indicates that you can double-click to see the details behind the number on the report.

After you double-click the number, QuickZoom displays a Transaction Detail By Account report (see Figure 5-25) that shows the details of each transaction in the account that you zoomed in on.

Transaction Detail By Account								▼ How Do I? ⏷□✕	
Modify Report...	Memorize...	Print...	Excel...	Hide Header	Refresh				
Dates Custom ▼	From 01/01/2002	To 02/28/2002	Total By Account list ▼	Sort By Default ▼					

Academy Glass
Transaction Detail By Account
January through February 2002

Type	Date	Num	Name	Memo	Class	Clr	Split	Amount	Balance
Product Sales									
▸ Invoice	01/08/2002	2002-103	Young, Bill:Windo...	Custom Win...	Walnut ...		Accounts Re...	477.60	477.60 ◂
Invoice	01/13/2002	2002-105	Young, Bill:Windo...	10 ft. Sliding...	Walnut ...		Accounts Re...	720.00	1,197.60
Sales Rec...	01/25/2002	2002-101	Johnson, Helen	Skylight	San Jose		Undeposited...	485.00	1,682.60
Invoice	01/26/2002	2002-106	Mason, Bob	Skylight	San Jose		Accounts Re...	700.00	2,382.60
Invoice	01/26/2002	2002-107	Young, Bill:Windo...	Custom Win...	Walnut ...		Accounts Re...	795.00	3,177.60
Credit Me...	01/31/2002	2002-107C	Young, Bill:Windo...	Custom Win...	Walnut ...		Accounts Re...	-795.00	2,382.60
Credit Me...	01/31/2002	2001-101C	Mason, Bob	Skylight	San Jose		Accounts Re...	-384.00	1,998.60
Credit Me...	01/31/2002	2001-101C	Mason, Bob	Restocking...	San Jose		Accounts Re...	38.40	2,037.00
Total Product Sales								2,037.00	2,037.00
TOTAL								2,037.00	2,037.00

Figure 5-25 The Transaction Detail by Account report

The columns in this report show the transaction Type, Date, transaction Num(ber), Name, Memo, Class, Clr (cleared), Split, Amount, and Balance. You can customize the report to add or delete columns as needed. See *Building Custom Reports* on page 241 for details on how to customize.

The "Clr" column on these reports shows a checkmark when the transaction has cleared. If it's a bank account transaction, this means that it has cleared the bank. Some transactions, such as Invoices, Sales Receipts, and Credit Memos, will never have a checkmark in this field.

Check Detail Reports

The Check Detail report can be invaluable if you use Accounts Payable or Payroll. It is frequently necessary to see what expense account(s) are associated with a Bill Payment. However, the Register report only shows that Bill Payments are associated with Accounts Payable. That's because a Bill Payment only involves the Checking account and Accounts Payable. Similarly, Paychecks only show in the register report as "Split" transactions because several accounts are associated with each paycheck. The Check Detail report gives you the expense account information about these types of transactions.

To create a Check Detail report, follow these steps:

COMPUTER TUTORIAL

1 Select the **Reports** menu, choose **Banking**, and then choose **Check Detail**.

2 Set the *Dates* fields on the report to *From* "01/01/2002" and *To* "04/15/2002."

3 Scroll down until you see Bill Payment number 6004 (near the bottom of the report).

In Figure 5-26, notice Bill Payment number 6004. The report shows that QuickBooks split the total payment of $1,260.28 between $-25.72 to the Accounts Payable account and $1,286.00 to the Purchases account. $-25.72 is the discount that you took when you paid the Bill. Although this report doesn't show it, you coded this amount to Purchase Discounts.

4 Close all open report windows. Click **No** when QuickBooks prompts you to memorize the reports.

TIP

In order to make your Check Detail reports easier to read and understand, consider recording your purchase discounts differently. Instead of taking the discount on the Pay Bills screen (as you did in Chapter 3), you might want to record your purchase discounts using Bill Credits.

Figure 5-26 The Check Detail report

ACCOUNTS RECEIVABLE AND ACCOUNTS PAYABLE REPORTS

There are several reports that you can use to keep track of the money that your customers owe you (Accounts Receivable) and the money that you owe to your vendors (Accounts Payable).

Collections Report

COMPUTER TUTORIAL

The Collections Report is an Accounts Receivable report that shows each customer's outstanding Invoices along with the customer's telephone number and contact information.

1. Select the **Reports** menu, choose **Customers & Receivables**, and then choose **Collections Report**.

2. Enter a date of "03/31/2002" and press <TAB> (see Figure 5-27).

Collections Report

Modify Report...   Memorize...   Print...   Excel...   Hide Header   Refresh

Dates Custom   ▼   03/31/2002 ▦   Past due 1   Sort By Default   ▼

Academy Glass

Collections Report

As of March 31, 2002

Type	Date	Num	P. O. #	Terms	Due Date	Class	Aging	Open Balance
Mason, Bob								
Bob								
555-9811								
Invoice	01/09/2002	2002...		Net 30	02/08/2002	San Jose	51	2,330.40 ◀
Invoice	03/01/2002	FC 5			03/01/2002		30	24.13
Total Mason, Bob								2,354.53
Young, Bill								
Window Replacement								
Bill Young								
(510) 555-1111								
Nancy Young								
Invoice	01/05/2002	2002...		2% 10 N...	02/04/2002	Walnut ...	55	960.00
Invoice	01/08/2002	2002...		2% 10 N...	02/07/2002	Walnut ...	52	559.00
Invoice	01/13/2002	2002...		2% 10 N...	02/12/2002	Walnut ...	47	779.40
Invoice	03/01/2002	FC 6			03/01/2002		30	27.82
Total Window Replacement								2,326.22
Total Young, Bill								2,326.22
TOTAL								4,680.75

Figure 5-27 The Accounts Receivable Collections report

Customer Balance Detail Report

Use the Customer Balance Detail Report to see the details of each customer's transactions and payments. This report shows all transactions that use the Accounts Receivable account, including Invoices, Payments, Discounts, and Finance Charges.

① Select the *Reports* menu, choose **Customers & Receivables**, and then choose **Customer Balance Detail** (see Figure 5-28).

To view any of the transactions shown on this report, double-click on the transaction.

COMPUTER TUTORIAL

Type	Date	Num	Account	Class	Amount	Balance
Anderson Floors						
2nd Street Store						
Invoice	12/21/2001	2001...	Accounts Receiva...	Walnut ...	160.00	160.00 ◄
Payment	01/27/2002		Accounts Receiva...		-160.00	0.00
Total 2nd Street Store					0.00	0.00
Total Anderson Floors					0.00	0.00
Mason, Bob						
Invoice	12/18/2001	2001...	Accounts Receiva...	San Jose	415.68	415.68
Invoice	01/09/2002	2002...	Accounts Receiva...	San Jose	2,330.40	2,746.08
Invoice	01/26/2002	2002...	Accounts Receiva...	San Jose	1,057.75	3,803.83
Payment	01/27/2002	5256	Accounts Receiva...		-415.68	3,388.15
Payment	01/30/2002	5254	Accounts Receiva...		-1,036.59	2,351.56
Discount	01/30/2002	5254	Accounts Receiva...		-21.16	2,330.40
Credit Memo	01/31/2002	2001...	Accounts Receiva...	San Jose	-377.28	1,953.12
Check	01/31/2002	330	Accounts Receiva...	Walnut ...	377.28	2,330.40
Check	02/01/2002	Boun...	Accounts Receiva...		414.72	2,745.12
Invoice	02/01/2002	5256...	Accounts Receiva...	San Jose	10.00	2,755.12
Payment	02/04/2002	5288	Accounts Receiva...		-424.72	2,330.40
Invoice	03/01/2002	FC 5	Accounts Receiva...		24.13	2,354.53
Total Mason, Bob					2,354.53	2,354.53

Academy Glass
Customer Balance Detail
All Transactions

Figure 5-28 The Customer Balance Detail report

Vendor Balance Detail Report

The Vendor Balance Detail report is similar to the Customer Balance Detail report, but it shows types of transactions that use Accounts Payable, including Bills, Bill Credits, Bill Payments, and Discounts.

COMPUTER TUTORIAL

1 Select the *Reports* menu, choose **Vendors & Payable**s, and then choose **Vendor Balance Detail** (see Figure 5-29).

Academy Glass
Vendor Balance Detail
All Transactions

Type	Date	Num	Account	Amount	Balance
Ace Glass					
Bill	01/18/2002	2084	Accounts Payable	1,286.00	1,286.00
Bill Pmt -Check	01/20/2002	6002	Accounts Payable	0.00	1,286.00
Bill Pmt -Check	01/20/2002	6004	Accounts Payable	-1,260.28	25.72
Discount	01/20/2002	6004	Accounts Payable	-25.72	0.00
Total Ace Glass				0.00	0.00
Artigues Construction Rentals					
Check	02/10/2002	328	Accounts Payable	-200.00	-200.00
Deposit	02/15/2002	423	Accounts Payable	15.00	-185.00
Bill	02/15/2002	1352	Accounts Payable	185.00	0.00
Total Artigues Construction Rentals				0.00	0.00
National Bank					
Bill	02/28/2002	Feb ...	Accounts Payable	139.81	139.81
Total National Bank				139.81	139.81
Nellis Windows & Doors					
Bill	01/29/2002	5055	Accounts Payable	400.00	400.00
Credit	01/30/2002	5055C	Accounts Payable	-25.00	375.00
Bill Pmt -Check	01/30/2002	6005	Accounts Payable	-375.00	0.00
Total Nellis Windows & Doors				0.00	0.00

Figure 5-29 The Vendor Balance Detail report

Sales Tax Liability Report

COMPUTER TUTORIAL

The Sales Tax Liability report shows you how your sales break down by locality, and how much sales tax you have collected for the period you specify.

1 Select the *Reports* menu, choose **Vendors & Payables**, and then choose **Sales Tax Liability**.

2 Set the *Dates* fields to *From* "01/01/2002" and *To* "03/31/2002" and press <TAB> (see Figure 5-30).

	Total Sales	Non-Taxa...	Taxable S...	Tax Rate	Tax Colle...	Sales Tax... As of Mar ...
State Board of Equalization						
Contra Costa	▶ 2,199.60	◀ 1,002.00	1,197.60	8.25%	98.80	98.80
Santa Clara	3,599.80	2,798.80	801.00	8.25%	66.08	97.76
State Board of Equalizat...	0.00	0.00	0.00		0.00	105.30
Total State Board of Equa...	5,799.40	3,800.80	1,998.60		164.88	301.86
TOTAL	5,799.40	3,800.80	1,998.60		164.88	301.86

Academy Glass
Sales Tax Liability
January through March 2002

Figure 5-30 The Sales Tax Liability report

The Sales Tax Liability report shows total sales in each county (e.g., sales tax Item), and shows the taxable sales separately from the nontaxable sales. Also, you can see the tax rates and tax collected in each county. You use this information to prepare your sales tax return. The column to the far right shows how much you still owe of the tax you've collected. If you have made any sales tax payments, the amount due will reflect those payments.

> **NOTE**
>
> The Total Sales, Non-Taxable Sales and Taxable Sales columns will show different information depending on your sales tax preferences. If you select "As of Invoice date" in the **Owe Sales Tax** section of the sales tax preferences (see Figure 5-31), this report will show all sales, including Invoices that your customers have not paid. On the other hand, if you select "Upon receipt of payment" in the **Owe Sales Tax** section of the sales tax preferences, this report will only show those sales for which you have received payment. Check your state sales tax rules and set your sales tax preferences accordingly.

To see the detail of transactions that feed the sales Tax Liability report, double-click on any number in the report.

The **State Board of Equalization – Other** line on the report shows the opening balance in your Sales Tax Payable account, as well as any adjustments to Sales Tax payable.

3 Close all open report windows. Click **No** when QuickBooks prompts you to memorize the reports.

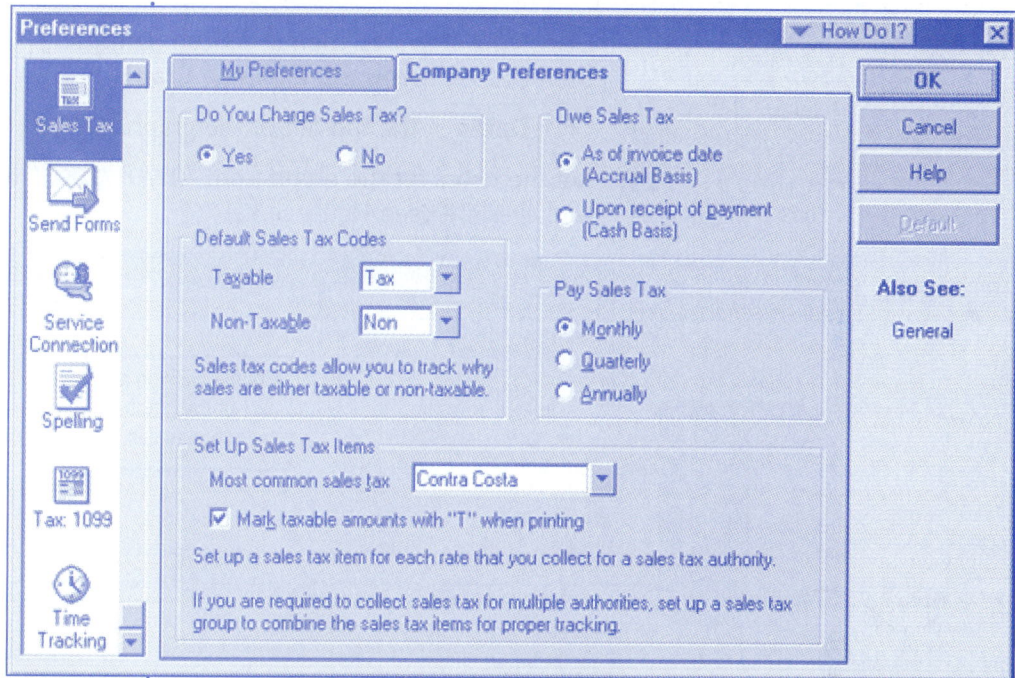

Figure 5-31 Set the Sales Tax Company Preferences

QUICKBOOKS GRAPHS

One of the best ways to quickly get information from QuickBooks is to create a graph. In some cases, it's faster for you to create your filtered reports by starting with a graph and zooming in on sections of the graph until QuickBooks creates the report you want. If you're having trouble filtering reports, try viewing a graph first.

COMPUTER TUTORIAL

① Select the *Reports* menu, choose **Company & Financial**, and then choose **Income & Expense Graph**.

② Click **Dates** at the top left of the graph.

③ Set the dates for the graph from "01/01/2002" to "02/28/2002" and click **OK** (see Figure 5-32).

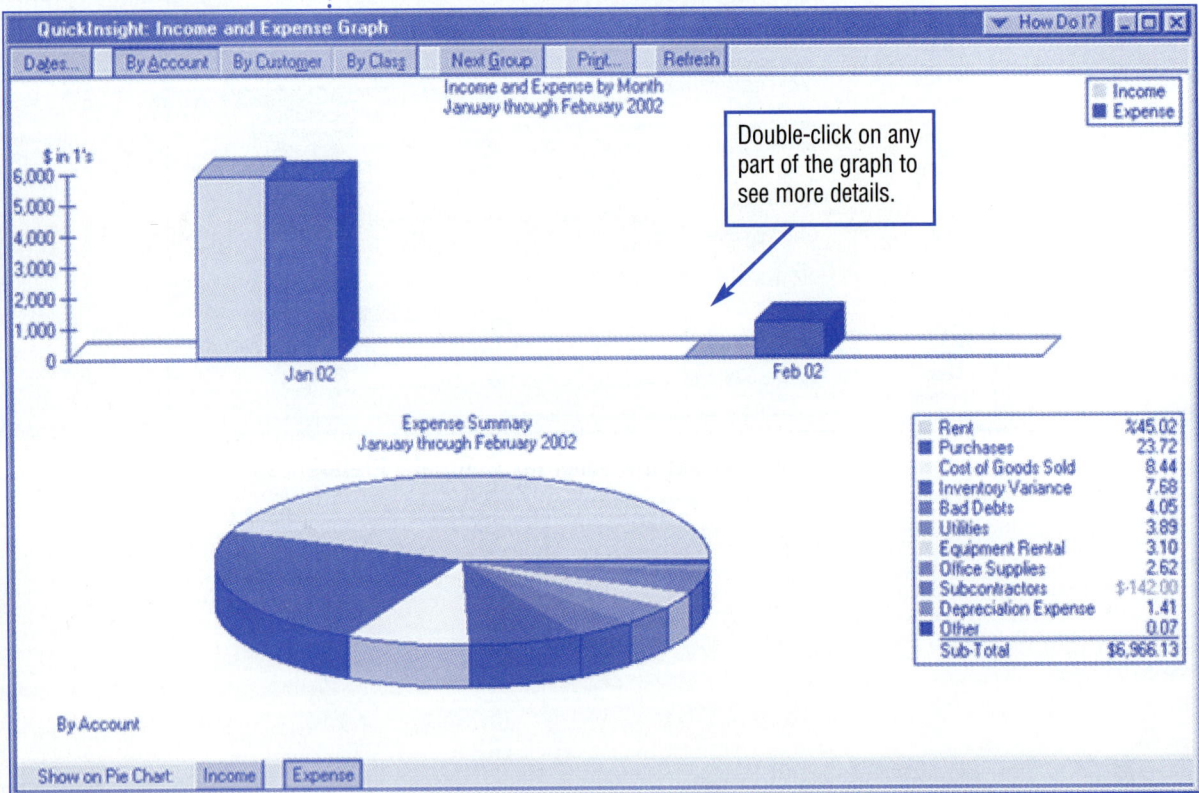

Double-click on any part of the graph to see more details.

Rent	%45.02
Purchases	23.72
Cost of Goods Sold	8.44
Inventory Variance	7.68
Bad Debts	4.05
Utilities	3.89
Equipment Rental	3.10
Office Supplies	2.62
Subcontractors	$-142.00
Depreciation Expense	1.41
Other	0.07
Sub-Total	$6,966.13

Figure 5-32 The Expense graphs

COMPUTER TUTORIAL

QuickBooks graphs highlight interesting facts about your company. For example, you can create a graph that shows which customers spent the most money on your services and products during January and February of 2002.

1 Select the *Reports* menu, choose **Sales**, and then choose **Sales Graph** (see Figure 5-33).

2 Click **Dates** and set the dates for the graph from "01/01/2002" to "02/28/2002." Click **OK**.

3 Click **By Customer**.

4 Close all open windows.

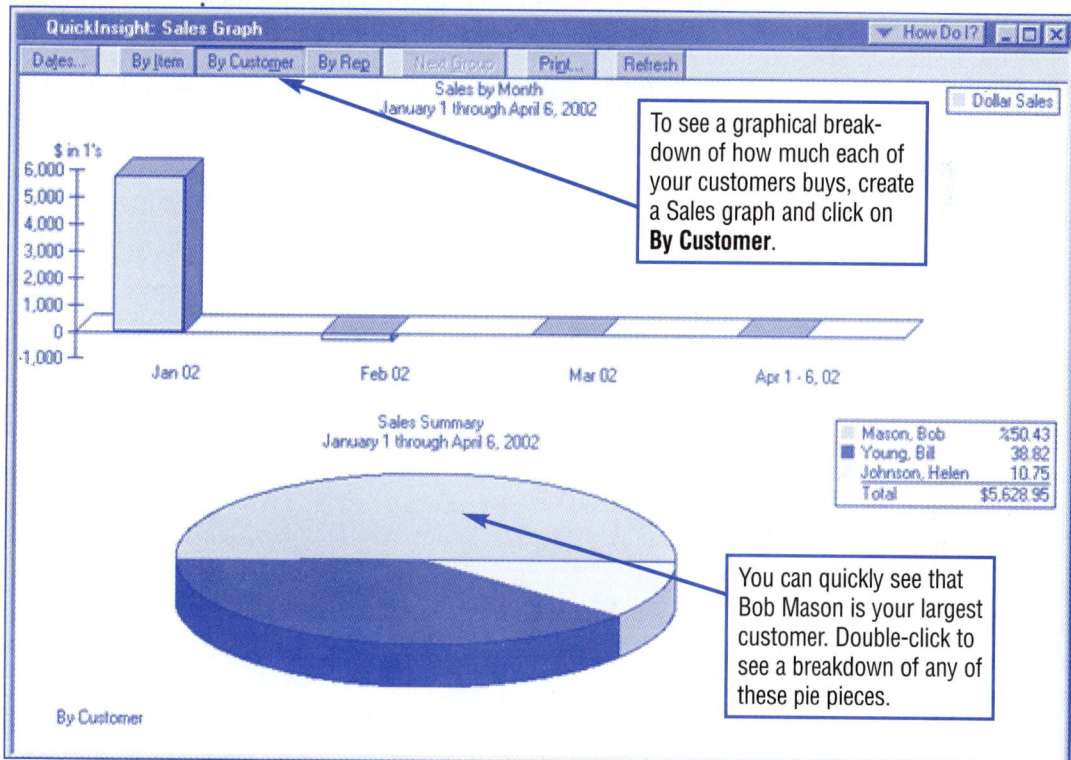

Figure 5-33 Create a Sales Graph by Customer.

CREATING BUDGETS AND BUDGET REPORTS

COMPUTER TUTORIAL

QuickBooks can help you track your budget by allowing you to enter budget amounts for each account, job, and class for each month of the year. Then, at any time, you can create a report of your actual income and expenses compared to your budgeted amounts.

1 Select the *Company* menu and choose **Set Up Budgets**.

2 Select "Product Sales" in the *Account* field.

You can also set a budget for each customer, job, or class by entering information in the additional fields.

3 Enter "3,000.00" in the *Jan 2002* field in the Budget Amount column as shown in Figure 5-34.

4 Click **Fill Down** so that QuickBooks will enter "3,000" for February through December as shown in Figure 5-34. On the Fill Down screen click **OK**.

In your own company, you will repeat Steps 2-4 for each of your income and expense accounts.

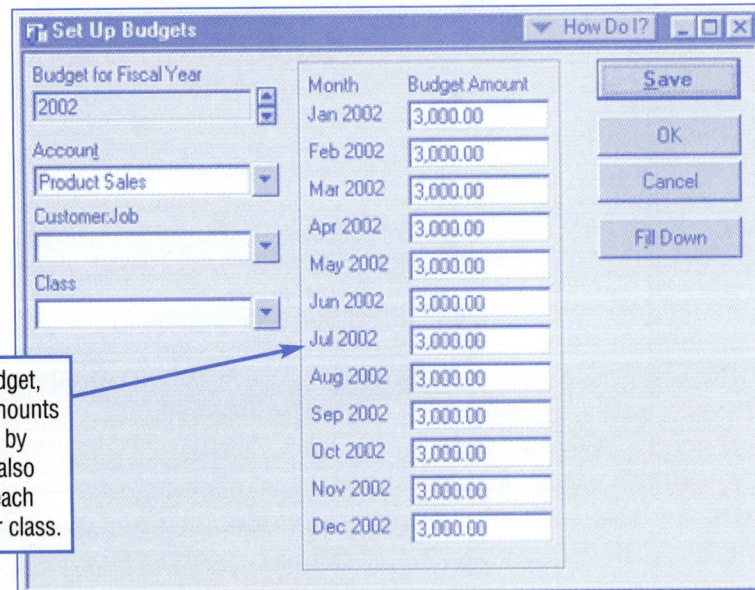

To track your budget, fill out budget amounts for each account by month. You can also set budgets for each customer, job, or class.

Figure 5-34 The Set Up Budgets screen

5 To save your budget, click **Save**.

6 Click the (**X**) in the top right of the Set Up Budgets screen to close the screen.

Then create a Budget vs. Actual report to compare your actual income and expenses to your budget.

NOTE

QuickBooks includes a variety of budget reports. Explore them all to see how they can help you manage income and expenses.

7 Select the **Reports** menu, choose **Budget**, and then choose **Profit & Loss Budget vs. Actual**.

8 Set the *Dates* fields to *From* "01/01/2002" and *To* "02/28/2002." Press <TAB> (see Figure 5-35)

9 Close all open report windows. Click **No** when QuickBooks prompts you to memorize the reports.

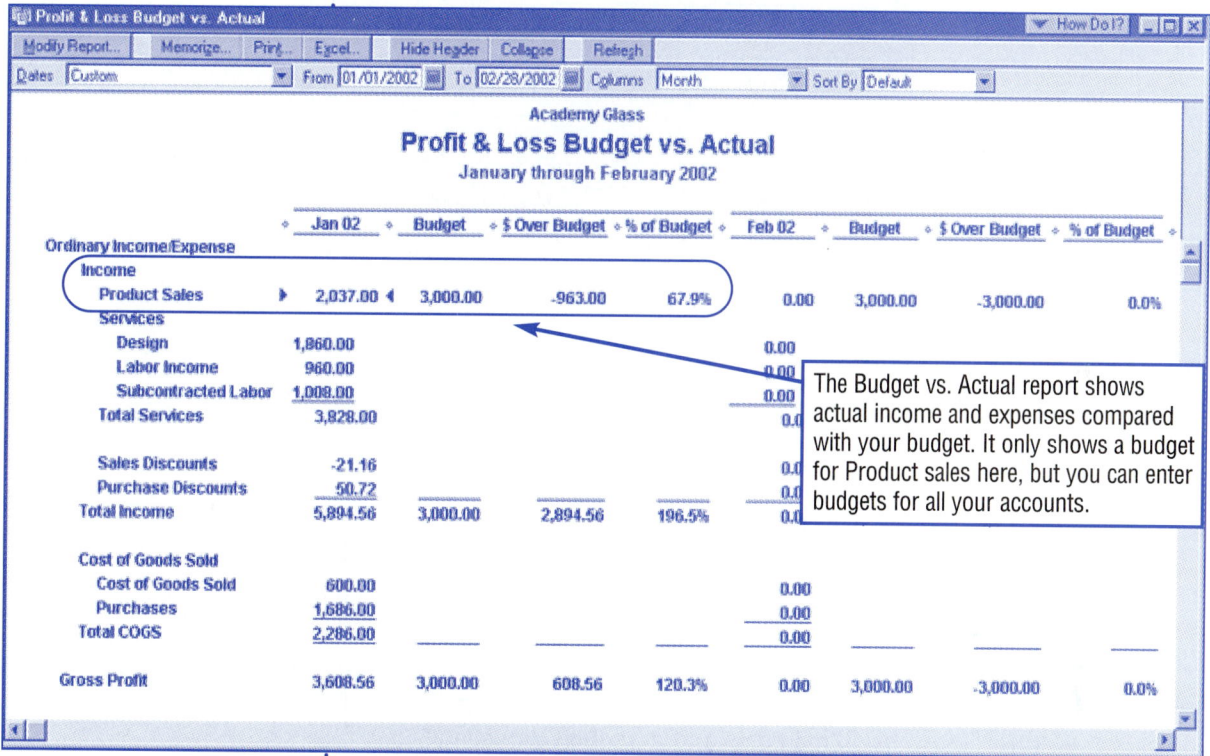

Figure 5-35 The Budget vs. Actual report

BUILDING CUSTOM REPORTS

To make your reports show only the information you want, you can *modify* (i.e., *customize*) the reports. All reports can be modified and filtered in some way, so familiarize yourself with Figure 5-36 and Figure 5-37 and learn how they affect different reports. In the next section, you'll create an example report using modifying and filtering.

Use the **Modify Report** button on any report to add or delete columns and change several other formats of the report.

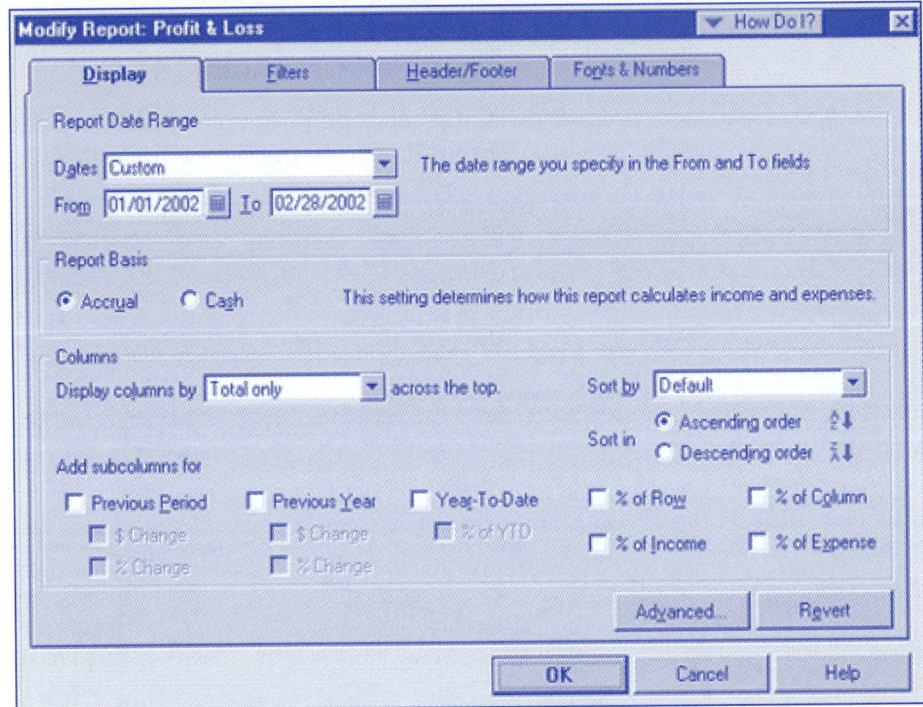

Figure 5-36 The Display tab of the Modify Report: Profit & Loss screen

Use the Filters tab on the Modify Report screen to narrow the contents of reports, so that you can analyze specific areas of your business. On the Filters tab, you can filter or choose specific accounts, dates, names, or Items to include on the report. Report filtering works similarly to the Find Command described on page 254.

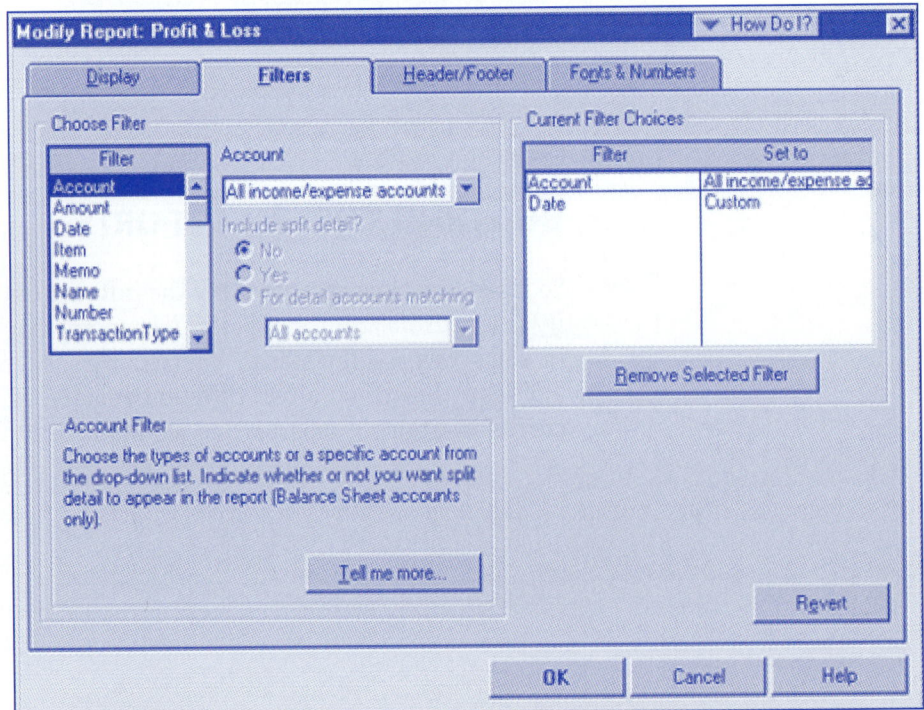

Figure 5-37 The Filters tab of The Modify Report: Profit & Loss screen

NOTE

Academy Glass uses Classes to track which store our customers buy from, but we want a report about where customers *live*. Therefore, we're not interested in the *Class* field for this report.

COMPUTER TUTORIAL

To practice modifying reports, suppose you want to get a report of all transactions that involve the Service Items that you sold during January and February of 2002 to customers who live in Walnut Creek. Also, you want the report sorted and totaled by customer. This report should include all sales transactions that include a service Item (Labor, Subcontracted Services, or Design).

Because you used a custom field on sales forms to track the *city* in which your Customers live, we can use a filter to narrow our report to include only those transactions with customers who live in Walnut Creek.

QuickBooks doesn't have a report for exactly what we're looking for, but you can start with a Custom Transaction Detail report and then modify the report so that it provides the information you need.

1 Select the **Reports** menu, and choose **Custom Transaction Detail Report**. The Modify Report: Custom Transaction Detail Report screen displays.

2 Set the *Dates* fields to From "01/1/2002" and To "02/28/2002" in the Display tab.

3 Select "Customer" from the *Total by* field drop-down menu. Click **OK**.

This report will now show all transactions during January and February totaled by customer (see Figure 5-38).

Figure 5-38 The Transaction Detail by Account report totaled by customer

There are several other settings that you can change on this screen. For example, you could change the basis on the report to Cash or Accrual, or you could set the sorting preferences. Click the **Advanced** button for even more settings. Explore these settings to learn how they affect your reports. For descriptions of each, use the Help menu in QuickBooks.

For your purposes, there are two problems with this standard report. First, it shows all transactions no matter what you sold. Secondly, the report does not show which Items you sold or in which city the customers lived.

You'll use the Modify function to select the columns you want displayed and to filter the report to include only the data you want.

④ Click **Modify Report**.

⑤ In the Columns section, notice that there are checkmarks by some of the fields (see Figure 5-39). The checkmarks indicate which columns show on the report. Select "City" and "Item" to turn those columns on. Then deselect "Memo," "Class," "Clr," "Split," and "Balance." You'll need to scroll up and down in the list to find each of the fields.

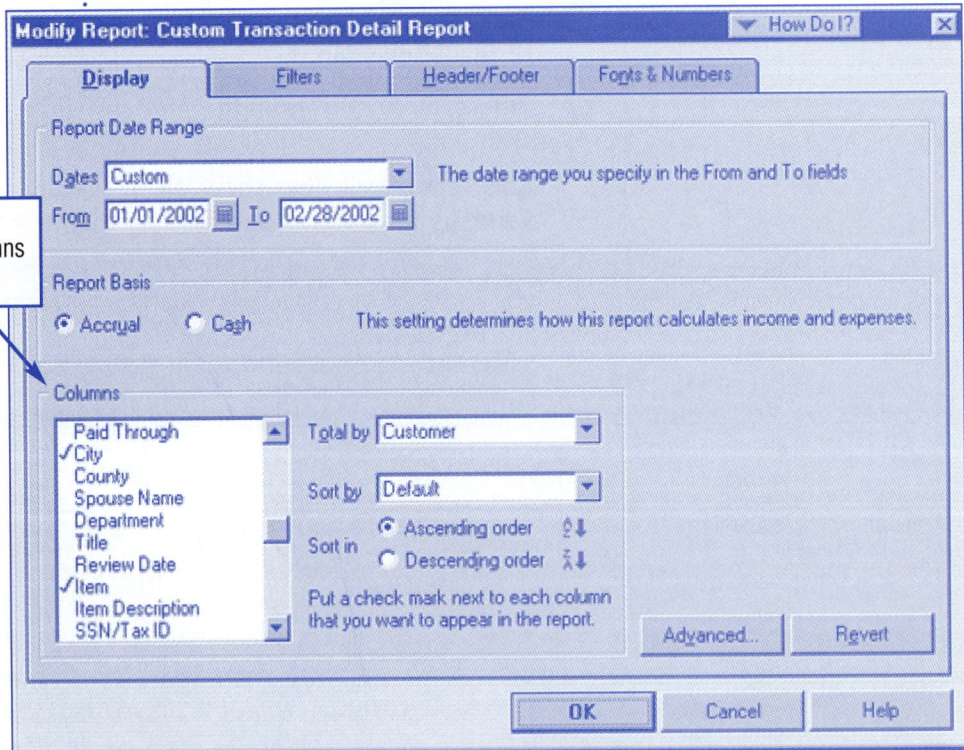

Figure 5-39 Modify columns by checking and unchecking selected ones in the Columns list

⑥ Click the Filters tab.

⑦ To filter the report so that it includes only service Items, select the Item filter in the Choose Filter section and choose "All services" from the *Item* field drop-down menu (see Figure 5-40).

⑧ To filter the report so that it includes only those customers who live in Walnut Creek, select the City filter in the Choose Filter section and enter "Walnut Creek" in the *City* field (see Figure 5-41).

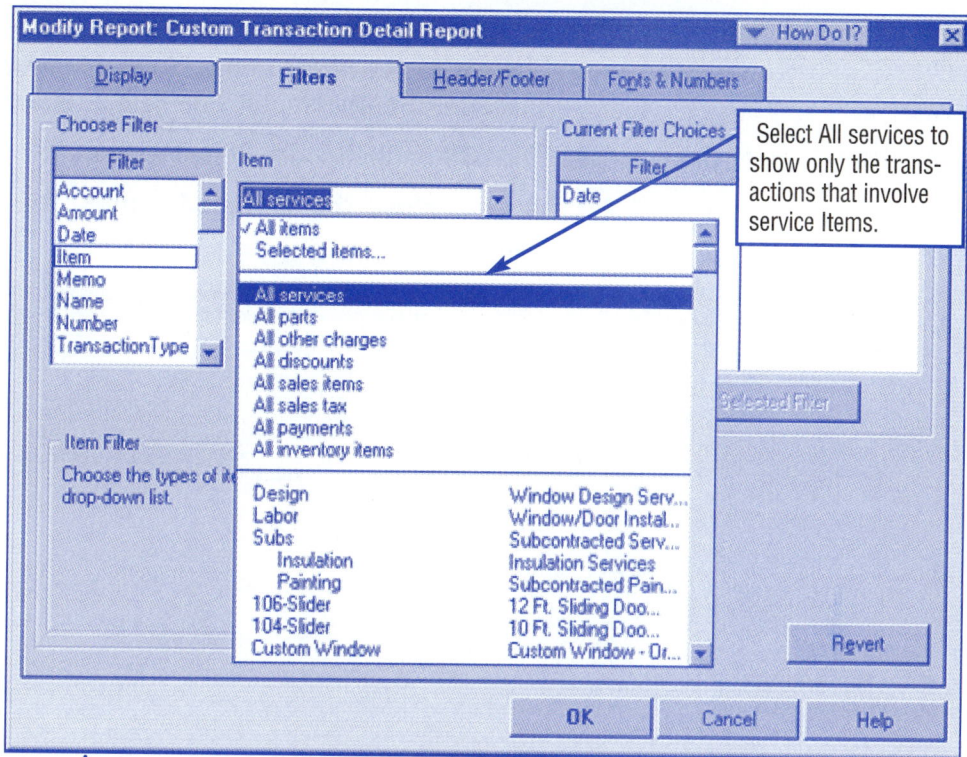

Figure 5-40 The Item drop-down list in the Filters screen

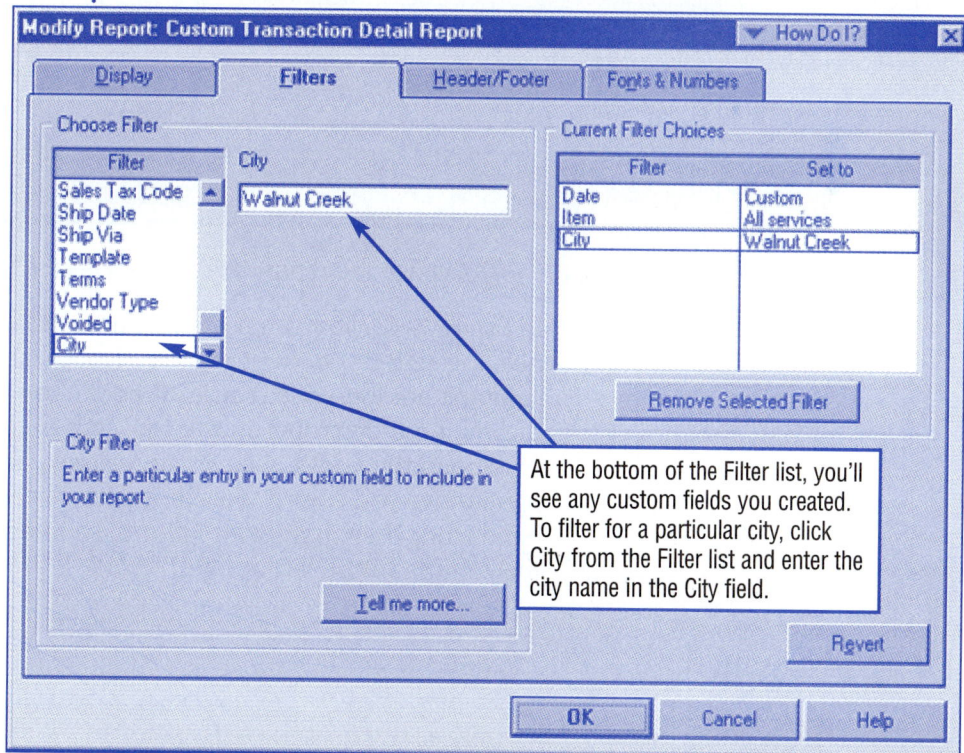

Figure 5-41 Click on the City Filter and enter "Walnut Creek."

⑨ Click the Header/Footer tab on the Modify Report screen.

10 To modify the title of the report so that it accurately describes the content of the report, enter "Sales of Services to Walnut Creek Customers" in the *Report Title* field as shown in Figure 5-42.

11 Click **OK** on the Modify Report screen.

12 **Do not close the modified report. You will use it in the next tutorial.**

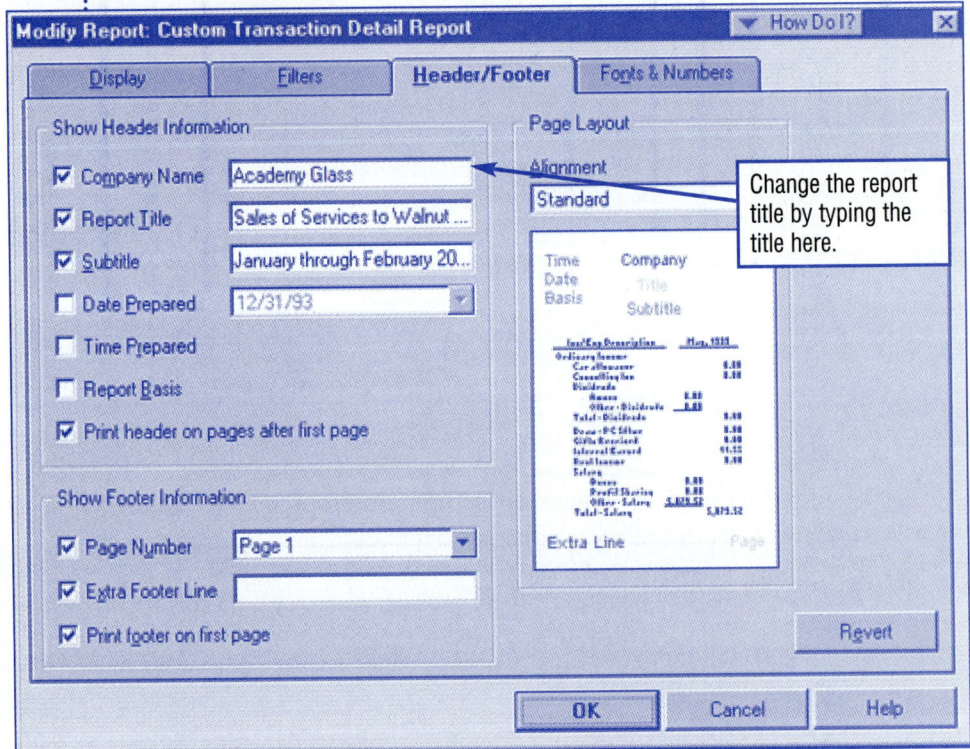

Figure 5-42 Change the report title on the Header/Footer tab.

In Figure 5-43, you can see your modified report. Notice that its heading reflects its new content. Notice also that some of the columns are too wide. You can modify the width of columns by dragging the diamond on the top right of the column to reduce or expand the width. Also, if you want to move a column left or right, move you curser over the column header until you see the hand icon. Then, hold your left mouse button down as you drag the column to the left or right.

To change the width of a column, drag this diamond to the right or left.

Academy Glass
Sales of Services to Walnut Creek Customers
January through February 2002

◇ Type ◇	Date ◇	Num ◇	Name	◇ City ◇	Item ◇	Account ◇	Amount ◇
Young, Bill							
Window Replacement							
Invoice	01/05/2002	2002-101	Young, Bill:Window Replacement	Walnut Creek	Design	Design	240.00 ◀
Invoice	01/05/2002	2002-101	Young, Bill:Window Replacement	Walnut Creek	Labor	Labor Income	240.00
Invoice	01/05/2002	2002-101	Young, Bill:Window Replacement	Walnut Creek	Labor	Labor Income	240.00
Invoice	01/05/2002	2002-101	Young, Bill:Window Replacement	Walnut Creek	Labor	Labor Income	240.00
Invoice	01/06/2002	2002-102	Young, Bill:Window Replacement	Walnut Creek	Subs:In...	Subcontracted...	288.00
Invoice	01/26/2002	2002-107	Young, Bill:Window Replacement	Walnut Creek	Labor	Labor Income	160.00
Total Window Replacement							1,408.00
Total Young, Bill							1,408.00
TOTAL							1,408.00

Figure 5-43 The customized report

MEMORIZING REPORTS

After you've modified a report, you can *memorize* the format and filtering so that you don't have to go through all of the modification steps the next time you want to use the same report configuration.

If you enter specific dates, QuickBooks will use those dates the next time you bring up this report. However, if you select a *relative* date range in the *Dates* field (e.g., Last Fiscal Quarter, Last Year, or This Year to Date) before memorizing a report, QuickBooks will use the relative dates the next time you create the report.

For example, if you memorize a report with the *Dates* field set to "Last Fiscal Quarter," that report will always use dates for the fiscal quarter prior to the current date (see Figure 5-44).

Figure 5-44 The Dates field showing a relative date range

COMPUTER TUTORIAL

1 Click **Memorize** at the top of the report.

2 In the Memorize Report window, the name for the report is automatically filled in for you. You can change it if you want.

QuickBooks uses the report title as the default name for the memorized report.

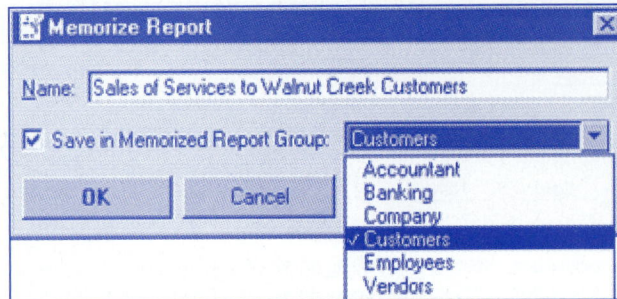

Figure 5-45 The Memorize Report screen

3 Click the "Save in Memorized Report Group" box and choose "Customers" from the drop-down menu (see Figure 5-45).

You can group your reports into similar types when you memorize them. This allows you to run several reports in a group by selecting them in the Process Multiple Reports screen. See following section.

4 Click **OK** and close the report.

The next time you want to see this report follow these steps:

5 Select the *Reports* menu, choose **Memorized Reports**, and then choose **Memorized Report List**.

Notice that QuickBooks displays the reports in groups according to how you memorized them.

6 Select the report you just memorized and click **Display**. Or double-click on the report in the list (see Figure 5-46).

Close all open windows.

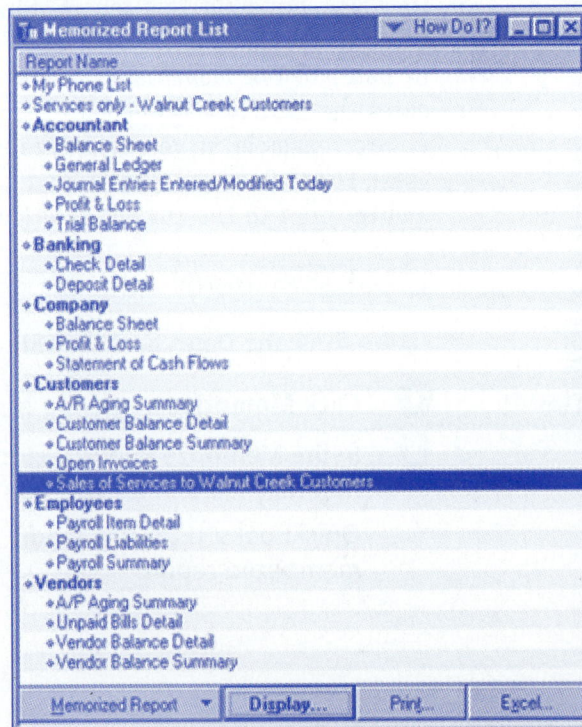

Figure 5-46 The Memorized Report List

REPORT GROUPS

QuickBooks allows you to combine several reports into a group, so that you can later display and/or print the reports in the group automatically.

As you can see in the Memorized Report list shown in Figure 5-46, you can have as many reports as you want in a group by memorizing the report and assigning it to the group. If you want to reassign a report to another group, click on the diamond to the left of the report in the Memorized Reports list and drag the mouse up or down until the report appears under the desired group. If you drag it to where it is no longer below a group name, it will not belong to any group.

Processing Multiple Reports

COMPUTER TUTORIAL

① Select the *Reports* menu and choose **Process Multiple Reports** (see Figure 5-47).

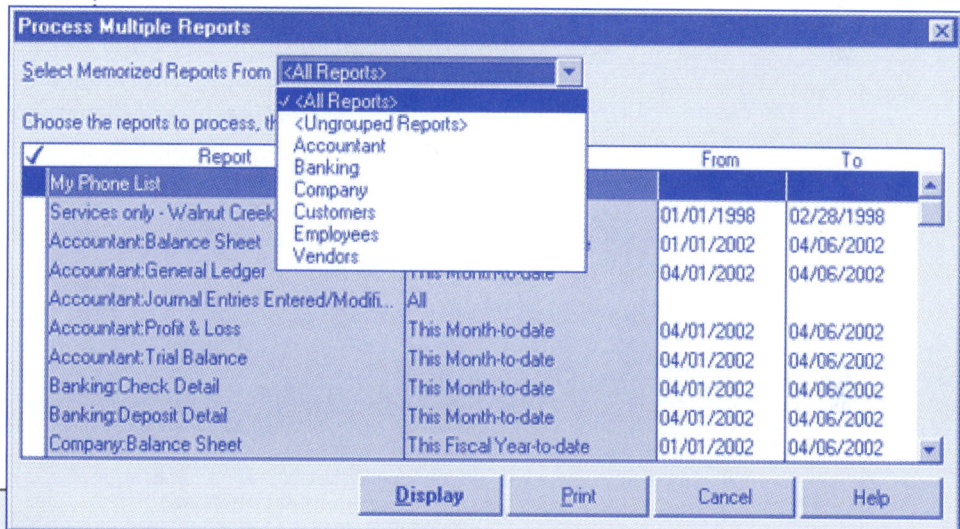

Process Multiple Reports				✕
Select Memorized Reports From	<All Reports> ▼			
Choose the reports to process, th				
✓ Report			From	To
My Phone List				
Services only - Walnut Creek			01/01/1998	02/28/1998
Accountant:Balance Sheet			01/01/2002	04/06/2002
Accountant:General Ledger			04/01/2002	04/06/2002
Accountant:Journal Entries Entered/Modifi...	All			
Accountant:Profit & Loss	This Month-to-date		04/01/2002	04/06/2002
Accountant:Trial Balance	This Month-to-date		04/01/2002	04/06/2002
Banking:Check Detail	This Month-to-date		04/01/2002	04/06/2002
Banking:Deposit Detail	This Month-to-date		04/01/2002	04/06/2002
Company:Balance Sheet	This Fiscal Year-to-date		01/01/2002	04/06/2002

Drop-down menu list:
- ✓ <All Reports>
- <Ungrouped Reports>
- Accountant
- Banking
- Company
- Customers
- Employees
- Vendors

Buttons: Display · Print · Cancel · Help

Figure 5-47 The Process Multiple Reports screen

② Select "Customers" from the *Select Memorized Reports From* field drop-down menu.

NOTE

Click in the column to the left of the reports you want to include when you print or display. If you print the same group of reports on a regular basis, combine them together in a Report Group and select the group name in the *Select Memorized Reports From* field.

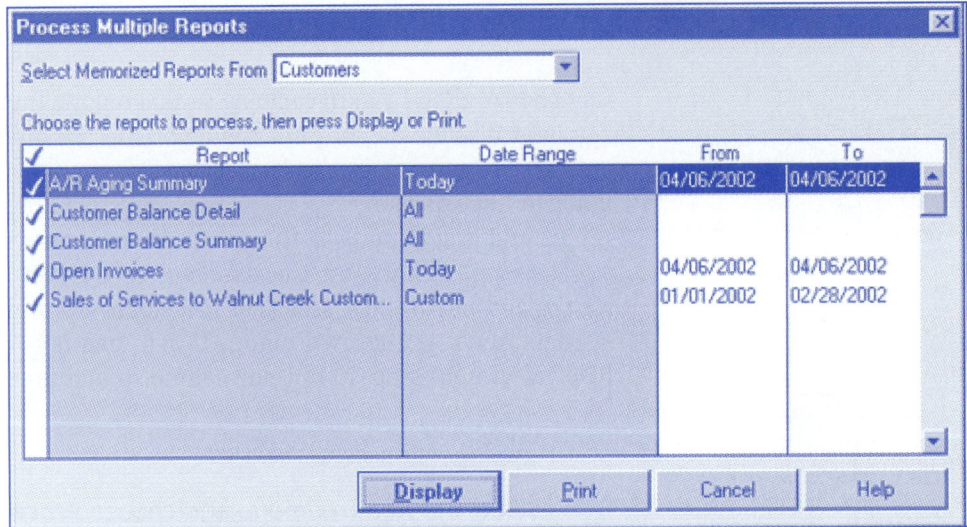

Figure 5-48 The Customers Report Group

3 If you don't want to display or print all the reports in the group (see Figure 5-49), click the checkmark in the left column to remove it and deselect each report that you want to omit. Click **Display** to show the reports on the screen (see Figure 5-49) or click **Print** to print all the reports.

4 Close all open report windows. Click **No** when QuickBooks prompts you to memorize the reports.

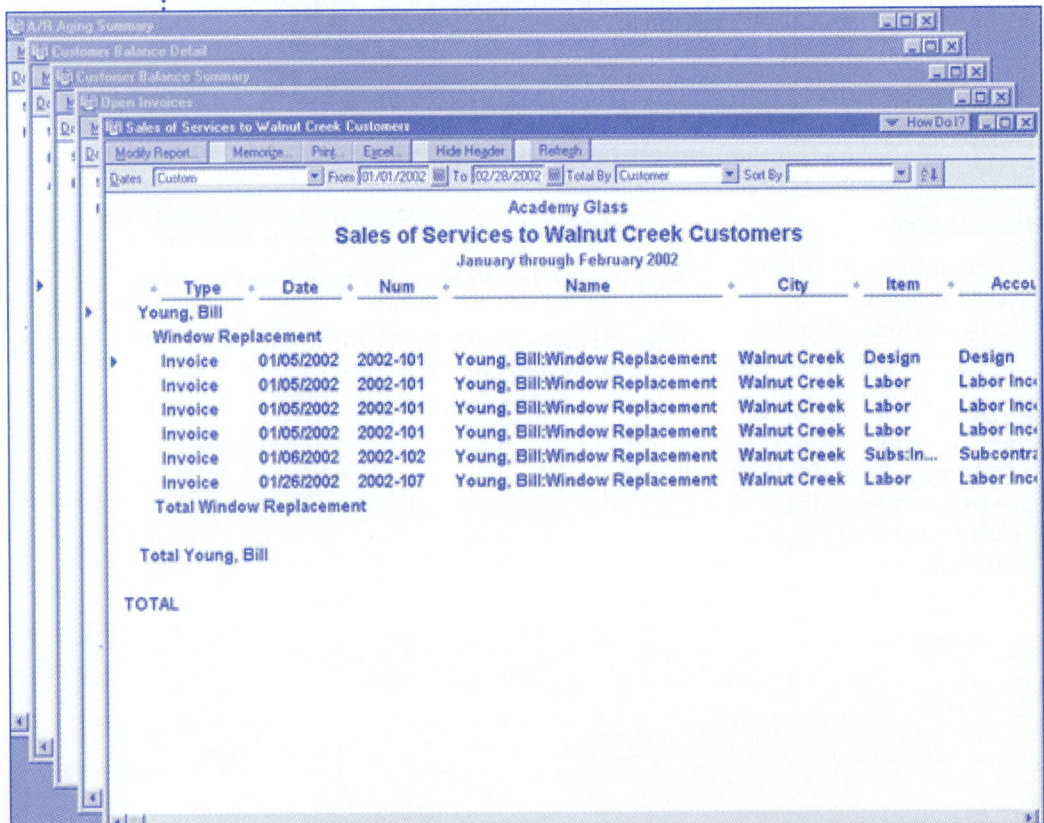

Figure 5-49 All the reports in the Customer report group

PRINTING REPORTS

Every report in QuickBooks is printable. When you print reports, QuickBooks allows you to specify the orientation (landscape or portrait) and page-count characteristics for the reports.

1 Create a Profit & Loss by Job report for 1/1/2002 to 3/31/2002 (see page 226).

2 To print the report, select the *File* menu and choose **Print Report**.

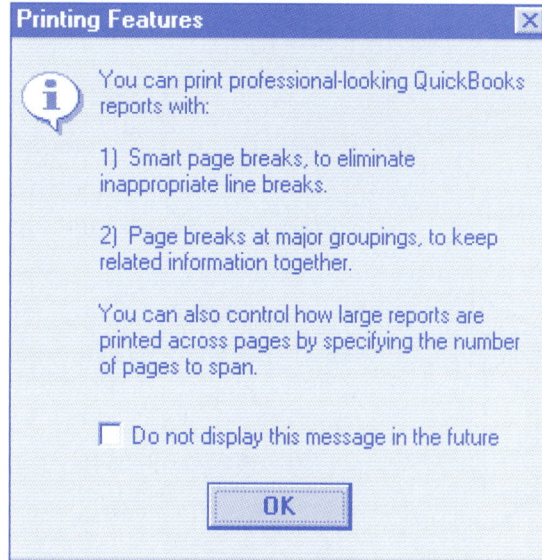

COMPUTER TUTORIAL

ANOTHER WAY

To print a report, press <CTRL+P> or click the **Print** button at the top of the report.

Printing Features

You can print professional-looking QuickBooks reports with:

1) Smart page breaks, to eliminate inappropriate line breaks.

2) Page breaks at major groupings, to keep related information together.

You can also control how large reports are printed across pages by specifying the number of pages to span.

☐ Do not display this message in the future

OK

Figure 5-50 The page-break message

3 The message displayed in Figure 5-50 may appear. As the message in Figure 5-50 says, you can control (to some extent) where page breaks occur on reports so that your pages don't break in inappropriate places. This feature is called *Smart page breaks*. Also, you can have QuickBooks break the pages after each major grouping of accounts. (See Figure 5-53 for both of these settings.) In the Profit & Loss report, this means that all Income and Cost of Goods Sold accounts will be on the first page (or pages), and all the Expense accounts will begin on a new page.

Click **OK**.

4 Notice the report settings on the Print Reports screen. On the Print Reports screen shown in Figure 5-51, you can set the orientation to Portrait or Landscape.

The Portrait setting (see Figure 5-52) makes the print appear from left to right across the 8½-inch dimension of the page ("straight up"), while the Landscape setting makes the print appear across the 11-inch side ("sideways").

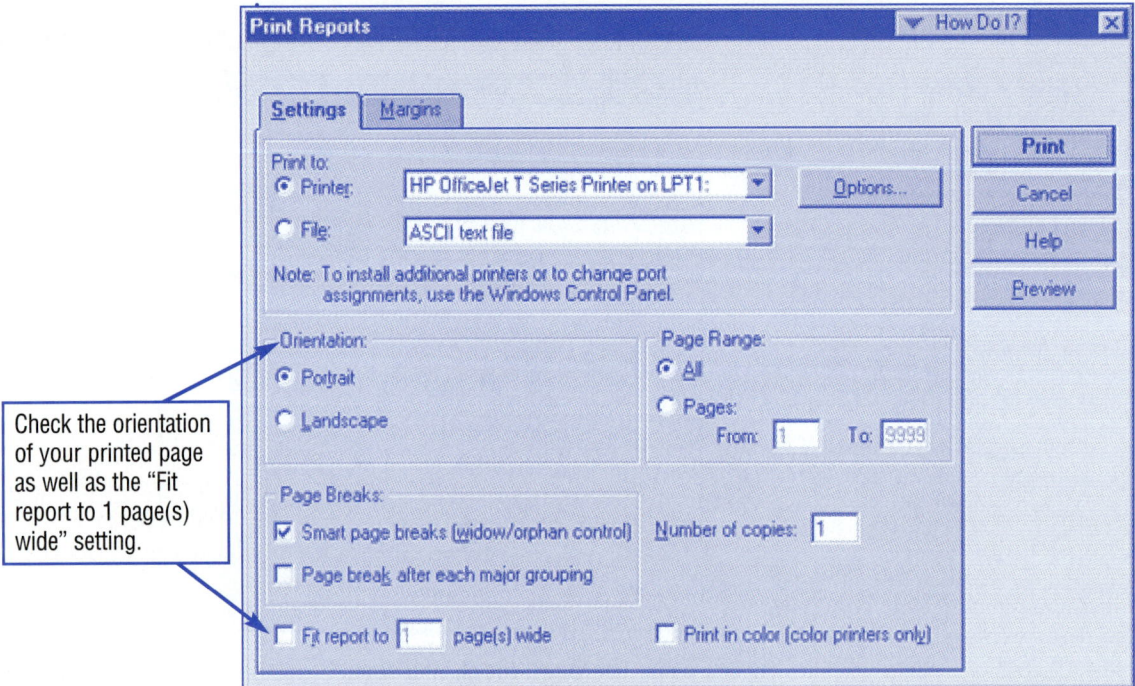

Check the orientation of your printed page as well as the "Fit report to 1 page(s) wide" setting.

Figure 5-51 The Print Reports screen

Figure 5-52 You can choose Portrait or Landscape orientation.

5 You can also set the Smart page breaks (widow/orphan control) setting (see Figure 5-53), which keeps related data from splitting across two pages.

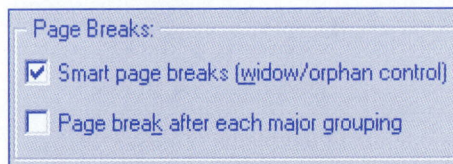

Figure 5-53 The Page Breaks setting

6 Select the "Fit report to 1 pages wide" option (see Figure 5-54). When you select this option, QuickBooks reduces the font size of the report so the width of all columns does not exceed 8½" (in portrait mode) or 11" (in landscape mode).

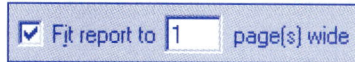

☑ Fit report to 1 page(s) wide

Figure 5-54 Select "Fit report to 1 page(s) wide"

7 Before you print any report, it's a good idea to preview the report to make sure it will print the way you want. Click the **Preview** button on the **Print Reports** screen.

8 If everything looks right, click **Print** to print the report.

9 Close all open report windows. Click **No** when QuickBooks prompts you to memorize the reports.

FINDING TRANSACTIONS

There are several ways to find transactions in QuickBooks, depending on what you're trying to find. Sometimes you only know the date of a transaction, and other times you know only the customer, the Item, or the amount. Here are a couple of different ways to search for transactions.

Finding Transactions in Registers

If you know that the transaction you're looking for is in the Checking account register, display the register and scroll up and down until you find it. Click the scroll box, hold down the left mouse button, and drag the scroll box up and down. As you do so, the date for the transaction displayed will show next to the scroll box.

To find transactions by scrolling, follow these steps:

COMPUTER TUTORIAL

1 Select the *Lists* menu, and choose **Chart of Accounts** (or press <CTRL+A>).

2 Double-click on the "Checking" account to display the register.

3 Click the scroll box on the far right of your screen. Hold down the left mouse button and drag the scroll box up until you see "01/04/2002" in the date display box (see Figure 5-55). Release the mouse button to allow the transaction to appear.

Close all open windows.

Date	Number	Payee		Payment	✓	Deposit	Balance
	Type	Account	Memo				
01/04/2002	326	Valley Gas & Electric		276.52	✓		17,663.08
	CHK	Utilities:Gas and Elec					
01/05/2002	327	Jones Office Supply		128.60	✓		17,534.48
	CHK	-split-					
01/05/2002	6001	Orlando Properties		3,200.00	✓		14,334.48
	CHK	Rent					
01/20/2002	6002	Ace Glass		0.00	✓		14,334.48
	BILLPMT	Accounts Payable					

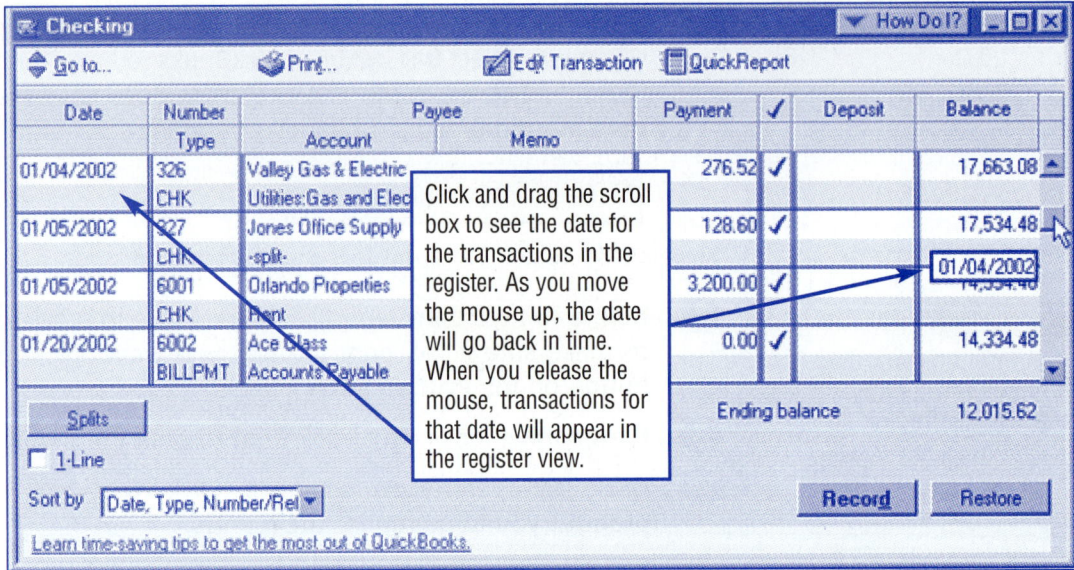

Figure 5-55 Search for a date by dragging the scroll box.

Using the Find Command

If you're looking for a transaction and you don't know which register to look in, or if you want to find more than just a single transaction, you can use the **Find** command. You can search by several criteria in order to find the transaction or transactions you want.

There are two tabs on the Find screen: Simple and Advanced. Use the Simple tab if you want to search for any of the following information: the transaction type, the Customer:Job name used on the transaction, the approximate date of the transaction, the number of the transaction (e.g., Invoice #) or the Amount. If you need to search based on any other criteria (e.g., account name, Item name, or memo), use the Advanced tab.

Using the Find Command to Find an Invoice

If you need to find a particular Invoice, many QuickBooks users will open the Invoice screen and click **Previous** until they find the Invoice they need. This is often a very time consuming and inefficient way to locate a specific transaction. Instead, to find an Invoice for $1,057.75 that you issued Bob Mason, use the Simple tab of the Find screen.

COMPUTER TUTORIAL

❶ Select the *Edit* menu and choose **Simple Find** (or press <CTRL+F>).

❷ "Invoice" is preselected in the *Transaction Type* field. Press <TAB>.

❸ Select "Mason, Bob" from the *Customer:Job* field drop-down menu and press <TAB>.

4 Since you do not know the exact date of the Invoice, but you know that you created the Invoice during the first quarter of 2002, enter "01/01/2002" and "03/31/2002" in the *Dates* fields. Press <TAB>.

5 Press <TAB> to skip the *Invoice #* field.

If you knew the Invoice number you could enter it in this field. For this tutorial we will assume that you do not know the number.

6 Enter "1,057.75" in the *Amount* field and press <TAB>.

7 Click **Find** to search for all Invoices for Bob Mason in the amount of $1,057.75 (see Figure 5-56).

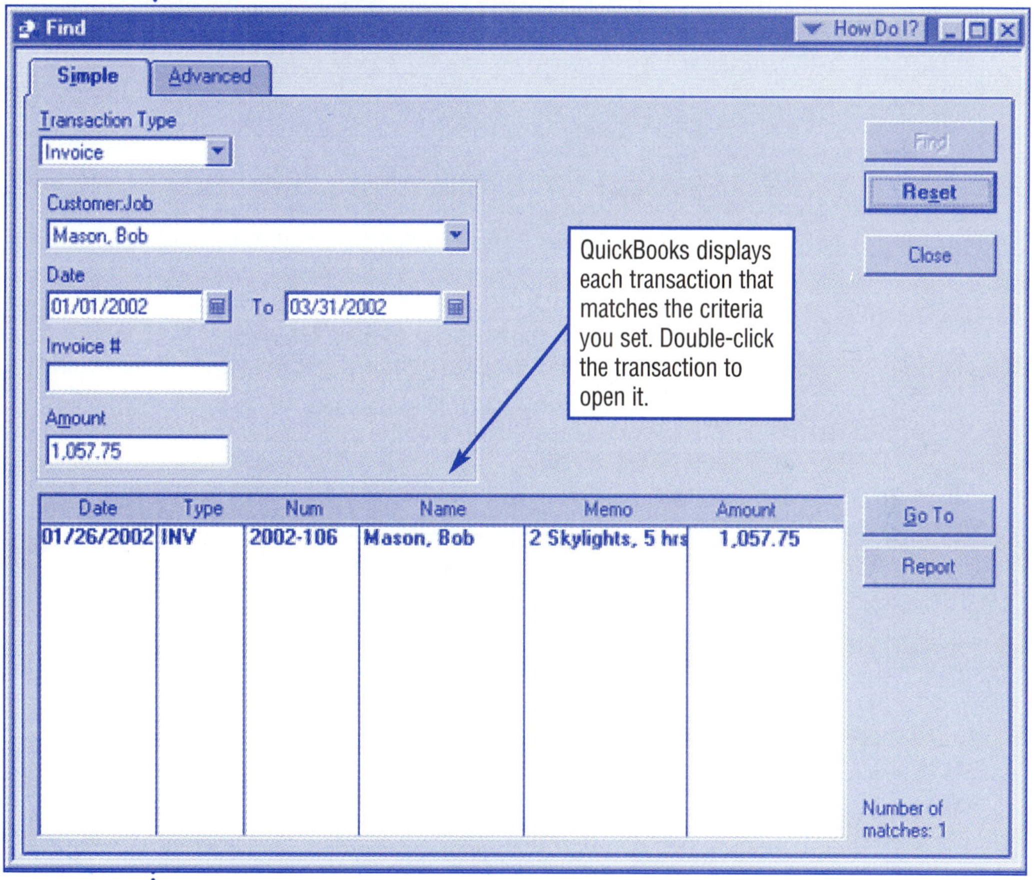

Figure 5-56 Use the Simple tab of the Find screen to locate an Invoice for Bob Mason.

COMPUTER TUTORIAL

To find all transactions that use the Skylight Item, use the Advanced tab of the Find screen.

1 Click the Advanced tab.

2 In the Filter section, select "Item." Then enter "Skylight" in the *Item* field (see Figure 5-57).

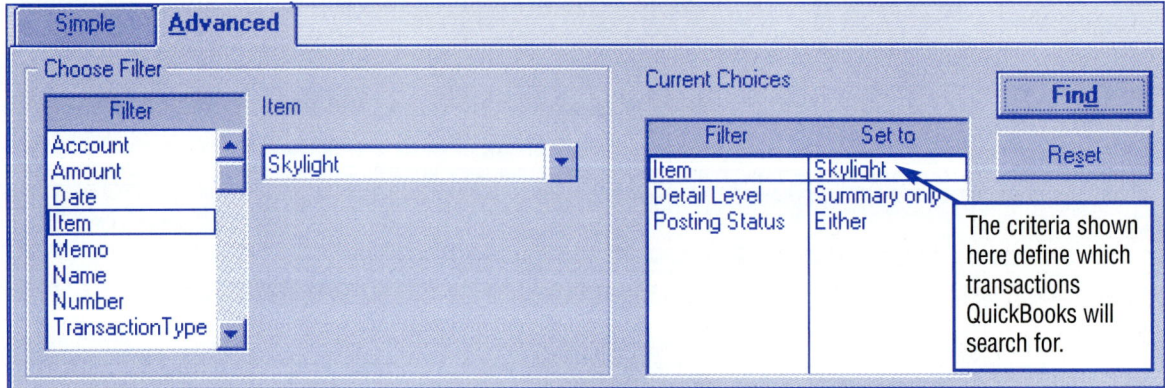

Simple	**Advanced**		

Choose Filter

Filter	Item	Current Choices		Find

Filter: Account, Amount, Date, **Item**, Memo, Name, Number, TransactionType

Item: Skylight

Filter	Set to
Item	Skylight
Detail Level	Summary only
Posting Status	Either

Reset

The criteria shown here define which transactions QuickBooks will search for.

Figure 5-57 Enter "Skylight" in the Item field.

3 Select Detail Level in the Filter column of the Current Choices section (see Figure 5-58). Then click "All" in the Detail Level section to the left (see Figure 5-59). This will remove the "Detail Level – Summary Only" criterion.

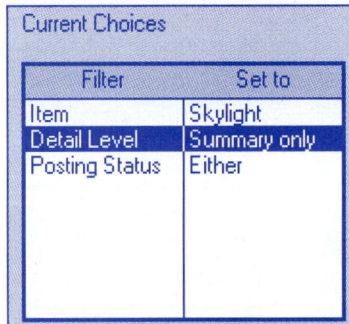

Current Choices

Filter	Set to
Item	Skylight
Detail Level	Summary only
Posting Status	Either

Figure 5-58 The Current Choices section

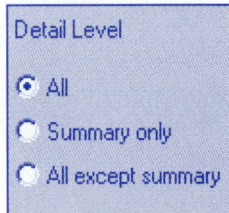

Detail Level

⦿ All
○ Summary only
○ All except summary

Figure 5-59 The Detail Level section

QuickBooks adds two criteria by default: "Posting status – Either," and "Detail Level – Summary Only." In almost all situations, it is best to remove the Detail Level criterion before beginning your search.

④ Click **Find**.

QuickBooks finds all of the transactions that match your criteria and then displays them at the bottom of the Find screen (see Figure 5-60).

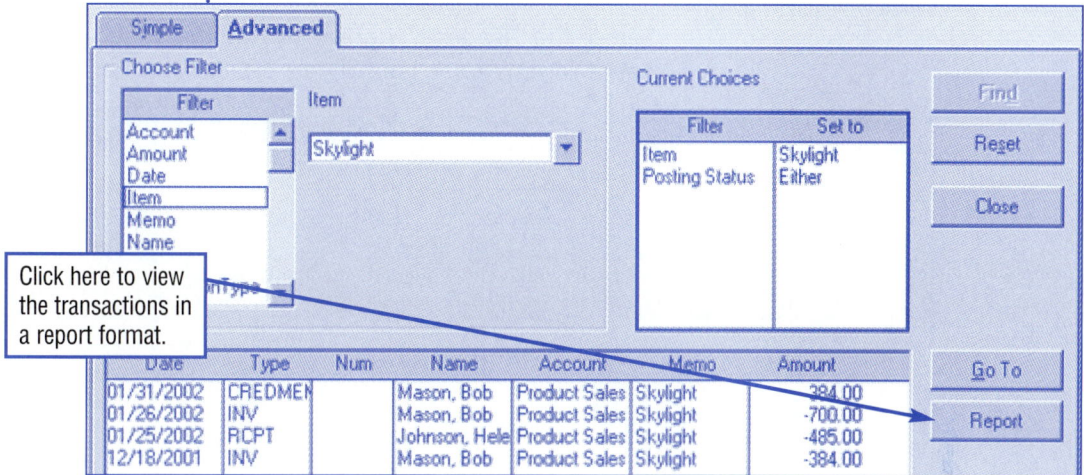

Simple	**Advanced**

Choose Filter

Filter
Account
Amount
Date
Item
Memo
Name

Item

Skylight

Click here to view the transactions in a report format.

Current Choices

Filter	Set to
Item	Skylight
Posting Status	Either

Find

Reset

Close

Date	Type	Num	Name	Account	Memo	Amount
01/31/2002	CREDMEM		Mason, Bob	Product Sales	Skylight	384.00
01/26/2002	INV		Mason, Bob	Product Sales	Skylight	-700.00
01/25/2002	RCPT		Johnson, Hele	Product Sales	Skylight	-485.00
12/18/2001	INV		Mason, Bob	Product Sales	Skylight	-384.00

Go To

Report

Figure 5-60 The Advanced tab of the Find screen

⑤ To view these transactions in a report format, click **Report**.

The report shown in Figure 5-61 shows all transactions that involve the skylight Item. If you want to look at one of these transactions, double-click on it in the report.

Close all open windows.

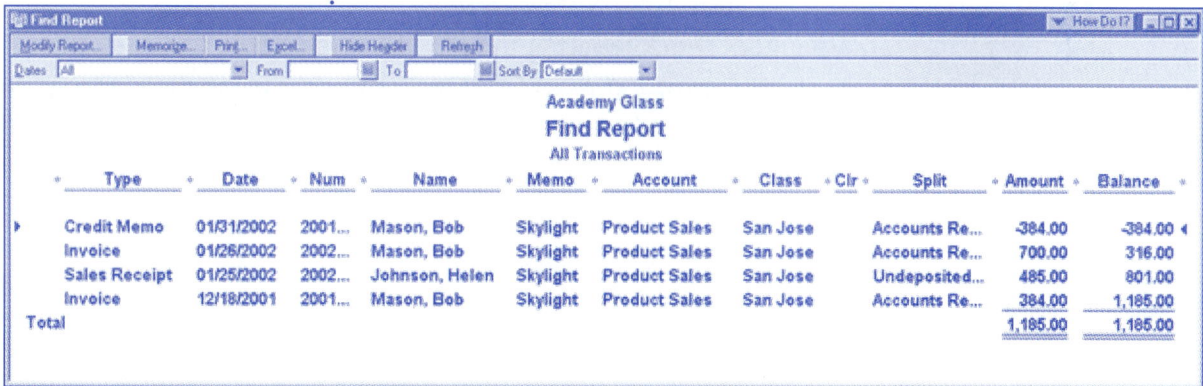

Find Report — How Do I? ▾

| Modify Report... | Memorize... | Print... | Excel... | Hide Header | Refresh |

Dates [All] From [ ] To [ ] Sort By [Default]

Academy Glass
Find Report
All Transactions

Type	Date	Num	Name	Memo	Account	Class	Clr	Split	Amount	Balance
Credit Memo	01/31/2002	2001...	Mason, Bob	Skylight	Product Sales	San Jose		Accounts Re...	-384.00	-384.00
Invoice	01/26/2002	2002...	Mason, Bob	Skylight	Product Sales	San Jose		Accounts Re...	700.00	316.00
Sales Receipt	01/25/2002	2002...	Johnson, Helen	Skylight	Product Sales	San Jose		Undeposited...	485.00	801.00
Invoice	12/18/2001	2001...	Mason, Bob	Skylight	Product Sales	San Jose		Accounts Re...	384.00	1,185.00
Total									1,185.00	1,185.00

Figure 5-61 The Find Report for Skylight Items

COMPUTER TUTORIAL

Using Register QuickReports to Find Transactions

To find all transactions in your Checking account for a particular name, follow these steps:

1 Display the Check register.

2 Select the "Bounce" transaction in the register for Bob Mason dated 02/01/2002 (see Figure 5-62).

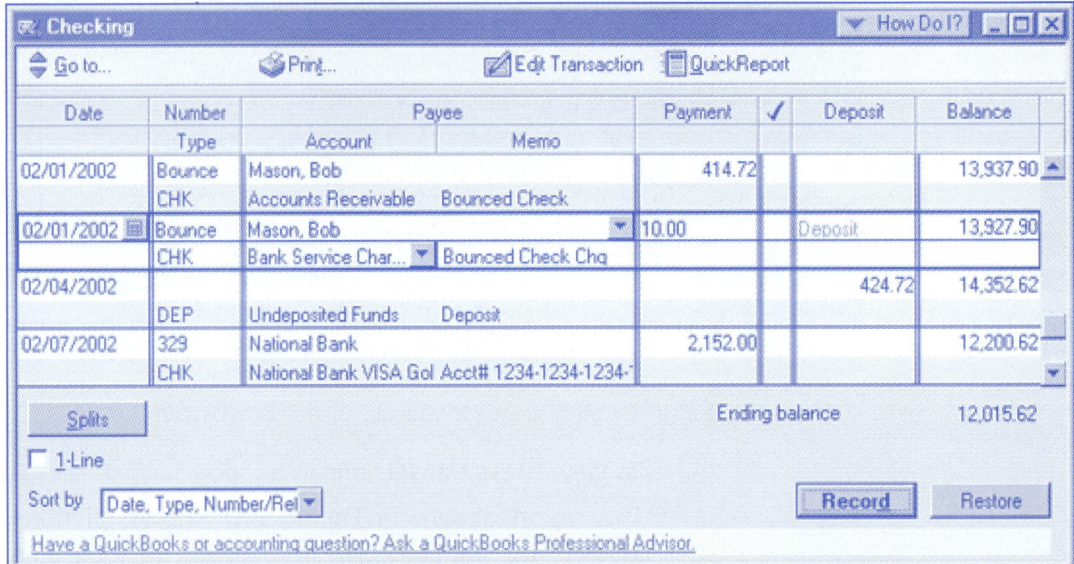

Checking								
♦ Go to...		🖶 Print...		📝 Edit Transaction	📋 QuickReport			▼ How Do I?
Date	Number	Payee			Payment	✓	Deposit	Balance
	Type	Account	Memo					
02/01/2002	Bounce	Mason, Bob			414.72			13,937.90
	CHK	Accounts Receivable	Bounced Check					
02/01/2002	Bounce	Mason, Bob			10.00		Deposit	13,927.90
	CHK	Bank Service Char... ▼	Bounced Check Chg					
02/04/2002							424.72	14,352.62
	DEP	Undeposited Funds	Deposit					
02/07/2002	329	National Bank			2,152.00			12,200.62
	CHK	National Bank VISA Gol Acct# 1234-1234-1234-1						

Splits			Ending balance	12,015.62

☐ 1-Line

Sort by [Date, Type, Number/Ref ▼]   [Record] [Restore]

Have a QuickBooks or accounting question? Ask a QuickBooks Professional Advisor.

Figure 5-62 Select the "Bounce" transaction for Bob Mason in the Checking register.

3 Click **QuickReport** at the top of the register.

This creates a report of all transactions using the same name as the selected transaction (see Figure 5-63). The transaction must appear in this register to be included in the QuickReport.

Close all open windows.

Register QuickReport							▼ How Do I?
Modify Report...	Memorize...	Print...	Excel...	Hide Header	Refresh		
Dates [All ▼]	From [ ]	To [ ]	Sort By [Default ▼]				

Academy Glass
Register QuickReport
All Transactions

◇ Type ◇	Date ◇	Num ◇	Memo ◇	Account ◇	Clr ◇	Split ◇	Amount ◇
Mason, Bob							
► Check	01/31/2002	330		Checking		Accounts Re...	-377.28 ◄
Check	02/01/2002	Boun...	Bounced Ch...	Checking		Accounts Re...	-414.72
Check	02/01/2002	Boun...	Bounced Ch...	Checking		Bank Service...	-10.00
Total Mason, Bob							**-802.00**
TOTAL							**-802.00**

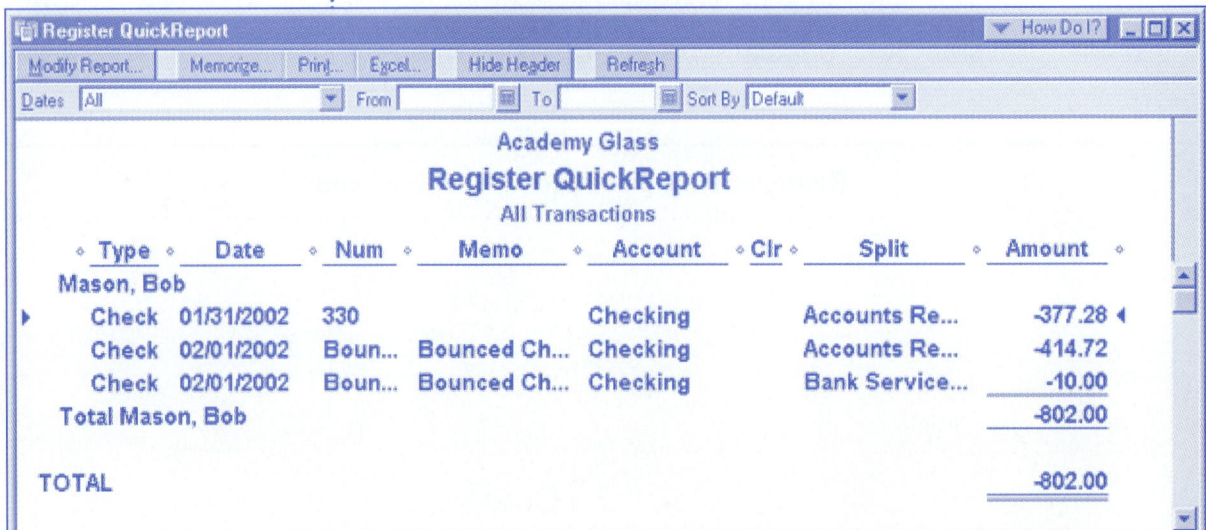

Figure 5-63 The Register QuickReport for the Checking register

EXPORTING REPORTS TO SPREADSHEETS

When you need to modify reports in ways that QuickBooks does not allow (e.g., changing the name of a column heading) you will need to export the report to a spreadsheet program.

Exporting a Report to Microsoft Excel

COMPUTER TUTORIAL

1 Select the *Reports* menu, choose **Sales**, and then choose **Sales by Customer Detail**.

2 Set the *Dates* fields to *From* "01/01/2002" and *To* "02/28/2002" and press <TAB> twice (see Figure 5-64).

Click Excel to export the report to a Microsoft Excel spreadsheet.

Figure 5-64 Click Excel to export the report to a Microsoft Excel spreadsheet.

3 Click **Excel** at the top of the report.

④ Click **OK** on the Export Report To Excel screen. QuickBooks will export your report directly to an Excel spreadsheet (Figure 5-65).

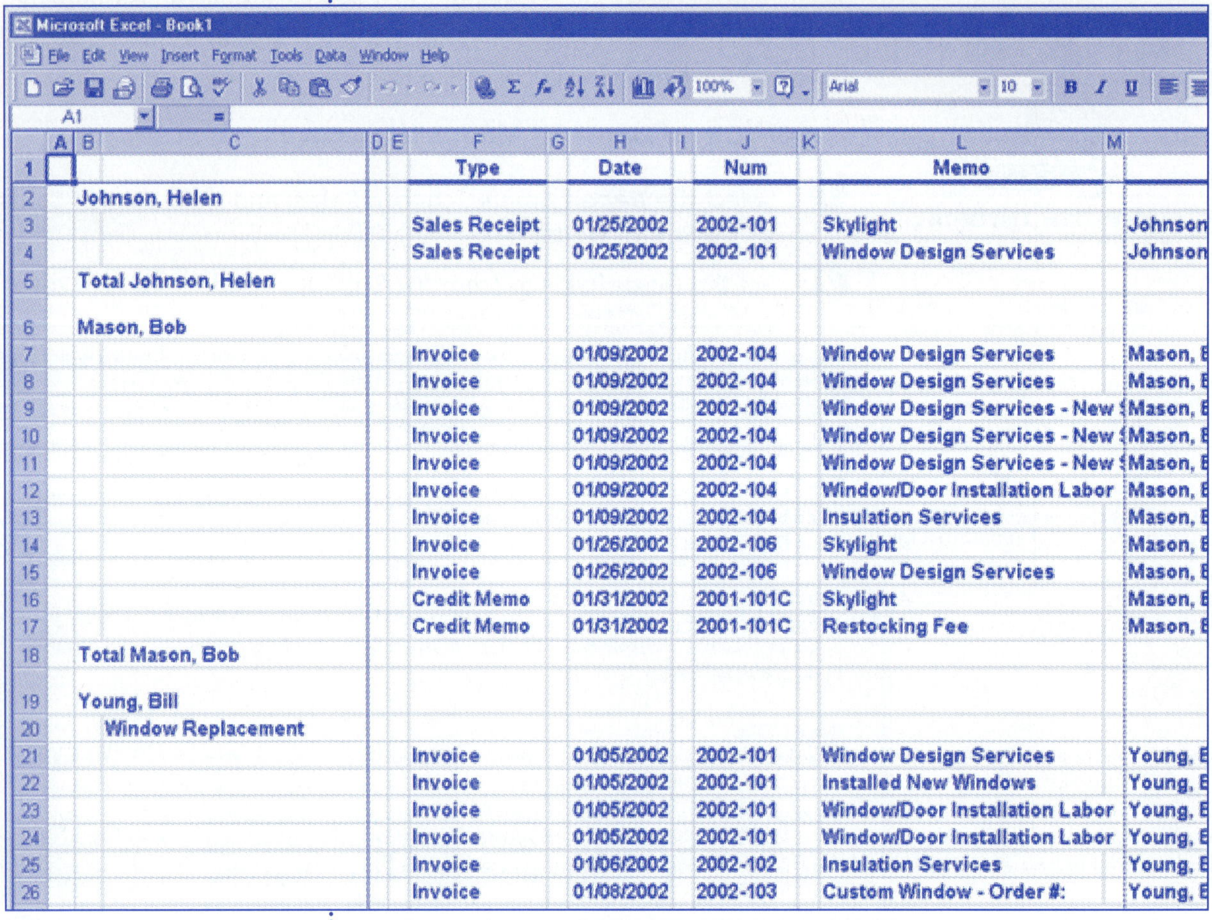

	Type	Date	Num	Memo	
Johnson, Helen					
	Sales Receipt	01/25/2002	2002-101	Skylight	Johnson
	Sales Receipt	01/25/2002	2002-101	Window Design Services	Johnson
Total Johnson, Helen					
Mason, Bob					
	Invoice	01/09/2002	2002-104	Window Design Services	Mason, B
	Invoice	01/09/2002	2002-104	Window Design Services	Mason, B
	Invoice	01/09/2002	2002-104	Window Design Services - New	Mason, B
	Invoice	01/09/2002	2002-104	Window Design Services - New	Mason, B
	Invoice	01/09/2002	2002-104	Window Design Services - New	Mason, B
	Invoice	01/09/2002	2002-104	Window/Door Installation Labor	Mason, B
	Invoice	01/09/2002	2002-104	Insulation Services	Mason, B
	Invoice	01/26/2002	2002-106	Skylight	Mason, B
	Invoice	01/26/2002	2002-106	Window Design Services	Mason, B
	Credit Memo	01/31/2002	2001-101C	Skylight	Mason, B
	Credit Memo	01/31/2002	2001-101C	Restocking Fee	Mason, B
Total Mason, Bob					
Young, Bill					
Window Replacement					
	Invoice	01/05/2002	2002-101	Window Design Services	Young, B
	Invoice	01/05/2002	2002-101	Installed New Windows	Young, B
	Invoice	01/05/2002	2002-101	Window/Door Installation Labor	Young, B
	Invoice	01/05/2002	2002-101	Window/Door Installation Labor	Young, B
	Invoice	01/06/2002	2002-102	Insulation Services	Young, B
	Invoice	01/08/2002	2002-103	Custom Window - Order #:	Young, B

Figure 5-65 The report is now an Excel spreadsheet.

COMPUTER TUTORIAL

Exporting to Other Spreadsheet Programs

1 With the Sales by Customer Detail report open, click **Print**.

2 In the Print to section of the Print Reports screen, click **File**.

3 Select "Tab delimited file" from the *File* field drop-down menu (see Figure 5-66).

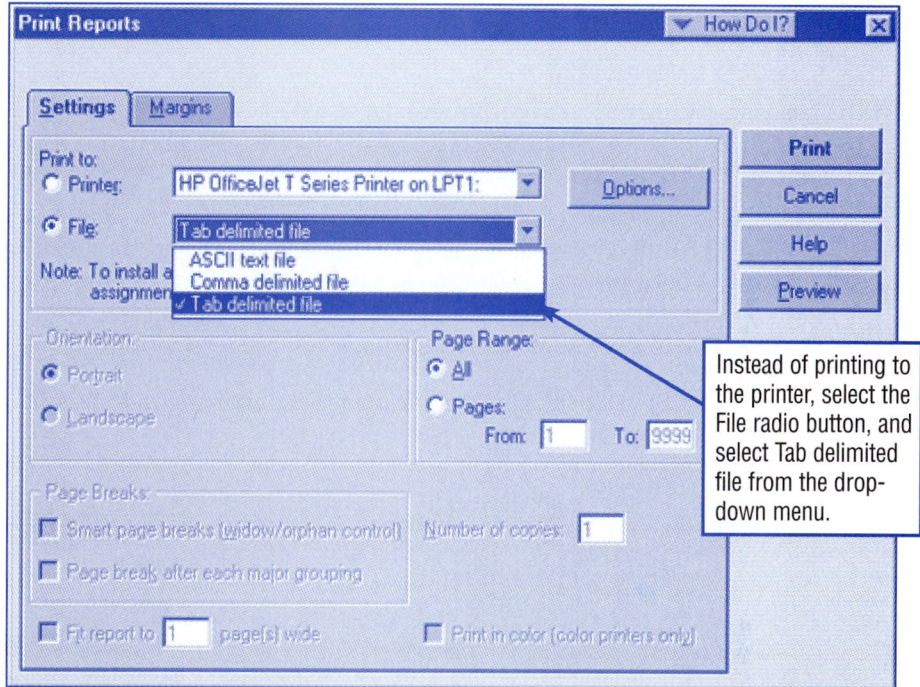

Instead of printing to the printer, select the File radio button, and select Tab delimited file from the drop-down menu.

Figure 5-66 The Settings tab of the Print Reports screen.

4 Then give the file a name that will be recognized by your spreadsheet program. Use the file extension your spreadsheet program uses (see Figure 5-67).

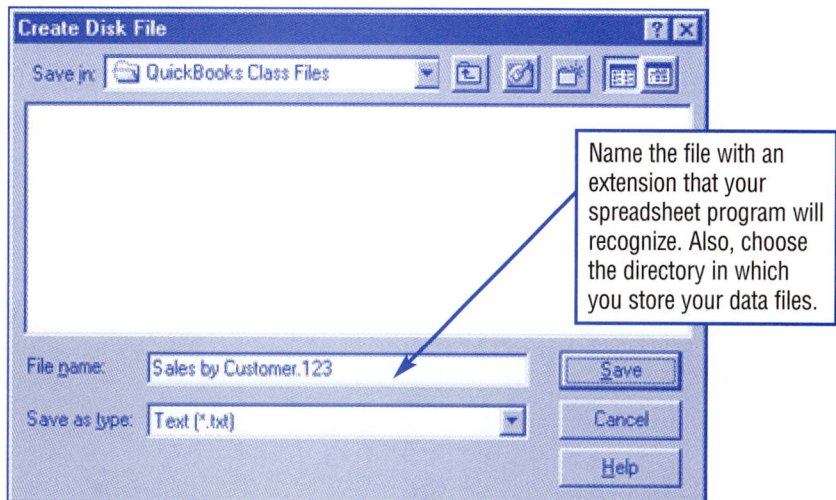

Name the file with an extension that your spreadsheet program will recognize. Also, choose the directory in which you store your data files.

Figure 5-67 Choose a file name and extension for the exported file.

⑤ Launch your spreadsheet program and open the file you just saved.

Once you have the data in your spreadsheet, you can manipulate it in any way you want. Close all open windows.

SUMMARY OF KEY POINTS

In this chapter, you learned about QuickBooks reports. There are literally thousands of reports that you can generate from QuickBooks by modifying the standard reports. You should now be familiar with how to use QuickBooks to do all of the following:

◆ Create several types of reports (Page 212)

◆ Use QuickZoom to see the numbers behind the numbers on reports (Page 230)

◆ Create graphs (Page 238)

◆ Customize the look of reports and filter the data on reports (Page 241)

◆ Memorize and group reports (Page 247)

◆ Print reports (Page 251)

◆ Use the Find command to find transactions (Page 254)

◆ Export reports to spreadsheets for further analysis (Page 259)

Name _____ **Date** _____

APPLY YOUR KNOWLEDGE

PROBLEM 5-1

> **Restore the Problem 5-1.QBB file from the CD-ROM and store it on your hard disk according to your instructor's directions.**

1. Print the reports listed below for Academy Glass.
   a. Customer phone list
   b. Check register with Transaction Details for January and February of 2002
   c. Customer QuickReport for Bill Young's Window Replacement Job for January and February 2002
   d. Profit & Loss report (standard) for January and February 2002

2. Create a budget for Academy Glass with the following data:

Account	Budget for Each Month in 2002
Product Sales	$2000.00
Serivces:Design Income	$2000.00
Services:Labor Income	$2000.00
Services:Subcontracted Labor Income	$1000.00
Purchases	$1500.00

3. Create and print a Profit & Loss Budget vs. Actual report for January and February of 2002. Print the report in Landscape mode and fit the report to one page wide.

4. Create a custom report showing the sales of all services to customers who live in Morgan Hill. Make your report match the one shown in Figure 5-68.

Custom Transaction Detail Report							How Do I? _ □ ×

Modify Report... | Memorize... | Print... | Excel... | Hide Header | Refresh

Dates | Custom ▼ | From 01/01/2002 📅 To 02/28/2002 📅 Total By Item detail ▼ | Sort By Default ▼

Academy Glass
Sales of Services to Morgan Hill Customers
January through February 2002

Type	Date	Num	Name	Memo	City	Amount
Service						
Design						
Invoice	01/09/2002	2002-104	Mason, Bob	Window Desig...	Morgan Hill	240.00 ◄
Invoice	01/09/2002	2002-104	Mason, Bob	Window Desig...	Morgan Hill	240.00
Invoice	01/09/2002	2002-104	Mason, Bob	Window Desig...	Morgan Hill	300.00
Invoice	01/09/2002	2002-104	Mason, Bob	Window Desig...	Morgan Hill	120.00
Invoice	01/09/2002	2002-104	Mason, Bob	Window Desig...	Morgan Hill	300.00
Invoice	01/26/2002	2002-106	Mason, Bob	Window Desig...	Morgan Hill	300.00
Total Design						1,500.00
Labor						
Invoice	01/09/2002	2002-104	Mason, Bob	Window/Door...	Morgan Hill	240.00
Total Labor						240.00
Subs						
Insulation						
Invoice	01/09/2002	2002-104	Mason, Bob	Insulation Se...	Morgan Hill	720.00
Total Insulation						720.00
Total Subs						720.00
Total Service						2,460.00
TOTAL						2,460.00

Figure 5-68 Customize your report to look like this.

5. Print the report you created in step 4 and then memorize it in the Customers report group.

6. Create and print a Graph of your Income and Expenses for January and February 2002.

Name _____ Date _____

Workplace Applications

DISCUSSION QUESTIONS

These questions are designed to help you apply what you are learning about QuickBooks to your own organization. Use your notebook to record your answers and your thoughts about how your company could use QuickBooks to organize information and track performance.

1. Reports generally fall into two categories—operational and managerial. Operational reports are used on a day-to-day basis in running the company. Managerial reports are used to guide policies, to set prices, and to prepare plans and budgets. What kinds of operational reports does your company produce? What kinds of managerial reports are produced?

2. Select some operational reports and identify who uses them. How are they used in running the organization? How are they used in managing your relationships with your clients?

3. How does your company set prices on the products and services it offers? What kinds of information would you need in order to understand how to set prices? What are some kinds of information that could be available in QuickBooks? What are some kinds of information that would not be in QuickBooks?

ACTIVITY

1. Select some managerial reports and identify who uses them. Explain in writing how they are used in guiding the organization's operations.

2. Write an essay on the purpose and use of the Profit & Loss, A/P Aging and A/R Collections reports.

CASE STUDY

SOFTWARE SUPPORT, INC.

Software Support, Inc. is a company that provides computer consulting services for clients throughout the Chicago metropolitan area. The company provides computer setup, training, and troubleshooting services for small business clients.

They track their income and expenses separately for each area of the business using classes. The classes are Training, Consulting, and Troubleshooting.

The owners of the company have contracted you to help them analyze their business, and they've asked you to create reports from their QuickBooks file to help them.

Questions

These questions are designed to help you apply what you are learning about QuickBooks to this case study. Use your notebook to record your answers and your thoughts.

1. Which reports would you use to present the financial position of the company at the end of last month?

2. Which report would you use to show all income and expenses separately for each class?

3. Which report would you use to show a list of open invoices, sorted by customer and totaled at the bottom?

4. Which report would you use to show which bills were paid with bill payments in the check register?

inter**NET** CONNECTION

Publicly traded companies often provide annual reports on their web sites. Use the following web addresses to review the financial statements for these corporations. What similarities do you find? How do the presentations vary? What notes accompany the financial statements?

Gannet Co.: **www.gannett.com/street/ann.htm**
SaraLee: **www.saralee.com/investor_relations/financial_reports.htm**

Inventory

After completing this chapter, you should be able to:

1. Activate the Inventory function in QuickBooks preferences.
2. Set up inventory part Items in the Item list.
3. Use QuickBooks to calculate the average cost of inventory.
4. Use QuickBooks to record inventory sales.
5. Use purchase orders to purchase inventory.
6. Receive inventory and match the receipt with a purchase order.
7. Work with item receipts and bills for inventory parts.
8. Adjust inventory quantities and values.
9. Create and print several reports for inventory.

RESTORE THIS FILE

This chapter uses Chapter 6.QBB. To open this file, restore the file called **Chapter 6.QBW** to your hard disk. See page 7 for instructions on restoring files.

n this chapter, you'll learn how to set up inventory parts, and handle all transactions involving them.

Table 6-1 shows an overview of the **accounting behind the scenes** of different business transactions that involve inventory. Familiarize yourself with this table, and refer to it when you encounter business transactions with inventory purchases or sales.

Business Transaction	QuickBooks Transaction	Accounting Entry	Comments
Purchasing Inventory with Purchase Orders	**Create Purchase Order**	Purchase orders do not post to the General Ledger. The Purchase Orders account shows all purchase orders.	You don't have to use purchase orders, but if you do, QuickBooks tracks the status of your orders and matches them with the bill from your vendor.
Receiving Inventory (no Bill from Vendor)	**Receive Items**	Increase (debit) Inventory, increase (credit) Accounts Payable. Increase inventory counts for each item received.	Use this transaction when you receive inventory items that are not accompanied by a bill. This transaction enters an "item receipt" in the Accounts Payable account. Although it increases A/P, no bill shows in the Pay Bills screen.
Receiving Inventory (with Bill from Vendor)	**Receive Items and Enter Bill**	Increase (debit) Inventory, increase (credit) Accounts Payable. Increase inventory counts for each item received.	Use this transaction when you receive inventory accompanied by a Bill from the vendor.
Entering a Bill for Previously Received Inventory Items	**Enter Bill for Received Items**	No change in debits and credits. This transaction only changes an Item Receipt transaction into a bill.	When an item receipt is turned into a bill, QuickBooks shows the bill in the Pay Bills screen. In addition, the bill shows in the Pay Bills screen.
Purchase Inventory with Check or Cash	**Write Checks**	Increase (debit) Inventory, decrease (credit) Checking.	Use this transaction when you buy inventory with a check. If you use cash to buy inventory, use the Write Checks function using a Petty Cash account.
Purchase Inventory with Credit Card	**Enter Credit Card Charges**	Increase (debit) Inventory, increase (credit) Credit Card Liability.	Use this transaction if you use a credit card to purchase Inventory and you track that credit card with a QuickBooks Credit Card account.

Table 6-1 Summary of inventory transactions

TRACKING INVENTORY WITH QUICKBOOKS

When you use inventory part Items to track your inventory, QuickBooks handles all the accounting for you automatically, according to how you set up your inventory part Items in the Item list. QuickBooks keeps a **perpetual** inventory, meaning that every purchase and every sale of inventory immediately updates all your reports.

When QuickBooks calculates the cost of inventory, it uses the weighted-average cost method, (explained on page 277). QuickBooks does not support the first-in, first-out (FIFO) or last-in, first-out (LIFO) methods.

> **KEY TERM**
>
> **Perpetual Inventory**
> A continuous record of increases, decreases, and balance on hand of inventory items.

SETTING UP INVENTORY ITEMS

To set up an inventory part in the Item list, follow these steps:

1 Select the *Lists* menu and choose **Item List**.

2 Select the *Item* menu at the bottom of the list, and then choose **New**.

3 Select "Inventory Part" from the Type drop-down list (see Figure 6-3). Then press <TAB>.

4 Enter "106-Slider" in the *Item Name/Number* field, and press <TAB>.

You might want to give each item in your inventory a part number, and then use the part numbers in the *Item Name/Number* field.

5 Skip the *Subitem of* field by clicking <TAB>.

This field allows you to create subitems of items. If you use subitems, the Sales by Item reports and graphs will show totals for all sales and costs of the subitems.

6 Enter "12 ft. Sliding Door – Wood Frame" in the *Description on Purchase Transactions* field, and press <TAB>.

The description you enter here appears as the default description when you use this Item on purchase orders and bills.

Notice that there are three account fields on the New Item screen (COGS Account, Income Account, and Asset Account). In each of these fields, enter the accounts that QuickBooks should use when you purchase, hold, or sell this item. You're specifying how QuickBooks should treat the accounting when you use this item. Each field is covered separately in this chapter.

Figure 6-3 The completed New Item screen

7 Enter "350.00" in the *Cost* field, and then press <TAB>.

Use this field to track the price you pay to your vendor for the item. QuickBooks takes this amount as the default price when you put this Item on purchase orders and bills. If the price changes, you can override the amount on the purchase orders and bills or you could edit the amount here.

8 In the *COGS Account* field "Cost of Goods Sold" is preselected. Press <TAB>.

QuickBooks uses the **COGS Account** to record the average cost of this item when you sell it. For more information on average cost, see page 277.

9 Select "Ace Glass" from the *Preferred Vendor* drop-down list, and then press <TAB>.

The *Preferred Vendor* field is used to associate the item with the vendor from whom you normally purchase this part. It's an optional field and you can leave it blank without compromising anything.

10 Press <TAB> to leave the *Description on Sales Transactions* field unchanged. The text in this field defaults to whatever you entered in the *Description on Purchase Transactions* field.

QuickBooks allows you to have two descriptions for this Item: one for purchase orders and one for sales forms. You can use your vendor's description when ordering the item and a more customer-oriented description on your Invoices and Sales Receipt forms.

11 Press <TAB> to accept the preselected sales price of 420.00 in the *Sales Price* field.

The *Sales Price* field automatically calculates based on the cost of the item plus the markup percentage entered in the company preferences. To modify this markup percentage, go to the company preferences for sales and customers.

The *Sales Price* field is where you enter how much you normally charge your customers for the Item. If the price changes, you can override it on sales forms.

12 The "Tax" *Tax Code* is preselected. Press <TAB>.

Tax Codes determine the default taxable status of the Item. Since the Tax Code called "Tax" is taxable, QuickBooks calculates sales tax on this Item when it appears on Sales Receipts and Invoices. You can override the default Tax Code on each sales form.

13 Select "Product Sales" from the Income Account drop-down list. Press <TAB>.

Choose the income account that should track sales of this item.

14 In the *Asset Account* field, "Inventory Asset" is preselected. Press <TAB>.

The Inventory Asset account is the account that tracks the cost of your inventoried products between the time you purchase them and the time you sell them.

> **NOTE**
>
> When you sell an inventory part, QuickBooks increases (credits) the income account defined for the item sold on the Invoice or Sales Receipt form.

> **NOTE**
>
> When you purchase inventory, QuickBooks increases (debits) the Inventory Asset account for the amount of the purchase price. When you sell inventory, QuickBooks decreases (credits) the Inventory Asset account and increases (debits) the COGS account for the average cost of that item at the time it is sold. For details on how QuickBooks calculates average cost, see page 277.

⑮ Enter "5" in the *Reorder Point* field, and press <TAB> (see Figure 6-4).

The QuickBooks Reminders list shows all inventory items that need to be reordered.

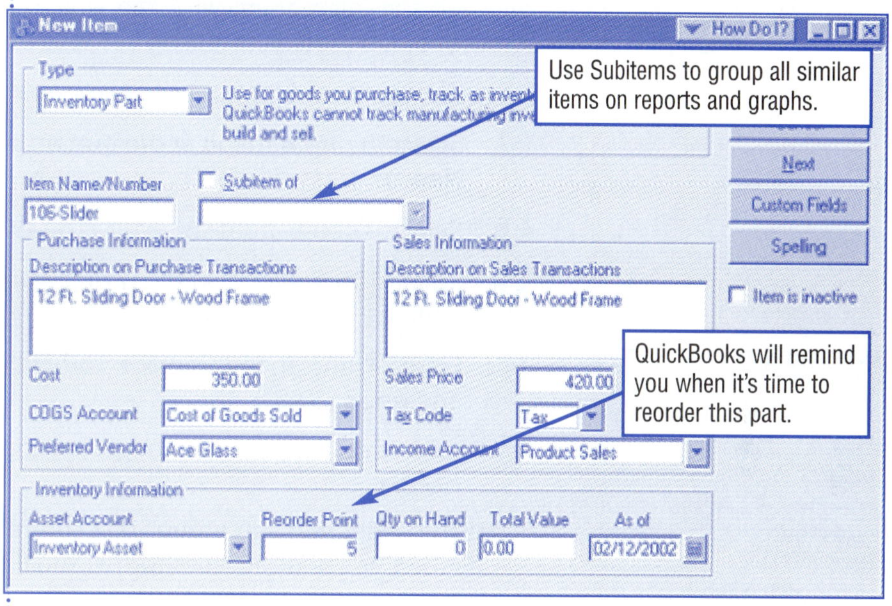

Figure 6-4 When inventory drops below the reorder point, QuickBooks reminds you to reorder.

⑯ Leave the *Qty on Hand*, *Total Value*, and *As of* fields unchanged.

⑰ Click **OK** to save the new item, and close the Item List.

NOTE

The *Qty on Hand*, *Total Value*, and *As of* fields are used during the original setup of the template file. If you enter a quantity and value on this screen, QuickBooks increases (debits) Inventory for the total value, and increases (credits) Opening Balance Equity.

However, even if you are setting up the template file it is better to leave the *Qty on Hand* and *Total Value* fields set to zero when you set up the item.

SETTING UP GROUP ITEMS

Sometimes, you sell items in bundles. For example, every time Academy Glass sells a 106-Slider Item, they also install that window. Therefore, they sell the labor along with the window. Academy Glass uses Group Items to bundle products and/or services on sales forms.

COMPUTER TUTORIAL

1 Choose **Item List** from the *Lists* menu.

2 Select the *Item* menu at the bottom of the Item list. Then choose **New** or press <Ctrl+N>.

3 Select "Group" from the Type drop-down list, and press <TAB>.

4 Enter "106 Replace" in the *Group Name/Number* field, and press <TAB>.

5 Enter "Remove and Replace 106-Slider" in the *Description* field, and press <TAB>.

6 Click the "Print items in group" box (see Figure 6-5). Press <TAB>.

The "Print items in group" box controls whether the items in the group will print on sales forms. You'll always see the items in this group on the screen version of the sales form, but the printed form shows the detail only if this box is checked.

> **NOTE**
>
> The New Item screen in Figure 6-5 does not include a *Sales Price* field. When you enter a Group item on sales forms, QuickBooks uses the sales prices of the Items within the group to calculate a total price for the group. You can override the price of each item within the group directly on the sales form.

Click this box to have your printed Invoices show the detail of each item in the group. The screen invoice will always show each individual item in the group.

List each item that is included with this group. At the right, indicate the quantities of each item. This is like defining a bill of materials for this group Item.

Figure 6-5 Specify Items in the group and whether to print Items on the sales form

7 On the first line at the bottom of the screen, select "106-Slider" from the Item drop-down list. Press <TAB>.

8 In the Qty column, enter "1." Press <TAB>.

The Qty column indicates how many of each item is included in the group.

9 On the second line at the bottom of the screen, select "Labor" from the Item drop-down list. Press <TAB>.

10 In the Qty column, enter "8."

11 Click **OK** to save the Group Item, and close all open screens.

CALCULATING AVERAGE COST OF INVENTORY

When you use an inventory Item on a purchase form (e.g. a Bill), QuickBooks increases (debits) the Inventory Asset account for the actual cost of the inventory purchase. At the same time, it recalculates the **average cost** of all Items in inventory.

When you use an inventory Item on a sales form (e.g., an Invoice), QuickBooks increases (debits) Cost of Goods Sold and decreases (credits) Inventory Asset for the average cost of the items.

Table 6-3 shows how QuickBooks calculates the average cost of inventory Items.

Situation	Calculation
You have ten 104-Sliders in stock. Each originally cost $300.	10 units x $300 per unit = $3,000 total cost
You buy three new items at $325 each.	3 units x $325 per unit = $975 cost
The combined cost in inventory.	$3,000 + $975 = $3,975
The average cost per unit is equal to the total cost of inventory divided by the total units in inventory.	$\dfrac{\text{total cost}}{\text{total units}} = \text{average cost per unit}$ $\dfrac{\$3,975}{13} = \$305.77$ average cost per unit

Table 6-3 QuickBooks calculates the average cost of inventory items.

Each time you sell inventory Items, the average cost per unit is multiplied by the number of units sold. Then this amount is deducted from the Inventory Asset account and added to the Cost of Goods Sold account.

INVOICING FOR INVENTORY ITEMS

COMPUTER TUTORIAL

Selling Inventory Items Using an Invoice Form

① Enter the Invoice as shown in Figure 6-6, recording a sale of two 104-Sliders.

Figure 6-6 Enter this data in your Invoice.

② Click **Save & New** to save the Invoice.

Creating a Transaction Journal Report

To see how this Invoice affects the General Ledger, use a Transaction Journal report.

COMPUTER TUTORIAL

① Display the invoice shown in Figure 6-6.

② Select the *Reports* menu, and then choose **Transaction Journal**. An example of this report is shown in Figure 6-7.

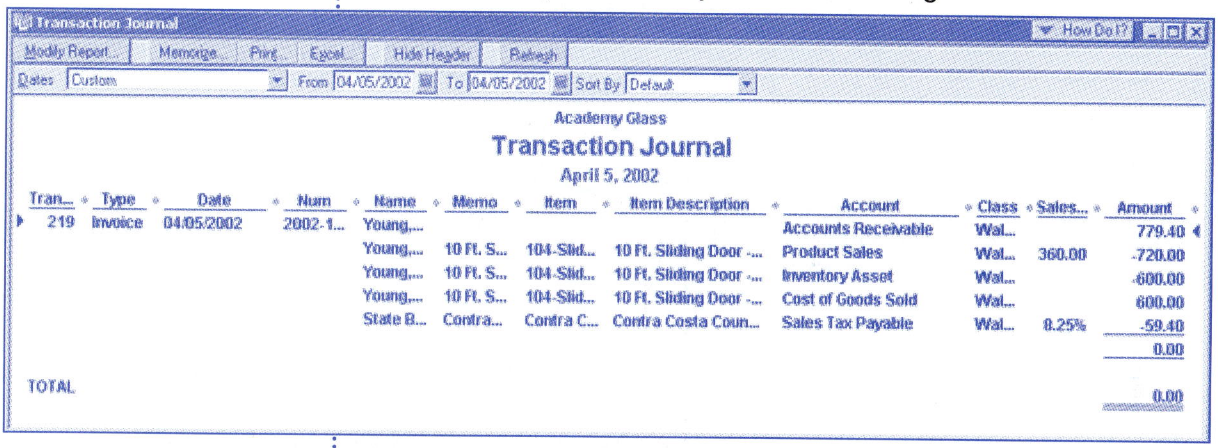

Figure 6-7 The Transaction Journal report

— ▶ **ANOTHER** ▶—
◀ **WAY** ◀—

To display the Transaction Journal, press <Ctrl+Y>.

③ To display Debit and Credit columns on this report, click **Modify Report**.

④ Scroll to the bottom of the list in the Columns section, and click the Debit and Credit lines. Also, remove the checkmarks next to Class, Memo, Sales Price and Amount (see Figure 6-8).

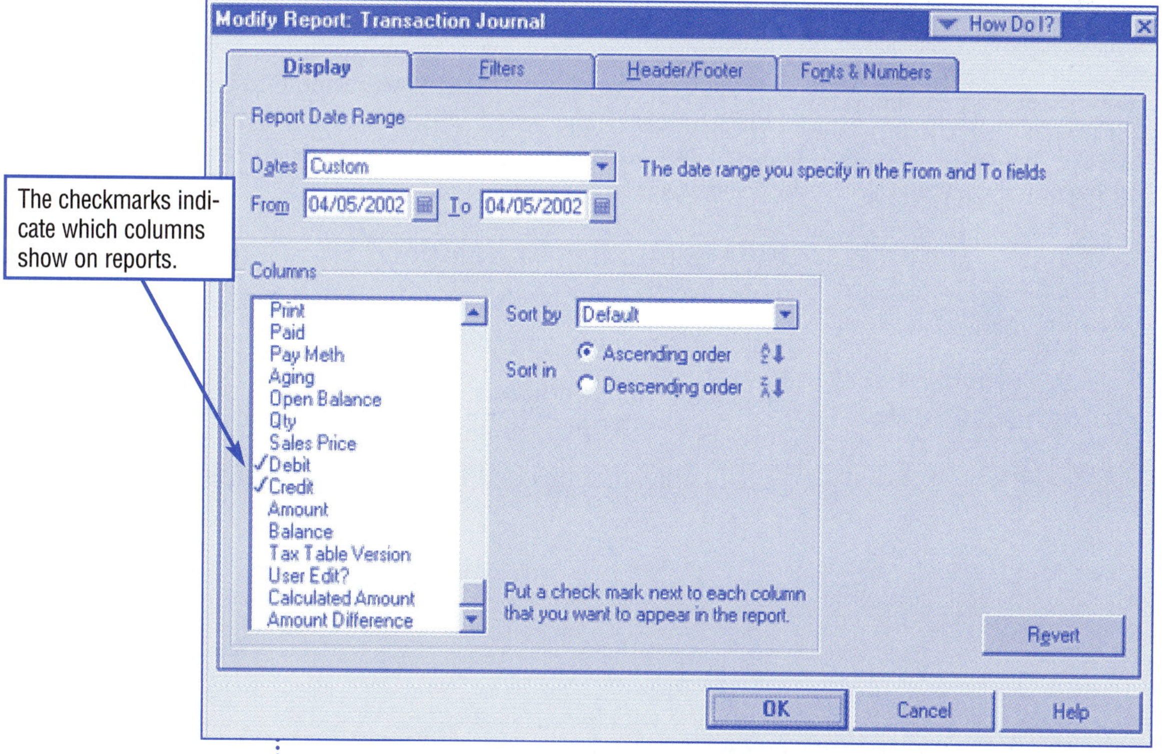

Figure 6-8 Select the columns to include on the report.

⑤ Click **OK** to see your report with Debit and Credit columns (see Figure 6-9).

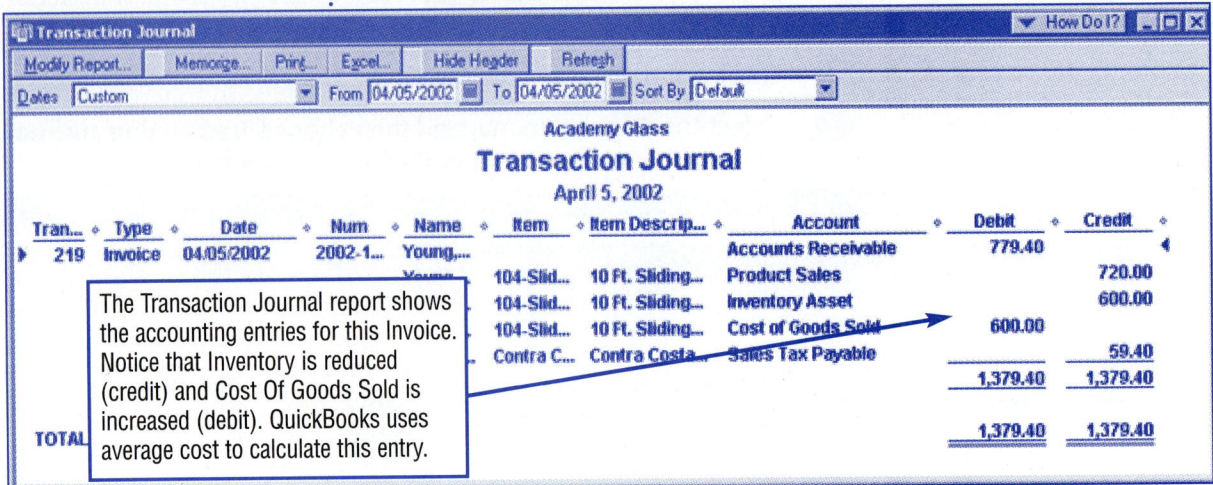

The Transaction Journal report shows the accounting entries for this Invoice. Notice that Inventory is reduced (credit) and Cost Of Goods Sold is increased (debit). QuickBooks uses average cost to calculate this entry.

Figure 6-9 The Transaction Journal report with Debit and Credit columns

⑥ Close the report by clicking the close box (**X**) in the upper right corner. Click **No** when prompted to memorize the report.

NOTE

You can enter or modify reorder quantities in the Edit Item screen for each Inventory item. To access the Edit Item screen, choose Item List from the *Lists* menu. Then choose **Edit** from the *Item* menu at the bottom of the Item List.

COMPUTER TUTORIAL

USING PURCHASE ORDERS

In order to track inventory purchases by item and to easily determine which items you have on order, use purchase orders when you purchase inventory.

If you use purchase orders, you'll be able to create reports that show what is on order and when it is due to arrive from your supplier. Also, you can see which purchase orders are open, even if you've partially received items on the order.

Using Reminders to Reorder

Because you sold two 104-Sliders and inventory fell below five units, QuickBooks reminds you that it's time to reorder.

① Select the *Company* menu, and then select **Reminders** (see Figure 6-10).

② Double-click on the Inventory to Reorder line.

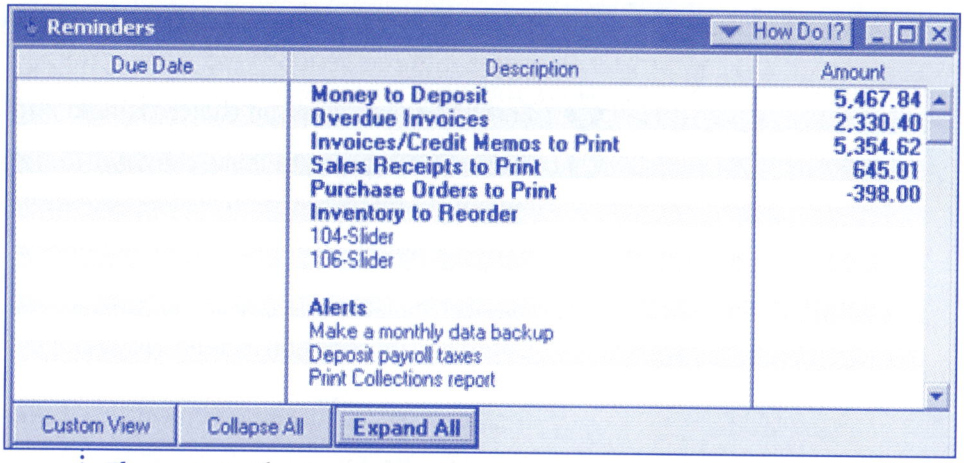

Figure 6-10 The Reminders List

Creating Purchase Orders

Create a Purchase Order to reorder inventory, filling out each item and quantity. Purchase orders do not post to the Chart of Accounts. However, QuickBooks tracks Purchase Orders in a non-posting account called **Purchase Orders**. You can see this account at the bottom of your Chart of Accounts.

COMPUTER TUTORIAL

❶ Select the **Vendors** menu and then choose **Create Purchase Orders** (see Figure 6-11).

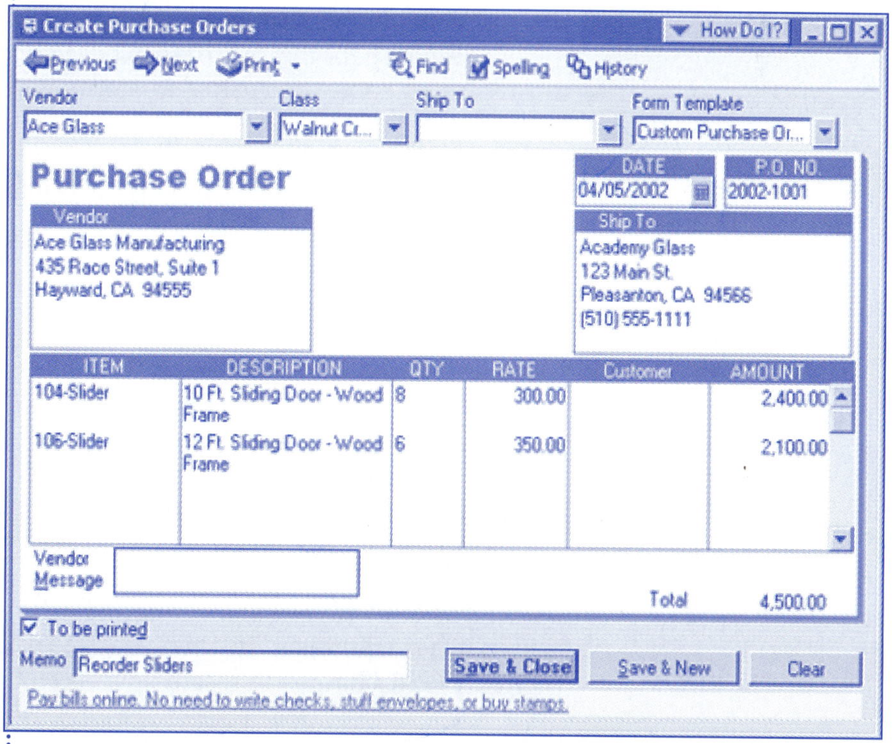

NOTE

Since Purchase Orders are non-posting, QuickBooks does not include Purchase Orders on the Reminders or Pay Bills screens. See page 287 for more information on tracking Purchase Orders in QuickBooks.

Figure 6-11 The Create Purchase Orders screen

2 Select "Ace Glass" from the Vendor drop-down list or type the name into the *Vendor* field. Press <TAB>.

3 Enter "Walnut Creek" in the *Class* field and press <TAB>.

4 Press <TAB> twice to leave the *Ship To* field blank and to accept "Custom Purchase Order" as the default form template.

If you wanted the order shipped directly to one of your customers, you would enter the customer in the *Ship To* field. By default, QuickBooks enters your company's address from the Company Information screen. To change your Ship To address, you could override it here or select the **Company** menu, and then choose **Company Information**. Then click **Ship** to address.

5 Enter "04/05/2002" in the *Date* field, and press <TAB>.

6 Press <TAB> to accept the default Purchase Order number of "2002–1001."

QuickBooks automatically numbers your Purchase Orders in the same way it numbers Invoices. It increases the number by one for each new purchase order. However, you can override this number if necessary.

7 Press <TAB> twice to accept the preselected vendor address and ship-to address.

8 Enter the 104-Slider and 106-Slider items in the body of the purchase order, as shown in Figure 6-11.

The Customer column allows you to associate your purchases with the customer or job to which you want to assign the expense for this purchase. Since you're purchasing inventory, you don't know the customer information, so don't use this column.

9 Enter "Reorder sliders" in the *Memo* field, and press <TAB>.

10 Click the **Print** icon to print the purchase order on blank paper.

11 When you have finished printing it, click **Save & Close** to save the Purchase Order.

RECEIVING INVENTORY

There are several ways to record the receipt of inventory in QuickBooks. How you record the receipts depends on when you receive the inventory and how you pay for it.

You could pay for items at the time you receive them. For example, you may be at your vendor's store and write a check or charge your credit card for the items. In this case, you'll use **Write Checks** or **Enter Credit Card Charges** to record your receipt of inventory.

In another example, you could issue a purchase order and later receive part or all of the order, but the bill doesn't accompany the shipment. In this case, you'll use the **Receive Items** function. When the bill comes, you'll use the **Enter Bill for Received Items** function. If you receive the bill when you receive the order, you'll use the **Receive Items and Enter Bill** function.

The Receive Items and the Receive Items and Enter Bill functions both record transactions that are connected to Purchase Orders. This connection is used by QuickBooks to track which purchase orders are open and which purchase orders are closed.

Purchasing Inventory at Retail with Check or Credit Card

If you buy inventory at a retail store, use the **Write Checks** or **Enter Credit Card Charges** functions to record the purchase. Make sure you record which items you purchase using the Items tab at the bottom of the check or credit card charge (see Figure 6-12).

> **DON'T ENTER THE TRANSACTION SHOWN IN FIGURE 6-12. IT IS FOR REFERENCE ONLY.**

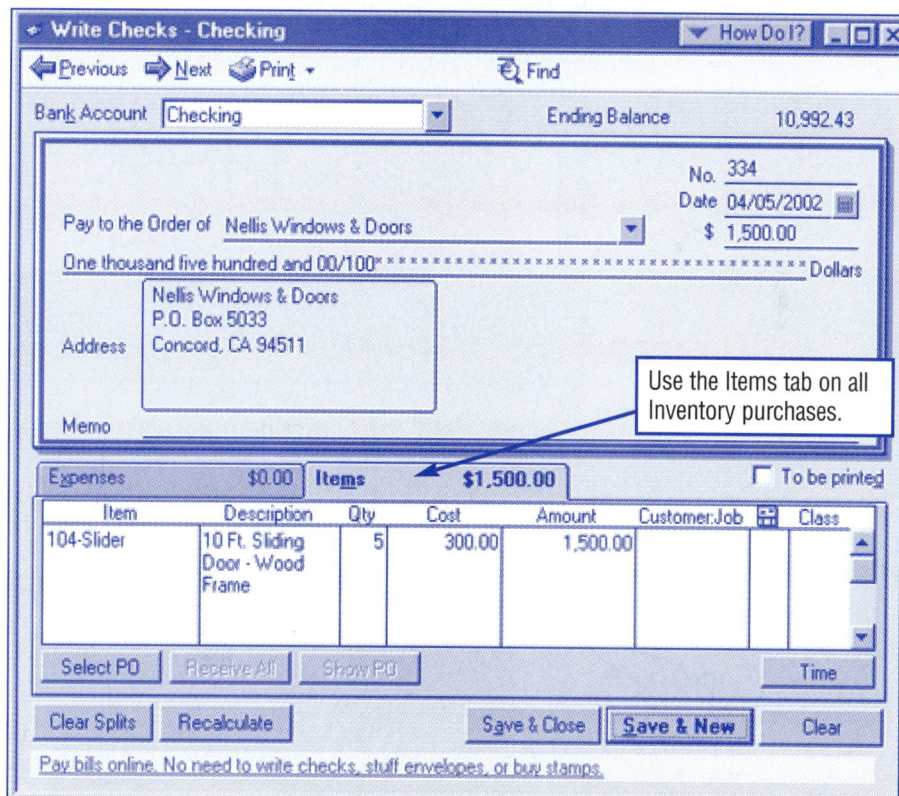

Figure 6-12 Use the Items tab to record a purchase.

COMPUTER TUTORIAL

Receiving Shipments

If you use Purchase Orders and you receive a partial or full shipment without a Bill, follow these steps:

① Select the *Vendors* menu, and then choose **Receive Items**. The Create Item Receipts screen opens.

② Enter "Ace Glass" in the *Vendor* field (see Figure 6-13) and press <TAB>.

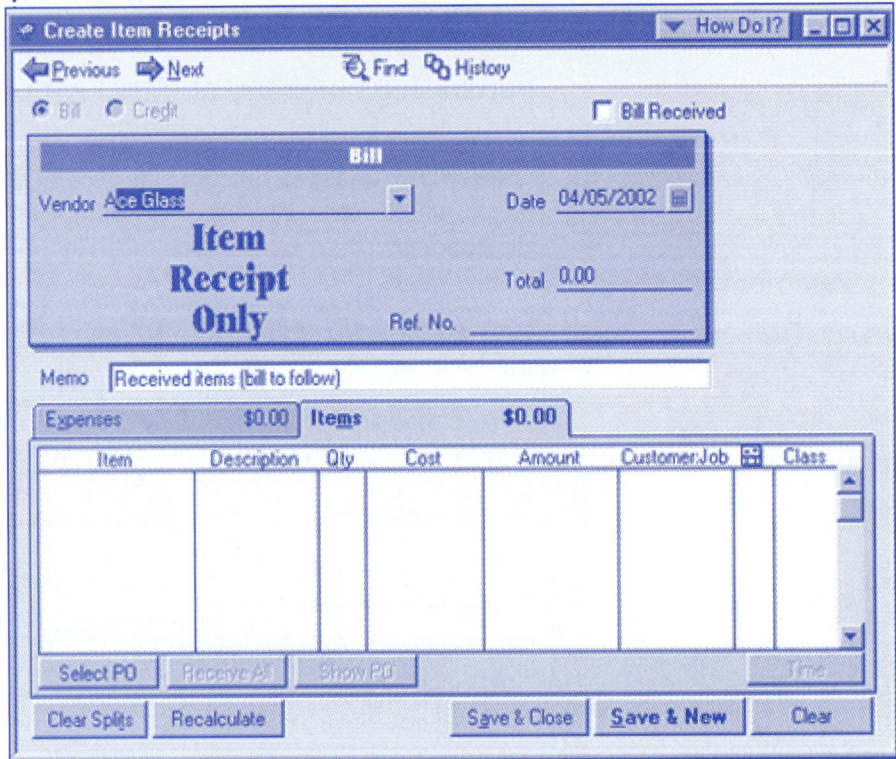

Figure 6-13 The Create Item Receipts screen

③ Since there is an open Purchase Order for this vendor, QuickBooks displays the message in Figure 6-14. Click **Yes**.

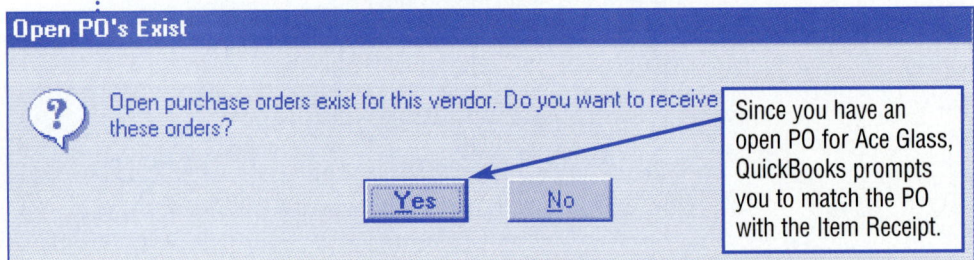

Since you have an open PO for Ace Glass, QuickBooks prompts you to match the PO with the Item Receipt.

Figure 6-14 QuickBooks displays an Open POs Exist message, if applicable.

④ Select the Purchase Order you're receiving against from the list in Figure 6-15 by clicking in the √ column, and click **OK**.

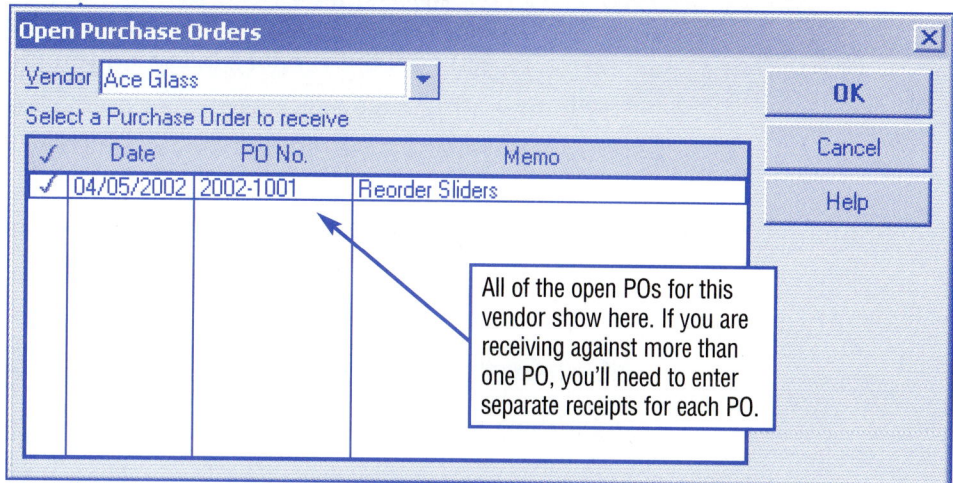

Figure 6-15 The Open Purchase Orders screen

⑤ QuickBooks automatically fills in the Item Receipt with the information from the Purchase Order as shown in Figure 6-16.

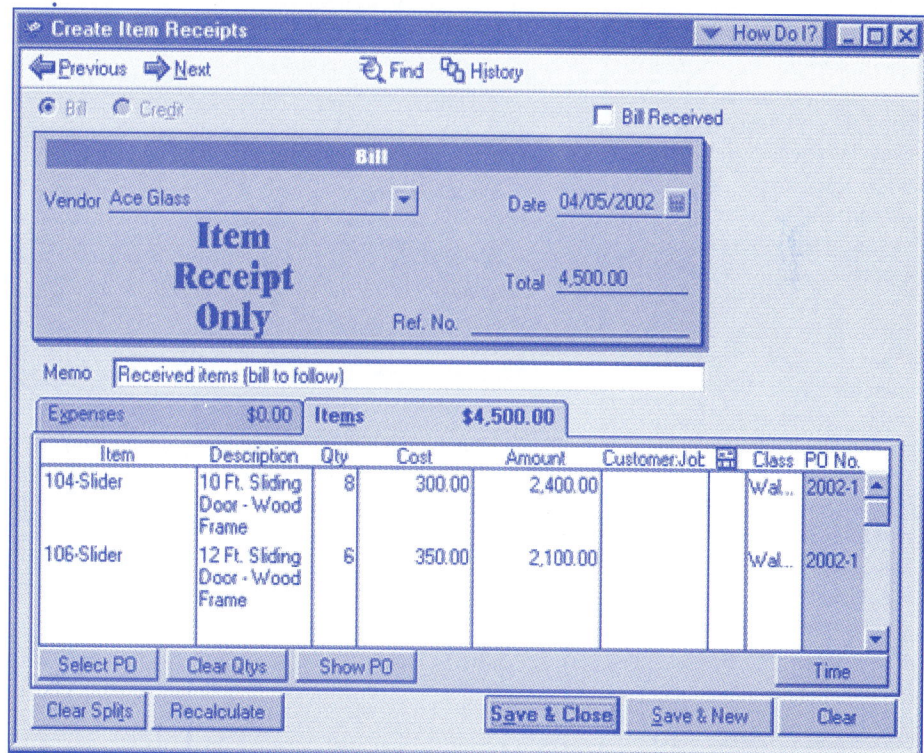

Figure 6-16 The Create Item Receipts screen is automatically filled in.

⑥ Enter "04/05/2002" in the *Date* field. Press <TAB> twice.

7 Enter "4431" in the *Ref. No.* field (see Figure 6-17).

In the Ref. No. field you enter the shipper number on the packing slip that accompanies the shipment. This helps you match the receipt with the vendor's bill when you receive it.

8 Tab to the Qty column. Change the quantity to "4" for the 104-Slider, and to "3" for the 106-Slider (see Figure 6-17).

Do not worry about the Cost column. You haven't received the bill yet, so QuickBooks uses the amounts you put on the Purchase Order. When you get the actual bill for this shipment, you'll correct or adjust the Cost column.

NOTE

Although you haven't received the bill yet, QuickBooks adds the amount from this Item Receipt to the balance of Accounts Payable. This transaction keeps your General Ledger in balance. Remember, the accounting equation states that Assets = Liabilities + Equity and because you increased an asset by receiving the inventory, QuickBooks increases a liability to keep the balance. The transaction increases (debits) Inventory (for the actual cost) and increases (credits) Accounts Payable. Also, because you received only part of the order, the Purchase Order remains "open."

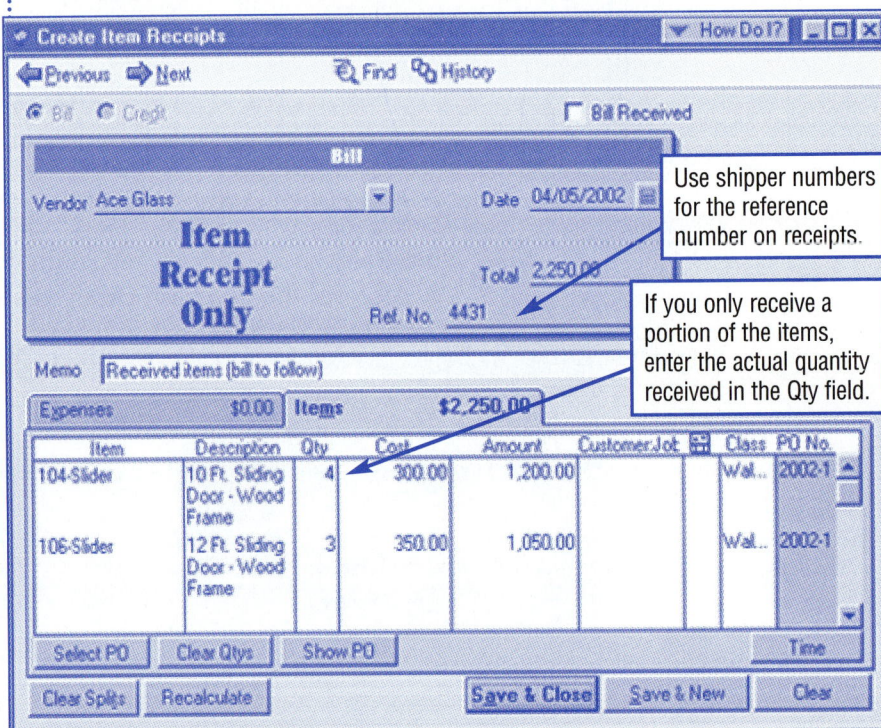

Figure 6-17 Use the shipper number in the Ref. No. field.

9 To save the Item Receipt, click **Save & Close**.

You have now recorded the receipt of inventory and QuickBooks has updated your inventory on hand as well as your Accounts Payable balance.

COMPUTER TUTORIAL

Creating Open Purchase Orders Reports

1 Select the *Reports* menu, choose **Purchases**, and then choose **Open Purchase Orders**.

This report (see Figure 6-18) shows the total dollar amount for *all* open purchase orders, not just the open balance of each Purchase Order. To see the open balance on a Purchase Order, double-click on it from this report.

Although you've partially received on this PO, it is still "open." Double-click on the PO to see more detail.

Academy Glass
Open Purchase Orders
All Transactions

Type	Date	Name	Num	Deliv Date	Amount
Purchase Order	04/05/2002	Ace Glass	2002-1001	04/05/2002	4,500.00
▶ Total					4,500.00

Figure 6-18 The Open Purchase Orders report

COMPUTER TUTORIAL

Checking Purchase Order Status

To check the status of a purchase order or to change or cancel a purchase order, edit the purchase order directly.

1 Display the Purchase Order by double-clicking on it from the Open Purchase Orders report shown in Figure 6-18, or by selecting it from the list that displays when you choose **Purchase Orders List** from the *Vendors* menu.

2 Review the quantity of each Item in the Rcv'd column.

NOTE

If you know you won't be receiving items on a Purchase Order, you can close specific line items or close the whole order. To *close* any line of the order, click in the Clsd column. To *close* the whole order and cancel the rest of the order, click the "Closed" box at the bottom left.

If you cancel an order, don't forget to notify your vendor.

On the screen in Figure 6-19, you can see that Academy Glass has received four 104-Sliders and three 106-Sliders.

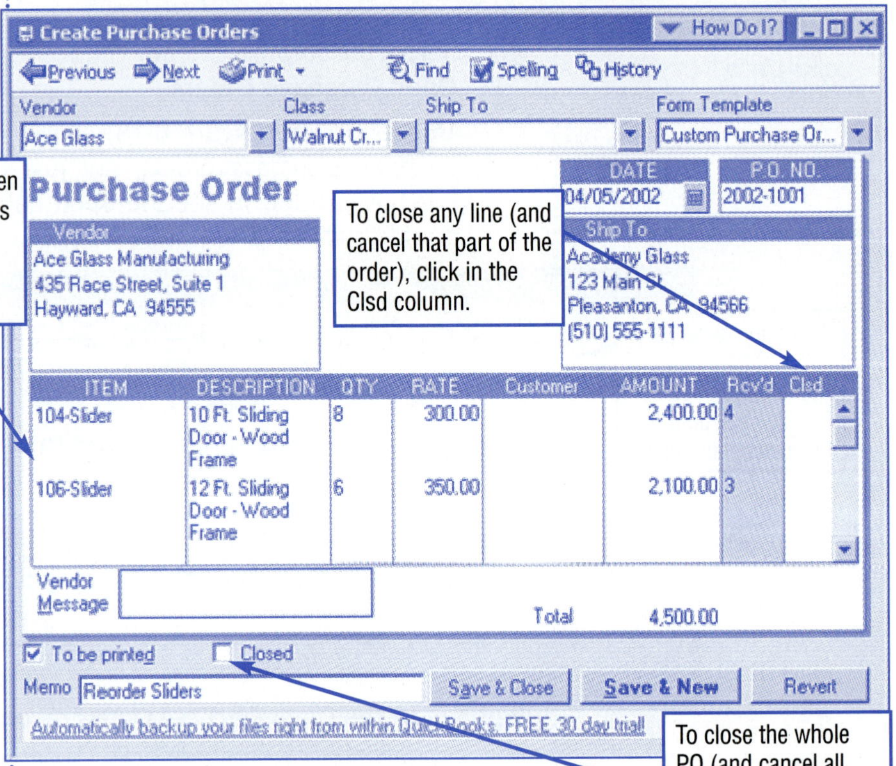

You can see what's been received already on this PO. The whole PO remains "open" until all items are received.

To close any line (and cancel that part of the order), click in the Clsd column.

Figure 6-19 Edit the purchase order as necessary.

To close the whole PO (and cancel all outstanding orders), click the Closed box.

> **NOTE**
>
> Although QuickBooks tracks the status of your back-ordered purchases, (holding open the Purchase Orders until the whole order is received), it does not have any features to help you track back orders for your customers. That is, you are not able to take an "order" in QuickBooks, ship part of it, and have QuickBooks track the unshipped portion.

3 Close the screen without making any changes to the purchase order.

COMPUTER TUTORIAL

Entering the Final Shipment

① Select the *Vendors* menu, and choose **Receive Items**. The Create Item Receipts screen opens.

② Enter "Ace Glass" in the *Vendor* field, and press <TAB> (see Figure 6-20).

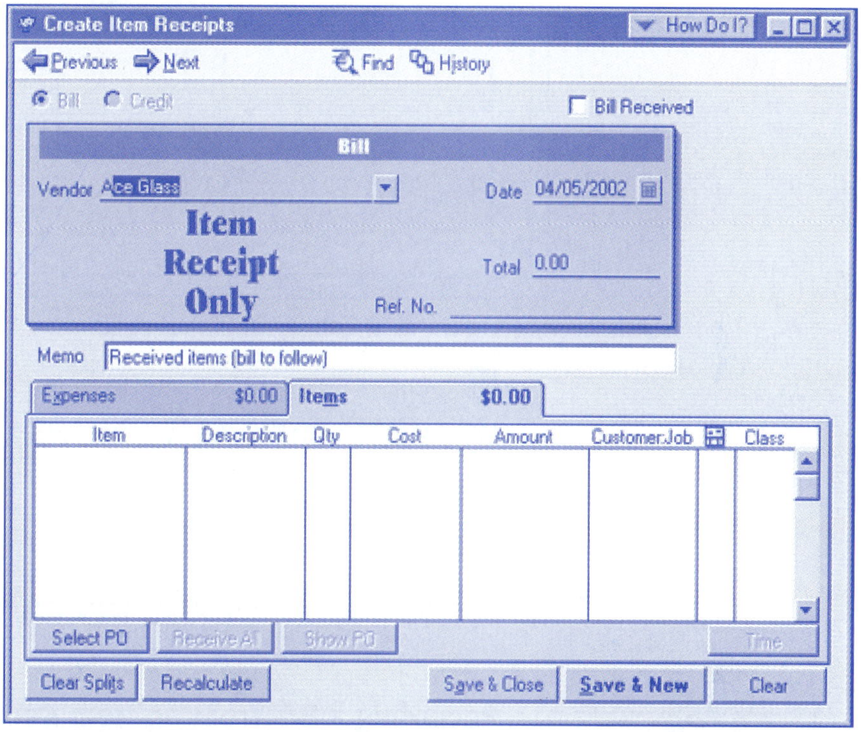

Figure 6-20 Enter the Vendor name in the Create Item Receipts screen.

③ Because there is an open Purchase Order for this vendor, QuickBooks displays the message shown in Figure 6-21. Click **Yes**.

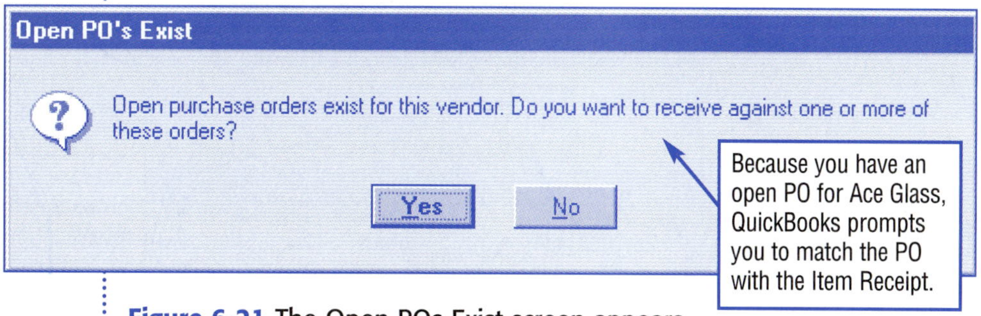

Because you have an open PO for Ace Glass, QuickBooks prompts you to match the PO with the Item Receipt.

Figure 6-21 The Open POs Exist screen appears.

4 Select the Purchase Order you're receiving against from the list (see Figure 6-22) and click **OK**. QuickBooks automatically fills in the item receipt with the information from the purchase order.

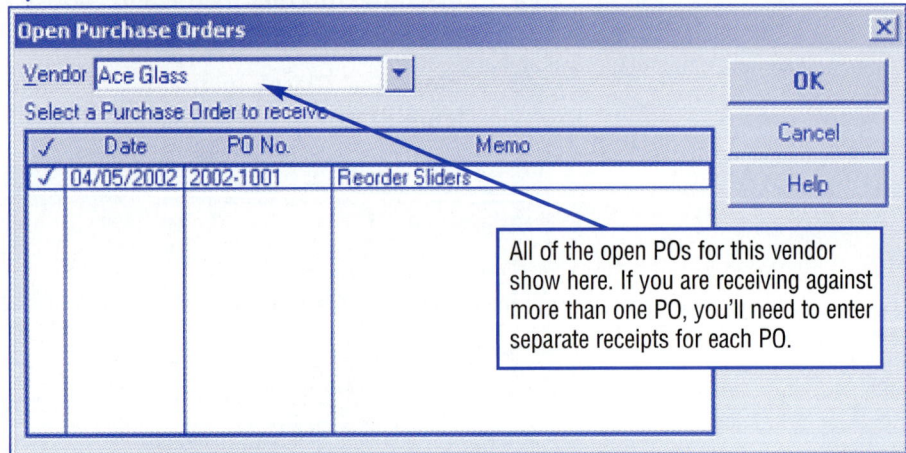

Open Purchase Orders

Vendor: Ace Glass

Select a Purchase Order to receive

✓	Date	PO No.	Memo
✓	04/05/2002	2002-1001	Reorder Sliders

OK

Cancel

Help

All of the open POs for this vendor show here. If you are receiving against more than one PO, you'll need to enter separate receipts for each PO.

Figure 6-22 The Open Purchase Orders screen

5 Enter "04/05/2002" in the *Date* field.

6 Enter "4441" in the *Ref. No.* field.

7 Click **Save & Close** to record the receipt.

ENTERING BILLS FOR RECEIVED INVENTORY

COMPUTER TUTORIAL

Recording a Bill from an Item Receipt

1 Select the ***Vendors*** menu, and then choose **Enter Bill for Received Items**.

2 Enter "Ace Glass" in the *Vendor* field and press <TAB>.

Select Item Receipt   ▼ How Do I?

Vendor: Ace Glass

Choose the Item Receipt which corresponds to your bill

OK

Cancel

Date	Ref No.	Memo
04/05/2002	4431	Received items (bill to follow)
04/05/2002	4441	Received items (bill to follow)

Enter the vendor name and press <TAB> to see a list of shipments received from this vendor.

Select one shipment at a time to record the amount of the bill for each.

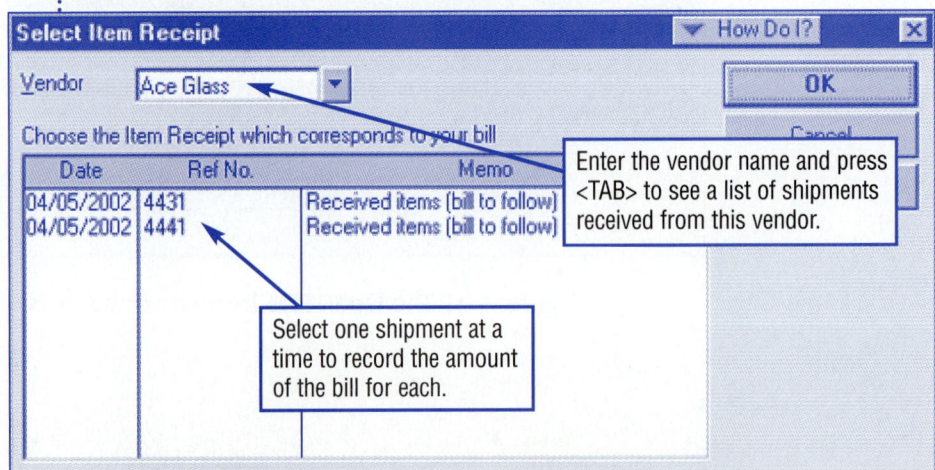

Figure 6-23 Select one shipment at a time.

③ Select the first line on the screen shown in Figure 6-23, and click **OK**.

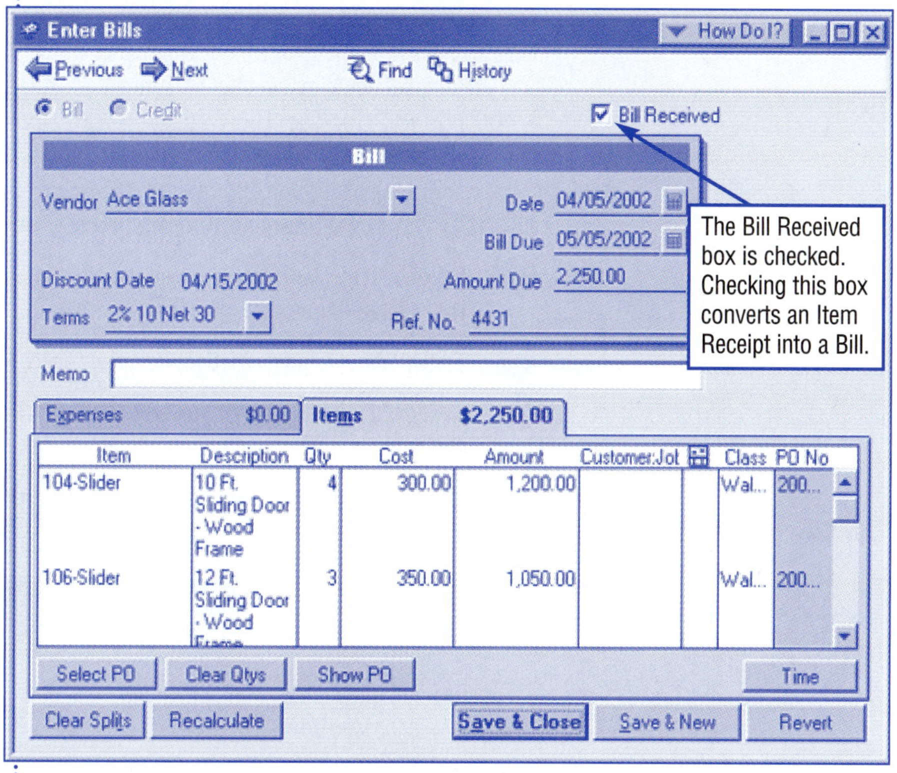

The Bill Received box is checked. Checking this box converts an Item Receipt into a Bill.

Figure 6-24 The Enter Bills screen

④ QuickBooks displays the Item Receipt and automatically checks the "Bill Received" box (see Figure 6-24). Checking the "Bill Received" box converts the Item Receipt into a Bill. Verify that the Bill matches your records and make changes to price, terms, due date, or any other field that doesn't match the vendor's bill. If you have a discrepancy, see *Handling Overshipments or Handling Vendor Overcharges* (page 293).

⑤ Click **Save & Close** to record the bill.

⑥ Click **Yes** when you see the Recording Transaction message.

NOTE

QuickBooks doesn't add a new transaction when you use the Enter Bill for Received Items function. That's because you've already recorded an Item Receipt, which increases Inventory and Accounts Payable. This function simply converts your Item Receipt into a Bill.

Adding Freight Charges When Receiving Inventory

Assume that the freight charges for Item Receipt #4441 were $126.00. For this example, you'll allocate the freight cost to the items proportionally to the weight of each product.

The total weight of the shipment is 800 pounds (for the 104-Sliders) + 400 pounds (for the 106-Sliders) = 1200 pounds. The 104-Sliders should therefore absorb eight-twelfths (8 ÷ 12 = 67%) of the total freight cost. The allocation of total freight to the 104-Sliders is $84.42 ($126 x 67% = $84.42). The 106-Sliders should absorb the remainder of the cost ($41.58).

COMPUTER TUTORIAL

❶ Select the **Vendors** menu, and then choose **Enter Bill for Received Items**.

❷ Enter "Ace Glass" in the *Vendor* field and press <TAB>.

❸ Select "Ref No. 4441" in the Select Item Receipt screen, and click **OK**.

❹ QuickBooks displays the Item Receipt and automatically checks the "Bill Received" box (see Figure 6-25).

Figure 6-25 The Enter Bills screen for Item Receipt #4441

❺ Add the freight allocations to each item in the Amount column. Manually override the Amount column on each line of the bill as shown on the screen in Figure 6-26. This forces a recalculation of the Cost column. Notice that QuickBooks recalculates the cost to the nearest tenth of a cent.

❻ Click **Recalculate** to update the *Amount Due* field.

❼ Click **Save & Close** to record the bill.

NOTE

Adding the freight charges to each inventory part Item as shown, increases the total cost (and average cost) of each item in inventory. This method of proportionally adding freight-in charges to each inventory part is known as *capitalizing freight-in.*

8 When the Recording Transaction message appears, click **Yes**.

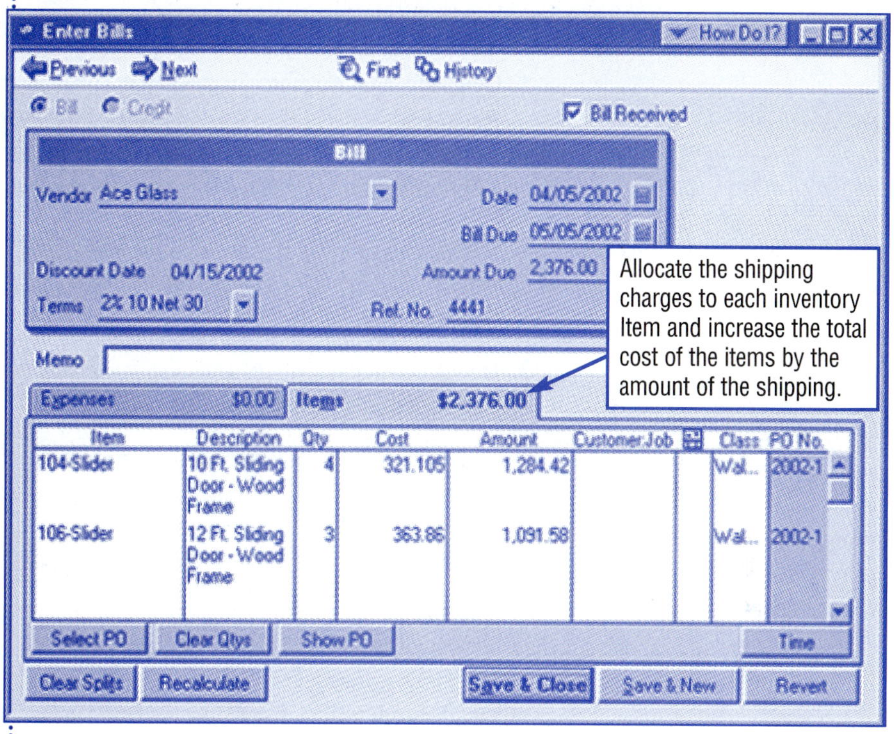

Allocate the shipping charges to each inventory Item and increase the total cost of the items by the amount of the shipping.

Figure 6-26 Add the freight charge to the Amount column.

Handling Overshipments

If your vendor ships more than you ordered on a Purchase Order, you have three choices. First, you could refuse the extra shipment and send it back to the vendor without recording anything in QuickBooks. Second, you could receive the extra shipment into inventory and keep it (and pay for it). Third, you could receive the extra shipment into inventory, and then send it back and record a bill credit in QuickBooks.

Don't perform these steps now. They are for reference only.

If you keep the overshipment (and pay for it):

1. Override the number in the Qty column on the Item Receipt so that it exceeds the quantity on your Purchase Order. This increases the Inventory Asset and Accounts Payable accounts for the total amount of the shipment, including the overshipment.

2. When the bill arrives from the vendor, match it with the Item Receipt and pay the amount actually due. Unless you edit the Purchase Order, it will not match the Item Receipt or Bill. This may be important later when you look at Purchase Orders and actual purchase costs, so consider updating your Purchase Order to match the actual costs.

> **Don't perform these steps now. They are for reference only.**

If you send the overshipment back after receiving it into inventory:

1. Override the number in the Qty column on the Item Receipt so that it exceeds the quantity on your Purchase Order. This increases the Inventory Asset and Accounts Payable accounts for the total amount of the shipment, including the overshipment.

2. When you return the excess items, create a Bill Credit for the vendor. On the Bill Credit, enter the quantity returned and the cost for each item.

3. If you receive a refund from the vendor, record the refund as explained in Chapter 3.

4. To apply the Bill Credit to an unpaid bill for that vendor, use the Pay Bills screen as explained in Chapter 3.

Handling Vendor Overcharges

If you have a discrepancy between your purchase order and the vendor's bill, there are several ways to handle it.

If the vendor overcharged you, the vendor might agree to revise the bill and send you a new one. In this case, wait for the new bill before recording anything in QuickBooks.

On the other hand, you might decide to pay the incorrect bill and have the vendor adjust the next bill. In that case, use the Expenses tab on the Bill to track the error.

COMPUTER TUTORIAL

1. Select the *Vendors* menu and then choose **Enter Bills**.

2. Click **Previous** on the Enter Bills screen to retrieve Bill #4441.

3. Select the Expenses tab to record a $48.00 overcharge from the vendor. Use the Miscellaneous expense account to track the overcharge (see Figure 6-27).

4. Click **Recalculate** to update the *Amount Due* field.

5. Click **Save & Close**. Click **Yes** on the Recording Transaction message screen.

   Since the Bill in Figure 6-27 is $48.00 more than the vendor's records, the vendor will issue you a refund check or will apply the overpayment to a future bill.

Figure 6-27 Record a vendor overcharge in the Expenses tab.

> Depending on the vendor's action, do one of the following:
>
> ◆ If the vendor *refunds* your money, add the refund directly onto your next deposit, as explained in Chapter 3.
>
> ◆ If the vendor sends you a *credit memo*, enter a Bill Credit as explained in Chapter 3.

ADJUSTING INVENTORY

QuickBooks automatically adjusts inventory each time you purchase or sell inventory Items. However, it may be necessary to manually adjust inventory after a physical count of your inventory, or in case of an increase or decrease in the value of your inventory on hand. For example, you might decrease the value of your inventory if it has lost value due to new technology trends.

Adjusting the Quantity of Inventory on Hand

COMPUTER TUTORIAL

① Select the *Vendors* menu, choose **Inventory Activities**, and then choose **Adjust Quantity/Value on Hand** (see Figure 6-28).

② Enter "04/30/2002" in the *Adjustment Date* field, and press <TAB>.

③ Enter "2002–1" in the *Ref. No.* field, and press <TAB>.

④ Enter "Inventory Variance" in the *Adjustment Account* field, and press <TAB>.

QuickBooks uses the Adjustment Account to offset the change in your Inventory Asset due to this adjustment. Inventory Variance is a commonly used expense account, but you can use whatever account is best for your records.

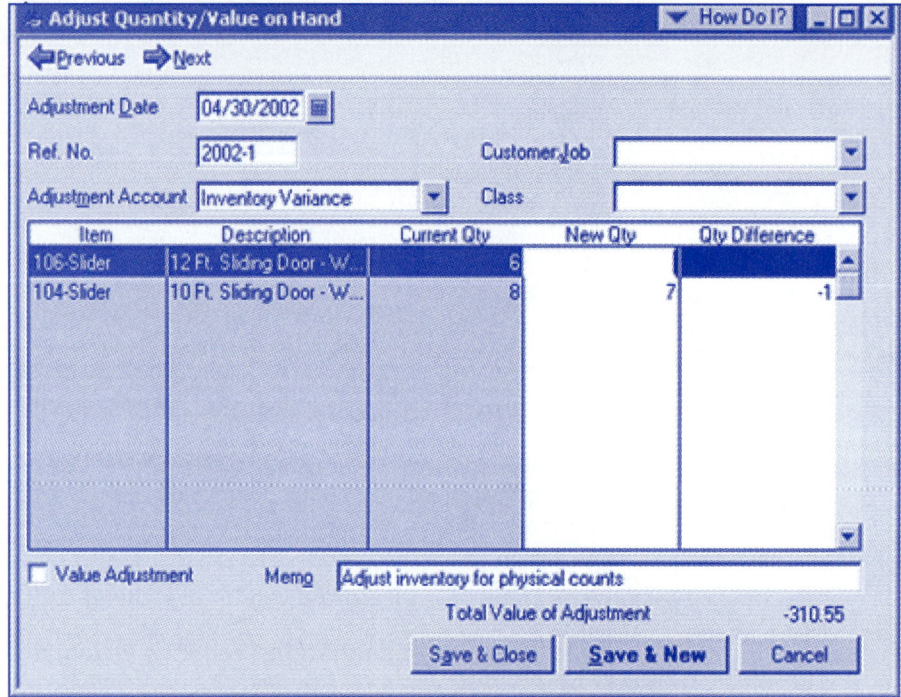

Figure 6-28 The Adjust Quantity/Value on Hand screen

⑤ Skip to the New Qty column. Enter "7" on the 104-Slider line, and press <TAB>.

Notice that QuickBooks calculates the quantity difference (-1) in the Qty Difference column. Also, notice that QuickBooks automatically calculates the Total Value of Adjustment in the bottom right corner. QuickBooks uses the *average cost method* to calculate this value. Look at the Inventory Valuation Detail report later in this chapter to see how the average cost changes each time you purchase or adjust inventory in this way.

⑥ To save the adjustment, click **Save & New**.

COMPUTER TUTORIAL

Adjusting the Value of Inventory

1 At the bottom left of the Adjust Quantity/Value on Hand screen, click on the "Value Adjustment" box (see Figure 6-29).

Figure 6-29 Click on the Value Adjustment box to change inventory value.

2 Enter "1,800.00" in the New Value column on the 106-Slider line and press <TAB>.

Notice that QuickBooks calculates the Total Value of Adjustment.

3 Click **Save & Close** to save the adjustment.

QuickBooks will post the amount of this adjustment ($1,800) to the General Ledger. Since this adjustment lowers the value of the 106-Sliders, it reduces the average cost of each unit on hand. Therefore, the next time you sell a 106-Slider, QuickBooks will transfer the new (lower) average cost out of Inventory and into Cost of Goods Sold.

NOTE

Inventory adjustments always affect your Inventory Asset account. If the Total Value of Adjustment is a positive number, the Inventory account increases (debit) by that amount, and the Adjustment Account decreases (credit). If the Total Value of Adjustment is a negative number, the debits and the credits are reversed.

CREATING INVENTORY REPORTS

QuickBooks provides several reports for inventory analysis, all of which are customizable in similar ways to other reports.

For daily management of inventory, use the Stock Status by Item report, the Stock Status by Vendor report, or the Inventory Valuation Summary report. These reports give a quick overview of inventory counts, inventory values, and pending orders.

For detailed research about transactions involving Inventory, use the Inventory Item QuickReport, or the Inventory Valuation Detail report.

Inventory Item QuickReport

The Inventory Item QuickReport is useful for seeing all transactions involving an inventory part.

COMPUTER TUTORIAL

① From the *Lists* menu, choose **Item List**.

② Click on the **104-Slider** Item.

③ Select "QuickReport: 104-Slider" from the *Reports* menu at the bottom of the Item list.

④ Set the *From* date to "01/01/2002" and the *To* date to "04/30/2002." Then press <TAB> (see Figure 6-30).

⑤ Close the report by clicking the close box (**X**) in the upper right corner of the screen.

```
Inventory Item QuickReport                              ▼ How Do I?  _ □ ✕

 Modify Report...   Memorize...   Print...   Excel...    Hide Header    Refresh
 Dates  Custom              ▼   From 01/01/2002 ▦  To 04/30/2002 ▦  Sort By  Default       ▼

                               Academy Glass
                        Inventory Item QuickReport
                            As of April 30, 2002
```

Type	Date	Num	Name	Memo	Qty
104-Slider					
On Hand As Of 12/31/2001					6
Invoice	01/13/2002	2002-99	Young, Bill:Win...	10 ft. Sliding...	-2 ◄
Invoice	02/28/2002	2002-109	Garrison, John...	10 Ft. Slidin...	-2
Invoice	04/05/2002	2002-112	Young, Bill:Win...	10 Ft. Slidin...	-2
Bill	04/05/2002	4431	Ace Glass	10 Ft. Slidin...	4
Bill	04/05/2002	4441	Ace Glass	10 Ft. Slidin...	4
Inventory...	04/30/2002	2002-1		104-Slider In...	-1
Tot On Hand As Of 04/30/2002					7
On Order As Of 12/31/2001					0
Purchase...	04/05/2002	2002-1001	Ace Glass	10 Ft. Slidin...	0
Tot On Order As Of 04/30/2002					0
TOTAL As Of 04/30/2002					7

Figure 6-30 The Inventory Item QuickReport

Inventory Stock Status by Item Report

The Stock Status by Item report is useful for getting a quick snapshot of each inventory part and the number of units on hand and on order. Also, this report gives you information about your inventory turnover, showing a sales per week column.

COMPUTER TUTORIAL

1 Select the *Reports* menu, choose **Inventory**, and then choose **Inventory Stock Status by Item**.

2 Set the *From* date to "01/01/2002" and the *To* date to "04/30/2002." Then press <TAB>(see Figure 6-31).

3 To close the report, click the close box (**X**) at the top right corner of the screen. Click **No** when you are prompted to memorize the report.

	Item Description	Pref Vendor	Reorder Pt	On H...	Order	On Order	Next D...	Sales/Week
106-Slider ▸	12 Ft. Sliding Doo...	Ace Glass	5	6		0		0
104-Slider	10 Ft. Sliding Doo...	Ace Glass	5	7		0		0.4

Academy Glass
Inventory Stock Status by Item
January through April 2002

Figure 6-31 The Inventory Stock Status by Item report

Inventory Stock Status by Vendor Report

COMPUTER TUTORIAL

The Stock Status by Vendor report gives you information about your inventory parts, including how many are on hand, and how many are on order. This report is sorted by the Preferred Vendor field in the item.

1 Select the **Reports** menu, choose **Inventory**, and then choose **Inventory Stock Status by Vendor**.

2 Set the *From* date to "01/01/2002" and the *To* date to "04/30/2002." Then press <TAB> (see Figure 6-32).

3 To close the report, click the close box (**X**) at the top right corner of the screen. Click **No** when you are prompted to memorize the report.

	Inventory Stock Status by Vendor						How Do I?
Modify Report...	Memorize...	Print...	Excel...	Hide Header	Refresh		
Dates	Custom		From	01/01/2002	To	04/30/2002	

Academy Glass
Inventory Stock Status by Vendor
January through April 2002

	Item Description	Reorde...	On Hand	Order	On Order	Next D...	Sales/Week
Ace Glass							
104-Slider ▶	10 Ft. Sliding Doo...	5	7		0		0.4 ◄
106-Slider	12 Ft. Sliding Doo...	5	6		0		0
Total Ace G..			13		0		0.4

Figure 6-32 The Inventory Stock Status by Vendor report

Inventory Valuation Summary Report

COMPUTER TUTORIAL

The Valuation Summary report gives you information about the value of your inventory Items on a certain date. This report shows each item in inventory, the quantity on-hand, the average cost, and the retail value of each item.

1 Select the **Reports** menu, choose **Inventory**, and then choose **Inventory Valuation Summary**.

2 Set the *Date* field to "04/30/2002" and press <TAB> (see Figure 6-33).

	Inventory Valuation Summary					How Do I?
Modify Report...	Memorize...	Print...	Excel...	Hide Header	Refresh	
Dates	Custom		04/30/2002			

Academy Glass
Inventory Valuation Summary
As of April 30, 2002

	Item Description	On Hand	Avg Cost	Asset Value	% of Tot Asset	Sales Price	Retail Value	% of Tot Retail
106-Slider ▶	12 Ft. Sliding Doo...	6	300.00	1,800.00	45.3%	420.00	2,520.00	50.0% ◄
104-Slider	10 Ft. Sliding Doo...	7	310.55	2,173.87	54.7%	360.00	2,520.00	50.0%
TOTAL		13		3,973.87	100.0%		5,040.00	100.0%

Figure 6-33 The Inventory Valuation Summary report

3 To close the report, click the close box (**X**) at the top right corner of the screen. Click **No** when you are prompted to memorize the report.

Inventory Valuation Detail Report

The Inventory Valuation Detail report gives you information about the value of your inventory Items over a date range.

COMPUTER TUTORIAL

1 Select the *Reports* menu, choose **Inventory**, and then choose **Inventory Valuation Detail**.

2 Set the *Date* fields to "01/01/2002" through "04/30/2002" and press <TAB> (see Figure 6-34).

	Inventory Valuation Detail						▼ How Do I? _ □ ×
Modify Report...	Memorize...	Print...	Excel...	Hide Header	Refresh		
Dates Custom	▼	From 01/01/2002 ■ To 04/30/2002 ■ Sort By Default ▼					

Academy Glass
Inventory Valuation Detail
January through April 2002

Type	Date	Name	Num	Qty	Cost	On Hand	Avg Co...	Asset Va...
106-Slider								
Bill	04/05/2002	Ace Glass	4431	3	1,050.00	3	350.00	1,050.00 ◄
Bill	04/05/2002	Ace Glass	4441	3	1,091.58	6	356.93	2,141.58
Invent...	04/30/2002		2002-2	0		6	300.00	1,800.00
Total 106-Slider						6		1,800.00
104-Slider								
Invoice	01/13/2002	Young, Bi...	2002-99	-2		4	300.00	1,200.00
Invoice	02/28/2002	Garrison,...	2002-109	-2		2	300.00	600.00
Invoice	04/05/2002	Young, Bi...	2002-112	-2		0	300.00	0.00
Bill	04/05/2002	Ace Glass	4431	4	1,200.00	4	300.00	1,200.00
Bill	04/05/2002	Ace Glass	4441	4	1,284.42	8	310.55	2,484.42
Invent...	04/30/2002		2002-1	-1		7	310.55	2,173.87
Total 104-Slider						7		2,173.87
TOTAL						13		3,973.87

Figure 6-34 The Inventory Valuation Detail report

3 To close the report, click the close box (**X**) at the top right corner of the screen. Click **No** when you are prompted to memorize the report.

It is crucial to think through your company's information needs before tackling inventory. New users sometimes try to use inventory parts to track products that don't really need to be tracked in detail. Notice from the chapter examples that you must separately enter every purchase and sale for each inventory part. That might not seem like too much work at first, but if you have hundreds of small products with even a moderate turnover, you might overwhelm your bookkeeping system with detailed transactions.

SUMMARY OF KEY POINTS

In this chapter, you learned how to process payroll in QuickBooks. You should now be familiar with how to use QuickBooks to do all of the following:

◆ activate the Inventory function (page 271)

◆ set up Inventory Items in the Item list (page 273)

◆ use QuickBooks to calculate the average cost of inventory (page 277)

◆ sell inventory on sales forms (page 278)

◆ use purchase orders to order inventory (page 280)

◆ receive against purchase orders (page 282)

◆ add freight-in charges to the cost of each inventory part (page 292)

◆ adjust your inventory (page 295)

◆ create reports about inventory (page 298)

CHAPTER REVIEW AND APPLICATIONS

Comprehension **QUESTIONS**

In your notebook, record answers to the following questions.

1. Describe the purpose of the Inventory Asset and Cost of Goods Sold Accounts in QuickBooks.

2. Discuss three ways you could handle an overshipment of goods from a vendor.

3. Name three inventory reports QuickBooks provides for daily management of inventory and explain what information is available on each.

Multiple-Choice **QUESTIONS**

In your notebook, record the best answer for each of the following questions.

1. _d_ To activate QuickBooks inventory:
   a. select the File menu and then choose Preferences.
   b. turn off Inventory tracking, Select Purchases – Vendors.
   c. consult your accountant to determine the proper inventory method.
   d. select the Edit menu, then choose Preferences, then click on Purchases & Vendors, and then click the Company Preferences tab.

2. _d_ The inventory asset account:
   a. tracks open purchase orders of inventory items.
   b. decreases when inventory is purchased.
   c. increases when inventory is sold.
   d. tracks the cost of each inventory item purchased.

3. _b_ QuickBooks inventory can do all of the following except:
   a. provide reports on the status of each item in inventory, including how many are on hand and how many are on order.
   b. use the LIFO or FIFO method of determining inventory cost
   c. calculate gross profit on inventory sold.
   d. track the cost of each inventory item purchased.

4. _c_ The best way to record inventory purchases by item is to:
   a. list the items ordered on a sheet and review it each morning.
   b. analyze your transaction journal report monthly.
   c. use a purchase order for all inventory purchases.
   d. hire an outside consultant to monitor your inventory levels.

5. *b* Which of the following statements is false regarding Purchase Orders?
   a. POs are held in a special non-posting account until you receive the item(s) ordered.
   b. POs that include inventory items are posted to the inventory account at the end of each month.
   c. You can list your open purchase orders at any time.
   d. You may close a purchase order in part or in full at any time.

6. *c* To display the screen used to record inventory adjustments in QuickBooks:
   a. select the Company menu and then choose Adjust Inventory for actual counts.
   b. no adjustments should be made. QuickBooks automatically adjusts inventory each time you purchase or sell inventory items.
   c. select the Vendors menu, choose Inventory Activities, and then choose Adjust Quantity/Value on Hand.
   d. perform a physical inventory count.

7. *d* QuickBooks maintains the cost of inventory under which method?
   a. First in First Out, FIFO
   b. Last in First Out, LIFO
   c. Cost/retail method of inventory
   d. Average Cost

8. *a* Which of the following is NOT a report available through QuickBooks?
   a. Inventory Backorder Sales by Item
   b. Inventory Stock Status by Item
   c. Inventory Valuation Summary
   d. Item Quick Report

9. *c* Which of the following statements is false regarding the recording of receipts of inventory items?
   a. How you record inventory received depends on how you pay for the items.
   b. Directly writing checks for inventory purchases is not generally advised.
   c. You must receive all the items ordered before you can process the purchase order and record the items to inventory.
   d. You may enter the receipt of inventory items before entering the bill from the vendor.

Name _Michele Hall_   **Date** _____

Completion
STATEMENTS

In the space provided, write the word(s) that best complete each statement.

1. The _Stock Status_ Report is useful for getting a quick snapshot of each inventory part and the number of units on hand and on order. Also, this report gives you information about your inventory turnover, showing a sales per week column.

2. In order to track inventory purchases by item and to easily determine which items you have on order, use _Inventory Stock Status_ when you purchase inventory.

3. QuickBooks keeps a _Perpetual_ inventory, meaning that every purchase and every sale of inventory immediately updates all your reports.

4. For detailed research about transactions involving inventory, use the _Quick Report_ or the _Valuation Detail_ report.

5. The _Valuation Summary_ Report gives you information about the value of your inventory items on a certain date. This report shows all values and average cost of items as of the date of the report.

APPLY YOUR KNOWLEDGE

PROBLEM 6-1

✳ *Done*

> Restore the Problem 6-1.QBB file and store it on your hard disk according to your instructor's directions.

1. Create a new Inventory Item in the Item list with the following data.

Item Type	Inventory Part
Item Name	538 Skylight
Purchase Description	5x8 Skylight
Cost	$448.00
COGS Account	Cost of Goods Sold
Preferred Vendor	Ace Glass
Sales Description	5x8 Skylight
Price	$537.60 (automatically calculates)
Tax Code	Tax
Income Account	Product Sales
Asset Account	Inventory Asset
Reorder Point	3
Qty on Hand	Leave zero
Total Value	Leave zero
As of	Leave current date

2. Enter a Purchase Order (#2002-1002) on 4/5/2002 to Ace Glass (Class: Walnut Creek) for the purchase of eight 104-Sliders ($300 each), six 106-Sliders ($350 each), and four 538 Skylights ($448 each). Leave the Ship To drop-down field at the top blank. Print the purchase order on blank paper.

3. Enter a partial receipt (#3883) against Purchase Order #2002-1002 on 4/10/2002 of four 104-Sliders, three 106-Sliders, and four 538 Skylights from Ace Glass. No bill was received, so use the Receive Items function.

4. Enter a receipt (#7622) on 4/15/2002 of the remaining items from Purchase order #2002-1002 from Ace Glass. No bill was received, so use the Receive Items function.

5. Enter an Invoice (#2002-113) recording the sale of two 538 Skylights ($537.60 each) to Bill Young's Window Replacement Job in the Walnut Creek class on 4/17/2002.

Name _____   **Date** _____

6. Enter a bill dated 4/20/2002 from Ace Glass for shipper #3883. On the bill, record freight-in charges of $225. Allocate $100 in freight to the cost of the 104-Sliders, $70 to the cost of the 106-Sliders, and $55 to the cost of the 538 Skylights. The total of the bill is $4,267.00.

7. Enter another bill dated 4/20/2002 from Ace Glass for shipper #7622. The total of the bill is $2,250.00.

8. On 4/30/2002, enter an Inventory adjustment to adjust for one broken 538 Skylight. Use the Inventory Variance account to record the cost of the adjustment. Inventory Adjustment Reference # 6.

9. Create and print the following reports:

Report	For the period of
104-Slider Item QuickReport	1/1/2002 through 4/30/2002
Inventory Stock Status by Item	1/1/2002 through 4/30/2002
Inventory Valuation Detail	1/1/2002 through 4/30/2002
Inventory Valuation Summary	as of 4/30/2002

EXTEND YOUR KNOWLEDGE

PROBLEM 6-2

Restore the Problem 6-2.QBB file and store it on your hard disk according to your instructor's directions.

1. Add the following Inventory items to the Item list

Type	Inventory Part
Item Name	240 Window
Purchase Description	Window – 2x4
Cost	$50.00
COGS Account	Cost of Goods Sold
Preferred Vendor	Nellis Windows and Doors
Sales Price	$150.00 (**Hint:** Override the default sales price)
Tax Code	Tax
Income Account	Product Sales
Asset Account	Inventory Asset
Reorder Point	2
Qty on Hand	Leave zero
Total Value	Leave zero
As of	Leave current date

Type	Inventory Part
Item Name	460 Window
Purchase Description	Window – 4x6
Cost	$80.00
COGS Account	Cost of Goods Sold
Preferred Vendor	Nellis Windows and Doors
Sales Price	$175.00 (**Hint:** Override the default sales price)
Tax Code	Tax
Income Account	Product Sales
Asset Account	Inventory Asset
Reorder Point	2
Qty on Hand	Leave zero
Total Value	Leave zero
As of	Leave current date

Name _____ **Date** _____

2. Record the transactions below. On the transactions, unless you're told differently, keep all defaults on transactions for prices, address, sales tax item, and others.

May 2, 2002	Create Purchase Order for six 104-Sliders. Purchase from Ace Glass. Class: San Jose. Leave the Ship To field (drop-down) at the top blank. Purchase Order #2002-1003. The price is $300 per window. Do not assign the purchase to a job.
May 5	Create Purchase Order for four 240 Windows ($50 each) and six 460 Windows ($80 each). Purchase from Nellis Windows and Doors. Class: Walnut Creek. Leave the Ship To field (drop down) at the top blank. Purchase Order #2002-1004. Do not assign the purchase to a job.
May 5	Invoiced Bob Mason (Inv #2002-114) for two 104-Slider Replacements (104 Replace). Class San Jose Sales Tax: Santa Clara. Invoice total is $1,419.40. Terms are 2% 10, Net 30.
May 7	Received four 240 Windows and three 460 Windows from Nellis Windows and Doors against PO #2002-1004. The product came without a bill, but the shipper number was 812.
May 7	Create Purchase Order (#2002-1005) for six 106-Sliders at $350 each. Purchase from Ace Glass. Class: San Jose.
May 7	Received six 104 –Sliders from Ace Glass against PO # 2002-1003. The product came without a bill, but the shipper number was 4102.
May 9	Received six 106-Sliders from Ace Glass for PO # 2002-1005. The product came without a bill, but the shipper number was 4111.
May 12	Received bill from Ace Glass for shipper #4102. Total bill was $1,800.00. Terms are 2%10, Net 30.
May 13	Received the three remaining 460 Windows from Nellis Windows and Doors against PO #2002-1004. The product came without a bill, but the shipper number was 815.

3. Create and print the following reports for the period of May 1, 2002 through May 15, 2002:
   a) 240 Window Item QuickReport
   b) Inventory Stock Status by Item
   c) Inventory Valuation Detail

BROADEN YOUR KNOWLEDGE

PROBLEM 6-3

> Restore the Problem 6-3.QBB file and store it on your hard disk according to your instructor's directions.

1. Record the transactions below. On the transactions, unless you're told differently, keep all defaults on transactions for prices, address, sales tax item, and others.

May 16, 2002	Received bill from Nellis Windows and Doors for #812. Allocate $17 of freight charges to the 240 Windows and $22 to the 460 Windows. Class: Walnut Creek. Total amount of the bill was $479. Terms are Net 30.
May 18	Received bill from Ace Glass for shipper #4111. Total bill was $2,100.00. Terms are 2%10, Net 30.
May 19	Invoiced Jerry Leonard (#2002-115) for two 240 Windows. Class: Walnut Creek, Contra Costa Sales Tax. Terms were Net 30. Total invoice was $324.75.
May 19	Received bill from Nellis Windows and Doors for shipper #815. The bill includes three 460 windows and freight charges of $22. The total amount of the bill was $262. Terms were Net 30.
May 21	Invoiced Ron Berry (#2002-116) for four 460 Windows ($150* each). Terms were Net 30. Class: San Jose. Santa Clara Sales tax. Total on the invoice was $649.50. ***Note:** you must manually override the price on the 460 Window item.
May 23	Create Purchase Order (#2002-1006) for four 460 Windows. Purchase from Nellis Windows and Doors. Class: Walnut Creek.
May 31	Enter an inventory adjustment (#2002-7) to adjust for one broken 460 Window. Use the Inventory Variance account and the San Jose Class.

2. Create and print the following reports for the month of May 2002:
   a) 460 Window Item QuickReport
   b) Inventory Stock Status by Item
   c) Inventory Valuation Detail
   d) Open Purchase Orders

Name _____ **Date** _____

Workplace
Applications

DISCUSSION QUESTIONS

These questions are designed to help you apply what you are learning about QuickBooks to your own organization. Use your notebook to record your answers and your thoughts.

1. How many different items does your organization have in inventory? What is the total number of pieces in your organization's inventory? What is the highest priced item? What is the lowest? What is the total value of your inventory?

2. How do you currently determine when it is time to re-supply each of these items? Does going below a certain amount on-hand trigger an order? Or do you order items after you make a sale that requires them?

ACTIVITY

Search the Internet using www.google.com. Enter the search keywords "Weighted Average Cost of Inventory." Print one of the web pages or articles you found that describes and defines this term.

CASE STUDY

FANS 4 FANS, INC.

Fans 4 Fans, Inc. is a small company in Oakland, California, that specializes in selling and installing home ceiling fans with professional sports team logos on them. The company purchases the parts to build the fan from two different vendors. The logo parts, including team helmets that appear to sit on top of the fan, are purchased from the official respective sports associations, and the rest of the fan assembly is purchased from a hardware supply company.

The assembly parts are stocked under two separate SKUs (Stock-Keeping Units) called Helmet and Fan.

The company keeps the assembly parts in stock and assembles the fans shortly before they are installed at the customer location. Because of the need to ensure the fan is properly assembled and safe, they do not let customers install their own fans. All labor is included in the purchase price of the fan.

Questions

These questions are designed to help you apply what you are learning about QuickBooks to this case study. Use your notebook to record your answers and your thoughts.

1. What items should the company use to track the **Helmet** and **Fan** inventory?

2. A company has been so impressed with the Fans 4 Fans Company that it has offered to purchase the company. Marcus is required to find the value of the inventory on hand before further discussion of selling the business. What reports should he use?

3. If each fan requires the bundling of 4 hours of labor with the item, discuss how Marcus should set up a Group Item to track the sales of the fans.

*inter*NET CONNECTION

Inquisitive about inventory? Explore the inventory topic on Internet search engines such as http://www.yahoo.com or http://www.google.com. A wide variety of articles on inventory is available.

Payroll Setup

OBJECTIVES

After completing this chapter, you should be able to:

1 Activate the Payroll function in Preferences.

2 Use the Payroll Setup Wizard to set up payroll items, payroll vendors, employee defaults, employee records, and year-to-date amounts.

3 Use the Payroll Checkup function to ensure that your setup is correct.

4 Add new payroll items using the Custom Setup of payroll items.

5 Edit payroll items to modify how they affect accounts or taxes.

6 Release or deactivate employees.

RESTORE THIS FILE

This chapter uses Chapter 7.QBW. To open this file, restore the tutorial template called **Chapter 7.QBB** to your hard disk. (See page 7 for instructions on restoring files.)

In this chapter, you'll learn how to set up QuickBooks to track your payroll. If you plan to use QuickBooks to help you track your payroll, you must properly set up all your lists (payroll accounts, payroll items, employees) and opening balances.

If you want to prepare your own payroll, you can do so with QuickBooks, but before using QuickBooks payroll, you must at least subscribe to the Intuit Basic Payroll Service. You can also subscribe to Intuit's Deluxe or Premier Payroll service. The Deluxe Payroll service provides payroll tax preparation in addition to the tax tables, and the Premier Payroll service provides for the complete outsourcing of your payroll. For detailed information on the differences between these options, select **Learn About Payroll Options** from the *Employees* menu.

In this text, we'll assume you are using QuickBooks with the Basic Payroll Service to prepare your own payroll.

CHECKLIST FOR SETTING UP PAYROLL

The setup of your payroll, just like the setup of your company file itself, is the most important factor in getting it to work well for you. Here is a checklist for your payroll setup. Make sure you don't skip steps unless they really don't apply.

1. Gather information about each of your employees, including name, address, Social Security Number and W-4 information.
2. Activate the Payroll function in Preferences.
3. Set up payroll accounts in the Chart of Accounts. Example accounts: Gross Wages, Payroll Tax Expense, and Federal Withholding.
4. Using the Payroll Setup Wizard, set up payroll items, payroll vendors, employee defaults, employee records, and year-to-date payroll figures.
5. Add additional payroll items not included in the setup by the Payroll Wizard.
6. Edit payroll items to modify the vendor information and the way the items affect the chart of accounts.
7. If setting up mid-year, enter year-to-date information for each employee and enter year-to-date liability payments.
8. Verify every payroll item setup, employee setup, and the vendor list.
9. Proof your setup. Use the Payroll Checkup function and compare reports with your accountant's or payroll service's reports.

About Your Tutorial Template – The tutorial template provided with this course comes with the Basic Payroll Service Subscription activated, so you won't have to pay for a subscription. As Intuit updates the tax tables, you will be able to download them, so that the calculations on your paychecks are correct for your current tax rates. Therefore, you might find that some of the calculations on your paychecks differ slightly from the screenshots in the book. Ignore these differences and allow QuickBooks to calculate the checks using the new table information.

When you set up payroll for your own file, you must subscribe to one of Intuit's Payroll Services (Basic, Deluxe, or Premier).

Do Not Use The Tutorial Template to Prepare Your Own Payroll. Also, do not attempt to sign up for any Intuit Payroll Service with this file "open." It is registered as a separate company with the payroll service.

COMPUTER TUTORIAL

Activating Payroll

1 Select the *Edit* menu and then choose **Preferences**.

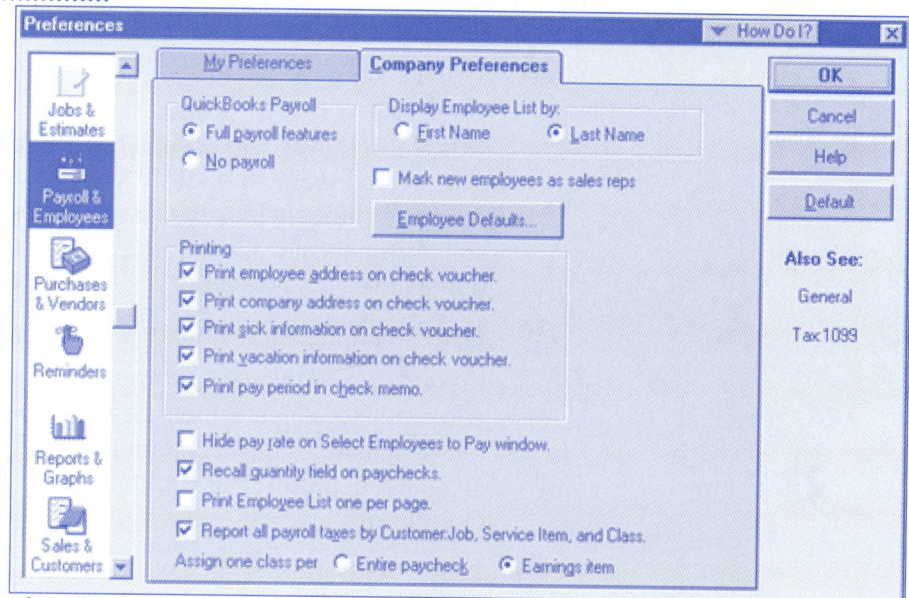

Figure 7-1 Company Preferences tab for Payroll & Employees

2 Scroll down and click **Payroll & Employees**.

3 Click the tab labeled Company Preferences, as shown in Figure 7-1.

4 Leave "Full payroll features" selected.

In the tutorial template, the Payroll function is already activated. In your company file, choose "Full payroll features" if you want to calculate paychecks, print paychecks, track liabilities by Payroll Item, or prepare Forms 941, 940, W-2, and W-3.

5 Leave all of the boxes checked in the Printing section.

You can customize what will print on paycheck vouchers by clicking the appropriate boxes. If you plan to track sick and vacation pay in QuickBooks, these should all be turned on as shown in Figure 7-1. QuickBooks prints sick and vacation hours used and available on each paycheck if these options are set.

6 Leave the "Hide pay rate on Select Employees to Pay" window box unchecked.

If you don't want to see the employee pay rates when selecting employees to pay, check this box. You might want to check this if you are concerned about people looking over your shoulder when you are paying your employees.

7 Leave the "Recall quantity" field on paychecks box checked.

If you check this box, QuickBooks remembers the quantities you entered on the last paycheck, and prefills those quantities on each new paycheck. This includes hours worked (if you don't transfer time to paychecks), and quantities for additions, deductions, and company contributions.

8. Leave the "Print Employee List one per page" box unchecked.

This setting makes it easy to file hardcopy employee records separately by employee name.

9. Leave the "Report all payroll taxes by Customer:Job, Service Item, and Class" box checked.

This feature gives you the ability to track payroll taxes by job and class. If you want to allocate your payroll taxes as well as gross wages to multiple jobs or classes, check this box and QuickBooks will automatically allocate the payroll taxes in the same proportion as the gross wages.

10. Leave "Earnings item" next to "Assign one class per" selected.

If you have employees who work in different departments and you want to allocate their payroll expenses to separate departments (classes), select "Earnings item." Classes allow you to track separate departments, profit centers, or store locations in one QuickBooks file.

11. Leave "Last Name" in the Display Employee List by: section selected.

12. Verify that your screen matches Figure 7-1. Click **OK** to save.

Federal and State Employer IDs

If you haven't already set up your Federal Employer Identification Number (FEIN), you won't be able to complete the signup process for any of the payroll service options. QuickBooks will automatically enter your Federal Employer ID in the payroll signup screens. To set up your taxpayer ID, select the *Company* menu and then choose **Company Information** (see Figure 7-2).

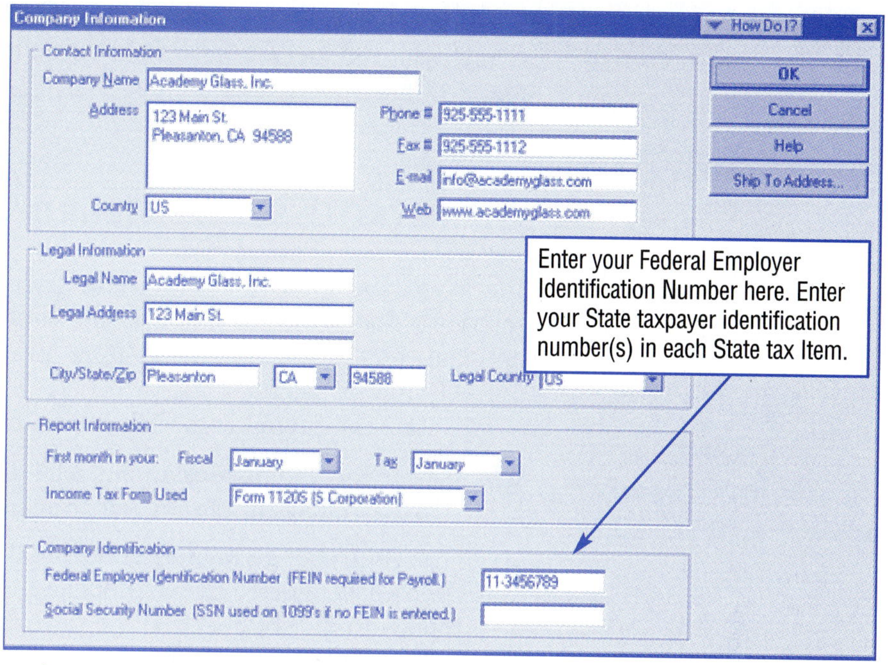

Figure 7-2 The Company Information screen

Your State taxpayer ID must be entered on each State Payroll Item, such as Withholding or Unemployment. These are discussed below.

Payroll Accounts

In your Chart of Accounts, confirm that you have all of the accounts you want to see on your Balance Sheet and Profit and Loss reports. Academy Glass uses the following accounts for payroll. The tutorial template file already contains these accounts.

◇ Payroll Liabilities	Other Current Liability
◇ Federal PR Taxes	Other Current Liability
◇ State PR Taxes	Other Current Liability
◇ Other Payroll Liabilities	Other Current Liability

Figure 7-3 Payroll Liability Accounts

◇ Payroll Expenses	Expense
◇ Benefits	Expense
◇ Gross Wages	Expense
◇ Officer's Compensation	Expense
◇ Payroll Taxes	Expense

Figure 7-4 Payroll Expense Accounts

If you're not sure which accounts you should have, talk with your accountant. However, as a general rule you should have only a few subaccounts of the Payroll Liabilities account and a few subaccounts of the Payroll Expenses account. Don't add unnecessary accounts and subaccounts to the Chart of Accounts, since the detailed tracking of payroll comes from Payroll Items, not accounts.

If your Chart of Accounts already has too many accounts or subaccounts, you can merge some of the accounts. See Merging Accounts on page 517 for more details.

THE PAYROLL SETUP WIZARD

The Payroll Setup Wizard is a set of screens similar to the Easy Step Interview that walk you through the setup of payroll. This Wizard is optional, but if you're starting from scratch (as shown here), you'll probably find it helpful.

To start the Payroll Setup Wizard, follow these steps:

COMPUTER TUTORIAL

1. Select the *Employees* menu and then choose **Set up Payroll**. The Payroll Setup Wizard will appear as shown in Figure 7-5.

   The **Add/change payroll option** and **Sign up for payroll service** steps have already been completed for you, so the Payroll Wizard points to the third step in the payroll setup process, which is the setup of company information.

> **IMPORTANT**
>
> If you don't already have a payroll service key entered into your tutorial template, you'll see a screen prompting you to click either **Add Company** or **Payroll Options**. To learn more about the payroll services before you purchase, click **Payroll Options**. If you are already familiar with the Payroll Services, click **Add Company** to subscribe. When you click **Add Company**, QuickBooks will log on to the Internet. Select a Payroll Service option (Basic, Basic with Direct Deposit or Deluxe Payroll service), provide a credit card number, and download the current tax tables.

Payroll Items

The next step in your setup is to add the payroll items you'll need for your company, such as payroll taxes, wages, benefits and others.

Setting up payroll taxes

2 Click on **Set up company information** (see Figure 7-5).

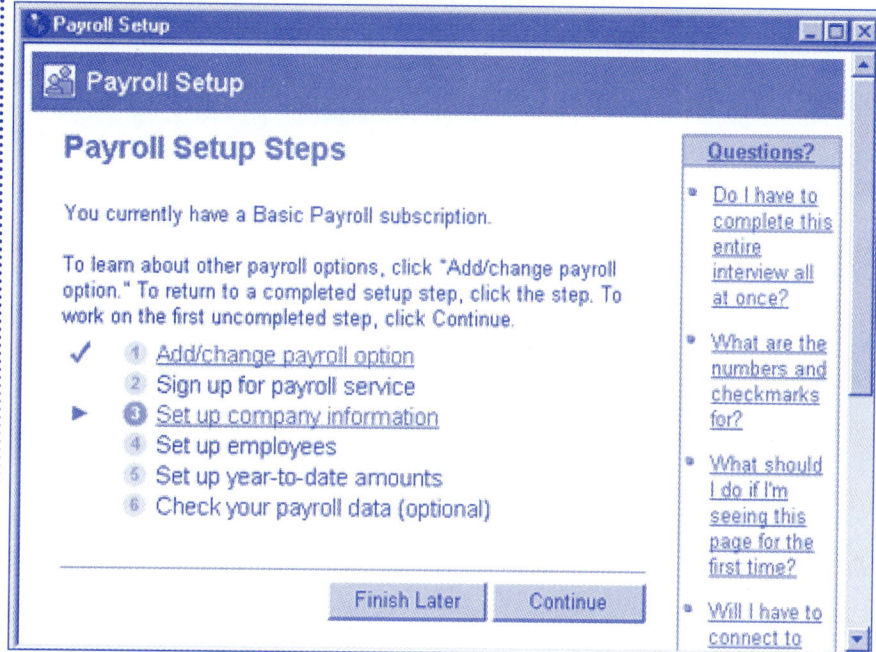

Figure 7-5 Payroll Setup Wizard

3 Click on **Set up payroll taxes** (see Figure 7-6).

You may have to resize your Payroll Setup screen or scroll down to see the Continue button.

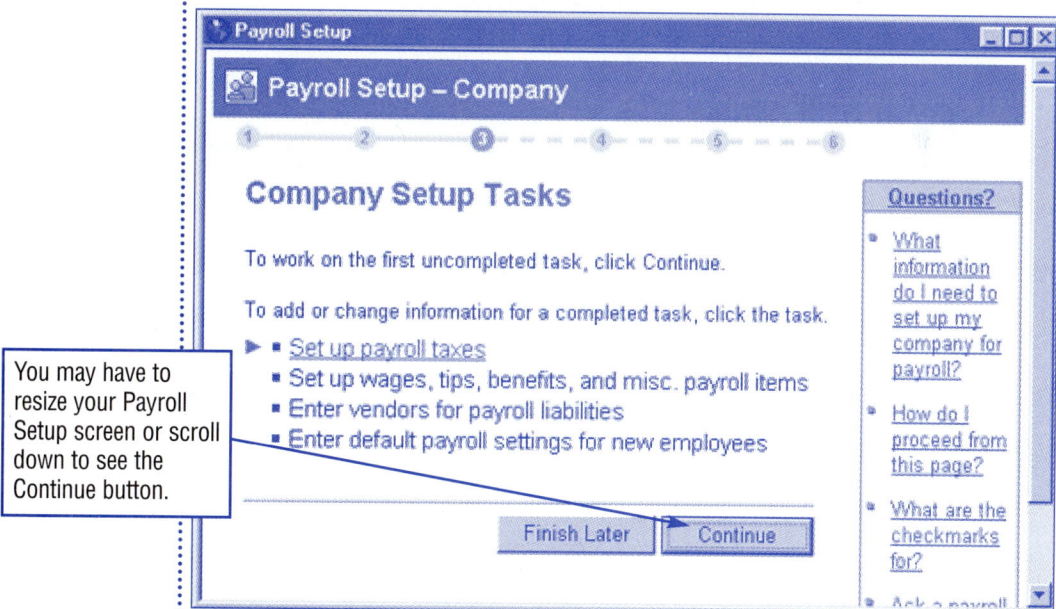

Figure 7-6 The Company Setup Tasks screen

④ Check the box next to "California," and then click **Continue**. You can select the States where your employees reside from the list in Figure 7-7.

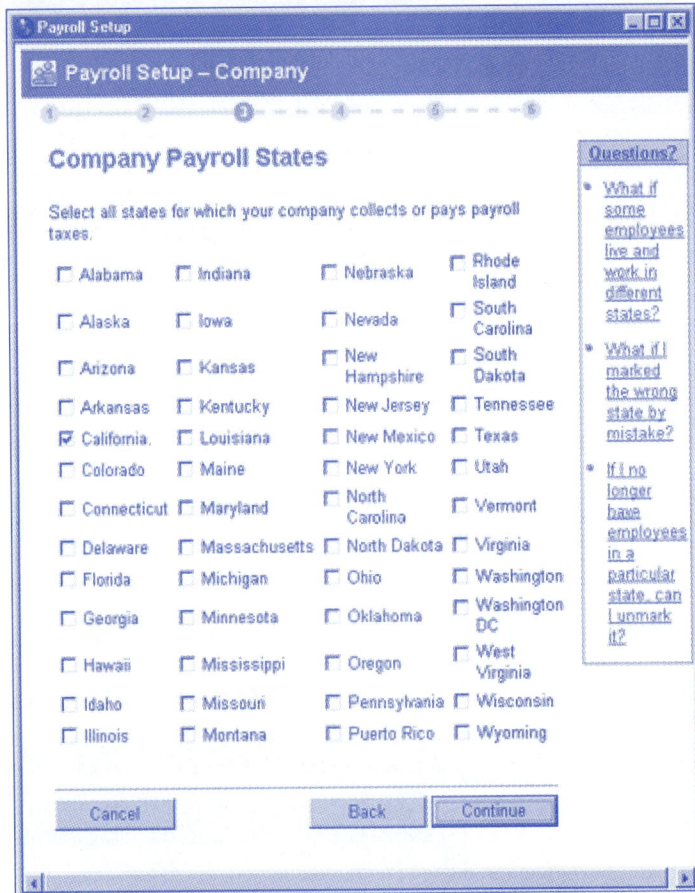

Figure 7-7 The Company Payroll States screen

⑤ Click **Continue** on the Federal Payroll Taxes screen (see Figure 7-8).

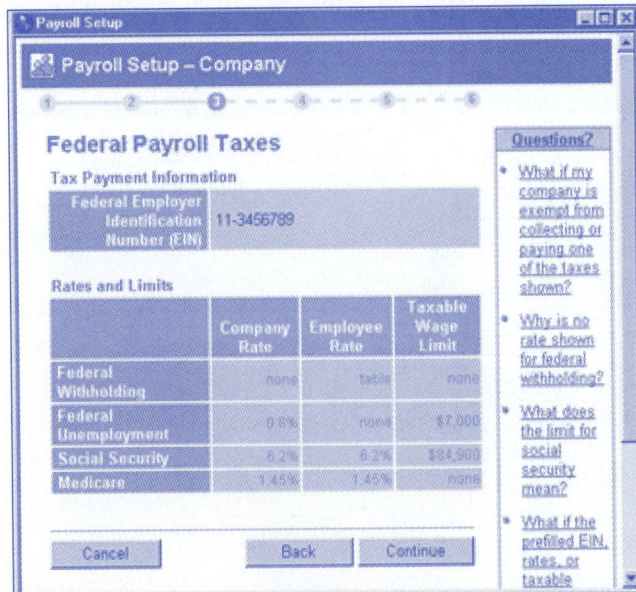

Figure 7-8 The Federal Payroll Taxes screen

6 On the State Payroll Taxes screen, enter "123-4567-8" in the *California EDD Employer Account Number* field, and enter "3.4" in each of the *CA Unemployment Company* fields (see Figure 7-9).

Note that each State will have different fields on this screen.

7 After you have finished entering data as shown in Figure 7-9, click **Continue**.

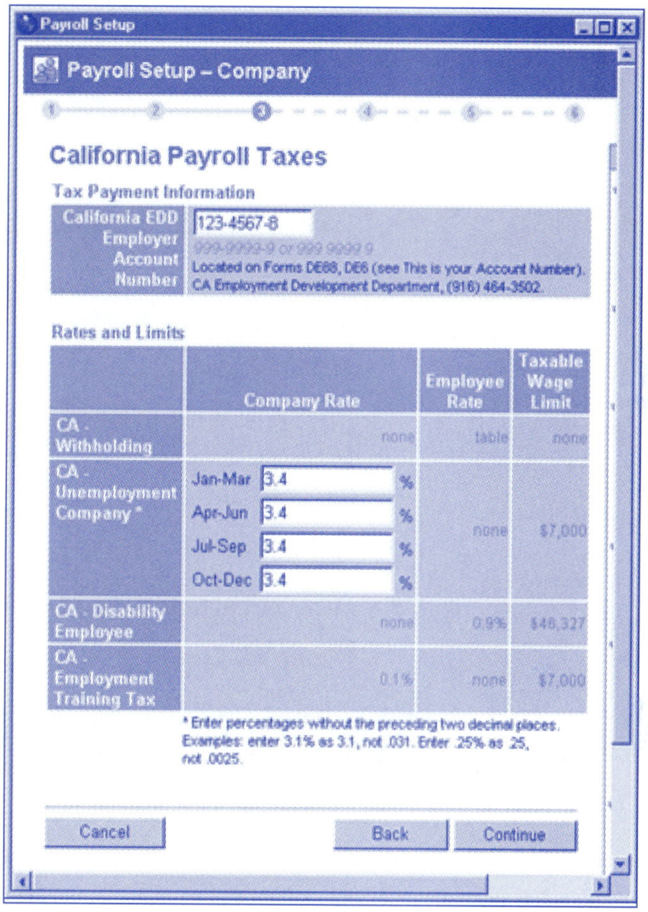

Figure 7-9 The State Payroll Taxes screen

Setting up wages, benefits, and misc. payroll items

⑧ To set up all your wage items and taxable fringe benefits, click **Continue** on the screen shown in Figure 7-10.

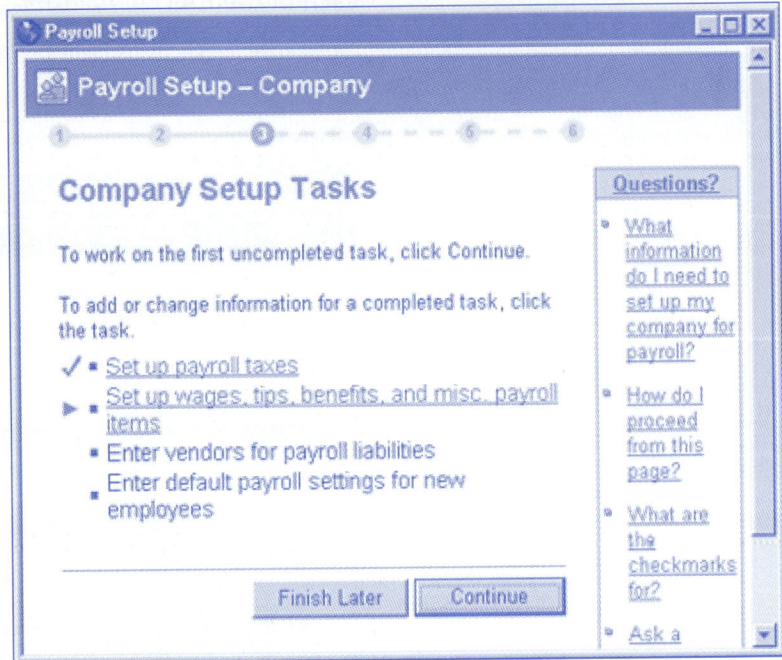

Figure 7-10 Federal and State Tax items completed

⑨ Click on each item you'll need as shown in Figure 7-11.

⑩ Then click **Create** on the screen shown in Figure 7-11.

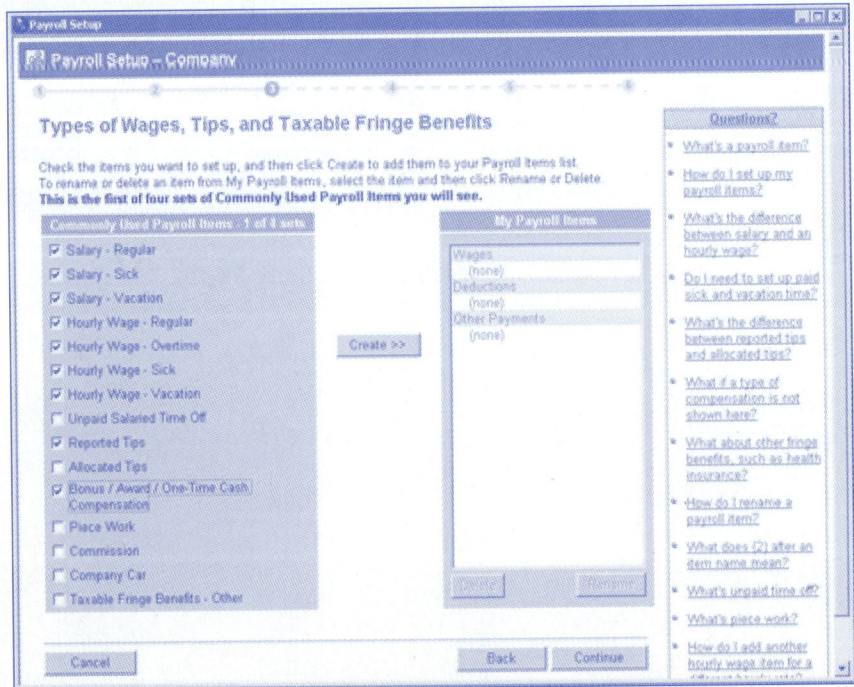

Figure 7-11 Types of Wages, Tips, and Taxable Fringe Benefits

⑪ When QuickBooks creates the payroll items in the My Payroll Items section, notice that the names are different from those shown in the Commonly Used Payroll Items section in Figure 7-12. Click each Item in the My Payroll Items section, and then click **Rename** to change all the names as follows.

Commonly Used Payroll Item Name	Rename to
Hourly Rate	Hourly Regular
Overtime Hourly Rate	Hourly Overtime
Salary	Salary Regular
Sick Hourly Rate	Hourly Sick
Sick Salary	Salary Sick
Vacation Hourly Rate	Hourly Vacation
Vacation Salary	Salary Vacation
Reported Tips Out	Tips (Deduction)
Bonus (one-time cash award)	Bonus
Reported Tips In	Tips (Addition)

IMPORTANT

When setting up these earnings items, QuickBooks creates regular pay items, sick pay items, and vacation pay items. The item names indicate the type. For example, the "Hourly Rate" item is a regular pay item and the "Sick Hourly Rate" item is a sick pay item. Therefore, you must rename the items so that they still indicate the type of pay. For example, rename "Hourly Rate" to "Hourly Regular" and "Sick Hourly Rate" to "Hourly Sick."

⑫ Click **Continue** in the Rename Payroll Item screen to save your changes.

⑬   My Payroll Items should now match Figure 7-12. Click **Continue**.

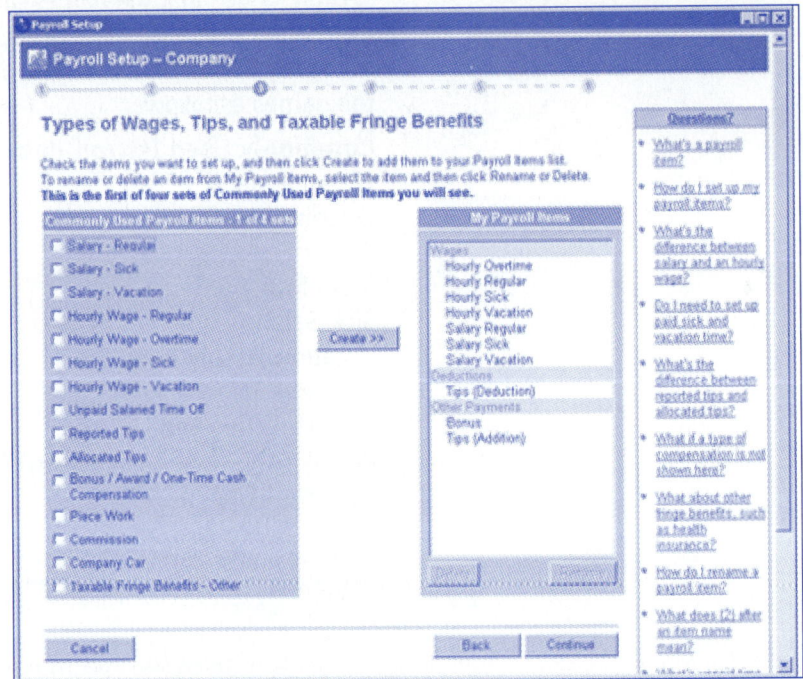

Figure 7-12 Names for Earnings items

⑭   On the Insurance Benefits screen (see Figure 7-13), select the items shown and click **Create**.

You could add many more common payroll items, such as a Section 125 health insurance deduction, on this screen.

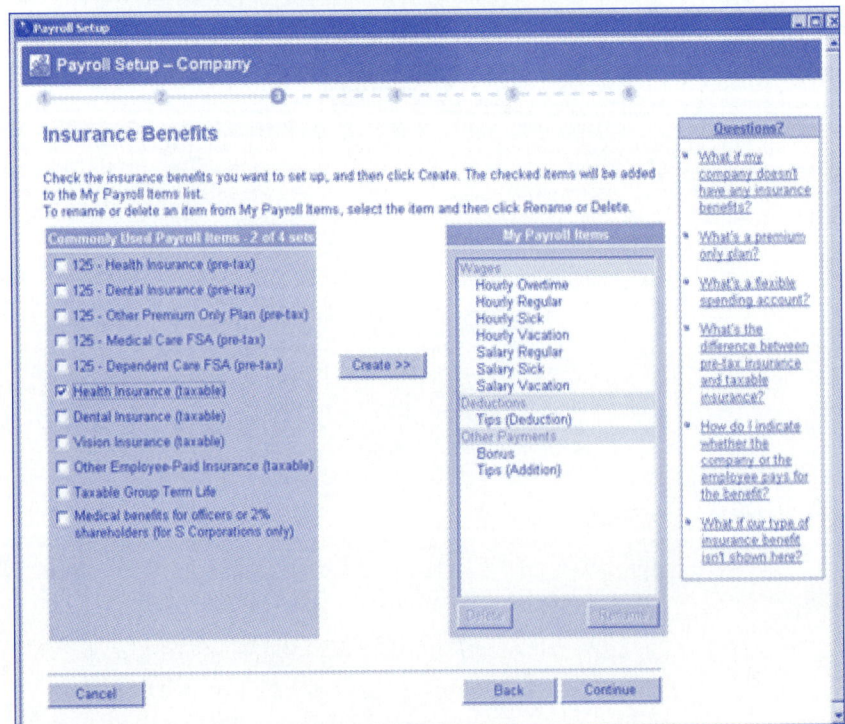

Figure 7-13 Insurance Benefits items

15 Rename the Health Insurance (taxable) item to "Medical Insurance" as shown in Figure 7-14 and click **Continue**. Click **Continue** again to proceed to the next screen.

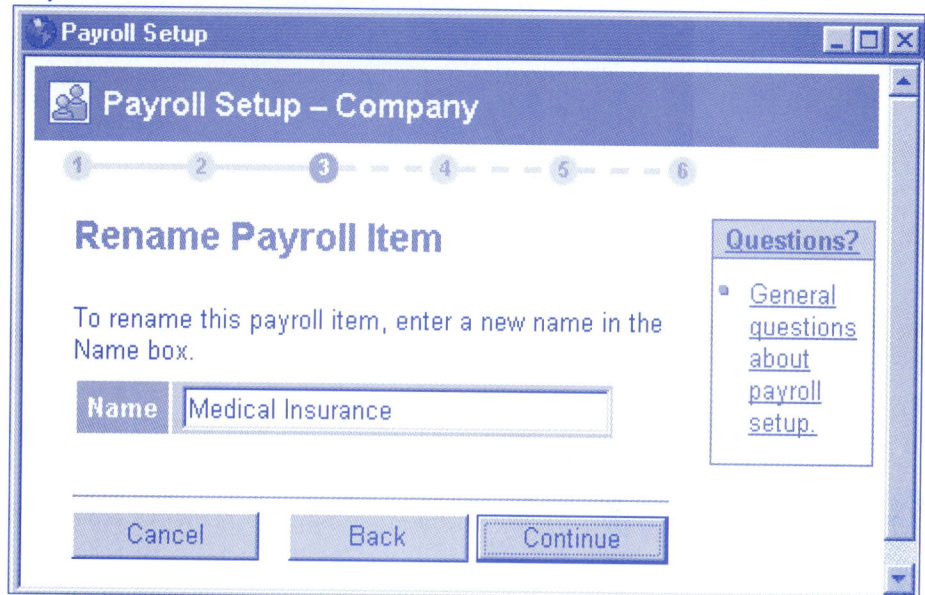

Figure 7-14 Renaming an Insurance Benefit item

16 Check the two 401(k) boxes as shown in Figure 7-15 and click **Create**.

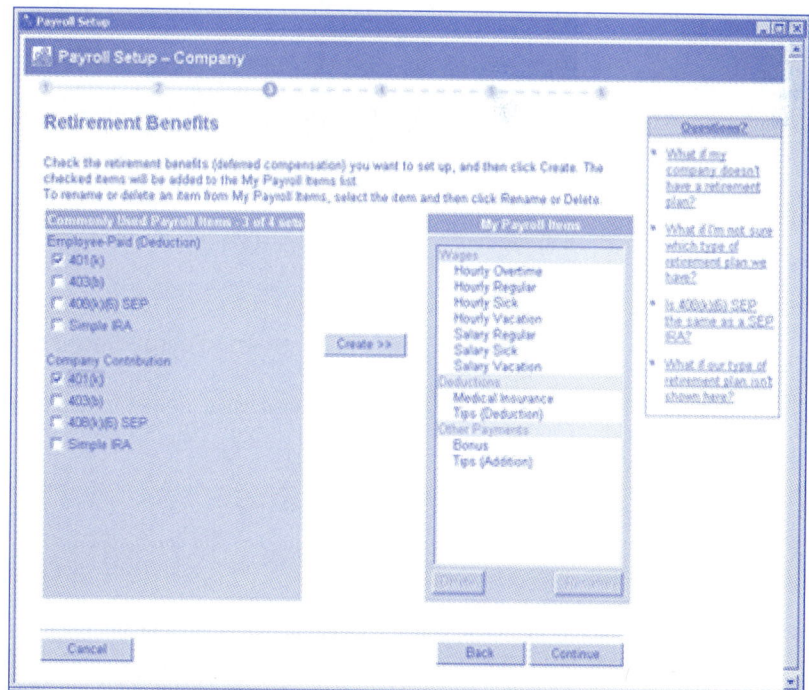

Figure 7-15 Selecting Retirement Benefits

17 Rename "401(k) Emp." to "401(k) Deduction" (see Figure 7-16) and click **Continue**. Rename "401(k) Co. Match" to "Match 401(k)" (see Figure 7-17) and click **Continue**.

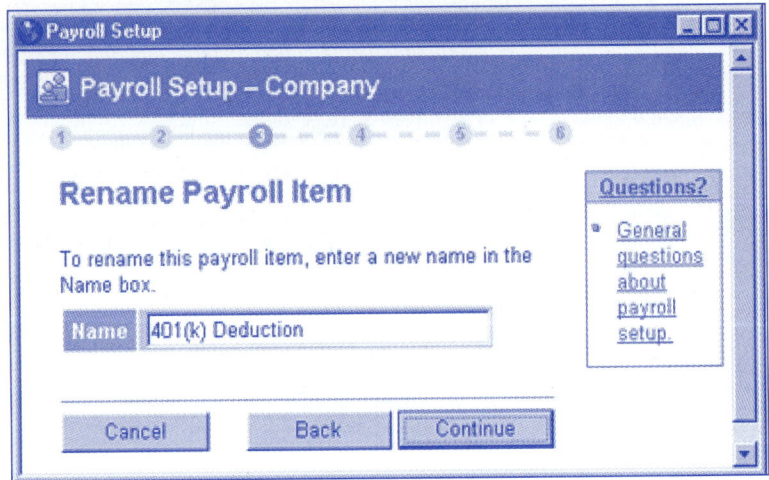

Figure 7-16 Renaming a Retirement Benefit item

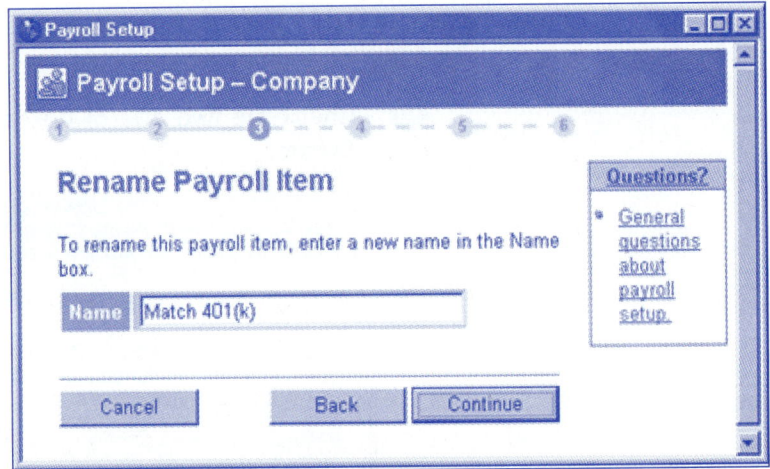

Figure 7-17 Rename Payroll Item screen

18 Click **Continue** again to proceed to the next screen.

19 Select "Union Dues" from the Other Payments and Deductions screen as shown in Figure 7-18, and click **Create**.

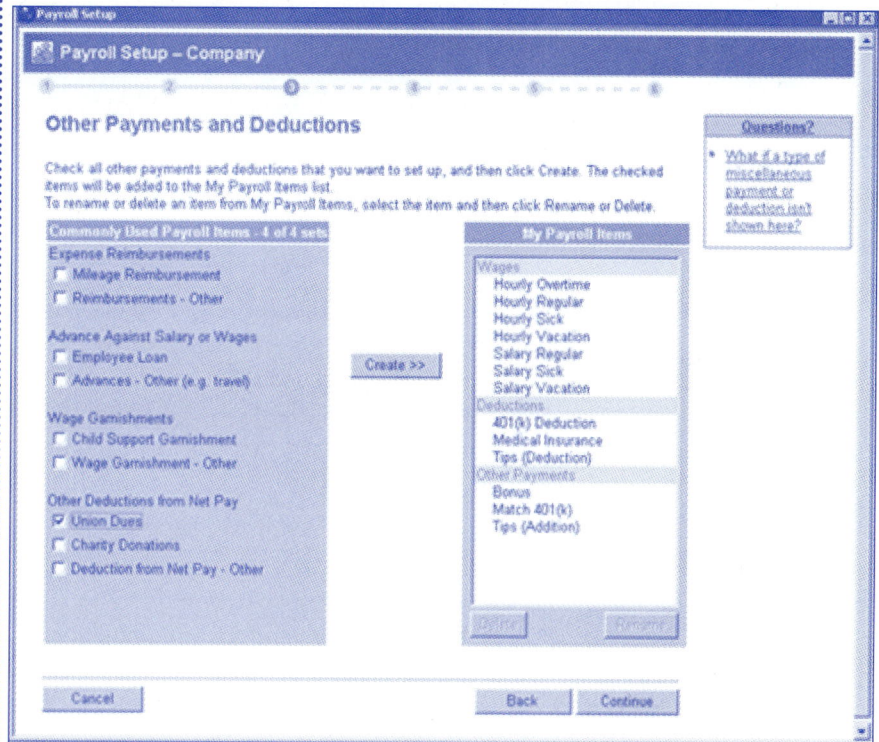

Figure 7-18 Selecting Other Payments and Deductions

20 Leave the names as shown on the screen in Figure 7-19 and click **Continue**.

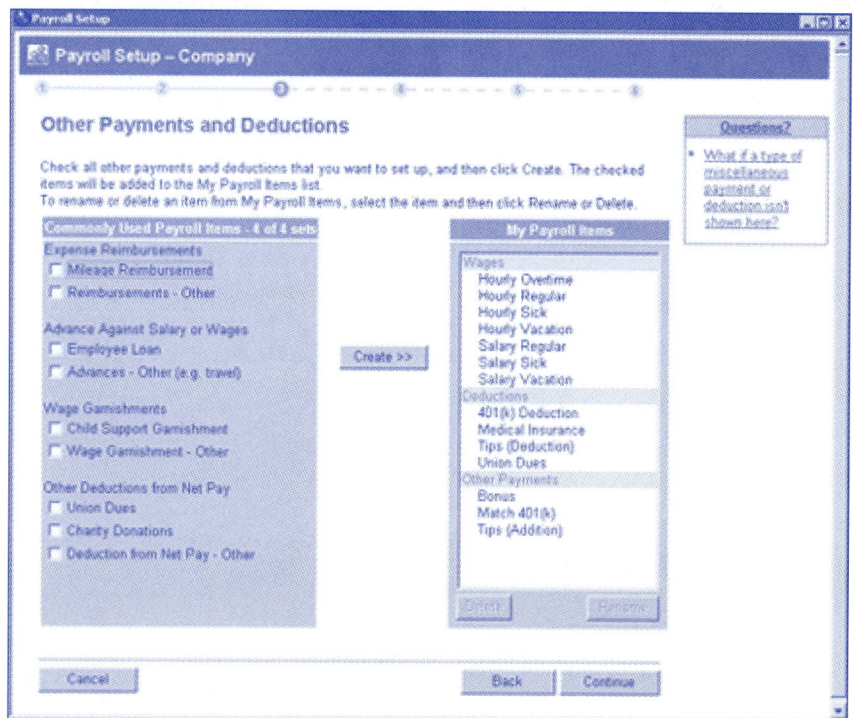

Figure 7-19 Names for Other Payments and Deductions

Entering vendors for payroll liabilities

㉑ To set up vendors for payroll liabilities, click **Continue** on the Company Setup Tasks screen (see Figure 7-20).

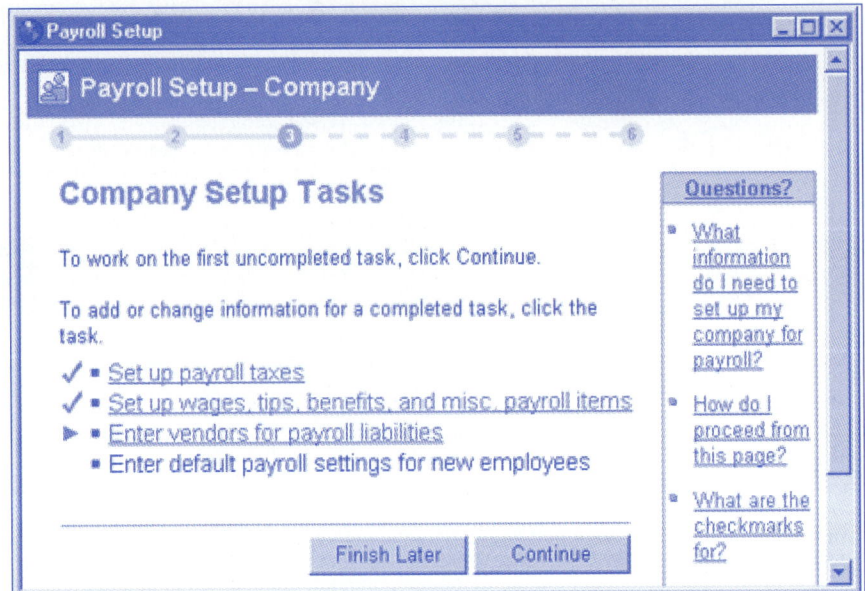

Figure 7-20 Enter vendors and liabilities

Entering Vendors for Payroll Items

㉒ From the "Paid to:" drop-down menu in the Tax Payment Information screen, select "EFTPS" as the vendor you use to pay your liabilities for Federal taxes, and leave "EDD" as the agency to which you pay your State withholding taxes (see Figure 7-21). Then click **Continue**.

If the vendor you use for payroll items is not already set up in your vendor list, select "Add New" from the drop-down list and add the new vendor.

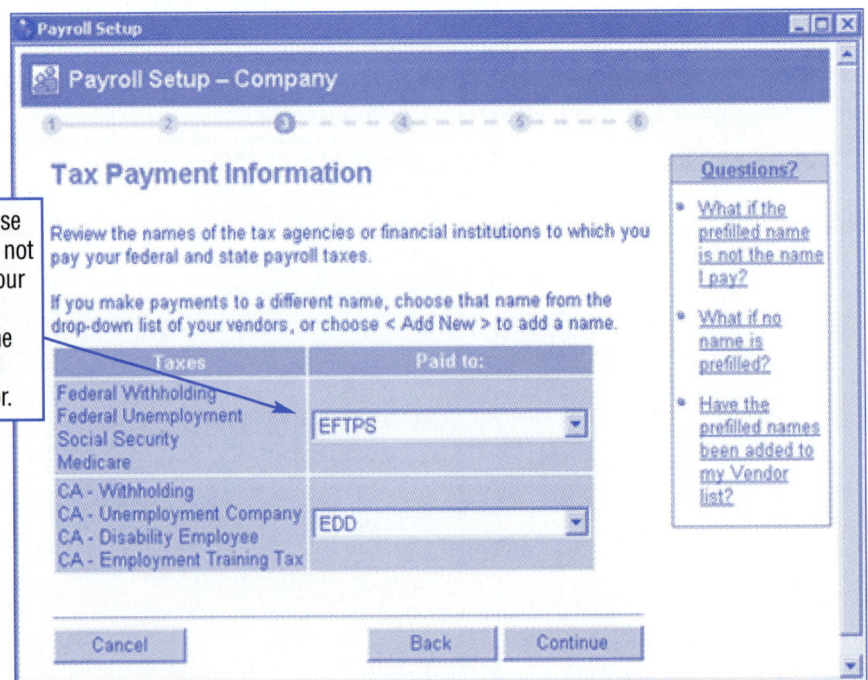

Figure 7-21 Vendors for tax payments

㉓ In the Payee Information for Benefits and Misc. Liabilities screen (see Figure 7-22), select "Merrill Lynch" in the Payable to Vendor column for both 401(k) Deduction and Match 401 (k), and enter "99-1133334" in the corresponding *Account No. with Vendor* fields.

Leave "none" in the Payable to Vendor column for Medical Insurance, and leave blank the corresponding *Account No. with Vendor* fields for these items.

On the Union Dues line, select "Carpenter's Union" in the Payable to Vendor column, and enter "See Attached" in the corresponding *Account No. with Vendor* field.

Then click **Continue**.

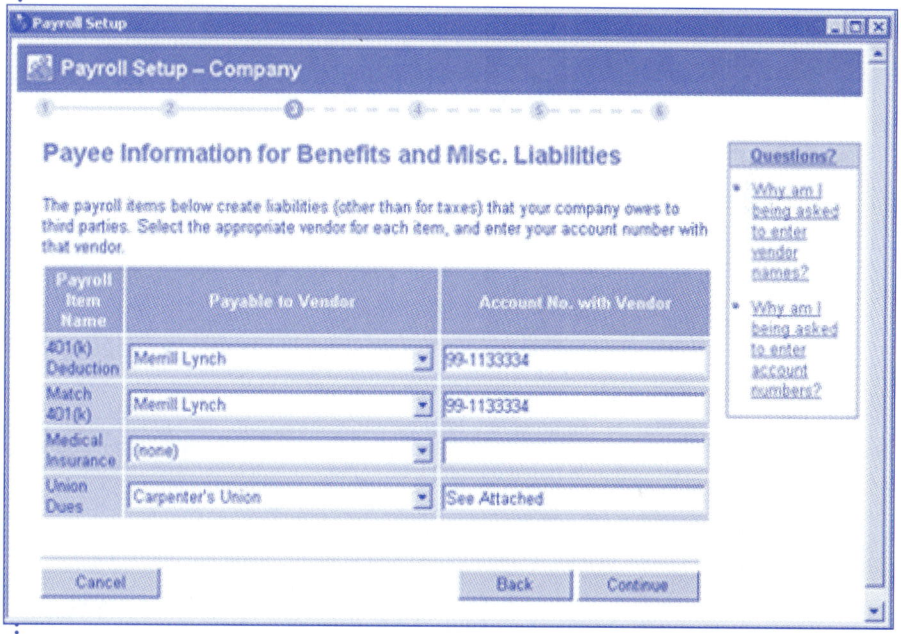

Figure 7-22 Vendor names for Benefits and Misc. Liabilities

Setting Up Employee Defaults

Before you set up your employees in the Employee list, you might want to set up Employee Defaults. The Employee Defaults feature allows you to define defaults for your employee records, so that each time you add a new employee, you don't have to enter the same information over and over. For example, if you pay all your employees weekly, you can set up the defaults for weekly payroll, and that way you won't have to enter the pay period on each new employee record. You don't have to use the Employee Defaults, but if you do, it will save you time and reduce the likelihood of errors.

24 You're now ready to enter your default settings and add your employees. Click **Continue** on the screen shown in Figure 7-23.

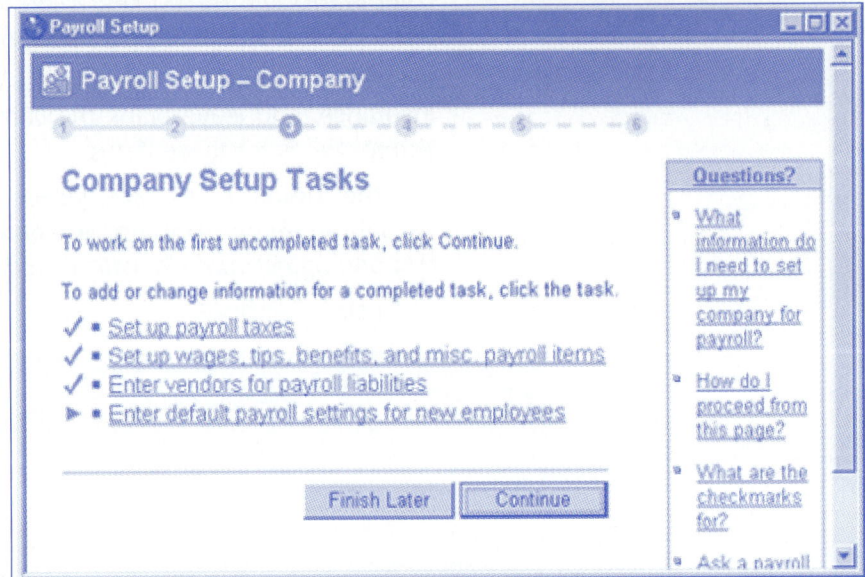

Figure 7-23 Enter default settings and new employees

25 On the screen shown in Figure 7-24, click **Edit** to edit your employee defaults.

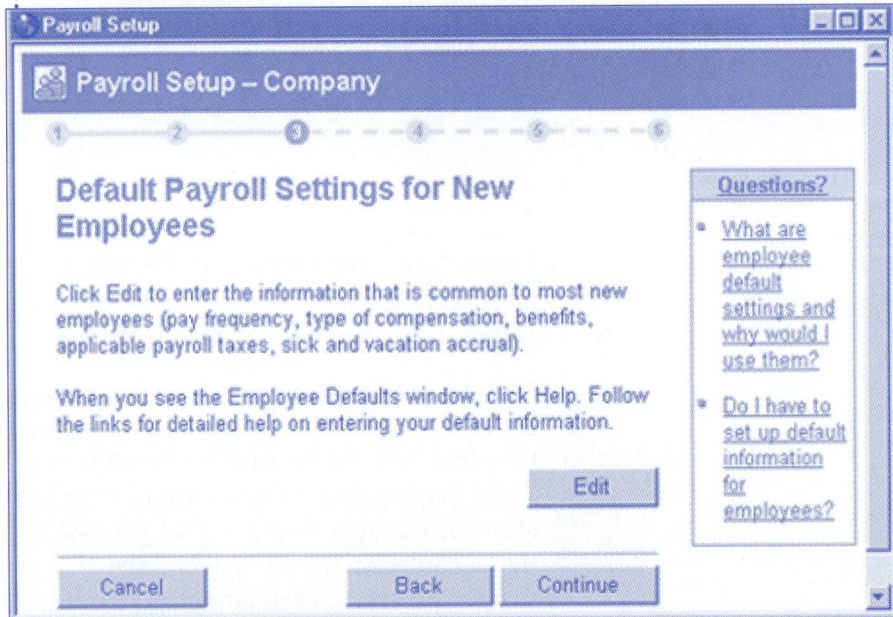

Figure 7-24 Default settings

26. On the Employee Defaults screen, select "Semimonthly" from the drop-down menu in the *Pay Period* field, and leave the *Class* field blank. Enter the "401(k) Deduction," "Match 401(k)," and "Medical Insurance" items in the Additions, Deductions and Company Contributions section. Then enter the amounts and limits as shown in Figure 7-25 and check the box labeled "Employee is covered by a qualified pension plan."

Use the Employee Defaults screen to set up the payroll information that most of your employees have in common. In the *Pay Period* field, enter how often most employees are paid. These are only defaults, so entering something here does not preclude you from overriding your choices for an individual employee.

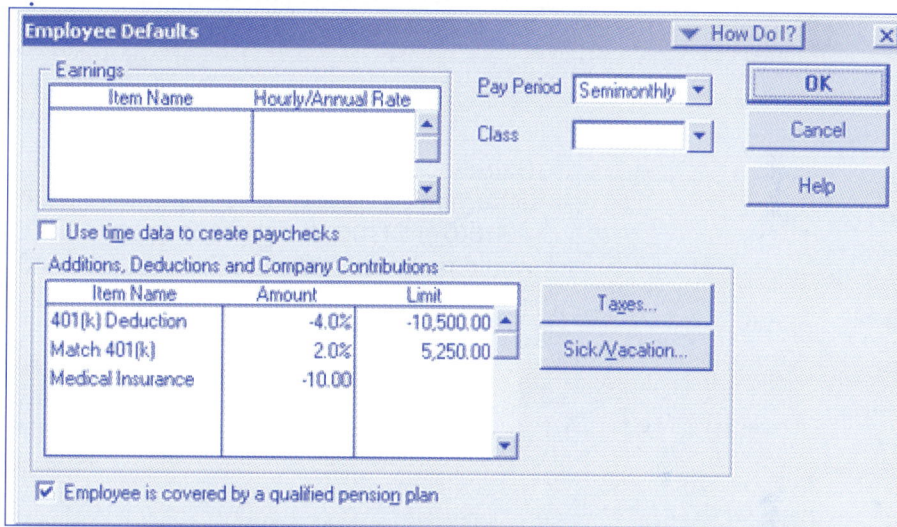

Figure 7-25 Employee Defaults screen

Check Item Order on Additions, Deductions and Contributions

27 Verify that your screen matches Figure 7-25, and then click **Taxes**.

This is a good time to consider a fundamental concept: how the order in which you enter Additions, Deductions and Company Contributions affects how they calculate on paychecks.

Example

If an employee has earnings of $1000, an addition to gross of $100, and a 2% deduction from gross, the 2% deduction will calculate differently depending on where it shows in the list of Additions, Deductions and Company Contributions.

If you enter the addition before the deduction...	Salary	$1,000.
	Tips Addition	$100.
	(Addition to Gross)	
	401(k)	2%
	(Deduction from Gross)	
QuickBooks calculates the 2% deduction on a gross of $1000 + $100, or $1100. The deduction would be $1100 * 2% = $22.	Salary	$1,000.
	Tips Addition	$100.
	Total Gross	$1,100.
	401(k) (2%)	**$22.**

However,

If you enter the addition after the deduction...	Salary	$1,000.
	401(k)	2%
	(Deduction from Gross)	
	Tips Addition	$100.
	(Addition to Gross)	
QuickBooks calculates the 2% deduction on a gross of $1000. The deduction would be $1000 * 2% = $20.	Salary	$1,000.
	401(k) (2%)	**$20.**
	Tips Addition	$100.

Table 7-1 Example of how order affects Additions, Deductions, and Contributions

Default settings for taxes

28 In the Taxes Defaults screen, leave the default Federal tax settings as shown in Figure 7-26 and click the State tab.

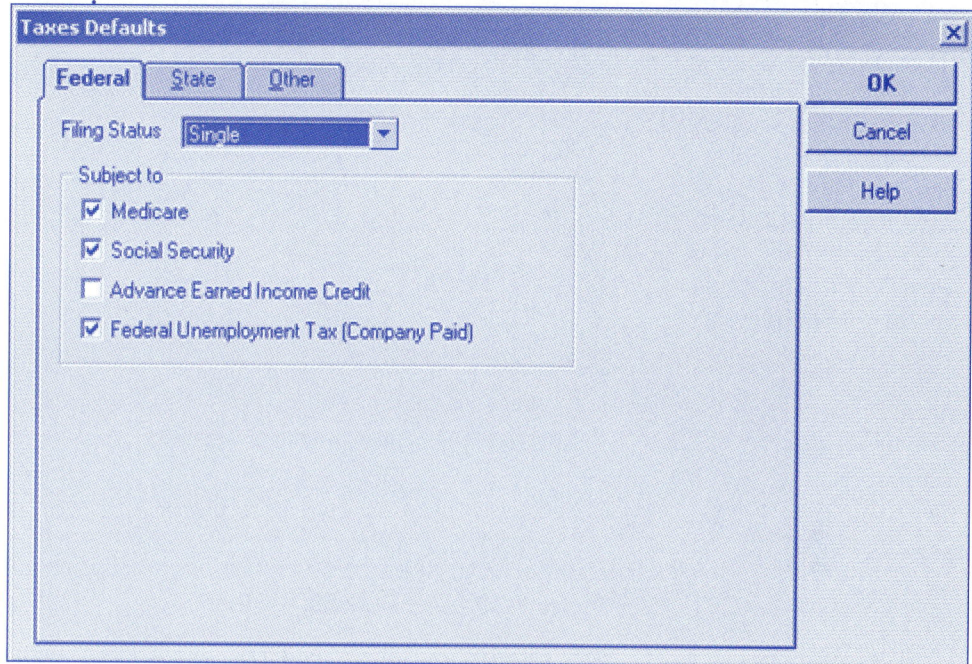

Figure 7-26 Taxes Defaults – Federal

29 On the State taxes default screen, select "CA" from the State drop-down menu in both the State Worked and State Lived sections. Then click the Other tab.

If your State has local taxes, click the Other tab and indicate the local taxes to which your employees are subject.

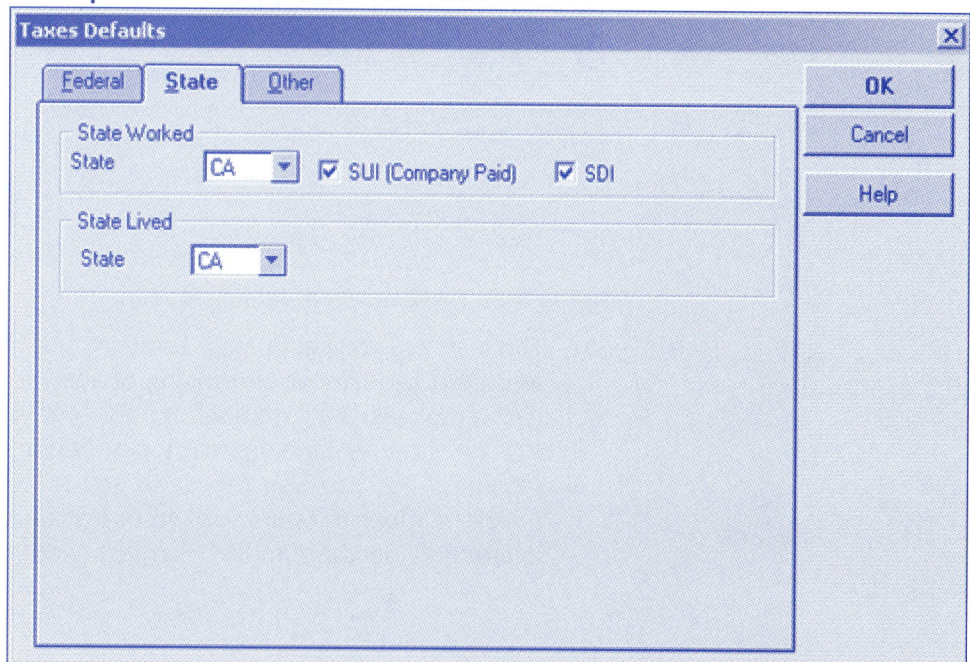

Figure 7-27 Taxes Defaults – State

NOTE

If your employees are subject to any of the local taxes that are supported by QuickBooks, you can add those taxes here. If your local tax is not supported directly by QuickBooks, you should set up a "User Defined" Other tax.

③⓪ Enter "CA – Employment Training Tax" in the Item Name section as shown in Figure 7-28. Then click **OK**.

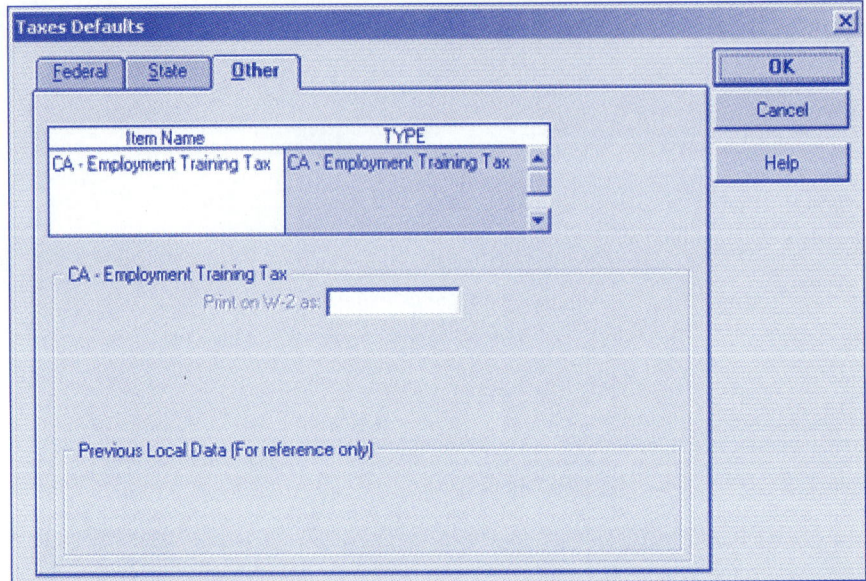

Figure 7-28 Taxes Defaults – Other

Default settings for sick/vacation time

③① On the Employee Defaults screen, click **Sick/Vacation** (see Figure 7-29).

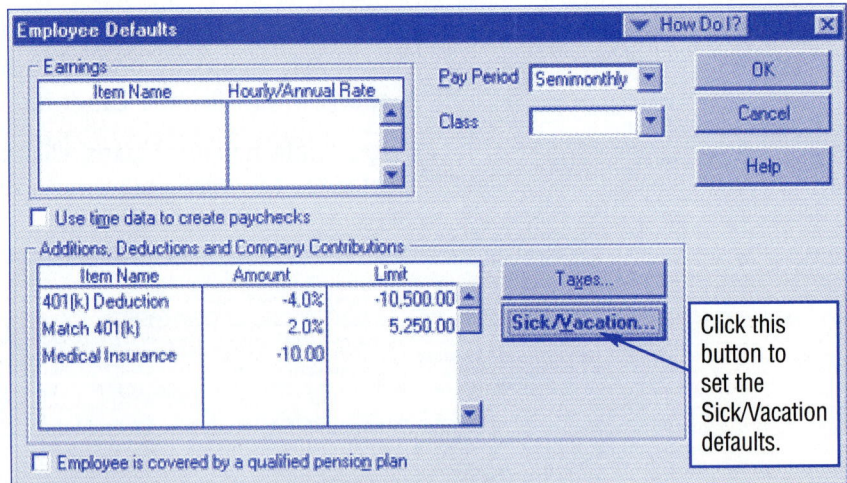

Figure 7-29 The Employee Defaults screen

This is where you set up your company policy for sick and vacation time. You can choose "Beginning of year" if your policy is to give each employee a set number of hours per year. If employees earn sick or vacation time for each pay period, then choose "Every paycheck." You can also choose to accrue sick and vacation based on the number of hours worked or just once per year. Select the appropriate option from the "Accrual period" drop-down menu.

32 In the Sick & Vacation Defaults screen, select "Every paycheck" from the "Accrual period" drop-down menu of the Sick section to indicate how often you want Sick Hours accrued (see Figure 7-30).

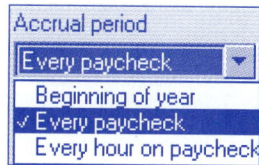

Figure 7-30 Accrual periods for sick and vacation time

33 Enter "1.00" in the *Hours accrued per paycheck* field and press <TAB>.

This is how many hours will accrue for each pay period.

34 Enter "20.00" in the *Maximum number of hours* field and press <TAB>.

QuickBooks will stop accruing hours after an employee reaches this maximum.

35 Check the "Reset hours each new year?" box.

Checking this box causes QuickBooks to set the balance of accrued sick hours to zero at the end of each year. This means that when employees don't use their sick time in a given year, they forfeit the remaining benefit.

36 Select "Every paycheck" from the "Accrual period" drop-down menu of the Vacation section to indicate how often you want vacation hours accrued (see Figure 7-31).

37 Enter "3.00" in the *Hours accrued per paycheck* field and press <TAB>.

38 Enter "200.00" in the *Maximum number of hours* field. Click **OK** to save your work on this screen, then click **OK** on the Employee Defaults screen to save your changes.

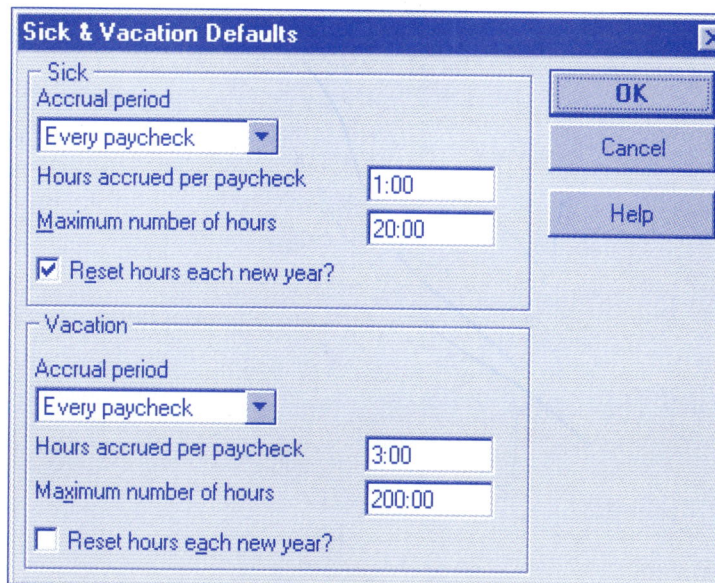

Figure 7-31 Sick and Vacation Defaults

39 After finishing the employee defaults, you'll be back in the Payroll Setup Wizard as shown in Figure 7-32. Click **Continue**.

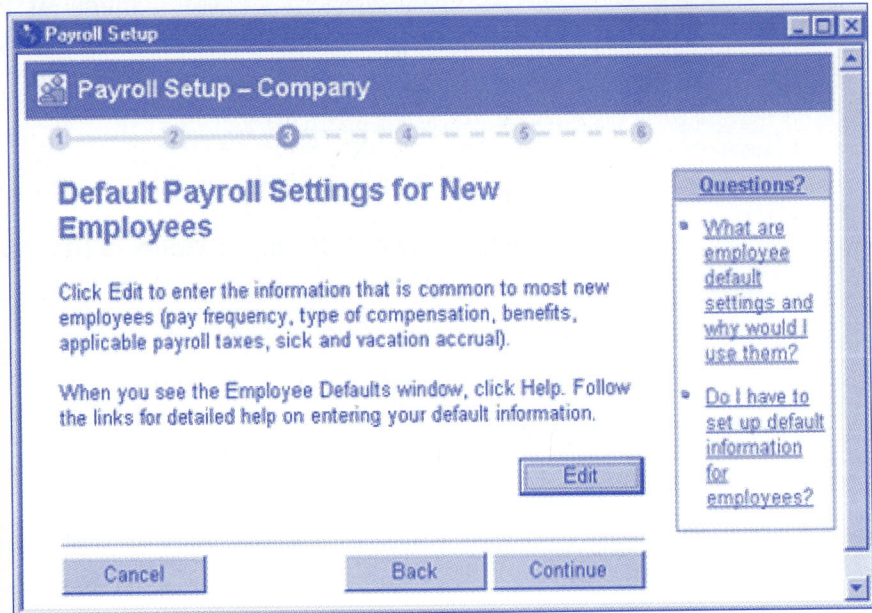

Figure 7-32 Payroll Setup after finishing Employee Defaults

40 Next you'll see the screen shown in Figure 7-33. Click **Done**.

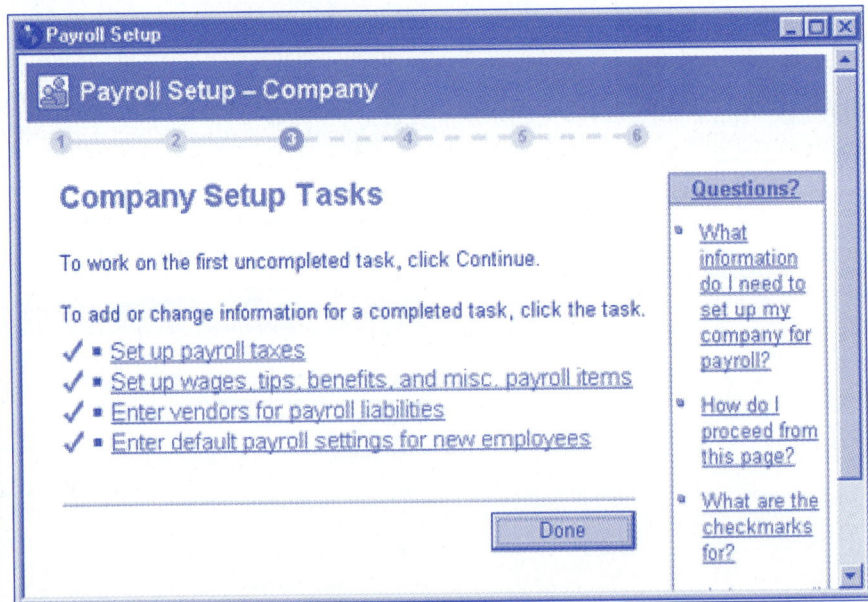

Figure 7-33 Payroll Setup Wizard tasks completed

SETTING UP EMPLOYEE RECORDS

COMPUTER TUTORIAL

After you have set up your Payroll Items and your Employee Defaults, you can set up each employee's payroll record.

1 On the Payroll Setup screen (Figure 7-34), click **Continue**.

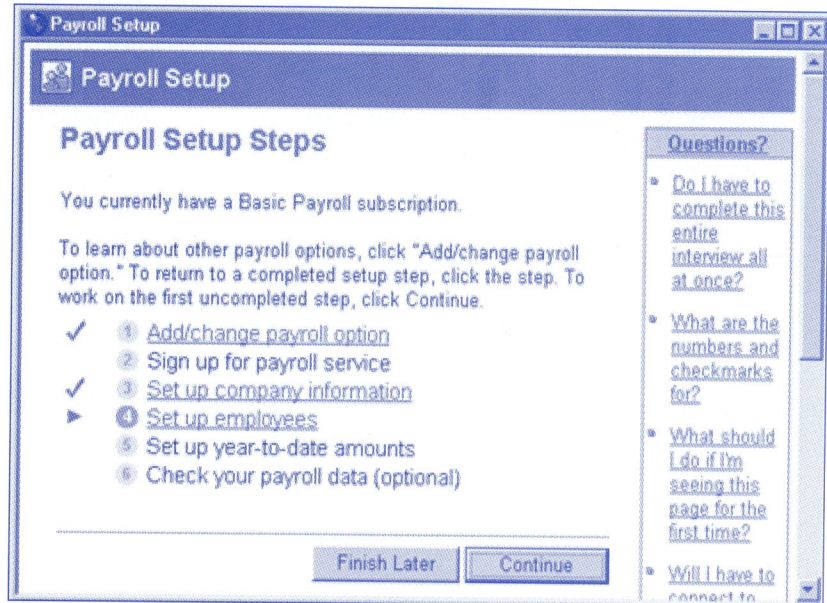

Figure 7-34 Set up employees

2 In the Employee Setup screen click **Add Employee** (Figure 7-35).

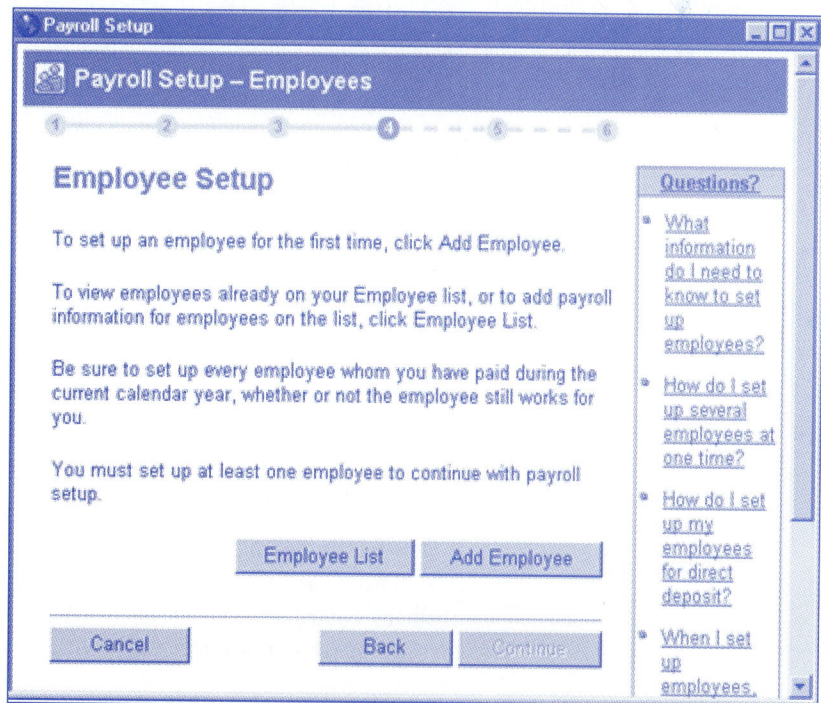

Figure 7-35 Employee Setup screen

NOTE

QuickBooks uses the
Employee name fields
(first name, middle
initial, then last name)
to distinguish between
employees. Therefore, if
two employees have the
same name, you must
not use their exact names
in the Employee list. If
necessary, add or omit a
middle initial to distin-
guish between different
employees with the
same name.

③ Enter the name and address information for Kati Reynolds as
shown in Figure 7-36, and then click the Additional Info tab.

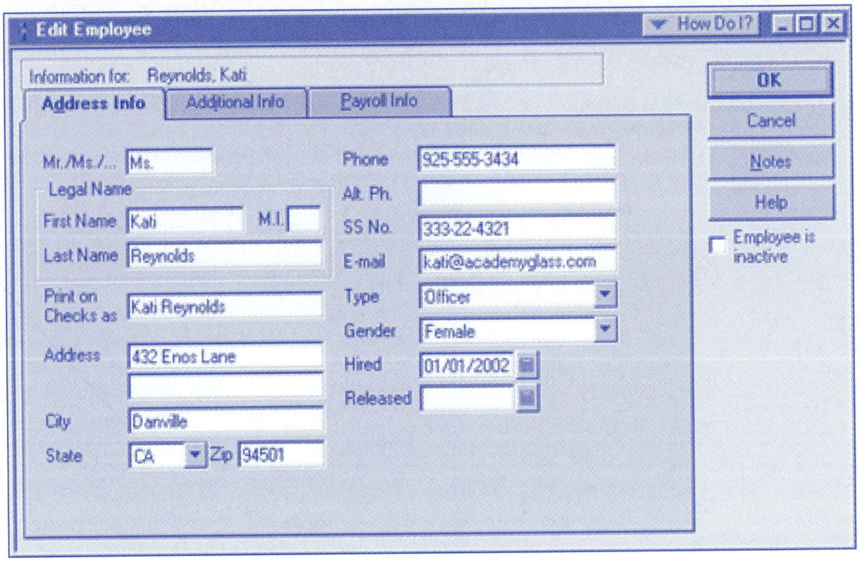

Figure 7-36 Adding an employee – Address Info tab

④ Enter the Additional information for Kati Reynolds as shown in
Figure 7-37.

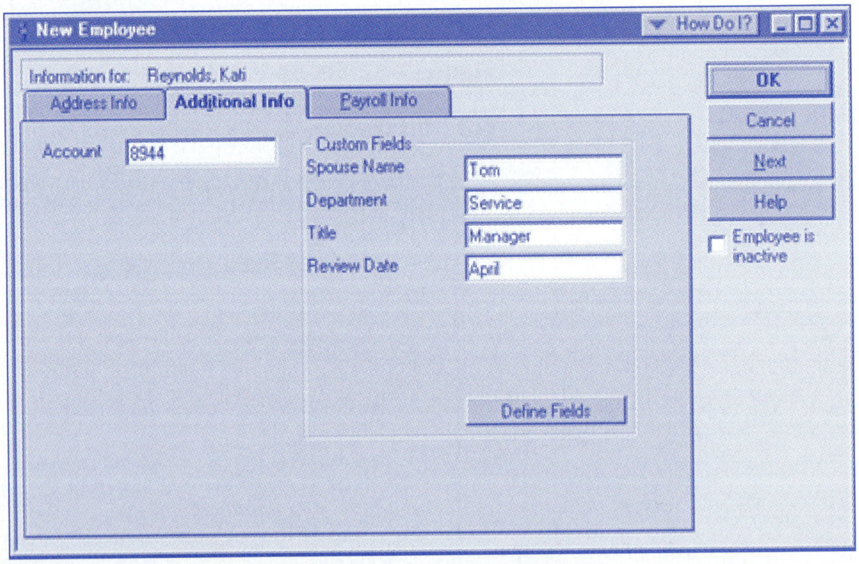

Figure 7-37 Adding an employee – Additional Info

Custom Fields for Payroll

If you want to track more detailed information about your employees,
use custom fields (see Figure 7-38). You can create up to 15 fields to be
used for customers, vendors, or employees. In the tutorial template file,
several custom fields have already been added.

⑤ Click **Define Fields**.

⑥ When you're finished reviewing the field names that are already
entered in your template file, click **OK**.

These fields allow you to create filtered list reports that focus on the value of one or more custom fields. For example, you could create a list of all employees whose review date is in March by creating an Employee list and filtering the review date field to March. For more details, see the Create a Customized Report section in Chapter 5.

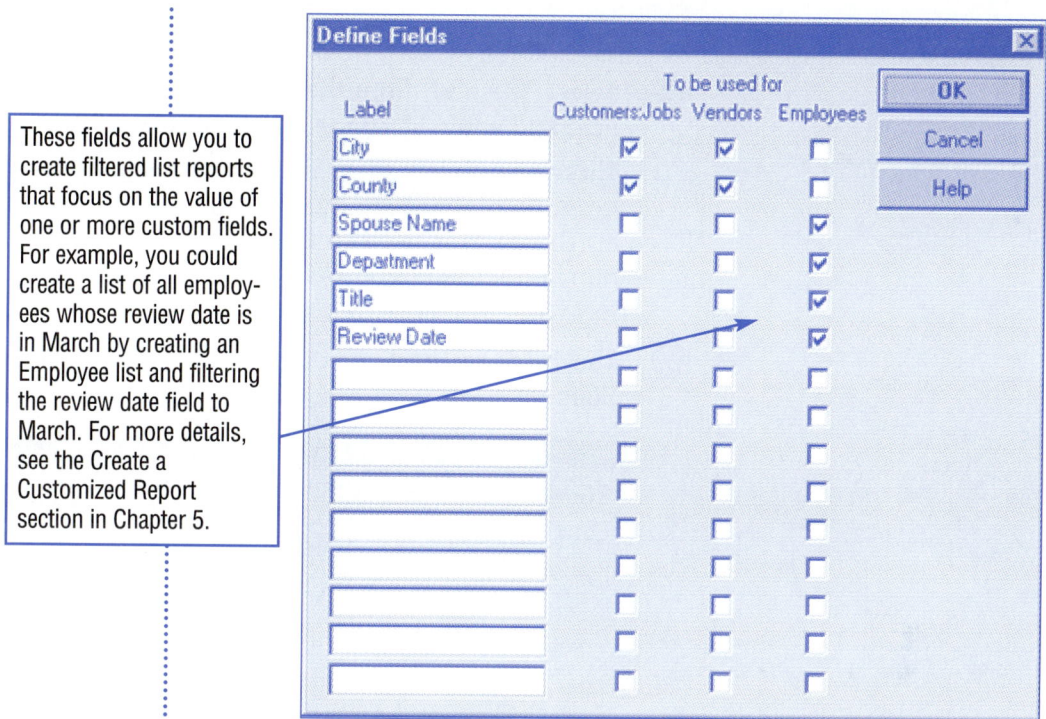

Figure 7-38 Defining custom fields

7 Click the Payroll Info tab.

8 Leave "Semimonthly" in the *Pay Period* field, and select "San Jose" from the drop-down menu in the *Class* field.

9 In the Earnings section of the Payroll Info screen, enter "Salary Regular" in the Item Name column, and "60,000.00" in the Hourly/Annual Rate column (see Figure 7-39).

On the Payroll Info screen, set up the specific payroll information for your employees. In the Earnings section, indicate which payroll items are used to pay a given employee.

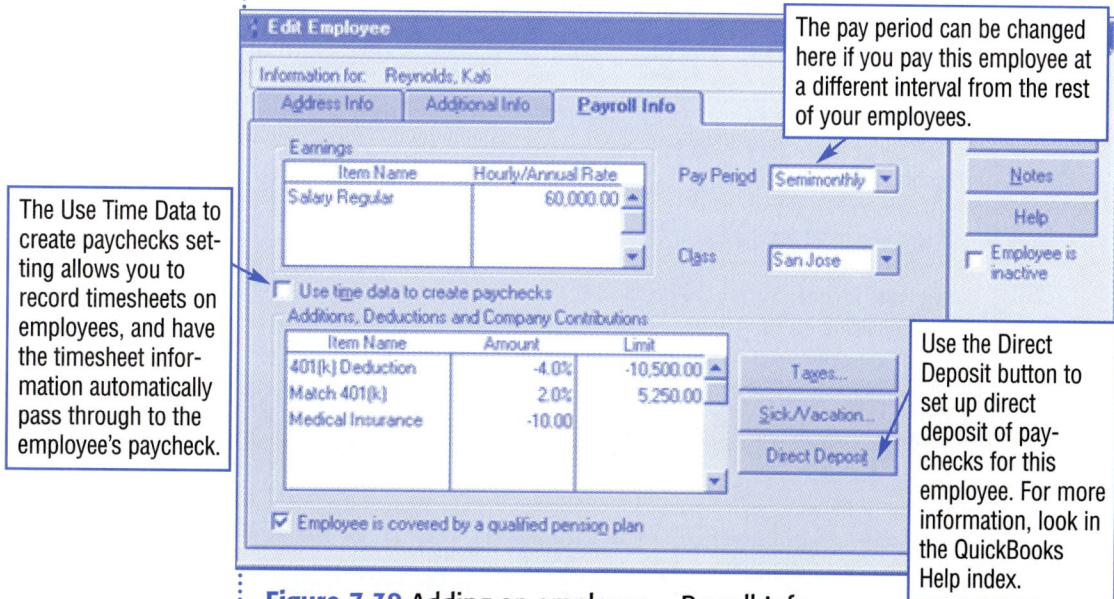

The pay period can be changed here if you pay this employee at a different interval from the rest of your employees.

The Use Time Data to create paychecks setting allows you to record timesheets on employees, and have the timesheet information automatically pass through to the employee's paycheck.

Use the Direct Deposit button to set up direct deposit of paychecks for this employee. For more information, look in the QuickBooks Help index.

Figure 7-39 Adding an employee – Payroll Info

⑩ Click **Taxes**.

⑪ Select "Married" from the drop-down menu in the *Filing Status* field and enter "2" in the *Allowances* field (see Figure 7-40).

These two fields affect the tax calculations for Federal payroll taxes. Each employee must submit IRS form W-4 to the employer. This form is used to calculate and report marital status and number of exemptions (allowances). Use the information on this form for each employee's record.

⑫ The fields in the Subject to section are pre-selected. Click the State tab.

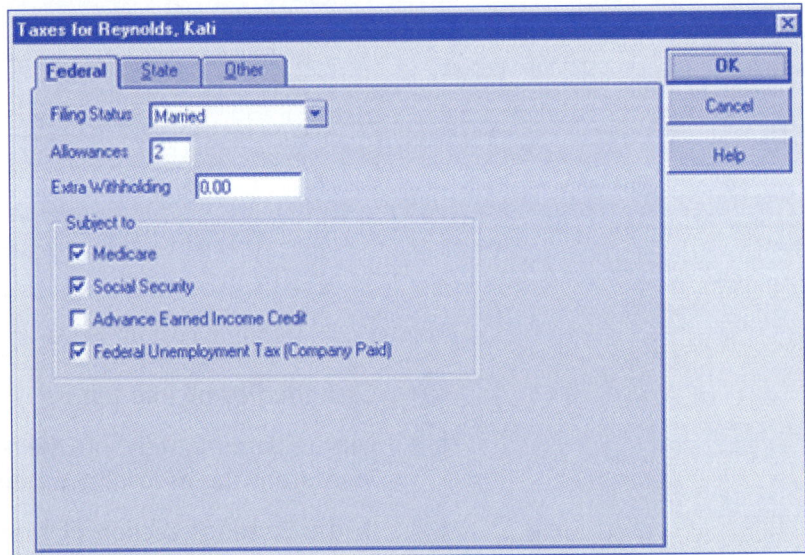

Figure 7-40 Federal taxes for Kati Reynolds

⑬ On the State screen, notice that the defaults from the employee defaults screen are already entered. Select "Married (two incomes)" from the drop-down menu in the *Filing Status* field and enter "2" in the *Allowances* field (see Figure 7-41). Then click the Other tab.

The State Lived and State Worked sections are very important. In order for SUI or SDI to calculate automatically, you must set the State Worked section as shown here. In order for State withholding tax to work correctly, you must set the State Lived section as shown here.

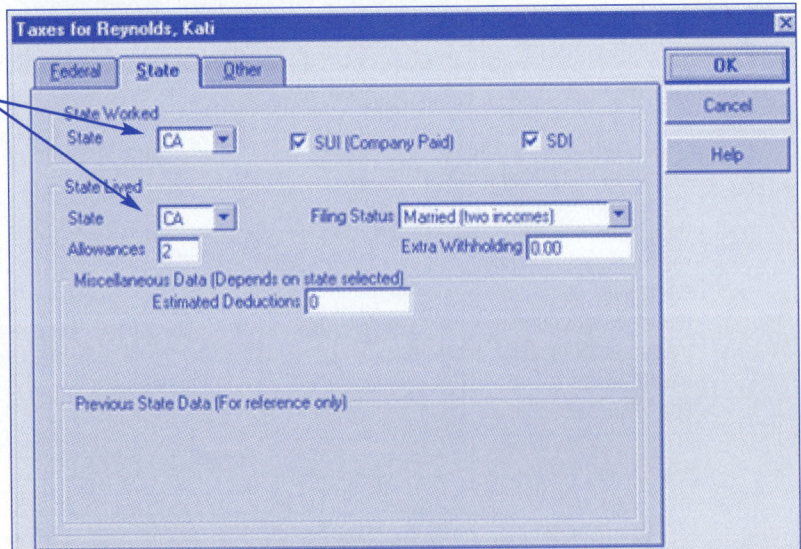

Figure 7-41 State Taxes for Kati Reynolds

14 Leave "CA – Employment Training Tax" in the Item Name column (see Figure 7-42). Then click **OK**.

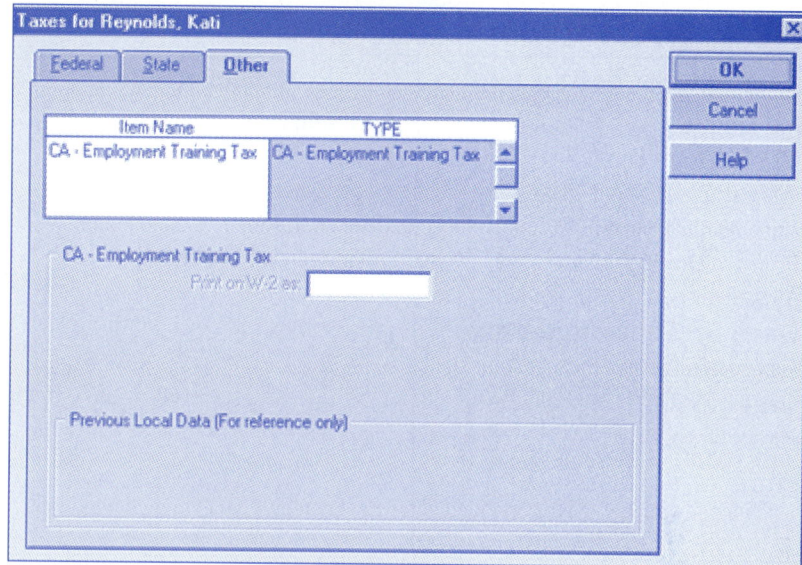

Figure 7-42 Other taxes for Kati Reynolds

15 Next, from the Payroll Info tab of the New Employee screen (see Figure 7-39), click **Sick/Vacation**.

16 Confirm that your screen has the information shown in Figure 7-43 and then click **OK**. This information automatically fills in from the Employee Defaults.

If your employees have accrued sick and/or vacation time as of your setup date, you can enter the balance of hours available for each in the Sick/Vacation screen.

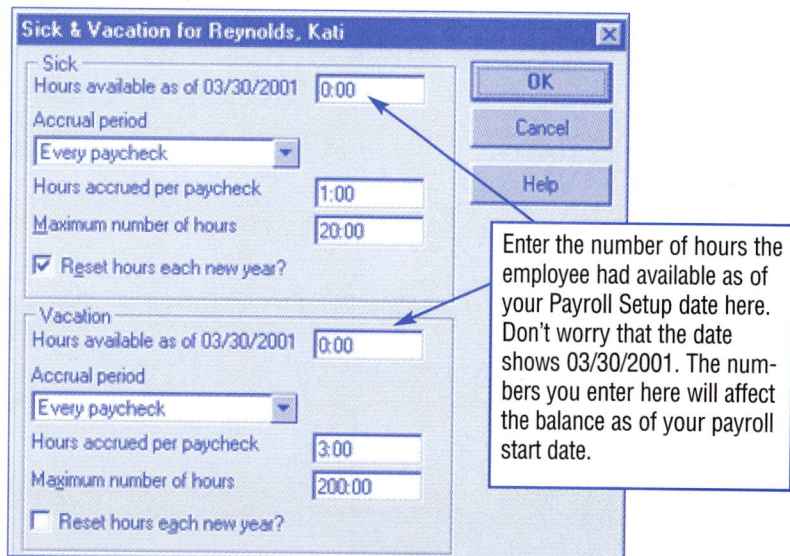

Enter the number of hours the employee had available as of your Payroll Setup date here. Don't worry that the date shows 03/30/2001. The numbers you enter here will affect the balance as of your payroll start date.

Figure 7-43 Sick & Vacation for Kati Reynolds

17 To save the new employee record, click **OK** on the New Employee screen.

⑱ Then click **Continue** on the Payroll Setup Wizard.

⑲ Next, add another employee by clicking **Add Employee** and enter the information shown in Table 7-2.

Employee Address Info	Additional Info	Payroll Info
Mr. Jim Moen 123 Hillsboro Lane Walnut Creek, CA 94569 Print As: Jim Moen Phone: 925-555-1233 SS No: 111-22-3333 Email: jim@academyglass.com Type: Regular Gender: Male Hired: 1/1/2002	Acct: 4683 Spouse: Kim Dept: Sales Title: Manager Review Date: March	Hourly Regular: 24.00 Hourly Sick: 24.00 Hourly Vacation: 24.00 Hourly Overtime: 36.00 √ Use Time data to create paychecks 401(k) Deduction 4% Limit $10,500 Match 401(k) 2% Limit $5,250 Medical Insurance$10.00 Pay Period: Semi Monthly Class: Walnut Creek √ Employee is covered by a qualified pension plan Use Sick and Vacation Defaults
Taxes – Federal	**Taxes – State**	**Taxes – Other**
Filing Status: Married Allowances: 2 Extra Withholding: 0 Subject to: √ Medicare √ Social Security √ Federal Unemployment Tax	State Worked: CA √ Subject to SUI √ Subject to SDI State Lived: CA Allowances: 2 Filing Status: Married (2 incomes) Extra withholding: 0	CA – Employment Training Tax

Table 7-2 New Employee information – Jim Moen

⑳ After adding the second employee, click **Continue** in the Payroll Setup Wizard until you reach the screen shown in Figure 7-44. Then click **Continue**.

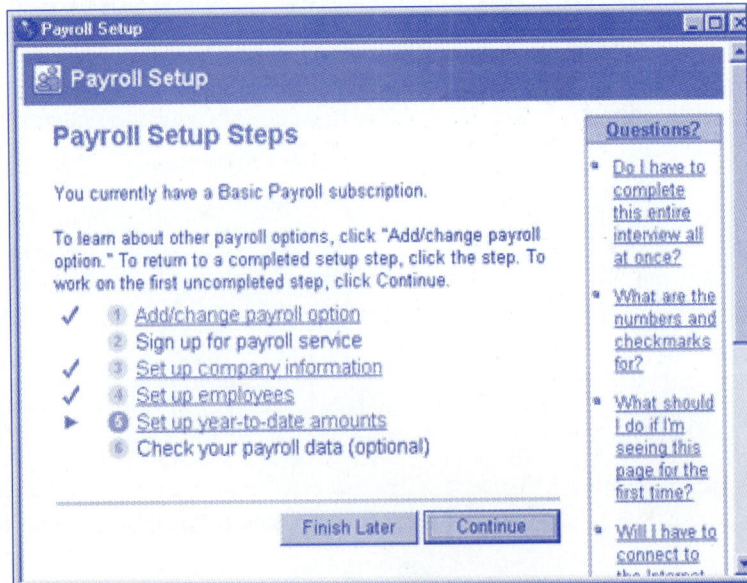

Figure 7-44 Setting up employees completed

COMPUTER TUTORIAL

SETTING UP YEAR-TO-DATE PAYROLL AMOUNTS

① Click **Continue** on the Enter Year-to-Date Payroll Amounts in QuickBooks screen.

If you were setting up your own payroll in the middle of the year, you would click **Set Up YTD Amounts** as shown in Figure 7-45. However, our example assumes that you're setting up payroll at the beginning of the year, so click **Continue**.

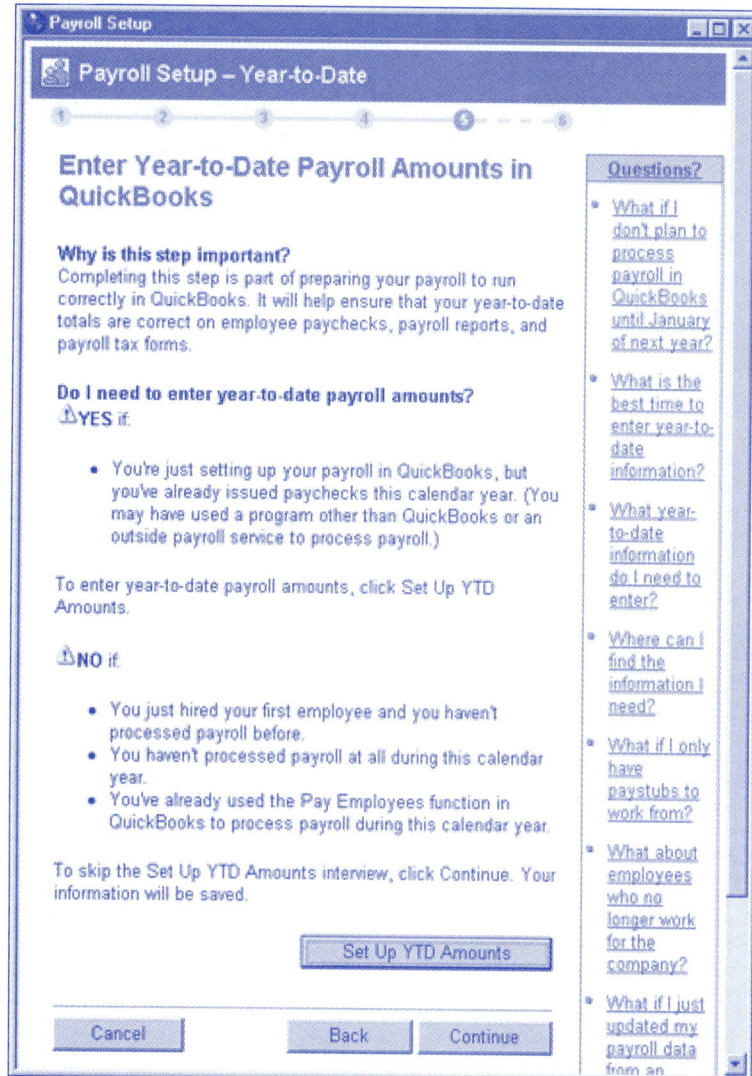

Figure 7-45 Entering YTD Payroll Amounts

2 On the screen shown in Figure 7-46, click **Continue**.

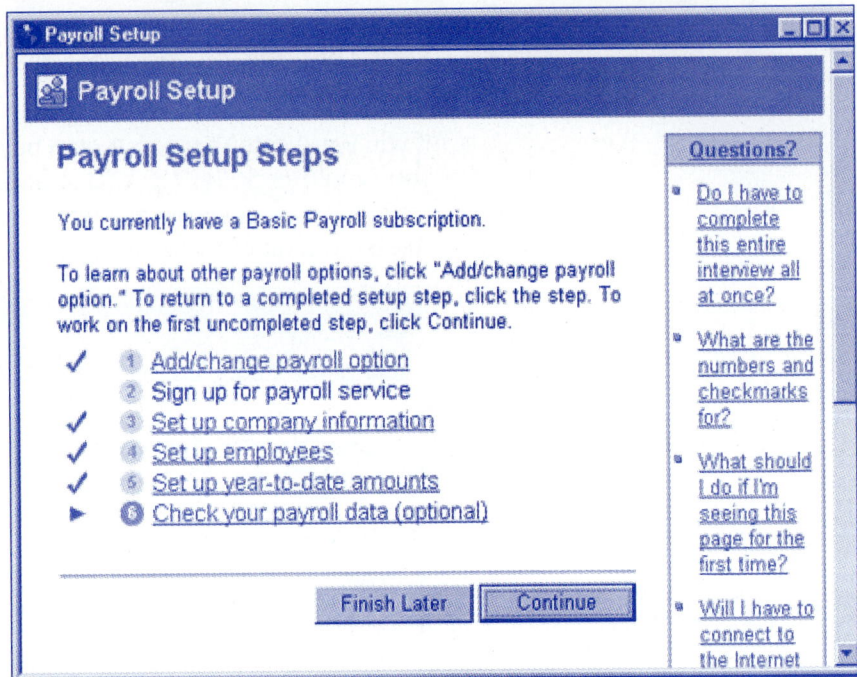

Figure 7-46 YTD Payroll Amounts completed

PAYROLL CHECKUP

COMPUTER TUTORIAL

1 Next, QuickBooks will run a check on your payroll setup. Click **Continue** (see Figure 7-47).

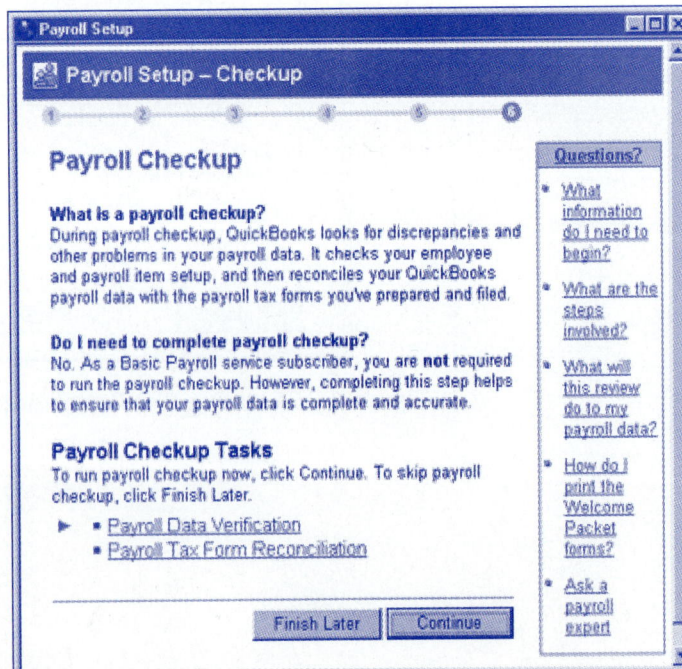

Figure 7-47 Payroll Checkup screen

2 Click **Continue** on the Payroll Checkup screen (see Figure 7-48).

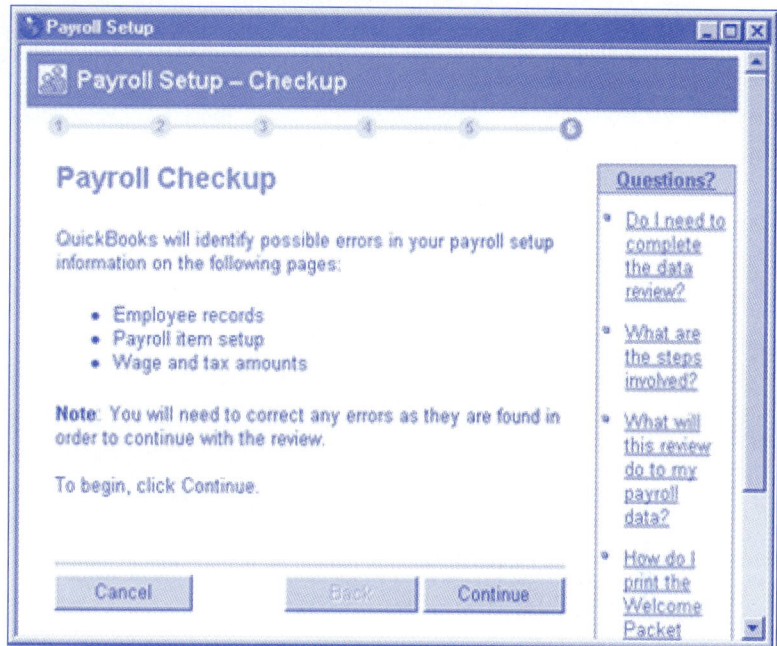

Figure 7-48 The Payroll Checkup screen before you begin data verification

3 After QuickBooks reviews all your employees and payroll items, it will generate a report similar to the one shown in Figure 7-49.

This report shows that there is no year-to-date payroll information for either of our employees. In our case this is normal, so you don't need to do anything. However, if you were setting up in the middle of the year, you would need to click **Edit** on each employee to enter his or her year-to-date earnings as well as the year-to-date payroll tax payments.

4 Click **Continue** on the screen shown in Figure 7-49.

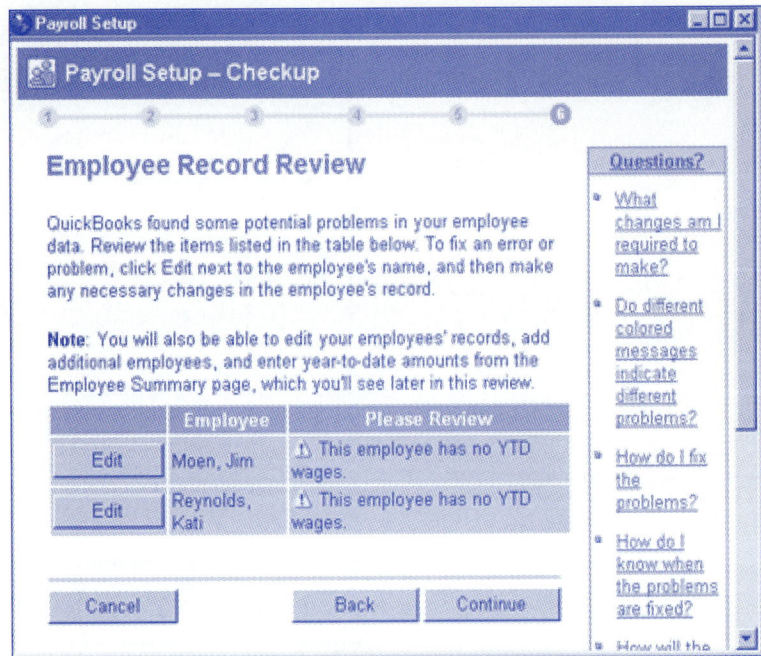

Figure 7-49 The Employee Record Review screen

5 In Figure 7-50, QuickBooks allows you to review each employee that is enrolled in a qualified pension plan. Leave both boxes checked and then click **Continue**.

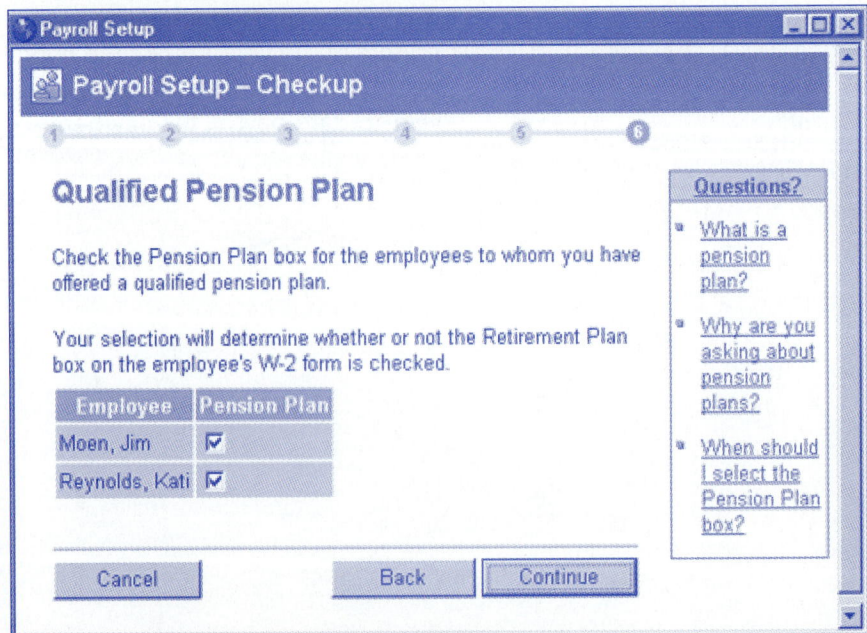

Figure 7-50 The Qualified Pension Plan screen

6 In the Employee Summary screen (Figure 7-51), QuickBooks displays some of the information for each employee. If any of this information is incorrect, click **Edit** and fix it. Then return to this screen and click **Continue**.

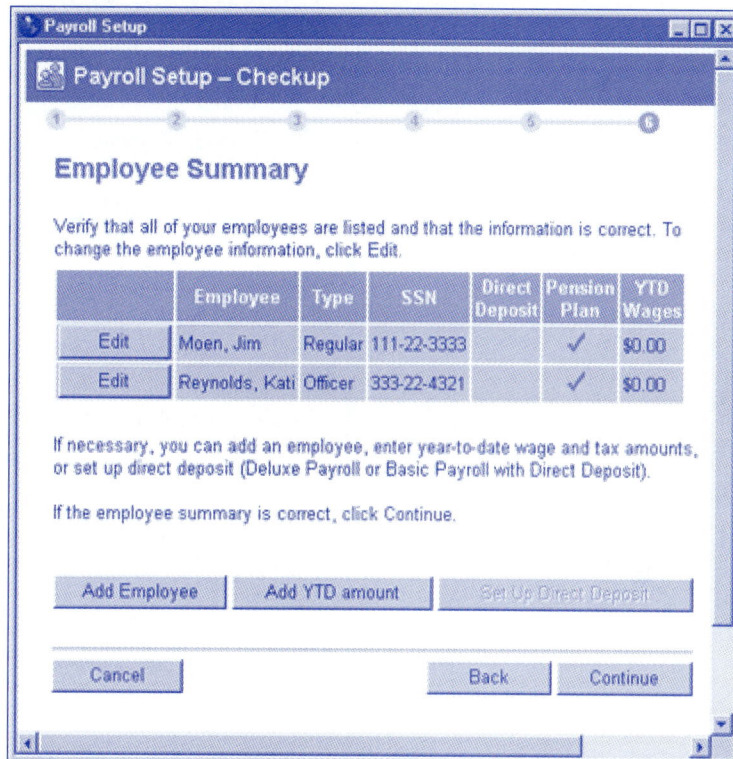

Figure 7-51 The Employee Summary screen

7 In the Employee Benefits screen (see Figure 7-52), leave all checkboxes blank and click **Continue**.

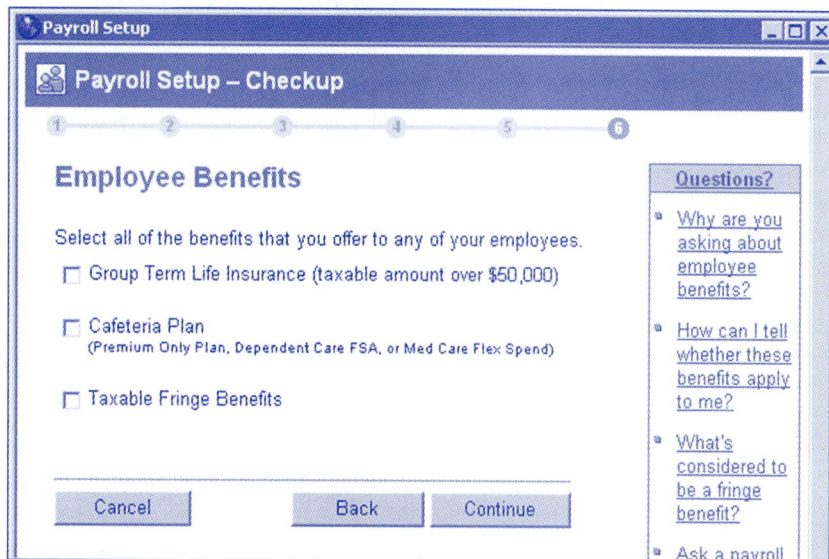

Figure 7-52 The Employee Benefits screen

8 QuickBooks will then review the setup of your Payroll items and display a report as shown in Figure 7-53.

Although the report shows that QuickBooks found some problems, your setup is correct if your screen matches the one in Figure 7-53. Click **Continue**.

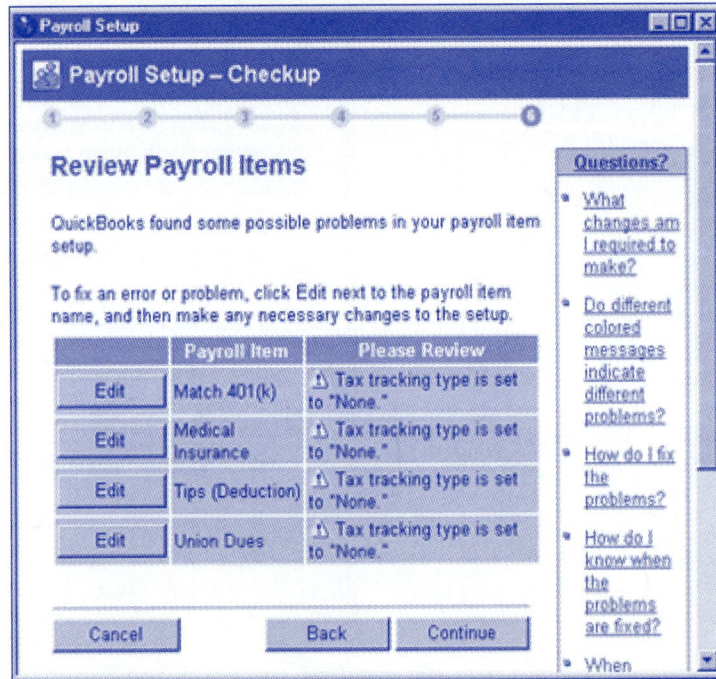

Figure 7-53 The Review Payroll Items screen

9 On the Wage and Tax Verification screen (see Figure 7-54), click **Continue**, and then click **Continue** again on the verification results screen.

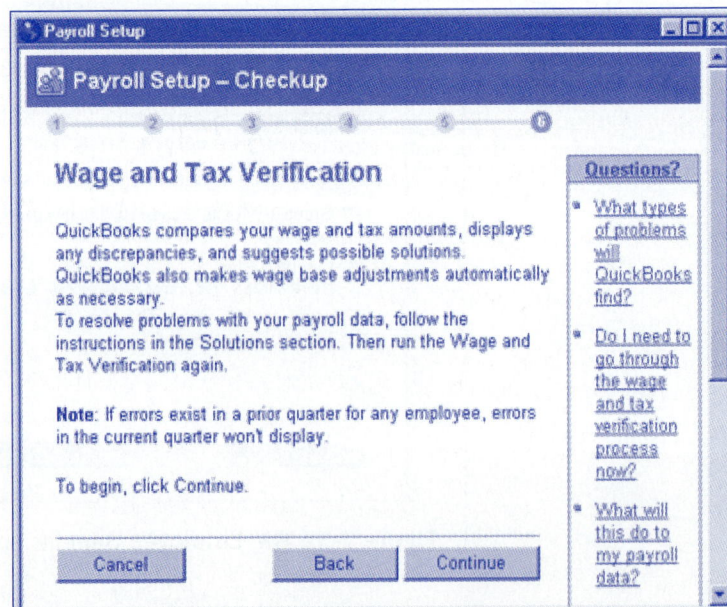

Figure 7-54 The Wage and Tax Verification screen

⑩ You will then see the screen shown in Figure 7-55. Click **Continue**.

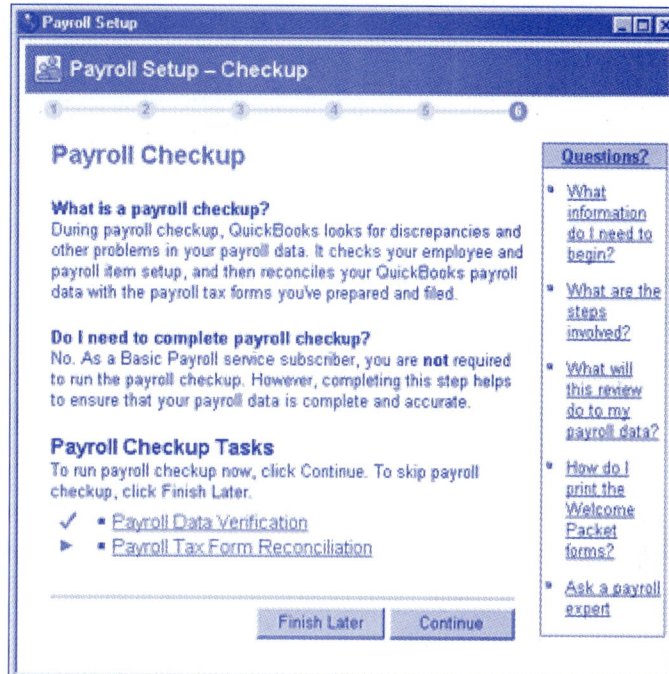

Figure 7-55 The Payroll Checkup screen

QuickBooks then does a checkup to see that your previously filed tax forms agree with your data.

Since you're setting up at the beginning of the year, click **Continue** through these screens. If you were setting up in the middle of the year, you would enter data from your payroll tax forms, so that QuickBooks could check to see that you entered the data correctly.

⑪ Click **Continue** on the screen shown in Figure 7-56.

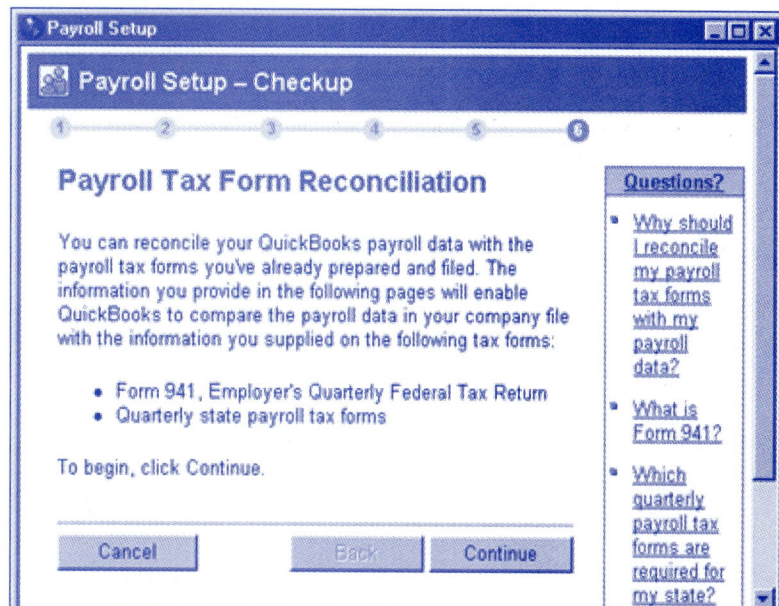

Figure 7-56 The Payroll Tax Form Reconciliation screen

⑫ Select "Yes" on the screen shown in Figure 7-57 and then click **Continue**.

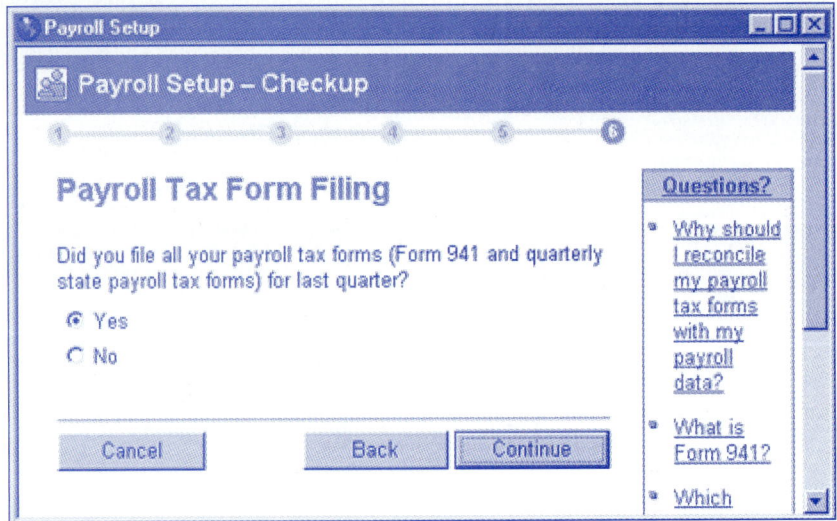

Figure 7-57 The Payroll Tax Form Filing screen

⑬ Leave numbers as shown in Figure 7-58 and click **Continue**.

> **NOTE**
>
> The next two screens change as your Windows system date changes. If you run the checkup prior to the end of the first quarter, QuickBooks won't display the screens shown in Figure 7-58 and Figure 7-59. However, if you run the checkup after the end of the first quarter, you'll see these screens with a column for each quarter during the year.

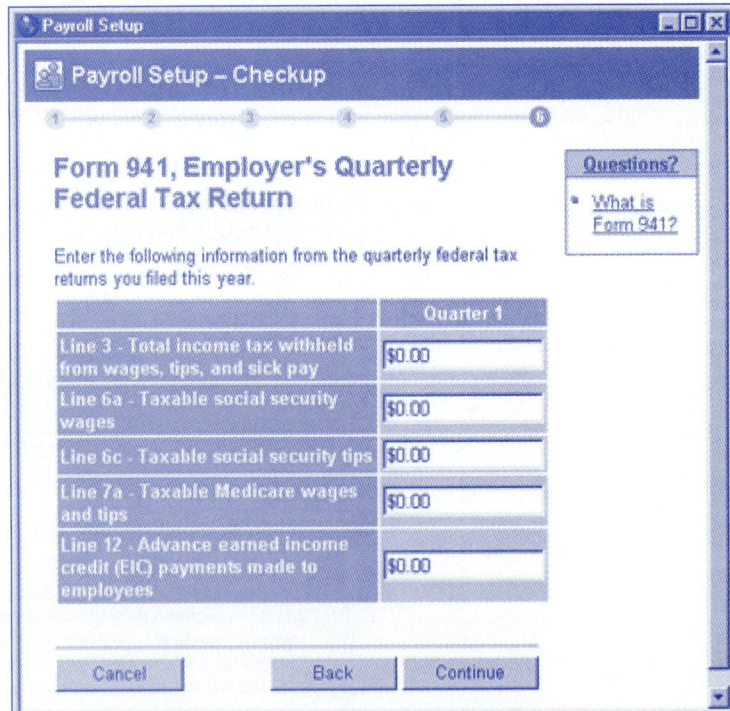

Figure 7-58 The Form 941 Return screen

⑭ Leave numbers as shown in Figure 7-59 and click **Continue**.

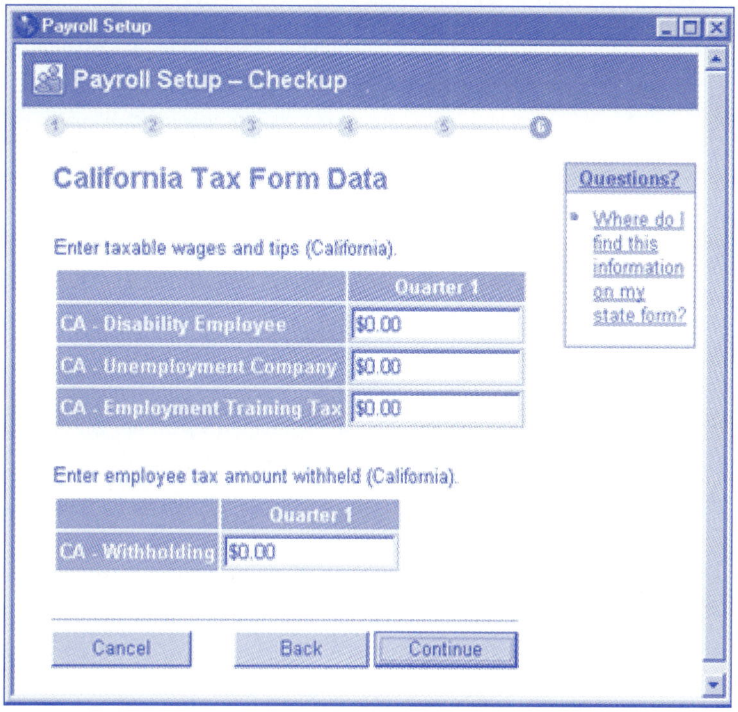

Figure 7-59 The California Tax Form Data screen

⑮ After comparing your data, QuickBooks will display the screen shown in Figure 7-60. Click **Continue**.

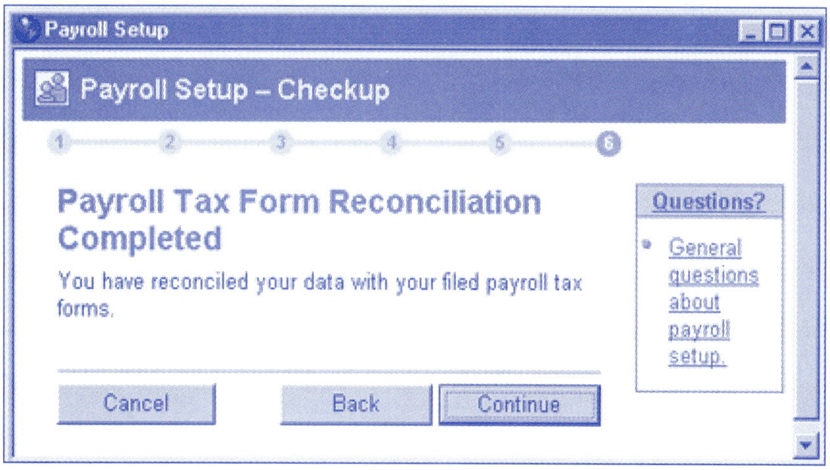

Figure 7-60 The Payroll Tax Form Reconciliation Completed screen

16 When you've finished the payroll checkup, you'll see the screen shown in Figure 7-61. Click **Done**.

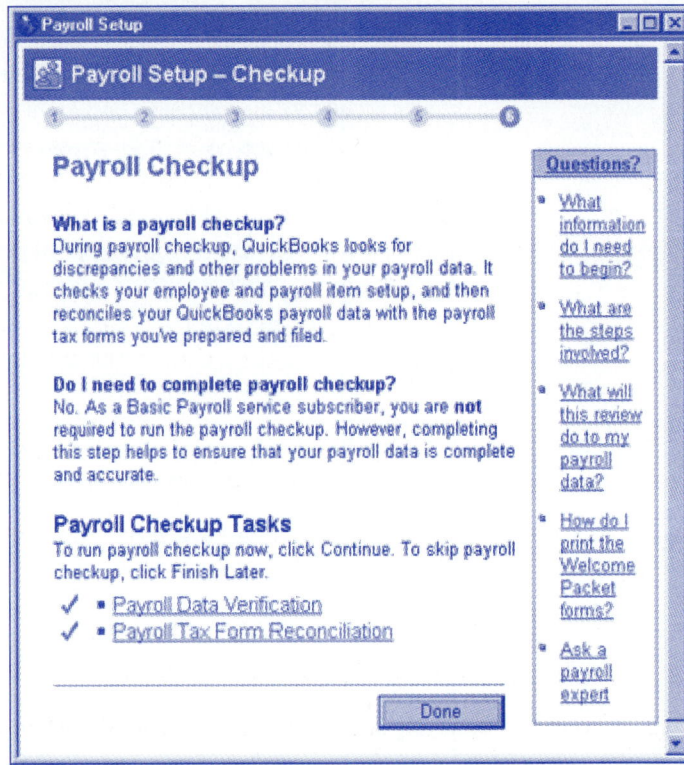

Figure 7-61 The Payroll Checkup screen

17 All the steps are now complete. Click **Done** on the screen shown in Figure 7-62.

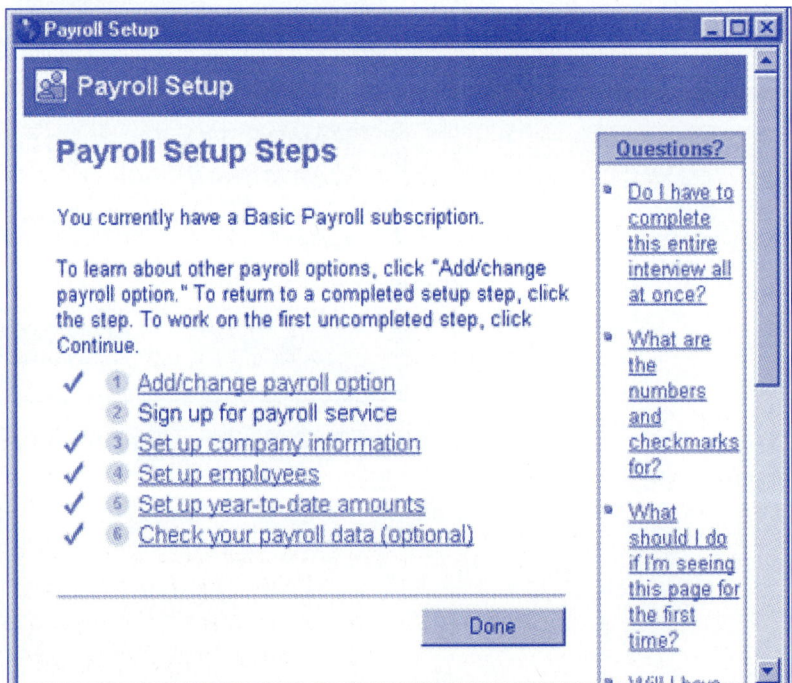

Figure 7-62 Final checklist

THE ACCOUNTING BEHIND THE SCENES – PAYROLL ITEMS

Now that you've finished with the Payroll Setup Wizard, consider the accounting behind the scenes involving payroll items.

Payroll Items define the relationship between Items you put on paychecks and the Chart of Accounts. Payroll Items are used by QuickBooks to track each kind of compensation, withholding tax, employer tax, addition, and deduction from paychecks. Using Payroll Items, QuickBooks tracks the detail it needs to calculate paychecks, look up taxes in the tax table, prepare detailed reports, and prepare your payroll tax forms.

Some Payroll Items accumulate payroll liabilities (withholdings and company taxes) into liability accounts according to which tax vendor collects the tax. For example, the Federal Withholding Item accumulates Federal taxes withheld into the Federal Payroll Taxes liability account. It also accumulates those taxes as being owed to the Payee (vendor) that you indicate in the Item.

Payroll Items are set up so that QuickBooks automatically makes all the accounting entries when you process paychecks and payroll liability payments.

Wage Items

> **NOTE**
>
> QuickBooks automatically accumulates sick and vacation hours, but it does not record a liability for this unpaid expense in the General Ledger. If you want to accrue expenses and liabilities for unpaid sick and vacation time, you'll need to make an adjustment using a General Journal entry. For more information about General Journal entries, see page 458.

There are two types of **Earnings Items: Salary Wage** Items and **Hourly Wage** Items. When you set up Earnings items, you indicate whether the Item tracks regular pay, sick, or vacation. For example, if you pay an employee for 50 regular hours and 10 hours of vacation, you'll use a regular pay Item and a vacation pay Item, with the corresponding number of hours for each.

Salary Wage

Salary Wage Items are used to track payments of gross wages to salaried employees. Since these Items represent company expenses, these Items increase (debit) an expense account, usually Gross Wages or Officer's Compensation expense.

Hourly Wage

Hourly Wage Items are used to track payments to hourly employees. Just like the Yearly Salary Items, these Items increase (debit) an expense account, usually Gross Wages or Officer's Compensation Expense.

Commission

Commission Items are used to track payments of commissions. These Items can be defined as a percentage of the number that you enter when you create paychecks. Commission Items increase (debit) an expense account, usually Gross Wages expense.

Addition

Addition Items are used to track amounts added to paychecks beyond gross wages. For example, you might set up an Addition Item to track bonuses or employee expense reimbursements. Additions increase (debit) an expense account.

Deduction

Deduction Items are used to track deductions from paychecks. You can create separate deduction items for each deduction you use on paychecks. For example, if you have a retirement plan with salary deferrals, you can create a 401(k) Deduction Item that calculates a percentage of the total gross wages to be deducted before QuickBooks calculates the Federal and State income tax. Since deductions are withheld from paychecks, they increase (credit) a liability account. The Item also accumulates a balance due to the vendor to whom the deductions are paid.

Company Contribution

Company Contribution Items are used to track additional money that the company contributes as a result of a paycheck. A company contribution is not paid to the employee, but to a vendor on behalf of an employee. For example, if your company matches employees' 401(k) contributions, use a Company Contribution Item to track it. Since this Item represents additional company expense but is not paid directly to the employee, the Item increases (debits) an expense account and increases (credits) a liability account. The Item also accumulates a balance due to the vendor to whom the contribution is paid.

Federal Tax

Federal Tax Items are used to track Federal taxes that are withheld from paychecks or paid by the employer.

The following Federal Tax Items are employee taxes and are withheld from paychecks: **Federal Withholding**, **Social Security Employee**, and **Medicare Employee**. These Items are associated with a liability account and with the vendor to whom the tax is paid (usually the Internal Revenue Service or your bank).

The following Federal Tax Items are company taxes: **Federal Unemployment**, **Social Security Company**, and **Medicare Company**. These Items are company-paid taxes; they increase (debit) an expense account, usually Payroll Tax Expense, and increase (credit) a liability account, usually Federal Payroll Taxes.

State Tax

State Tax Items are used to track State taxes that are withheld from paychecks or paid by the employer. Each state has different taxes, so depending on your State, you might have a **State Withholding**, **State Disability**, and/or **State Unemployment Tax** Item.

State Withholding taxes are employee taxes and are withheld from paychecks. These Items are associated with a liability account and with the vendor to whom the tax is paid — usually the State Department of Revenue or Taxation.

State Disability taxes are usually employee taxes, but this varies by state.

State Unemployment taxes are usually company taxes, but this also varies by state.

Other Tax

Other Tax Items are used to track other State or local taxes that are withheld from paychecks or paid by the employer. Each locality has different taxes, so check in your State for which local taxes apply to payroll. If your local tax is not directly supported by QuickBooks (i.e., if you don't see the tax in the Other Tax List), you'll need to use a "User Defined" other tax to track it.

Based on Quantity

Deduction Items, Addition Items, and Company Contribution Items are used to withhold or contribute a fixed amount, or a percentage of gross or net pay. However, sometimes you want these Items to calculate a percentage of some other number. For example, a bonus might be a calculation of 5% of the gross profit for the company. In this case, the bonus Item is set up with the "Based on Quantity" box checked (see Figure 7-63). Then, when the bonus is added to a paycheck, you'll manually enter the amount (gross profit in this example) on which the calculation should be based.

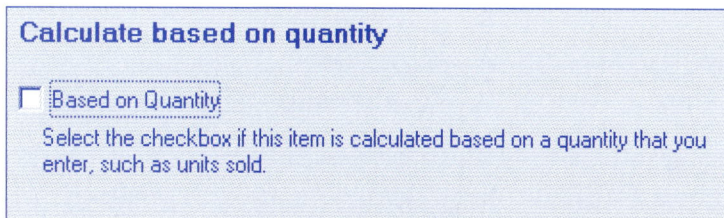

Calculate based on quantity

☐ Based on Quantity

Select the checkbox if this item is calculated based on a quantity that you enter, such as units sold.

Figure 7-63 Some items can be set up based on quantity.

ADDING NEW PAYROLL ITEMS

The Payroll Setup Wizard sets up most of your items, but you'll probably need to set up a few more on your own. Also, some of the items will need to be edited, so that they use the proper accounts you created in the section above.

If your company is a corporation, the IRS requires you to report compensation of officers separately from the rest of the employees. To track officers' compensation separately from the rest of your employees, you should create an additional compensation Payroll Item called Officer's Salary.

Adding a wage item:

COMPUTER TUTORIAL

1 Display the Payroll Items list by selecting the **Lists** menu and then choose **Payroll Item List**.

2 Since you haven't run your first payroll, QuickBooks asks if you want help setting up payroll (see Figure 7-64). Click **No**.

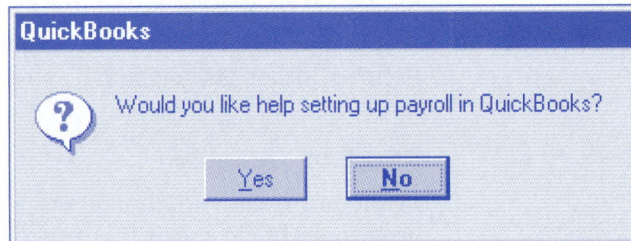

Figure 7-64 QuickBooks asks if you want help setting up Payroll.

3 The Payroll Item List (see Figure 7-65) shows all the items that you have set up using the Wizard.

Item Name	Type
Salary Regular	Yearly Salary
Salary Sick	Yearly Salary
Salary Vacation	Yearly Salary
Hourly Overtime	Hourly Wage
Hourly Regular	Hourly Wage
Hourly Sick	Hourly Wage
Hourly Vacation	Hourly Wage
Bonus	Addition
Tips (Addition)	Addition
401(k) Deduction	Deduction
Medical Insurance	Deduction
Tips (Deduction)	Deduction
Union Dues	Deduction
Match 401(k)	Company Contribution
Advance Earned Income Credit	Federal Tax
Federal Unemployment	Federal Tax
Federal Withholding	Federal Tax
Medicare Company	Federal Tax
Medicare Employee	Federal Tax
Social Security Company	Federal Tax
Social Security Employee	Federal Tax
CA - Withholding	State Withholding Tax
CA - Disability Employee	State Disability Tax
CA - Unemployment Company	State Unemployment Tax
CA - Employment Training Tax	Other Tax

Figure 7-65 Payroll Item list

Adding an Officer's Salary wage item

4 To add a new item, select **New** from the *Payroll Item* menu at the bottom of the Payroll Item List, or press <Ctrl+N> (see Figure 7-66).

Figure 7-66 Select New from Payroll Item menu

5 Select "Custom Setup" on the Select setup method screen (see Figure 7-67) and click **Next**.

Since you're setting up an item (Officer's Salary) that isn't handled by the Easy Setup Wizard, you'll have to use the custom setup.

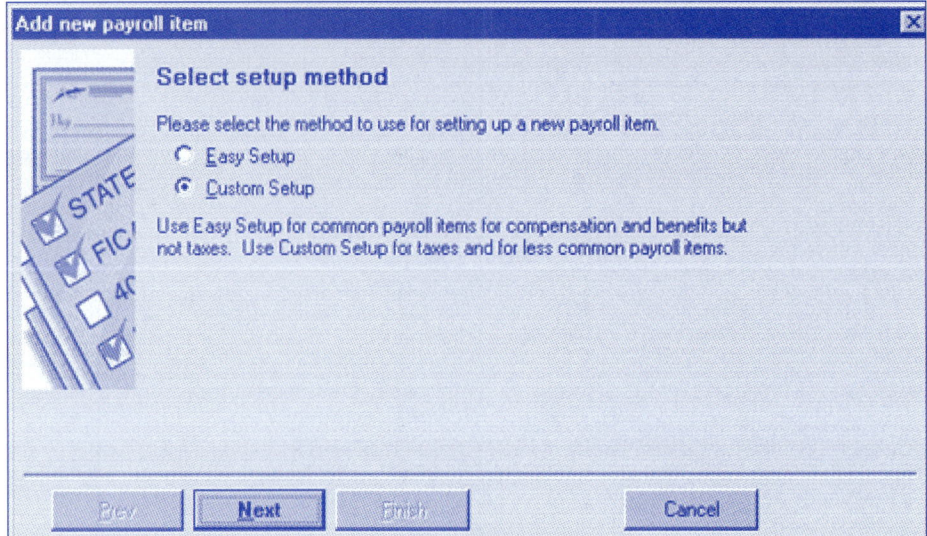

Figure 7-67 The Select setup method screen

6 Select "Wage" on the Payroll item type screen and click **Next** (see Figure 7-68).

QuickBooks provides a guided process for setting up Payroll Items. Click **Next** or **Prev** to navigate between screens.

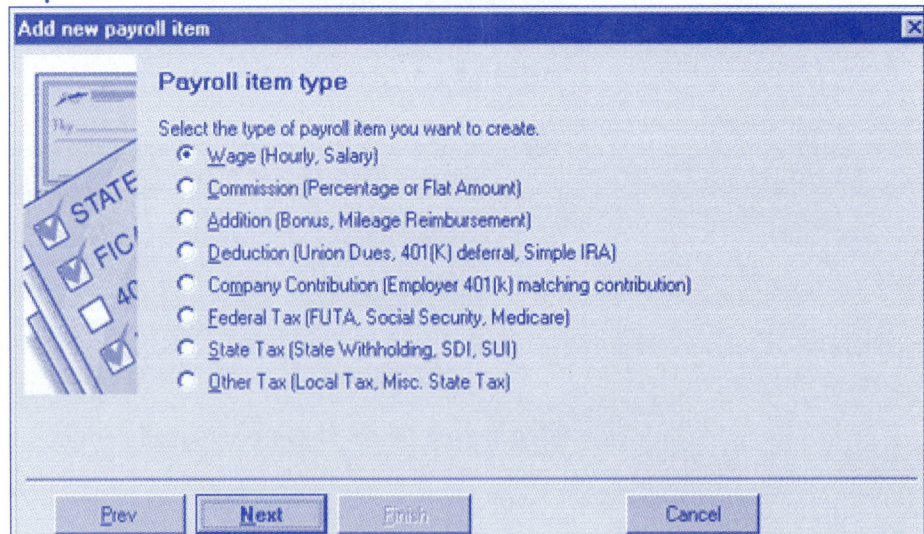

Figure 7-68 Payroll Item types

7 Leave "Salary Wages" and "Regular Pay" selected on the Wages screen (see Figure 7-69) and click **Next**.

You can set up hourly wage items on this screen too. Also, each Wage Item can be for regular pay, sick pay, or vacation pay. When you pay an employee for sick or vacation time, you'll use a Sick or Vacation Pay Item in addition to the regular pay item.

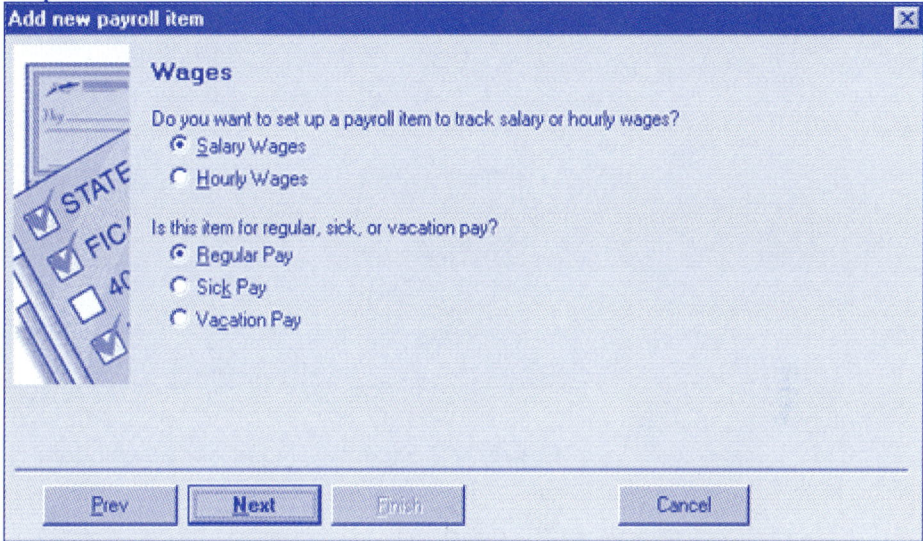

Figure 7-69 Use this screen to set up salary and hourly wages.

8 Enter "Officer's Salary" on the Name used in paychecks and payroll reports screen and click **Next** (see Figure 7-70).

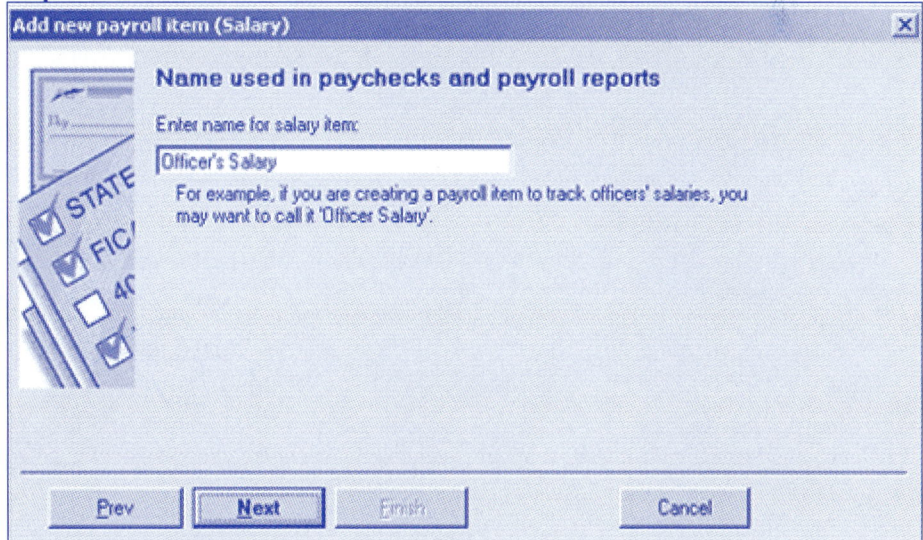

Figure 7-70 Use this screen to name the Item.

9 Select "Payroll Expenses:Officer's Compensation" on the Expense account screen and click **Finish** (see Figure 7-71).

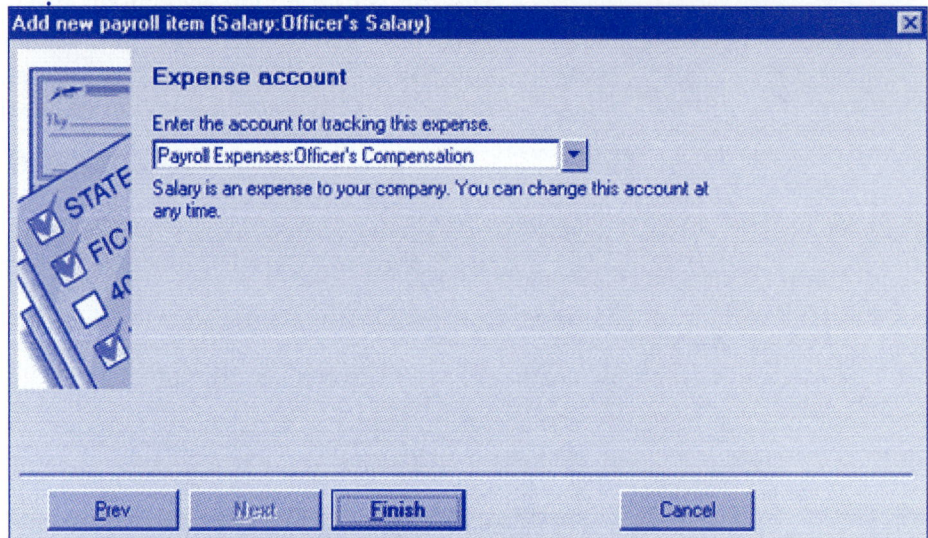

Figure 7-71 Expense account for payroll item

10 Create two more Salary Items like the one shown in Figure 7-70. Create one that tracks sick pay (called Officer's Salary Sick) and one that tracks vacation pay (called Officer's Salary Vacation). They both should be expensed to "Payroll Expenses:Officer's Compensation."

Close the Payroll Item List.

Adding a Commissions Item

COMPUTER TUTORIAL

If you pay commissions to your employees, you can set up a Commission Item to track payments for commissions. You might need several of these Items if you track different kinds of commissions.

① Select *Lists* and choose **Payroll Item List**.

② Click **No** on the QuickBooks screen that asks if you need help with payroll setup.

③ Select **New** from the *Payroll Item* menu at the bottom of the Payroll Item list.

④ Select "Custom Setup" on the Select setup method screen.

⑤ Select "Commission" from the Payroll item type screen and click **Next** (see Figure 7-72).

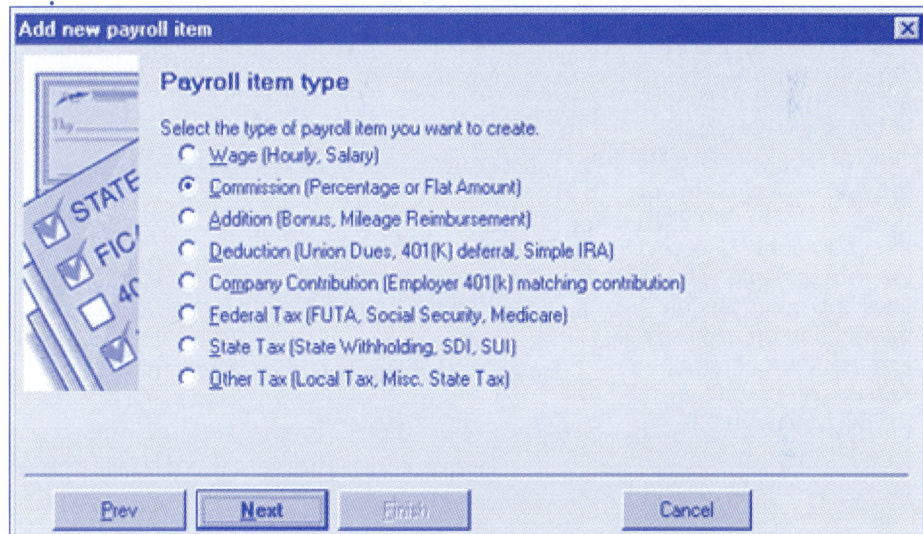

Figure 7-72 Payroll item type screen with Commission Selected

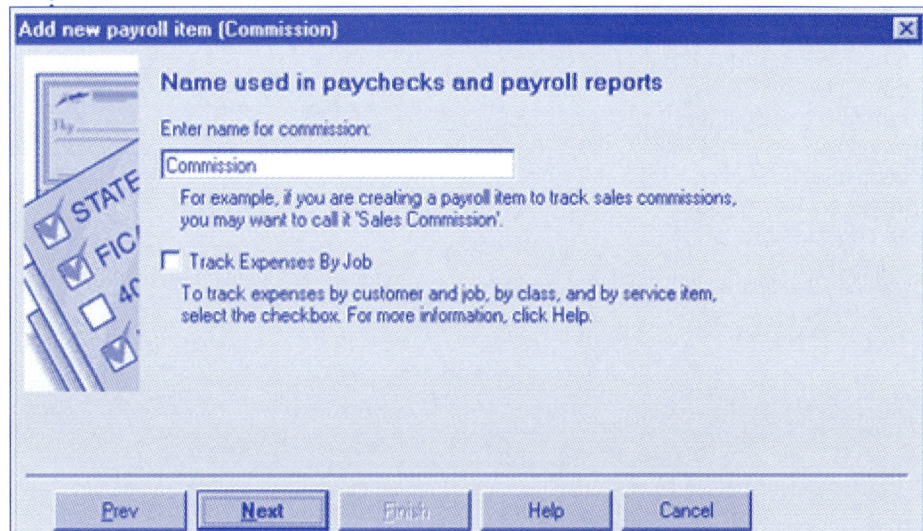

Figure 7-73 Name used in paychecks and payroll reports screen

It is not possible to assign commissions to a particular job unless all of the wages on the paycheck are assigned to that one job.

If you want to allocate commissions to specific jobs for employees who work on more than one job, it's better to set up an hourly wage item called "Commission." Then use this item on paychecks to record the commission by entering the rate of commission (e.g., percentage) in the rate column. Then enter the sales dollars in the hours column. QuickBooks will calculate the rate multiplied by the hours. Then, to apply different amounts to each job, use multiple split lines and enter the job information on each split line. For more information on job-costing payroll, see page 399.

TIP

If you pay commissions to contract employees (i.e., 1099 contractors), don't use the Payroll function to calculate or pay those commissions. Instead, use Service Items on Bills to track all commissions of the same type.

6 Enter "Commission" in the Name used in paychecks and payroll reports screen and click **Next**.

Do not check the "Track Expenses By Job" box (see Figure 7-73). If you chose "Track Expenses By Job" on a commission Item, QuickBooks would allocate commissions to jobs based on the proportion of wages for each job.

7 Select "Payroll Expenses:Gross Wages" on the Expense account screen and click **Next** (see Figure 7-74).

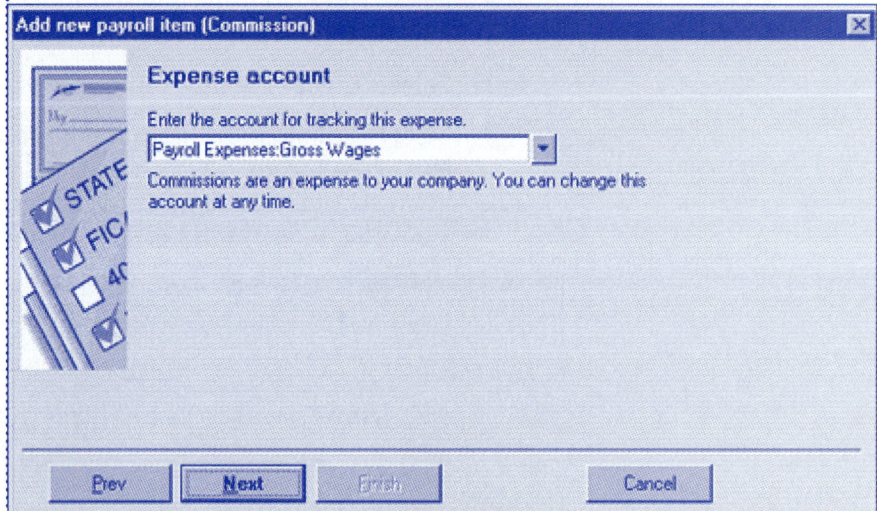

Figure 7-74 Expense Account screen

8 Enter "5.0%" in the Default rate screen and click **Finish** (see Figure 7-75). This sets the default rate when you add this Item to an employee record.

Close the Payroll Itme List.

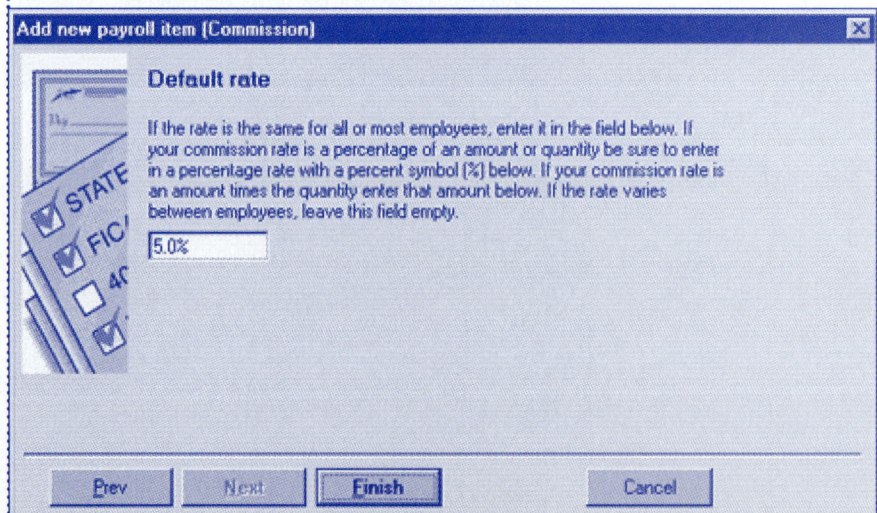

Figure 7-75 Set the default commission rate.

EDITING PAYROLL ITEMS

You will need to edit several of the items created by the Payroll Setup Wizard so that they will affect the appropriate accounts in the Chart of Accounts. For example, the Federal withholding tax is set up to affect the Payroll Liabilities account instead of one of its subaccounts (Federal PR Taxes).

Editing the Federal Withholding item

COMPUTER TUTORIAL

1 Display the Payroll Items list by selecting the *Lists* menu, then choose **Payroll Item List** (see Figure 7-76).

Figure 7-76 The Payroll Item list

2 Double-click on the **Federal Withholding** payroll item.

3 Click **Next** on the Name used in paychecks and payroll reports screen.

④ On the following screen (see Figure 7-77), choose which liability account you want this Item to affect. In this example, select "Payroll Liabilities:Federal PR Taxes" from the "Liability account" drop-down menu.

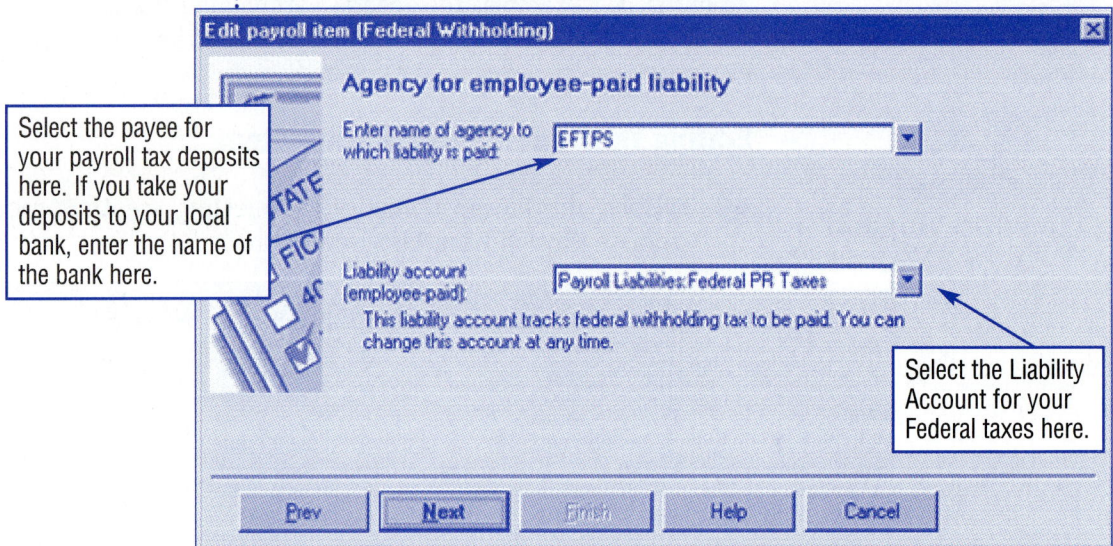

Select the payee for your payroll tax deposits here. If you take your deposits to your local bank, enter the name of the bank here.

Select the Liability Account for your Federal taxes here.

Figure 7-77 Edit the Liability Account for Federal Withholding item.

⑤ Click **Next** twice and then click **Finish** to save the change.

COMPUTER TUTORIAL

Editing the Federal Unemployment item

① To modify the Federal Unemployment item, double-click on the **Federal Unemployment** item in the Payroll Item List.

② On the Agency for company-paid liability screen of the Edit Payroll Item Wizard, change the account information as shown in Figure 7-78. Then click **Next**.

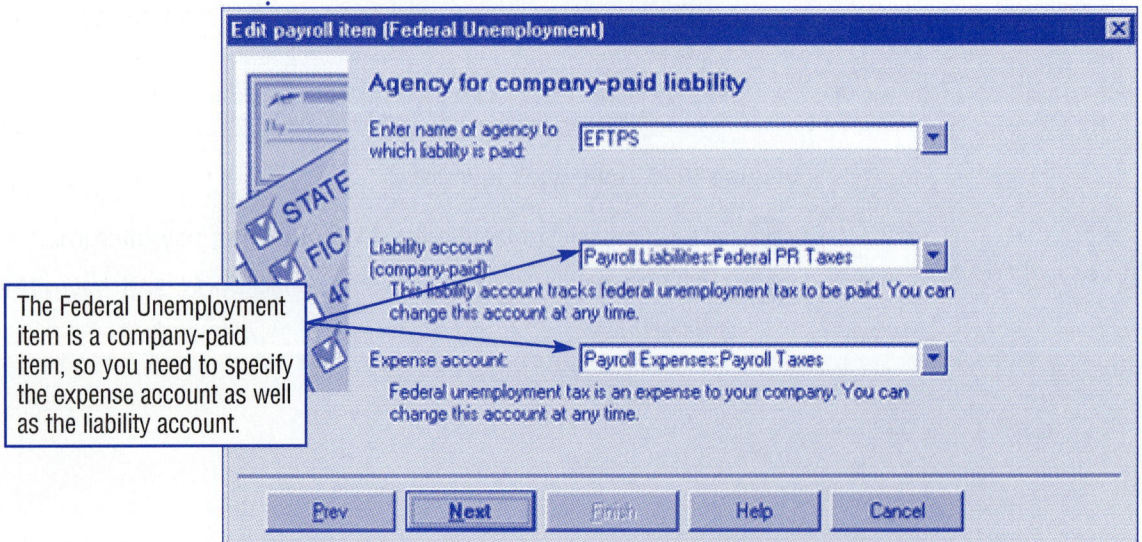

The Federal Unemployment item is a company-paid item, so you need to specify the expense account as well as the liability account.

Figure 7-78 Edit the Federal Unemployment Item's accounts.

Since Federal Unemployment is an employer-paid tax, you need to enter two account names, one for the liability account and one for the expense account.

3 The tax rate of "0.8%" is already selected (see Figure 7-79). Click **Next** twice and then click **Finish**.

If your State has a State Unemployment Tax you may be eligible for a FUTA tax reduction, making your FUTA tax 0.8% instead of 6.2%. Select the appropriate button on this screen. If you're not sure if you're eligible for this reduction, ask your accountant.

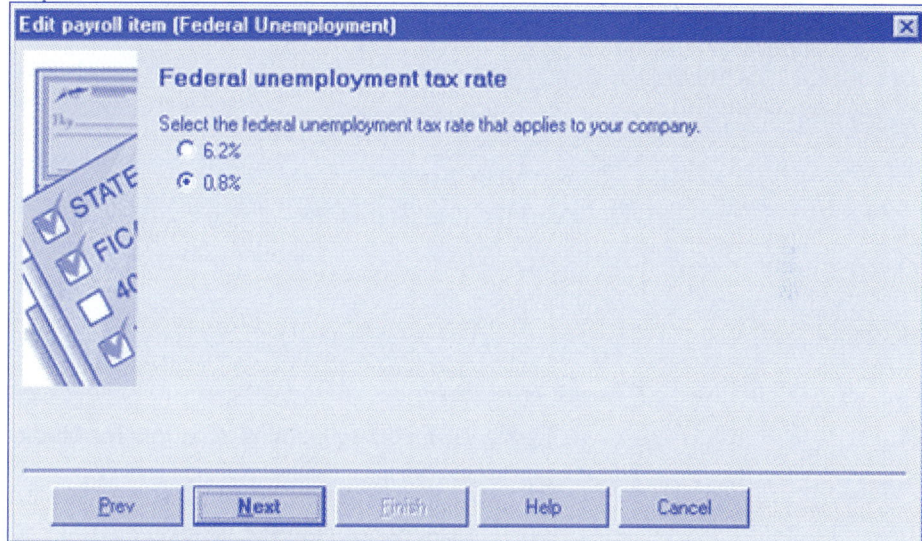

Figure 7-79 Setting the Unemployment tax rate

In the Payroll Item List, there are two Medicare and two Social Security items (see Figure 7-80). These two items for each withholding are grouped together in QuickBooks and are modified using a single edit screen. This means that, when you change the Medicare Company account, the Medicare Employee account is automatically updated and vice versa. The same applies to the Social Security accounts.

Figure 7-80 Medicare and Social Security tax items

Editing the Social Security and Medicare items

1 Modify all four of the Medicare and Social Security Items to indicate the liability account for the employer- and employee-paid portions as shown in Figure 7-81.

Notice that both the employee and employer information are displayed on the Liability agency screen.

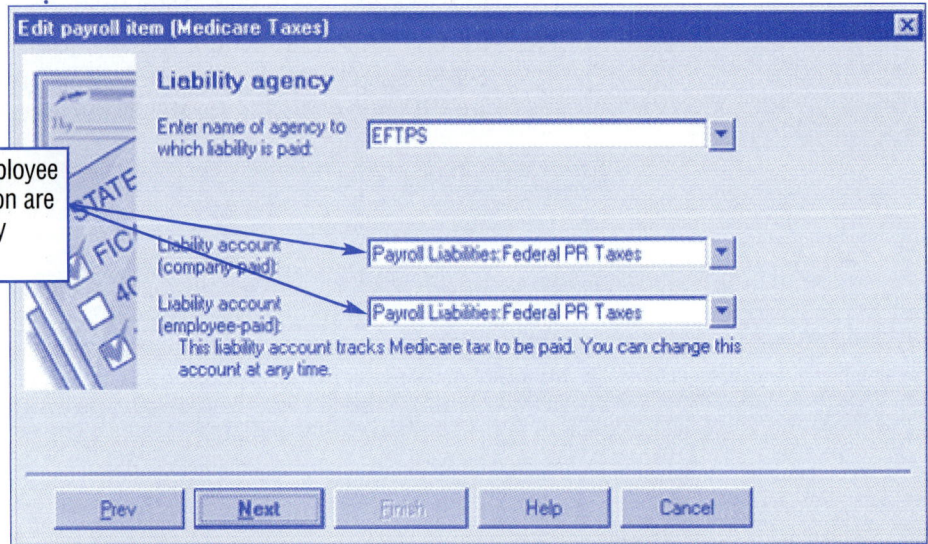

Figure 7-81 Editing Liability accounts for Medicare item

2 On the Expense account screen for both the Medicare and the Social Security items, select "Payroll Expenses:Payroll Taxes" from the drop-down menu in the *Enter the account for tracking this expense* field (see Figure 7-82). Then click **Next** through the remaining screens and click **Finish** on the last screen.

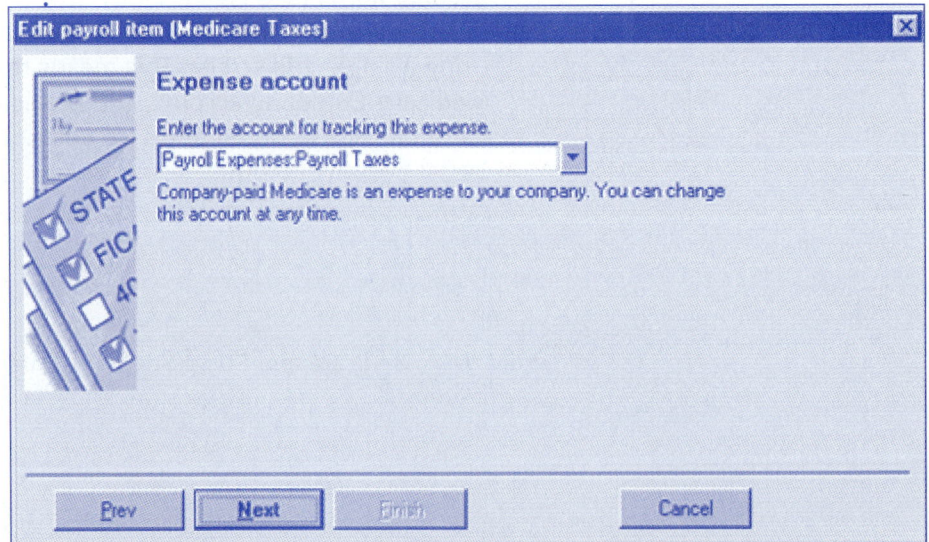

Figure 7-82 Enter the Expense account.

COMPUTER TUTORIAL

Editing the State Withholding item

1 To modify the State Withholding Item, double-click on "CA-Withholding" in the Payroll Item List.

2 Click **Next**.

3 On the Agency for employee-paid liability screen, change the *Liability account (employee-paid)* by selecting "Payroll Liabilities: State PR Taxes" from the drop-down menu. Your screen should look like Figure 7-83.

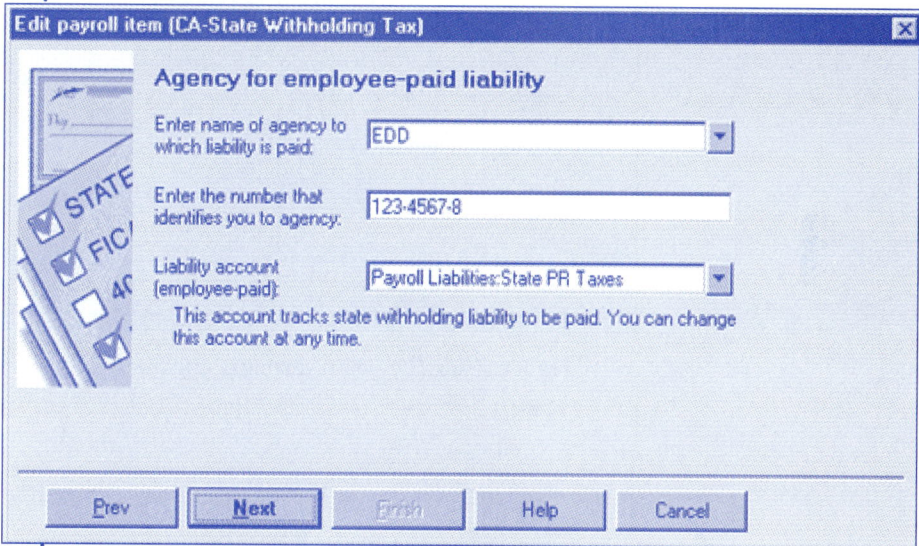

Figure 7-83 Editing the State Withholding item

4 Click **Next**.

5 On the Taxable compensation screen, QuickBooks automatically checks each of the Wage Items that are subject to State withholding. Leave these all checked (see Figure 7-84). Click **Next**.

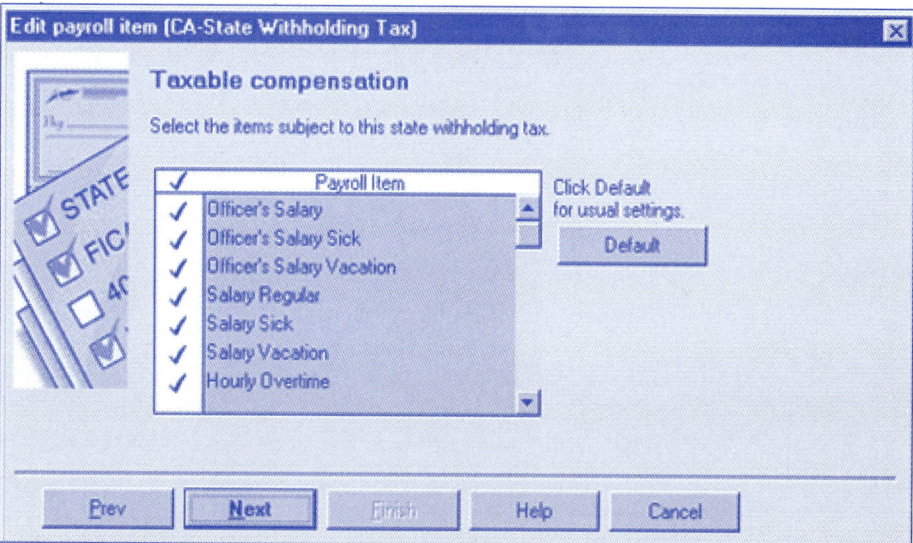

Figure 7-84 Leave these items checked.

6 On the Pre-tax deductions screen, QuickBooks automatically checks all of the Deduction Items that should be deducted before calculating State withholding. Leave this Item checked.

7 Click **Finish** (see Figure 7-85).

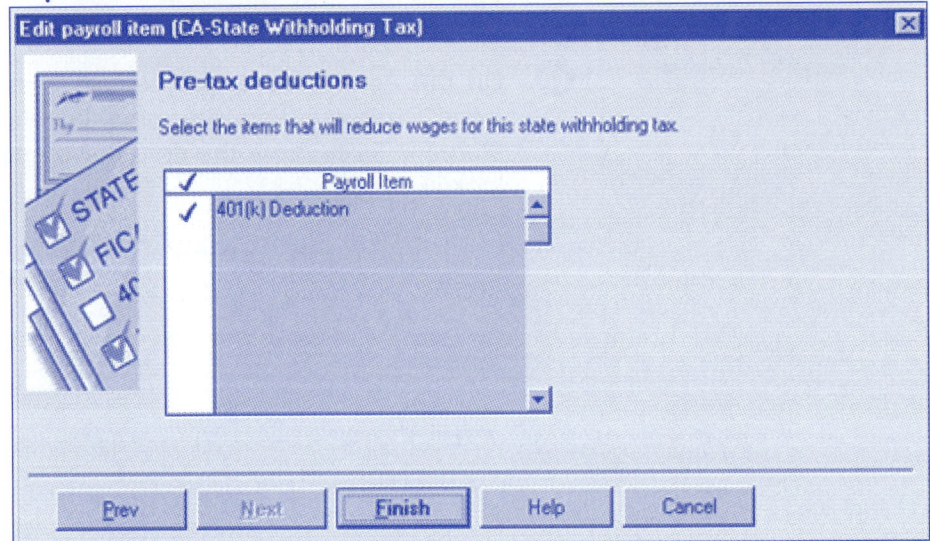

Figure 7-85 This item remains checked.

Editing the State Disability Item

QuickBooks creates a State Disability Item only if your State collects disability tax. Since California collects State Disability tax, the Payroll Setup Wizard created a State Disability Item. You'll now need to edit the item to make it affect the appropriate accounts.

COMPUTER TUTORIAL

① Double-click **CA – Disability Employee** in the Payroll Item List, and then click **Next**.

② In the *Liability account (employee-paid)* field, select "Payroll Liabilities:State PR Tax" from the drop-down menu. Your screen should look like Figure 7-86.

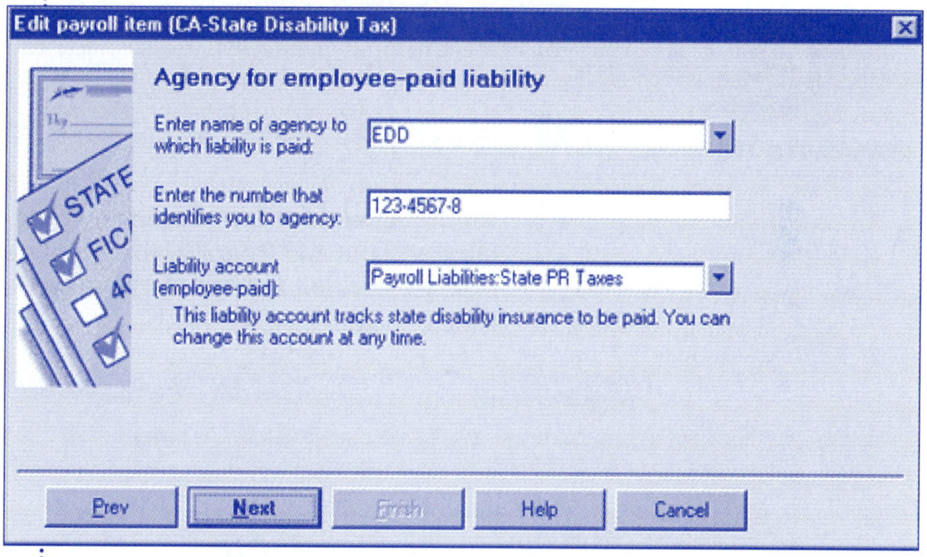

Edit payroll item (CA-State Disability Tax)

Agency for employee-paid liability

Enter name of agency to which liability is paid: EDD

Enter the number that identifies you to agency: 123-4567-8

Liability account (employee-paid): Payroll Liabilities:State PR Taxes

This liability account tracks state disability insurance to be paid. You can change this account at any time.

Prev   Next   Finish   Help   Cancel

Figure 7-86 Change the liability account for the disability item.

③ Click **Next** when you have finished entering this data.

④ On the Employee tax rate screen, QuickBooks automatically fills in the rate from the tax table (see Figure 7-87). You cannot change this amount. Click **Next**.

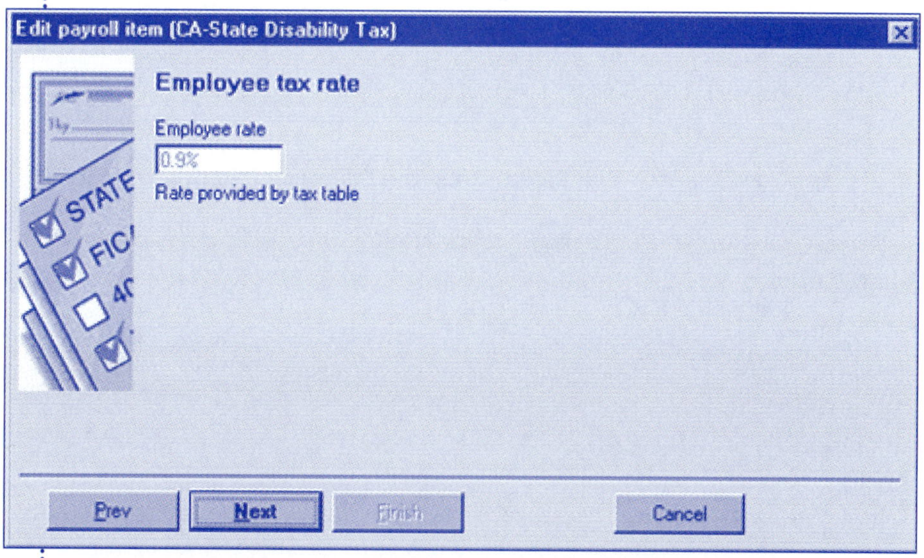

Edit payroll item (CA-State Disability Tax)

Employee tax rate

Employee rate
0.9%

Rate provided by tax table

Prev   Next   Finish   Cancel

Figure 7-87 QuickBooks supplies the tax rate from tax tables.

⑤ On the Taxable compensation screen, QuickBooks automatically checks all of the Wage items that are subject to State Disability tax. Leave all of these checked. Click **Next**.

⑥ On the Pre-tax deductions screen, QuickBooks automatically checks all of the Deduction Items that should be deducted before calculating State Disability. Leave this unchecked and click **Finish**.

Editing the State Unemployment item

For State Unemployment, you'll also need to edit the payroll item to make it affect the proper accounts.

① Double-click the **CA – Unemployment Company** item. Then click **Next**.

② On the Agency for company-paid liability screen, change the liability account to "Payroll Liabilities:State PR Taxes." Change the expense account to "Payroll Expenses:Payroll Taxes." Your screen should look like Figure 7-88.

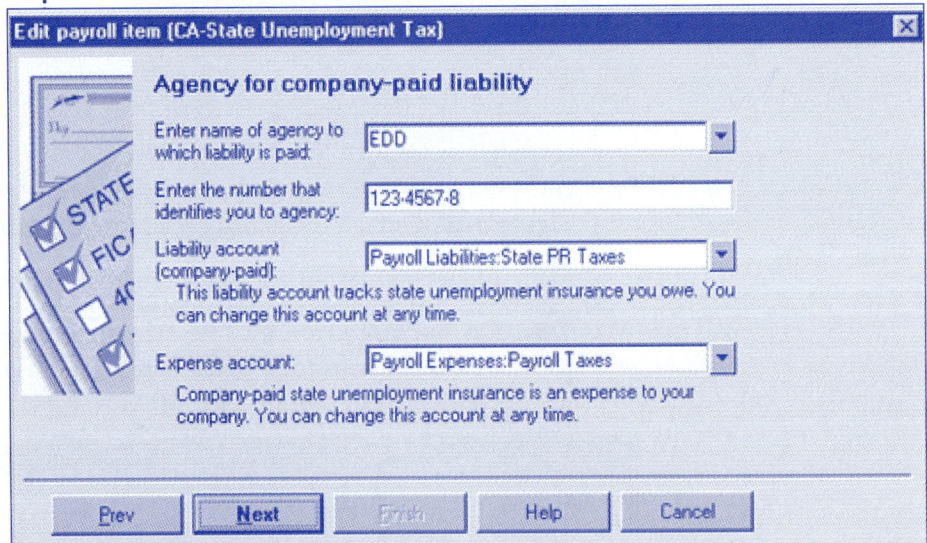

Figure 7-88 The Edit payroll item screen for the State Unemployment Tax

③ Click **Next**.

4. On the Company tax rates screen (Figure 7-89), leave the tax rates as you entered them in the Payroll Setup Wizard, or change them here if necessary. Click **Next**.

   If your State unemployment tax rate changes, return to this screen to make the necessary update.

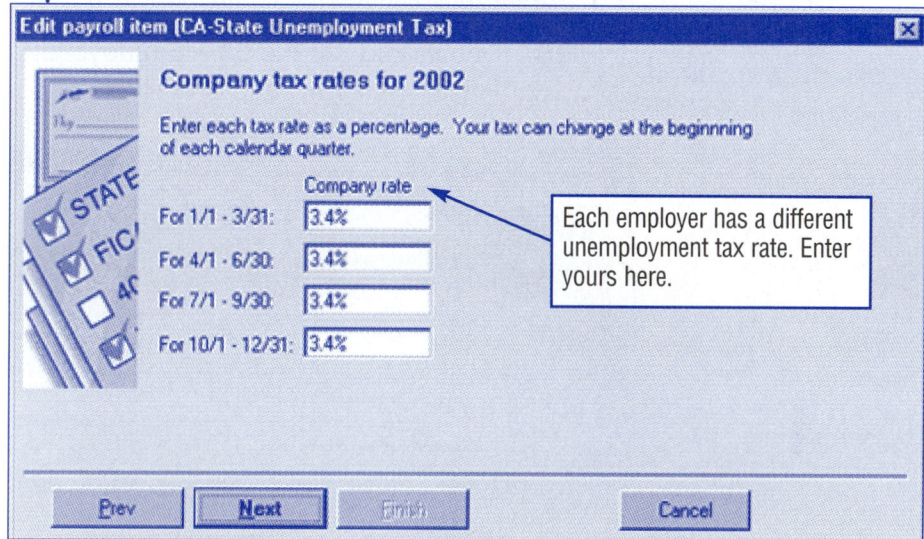

Edit payroll item (CA-State Unemployment Tax)

Company tax rates for 2002

Enter each tax rate as a percentage. Your tax can change at the beginning of each calendar quarter.

	Company rate
For 1/1 - 3/31:	3.4%
For 4/1 - 6/30:	3.4%
For 7/1 - 9/30:	3.4%
For 10/1 - 12/31:	3.4%

Each employer has a different unemployment tax rate. Enter yours here.

Prev | Next | Finish | Cancel

Figure 7-89 Unemployment tax rates

5. On the Taxable compensation screen, QuickBooks automatically checks all of the Wage Items that are subject to State unemployment tax. Leave them all checked. Click **Next**.

6. On the Pre-tax deductions screen, leave the 401(k) Deduction Item unchecked and click **Finish**.

Editing Other Tax items

If you have other State-specific taxes or local taxes, set up Other Tax items. For example, in California set up an Other Tax Item to track California Employment Training Tax (ETT).

You created the Employment Training Tax item in the Payroll Setup Wizard. Now follow these steps to edit it:

COMPUTER TUTORIAL

1 Double-click on the **CA – Employment Training Tax** item in the Payroll Item List. Then click **Next**.

Edit payroll item [CA - Employment Training Tax]

Agency for company-paid liability

Enter name of agency to which liability is paid: EDD

Enter the number that identifies you to agency: 123-4567-8

Liability account (company-paid): Payroll Liabilities:State PR Taxes
This liability account tracks other tax to be paid. You can change this account at any time.

Expense account: Payroll Expenses:Payroll Taxes
Company-paid other tax is an expense to your company. You can change this account at any time.

Prev | Next | Finish | Help | Cancel

Figure 7-90 Edit the liability and expense account for the ETT tax item.

2 On the Agency for company-paid liability screen, change the liability account to "Payroll Liabilities:State PR Taxes." Change the expense account to "Payroll Expenses:Payroll Taxes." Your screen should look like Figure 7-90. Click **Next**.

3 On the Taxable compensation screen, QuickBooks automatically checks all of the Wage items that are subject to this local tax. Leave all of these checked. Click **Next**.

4 On the Pre-tax deductions screen, leave the 401(k) Deduction Item unchecked and click **Finish**.

MEDICAL INSURANCE DEDUCTION

If you provide benefits, there are three options for allocating the costs between the company and the employee. First, the company could pay the entire expense; second, the company and employee could share the expense; and third, the employee could pay the entire expense.

NOTE

The Accounting Behind the Scenes. When you pay your health insurance, enter a bill coded to the Health Insurance Expense account and then proceed with your normal bill-paying process. The bill increases (debits) the Health Insurance Expense account. When you use the Medical Insurance Deduction Item on a paycheck, it reduces (credits) the Health Insurance Expense account. The net amount left in the expense account represents the company portion for health insurance.

If your company pays the entire expense, payroll is usually not involved. However, you might need to adjust the W-2s to include the benefits. To directly add benefits like these to a W-2, see *Processing W-2s* beginning on page 436.

If the costs are shared between the company and the employees, or if the employees pay the entire cost via payroll deductions, use a Deduction Item to track the deductions.

The following method is the simplest way to handle this type of deduction in payroll.

1. When you receive the bill from the provider of benefits, enter it in QuickBooks just like any other bill. Code the bill to the appropriate expense account, (in this example Health Insurance Expense). Then just pay this bill normally.

2. Set up a Payroll Deduction Item for the benefit, (in this case Medical Insurance as shown below). This deduction reduces the Health Insurance Expense account each time you withhold from employees' paychecks.

In the Easy Setup process, you already created a payroll item to track medical insurance. However, QuickBooks set it up to use a liability account instead of an expense account. Therefore, you'll need to modify the item to make it work as described above.

COMPUTER TUTORIAL

Modifying the Medical Insurance Deduction Item

① Double-click on the **Medical Insurance** deduction item in the Payroll Item List (see Figure 7-91). Leave the name for deduction the same and click **Next**.

Edit payroll item [Deduction:Medical Insurance]

Name used in paychecks and payroll reports

Enter name for deduction:

Medical Insurance

For example, if you are creating a deduction for employee 401(k) plan, you may want to call it '401(k)'.

☐ Payroll item is inactive

To hide this item on the Payroll Item list, select the checkbox.

Prev | **Next** | Finish | Cancel

Figure 7-91 Medical Insurance Deduction item

2 On the Agency for employee-paid liability screen, do not enter any information in the fields labeled *Enter name of agency to which liability is paid:* or *Enter the number that identifies you to agency:* (see Figure 7-92).

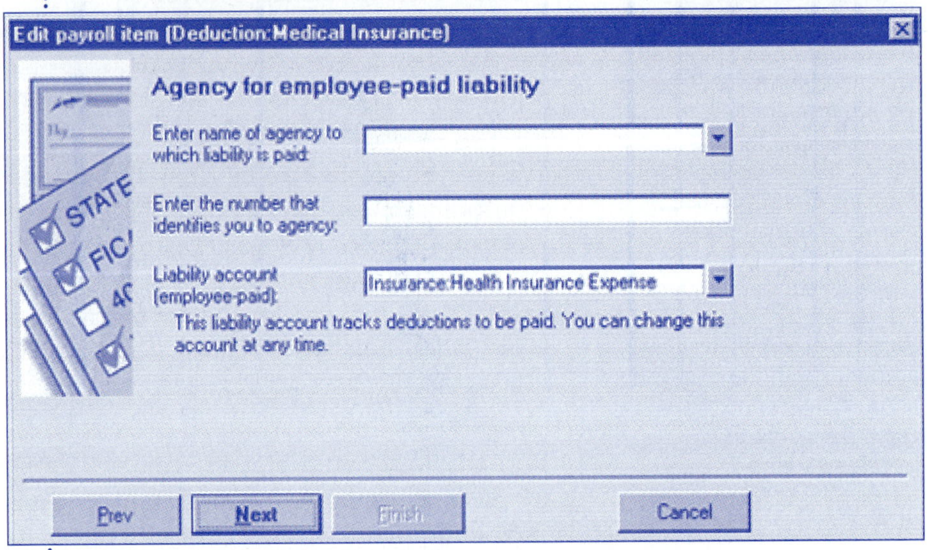

Edit payroll item (Deduction:Medical Insurance)

Agency for employee-paid liability

Enter name of agency to which liability is paid:

Enter the number that identifies you to agency:

Liability account (employee-paid): Insurance:Health Insurance Expense

This liability account tracks deductions to be paid. You can change this account at any time.

Prev   Next   Finish   Cancel

Figure 7-92 Editing the Medical Insurance Deduction item

3 Change the field labeled *Liability account (employee-paid):* to "Insurance:Health Insurance Expense." Then click **Next**.

4 "None" is preselected in the "Tax tracking type" drop-down menu. Click **Next**.

5 Leave all of the Items on the Taxes screen unchecked. Click **Next**.

6 Leave the "Based on Quantity" box unchecked and click **Next**.

7 On the Gross vs. net screen, "net pay" is preselected (see Figure 7-93). Click **Next**.

Health insurance premiums are withheld from the employees' net pay. This is an "after-tax" deduction.

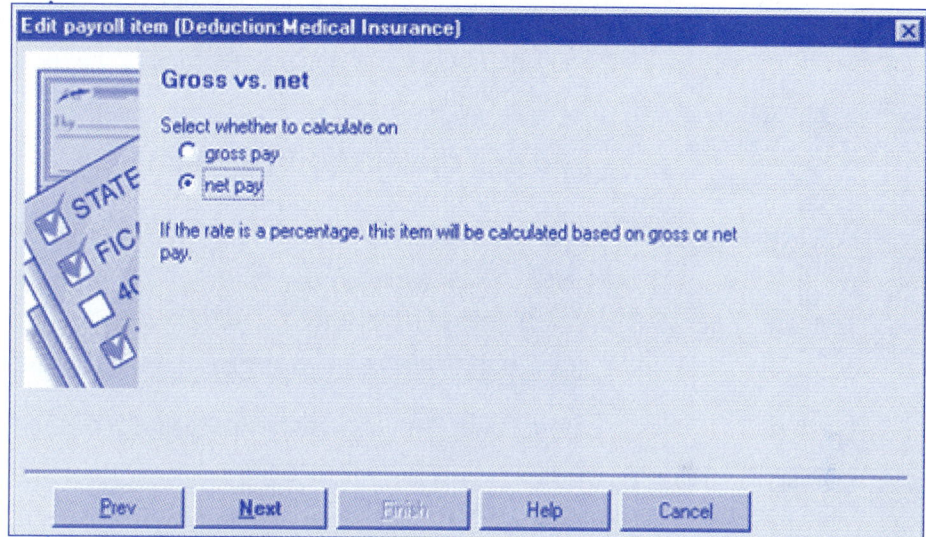

Figure 7-93 Gross vs. net screen

8 On the Default rate and limit screen, enter "10.00" in the top field and leave the bottom field blank. Then click **Finish**.

401(k) EMPLOYEE DEDUCTION AND COMPANY MATCH ITEMS

If you have a 401(k) plan, you can set up a deduction item to track the employee contributions (salary deferral) to the plan.

The 401(k) payroll deduction item was created during the Easy Setup process, but you'll need to edit the item to connect it to the correct liability account.

Editing the 401(k) Deduction Item

COMPUTER TUTORIAL

1 Double-click the **401(k) Deduction** item in the Payroll Item List.

2 Click **Next** on the Name used in paychecks and payroll reports screen (see Figure 7-94).

Figure 7-94 Editing the 401(k) Deduction item

3 On the screen shown in Figure 7-95, change the *Liability account (employee-paid):* field to Payroll Liabilities:Other Payroll Liabilities.

4 Click **Next** on each of the three screens that follow.

> **NOTE**
>
> If you have 401(k) deductions for several employees, you'll probably want to set up separate Deduction Items for each employee. Enter the employee's account number in the *Enter the number that identifies you to agency* field. That way, when you pay your liabilities, the voucher of the liability check lists deductions separately for each employee. Alternatively, you could use just one Deduction Item and send a printout of your Payroll Summary report with your payment to the 401(k) administrator. Filter that report to show only the 401(k) Deduction and the 401(k) company match items. You'll have to handwrite the account numbers for each employee on the report.

5 Then click **Finish**.

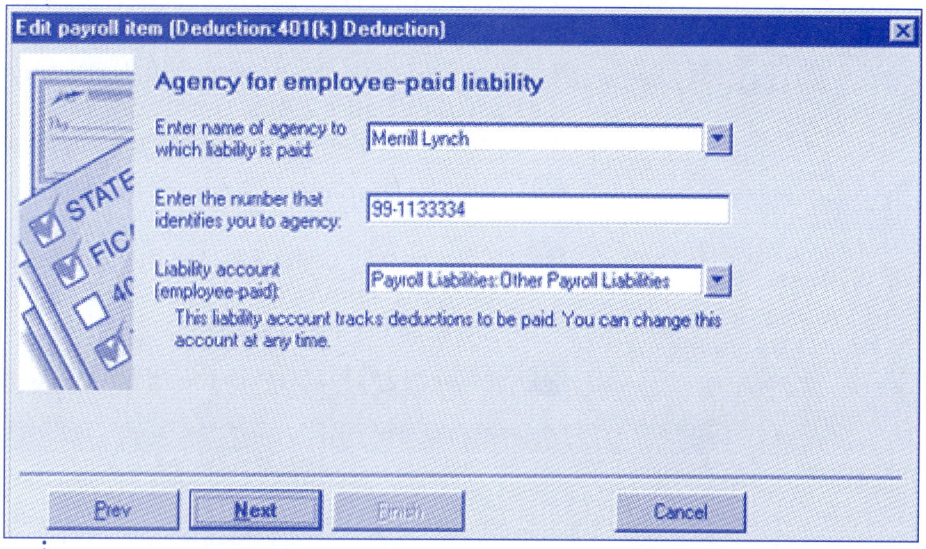

Figure 7-95 Agency for 401(k) Deduction item

Next, you'll need to make the same change to the Match 401(k) company contribution item.

Editing the 401(k) Company Contribution Item

Using the Match 401(k) item, follow steps 1 through 3 as shown for the 401(k) Deduction item. Then continue below.

COMPUTER TUTORIAL

1 In the *Expense account* field of the Agency for company-paid liability screen, select "Payroll Expenses:Benefits" from the drop-down menu, as shown in Figure 7-96. Click **Next**.

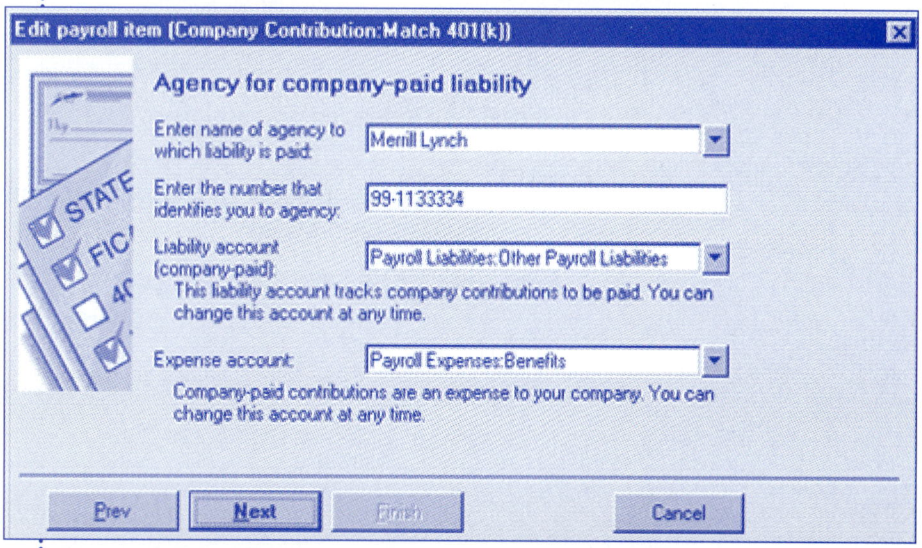

Figure 7-96 The Match 401(k) payroll item settings

2 Click **Next** on each of the three screens that follow, and then click **Finish**.

RELEASING EMPLOYEES

COMPUTER TUTORIAL

When you release an employee, edit the employee record and fill in the *Released* field with the date on which the employee separated from the company (see Figure 7-97). This causes this employee to stop appearing in the Select Employees to Pay screen when you run your payroll.

1. Choose **Employee List** from the *Lists* menu.

2. Click on the name row for that employee and then choose **Edit** from the *Employee* menu at the bottom of the screen, or double-click on the name row.

3. Enter "12/31/2002" in the *Released* field of the Address Info tab.

Edit Employee How Do I?

Information for: Moen, Jim

| Address Info | Additional Info | Payroll Info |

OK
Cancel
Notes
Help

Mr./Ms./... Mr.

☑ Employee is inactive

To deactivate an employee, click here.

Legal Name

First Name Jim M.I.

Last Name Moen

Phone 925-555-1233

Alt. Ph.

SS No. 111-22-3333

E-mail jim@academyglass.com

Print on Checks as Jim Moen

Type Regular

Gender Male

Address 123 Hillsboro Lane

Hired 01/01/2002

Released 12/31/2002 ☐ Deceased

When an employee separates from the company, enter the separation date in the *Released* field.

Figure 7-97 Releasing an employee

4. Click **OK** if you see a QuickBooks warning message regarding the released employee.

5. Click **OK** to save your changes.

DEACTIVATING EMPLOYEES

If an employee's name is used in any transactions (e.g., paychecks), or if the name is used in the *Rep* field on any customer records or sales, you won't be allowed to delete the employee from the Employee list. However, you can "deactivate" the employee by checking the box next to "Employee is inactive" in the Address Info screen (see Figure 7-97). This removes the employee from the list, but it doesn't delete the employee from your company file.

To reactivate an employee, click on the "**X**" icon in the Employee List as shown in Figure 7-98 (or edit the employee record and uncheck the "Employee is inactive" box).

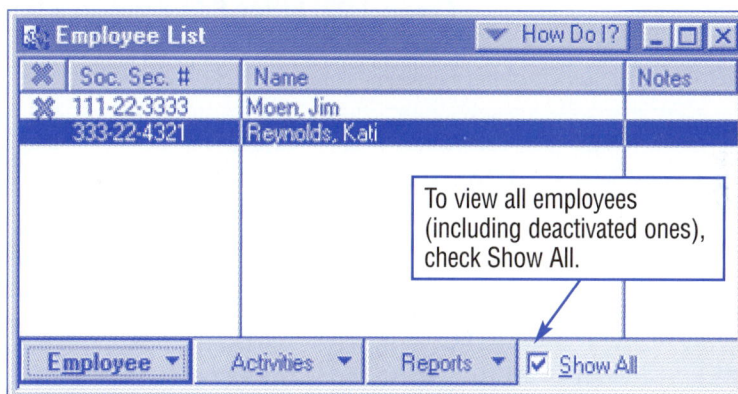

Figure 7-98 Deactivated employees show an "X" icon.

THE EMPLOYEE CONTACT LIST REPORT

COMPUTER TUTORIAL

To view all employees, including deactivated employees, display the Employee list and check the "Show All" box (see Figure 7-98). You can print a list of employees by following the steps below.

1 Select the *Reports* menu, choose **List**, and then **Employee Contact List** (see Figure 7-99).

> **IMPORTANT**
>
> If you made "Jim Moen" inactive in the preceding section, you will need to reactivate his record so that your report matches Figure 7-99. In the Edit Employee screen, uncheck the "Employee is inactive" box.

Employee Contact List							▼ How Do I? _ □ ✕
Modify Report...	Memorize...	Print...	Excel...	Hide Header	Refresh	Sort By Default ▼	

Academy Glass, Inc.
Employee Contact List
February 6, 2002

Employee	SS No.	Address	Phone
Moen, Jim	111-22-3333	Jim Moen 123 Hillsboro Lane Walnut Creek, CA 94569	925-555-1233
Reynolds, Kati	333-22-4321	Kati Reynolds 432 Enos Lane Danville, CA 94501	925-555-3434

Figure 7-99 The Employee Contact List

2 Click **Print** at the top of the report and follow the screens to print the report and close the window.

MID-YEAR PAYROLL SETUP

If your payroll start date is not December 31, you'll need to enter the year-to-date payroll information for each of your employees before entering your first paychecks.

To make your payroll setup easier, it is strongly recommended that you start processing your payroll through QuickBooks at the beginning of a calendar year. If you need to start in the middle of a calendar year, consider contacting your accountant or QuickBooks consultant for assistance.

SUMMARY OF KEY POINTS

In this chapter, you learned how to set up payroll in QuickBooks. You should now be familiar with how to use QuickBooks to do all of the following:

◆ Activate the payroll feature and configure payroll preferences (Page 315)

◆ Set up payroll accounts in the Chart of Accounts (Page 317)

◆ Use the Payroll Setup Wizard to add payroll items, vendors, employee defaults, employee records, and year-to-date amounts (Page 318)

◆ Understand the Accounting Behind the Scenes of Payroll Items (Page 353)

◆ Add new Payroll Items using the Custom Setup method (Page 356)

◆ Edit payroll items (Page 363)

◆ Release and deactivate employees (Page 378)

> **CHAPTER REVIEW AND APPLICATIONS**

Comprehension QUESTIONS

In your notebook, record answers to the following questions.

1. What type of payroll item should be set up to track additional money contributed by the company as a result of a paycheck?

2. Why do you need to edit several of your payroll items (e.g., Federal Withholding) after setting up your payroll accounts?

3. Name a payroll item that should be "Based on Quantity."

Multiple-Choice QUESTIONS

In your notebook, record the best answer for each of the following questions.

1. *b* In the Payroll Preferences screen, if you select "Hide pay rate on Select Employees to Pay window,"
   a. the employee's pay rate will not be printed on the paycheck voucher.
   b. the pay rate will not appear on the screen where you select employees to pay.
   c. you will not be able to calculate gross earnings.
   d. you will not be able to calculate sick and vacation pay hours.

2. *a* Use a Payroll Deduction Item to track medical insurance costs when:
   a. the employees pay part of the cost.
   b. costs exceed $100 per month for the employee.
   c. the employer pays the total cost.
   d. medical insurance costs are not tracked as a Payroll Deduction Item.

3. *d* Which of the following would be excluded from taxable earnings when calculating Federal withholding?
   a. Vacation salary
   b. Sick leave salary
   c. Overtime earnings
   d. Employee contributions to a 401(k)

4. *a* Why are there two Medicare and two Social Security items in the Payroll Items list?
   a. The employee and employer portions are tracked separately.
   b. Different tax rates apply to employee and employer portions.
   c. Separate accounts are used because separate checks must be written for employee and employer portions.
   d. Separate ledger accounts are maintained for the two portions of each tax.

5. *c* Which of the following payroll periods is not an option in QuickBooks?
   a. Quarterly
   b. Biweekly
   c. Daily
   d. Semiannually

Name _Michele Hall_ **Date** _____

Multiple-Choice
QUESTIONS
(Continued)

6. _b_ Which of the following is not a feature of QuickBooks payroll?
   a. Tracks individual employees for hours worked and gross pay.
   b. Writes and prints paychecks on standard checks.
   c. Calculates and electronically remits Federal payroll tax liabilities using EFTPS.
   d. Payroll tax tables for all Federal, State and some local taxes are supplied through the QuickBooks Basic Payroll Service.

7. _d_ Payroll items are used by QuickBooks to:
   a. accumulate payroll liabilities.
   b. track each different kind of compensation.
   c. define the relationship between items you put on paychecks and the chart of accounts.
   d. All of the above.

Completion
STATEMENTS

In the space provided, write the word(s) that best complete each statement.

1. The _Employee Defaults_ feature allows you to define defaults for your employee records, so that you do not have to enter the same information each time you add a new employee.

2. To set up custom fields for adding more detailed information about your employees, click the _define field_ button on the Additional Information tab of the New Employee screen.

3. _Payroll_ items are used to track payments of gross wages to salaried employees. Since these payroll items represent company expenses, these items debit an expense account such a Gross Wages or Officer's Compensation Expense.

4. When you release an employee, edit the employee record and fill in the _Released_ field with the date on which the employee separated from the company. This causes this employee to stop appearing in the Select Employees to Pay window.

APPLY YOUR KNOWLEDGE

PROBLEM 7-1

Done

> **Restore the Problem 7-1.QBB file and store it on your hard disk according to your instructor's directions.**

1. Modify the payroll preferences to print the vacation information on check vouchers and to assign one class per earnings Item.

2. Verify that your Chart of Accounts is properly set up for Payroll tracking. Make sure you have the accounts shown in the screens below. These accounts have already been set up for you in the problem template. You'll learn how to set up accounts in Chapter 10.

◆ Payroll Liabilities	Other Current Liability
◆ Federal PR Taxes	Other Current Liability
◆ State PR Taxes	Other Current Liability
◆ Other Payroll Liabilities	Other Current Liability
◆ Union Dues Payable	Other Current Liability

◆ Payroll Expenses	Expense
◆ Benefits	Expense
◆ Gross Wages	Expense
◆ Officer's Compensation	Expense
◆ Payroll Taxes	Expense

Name _____ Date _____

> **3.** Using the Payroll Setup Wizard, add the following payroll items. The order of the items in this list corresponds to the order in which they appear in the Wizard. However, the item names must be changed in the Wizard to match the "Item Name" column below. Set up the items in the Wizard and then modify them as appropriate from the payroll item list.

Item Name	Setup Notes
California State Items	Using the Wizard, set up all of the necessary payroll items for California Payroll Taxes. Set all State tax items to point to the State PR Taxes liability account. California Tax ID: 123-4567-8 State Unemployment Rate for all four quarters: 4.5%
Salary Regular	
Salary Sick	
Salary Vacation	
Hourly Regular	
Hourly Overtime	
Hourly Sick	
Hourly Vacation	
Commission	Add a 4% commission item.
Health Insurance	Use Health Insurance (taxable) item to set up this item. Leave the payee and account number fields blank. Use "Health Insurance Expense" to track the withholding.
408(k) – SEP Employee	Payee is Merrill Lynch. Account number with Merrill Lynch is "99-1133335." Liability account is "Other Payroll Liabilities," Tax Tracking type is "408(k)(6) SEP," and the Item should deducted before calculating Federal and State income tax. Maximum annual deduction is $10,500.00.
Match 408(k)	Track this expense by Job. Payee is Merrill Lynch, Account number is "99-1133335." Liability account is "Other Payroll Liabilities." Expense account is "Benefits." Tax Tracking type is "None." Maximum annual deduction is $5,250.00.
Child Support Garnishment	This garnishment is payable to Contra Costa County Commissioner (set up new vendor), vendor and the Account number should read "Case #23453."

Table 7-3 Add these payroll items.

4. Modify the items to point to the accounts shown in both Table 7-4a and Table 7-4b, and set the items in Table 7-4b to use the tax agencies (vendors) as shown:

Item Name	Setup Notes
Salary Regular	This item should point to Gross Wages Expense, a subaccount of the Payroll Expenses account.
Salary Sick	This item should point to Gross Wages Expense, a subaccount of the Payroll Expenses account.
Salary Vacation	This item should point to Gross Wages Expense, a subaccount of the Payroll Expenses account.
Hourly Regular	This item should point to Gross Wages Expense, a subaccount of the Payroll Expenses account.
Hourly Overtime	This item should point to Gross Wages Expense, a subaccount of the Payroll Expenses account.
Hourly Sick	This item should point to Gross Wages Expense, a subaccount of the Payroll Expenses account.
Hourly Vacation	This item should point to Gross Wages Expense, a subaccount of the Payroll Expenses account.
Commission	This item should point to Gross Wages Expense, a subaccount of the Payroll Expenses account.

Table 7-4a Modify these payroll items.

Name _____ Date _____

Item Name	Account: Set the items to point to the accounts shown below.	Vendor: Set up all of the Federal items to use one vendor in the Setup Wizard, and then edit them later to assign them to different vendors. Do the same with the State items.
Social Security	Federal PR Taxes (Subaccount of Payroll Liabilities)	EFTPS **Note:** EFTPS is not in the vendor list. You will need to add this vendor.
Medicare	Liability Account: Federal PR Taxes (Subaccount of Payroll Liabilities) Expense Account: Payroll Taxes (Subaccount of Payroll Expenses)	EFTPS
Federal Unemployment	Liability Account: Federal PR Taxes (Subaccount of Payroll Liabilities) Expense Account: Payroll Taxes (Subaccount of Payroll Expenses)	EFTPS *Federal Unemployment Tax Rate is 0.8%.*
CA – Withholding **CA – Disability**	Account: State PR Taxes (Subaccount of Payroll Liabilities)	EDD
CA – Unemployment **CA – Employment Training Tax**	Liability Account: State PR Taxes (Subaccount of Payroll Liabilities) Expense Account: Payroll Taxes (Subaccount of Payroll Expenses)	EDD
Health Insurance	Health Insurance Expense (Subaccount of Insurance)	No Vendor, no Account number.
408(k) SEP Employee	Other Payroll Liabilities (Subaccount of Payroll Liabilities)	Merrill Lynch Account number with Merrill Lynch is "99-1133335." **Note**: Tax Tracking type is "408(k)(6) SEP", and the Item should be deducted before calculating Federal and State withholding. Maximum annual deduction is $10,500.00.
Match 408(k)	Liability Account: Other Payroll Liabilities (Subaccount of Payroll Liabilities) Expense Account: Benefits Subaccount of Payroll Expenses)	Merrill Lynch Account number is "99-1133335", **Note** : Track this expense by job. Tax Tracking type is "None." Maximum annual deduction is $5,250.00
Child Support Garnishment	Other Payroll Liabilities (Subaccount of Payroll Liabilities)	Contra Costa County Commissioner Account #: Case #23453

Table 7-4b Modify these payroll items.

5. In the Payroll Setup Wizard, set up your Employee Defaults for the following:

Field Name	Setup Notes
Payroll Period	Weekly
Additions, Deductions and Company Contributions	408(k) SEP Employee (4%), Maximum $10,500.00 Match 408(k) (2%), Maximum $5,250.00 Health Insurance ($2 per paycheck)
Pension Plan	Employees are covered by a qualified pension plan.
Federal Taxes	Filing Status: Single Subject to: Social Security, FUTA, Medicare
State Taxes	Default State Worked: CA Default State Lived: CA
Other Taxes	CA – Employment Training Tax
Sick Hours Accruals	Accrual Period: Beginning of Year Hours Accrued at Beginning of Year: 40 Maximum number of hours: 40 Reset hours each new year
Vacation Hours Accruals	Accrual Period: Beginning of Year Hours Accrued at Beginning of Year: 80 Maximum number of hours: 240 Do not reset hours each new year.

Table 7-5 Employee default settings

6. Edit the Federal and State tax items to ensure that they point to the correct accounts as indicated in Step 4.

7. Edit all of the Earnings items to ensure that they point to Gross Wages as indicated in Step 3.

8. Create a Payroll Item Listing report (Select the **Reports** menu, then choose **List** and then choose **Payroll Item Listing**. Modify the report to include the Payable to column and then print the report. Set the report to print on 1 page wide).

Name _____ **Date** _____

EXTEND YOUR KNOWLEDGE

PROBLEM 7-2

> **Restore the Problem 7-2.QBB file and store it on your hard disk according to your instructor's directions.**

1. Use the Payroll Setup wizard to set up a new employee with the following information:

Field	Data
Mr./Ms./...	Ms.
First Name	Cynthia
M.I.	
Last Name	Plum
Printed on check as	Cynthia Plum
Address	555 Adams Ave. Pleasanton, CA 94555
Phone	925-555-6352
Alt Ph.	
SS No.	123-12-3123
Email	cyndy@academyglass.com
Type	Regular
Gender	Female
Hire Date	01/01/1999
Release Date	
Employee #	4466 **Hint:** use the "Account" field on the Additional Info tab for this number.
Spouse Name	Craig
Department	Sales
Title	Sales Rep
Review Date	January
Earnings	Hourly Regular – Rate $32 per hour
Time Data	Use Time Data to Create Paychecks
Additions, Deductions, and Company Contributions	408(k) SEP Employee (4%), limit $10,500 Match 408(k) (2%), limit $5,250 Health Insurance ($2)
Pay Period	Weekly
Class	San Jose
Marital Status	Married, 2 Allowances, Subject to Social Security, FUTA, Medicare
State Worked	CA – Subject to SUI, Subject to SDI
State Lived	CA – Filing Status Married (one income) 2 allowances
Other Taxes	CA – Employment Training Tax
Sick/Vacation Settings	Default Sick and Vacation settings
Qualified Pension Plan	Yes

2. Finish the Payroll Setup Wizard and select all of the remaining defaults. Do not set up any YTD amounts. Indicate that you paid all your taxes for last quarter, and that all the amounts were zero (both Federal and State).

3. Create an Officer's Salary item using custom setup through the Payroll Item List. Officer's Salary points to Officer's Compensation Expense.

4. Create a Payroll Item Listing report (Select the *Reports* menu, then choose **List** and then **Payroll Item Listing**. Modify the report to include the Payable to column and then print the report. Set the report to print on 1 page wide.)

5. Create an Employee Withholding list and print it.

DISCUSSION QUESTIONS

These questions are designed to help you apply what you are learning about QuickBooks to your own organization. Use your notebook to record your answers and your thoughts.

1. How many employees are there in your organization? Of these, how many are paid hourly wages, and how many are paid by salary?

2. What benefits does your company offer that are paid for by the employees? What benefits are offered and paid for by the company? What benefits are offered where the cost is shared by the employees and the company?

3. What payroll taxes does your organization have to pay? Are there different taxes or tax rates for different cities, counties, states, or countries in which your company operates? List some of the taxes and the rates that apply.

ACTIVITY

Go to the IRS Web site and find form W-4. Fill out the form by following the directions on the form. What is the total number of allowances you claim? Discuss how this form affects employees' net paychecks.

Workplace Applications

Name _____ **Date** _____

CASE STUDY

HARDWARE EASYCARE, INC.

Hardware Easycare, Inc. is a new hardware service company that travels to your work location and performs routine maintenance on computer hardware. They respond within thirty minutes on all service calls within a 10-mile radius of the company headquarters. There are 3 salaried employees and 8 service technicians (hourly employees) who will come to your home or office. All salaried employees get a quarterly bonus of 1% of net profit.

The company has a 401(k) program in which all employees can participate.

Questions

These questions are designed to help you apply what you are learning about QuickBooks to this case study. Use your notebook to record your answers and your thoughts.

1. Advise Fran (the Payroll Accounting clerk) how to set up QuickBooks payroll if she wants to deduct 2% of gross pay from employees for 401(k) contributions.

2. How would Fran set up QuickBooks to track the bonus for salaried employees?

inter**NET** ·CONNECTION·

What do kids have to do with payroll? Some parents have child-support deductions directly taken from their wages. The U.S. Office of Child Support Enforcement has information about the implications of this payroll issue:
http://www.acf.dhhs.gov/programs/cse/fctdsc.htm

Payroll Processing

OBJECTIVES

After completing this chapter, you should be able to:

1. Update your payroll tax tables.

2. Create paychecks for hourly and salaried employees.

3. Pay commissions to sales reps through payroll.

4. Print paychecks and paystubs.

5. Pay payroll liabilities.

6. Create a variety of payroll reports.

7. Create and print payroll tax forms such as the 941, 940, and W-2.

8. Summarize your payroll information in Microsoft Excel.

RESTORE THIS FILE

This chapter uses Chapter 8.QBW. To open this file, restore the tutorial template called **Chapter 8.QBB** to your hard disk. (See page 7 for instructions on restoring files.)

In this chapter, you'll learn to process your payroll smoothly by completing the following steps:

Every Payday
- ◆ Verify that your payroll setup is correct as discussed in Chapter 7
- ◆ Verify that your tax tables are current, and update them if necessary
- ◆ Create, review and correct (if necessary) paychecks
- ◆ Print paychecks and paystubs

Every Tax Deposit Due Date (monthly or semi-weekly)
- ◆ Create, review and correct (if necessary) liability payments
- ◆ Print liability payment checks

Every Quarter (after the end of the quarter)
- ◆ Verify accuracy of all payroll transactions for the previous quarter
- ◆ Create payroll reports for the previous quarter, and year-to-date
- ◆ Create payroll tax returns (Federal Form 941 and State Quarterly Returns)

Every January
- ◆ Verify accuracy of all payroll transactions for the entire previous year
- ◆ Create payroll reports for the previous quarter and year-to-date
- ◆ Create payroll tax returns (Federal Form 941, 940, and State Quarterly and Yearly Returns)

KEY TERM

Payroll Tax Tables
include the tax rates
necessary to calculate
an employee's paycheck.
This calculation affects
the amounts of taxes
that are withheld from
an employee's check
(e.g., Federal and State
income tax), as well as
the amounts of taxes
the company must pay
for the employee (e.g.,
Federal Unemployment).

PAYROLL TAX TABLES

In order for your paychecks to calculate properly, you must have current payroll tax tables. QuickBooks recommends that you connect to their Web site frequently to ensure that you're using the latest tax tables. To download the latest tax tables from the Internet, use the **Get Payroll Updates** function.

The tutorial template already has a unique key entered in it that allows you to download the tax tables without signing up or paying for the Basic or Deluxe Payroll service. Please note that you should never use the sample data file to create paychecks for a real business. It is only for use with this book.

If you are unable to download tax table updates from the Internet, you will have to manually enter the Federal and State taxes on paychecks, so that your screen matches the figures in this chapter.

The paychecks in this chapter are all dated in 2002, so the tax amounts may not match with paychecks calculated using tax tables from other years.

Updating your tax tables

IMPORTANT

Skip this section if you cannot connect to the Internet. If you are not able to update your tax tables, the paycheck calculations may produce slightly different numbers. However, everything else about the process of calculating payroll will remain the same.

COMPUTER TUTORIAL

1 Select the *Employees* menu and then choose **Get Payroll Updates**.

2 To connect to the Internet and download the tax tables, click **Update**.

When QuickBooks finishes downloading the tax tables, you're ready to process your payroll.

IMPORTANT

If you have not downloaded the current tax tables, complete the computer tutorial practices using your currently installed QuickBooks tax table, or by manually entering the Federal and State taxes on each paycheck. Note that the figures in this book were calculated using tax table version 20202.

> **QuickBooks Payroll Information**   ▼ How Do I?   _ □ X
>
> You are using tax table version: 20202 ◄   Tax Table Info
> You are using payroll version: 01151231
>
> You must update before: 03/11/2002   Update
> ⦿ Download only changes and additions to currently installed payroll files.
> ○ Download entire payroll update. Select this option if you are having
>   trouble downloading your payroll update. This may take a few minutes.
>
> Subscription Number: 0000154369
> Subscription Status: Active   Account Info
> Federal EIN: 11-3456789
>
> Service Key: 4000-7844-0148-0901   Change
>
> Registration Number: 02002-2030-75305-1007   Register
>
> OK

Your tax table version may be different depending on whether or not you've downloaded new tax tables and when you downloaded them.

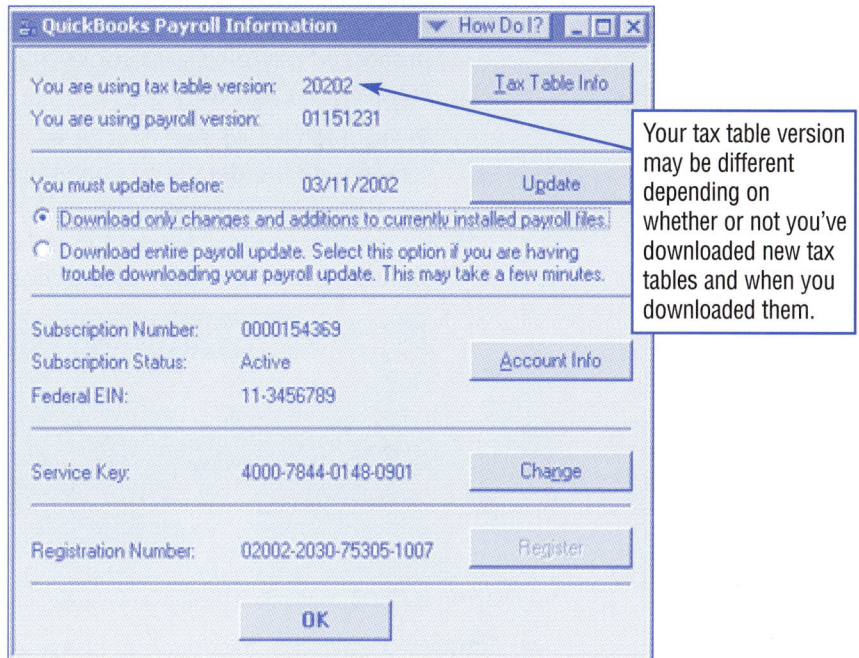

Figure 8-1 The QuickBooks Payroll Information screen

PAYING EMPLOYEES

Once your payroll records are completely set up, you can process your payroll.

Selecting the Employees to Pay

COMPUTER TUTORIAL

1 Select the *Employees* menu and then choose **Pay Employees**.

If you have *not* installed the payroll tax table update, QuickBooks may ask you to update your payroll subscription (see Figure 8-2). Click **No**.

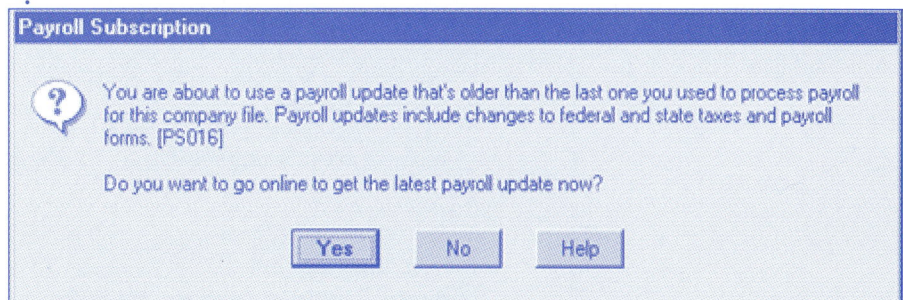

> **Payroll Subscription**
>
> (?) You are about to use a payroll update that's older than the last one you used to process payroll for this company file. Payroll updates include changes to federal and state taxes and payroll forms. [PS016]
>
> Do you want to go online to get the latest payroll update now?
>
> Yes   No   Help

Figure 8-2 The QuickBooks Payroll Subscription message

2 If you have installed a payroll tax table update since you last processed payroll, QuickBooks might display the screen shown in Figure 8-3. Click **No**.

If you had clicked **Yes**, QuickBooks would have shown a message screen with the details on changes made during the last payroll tax table update. When you are using QuickBooks to process payroll for your company, it is best to read this information thoroughly. You should also print a copy of the message for future reference.

Figure 8-3 Payroll Subscription Message Alert

3 The first time you process payroll, QuickBooks displays the screen shown in Figure 8-4. Click **No**.

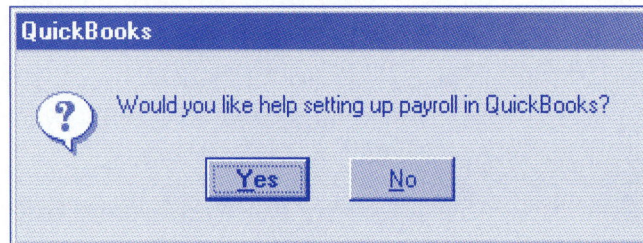

Figure 8-4 Offer of help in setting up payroll

4 The warning shown in Figure 8-5 appears only when processing your first payroll. Click **OK**.

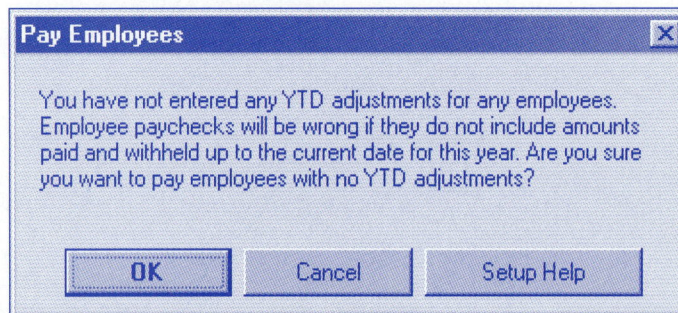

Figure 8-5 Year-to-date amounts warning

The check date on paychecks determines when the payroll expenses show up on all reports. For example, if you pay employees on the 16th of the month for wages earned during the first half of the month, the reports will show the expenses for that payroll on the 16th.

⑤ On the Select Employees To Pay screen, leave "Checking" in the *Bank Account* field, the "To be printed" box checked, and "Enter hours and preview check before creating" selected.

⑥ Enter "01/16/2002" in the *Check Date* field and enter "01/15/2002" in the *Pay Period Ends* field (see Figure 8-6).

The two date fields on this screen are very important. The first one sets the date of the actual paycheck, and the second one indicates the last day of the pay period included on the paychecks. Make sure you always check these dates before creating your paychecks.

Notice that the pay rate for each employee shows in Figure 8-6. If you don't want the pay rate to show here, you can hide it in the Payroll & Employees Company Preferences.

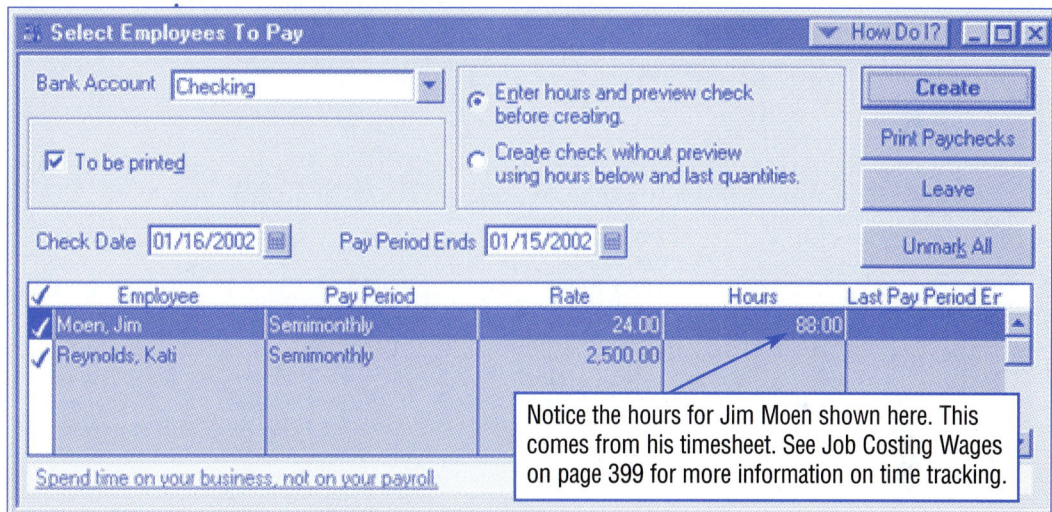

Figure 8-6 The Select Employees to Pay screen

⑦ Select both employees by clicking in the column to the left of each name (see in Figure 8-6). Then click **Create**. The Preview Paycheck screen appears.

Calculating Paychecks for Hourly Employees

In the Preview Paycheck screen, you see the detail of the paycheck for the first employee (see Figure 8-7).

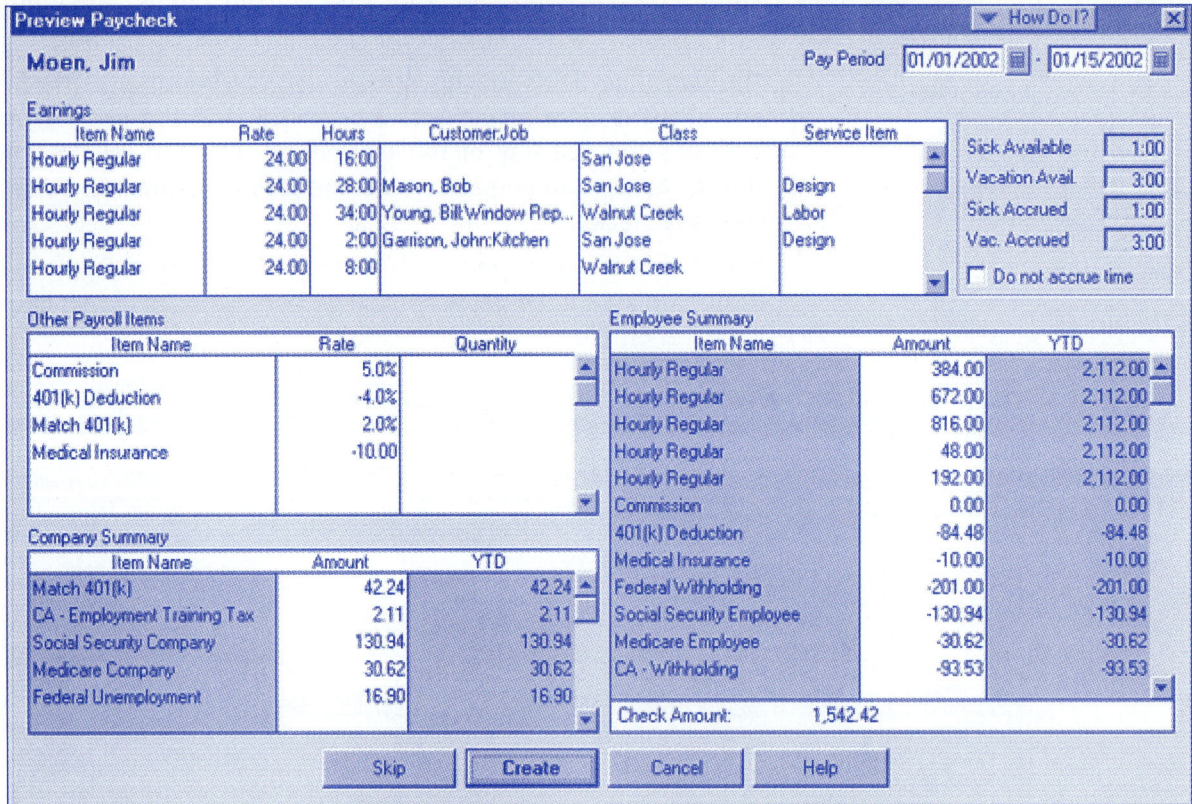

Figure 8-7 The Preview Paycheck screen

At the top right of the Preview Paycheck screen (see Figure 8-7), you will also see the dates for the pay period. The dates are already filled in to match the "Pay Period Ends" date on the Select Employees to Pay screen (see Figure 8-6). The Sick and Vacation hours available after this check are also shown on the right.

Earnings Section

In Chapter 7, this employee was set to "Use Time Data to Create Paychecks" (see page 342). This setting causes QuickBooks to automatically fill in the earnings section of the paycheck as shown in Figure 8-8.

Earnings				
Item Name	Rate	Hours	Customer:Job	Class
Hourly Regular	24.00	16:00		San Jose
Hourly Regular	24.00	28:00	Mason, Bob	San Jose
Hourly Regular	24.00	34:00	Young, Bill:Window Rep...	Walnut Creek
Hourly Regular	24.00	2:00	Garrison, John:Kitchen	San Jose
Hourly Regular	24.00	8:00		Walnut Creek

Figure 8-8 Earnings section of the Preview Paycheck screen

KEY TERM

Use Time Data to Create Paychecks
Notice that the timesheet information automatically entered the job and class information on the paycheck. This is automatic with QuickBooks when you set an employee's record to Use Time Data to Create Paychecks. However, if you didn't use the timesheets, you can manually allocate job and class information directly on the paycheck.

You can override any of the information that was automatically copied from the timesheet. However, any changes you make here will not change the original timesheet. So you might want to correct the timesheet before creating the paycheck.

Job-Costing Wages

To manually allocate this employee's wages to each of the jobs and classes that he worked on, enter splits for each combination of Payroll Item (Name), Rate, Hours, Customer:Job, and Class. QuickBooks calculates the amount of gross wages that should be allocated to each job and class based on the total pay for each Payroll Item. In addition, QuickBooks allocates the *payroll taxes*, *company contributions*, and *additions* for this paycheck based on the proportion of wages assigned to each job and class.

> **IMPORTANT**
>
> QuickBooks does not job cost any of the Items in the Other Payroll Items section of paychecks except commissions if the Item is set up to track by job. See *Adding a Commissions Item* on page 361.

Other Payroll Items Section

In the Other Payroll Items section, QuickBooks adds the Additions, Deductions, and Company Contributions as defined in this employee's record.

Paying Employee Commissions

If you pay commission to your employees, you would need to set up a Commission item as shown on page 361, and add it to the employee's record in the "Other Payroll Items" section.

COMPUTER TUTORIAL

① Enter "1,000.00" in the Quantity column on the Commission line in the Other Payroll Items section (see Figure 8-9). QuickBooks calculates the commission percentage – in this case 5% of $1,000, or $50. If you don't pay commissions as a percentage of sales, you can just enter a flat commission amount in the Rate column.

Other Payroll Items		
Item Name	Rate	Quantity
Commission	5.0%	1,000.00
401(k) Deduction	-4.0%	
Match 401(k)	2.0%	
Medical Insurance	-10.00	

Figure 8-9 The Other Payroll Items section

Company Summary Section

In the Company Summary section, QuickBooks calculates all of the company-paid taxes and contributions according to how the employee's record was set up (see Figure 8-10).

Company Summary		
Item Name	Amount	YTD
Match 401(k)	43.24	43.24
CA - Employment Training Tax	2.16	2.16
Social Security Company	134.04	134.04
Medicare Company	31.35	31.35
Federal Unemployment	17.30	17.30

Figure 8-10 The Company Summary section

Employee Summary Section

The Employee Summary is on the right side of the Preview Paycheck screen (see Figure 8-11). This section shows all of the earnings, additions, deductions, and net pay for this paycheck.

Employee Summary		
Item Name	Amount	YTD
Hourly Regular	384.00	2,112.00
Hourly Regular	672.00	2,112.00
Hourly Regular	816.00	2,112.00
Hourly Regular	48.00	2,1
Hourly Regular	192.00	2,1
Commission	50.00	
401(k) Deduction	-86.48	
Medical Insurance	-10.00	
Federal Withholding	-209.00	-2
Social Security Employee	-134.04	-1
Medicare Employee	-31.35	-31.35
CA - Withholding	-97.99	-97.99
Check Amount:	1,573.68	

Each payroll item that affects net pay shows as a separate line here. Total gross pay does not show here, but it does show on the paystub.

Figure 8-11 The Employee Summary section

QuickBooks automatically calculates all of the amounts in this section using the information from the Earnings section, the Other Payroll items section, and the Tax Tables.

> **NOTE**
>
> You can override the figures in the Amount column if necessary, but QuickBooks calculates the YTD column based on prior pay periods. You cannot change the figures in the YTD column. If you need to adjust any of the YTD amounts, use the Adjust Liabilities function discussed later in this chapter.

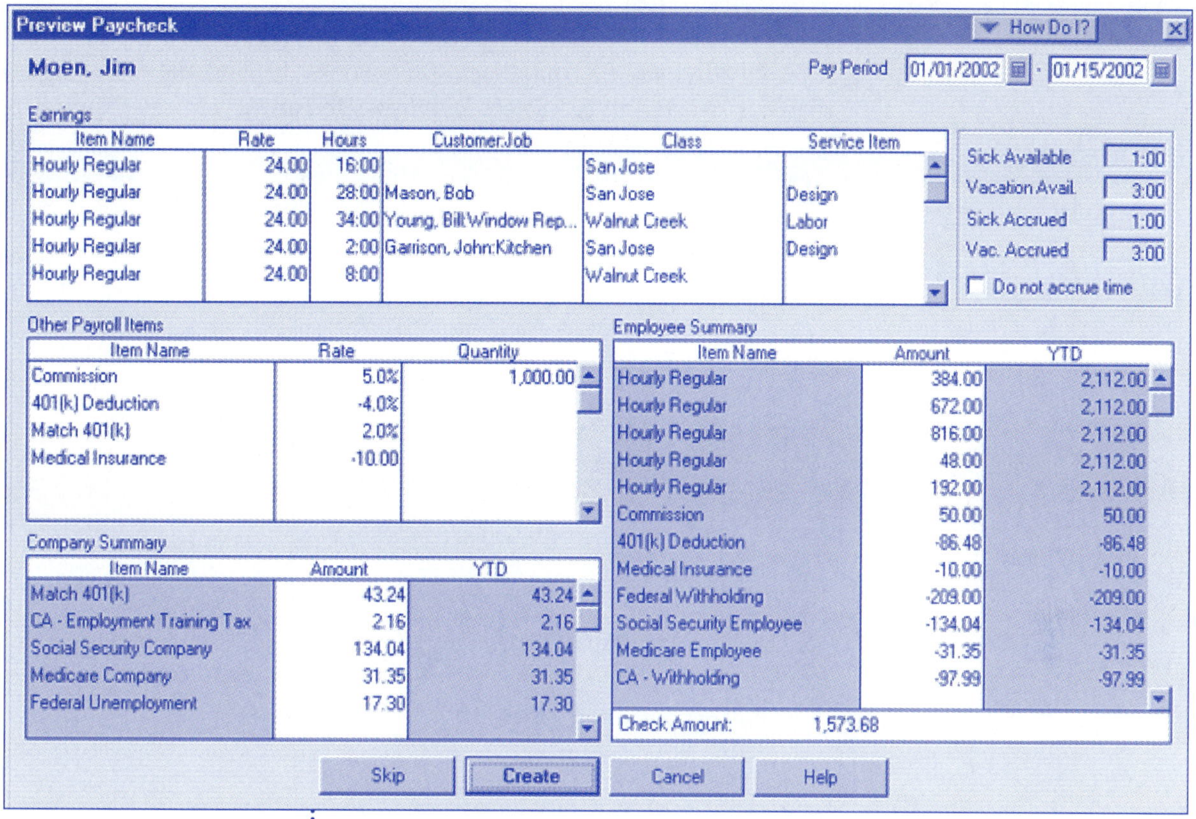

Preview Paycheck ▼ How Do I? ✕

Moen, Jim Pay Period 01/01/2002 ▦ · 01/15/2002 ▦

Earnings

Item Name	Rate	Hours	Customer:Job	Class	Service Item
Hourly Regular	24.00	16:00		San Jose	
Hourly Regular	24.00	28:00	Mason, Bob	San Jose	Design
Hourly Regular	24.00	34:00	Young, Bill:Window Rep...	Walnut Creek	Labor
Hourly Regular	24.00	2:00	Garrison, John:Kitchen	San Jose	Design
Hourly Regular	24.00	8:00		Walnut Creek	

Sick Available 1:00
Vacation Avail. 3:00
Sick Accrued 1:00
Vac. Accrued 3:00
☐ Do not accrue time

Other Payroll Items

Item Name	Rate	Quantity
Commission	5.0%	1,000.00
401(k) Deduction	-4.0%	
Match 401(k)	2.0%	
Medical Insurance	-10.00	

Employee Summary

Item Name	Amount	YTD
Hourly Regular	384.00	2,112.00
Hourly Regular	672.00	2,112.00
Hourly Regular	816.00	2,112.00
Hourly Regular	48.00	2,112.00
Hourly Regular	192.00	2,112.00
Commission	50.00	50.00
401(k) Deduction	-86.48	-86.48
Medical Insurance	-10.00	-10.00
Federal Withholding	-209.00	-209.00
Social Security Employee	-134.04	-134.04
Medicare Employee	-31.35	-31.35
CA - Withholding	-97.99	-97.99

Company Summary

Item Name	Amount	YTD
Match 401(k)	43.24	43.24
CA - Employment Training Tax	2.16	2.16
Social Security Company	134.04	134.04
Medicare Company	31.35	31.35
Federal Unemployment	17.30	17.30

Check Amount: 1,573.68

Skip   **Create**   Cancel   Help

Figure 8-12 Preview Paycheck screen – Hourly Employee

2 Verify that your screen matches Figure 8-12. Then click **Create**.

Calculating Paychecks for Salaried Employees

After creating the first paycheck, QuickBooks displays the next employee that was selected in the Select Employees to Pay screen (see Figure 8-13).

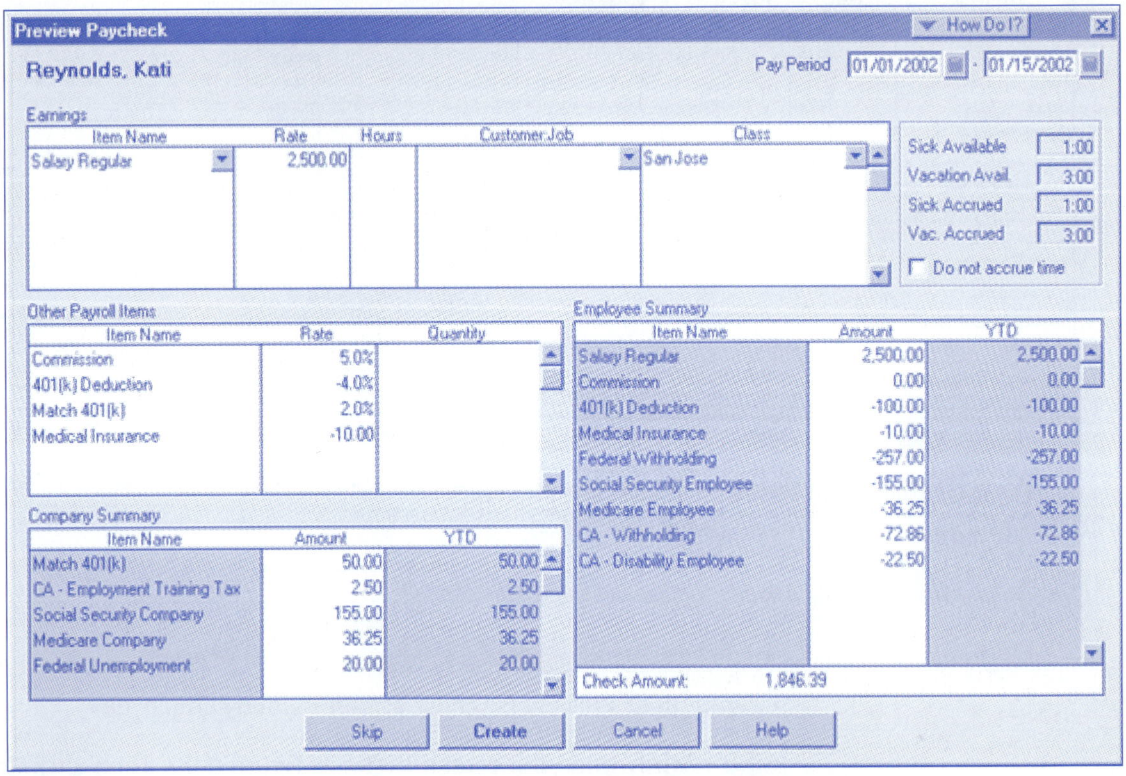

Figure 8-13 Preview Paycheck screen – Salaried Employee

COMPUTER TUTORIAL

① In the Earnings section, add a second line for Salary Vacation. Notice that the salary is split evenly between the two lines.

② Enter "85" in the Hours column for "Salary Regular" on the first line, and "3" in the Hours column for "Salary Vacation" on the second line (see Figure 8-14).

Since this is a salaried employee, QuickBooks calculates the total gross pay for the period and then divides that amount equally into each of the Earnings Items listed in the Earnings Section. To change this, enter the correct number for each line. QuickBooks will pro-rate the total salary amount to each line according to the number of hours on that line.

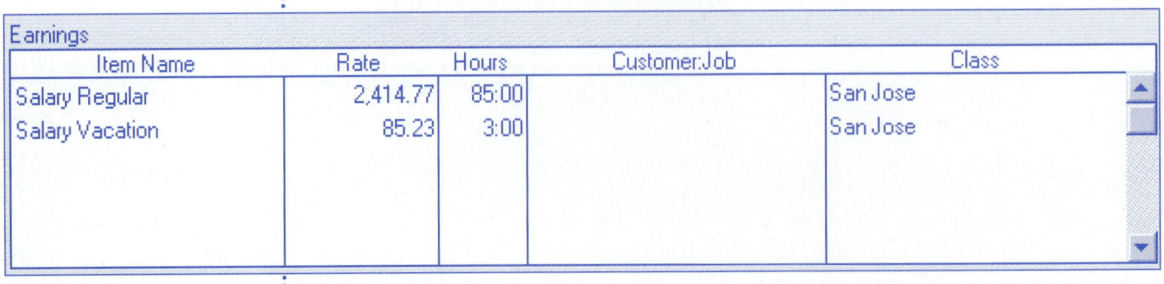

Figure 8-14 The Earnings section

3 Verify that your screen matches Figure 8-15 and click **Create**.

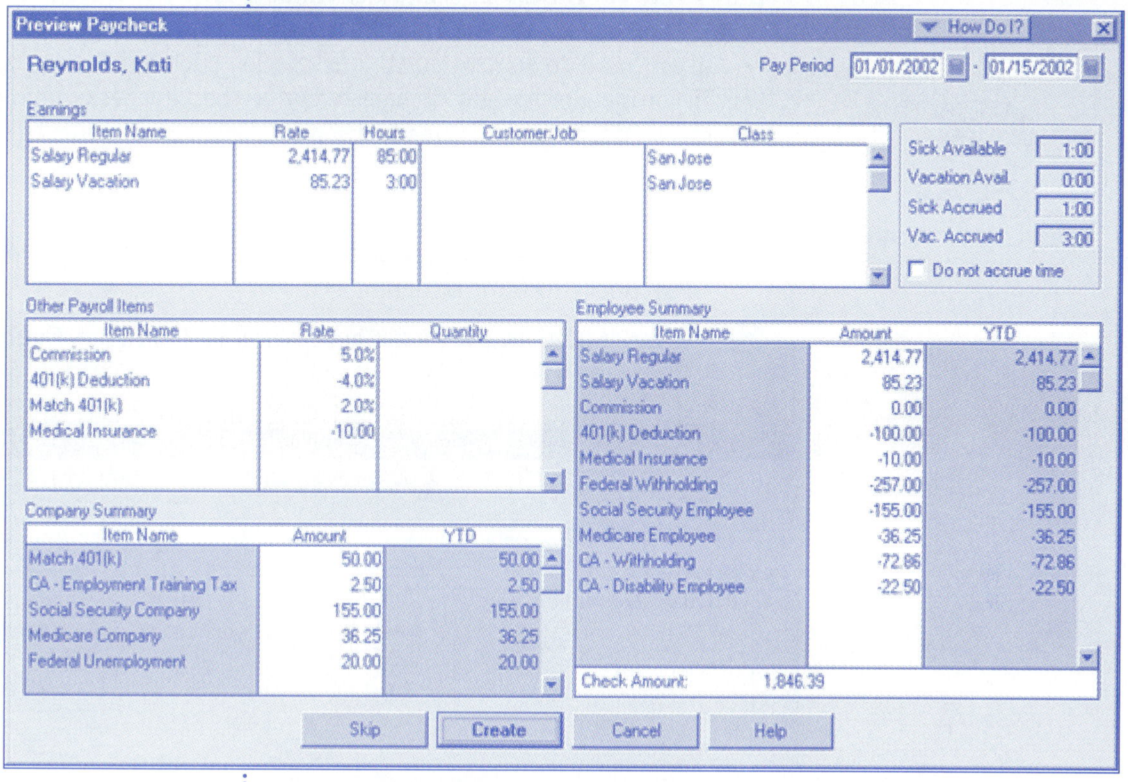

Figure 8-15 Preview Paycheck screen

Printing Paychecks

When you're finished creating all of the paychecks, QuickBooks displays the Select Employees to Pay screen again, but the program has updated the Last Pay Period Ends column with the ending period for each of the paychecks (see Figure 8-16).

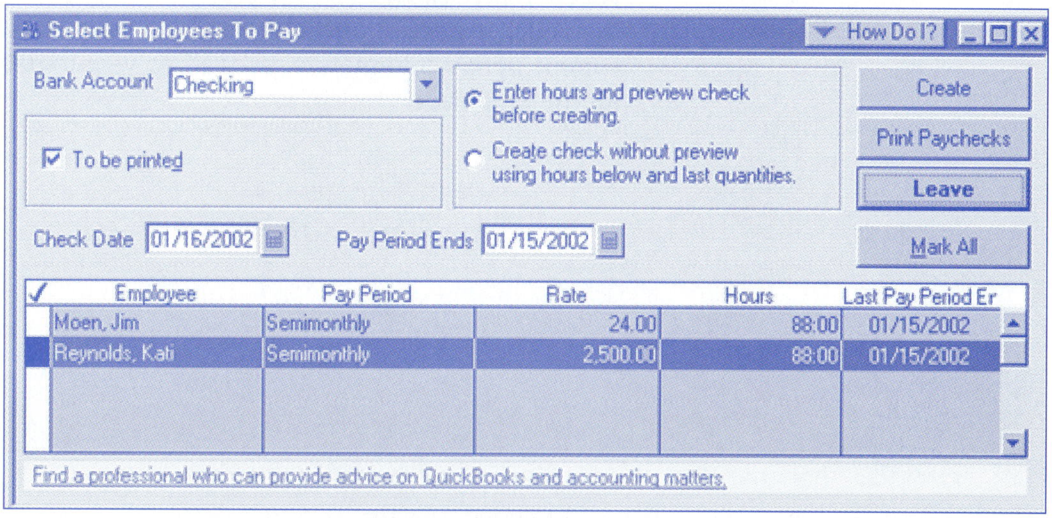

Figure 8-16 The Select Employees to Pay screen with updated Last Pay Period Ends column.

If you want to print the checks immediately after creating them, click **Print Paychecks** in the Select Employees to Pay screen (see Figure 8-16). Then follow steps 2 through 6 below.

If you want to wait to print your checks, click **Leave**. You would do this if you needed to edit or delete any of the paychecks before printing them. When you are ready to print paychecks, follow the steps below.

COMPUTER TUTORIAL

① Select the *File* menu, choose **Print Forms**, and then choose **Paychecks**. All the unprinted paychecks show in the Select Paychecks to Print screen.

② Enter "6004" in the *First Check Number* field (see Figure 8-17). Then click **OK**.

Select Paychecks to Print				☒
Bank Account [Checking ▼]		First Check Number [6004]		
Select Paychecks to print, then click OK.				
✓	Date	Employee	Amount	**OK**
✓	01/16/2002	Moen, Jim	1,573.68	Cancel
✓	01/16/2002	Reynolds, Kati	1,846.39	Help
				Select All
				Select None
Show:	⦿ Both	○ Paychecks	○ Direct Deposit	

Figure 8-17 Select the paychecks to be printed.

③ On the Print Checks screen, QuickBooks lets you know that there are two checks to print and gives the total amount of those checks (see Figure 8-18).

④ In the Print Checks screen, you can also select the check style. Select "Voucher" as your choice of check style. When you use voucher checks, QuickBooks prints the paystub information on the voucher portion of the checks. The paystub will include the current period information, as well as year-to-date information for the employee.

NOTE

For this class you'll print on blank paper instead of real checks. When you're printing on real checks, make sure you load the checks into the printer before you click **Print**.

⑤ Verify the printer settings and then click **Print**. Click **OK** if your checks printed correctly.

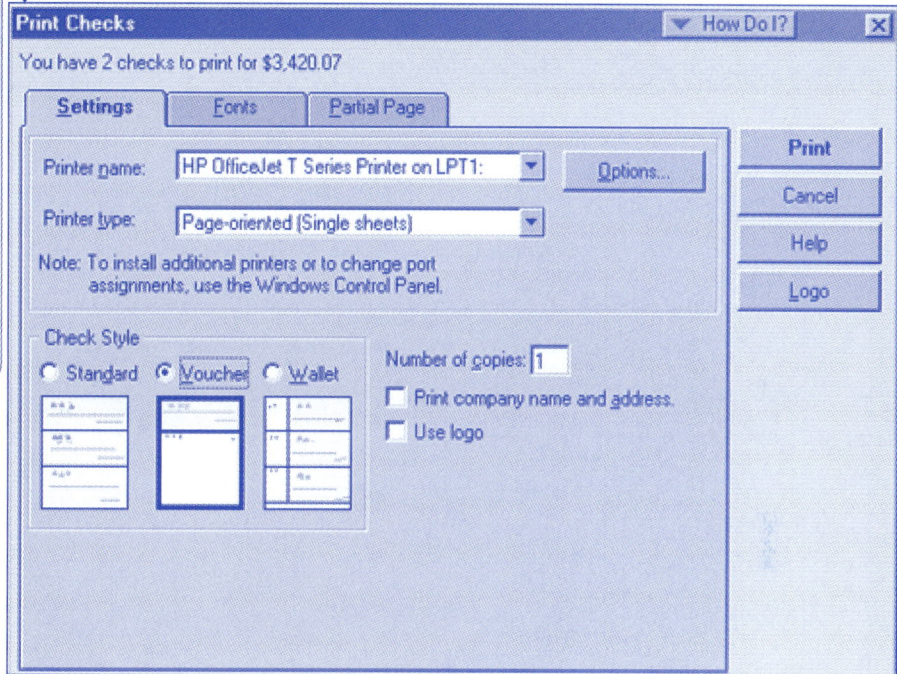

Figure 8-18 The Print Checks screen

Printing Paystubs

If you don't use voucher checks or if you don't print checks from QuickBooks, you can still print paystubs for your employees on blank paper.

① Select the *File* menu, choose **Print Forms**, and then choose **Paystubs** (see Figure 8-19). Enter the dates for the paystubs you want to print.

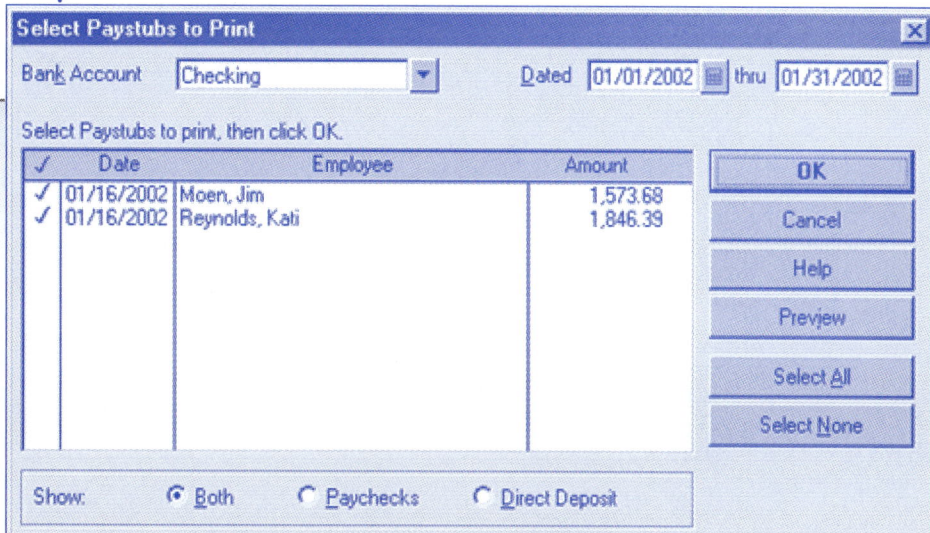

Figure 8-19 The Select Paystubs to Print screen

2 Click **Preview** to see what the paystubs look like when they print (see Figure 8-20). Paystubs print one per page.

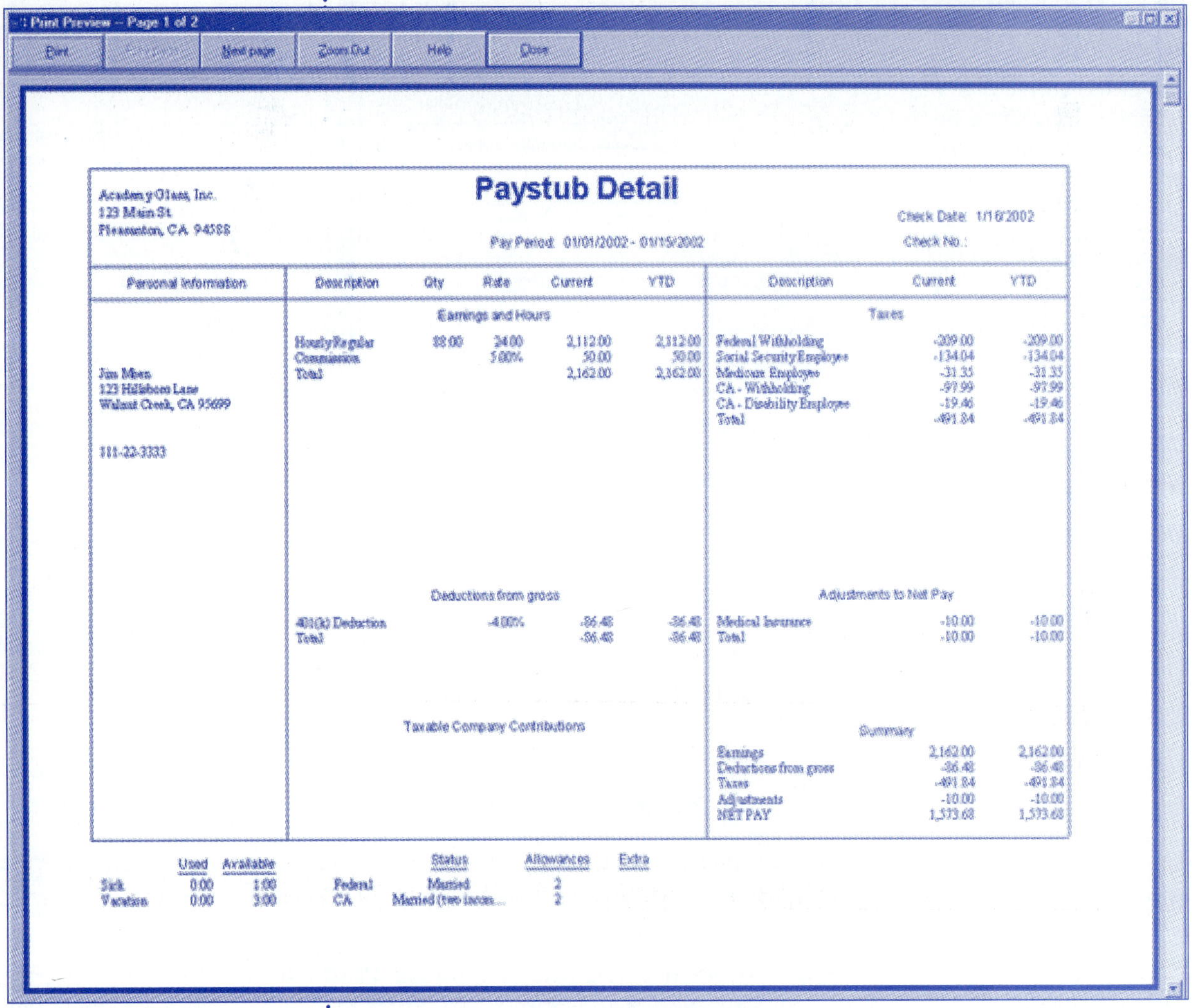

Figure 8-20 A preview of a paystub

3 After previewing the paystub, click **Print**.

EDITING, VOIDING, AND DELETING PAYCHECKS

If you find errors on paychecks, you can edit, void, or delete the paychecks. However, be careful when you do any of these actions because changing transactions may adversely affect your records. When in doubt, ask your accountant.

> **IMPORTANT**
>
> If you edit a paycheck that has already been printed, make sure your changes don't affect the net pay amount. Also, if this employee has other paychecks dated after this check, the changes you make may invalidate the tax calculations on the newer checks. It's best to avoid editing, voiding, or deleting any paycheck except the last paycheck for each employee. If you're unsure about an adjustment you need to make, check with your accountant.

Editing Paychecks

COMPUTER TUTORIAL

If you haven't printed the paycheck, you can edit the paycheck directly in the register.

1 Select the *Employees* menu and then choose **Edit/Void Paychecks**.

2 Set the *Show paychecks from* date to "01/01/2002" and the *through* date to "01/31/02." Then press <TAB>.

Edit/Void Paychecks	▼ How Do I?

Show paychecks from 01/01/2002 📅 through 01/31/2002 📅   Sort By Paycheck Date ▼

Paycheck Date	Employee	Memo	Net Amount
01/16/2002	Moen, Jim		1,573.68
01/16/2002	Reynolds, Kati		1,846.39

Edit	Void	Help	Done

Figure 8-21 The Edit/Void Paychecks screen

3 Press <TAB> to leave "Paycheck Date" in the *Sort By* field.

④ Highlight Jim Moen's paycheck dated 01/16/2002 and click **Edit** (see Figure 8-21).

⑤ To edit the items on the paycheck, click **Paycheck Detail** (see Figure 8-22).

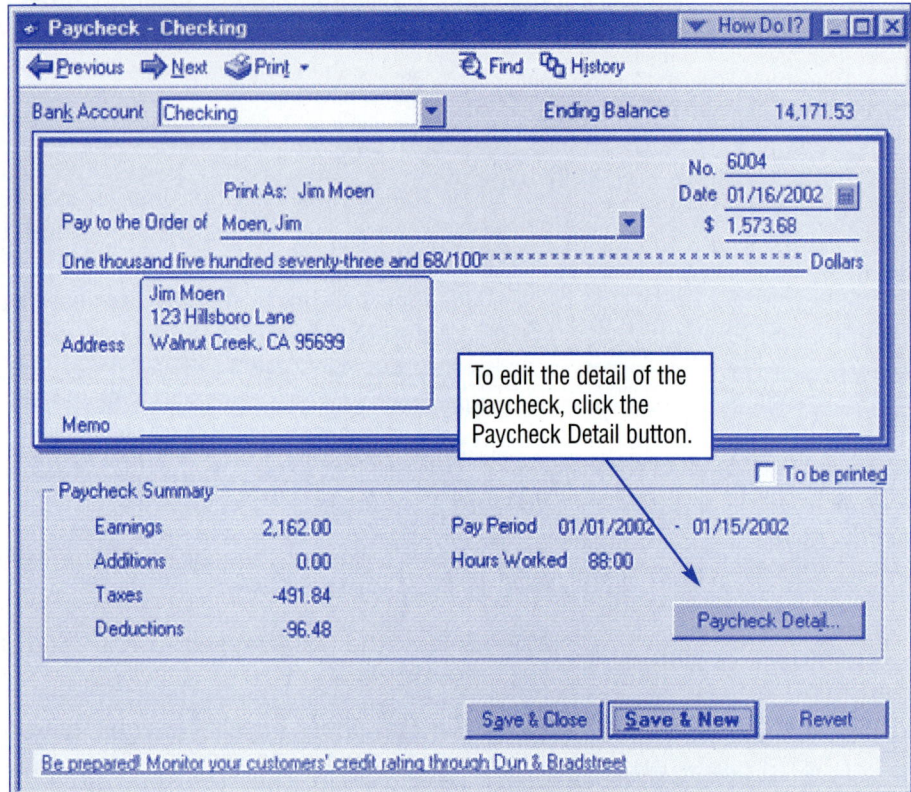

Figure 8-22 Click Paycheck Detail to edit the items on the paycheck.

Review Paycheck						▼ How Do I?	✕

Moen, Jim   Pay Period [01/01/2002] - [01/15/2002]

Earnings

Item Name	Rate	Hours	Customer:Job	Class	Service Item
Hourly Regular	24.00	16:00		San Jose	
Hourly Regular	24.00	28:00	Mason, Bob	San Jose	Design
Hourly Regular	24.00	34:00	Young, Bill:Window Rep...	Walnut Creek	
Hourly Regular	24.00	2:00	Garrison, John:Kitchen	San Jose	
Hourly Regular	24.00	8:00		Walnut Creek	

Sick Available [1:00]
Vacation Avail. [3:00]
Sick Accrued [1:00]
Vac. Accrued [3:00]
☐ Do not accrue time

> You can only modify fields with a white background.

Other Payroll Items

Item Name	Rate	Quantity
Commission	5.0%	1,000.00
401(k) Deduction	-4.0%	
Medical Insurance	-10.00	
Match 401(k)	2.0%	

Employee Summary

Item Name	Amount	YTD
Hourly Regular	384.00	2,112.00
Hourly Regular	672.00	2,112.00
Hourly Regular	816.00	2,112.00
Hourly Regular	48.00	2,112.00
Hourly Regular	192.00	2,112.00
Commission	50.00	50.00
401(k) Deduction	-86.48	-86.48
Medical Insurance	-10.00	-10.00
Federal Withholding	-209.00	-209.00
Social Security Employee	-134.04	-134.04
Medicare Employee	-31.35	-31.35
CA - Withholding	-97.99	-97.99

Company Summary

Item Name	Amount	YTD
Match 401(k)	43.24	43.24
CA - Employment Training Tax	2.16	2.16
Social Security Company	134.04	134.04
Medicare Company	31.35	31.35
Federal Unemployment	17.30	17.30

Check Amount: 1,573.68

OK	Cancel	Help

Figure 8-23 Any of the fields with a white background can be edited.

→ **ANOTHER** →
← **WAY** ←

Another way of editing paychecks is to double-click on the paycheck in the checking account register. Then continue from step 5 above.

6 Make whatever changes are necessary on the screen shown in Figure 8-23, just as you did when you originally created the paycheck. At this point, you won't actually make any changes to your paychecks, but this is the screen where you would make changes if necessary.

7 Click **Cancel** and then click **Save & Close** to leave the check unchanged.

TIP

The reason you don't void the original transaction and create a new paycheck is a little tricky to understand. In the event that the paycheck to be replaced was not the very last paycheck for that employee, QuickBooks would not be able to recreate the check exactly as the original. That's because the year-to-date information is calculated on each paycheck by taking all paychecks (regardless of their date) and adding their amounts together. The method shown here avoids this problem by simply reprinting the original paycheck on a new check number.

Replacing Lost or Stolen Checks

Don't perform these steps now. They are for reference only.

1. Find the check in the Checking Register, edit the check, and click the "To be printed" box in the Paycheck screen to deselect it.
2. Click **Save and Close** and then **Yes** to save your change.
3. Reprint the check and give it a new check number.
4. Enter a new check directly in the check register with the same date, payee, amount, and check number as the lost check. Code it to the miscellaneous expense account.
5. Void the new check you just created. This converts the check into a voided check with the same date, payee, amount and check number as the lost or stolen check.

Voiding Paychecks

If you need to void a paycheck, make sure it's the most recent paycheck for this employee.

Don't perform these steps now. They are for reference only.

1. Select the *Employees* menu and then choose **Edit/Void Paychecks**.
2. Set the *from* date to "01/01/2002" and the *through* date to "01/31/02." Then press <TAB>.
3. On the list of paychecks, select the paycheck you want to void.
4. Click **Void**.
5. Type "YES" in the *Type YES to Confirm, then click Void* field. Then click **Void**.

ANOTHER WAY

Another way of voiding paychecks is to select the paycheck in the checking account register. Then select **Void Paycheck** from the *Edit* menu.

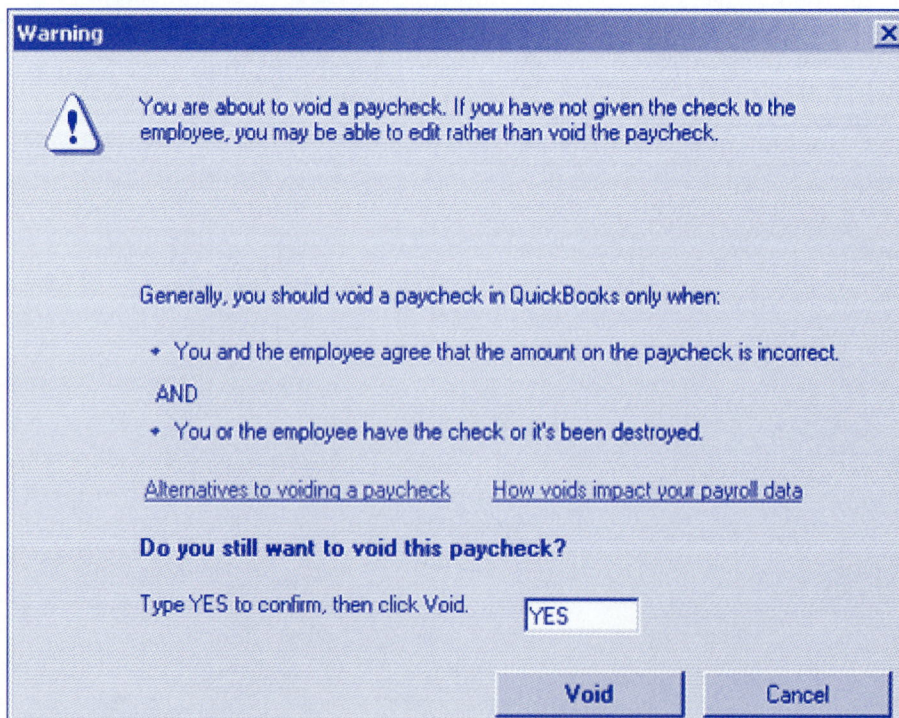

Figure 8-24 Void paycheck confirmation screen

This updates the employee's year-to-date payroll information. However, if this employee has paychecks already entered and dated after this paycheck, you won't see any changes to the year-to-date amounts on those paychecks. The next paycheck you create for this employee will show the correct year-to-date amounts, as will the payroll reports and tax forms.

If the paycheck you're voiding isn't the most recent paycheck, keep in mind that the year-to-date information on all paychecks dated after a voided paycheck will be incorrect. To avoid this problem, delete all the paychecks for this employee dated after the paycheck. Then, after you void the paycheck, recreate the paychecks that were dated after the voided paycheck. When you recreate those paychecks, QuickBooks recalculates all the year-to-date amounts and taxes. Make sure that all information on the new paychecks matches the original paychecks.

Before you start, make a backup of your file.

Deleting Paychecks

The only time you should delete a paycheck is when you created it in error and you haven't printed the check. Otherwise, you should void the paycheck so you can keep a record of it.

> **Don't perform these steps now. They are for reference only.**

> **→ ANOTHER →**
> **← WAY ←**
> Another way of deleting paychecks is to select the paycheck in the checking account register. Then select **Delete Paycheck** from the *Edit* menu.

1. Select the *Employees* menu and then choose **Edit/Void Paychecks**.
2. Set the *from* date to "01/01/2002" and the *through* date to "01/31/02." Then press <TAB>.
3. On the list of paychecks, click the paycheck you want to delete and click **Edit**.
4. Select the *Edit* menu and then choose **Delete Paycheck** (or press <Ctrl+D>).
5. Click **OK**.

PAYING PAYROLL LIABILITIES

An important part of keeping your payroll system working correctly is to make sure you pay the liabilities correctly.

When you pay the liabilities, don't just write a check for your taxes and code it to payroll liabilities because that won't involve the Payroll Items. To correctly pay your payroll liabilities, use the Pay Liabilities function. All payroll deductions, company contributions, and company taxes must be paid using the Pay Liabilities function.

QuickBooks requires that you use the Pay Liabilities function to record payments of all Payroll Items that increase (credit) liability accounts. If you don't use the Pay Liabilities function to record these payments, QuickBooks won't track your payments in the liabilities reports or tax forms such as the 941.

COMPUTER TUTORIAL

The IRS publication *Circular E, Employer's Tax Guide* specifies the rules for when your payroll taxes must be paid. Depending on the size of your payroll, you will be either a "Monthly" depositor or a "Semiweekly" depositor. Monthly depositors are required to pay all payroll liabilities by the 15th of the month following the payroll date. Semiweekly depositors are required to pay all payroll liabilities by the Wednesday after the payroll date if the payroll date is Wednesday, Thursday, or Friday. Semiweekly depositors are required to pay all payroll liabilities by the Friday after the payroll date, if the payroll date is Saturday, Sunday, Monday, or Tuesday.

Select the bank account you use to pay payroll taxes and set the payment date. QuickBooks assumes you want to show the liabilities you owe as of the end of last month. Change this date if necessary.

① Select the **Employees** menu and then choose **Pay Payroll Liabilities**.

② On the Select Date Range for Liabilities screen, set the *Show Liabilities from* field to "01/01/2002" and the *through* field to "01/16/2002" (see Figure 8-25).

Figure 8-25 The Select Date Range for Liabilities screen

③ Click **OK**.

On the Pay Liabilities screen, each Payroll Item shows along with the balance due as of the date shown in the *Show liabilities from... through...* date. This screen is similar to the Pay Bills screen, but it only shows payroll liabilities.

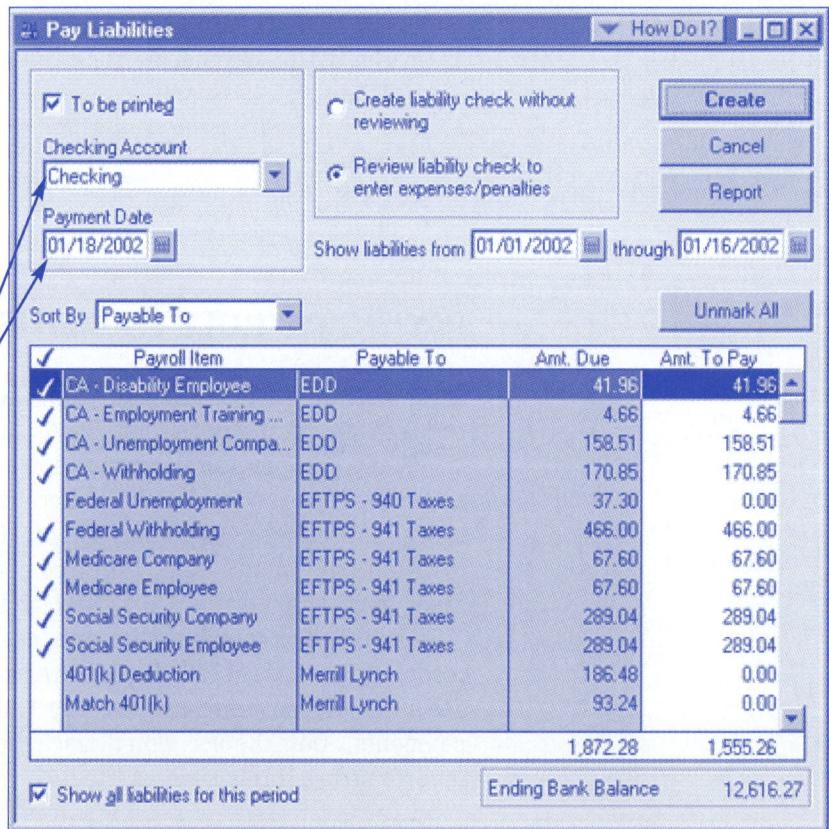

Figure 8-26 The Pay Liabilities screen

QuickBooks allows you to modify any amount in the Amt. to Pay column of the Pay Liabilities screen (Figure 8-26) but you should almost never do this. If you do, it will compound the problem of having incorrect payroll liabilities. Instead, if you need to make a small change to the amount you're paying (e.g., adjust for rounding), enter an adjustment on the liability check using the Expenses tab (see Figure 8-27). If you consistently have trouble in this area, contact your accountant or QuickBooks consultant for help.

If you find an error in the amount that QuickBooks suggests you owe, check each paycheck to see which one created the error. When you find the erroneous paycheck or paychecks, modify the Items on the paycheck. Of course, if you've already printed the paycheck, some adjustments won't be possible. In that case, you can use the Adjust Liabilities function discussed later in the chapter, or make an adjustment on the next check for the affected employees.

④ Leave the "To be printed" box checked, "Checking" in the *Checking Account* field, "Payable To" in the *Sort By* field, and the *Review liability check to enter expenses/penalties* field selected.

⑤ Set the *Payment Date* to "01/18/2002."

⑥ Then select the Payroll Items as shown in Figure 8-26. As with bill payments, QuickBooks adds all of the payments to the same vendor (*Payable To* field) onto one check.

⑦ Click **Create**. Click **Previous** or **Next** to locate the check shown in Figure 8-27, if it does not display automatically.

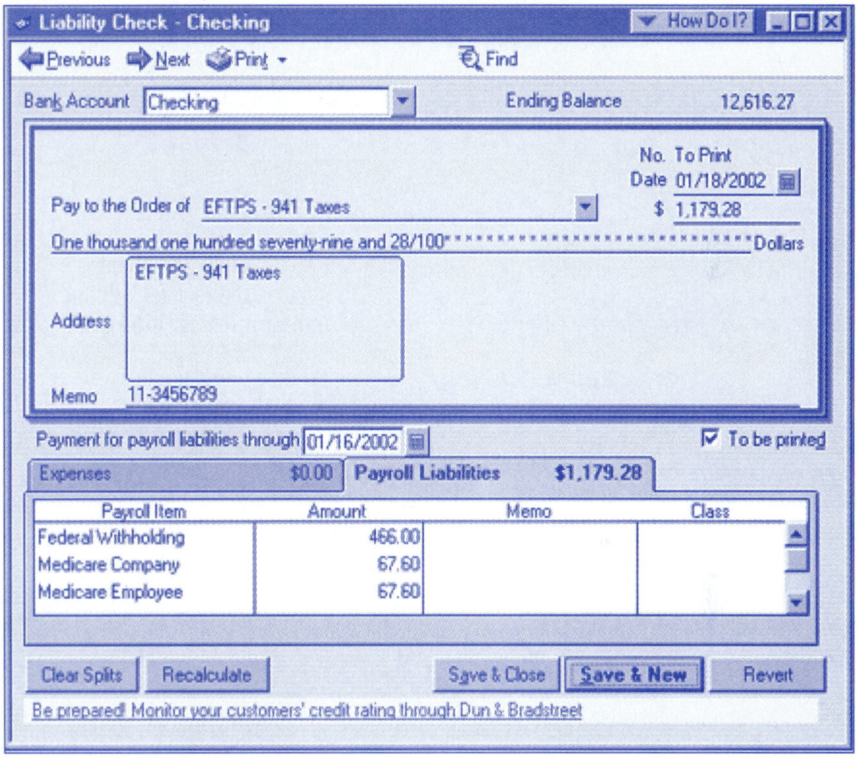

Figure 8-27 Reviewing the liability check before saving

In the screen shown in Figure 8-27, you can review the liability payments and make any necessary changes before recording them.

⑧ Click **Save & Close**.

⑨ Display the Checking account register by double-clicking it in the Chart of Accounts list.

Notice the transaction type is "LIAB CHK" as shown in Figure 8-28. The "LIAB CHK" transaction is the only type of transaction that properly records payment of payroll liabilities. That's because "LIAB CHK" transactions record the details of which payroll liabilities are paid by that check. Any other type of payment can't lower the balance due shown on the Payroll Liabilities report.

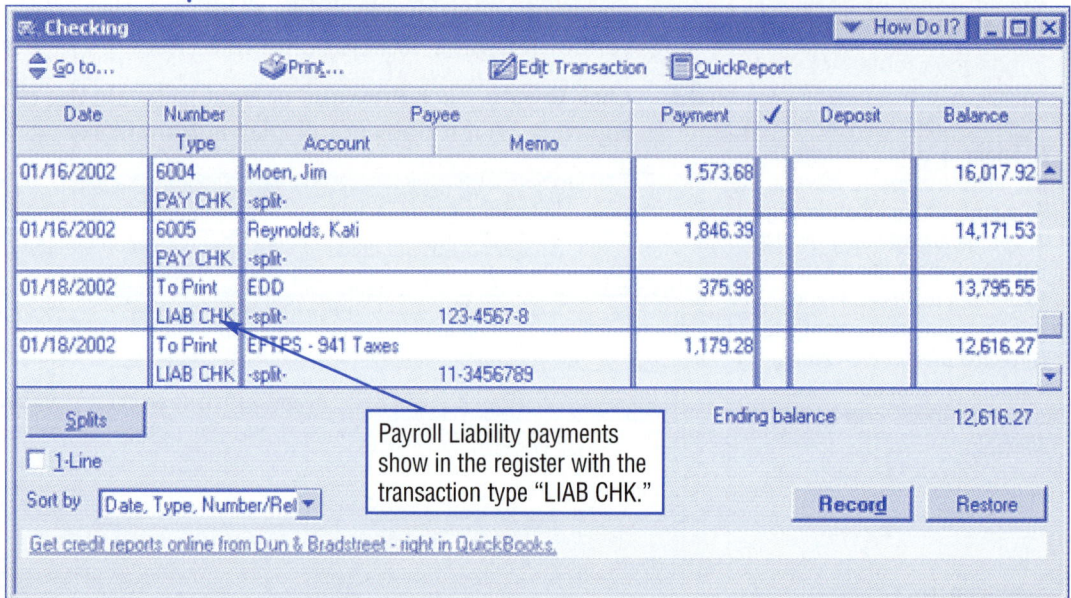

Figure 8-28 A payroll liability payment in the Check Register

NOTE

If your start date is December 31, there will probably be balances due for Federal and State payroll taxes on your start date. Use a journal entry on your start date to enter the amounts due for each of the liabilities, and don't use payroll to set up year-to-date amounts. Then, when you record the payments of liabilities from last year, enter regular checks in the Checking register to record those payments. This is the only time you'll use a check to record your liability payments instead of a Payroll Liability check.

Editing a Liability Payment

If you need to edit an existing liability payment, you can edit it as shown below. However, make sure you only do this if you haven't yet submitted the payment to the tax agency. If you have submitted the payment to the tax agency, you should use the Adjust Liabilities function instead of editing the payment.

Don't perform these steps now. They are for reference only.

1. Select the liability payment in the register and click **Edit Transaction**.
2. With the liability payment displayed (Figure 8-29), edit any of the fields on the check and then click **Save & Close**.

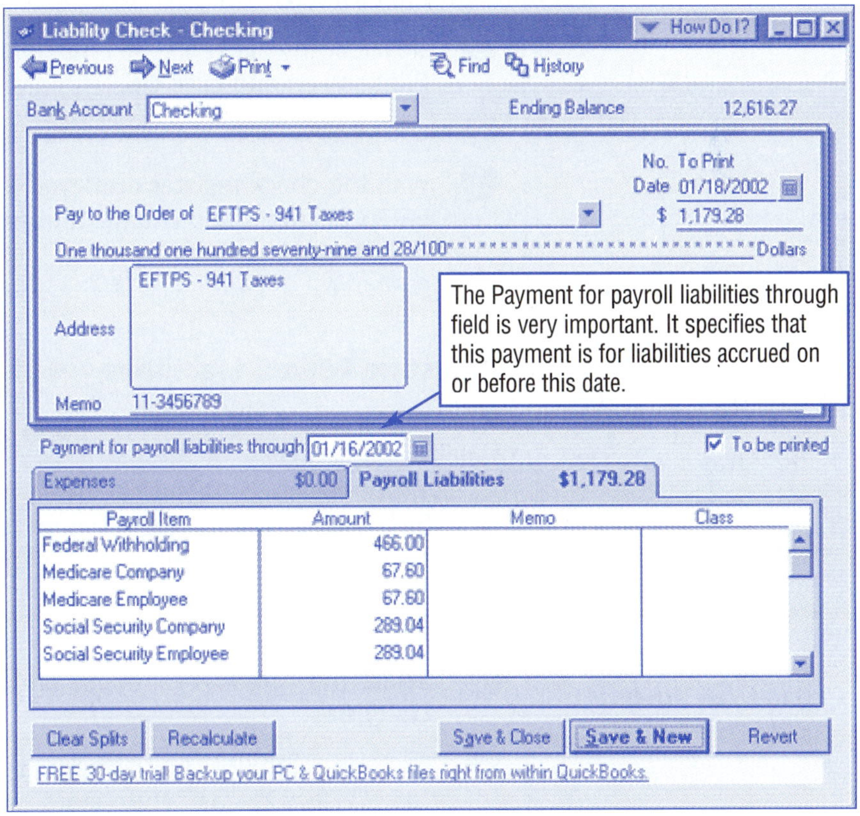

Figure 8-29 Edit a liability payment, if necessary.

COMPUTER TUTORIAL

Printing Payroll Liability Checks

You can continue paying your liabilities by printing the State Payroll Liability check and changing the check number on the EFTPS payment.

1 Select the *File* menu, choose **Print Forms**, and then choose **Checks**.

2 If you pay your liabilities electronically, for example with EFTPS (Electronic Federal Tax Payment System), don't print those checks. Instead, change the check number in the register to the last 11 digits of the approval code given to you by the EFTPS system when your payment is approved. Since we used EFTPS for the Federal payment, you'll only need to select the Employment Development Department transaction in the Select Checks to Print screen.

3 Deselect the "EFTPS – 941 Taxes" check in the Select Checks to Print screen and click **OK**.

4 Click **Print**. Then, click **OK** on the Did Check(s) print OK? screen.

5 With the check register displayed, edit the check number for the EFTPS payment and change it from "To Print" to "55-4354." Then click **Record**.

Adjusting Payroll Liabilities

If your payroll liabilities need adjusting, you can use the Adjust Liabilities function.

Adjusting payroll liabilities should be done with great care. You must fully understand all the accounting and tax implications of the adjustment to avoid significant tax penalties. Consult with your accountant or QuickBooks consultant if your payroll liabilities need adjusting.

COMPUTER TUTORIAL

1 Select the *Employees* menu and then choose **Adjust Payroll Liabilities**.

2 On the Liability Adjustment screen (Figure 8-30), enter "03/31/2002" as the *Date* for your adjustment and "03/31/2002" as the *Effective Date* of the adjustment.

The *Date* field is the date you actually enter the transaction. The *Effective Date* field is the date you want this adjustment to affect your liability balances in your liability reports. Make sure you use the *Memo* field to explain your adjustment.

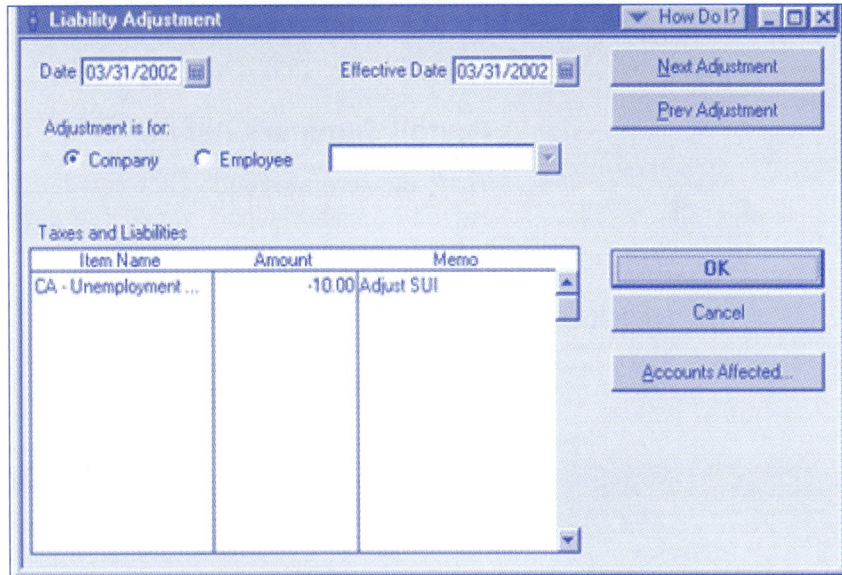

Figure 8-30 The Liability Adjustment screen

3 Leave "Company" preselected in the *Adjustment is for:* field. In the Taxes and Liabilities section, enter "CA – Unemployment Company " as the Item Name, "-10.00" in the Amount column, and "Adjust SUI" in the Memo column.

Use positive numbers to increase the balance of the Liability Item and negative numbers to reduce the balance of the Liability Item.

4 Click **Cancel** to prevent this adjustment from being saved. **Do not save the adjustment** shown in Figure 8-30. It is for illustration only.

If you're having trouble adjusting your payroll liabilities, click **How Do I?** on the Liability Adjustment screen shown in Figure 8-30 and select the appropriate topic from the drop-down menu. You can also press <F1> while the Liability Adjustment screen is open. This activates QuickBooks Help, where you can search for the exact payroll liability situation you are trying to resolve. There are many useful tips and hints in the Help system for solving problems related to payroll liabilities (see Figure 8-31).

> **DID YOU KNOW** You can press the <F1> key while viewing almost any screen in QuickBooks to open QuickBooks Help. The Help screen will default to topics related to the screen you are viewing.

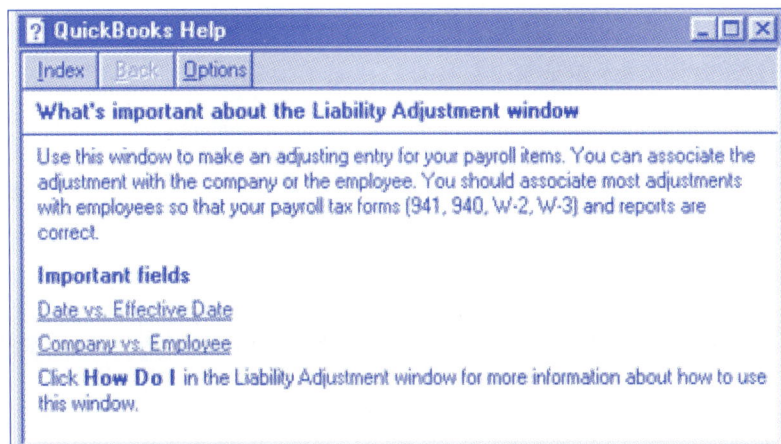

Figure 8-31 The QuickBooks Help screen

CREATING PAYROLL REPORTS

Payroll Summary Report

COMPUTER TUTORIAL

There are several reports that you can use to analyze your payroll. The Payroll Summary report shows the detail of each employee's earnings, taxes, and net pay.

1 Select the **Reports** menu, choose **Employees & Payroll**, and then choose **Payroll Summary**.

2 Set the date range from "01/01/2002" to "01/31/2002" and press <TAB>.

Payroll Summary		▼ How Do I? □ □ ☒
Modify Report... Memorize... Print... Excel... Hide Header Collapse Refresh		
Dates This Month-to-date ▼ From 01/01/2002 ▦ To 01/31/2002 ▦ Columns Employee ▼		

To modify the columns on this report, click Modify Report.

Academy Glass, Inc.
Payroll Summary
January 2002

	Moen, Jim			Reynolds, Kati			TOTAL		
	Hours ◇	Rate ◇	Jan 02 ◇	Hours ◇	Rate ◇	Jan 02 ◇	Hours ◇	Rate ◇	Jan 02 ◇
Employee Wages, Taxes and Ad...									
Gross Pay									
Salary Regular			0.00	85		2,414.77	85		2,414.77
Salary Vacation			0.00	3		85.23	3		85.23
Hourly Regular	88	24.00	2,112.00			0.00	88		2,112.00
Commission			50.00			0.00			50.00
Total Gross Pay			2,162.00			2,500.00			4,662.00
Deductions from Gross Pay									
401(k) Deduction			-86.48			-100.00			-186.48
Total Deductions from Gross Pay			-86.48			-100.00			-186.48
Adjusted Gross Pay			2,075.52			2,400.00			4,475.52
Taxes Withheld									
Federal Withholding			-209.00			-257.00			-466.00
Medicare Employee			-31.35			-36.25			-67.60
Social Security Employee			-134.04			-155.00			-289.04
CA - Withholding			-97.99			-72.86			-170.85
CA - Disability Employee			-19.46			-22.50			-41.96
Total Taxes Withheld			-491.84			-543.61			-1,035.45
Deductions from Net Pay									
Medical Insurance			-10.00			-10.00			-20.00
Total Deductions from Net Pay			-10.00			-10.00			-20.00
Net Pay			1,573.68			1,846.39			3,420.07

Figure 8-32 The Payroll Summary report

The Payroll Summary report (see Figure 8-32) shows columns for each employee, along with the hours and rate of pay. If you want to see more employees on a page, you can customize this report not to show the Hours and Rate columns.

3 Click **Modify Report** at the top of the Payroll Summary report.

4 Then clear the "Hours" and "Rate" boxes and click **OK** (see Figure 8-33). Your report will now look like Figure 8-34.

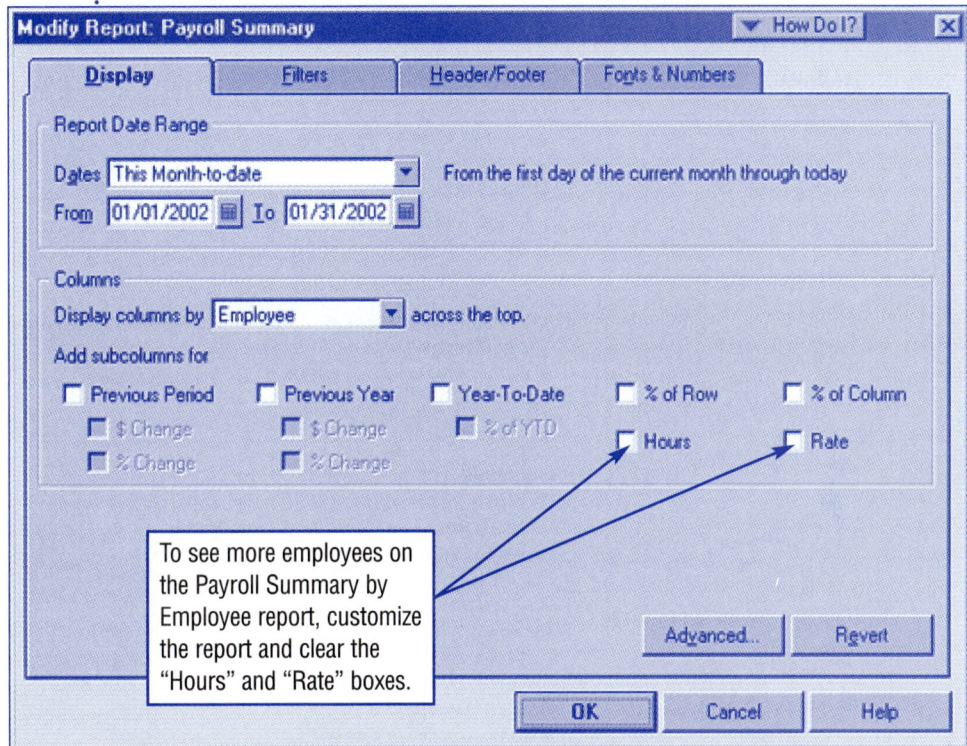

Modify Report: Payroll Summary ▼ How Do I? ✕

| **Display** | Filters | Header/Footer | Fonts & Numbers |

Report Date Range

Dates This Month-to-date ▼   From the first day of the current month through today

From 01/01/2002 To 01/31/2002

Columns

Display columns by Employee ▼ across the top.

Add subcolumns for

☐ Previous Period ☐ Previous Year ☐ Year-To-Date ☐ % of Row ☐ % of Column
☐ $ Change ☐ $ Change ☐ % of YTD ☐ Hours ☐ Rate
☐ % Change ☐ % Change

To see more employees on the Payroll Summary by Employee report, customize the report and clear the "Hours" and "Rate" boxes.

Advanced...   Revert

OK   Cancel   Help

Figure 8-33 The Modify Report screen

Payroll Summary		How Do I?	_ □ X
Modify Report...	Memorize... Print... Excel... Hide Header Collapse	Refresh	
Dates	This Month-to-date ▾ From 01/01/2002 To 01/31/2002	Columns	Employee

Academy Glass, Inc.
Payroll Summary
January 2002

	◆ Moen, Jim ◆	Reynolds, Kati ◆	TOTAL ◆
Employee Wages, Taxes and Adjustments			
Gross Pay			
Salary Regular	0.00	2,414.77 ▶	2,414.77 ◀
Salary Vacation	0.00	85.23	85.23
Hourly Regular	2,112.00	0.00	2,112.00
Commission	50.00	0.00	50.00
Total Gross Pay	2,162.00	2,500.00	4,662.00
Deductions from Gross Pay			
401(k) Deduction	-86.48	-100.00	-186.48
Total Deductions from Gross Pay	-86.48	-100.00	-186.48
Adjusted Gross Pay	2,075.52	2,400.00	4,475.52
Taxes Withheld			
Federal Withholding	-209.00	-257.00	-466.00
Medicare Employee	-31.35	-36.25	-67.60
Social Security Employee	-134.04	-155.00	-289.04
CA - Withholding	-97.99	-72.86	-170.85
CA - Disability Employee	-19.46	-22.50	-41.96
Total Taxes Withheld	-491.84	-543.61	-1,035.45
Deductions from Net Pay			
Medical Insurance	-10.00	-10.00	-20.00
Total Deductions from Net Pay	-10.00	-10.00	-20.00
Net Pay	**1,573.68**	**1,846.39**	**3,420.07**

Figure 8-34 Payroll Summary report without hours and rates

⑤ To print the report, click **Print**.

Reports Including Commission

If you pay your employees commission, you can create a Sales by Rep Summary or Sales by Rep Detail report.

① Select the *Reports* menu, choose **Sales**, and then choose **Sales by Rep Summary** (see Figure 8-35).

② Set the date range from "01/01/2002" to "01/31/2002" and press <TAB>.

> **IMPORTANT**
>
> The Sales by Rep Summary or Detail report requires you to first tag each sale with the employee who gets credit. To set this up, modify your Invoice and Sales Receipts template to include the *Rep* field. In the *Rep* field on each sales form, make sure you enter the initials of the employee that gets credit for the sale. The Sales by Rep report will show the total sales for each sales rep.

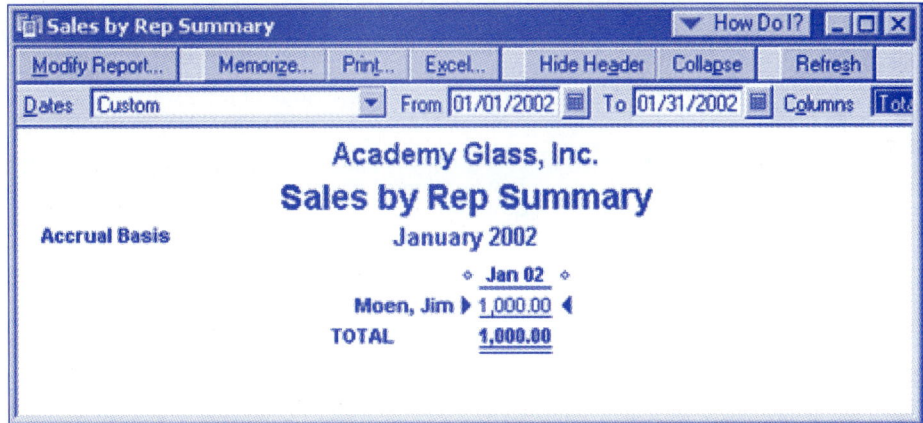

Figure 8-35 The Sales by Rep Summary report

Payroll Liabilities Report

The Payroll Liabilities report is used to track the status of your payroll liabilities by Item.

1 Select the **Reports** menu, choose **Employees & Payroll**, and then choose **Payroll Liabilities**.

2 Set the *From* date to "01/01/2002" and the *To* date to "03/31/2002." Then press <TAB> (see Figure 8-36).

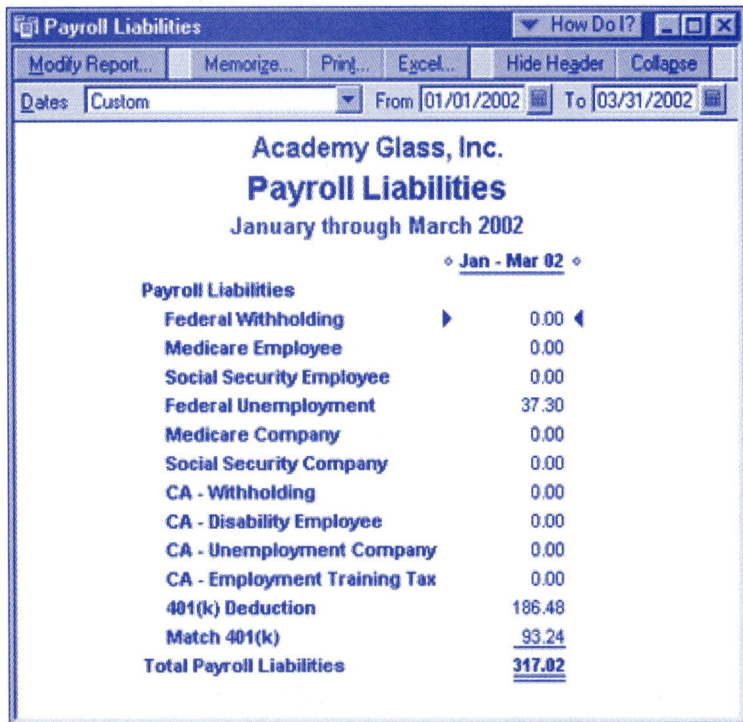

Figure 8-36 The Payroll Liabilities report

If you want to see accruals and payments for a range of time, set the "From" date to the beginning of the period and the "To" date to the end of the period. Choose "Week" in the *Columns* field to see accruals and payments for each week during the period (see Figure 8-37).

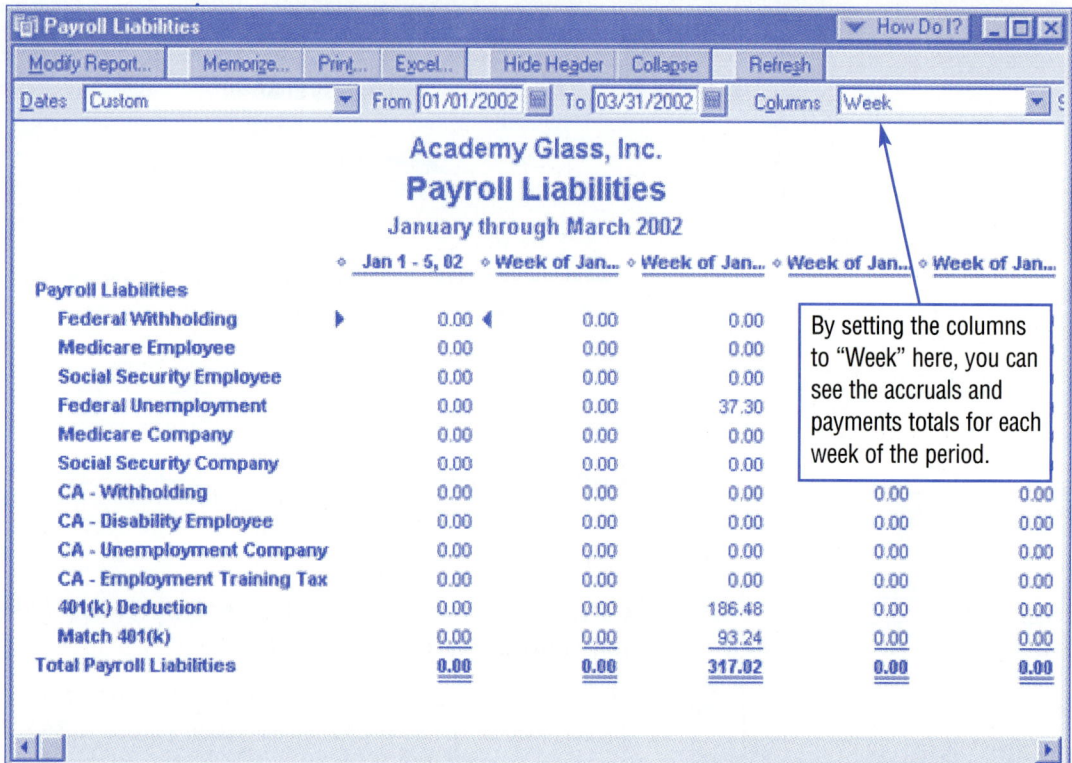

Figure 8-37 The Payroll Liabilities report showing accruals and payments by week

You can filter the report to show only certain liabilities. For example, if you only want to see the Federal liabilities, follow these steps.

③ Click **Modify Report**. Then click the Filters tab (see Figure 8-38).

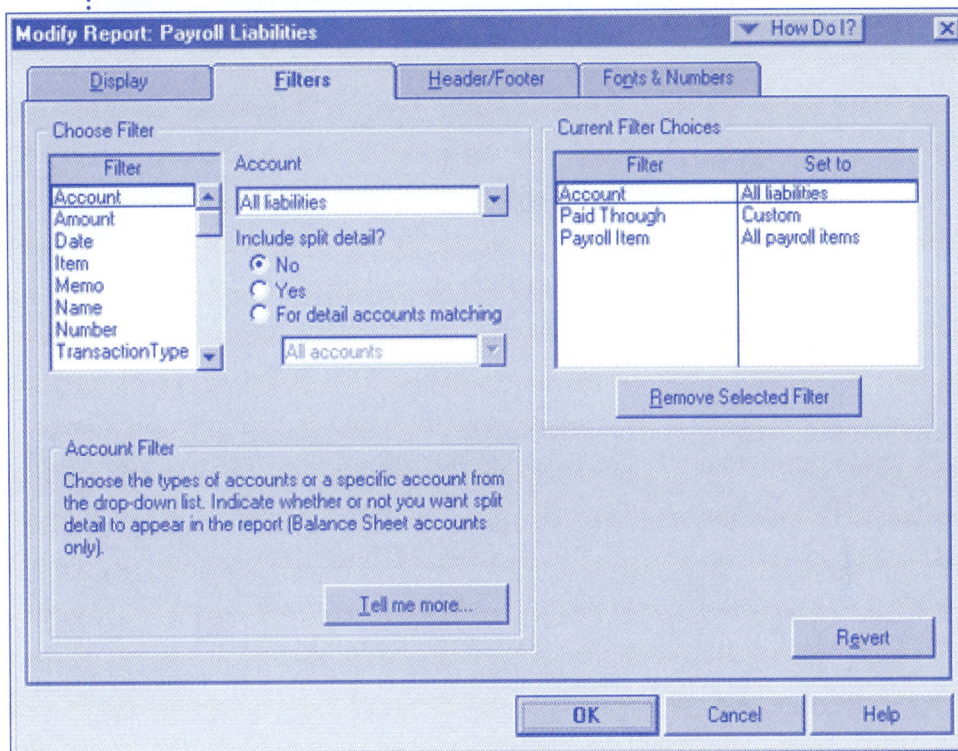

Figure 8-38 Modify Report – Filters Tab

④ Scroll down on the Filter list on the left side of the screen and select "Payroll Item."

⑤ Select "All Federal" from the Payroll Item drop-down menu in the center of the screen (see Figure 8-39).

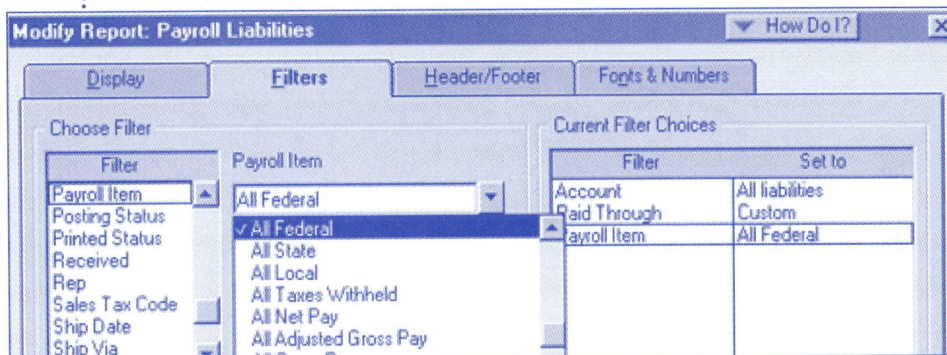

Figure 8-39 Payroll Item filter for all Federal items

To give the report a new title to match the filtered content of the report, follow these steps:

6 Click the Header/Footer tab.

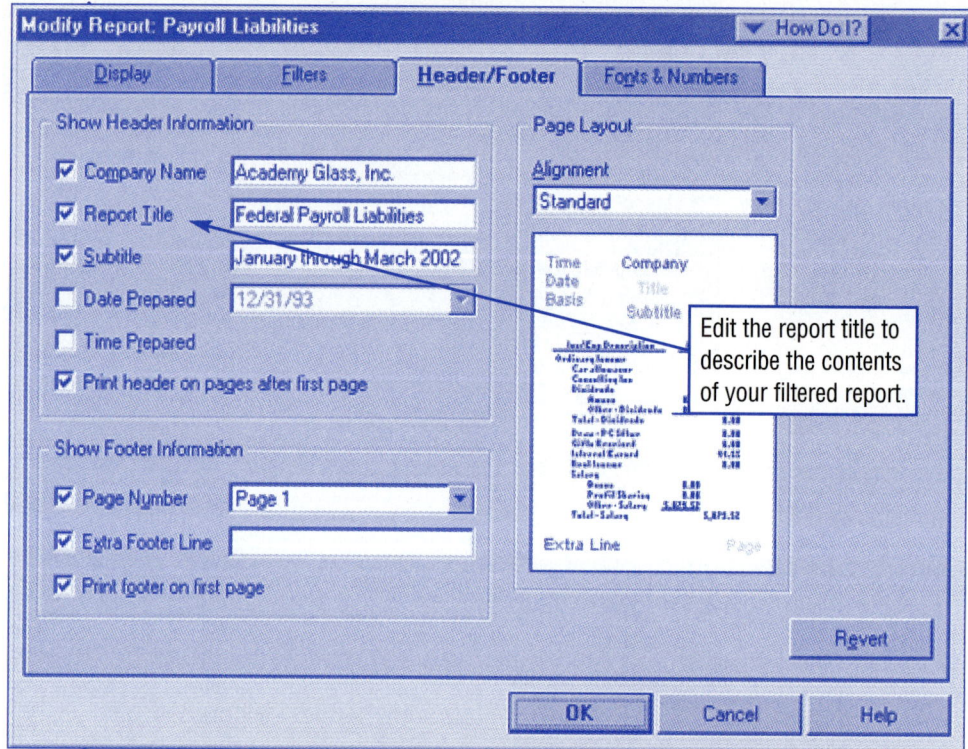

Figure 8-40 The Report Title field allows you to enter a new title.

7 Enter "Federal Payroll Liabilities" in the *Report Title* field and click **OK** (see Figure 8-40).

8 Verify that the *Columns* field shows "Total only."

Now the report title matches the content of the report.

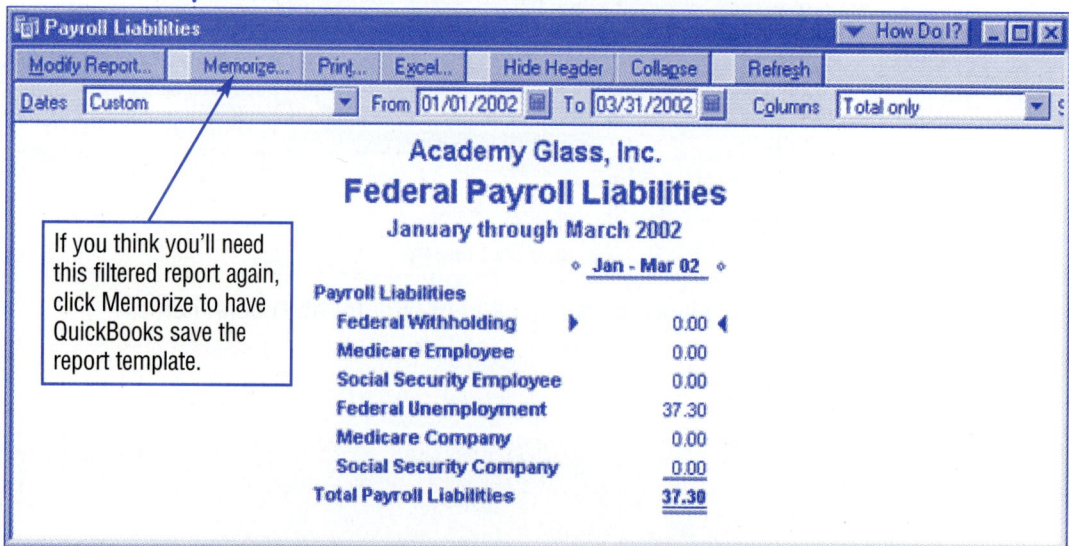

Figure 8-41 Custom Report called "Federal Payroll Liabilities."

To memorize this report so you can save the current settings, follow these steps:

⑨ Click the **Memorize** button shown in Figure 8-41.

⑩ QuickBooks uses the customized report header as the default name for the Memorized Report. Press <TAB> to accept the default name "Federal Payroll Liabilities."

⑪ Check the "Save in Memorized Report Group" box and select "Employees" from the drop-down menu. Then click **OK** (see Figure 8-42).

Figure 8-42 Enter the name of the report to memorize.

Then, to create this report again:

⑫ Select the *Reports* menu, choose **Memorized Reports**, and then choose **Memorized Report List**.

⑬ Double-click on the memorized report called Federal Payroll Liabilities or click on the report name and click **Display** (see Figure 8-43).

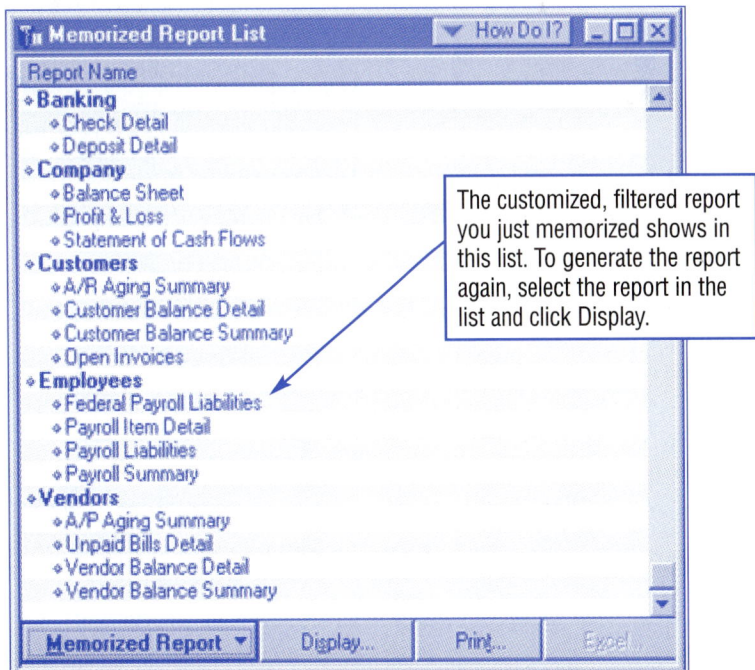

The customized, filtered report you just memorized shows in this list. To generate the report again, select the report in the list and click Display.

Figure 8-43 Select the report to create.

PREPARING PAYROLL TAXES

Processing Form 941 and Schedule B

To prepare the Federal quarterly payroll tax return known as Form 941, follow these steps:

1 Select the *Employees* menu and then choose **Process Payroll Forms**.

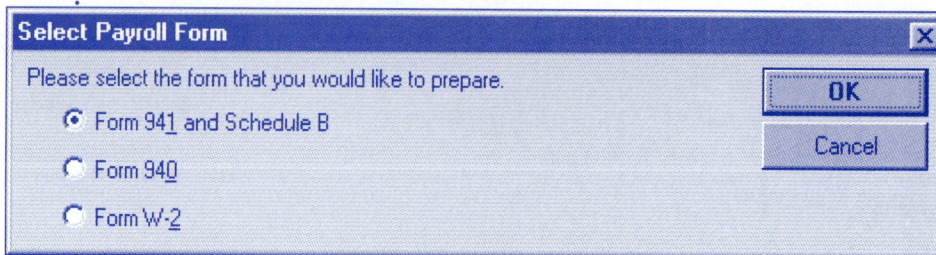

Select Payroll Form

Please select the form that you would like to prepare.

- Form 941 and Schedule B
- Form 940
- Form W-2

OK
Cancel

Figure 8-44 The Select Payroll Form screen

2 Select "Form 941 and Schedule B," and click **OK** (see Figure 8-44).

3 On the 941/Schedule B options screen (see Figure 8-45), select "Create Form for Quarter Ending" and enter "3/31/2002" in the *date* field. Then click **OK**.

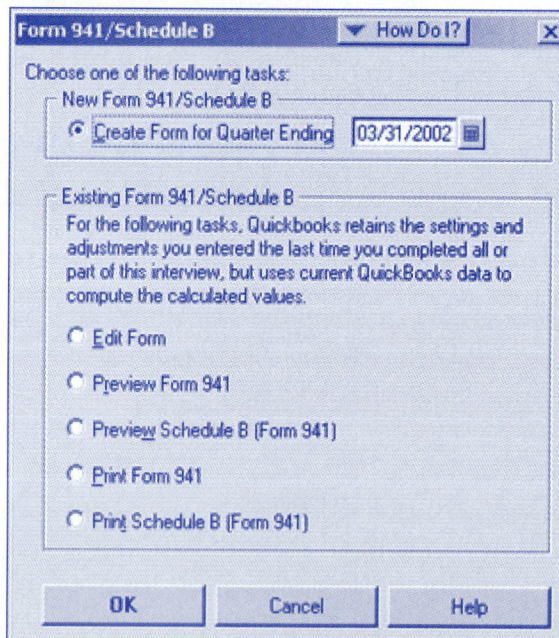

Form 941/Schedule B   ▼ How Do I?

Choose one of the following tasks:

New Form 941/Schedule B
- Create Form for Quarter Ending 03/31/2002

Existing Form 941/Schedule B
For the following tasks, Quickbooks retains the settings and adjustments you entered the last time you completed all or part of this interview, but uses current QuickBooks data to compute the calculated values.

- Edit Form
- Preview Form 941
- Preview Schedule B (Form 941)
- Print Form 941
- Print Schedule B (Form 941)

OK   Cancel   Help

Figure 8-45 The Form 941/Schedule B options screen

4 Choose "CA" from the "Enter state code for state in which deposits were made, if different than the state of your address" drop-down menu and click **Next** (see Figure 8-46).

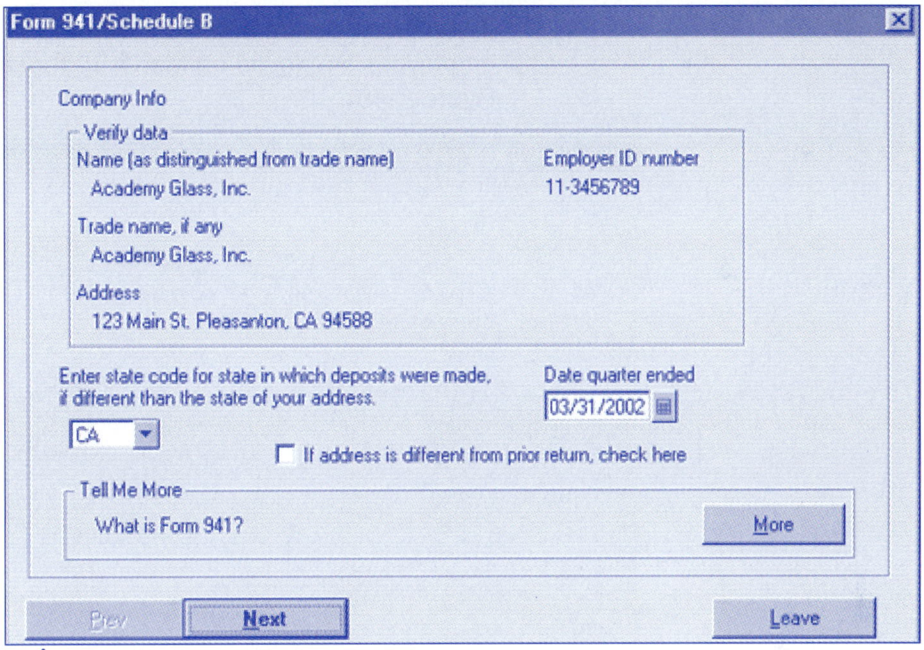

Form 941/Schedule B ☒

Company Info

Verify data

Name (as distinguished from trade name)   Employer ID number
Academy Glass, Inc.   11-3456789

Trade name, if any
Academy Glass, Inc.

Address
123 Main St. Pleasanton, CA 94588

Enter state code for state in which deposits were made,   Date quarter ended
if different than the state of your address.   `03/31/2002`

`CA ▼`
☐ If address is different from prior return, check here

Tell Me More

What is Form 941?   More

Prev   **Next**   Leave

Figure 8-46 Select the state code and verify the end of the quarter date

5 QuickBooks takes you through a series of screens that go through Form 941 from top to bottom. For the most part, this process is automatic, and all you need to do is verify that the calculations are correct. You should only need to make minor adjustments to the amounts. For example, you may need to correct rounding discrepancies. However, do not make any changes to the screen shown in Figure 8-47 at this time. Click **Next** to continue.

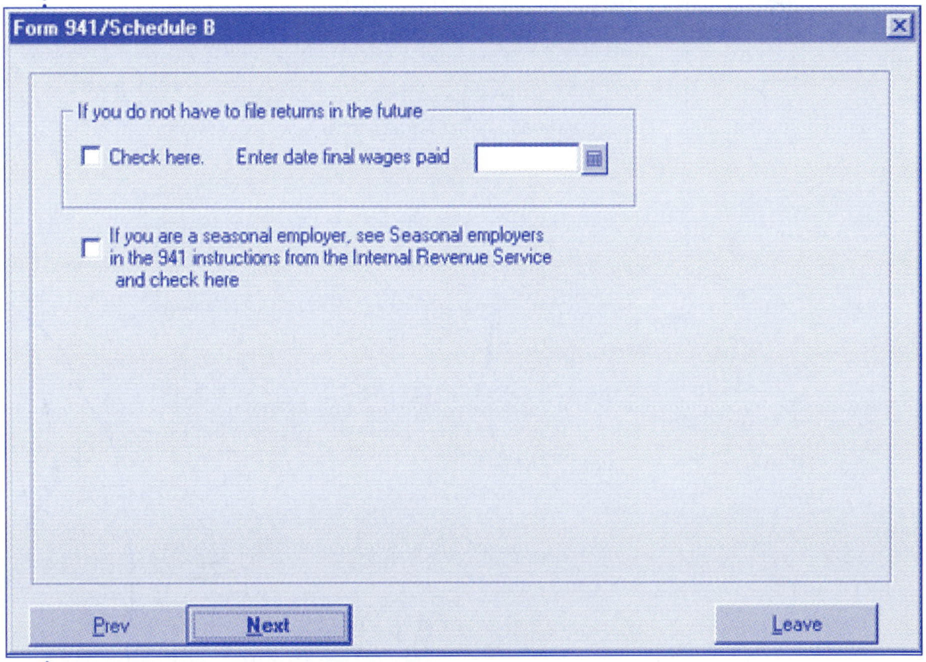

Form 941/Schedule B ☒

If you do not have to file returns in the future

☐ Check here.   Enter date final wages paid

☐ If you are a seasonal employer, see Seasonal employers
in the 941 instructions from the Internal Revenue Service
and check here

Prev   **Next**   Leave

Figure 8-47 Enter necessary information.

6 If you're preparing your first quarter 941, enter the number of employees employed on March 12 for *Line 1* and click **Next** (see Figure 8-48).

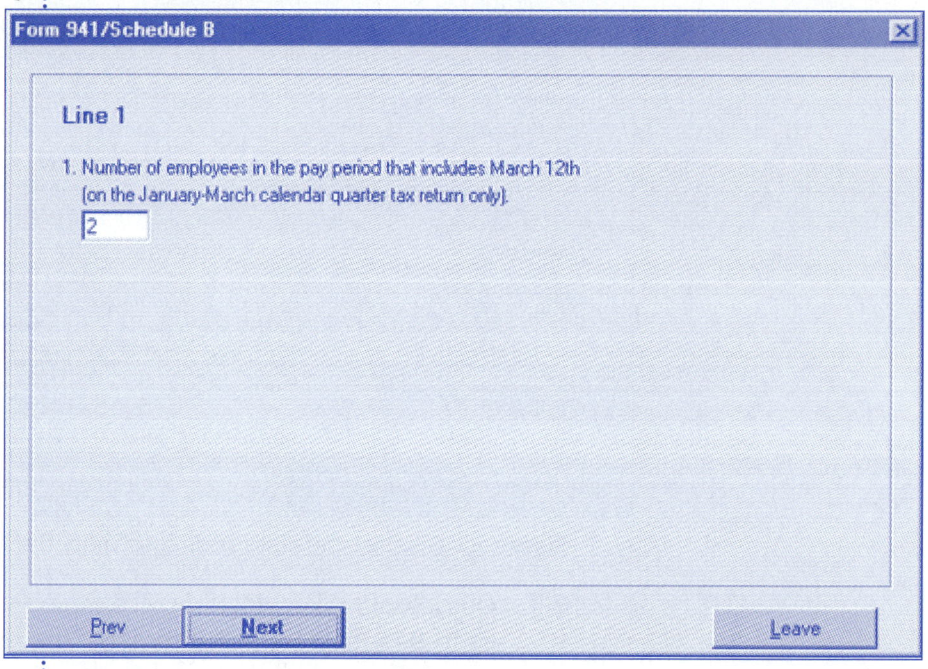

Figure 8-48 Enter the number of employees as of March 12.

7 Verify the numbers on each line and click **Next**. QuickBooks shows each line of form 941 as you go through these screens (see Figure 8-49 and Figure 8-50).

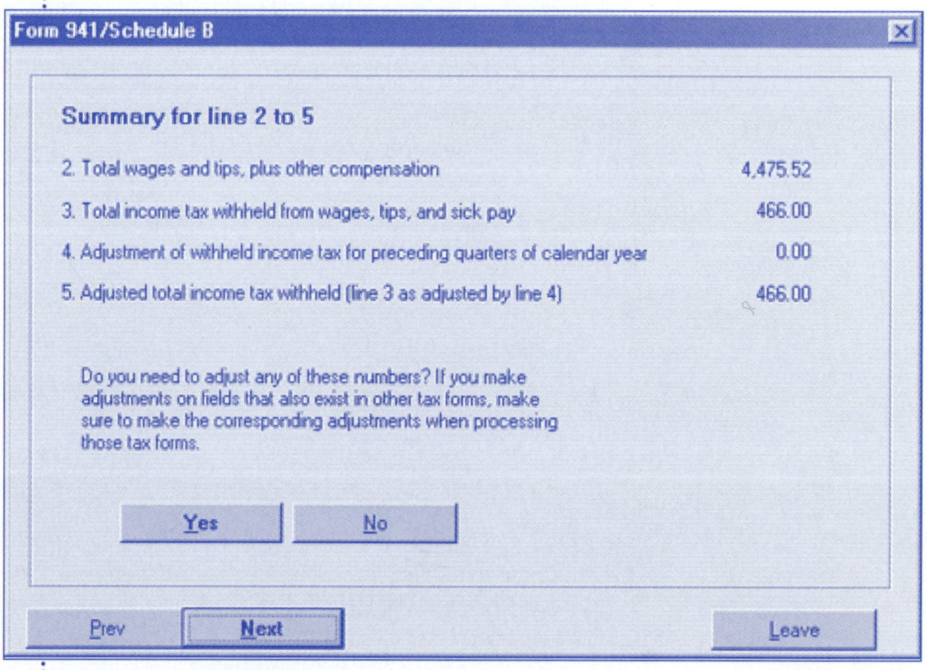

Figure 8-49 Verify calculations shown.

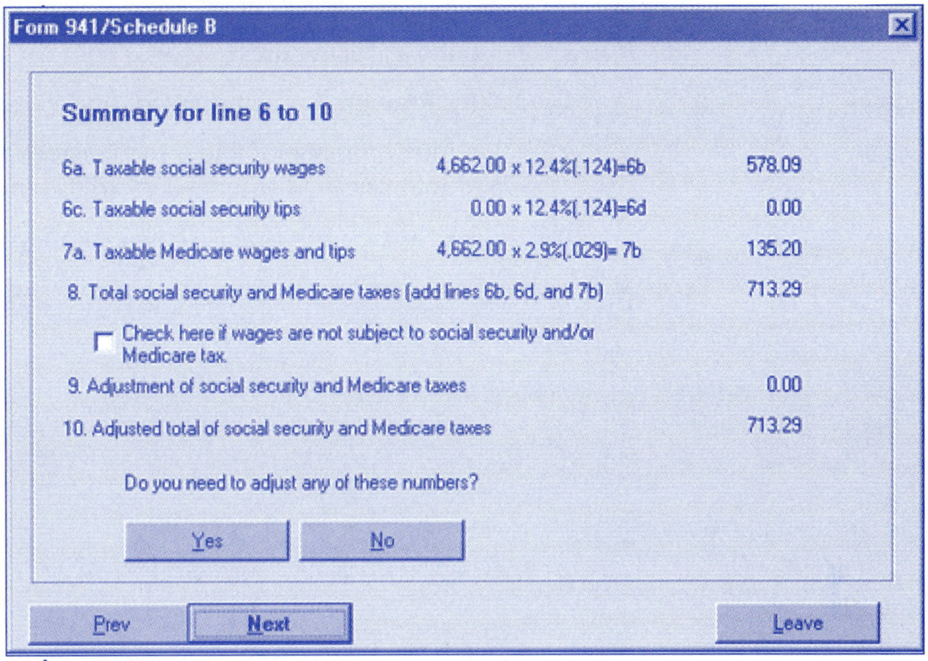

Figure 8-50 Verify calculations shown.

8 On the Summary for line 11 to 14 screen (see Figure 8-51), compare line 13 and line 14. Notice that these two figures don't match in Figure 8-51. These two numbers should match if you've deposited all your taxes by the time you create your 941. If the two numbers are close, but not equal, it's probably due to a rounding discrepancy.

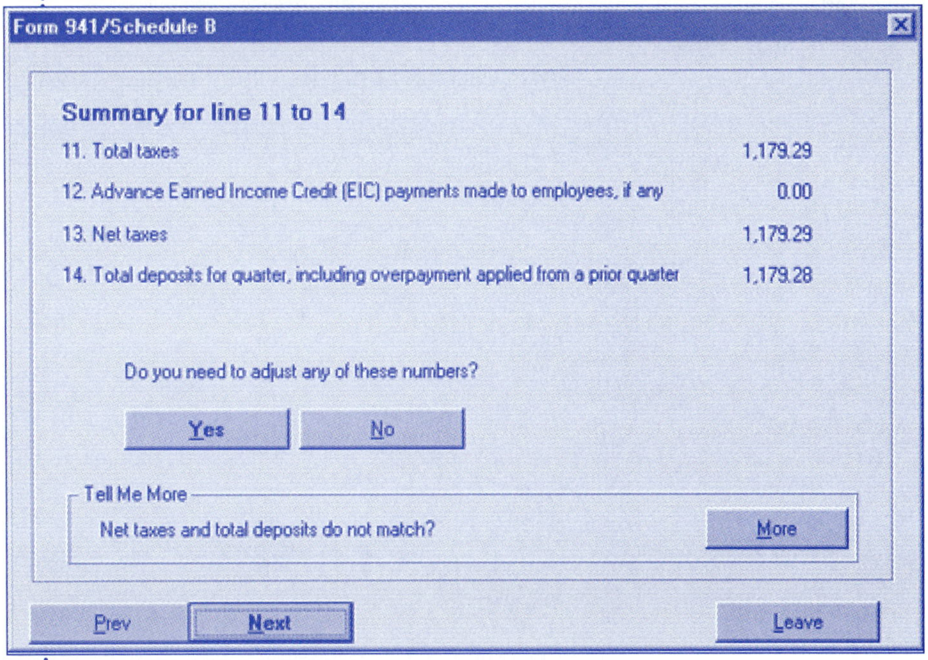

Figure 8-51 Compare lines 13 and 14.

To adjust for the rounding discrepancy between line 13 and line 14 above, follow these steps:

9. Click **Prev** on the Summary for line 11 to 14 screen.
10. On the Summary for line 6 to 10 screen, click **Yes** just below the text that says "Do you need to adjust any of these numbers?"
11. Click Next on the Line 6 screen (see Figure 8-52).

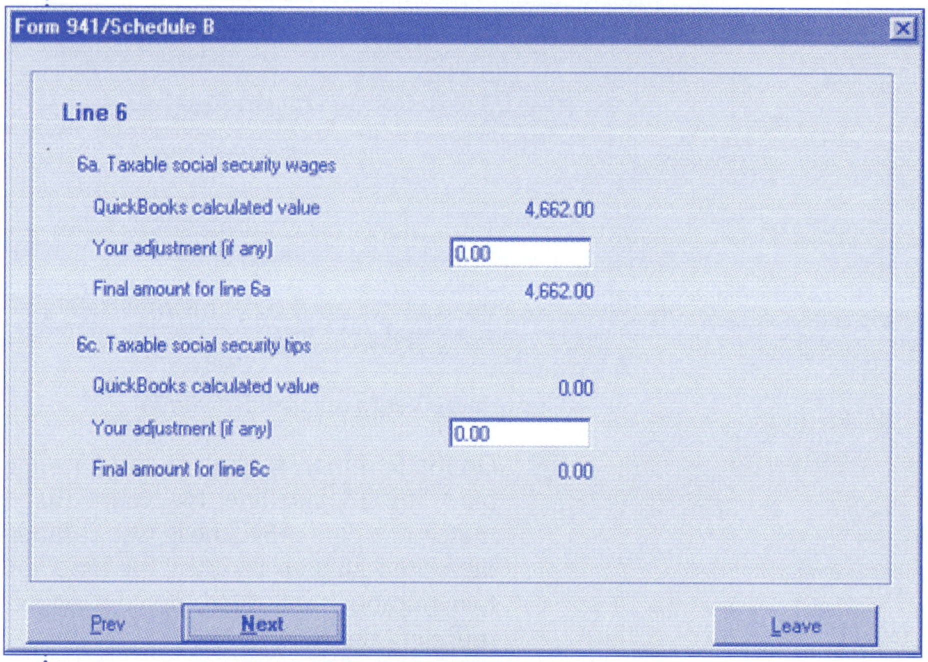
Form 941/Schedule B
Line 6
6a. Taxable social security wages
QuickBooks calculated value
4,662.00
Your adjustment (if any)
0.00
Final amount for line 6a
4,662.00
6c. Taxable social security tips
QuickBooks calculated value
0.00
Your adjustment (if any)
0.00
Final amount for line 6c
0.00
Prev
Next
Leave

Figure 8-52 Click Next on this screen.

12. Click **Next** on the Line 7 screen (see Figure 8-53).

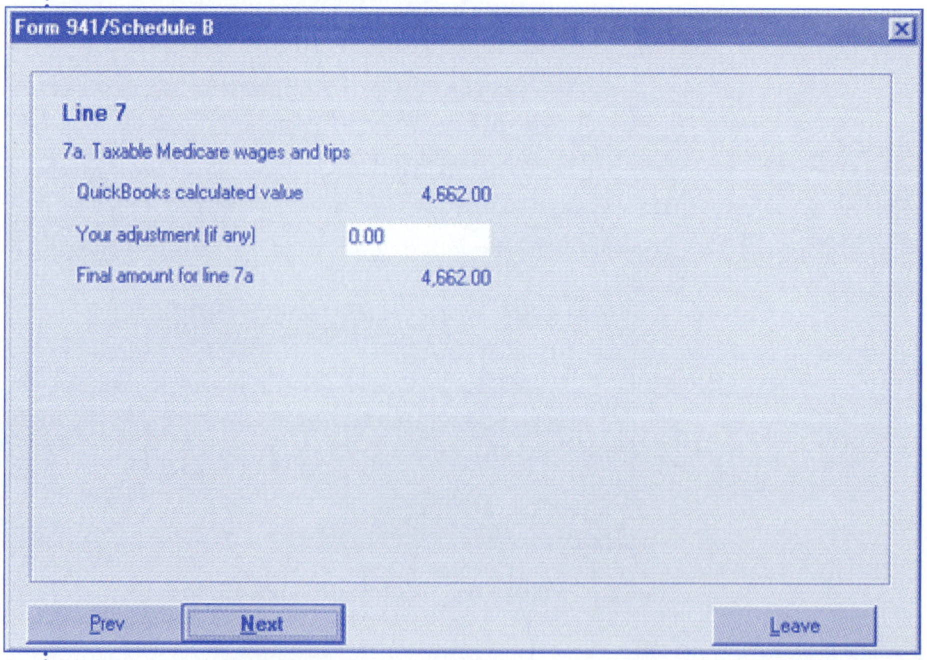
Form 941/Schedule B
Line 7
7a. Taxable Medicare wages and tips
QuickBooks calculated value
4,662.00
Your adjustment (if any)
0.00
Final amount for line 7a
4,662.00
Prev
Next
Leave

Figure 8-53 Click Next on this screen.

13 On the Line 9 screen, enter "-.01" in the *Fraction of Cents* field (see Figure 8-54) and click **Next**.

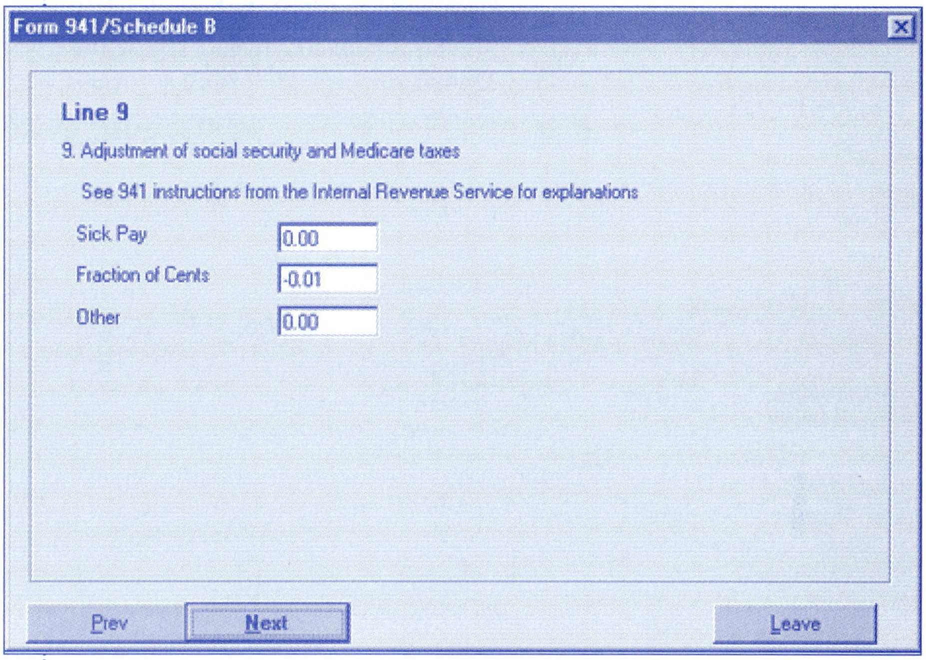

Form 941/Schedule B   ☒

Line 9

9. Adjustment of social security and Medicare taxes

   See 941 instructions from the Internal Revenue Service for explanations

   Sick Pay   [0.00]

   Fraction of Cents   [-0.01]

   Other   [0.00]

   Prev   Next   Leave

Figure 8-54 Enter "-.01" in the *Fraction of Cents* field.

14 Click **Next** on the Summary for line 6 to 10 screen.

15 Now the Summary for line 11 to 14 screen shows the adjustment to lines 11 and 13 (see Figure 8-55). Your 941 is now ready to print. Click **Next**.

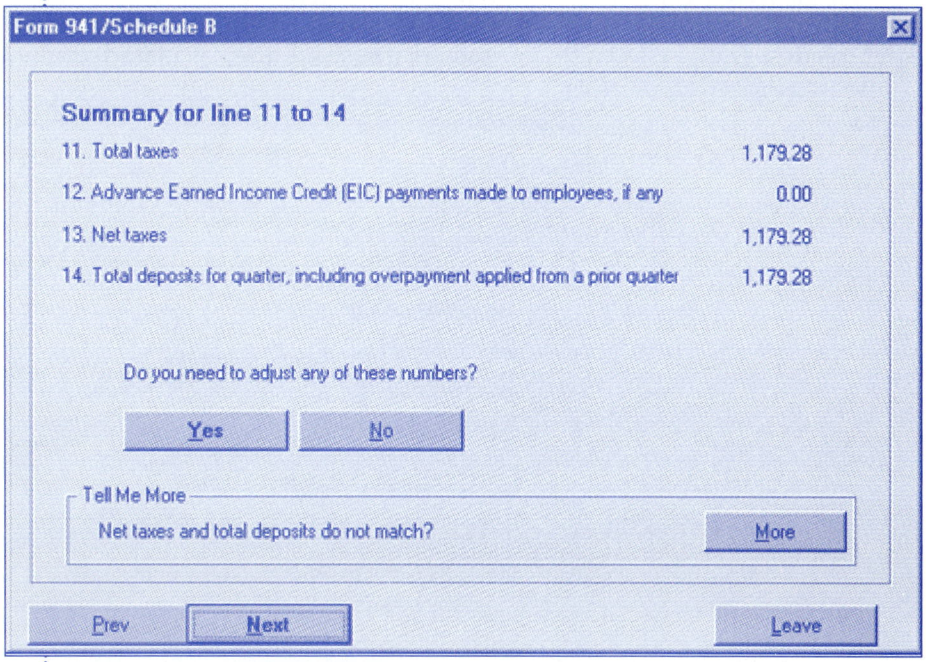

Form 941/Schedule B   ☒

Summary for line 11 to 14

11. Total taxes   1,179.28

12. Advance Earned Income Credit (EIC) payments made to employees, if any   0.00

13. Net taxes   1,179.28

14. Total deposits for quarter, including overpayment applied from a prior quarter   1,179.28

         Do you need to adjust any of these numbers?

              Yes   No

   ┌ Tell Me More ───
   │ Net taxes and total deposits do not match?   More

   Prev   Next   Leave

Figure 8-55 Verify the change in lines 11 and 13.

16 On the Line 15 and 16 screen, check the "Semiweekly depositor" box for line 16, and click **Next** (see Figure 8-56).

Check the appropriate box for whether you are a monthly or semiweekly depositor. If you check the "Semiweekly depositor" box, QuickBooks will print both Form 941 and Form 941 Schedule B.

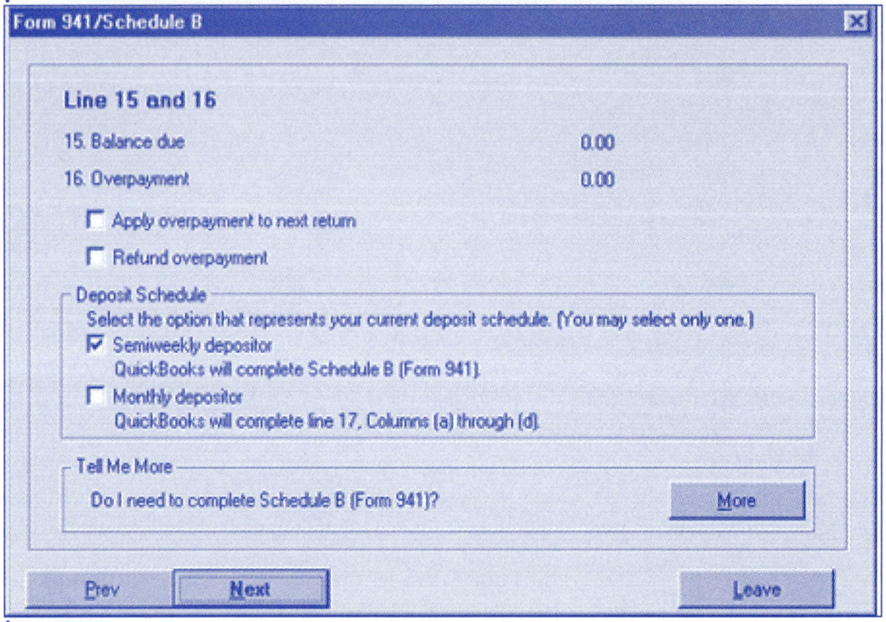

Figure 8-56 Complete the depositor type.

NOTE

If you select "Monthly depositor" on the Line 15 and 16 screen (see Figure 8-56), QuickBooks will show a breakdown of liability payments by month only. This breakdown will show on a single screen entitled "Line 17." You can make adjustments for actual liabilities on each month during the quarter. If you have to adjust, however, it's likely that you have problems with your setup. If you are a monthly depositor click **Next** on this screen and skip to Step 19.

17 On the next three screens you can make adjustments for actual liabilities on each day of each month during the quarter (see Figure 8-57). If you have to adjust, however, it's likely that you have problems with your setup. Click **Next** on these three screens to accept the calculated amounts.

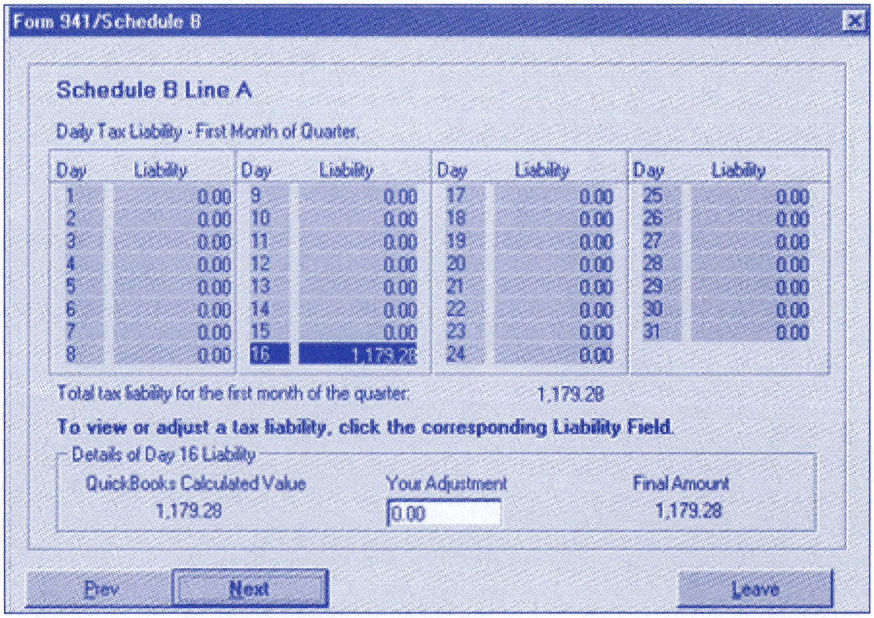

Figure 8-57 If you need to make adjustments, you may have setup problems.

18 The Schedule B (Form 941) Summary screen provides a summary of liability payments by month (see Figure 8-58). Click **Next**.

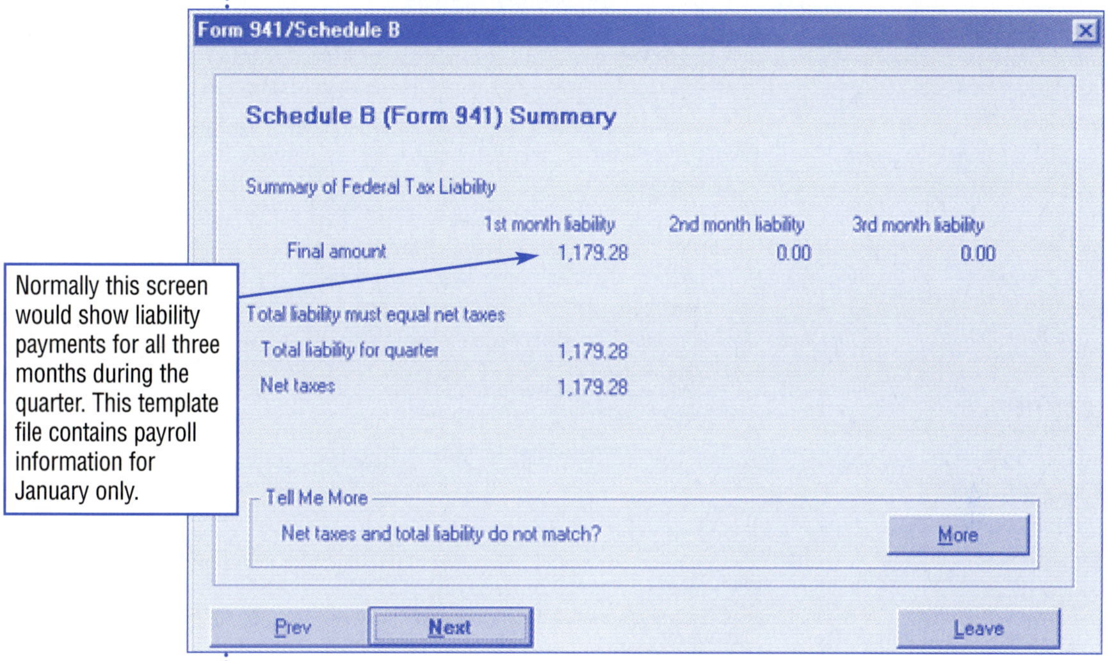

Normally this screen would show liability payments for all three months during the quarter. This template file contains payroll information for January only.

Figure 8-58 Form 941/Schedule B Summary

19 Finally, when you're finished with the Form 941 and Schedule B, you can print it on your printer (see Figure 8-59, Figure 8-60 and Figure 8-61) by clicking the **Print Form 941** and **Print Schedule B** buttons. The forms print on blank paper, suitable for filing with the IRS. There is no form to buy; you simply print the form, sign it, and send it in.

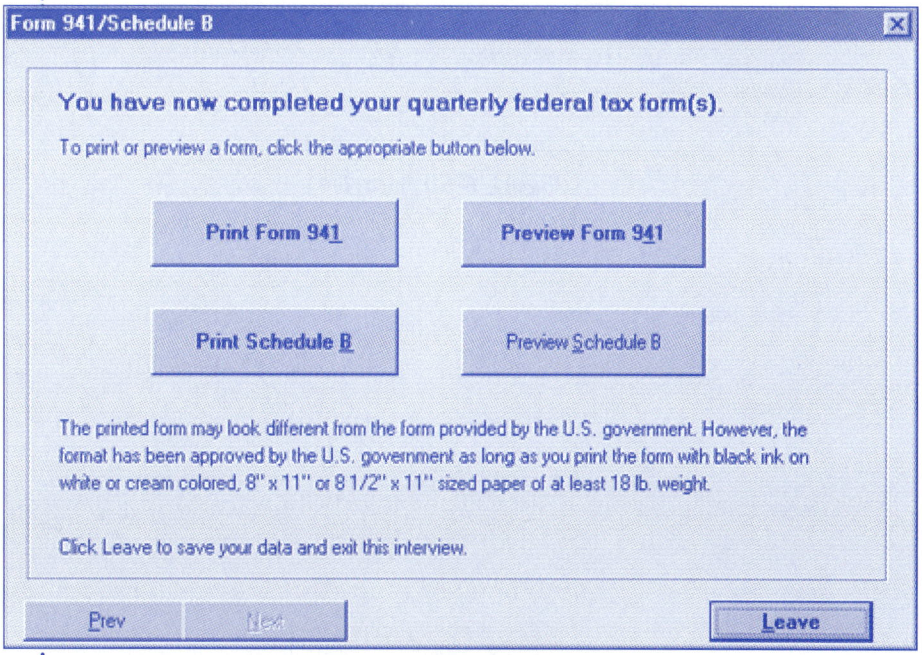

Figure 8-59 Print the form on blank paper.

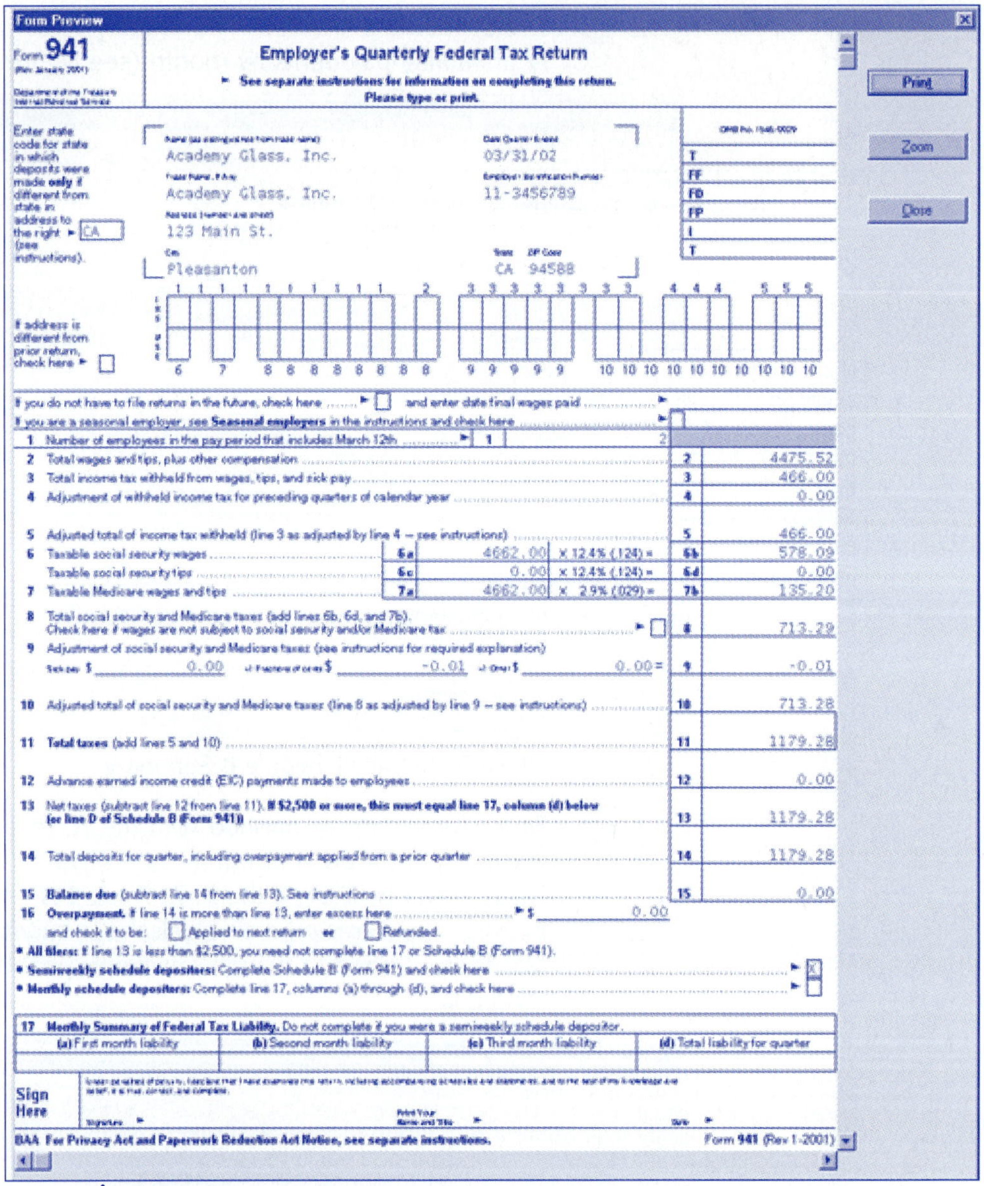

Form Preview

Form **941** (Rev. January 2001)

Department of the Treasury Internal Revenue Service

Employer's Quarterly Federal Tax Return

► **See separate instructions for information on completing this return.**
Please type or print.

Enter state code for state in which deposits were made **only** if different from state in address to the right ► CA (see instructions).

Name (as distinguished from trade name): Academy Glass, Inc.
Date quarter ended: 03/31/02
Trade name, if any: Academy Glass, Inc.
Employer identification number: 11-3456789
Address (number and street): 123 Main St.
City: Pleasanton
State: CA ZIP code: 94588

T / FF / FD / FP / I / T

If address is different from prior return, check here ► ☐

If you do not have to file returns in the future, check here ► ☐ and enter date final wages paid ►

If you are a seasonal employer, see **Seasonal employers** in the instructions and check here ► ☐

Line	Description		Amount
1	Number of employees in the pay period that includes March 12th ► 1		2
2	Total wages and tips, plus other compensation	2	4475.52
3	Total income tax withheld from wages, tips, and sick pay	3	466.00
4	Adjustment of withheld income tax for preceding quarters of calendar year	4	0.00
5	Adjusted total of income tax withheld (line 3 as adjusted by line 4 — see instructions)	5	466.00
6	Taxable social security wages 6a 4662.00 × 12.4% (.124) =	6b	578.09
	Taxable social security tips 6c 0.00 × 12.4% (.124) =	6d	0.00
7	Taxable Medicare wages and tips 7a 4662.00 × 2.9% (.029) =	7b	135.20
8	Total social security and Medicare taxes (add lines 6b, 6d, and 7b). Check here if wages are not subject to social security and/or Medicare tax ► ☐	8	713.29
9	Adjustment of social security and Medicare taxes (see instructions for required explanation) Sick pay $ 0.00 ± Fractions of cents $ -0.01 ± Other $ 0.00 =	9	-0.01
10	Adjusted total of social security and Medicare taxes (line 8 as adjusted by line 9 — see instructions)	10	713.28
11	**Total taxes** (add lines 5 and 10)	11	1179.28
12	Advance earned income credit (EIC) payments made to employees	12	0.00
13	Net taxes (subtract line 12 from line 11). **If $2,500 or more, this must equal line 17, column (d) below (or line D of Schedule B (Form 941))**	13	1179.28
14	Total deposits for quarter, including overpayment applied from a prior quarter	14	1179.28
15	**Balance due** (subtract line 14 from line 13). See instructions	15	0.00
16	**Overpayment.** If line 14 is more than line 13, enter excess here ► $ 0.00 and check if to be: ☐ Applied to next return **or** ☐ Refunded.		

• **All filers:** If line 13 is less than $2,500, you need not complete line 17 or Schedule B (Form 941).
• **Semiweekly schedule depositors:** Complete Schedule B (Form 941) and check here ► ☒
• **Monthly schedule depositors:** Complete line 17, columns (a) through (d), and check here ► ☐

17 Monthly Summary of Federal Tax Liability. Do not complete if you were a semiweekly schedule depositor.

(a) First month liability	(b) Second month liability	(c) Third month liability	(d) Total liability for quarter

Sign Here Under penalties of perjury, I declare that I have examined this return, including accompanying schedules and statements, and to the best of my knowledge and belief, it is true, correct, and complete.
Signature ► Print Your Name and Title ► Date ►

BAA For Privacy Act and Paperwork Reduction Act Notice, see separate instructions. Form **941** (Rev. 1-2001)

Figure 8-60 Form 941

Form Preview [×]

Schedule B
(Form 941)
(Rev November 1998)
Department of the Treasury
Internal Revenue Service

Employer's Record of Federal Tax Liability
► See Circular E for more information about employment tax returns.
► Attach to Form 941 or 941-SS.

OMB No. 1545-0029

[Print] [Zoom] [Close]

Name as Shown on Form 941 (or Form 941-SS)
Academy Glass, Inc.

Employer Identification Number
11-3456789

Date Quarter Ended
03/31/02

You must complete this schedule if you are required to deposit on a semiweekly schedule, or if your tax liability on any day is $100,000 or more.
Show tax liability here, not deposits. (The Internal Revenue Service gets deposit data from FTD coupons or EFTPS.)

A Daily Tax Liability – First Month of Quarter

1	0.00	8	0.00	15	0.00	22	0.00	29	0.00
2	0.00	9	0.00	16	1,179.28	23	0.00	30	0.00
3	0.00	10	0.00	17	0.00	24	0.00	31	0.00
4	0.00	11	0.00	18	0.00	25	0.00		
5	0.00	12	0.00	19	0.00	26	0.00		
6	0.00	13	0.00	20	0.00	27	0.00		
7	0.00	14	0.00	21	0.00	28	0.00		

A Total tax liability for first month of quarter .... ► A 1,179.28

B Daily Tax Liability – Second Month of Quarter

1	0.00	8	0.00	15	0.00	22	0.00	29	0.00
2	0.00	9	0.00	16	0.00	23	0.00	30	0.00
3	0.00	10	0.00	17	0.00	24	0.00	31	0.00
4	0.00	11	0.00	18	0.00	25	0.00		
5	0.00	12	0.00	19	0.00	26	0.00		
6	0.00	13	0.00	20	0.00	27	0.00		
7	0.00	14	0.00	21	0.00	28	0.00		

B Total tax liability for second month of quarter .... ► B 0.00

C Daily Tax Liability – Third Month of Quarter

1	0.00	8	0.00	15	0.00	22	0.00	29	0.00
2	0.00	9	0.00	16	0.00	23	0.00	30	0.00
3	0.00	10	0.00	17	0.00	24	0.00	31	0.00
4	0.00	11	0.00	18	0.00	25	0.00		
5	0.00	12	0.00	19	0.00	26	0.00		
6	0.00	13	0.00	20	0.00	27	0.00		
7	0.00	14	0.00	21	0.00	28	0.00		

C Total tax liability for third month of quarter .... ► C 0.00
D Total for quarter (add lines A, B, and C). This should equal line 13 of Form 941 (or line 10 of Form 941-SS) .... ► D 1,179.28

Figure 8-61 Form 941 Schedule B

Processing Form 940

To prepare Form 940, select the *Employees* menu, choose **Process Payroll Forms**, and then choose **Form 940**.

The process for creating Form 940 is nearly the same as for Form 941. You'll also print this form on blank paper suitable for filing with the IRS.

Processing W-2s

COMPUTER TUTORIAL

1. Select the *Employees* menu, choose **Process Payroll Forms** and then select "Form W-2."

Select Payroll Form

Please select the form that you would like to prepare.

- ○ Form 941 and Schedule B
- ○ Form 940
- ● Form W-2

OK

Cancel

Figure 8-62 Select Payroll Form screen

2. Click **OK**.

Process W-2s ▼ How Do I?

Year 2002 ▼   Unmark All

✓	Employee	SS No.	Reviewed	Printed
✓	Moen, Jim	111-22-3333		
✓	Reynolds, Kati	333-22-4321		

Review W-2   Print W-2s   Print W-3   Done

Figure 8-63 The Process W-2s screen

3. Enter "2002" in the *Year* field.

4. On the Process W-2s screen (see Figure 8-63), select all of the employees you want to review, and click **Review W-2**. You must review the W-2s onscreen before QuickBooks will allow you to print them.

You can adjust W-2s right onscreen (see Figure 8-64). For example, if you need to adjust any amount, double-click on the box and enter your adjustment.

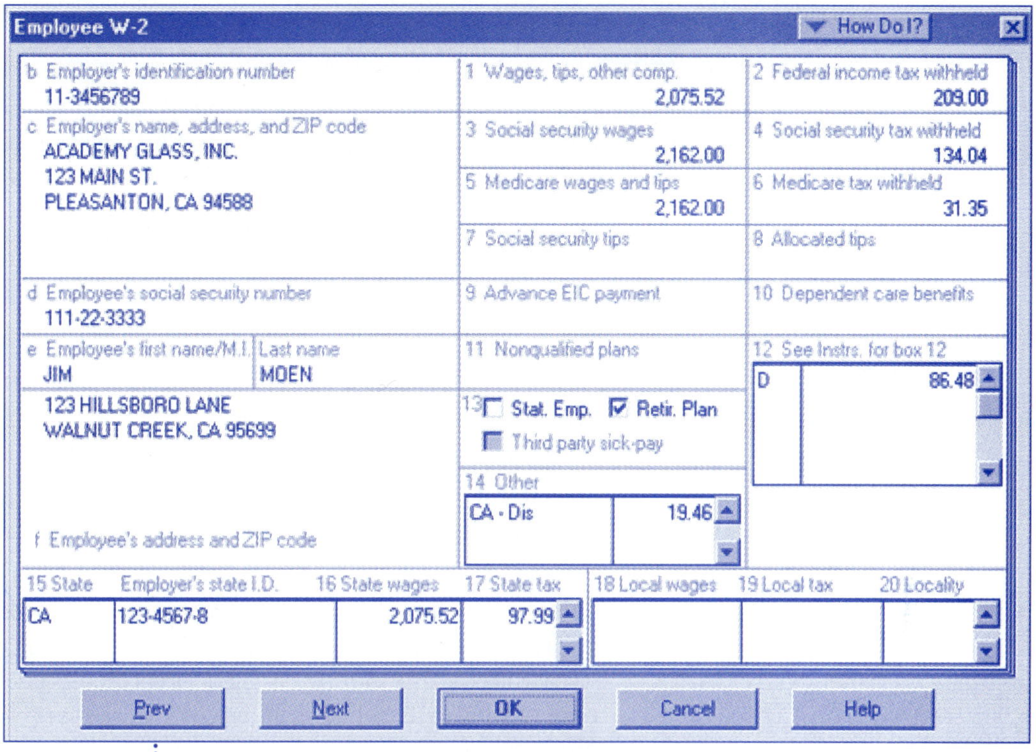

Figure 8-64 Adjust W-2s as necessary.

⑤ To review the next W-2, click **Next**.

⑥ When you have finished reviewing the W-2s (and adjusting if necessary), click **OK**.

⑦ Click **Print W-2s** on the Process W-2s screen (see Figure 8-65).

You'll print on blank paper for this class, but you can purchase W-2s from your local office supply or stationery store. They are available in multi-part forms, and you can get them for laser or inkjet printers. When you click **Print W-2s**, QuickBooks asks how many copies to print. It's best to print one copy at a time, separately loading a new W-2 each time.

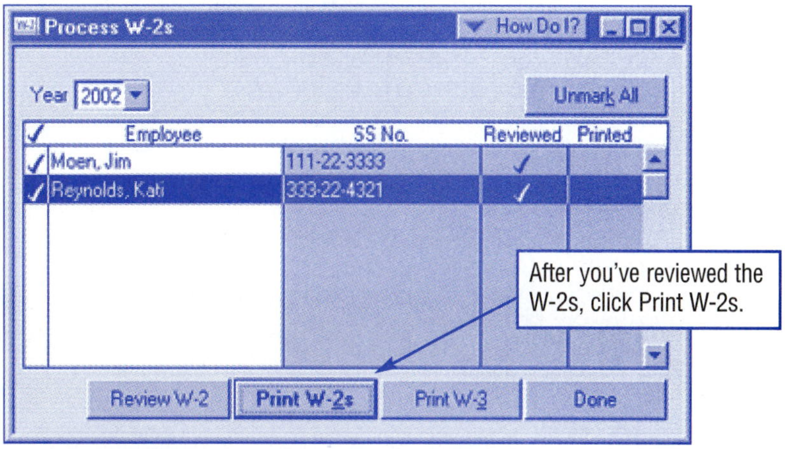

> **TIP**
>
> Before processing W-2s or Form 940, first upgrade your tax tables. Any necessary changes to the forms may be included in the most recent tax tables.

Figure 8-65 Print W-2s.

Creating Reports for Preparing State or Local Payroll Taxes

QuickBooks does not print any State payroll tax forms. However, you can create reports that help you prepare your State payroll tax returns, such as the Employee State Payroll Taxes Detail Report.

State Payroll Taxes Detail Report

COMPUTER TUTORIAL

① Select the *Reports* menu, choose **Employees & Payroll**, and then choose **Employee State Taxes Detail**.

② Set the *From* date to "01/01/2002" and the *To* date to "03/31/2002." Then press <TAB> (see Figure 8-66).

The Employee State Taxes Detail report allows you to see all of the State tax items summarized by employee. You can also see the employee's Social Security Number on this report (see Figure 8-66).

The Income Subject to Tax column is very important for many State payroll tax reports. For example, in California, you must report on the Quarterly Form DE-6 Subject Wages, PIT wages, and PIT withheld. The Subject Wages are calculated by filtering this report to include only the State Unemployment (SUI) item. Then report the total of the Income Subject to Tax column as Subject Wages on Form DE-6. The PIT Wages are calculated by filtering this report to include only the State Withholding item. Then, report the total of the Income Subject to Tax column as PIT Wages on Form DE-6. Finally, the PIT Withheld is the total of the Amount column in this report.

Figure 8-66 Employee State Taxes Detail report

Summarizing Payroll Information in Microsoft Excel

For some companies, the built-in payroll reports in QuickBooks do not provide all of the information needed to manage their employees and complete the necessary payroll tax forms. The Summarize Payroll Data in Excel function allows you to export all payroll information to an Excel spreadsheet where you can manipulate it to suit your company's unique needs.

COMPUTER TUTORIAL

① Select the *Employee* menu and then choose **Summarize Payroll Data in Excel**.

QuickBooks will launch Microsoft Excel and prompt you to enable Macros.

② Click **Enable Macros** (See Figure 8-67).

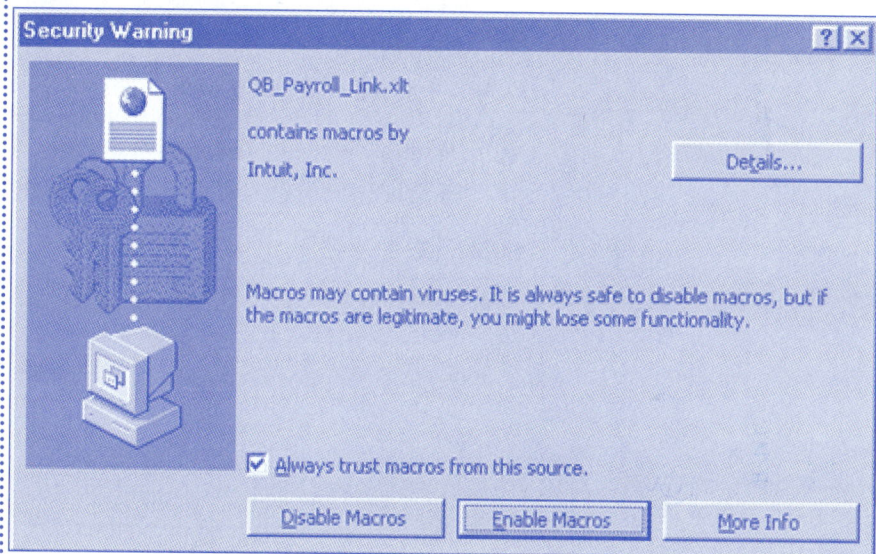

Figure 8-67 Enabling macros in Microsoft Excel

③ When Excel finishes launching the Pivot Table, you'll see the Welcome screen shown in Figure 8-68. Click **OK**.

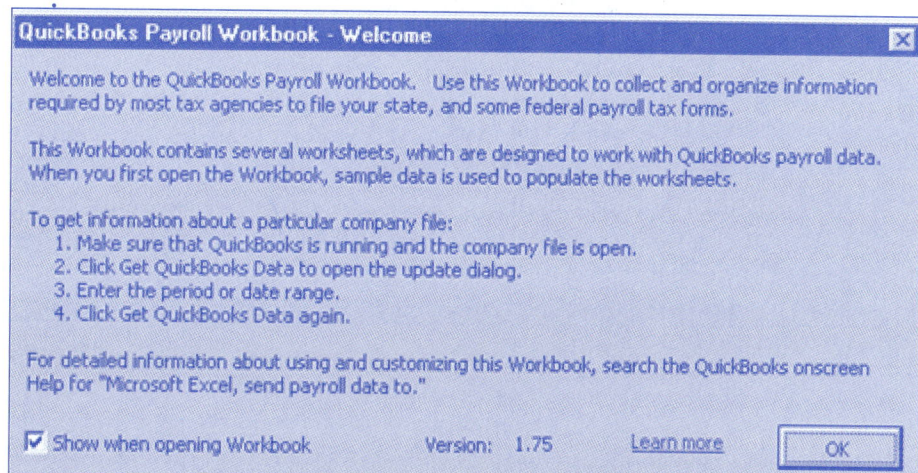

Figure 8-68 Pivot Table Welcome screen

④ To gather the data from QuickBooks, set the *From* date to "01/01/2002" and the *To* date to "03/31/2002" in the Options screen, and then click **Get QuickBooks Data** (see Figure 8-69).

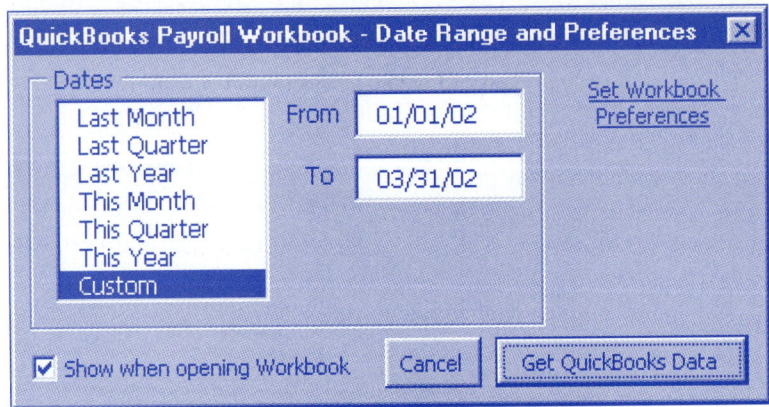

Figure 8-69 Set the dates and click Get QuickBooks Data.

⑤ When Excel finishes gathering the data from QuickBooks, you'll see the message shown in Figure 8-70. Click **OK**.

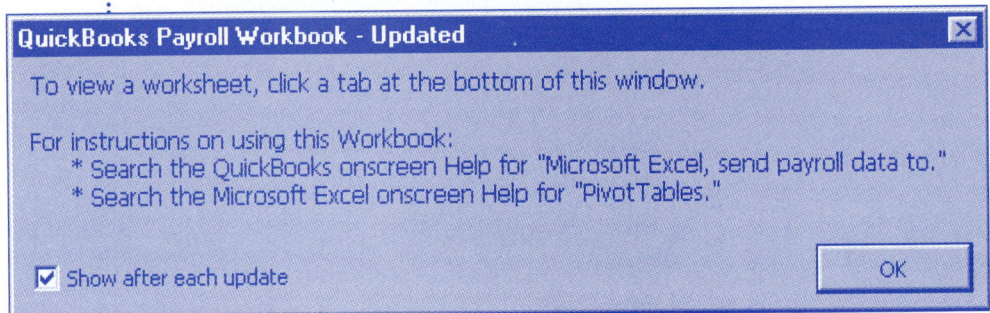

Figure 8-70 Pivot Table Reports Updated message

⑥ The Excel spreadsheet shown in Figure 8-71 shows details of your State wages and taxes.

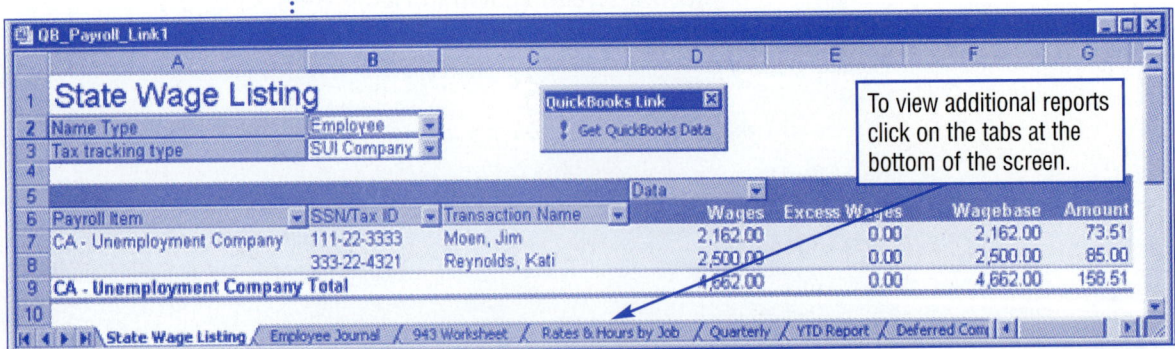

Figure 8-71 QuickBooks Payroll Data in Excel Pivot table – State Wage Listing

SUMMARY OF KEY POINTS

In this chapter, you learned how to process payroll in QuickBooks. You should now be familiar with how to use QuickBooks to do all of the following:

◆ Update your Payroll Tax Tables (Page 394)

◆ Create Paychecks and override default calculations (Page 395)

◆ Edit, Void, and Delete Paychecks (Page 407)

◆ Pay Payroll Liabilities (Page 411)

◆ Adjust Payroll Liabilities (Page 416)

◆ Create Payroll Reports (Page 418)

◆ Prepare Payroll Tax Form 941, 940, W-2s, and reports to help you prepare your State payroll tax returns (Page 426)

CHAPTER REVIEW AND APPLICATIONS

Comprehension QUESTIONS

Done

In your notebook, record answers to the following questions.

1. What menu option do you choose to update your payroll tax tables?

2. Can you override the Federal income tax withholding on a paycheck?

3. What type of checks (standard, voucher, or wallet) should you use for printing paychecks?

4. Should you ever delete a paycheck that has already been printed and given to the employee?

5. What menu do you choose to pay payroll liabilities?

6. Explain how to update your tax tables and the impact of failing to update them.

7. Discuss why you would not want to make changes to the Amt. to Pay column on the Pay Liabilities screen even though QuickBooks allows this.

Multiple-Choice QUESTIONS

Done

In your notebook, record the best answer for each of the following questions.

1. *d* In order for payroll liabilities to be posted correctly, which function (from the Employees menu) should you use?
   a. Write Checks
   b. Pay Bills
   c. Pay Employees
   d. Pay Payroll Liabilities

2. *d* The preprinted voucher checks you use for processing payroll may contain:
   a. earnings and tax withholdings.
   b. adjustments to Earnings.
   c. net pay.
   d. all of the above.

3. *b* The Payroll Liabilities Report identifies:
   a. liability payments made during the payment period.
   b. liability status by item.
   c. liabilities for employee deductions only.
   d. liabilities for employer taxes only.

4. *b* The payroll tax return that reports Social Security, Medicare, and Federal Income Tax is submitted quarterly on:
   a. Form 940.
   b. Form 941.
   c. W-2
   d. the Payroll Liabilities Report.

Name _____ Date _____

Multiple-Choice
QUESTIONS
(Continued)

5. *C* To begin processing your payroll, you may do any of the following except:
   a. choose Pay Employees from the Activities menu at the bottom of the Employee list.
   b. select the Employees menu and then choose Pay Employees.
   c. select the Payroll menu and then choose Process Payroll Items.
   d. choose Pay Employees from the Employee Navigator.

6. *a* QuickBooks automatically calculates paychecks using information from all of the following sources except:
   a. amounts on all previous paychecks.
   b. the employee's current earnings shown in the earnings section of the paycheck.
   c. the employee's tax settings in the employee record.
   d. the employee's expense report.

7. *b* Which statement is false?
   a. You can print paystubs at any time.
   b. Paystubs print two per page.
   c. You can edit, void, or delete paychecks.
   d. You do not have to print checks using QuickBooks.

8. *b* To correctly pay your payroll liabilities, choose one of the following options:
   a. Write a check for the taxes and code it to payroll liabilities.
   b. Use the Pay Payroll Liabilities function.
   c. Enter the tax authorities as active vendors.
   d. QuickBooks will automatically pay all taxes due.

9. *d* The payroll summary by employee report shows:
   a. the detail of each employee's earnings only.
   b. the YTD employee's earnings by job.
   c. the detail of each employee's biographical information.
   d. the detail of each employee's earnings, taxes, and net pay.

Completion
STATEMENTS

In the space provided, write the word(s) that best complete each statement.

1. To manually job-cost or classify wages, enter splits for each combination of Payroll Item, Rate, Hours, _Class_ , and _Customer Job_ .

2. Tracking income and expenses separately for each job is known as _Job-Costing_ .

3. In order to edit the items on paycheck, display the paycheck and click the _Paycheck Detail_ button.

Completion
STATEMENTS
(Continued)

4. QuickBooks does not print any State payroll tax forms. However, you can create reports that help you prepare your Sate payroll tax returns, such as *Employee State Payroll Tax Detail*

5. The *Summarize Payroll Data in Excel* function allows you to export all payroll information to an Excel spreadsheet where you can manipulate it to suit your company's unique needs.

Name _____ **Date** _____

APPLY YOUR KNOWLEDGE

PROBLEM 8-1

Done

> Restore the Problem 8-1.QBB file from the CD-ROM and store it on your hard disk according to your instructor's directions.

1. Process two paychecks for Jim Moen and Kati Reynolds with the information shown below.

Jim Moen's Paycheck

Field	Data
Check Date	1/31/2002
Pay Period Ends	1/31/2002
Earnings	Use data from timesheet that automatically posts to the paycheck.
Other Payroll Items (Deductions)	Commission, 5% of sales of $500 401(k) Employee, 4% Match 401(k), 2% Medical Insurance -$10
Company Summary	All taxes calculate automatically. Verify that taxes are calculating for all Items.
Employee Summary	All amounts and taxes calculate automatically. Verify that amounts and taxes calculate correctly.

Kati Reynolds' Paycheck

Field	Data
Check Date	1/31/2002
Pay Period Ends	1/31/2002
Earnings	Salary Regular, $2500.00, San Jose Class
Other Payroll Items (Deductions)	401k Employee, 4% Match 401k, 2% Medical Insurance -$10
Company Summary	All taxes calculate automatically. Verify that taxes are calculating for all Items.
Employee Summary	All amounts and taxes calculate automatically. Verify that amounts and taxes calculate correctly.

NOTE: The earnings and deductions for the employees are calculated automatically. Verify that the earnings and deductions match the amounts and percentages listed above; if not, make the necessary changes.

2. Print both paychecks on blank paper. Use voucher checks for the format of the printed checks. Assign the checks to number 6008 and 6009.

3. On 2/3/2002, pay the liabilities for all State and Federal taxes (except Federal Unemployment) and the 401(k) liabilities due from 1/1/2002 through 1/31/2002.

4. Assign the EFTPS payment to transaction #55-6800. **Hint:** Change the check number to this transaction number.

5. Print the payroll liability checks on blank paper, beginning with check number 6010.

EXTEND YOUR KNOWLEDGE

PROBLEM 8-2

> Restore the Problem 8-2.QBB file from the CD-ROM and store it on your hard disk according to your instructor's directions.

Done

1. Open the vendor list. Notice that there are two EFTPS vendors (EFTPS – 940 Taxes and EFTPS – 941 Taxes). Now display the Payroll Item list and go to the Edit payroll item (Federal Unemployment) screen. What is the name in the Agency to which liability is paid field?

2. Go to the Edit payroll item (Federal Withholding) screen. What is the name in the Agency to which liability is paid field?

3. Why is it useful to have two EFTPS vendors, one for Federal Unemployment and another for Federal Withholding, Social Security and Medicare?

4. Print a Payroll Summary report for the first quarter of 2002. In the Print Reports settings screen, select the option to fit the report to 1 page wide.

5. Process Form 941 and Schedule B for the first quarter of 2002. Use Line 9 to adjust for any round-off discrepancies. Academy Glass is a California Semiweekly Depositor, so indicate that on Form 941. Print all pages on blank paper.
   Hint: Check the Payroll Summary report for the number of employees.

6. Print a Balance Sheet for 3/31/2002.

7. Print a Payroll Liabilities Report for 1/1/2002 through 3/31/2002.

8. Print 2002 W-2s for Jim Moen and Kati Reynolds.

Name _____ **Date** _____

DISCUSSION QUESTIONS

These questions are designed to help you apply what you are learning about QuickBooks to your own organization. Use your notebook to record your answers and your thoughts.

1. What type of checks does your organization use to print pay-checks? If it does not use voucher checks, how does your organization print paystubs? How many paychecks does your company issue every week, every month, and every year?

2. Does your company keep track of payroll costs by job or project? How many different jobs or projects does your company track?

3. How often does your company make tax payroll deposits? Monthly? Semiweekly?

ACTIVITY

Search the IRS website (http://www.irs.gov) for how to apply for an Employer Identification Number (EIN) (also known as a Federal tax identification number).

What form must be submitted to the IRS to obtain an EIN?

CASE STUDY

SOFTWARE ANSWERS, INC.

Software Answers, Inc. is a company that sells and provides online support for over 200 software packages. The company also uses its expertise to write code for software solutions that customize other applications.

The company has 12 customer-support representatives earning hourly wages, and 4 founding members of the company who are salaried. The company pays a commission to its customer-support representatives for each software package they sell.

Questions

These questions are designed to help you apply what you are learning about QuickBooks to this case study. Use your notebook to record your answers and your thoughts.

1. How would you set up payroll items for employees on commission?

2. How would you ensure the commissions on software sales are correctly paid to the employees?

3. The senior management team requires a report that shows all sales made by each customer support representative. How would you produce this report?

inter**NET** CONNECTION

If you have a question about payroll, you can often find answers by joining a listserv. The computer listserv allows you to chat with others by e-mail.
Try the following listservs: **http://www.americanpayroll.org/mail.html** and **http://www.payroll-taxes.com/Payroll-List.html.**

Adjustments and Year-End Procedures

OBJECTIVES

After completing this chapter, you should be able to:

1. Set up, track, prepare, and print Form 1099.

2. Understand how and when to edit, void, and delete transactions.

3. Use General Journal Entries to adjust your General Ledger.

4. Track your fixed assets and record depreciation.

5. Track Loans Payable.

6. Memorize transactions.

7. Handle Owner's Drawing account and Owner's Investment account transactions.

8. Close Owner's Drawing and Owner's Investment into Owner's Equity.

9. Understand how QuickBooks closes the year.

10. Import and export data in QuickBooks.

RESTORE THIS FILE

This chapter uses Chapter 9.QBW. To open this file, restore the file called **Chapter 9.QBB** to your hard disk. See page 7 for instructions on restoring files.

In this chapter, you'll learn how to enter adjusting and closing transactions for closing the accounting period and the fiscal year. You will also learn about the maintenance of Fixed Assets and Long-Term Liability accounts.

PROCESSING FORM 1099S

NOTE

Your tax tables **may** need to be updated for the new year in order for your 1099s to print correctly. New versions of the tax table will include any changes in the layout of forms or threshold amounts for 1099s. To verify that you have the most current tax tables, select the *Employees* menu, and choose **Get Payroll Updates**. See page 394 for details on updating tax tables.

At the end of each year you must prepare, print, and send IRS Form 1099 to your vendors. The forms must be sent to your vendors no later than January 31.

Use Form 1099-Misc to report payments made to vendors who performed business-related services for your company. Generally, the term "services" includes work by an independent contractor, professional services, rent payments, commissions, and so on. If the vendor is a corporation or if total annual payments to each vendor do not equal or exceed $600, you are not required to prepare Form 1099-Misc. QuickBooks does not print Form 1099-Int, 1099-Div, or any other type of Form 1099.

QuickBooks automatically tracks the details of your payments to 1099 vendors. Each time you make a payment to a 1099 vendor, QuickBooks automatically adds the payment to the amount you must report on the vendor's Form 1099-Misc.

At the end of the year, you can view your 1099-related payments by creating a 1099 report or a 1099 Detail report. After verifying that the reports include the right vendors and cover the right accounts, you can print 1099s directly onto preprinted 1099 forms, ready to be filed with the IRS.

COMPUTER TUTORIAL

Setting up 1099 Preferences

① Select the *Edit* menu and choose **Preferences**.

② Scroll down and click on **Tax:1099**.

③ Click the Company Preferences tab.

Figure 9-1 Choose Selected accounts from the Account list.

4 Click in the Account column on the line labeled **Box 1: Rents**. Select "Rent" from the drop-down list.

This indicates that all payments to 1099 vendors, that are coded to Rent will show up in Box 1 on the 1099.

5 Click in the Account column on the line labeled **Box 7: Nonemployee Compensation**. Then select "Selected accounts" from the drop-down list (see Figure 9-1).

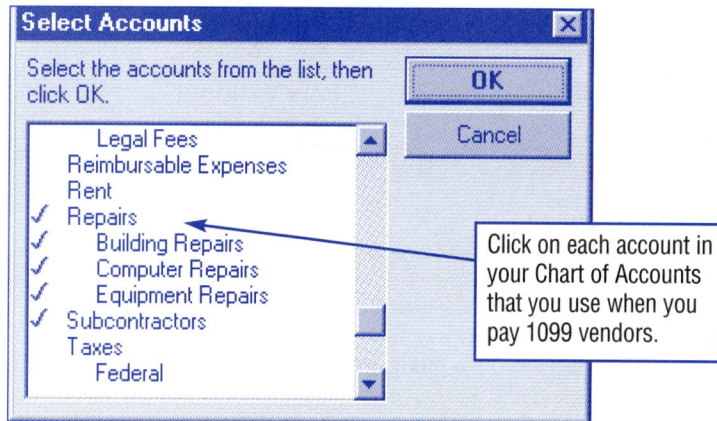

Click on each account in your Chart of Accounts that you use when you pay 1099 vendors.

Figure 9-2 The Select Accounts screen

6 In the Select Accounts window, specify which accounts are eligible for 1099 reporting. For this example, click on all of the **Repairs** subaccounts and on **Subcontractors** (see Figure 9-2). Click **OK** to record your selection, and click **OK** to close the Preferences window.

> **NOTE**
>
> When you use items to track your purchases, the item definition determines which QuickBooks account will be impacted. Therefore, if you use items to track payments to 1099 vendors, make sure you select the accounts to which those Items point.

Editing Vendors for 1099 Setup

Next, edit each of your 1099 vendors and verify that you have the full name, address and identification number (Social Security number or federal employer identification number) for the vendor. It's best to collect this data when you first start making payments to the vendor. Your vendors are required by law to provide you with this information.

COMPUTER TUTORIAL

1 Select the *Lists* menu, and choose **Vendor List**.

2 Double-click on "Boswell Insulation" to edit the Vendor record.

3 Verify that all the address information is correct so that the 1099 will print all the required fields (see Figure 9-3).

Make sure to fill out the name fields so that the 1099 will print all the information correctly on the form.

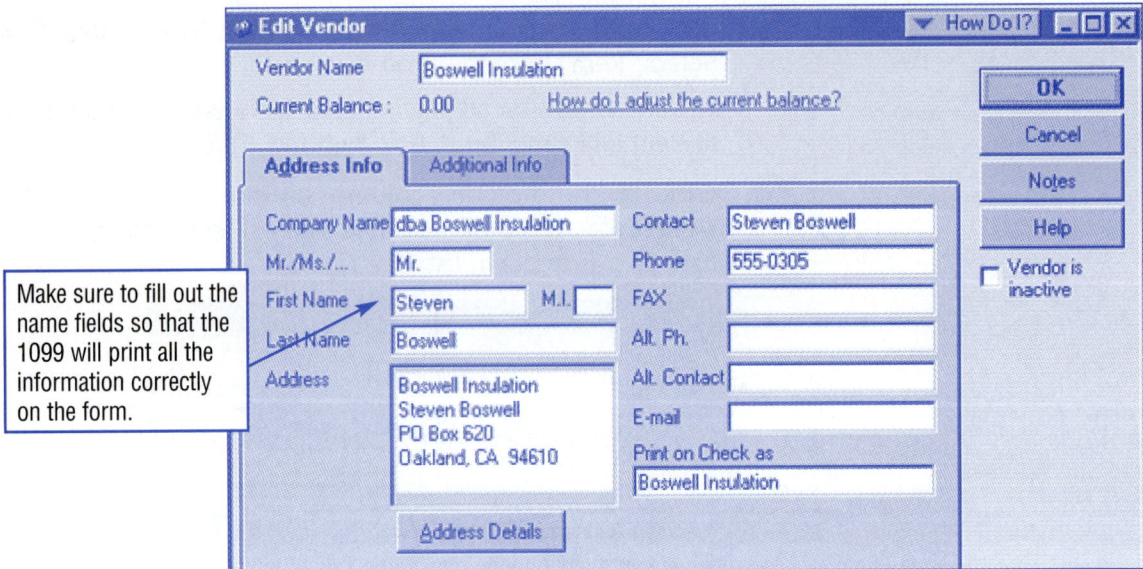

Figure 9-3 The Edit Vendor screen

④ Click the Additional Info tab.

⑤ Verify that "Vendor eligible for 1099" box is checked and that the Vendor's Social Security number (or taxpayer ID number) is in the *Tax ID* field (see Figure 9-4). Then click **OK**.

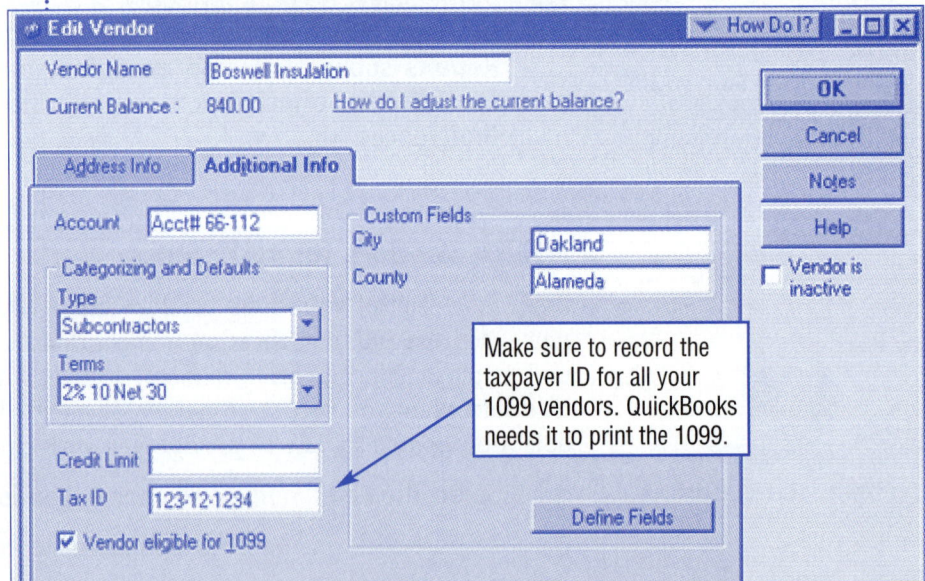

Make sure to record the taxpayer ID for all your 1099 vendors. QuickBooks needs it to print the 1099.

Figure 9-4 The Additional Information tab – Edit Vendor screen

Now that you've set your 1099 preferences and edited each of your 1099 Vendor records, QuickBooks automatically handles all of the tracking. Whenever payments to a 1099 vendor exceed the threshold set in the 1099 preferences ($600, in this example), a 1099 will be issued to that vendor at the end of the year.

To see how this preference works, pay one of your 1099 vendors so that the total payments exceed $600 for the year.

6 Select the *Vendors* menu, and then choose **Pay Bills**.

7 Click the "Show all bills" box.

8 Pay the Boswell Insulation bill as shown on the screen in Figure 9-5. Use "03/31/2002" as the Payment Date.

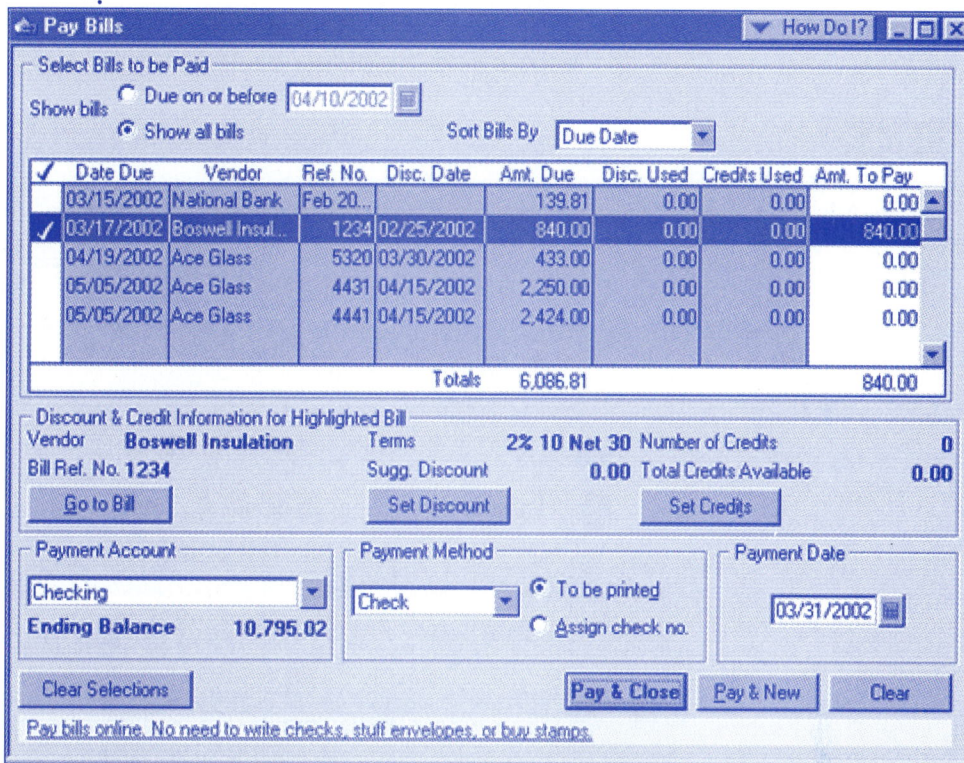

Figure 9-5 Use this data to pay the vendor.

9 Click **Pay & Close** to record the check.

COMPUTER TUTORIAL

Printing 1099s

1 Select the *File* menu, choose **Print Forms** and then choose **1099s**.

2 On the Printing 1099-MISC Forms screen (see Figure 9-6), set the Date fields to "01/01/2002" through "12/31/2002." Then click **OK**.

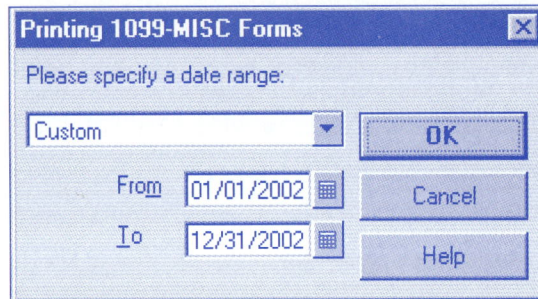

Printing 1099-MISC Forms

Please specify a date range:

Custom

From 01/01/2002

To 12/31/2002

OK   Cancel   Help

Figure 9-6 Set the Date fields for the 1099.

3 QuickBooks displays the list of 1099s to be printed (see Figure 9-7).

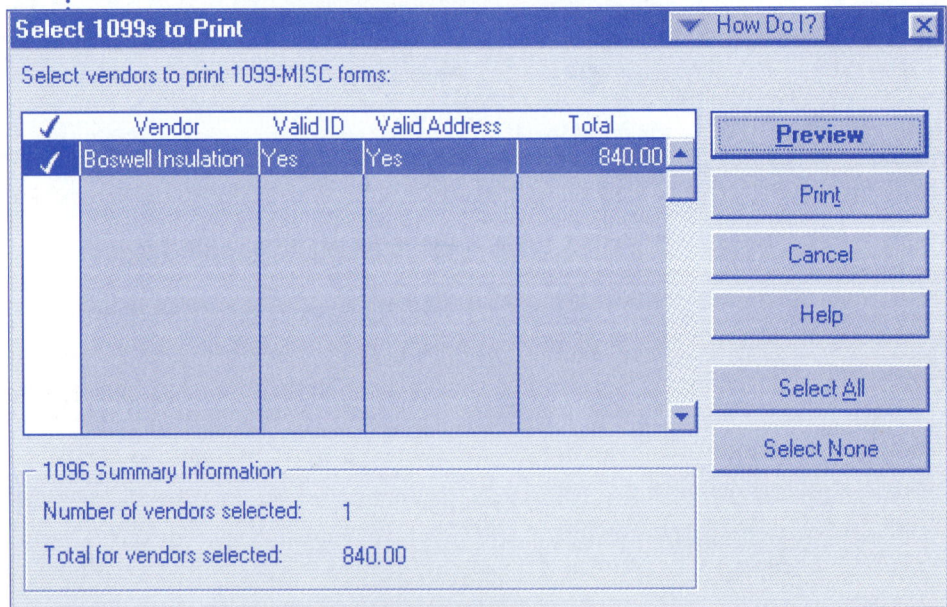

Select 1099s to Print   How Do I?

Select vendors to print 1099-MISC forms:

✓	Vendor	Valid ID	Valid Address	Total
✓	Boswell Insulation	Yes	Yes	840.00

Preview   Print   Cancel   Help   Select All   Select None

1096 Summary Information

Number of vendors selected: 1

Total for vendors selected: 840.00

Figure 9-7 The list of 1099s to print

4 Click **Preview** (Figure 9-8) to preview the 1099 before printing.

Print Preview -- Page 1 of 1

| Print | Prev page | Next page | Zoom Out | Help |

Academy Glass
123 Main St.
Pleasanton, CA 94566

> QuickBooks uses the name entered in the Company Name field of the vendor's record to complete this line of the 1099.

11-3456789   123-12-1234

Steven Boswell
dba Boswell Insulation
                                                840.00

PO Box 620

Oakland CA 94610

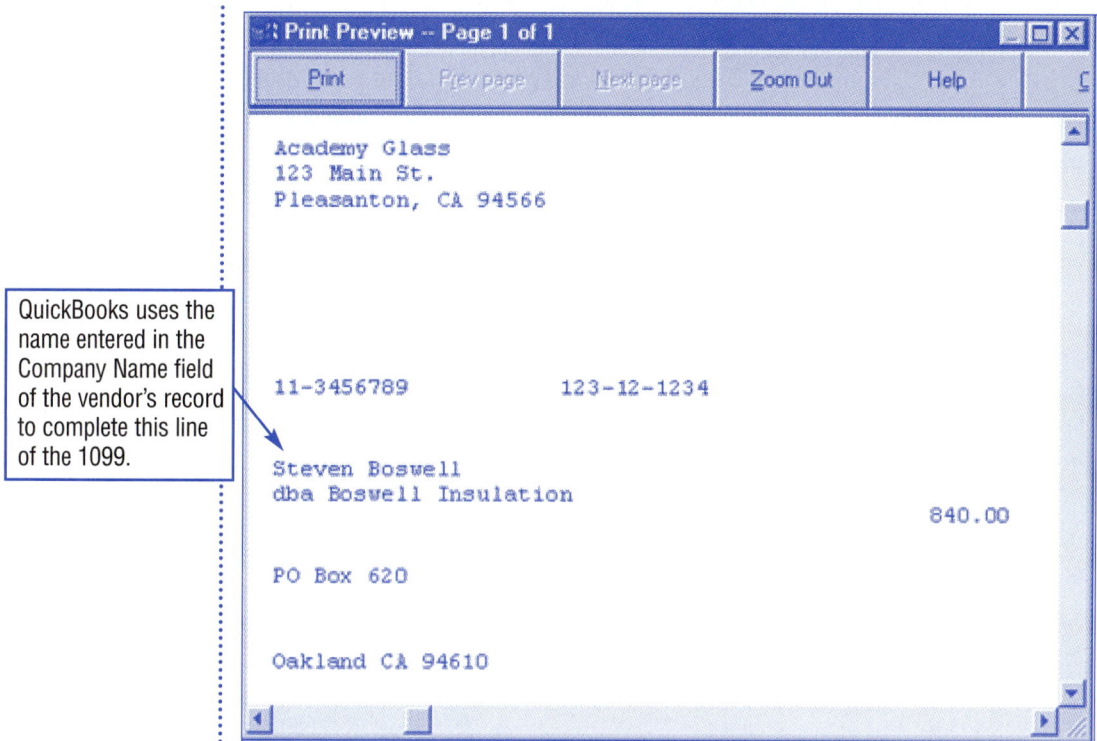

Figure 9-8 Preview the 1099 before printing.

⑤ Click **Print** to print the 1099s. Print the forms on blank paper for this example.

You can purchase preprinted 1099 forms in either tractor-feed or laser sheets from your local office supply store or from most forms providers.

EDITING, VOIDING, AND DELETING TRANSACTIONS

KEY TERM

A **closed accounting period** is a period for which you've already issued financial statements and/or tax returns.

Unlike many other accounting programs, QuickBooks allows you to change any transaction at any time. However, as explained in Chapter 4, you should almost never change transactions dated in closed accounting periods or transactions that have been reconciled with a bank statement.

When you change or delete a transaction, QuickBooks immediately updates the General Ledger with your change, regardless of the date of the transaction. Therefore, if you make a change to transactions in a closed accounting period, your QuickBooks financial statements will change for that period. That could put your QuickBooks data out of sync with your tax returns.

Some companies close their books monthly but other companies only close the books quarterly or annually. Make sure you know how often your company closes periods before you make changes to transactions that might affect those periods.

Editing Transactions

To edit (or modify) a transaction in QuickBooks, change the data directly on the form. For example, if you forgot to add a charge for 2 hours of labor to Invoice 2002-112, you will need to add a line in the Invoice.

COMPUTER TUTORIAL

❶ Display Invoice 2002-112, dated 4/5/2001 by selecting the *Customers* menu, choosing **Create Invoices** and then clicking **Previous** on the toolbar (see Figure 9-9).

Figure 9-9 Edit the transaction on the form.

❷ Click on the second line and enter "Labor" in the Item column. Press <TAB> twice.

❸ Enter "2" in the Quantity column, and press <TAB> (see Figure 9-10).

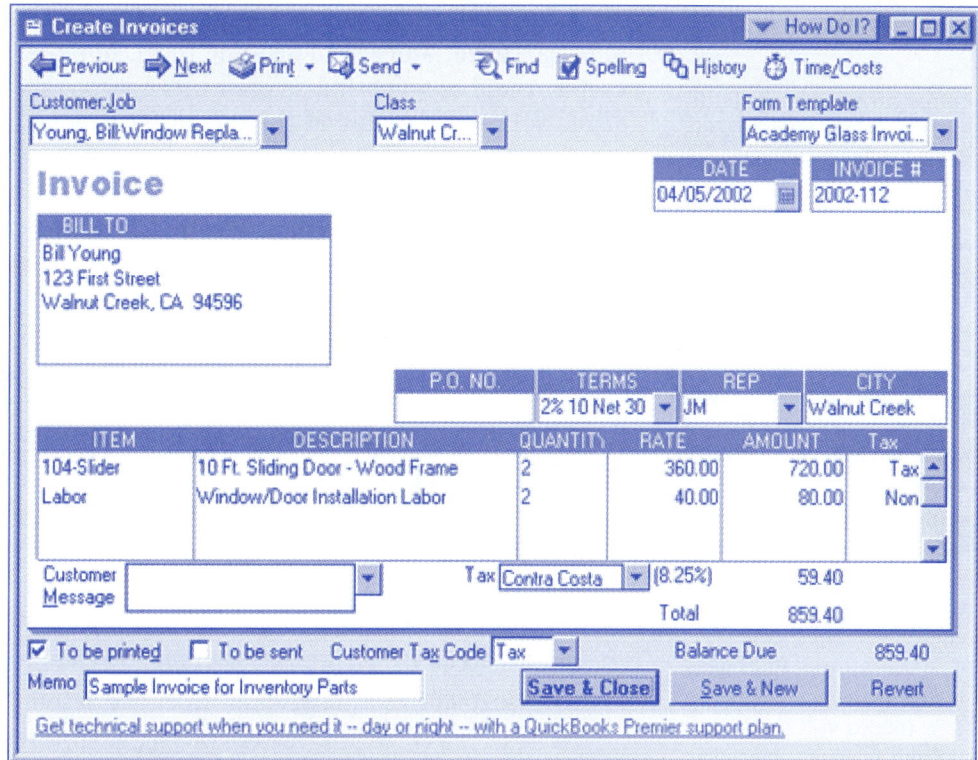

Figure 9-10 Add the labor Item to the Invoice.

④ Click **Save & Close** to save the Invoice.

⑤ On the Recording Transaction message screen, click **Yes**. This is just a warning to make sure you don't change transactions without meaning to (see Figure 9-11).

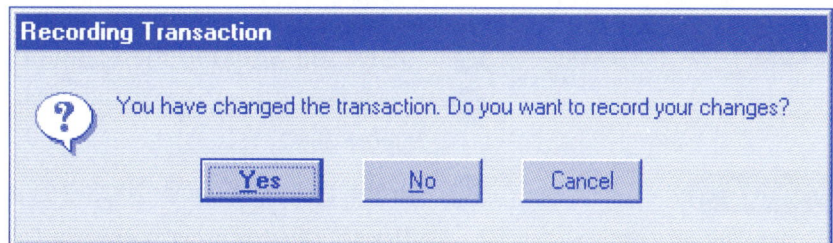

Figure 9-11 Recording Transaction screen

> **NOTE**
>
> Do not use this method of changing transactions if you have already sent the Invoice to the customer. In this case, you will need to create a new Invoice with the separate charge. Also, you should never change an Invoice transaction in a closed accounting period.

> **NOTE**
>
> If you have the Audit Trail activated in the Accounting Company Preferences, QuickBooks will show the deleted transaction on the Audit Trail report. For information about the audit trail, consult the QuickBooks online Help.

Voiding and Deleting Transactions

Unlike many accounting programs, QuickBooks allows you to void and delete transactions almost without restriction. Voiding and deleting transactions have the same effect on the General Ledger — to zero out the debits and the credits specified by the transaction.

There is one significant difference between voiding and deleting. When you void a transaction, QuickBooks keeps a record of the date, number, and detail of the transaction. When you delete a transaction, QuickBooks removes it completely from your file.

In general, it's a much better practice to void transactions that need to be cancelled rather than deleting them. In either case, make sure you keep a record of voids and deletions. The record should include the date of the void or deletion and the reason for it.

To **delete** a transaction:

1. Select the transaction in a register, or display the form.
2. Select the *Edit* menu and then choose **Delete**.

To **void** a transaction:

1. Select the transaction in a register, or display the form.
2. Select the *Edit* menu and then choose **Void**.

RECORDING ADJUSTMENTS AND GENERAL JOURNAL ENTRIES

Adjusting entries are transactions that adjust the balance of one or more accounts.

Here are a few examples of adjusting entries in QuickBooks:

◆ Recategorize a transaction from one class to another.

◆ Recategorize a transaction from one account to another.

◆ Allocate prepaid expenses to each month throughout the year.

◆ Record noncash expenses, such as depreciation.

◆ Close the Owner's Drawing account into the Owner's Equity account.

In most cases, you'll use a General Journal Entry to record adjustments.

Creating a General Journal Entry

① Select the *Banking* menu, and choose **Make Journal Entry**.

② Enter "01/31/2002" in the *Date* field and press <TAB> (see Figure 9-12).

③ In the *Entry No.* field, 2002-2 is already selected. Press <TAB>.

The very first time you enter a General Journal Entry, enter whatever number you want in the *Entry No.* field. Then, when you create your next General Journal Entry, QuickBooks increases the entry numbers sequentially.

④ On the top line of the General Journal Entry, enter "Journal Entries" in the Account column. Press <TAB> three times to leave the Debit and Credit columns blank for this line.

When you use an account called "Journal Entries" on the top line of each General Journal Entry, QuickBooks tracks all the General Journal Entries in a separate register on the Chart of Accounts. This separate register allows you to quickly look up and view previously entered General Journal Entries. Though you use this account in every General Journal Entry, you will never debit or credit the account. Therefore the account will never carry a balance. Set up a bank account called "Journal Entries" in your Chart of Accounts.

NOTE

General Journal Entries must *balance*. That is, the total of the Debits column must match the total of the Credits column.

5 Enter "Recategorize Expense" in the Memo column. Press <TAB>three times to leave the Name and Class columns blank for this line.

6 Enter the information on the next two lines as shown in Figure 9-12.

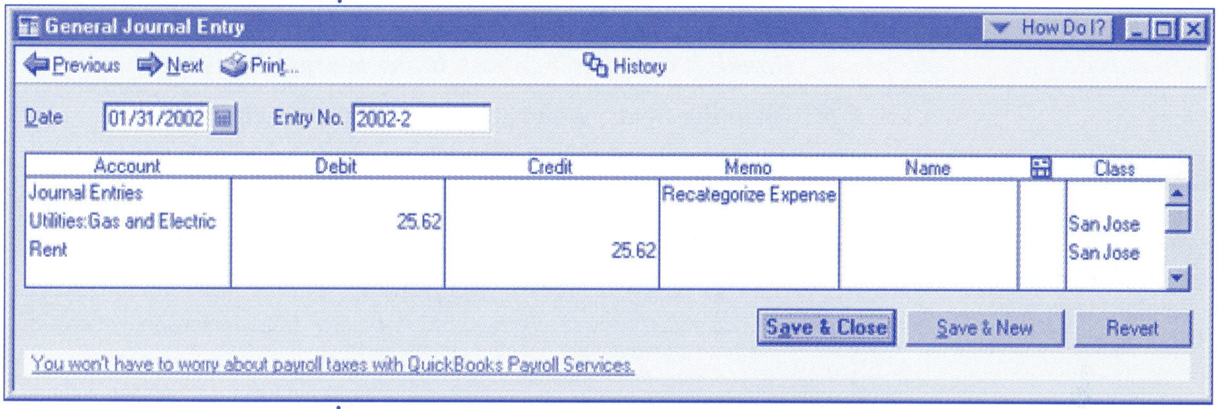

Figure 9-12 The General Journal Entry screen

7 Click **Save & Close** to save the transaction.

Making Adjustments for Prepaid Expenses

If you use the accrual basis of accounting, the goal is to properly match income and expenses to the period in which the income or expenses occur. However, sometimes you pay expenses in advance of when they are used. For example, if you pay your insurance yearly and you want to allocate the cost of the insurance to each month, set up an account called *Prepaid Expenses* (see Figure 9-13). The tutorial template file already includes the Prepaid Expenses account shown in Figure 9-13.

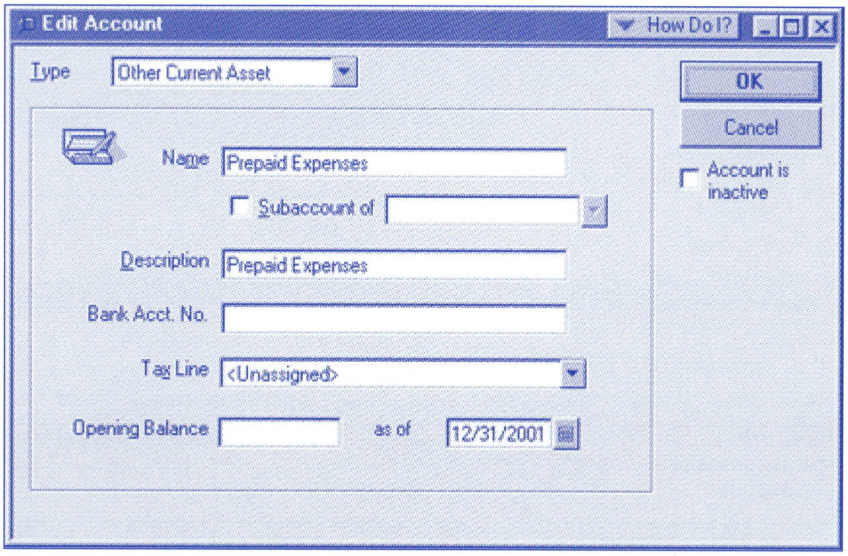

Figure 9-13 Set up a new account for Prepaid Expenses.

COMPUTER TUTORIAL

1 Select the *Banking* menu and choose **Write Checks**.

② Write a check for Sinclair Insurance as shown in Figure 9-14.

When you write a check for prepaid expenses, code the check to the Prepaid Expenses Other Current Asset account.

③ Click **Save & Close** to save the Check.

④ To allocate the expenses to each month of the year, enter a journal entry that records one-twelfth of the expenses. Select the *Banking* menu and choose **Make Journal Entry**.

⑤ Fill in the fields as shown on the screen in Figure 9-15.

⑥ Click **Save & Close** to save the transaction.

You might want to memorize this transaction and schedule it to automatically enter each month. See page 466 for details.

NOTE

This check decreases (credits) the Checking account and increases (debits) the Prepaid Expense asset account.

Code the check to Prepaid Expenses. It will show as an asset on your Balance Sheet.

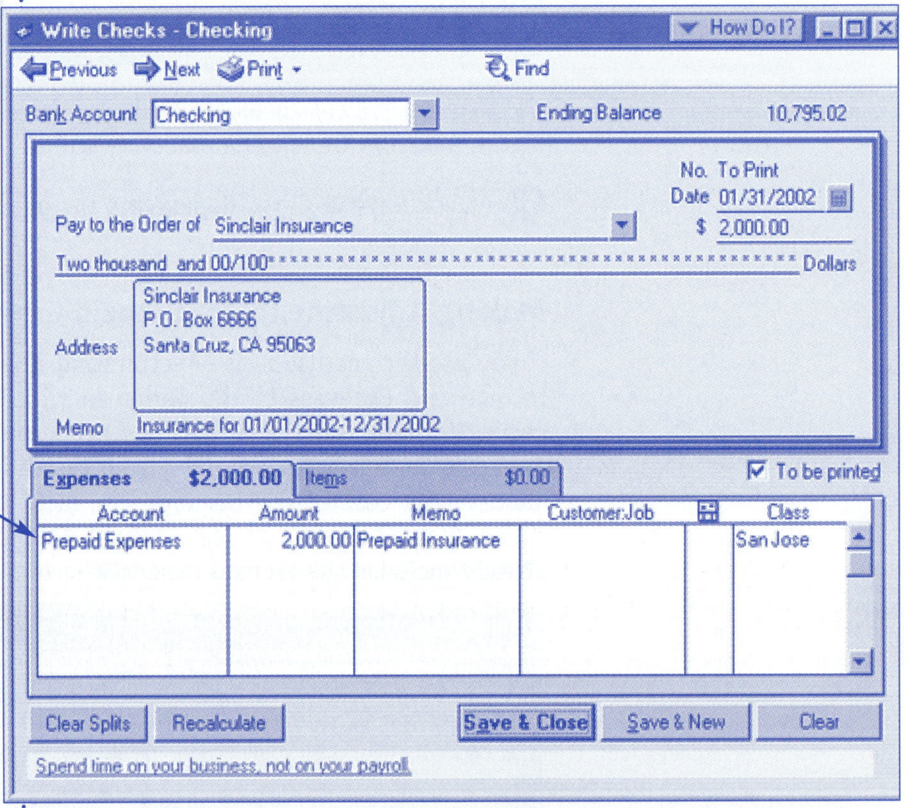

Figure 9-14 Code the check to the Prepaid Expenses account.

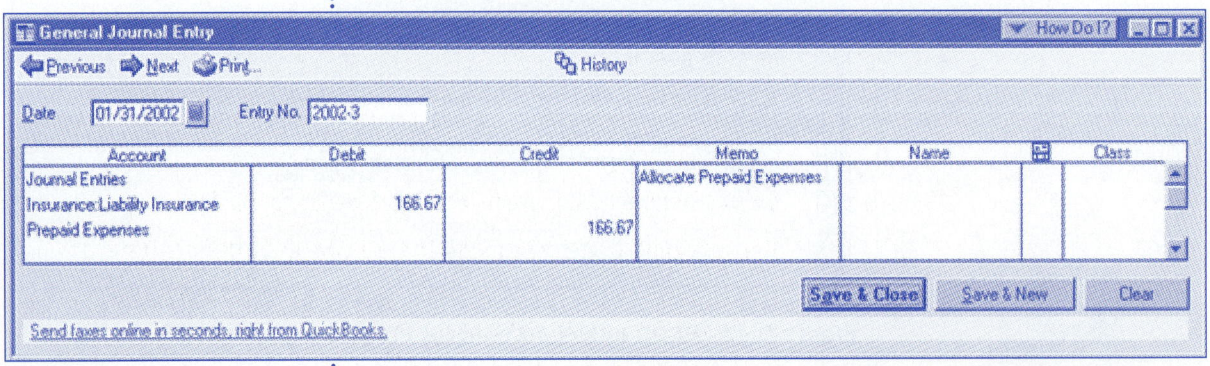

Figure 9-15 Use this data to complete the General Journal entry screen.

TRACKING FIXED ASSETS

When you purchase office equipment, buildings, computers, vehicles, or other assets that have useful lives of more than one year, you'll want to add them to your Balance Sheet and record the depreciation of the assets periodically. Check with your accountant if you need help deciding which purchases should be added to a fixed asset account.

Setting up Fixed Asset Accounts

COMPUTER TUTORIAL

To create Fixed Asset accounts for tracking asset cost and depreciation, follow these steps:

1 Display the **Chart of Accounts**.

2 Press <Ctrl+N> to create a new account.

3 Select "Fixed Asset" from the Type drop-down list.

4 Enter "Furniture and Equipment" in the *Name* field, and press <TAB> (see Figure 9-16).

Figure 9-16 Set up a new Account for a fixed asset.

5 The rest of the fields on this screen will be covered in detail later. For now, click **OK** to save the new account.

Add two subaccounts to each fixed asset. One subaccount tracks the cost of the asset, the other tracks accumulated depreciation. To create the Cost subaccount, follow these steps:

6 Press <Ctrl+N> to create a new account.

7 Select "Fixed Asset" from the Type drop-down list.

8 Enter "Cost" in the *Name* field and press <TAB>.

9 Check the "Subaccount of" box and enter "Furniture and Equipment" in the *Subaccount* field, as shown in Figure 9-17.

10 Click **OK** to save the new account.

⑪ Enter information on the **Accumulated Depreciation** account to match the screen in Figure 9-18.

⑫ In addition to the fixed asset accounts, you'll need an expense account called Depreciation Expense. This account is already set up in your Chart of Accounts.

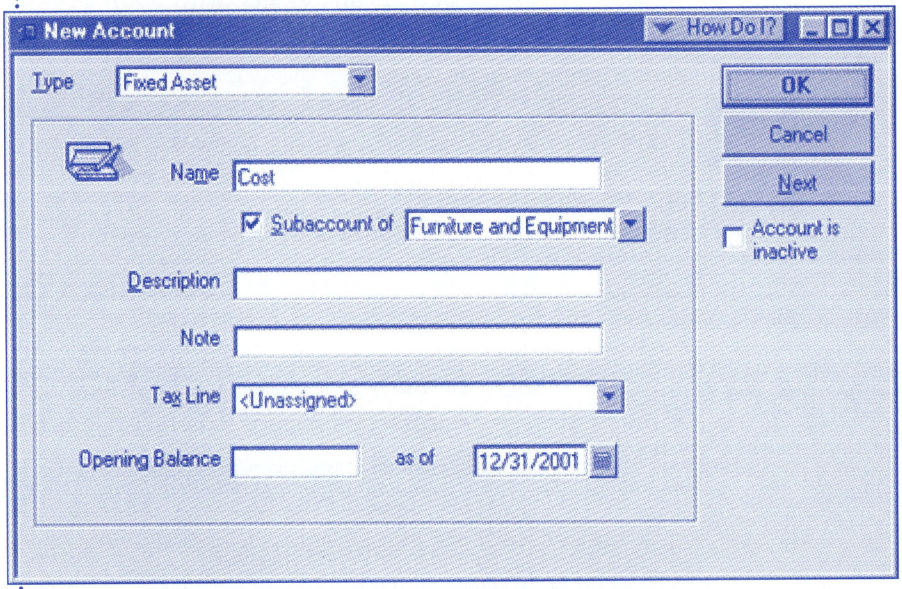

Figure 9-17 Create a subaccount to track the asset cost.

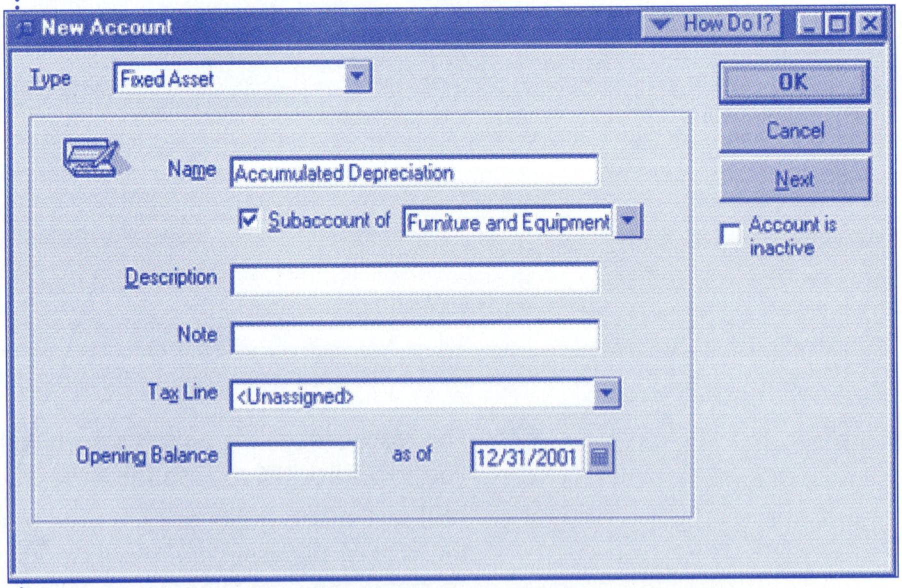

Figure 9-18 Create a subaccount to track accumulated depreciation.

Purchasing an Asset

When you purchase an asset, categorize the purchase to the appropriate asset Cost subaccount, such as Furniture and Equipment:Cost. If you want to track your assets by name, create names of your assets in the Other Names list.

To create names of assets in **the Other Names** list, follow these steps:

1 Select the *Lists* menu, and choose **Other Names List**.

2 Press <Ctrl+N> to add a new name.

3 Enter "Telephone System" in the *Name* field (see Figure 9-19).

You don't need to fill in the rest of the fields since you use this name only for reports about purchases and depreciation of your telephone system.

4 Click **OK**.

Figure 9-19 Add a new name to track your assets.

When you purchase the asset, enter a bill, check or credit card charge to record the purchase. For this exercise, enter a credit card charge.

5 Select the *Banking* menu and choose **Enter Credit Card Charges**.

6 Then enter the credit card charge with "Telephone System" in the *Purchased from* field. This allows you to track your asset purchases by name, so that you can create filtered reports that show all transactions with a particular asset, including purchases and depreciation. Code the transaction to the Furniture and Equipment:Cost account (see Figure 9-20).

7 Click **Save & Close** to save the transaction.

Figure 9-20 When purchasing assets, enter the asset name in the Purchased from field at the top of the transaction.

Recording Depreciation

QuickBooks does not calculate depreciation. You'll need to calculate the depreciation for your fixed assets and then use a journal entry to record the amount you've calculated. If you need help with the calculation, ask your accountant.

When you record depreciation, use the name of the asset in the Name column on the transaction as shown in Figure 9-21.

COMPUTER TUTORIAL

1 Select the *Banking* menu and then choose **Make Journal Entry**.

2 Fill out the General Journal Entry shown on the screen in Figure 9-21, and click **Save & Close** to save it.

Figure 9-21 Record depreciation as a General Journal Entry.

NOTE

When you purchase fixed assets, code the purchase to the Fixed Asset Cost account. This increases (debits) the Fixed Asset Cost account and decreases (credits) the Checking account (assuming you used a check). Then when you record depreciation, as shown on the General Journal Entry in Figure 9-21, you increase (debit) the Depreciation Expense account and decrease (credit) the Accumulated Depreciation account. The Accumulated Depreciation account is known as a "Contra-Asset" account because its balance is always a credit balance.

TRACKING LOANS

If your business takes out a loan, set up a long term liability account to track it. There is already a Loan Payable account in your template file. When you make your loan payments, split the payment between principal and interest manually. QuickBooks doesn't automatically calculate interest on loans, so you'll have to calculate the interest portion and manually enter it.

COMPUTER TUTORIAL

❶ Select the *Banking* menu and then choose **Write Checks**.

❷ Fill out your check as shown in Figure 9-22.

This reduces your loan balance for the principal amount and records interest expense for the interest portion.

3 Click **Save & Close** to save the transaction.

Figure 9-22 Record a loan payment on separate lines.

MEMORIZING JOURNAL ENTRIES

If you want QuickBooks to automatically enter the depreciation journal entry each month, you can memorize the transaction and then schedule it to automatically enter.

Scheduling Memorized Transactions

COMPUTER TUTORIAL

1 Display the entry you want to memorize. Select the *Banking* menu and choose **Make Journal Entry**. Then click **Previous** on the toolbar until you see General Journal Entry #2002-4 (the depreciation entry).

2 Select the *Edit* menu and then choose **Memorize General Journal**.

3 Enter "Telephone Depreciation" in the *Name* field.

Use names that you'll recognize so that you can recognize this transaction in the Memorized Transaction list.

4 Set the fields as shown in Figure 9-23 to indicate when and how often you want the transaction entered. Then click **OK**.

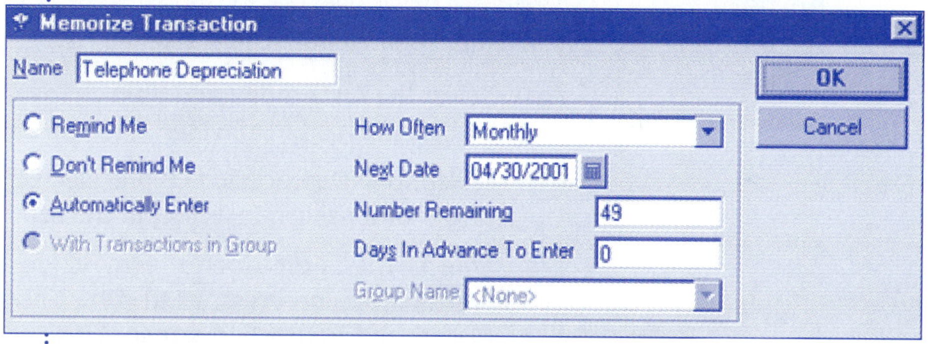

Figure 9-23 Enter this data to memorize the transaction.

> **DID YOU KNOW** You can memorize *any* transaction in QuickBooks except Bill Payments and payments from customers.

5 Close all your open windows by clicking the close box (**X**) in the upper left corner.

Now, every time you launch QuickBooks, it checks your Memorized Transaction list for transactions it needs to automatically enter. If the system date is on or after the date in the *Next Date* field (minus the number in the *Days In Advance To Enter* field), QuickBooks will ask you if you want to enter the memorized transaction (see Figure 9-24).

If you click **Now**, QuickBooks will automatically enter the transaction.

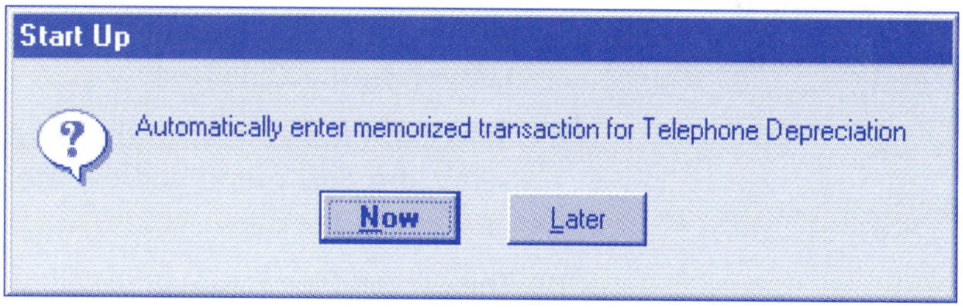

Figure 9-24 On or after April 30, QuickBooks will ask if you want to enter the memorized transaction.

Deleting, Rescheduling and Editing Memorized Transactions

COMPUTER TUTORIAL

Deleting Memorized Transactions

1 Select the *Lists* menu and then choose **Memorized Transaction List**, or press <Ctrl+T> (see Figure 9-25).

2 "Telephone Depreciation" is preselected because it is the first and only Memorized Transaction in the list.

3 Select the *Edit* menu and choose **Delete Memorized Transaction**, or press <Ctrl+D>. Click **Cancel** on the Delete Memorized Transaction screen. Close all open screens.

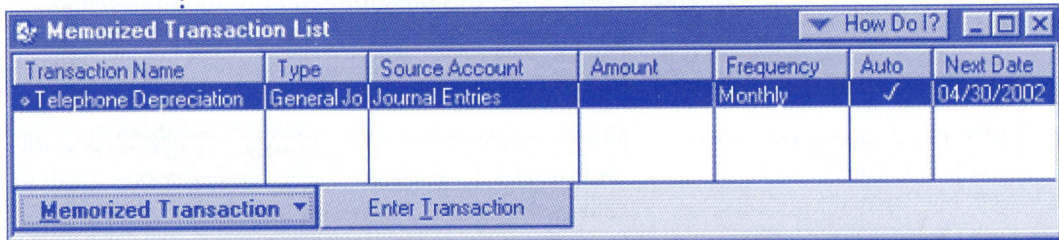

Transaction Name	Type	Source Account	Amount	Frequency	Auto	Next Date
◇ Telephone Depreciation	General Jo	Journal Entries		Monthly	✓	04/30/2002

Memorized Transaction ▼   Enter Transaction

Figure 9-25 The Memorized Transaction List screen

COMPUTER TUTORIAL

Rescheduling or Renaming Memorized Transactions

1 Select the *Lists* menu and then choose **Memorized Transaction List**, or press <Ctrl+T>.

2 Select the transaction in the **Memorized Transaction** list. Then select the *Edit* menu and choose **Edit Memorized Transaction**, or press <Ctrl+E>.

3 This screen (see Figure 9-26) allows you to reschedule or rename the transaction, but it does not allow you to edit the actual transaction.

4 Click **Cancel**. Close all open screens.

Schedule Memorized Transaction

Name Telephone Depreciation

- ○ Remind Me
- ○ Don't Remind Me
- ⦿ Automatically Enter
- ○ With Transactions in Group

How Often Monthly
Next Date 04/30/2002
Number Remaining 49
Days In Advance To Enter 0
Group Name <None>

OK   Cancel

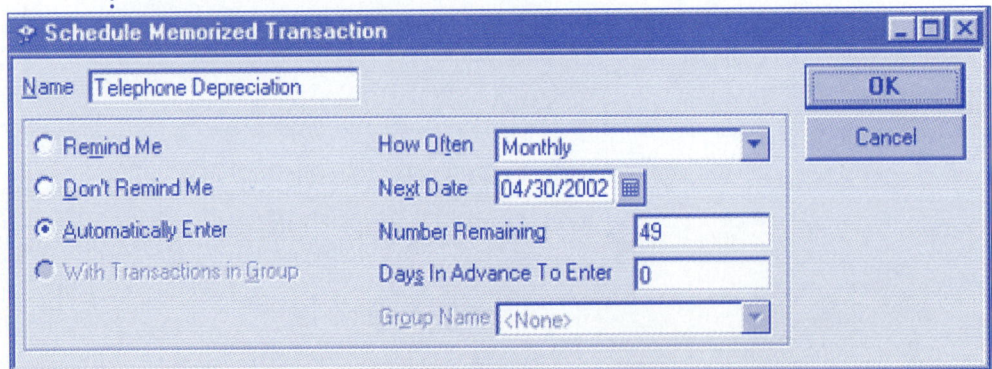

Figure 9-26 The Schedule Memorized Transaction screen

COMPUTER TUTORIAL

Editing Memorized Transactions

① Select the *Lists* menu and then choose **Memorized Transaction List**, or press <Ctrl+T>.

② Double-click the memorized transaction you want to edit in the **Memorized Transaction List**.

This displays a new transaction (see Figure 9-27) with the contents of the memorized transaction. You can change anything on the transaction and then rememorize it.

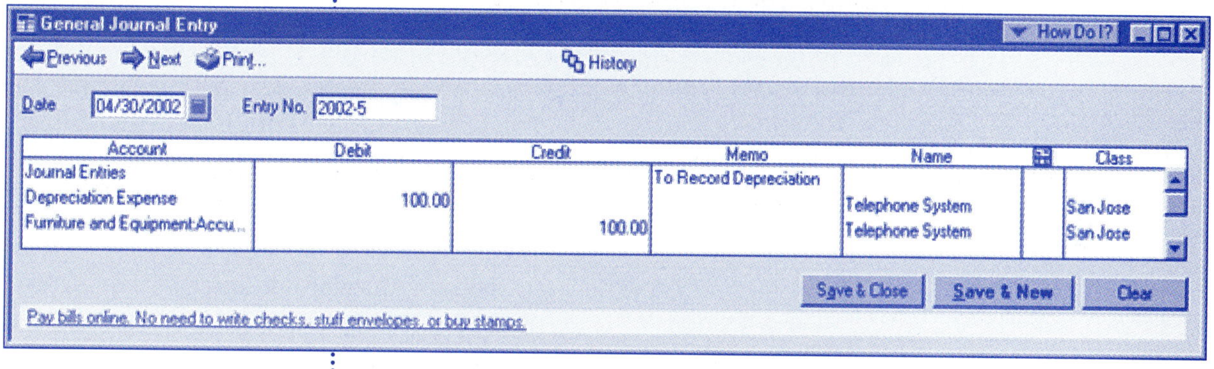

General Journal Entry

⬅ Previous   ➡ Next   🖨 Print...   🔲 History

Date 04/30/2002   Entry No. 2002-5

Account	Debit	Credit	Memo	Name		Class
Journal Entries			To Record Depreciation			
Depreciation Expense	100.00			Telephone System		San Jose
Furniture and Equipment:Accu...		100.00		Telephone System		San Jose

Save & Close   Save & New   Clear

Pay bills online. No need to write checks, stuff envelopes, or buy stamps.

Figure 9-27 Edit the transaction, as necessary.

③ Change the Memo on the first line to "To Record Telephone Depreciation." **Do not save the transaction.**

④ Select the *Edit* menu and then choose **Memorize General Journal**, or press <Ctrl+M>.

⑤ To save your edited transaction in the Memorized Transaction list (see Figure 9-28), click **Replace**.

⑥ Close the General Journal Entry window and then click **No** on the Recording Transaction message screen to prevent it from being saved.

Replace Memorized Transaction

(?) Telephone Depreciation is already in the Memorized Transaction list. Would you like to replace it or add a new one?

Replace   Add   Cancel

Figure 9-28 The Replace Memorized Transaction message.

CLOSING THE YEAR

At the end of each year, QuickBooks automatically enters an adjusting entry to your income and expense accounts, posting the net income into Retained Earnings (or Owner's Equity). This entry is known as the *closing entry*.

NOTE

Sole Proprietorships should *rename* the Retained Earnings account to "Owner's Equity."

In fact, QuickBooks never *really* creates a transaction for the closing entry, but when you create a Balance Sheet, QuickBooks calculates the balance in Retained Earnings by adding together the total net income for all prior years. At the end of your company's fiscal year, QuickBooks automatically transfers the net income into Retained Earnings.

On the left side of the example in Table 9-1, notice that the Balance Sheet for 12/31/2001 shows net income for the year is $100,000.00. The right side shows the same Balance Sheet, but for the next day (January 1, 2002). Since January is in a new year, last year's net income has been automatically transferred to the Retained Earnings account.

Equity on Dec 31, 2001		Equity on Jan 1, 2002	
Opening Bal Equity	0.00	Opening Bal Equity	0.00
Preferred Stock	50,000.00	Preferred Stock	50,000.00
Common Stock	75,000.00	Common Stock	75,000.00
Retained Earnings	100,000.00	Retained Earnings	200,000.00
Net Income	100,000.00	Net Income	0.00
Total Equity	325,000.00	Total Equity	325,000.00

Table 9-1 Example of QuickBooks closing entry.

There are two advantages to QuickBooks' automatically closing the year for you. First, you don't have to create the year-end entry, which can be time-consuming. Second, the details of your income and expenses are not erased each year, as some programs require.

Closing the Accounting Period

Following is a list of actions you should take at the end of each accounting period. Perform these steps as often as you close your company's books. Many companies close monthly or quarterly, while some close yearly. No matter when you close, these steps are meant to help you create proper reports that incorporate many noncash transactions, such as depreciation entries, prepaid expense allocations, and adjusting entries to equity accounts, to properly reflect that the books are closed.

At the end of the year, consider doing some or all of the following:

1. Enter depreciation entries.
2. Reconcile cash and loan accounts with the year-end statements.
3. If your business is a partnership, enter a General Journal Entry to distribute net income for the year to each of the partner's capital accounts. If your business is a sole proprietorship, enter a General Journal Entry closing Owner's Drawing and Owner's Investments into Owner's Equity.
4. Run reports for the year and verify their accuracy. Enter adjusting entries as necessary and rerun the reports.

NOTE

Condensing is not covered in this book. For information on condensing, consult the QuickBooks online Help.

5. Print and file the following reports as of your closing date: General Ledger, Balance Sheet Standard, Statement of Cash Flows, Inventory Valuation Summary, and Profit & Loss Standard for the year.

6. Back up your data file on a special backup diskette, zip disk, or CD-ROM that will never be touched.

7. Set the closing date to the last day of the period you are closing. See page 475 for details on setting the closing date.

8. Consider condensing the data file.

Recording Closing Entries for Sole Proprietorships and Partnerships

If your company is a sole proprietorship or partnership, the owners of the company put money into the company and occasionally take money out. Owners are not employees, so you won't use payroll to pay the owners.

Sole proprietorships have the following accounts in the Equity section of the Chart of Accounts (see Figure 9-29).

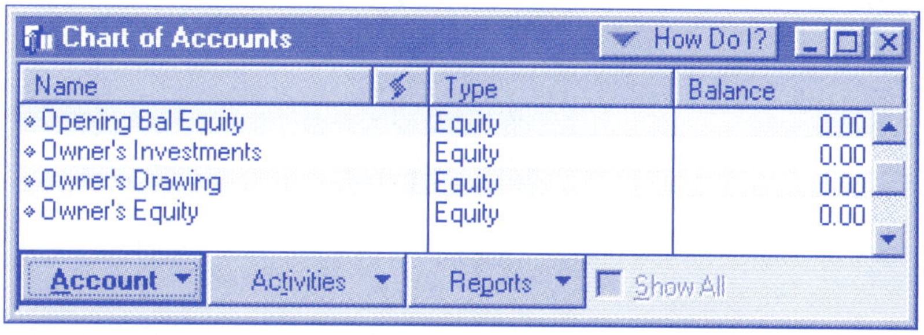

NOTE

You won't enter the transactions in this section. But do familiarize yourself with these issues, so that you can properly close the year in a sole proprietorship or partnership company.

Figure 9-29 Sample Equity Section – Sole Proprietorships

Partnerships have the following accounts (or similar accounts) in the Equity section of the Chart of Accounts (see Figure 9-30).

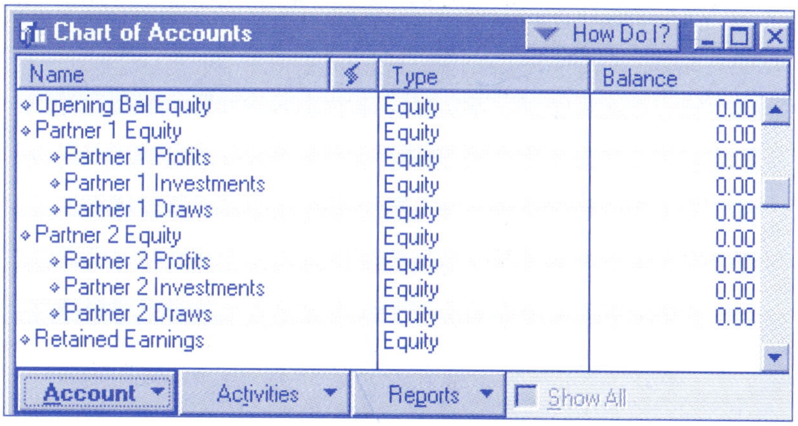

Figure 9-30 Sample Equity section – Partnerships

Throughout the year, as owners put money into and take money out of the business, you'll add transactions that increase and decrease the appropriate equity accounts. In a sole proprietorship, you'll use the Owner's Investments and Owner's Drawing accounts. In a partnership, you'll use the Drawing and Investment accounts for each partner.

To record owner's investments in the company, enter a deposit transaction in your Checking account (or the account to which you deposit), and enter "Owner's Investments" in the *From Account* field (see Figure 9-31).

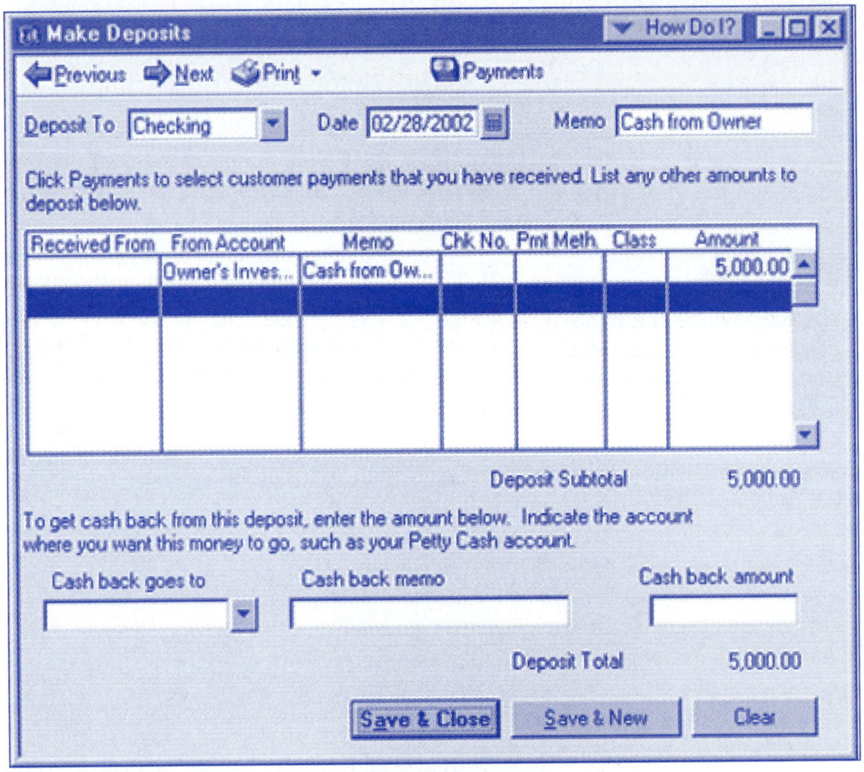

Figure 9-31 Record owner's investments in the Make Deposits screen

To record owner's withdrawals from the company, enter a check transaction in the Checking account (or the account from which the owner draws money), and enter "Owner's Drawing" in the *Account* field (see Figure 9-32).

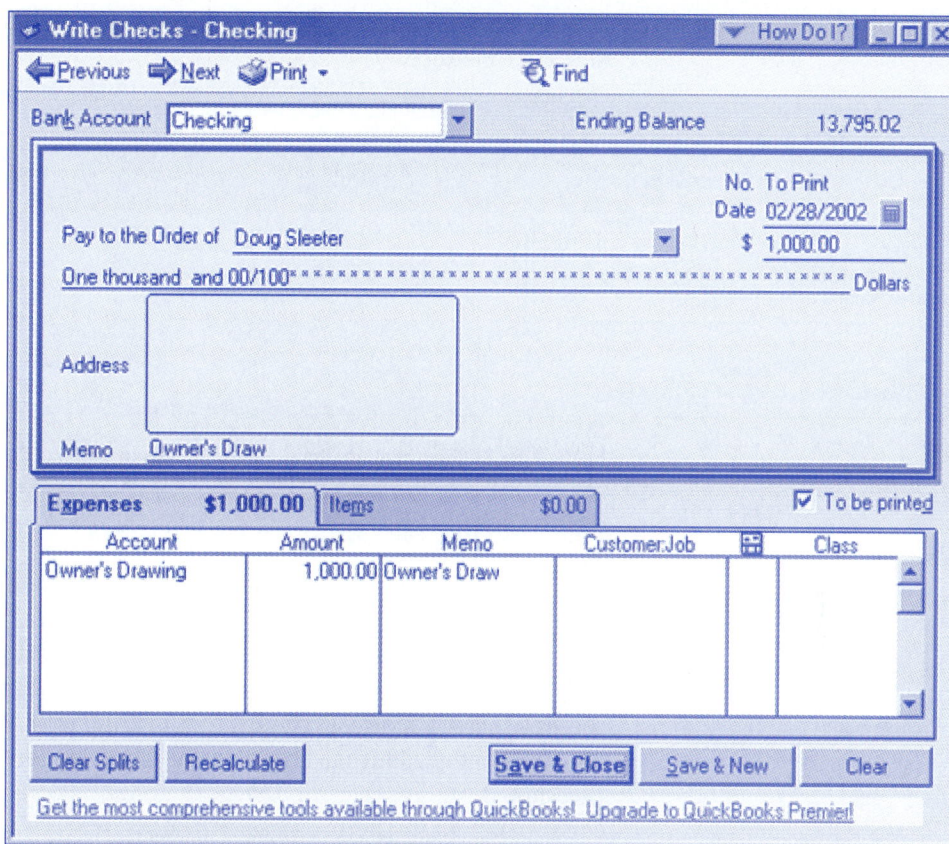

Figure 9-32 Record owner's withdrawals as a check transaction

At the end of each year, you'll create a General Journal Entry to zero out the Owner's Drawing account and close it into Owner's Equity (see Figure 9-33).

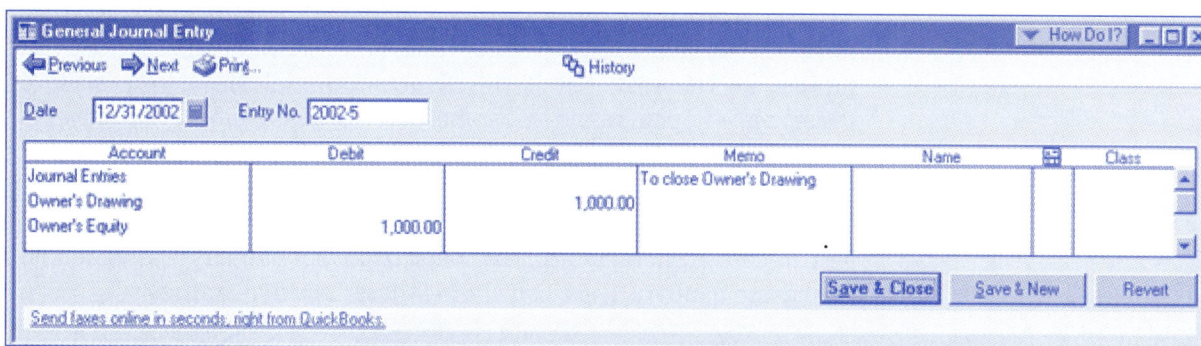

Figure 9-33 General Journal Entry to close Owner's Drawing

> **NOTE**
>
> If the balance in Owner's Drawing is larger than the balance in Owner's Investments, debit the Owner's Equity account for whatever amount is necessary to make this General Journal Entry balance.

To find the amounts for this General Journal Entry, create a Trial Balance report for the end of the year. Note the balance in the Owner's Drawing account and use this balance on a General Journal Entry to close the account. For example, if your Trial Balance shows a *debit* balance of $5000.00 in Owner's Drawing, enter $5000.00 in the *credit* column on the Owner's Drawing line of this General Journal Entry. Then enter the necessary debit or credit to the Owner's Equity account to make the entry balance.

To close the Partner's Draws accounts into each Partner's Profits account, use a General Journal Entry like the one shown in Figure 9-34.

Use the same process explained above to get the numbers from the year-end Trial Balance.

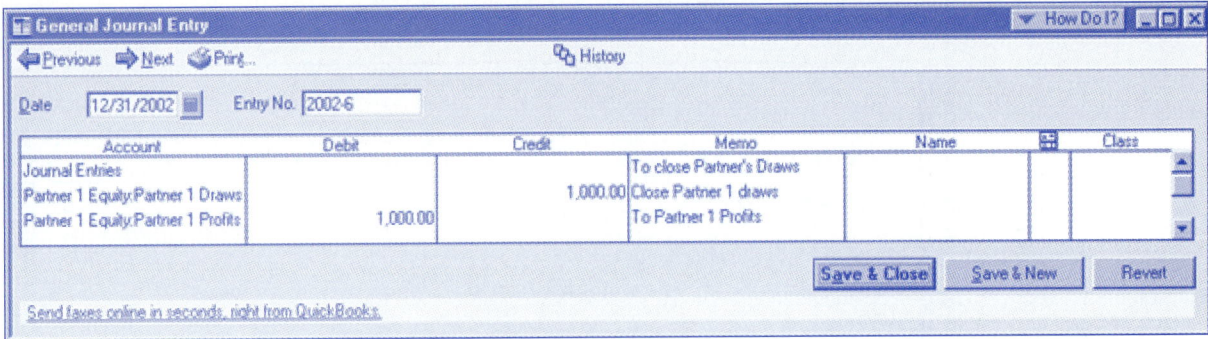

Figure 9-34 General Journal Entry to close partner's drawing accounts

Distributing Net Income to Partners

With partnerships, you need to use a General Journal Entry to distribute the profits of the company into each of the partner's profit accounts. After making all adjusting entries for depreciation, prepaid expenses, and any other accounts, create a Profit & Loss report for the year. Use the Net Income figure at the bottom of the Profit and Loss report to create the General Journal Entry, in Figure 9-35. In this example, assume the shown net income for the year is $50,000, and that there are two equal partners in the business.

Note that this General Journal Entry uses Retained Earnings for the debit. That's because QuickBooks automatically closes net income into Retained Earnings each year. So this is the entry you'll make each year to distribute the net income to the partners.

Also, note that the General Journal Entry is dated January 1. That's because there is no "after-closing" Balance Sheet in QuickBooks. We want the December 31 Balance Sheet to show "undistributed" net income for the year, but if this General Journal Entry were made on December 31, you would never be able to see a proper December 31 Balance Sheet. Therefore, to preserve the 12/31 Balance Sheet, use January 1 for this closing entry. If you ever want to see an "after closing" Balance Sheet, use January 1 for that Balance Sheet. It would be best to date all normal business transactions for January 1 as of January 2, and use January 1 exclusively for these "closing" entries.

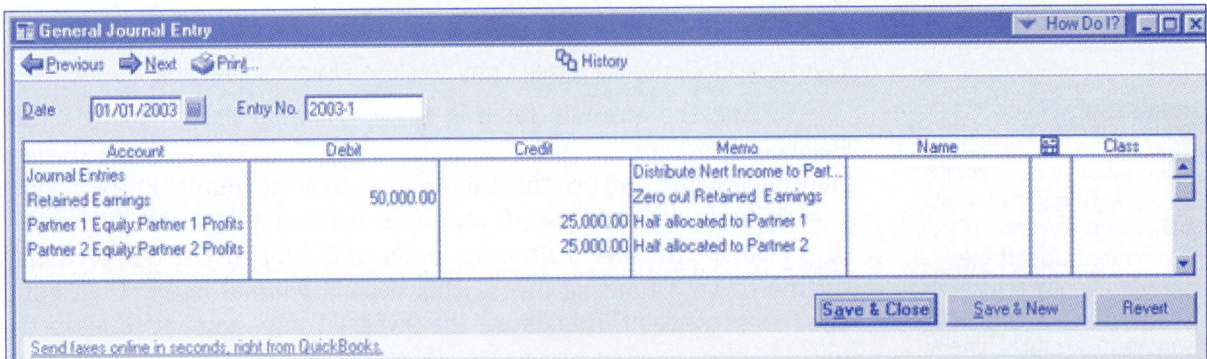

Figure 9-35 Use a General Journal entry to distribute partner's profits

SETTING THE CLOSING DATE TO "LOCK" TRANSACTIONS

COMPUTER TUTORIAL

QuickBooks allows you to set a closing date that effectively locks the file so that no one can make changes to the file on or after a specified date.

To set or modify the closing date and closing date password, follow these steps:

1 Select the *Company* menu and then choose **Set up Users**.

2 If you haven't set up an Administrator for the file yet, enter "Doug" in the *Administrator's Name* field. Enter "1234" in the *Administrator's Password* and *Confirm Password* fields (see Figure 9-36). Click **OK**.

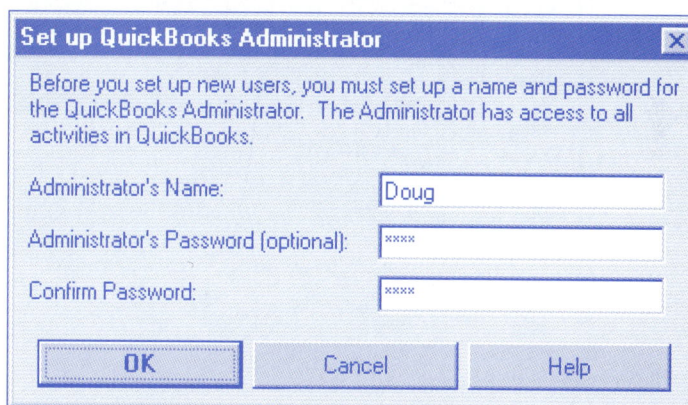

Figure 9-36 The Set up QuickBooks Administrator screen

3 Click **Closing Date** in the User List screen (Figure 9-37).

Clicking **Closing Date** opens the Accounting Company Preferences screen that includes a Closing Date section.

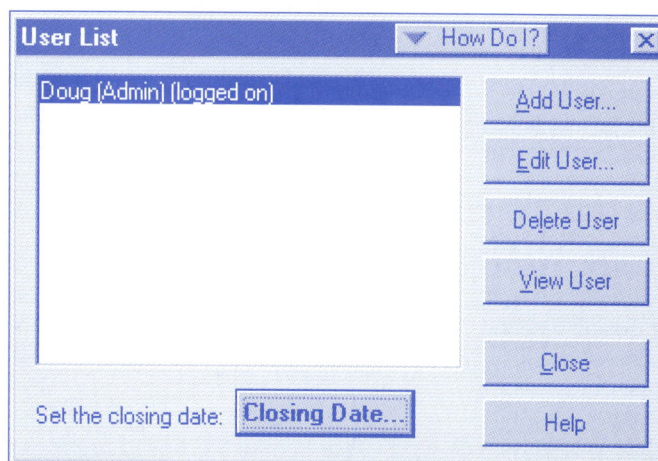

Figure 9-37 Access the Closing Date button from the User List screen.

④ Enter "12/31/2001" in the *Date through which books are closed* field (see Figure 9-38).

The date you enter specifies that all transactions dated on or before that date are "locked." QuickBooks disallows additions, changes, or deletions to any transactions with a date on or before this date.

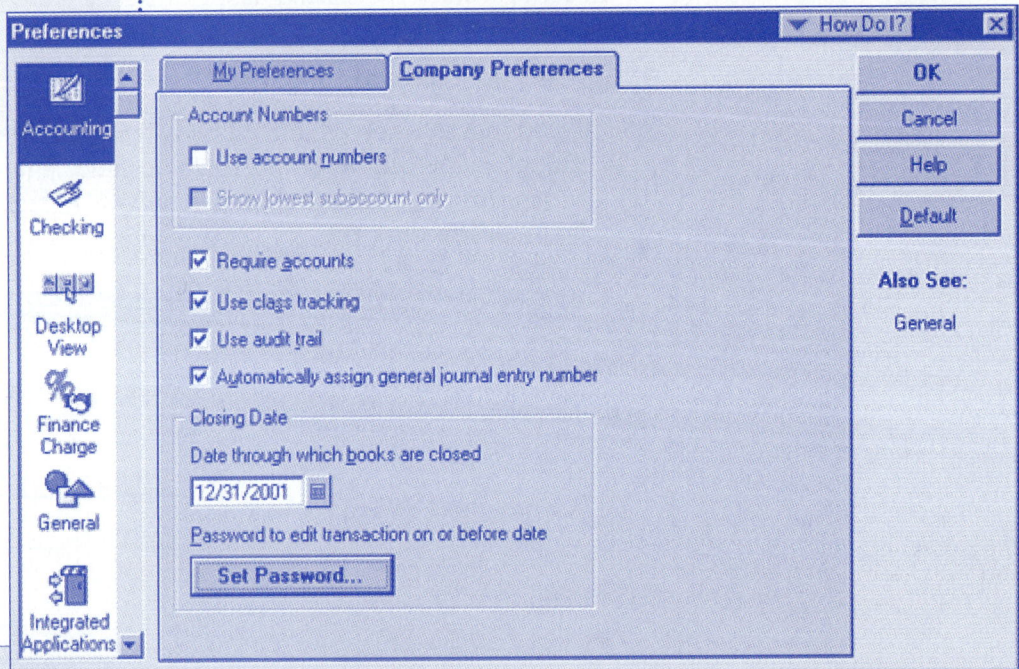

Figure 9-38 Enter 12/31/2001 in the Date through which books are closed section.

⑤ Click **Set Password**.

⑥ Enter "5678" in the *Password* and *Confirm Password* fields, then click **OK** on the Preferences screen and **Close** on the User List screen.

QuickBooks will now require all users to enter this password when attempting to add, change or delete transactions dated on or before the Closing Date.

TIP

The user's set up affects his or her ability to add, change or delete closed ("locked") transactions. When setting up new users, always choose the setting that prevents them from making additions, changes or deletions to transactions recorded on or before the closing date. Unless the Closing Date Password is set, the Administrator of the file can always bypass the closing date with a simple warning screen. To better protect the closing date in your QuickBooks file, require all users, including the Administrator, to enter a Closing Date Password.

IMPORTING AND EXPORTING DATA

With QuickBooks, you can import and export some of your data. In Chapter 5 you learned how to export reports to spreadsheets for further analysis. In addition, you can export your lists (Chart of Accounts, Customers, Vendors, etc.) to a file that can then import into another application such as Word or Excel. You can also import the lists into another QuickBooks data file.

Exporting Lists

Sometimes you may find it necessary to start a new QuickBooks data file. For example, if the data in the file contains numerous data entry errors, fixing the mistakes make take too much time. In this case it is usually best to create a new data file for your company.

The good news is that starting a new file does not have to include setting up your lists all over again. You can export all your lists to a special file (called an "IIF" file) and then import the lists into a new, blank company file.

COMPUTER TUTORIAL

NOTE

QuickBooks saves exported lists with an .IIF extension. The folder in which you save the .IIF file is not important, though it is best to choose a folder that you can find easily, for example My Documents or the Windows Desktop.

1 Select the **File** menu, choose **Utilities**, and then choose **Export** (see Figure 9-39).

2 Click in the "Customer List" and "Vendor List" boxes. Click **OK**.

3 Browse to the C:\My Documents folder and enter "My Lists" in the *File Name* field. Click **Save** (see Figure 9-40). Click **OK** on any subsequent QuickBooks messages.

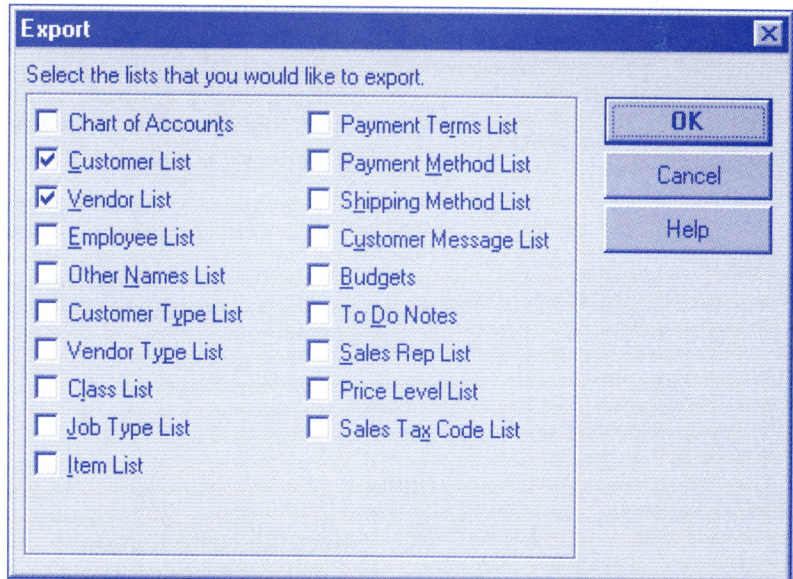

Figure 9-39 Click the lists to export.

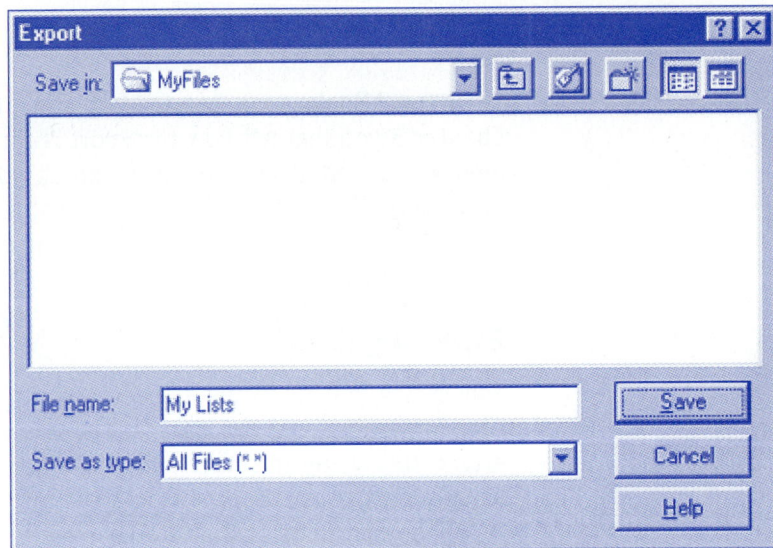

Figure 9-40 Name the export file.

NOTE

QuickBooks Pro allows you to synchronize your contacts with Microsoft Outlook or ACT! See the QuickBooks Pro online Help for details.

COMPUTER TUTORIAL

Exporting Lists to Other Programs

QuickBooks does not allow you to export your transaction data (invoices, checks, deposits, etc.) to other programs except by creating reports and printing the reports to files, as explained in Chapter 5. However, if you want to export any of your *address* lists to another program, you can use the Export Addresses command.

To export your Customers, Vendors, and/or Employee lists so that you can transfer the names into another program such as a database or word processor, follow these steps:

❶ Select the *File* menu, choose **Utilities**, and then choose **Export Addresses** (see Figure 9-41).

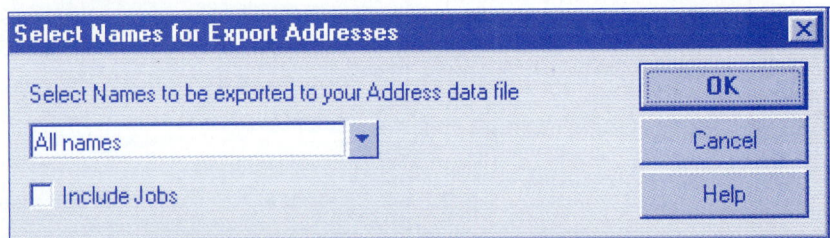

Figure 9-41 The Select Names for Export Addresses screen

❷ Select "All customers/jobs" from the Select Names to be exported to your Address data file drop-down list (see Figure 9-42).

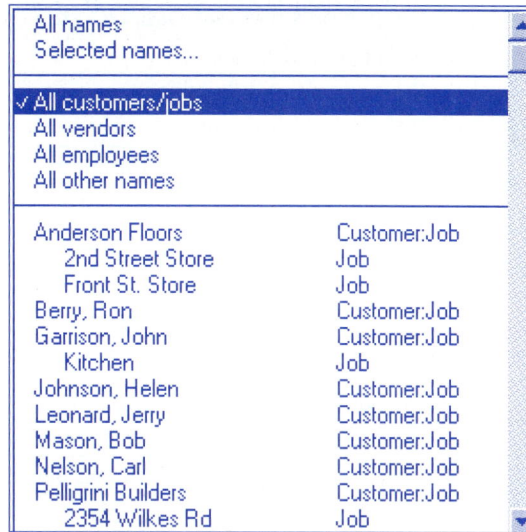

Figure 9-42 Select the names to be exported.

③ Click **OK** to create an export file.

④ On the Save Address Data File screen, browse to the C:\My Documents folder and enter "Company Addresses" in the *File name* field (see Figure 9-43).

⑤ Click **Save**. Click **OK** on any subsequent QuickBooks messages.

This tab-delimited .TXT file contains name and address information for the Customer and Job records in your QuickBooks file. You can now import this file into a word processing program (for mail merging), a spreadsheet program, or a database program.

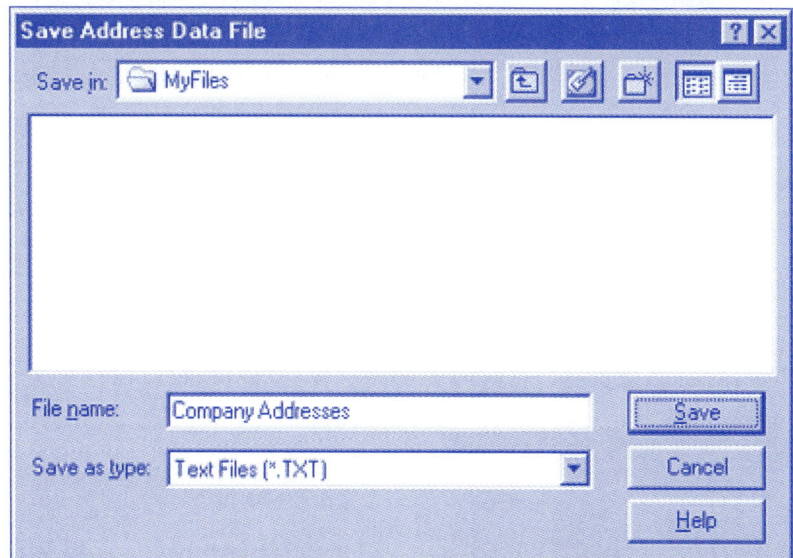

Figure 9-43 Name the export file.

Salutation	The person's title (Mr., Ms., Dr., etc.)
First Name	The person's first name
M.I.	The person's middle initial
Last Name	The person's last name
Company Name	The name of the person's company.
City	The city name in the address. For a customer, the city name comes from the customer's billing address
State	The state in the address. For a customer, the state comes from the customer's billing address
Zip	The Zip Code in the address. For a customer, the zip code comes from the customer's billing address
Country	The name of the country where the customer's business is located
Contact	The name of your main contact person at a company
Alt Contact	The name of an alternate contact person at a company
Address 1 through Address 5	A line in the person's or company's address. QuickBooks exports a separate field for Address 1 through Address 5. For a customer, the address lines come from the customer's billing address
Shipping Address 1 through Shipping Address 5	A line in the customer's shipping address. QuickBooks exports a separate field for Shipping Address 1 through Shipping Address 5 for each line in the address
Shipping City	The city in the customer's shipping address
Shipping State	The state in the customer's shipping address
Shipping Zip	The zip code in the customer's shipping address
Shipping Country	If applicable, the country in the customer's shipping address

Table 9-2 The fields of the exported file

COMPUTER TUTORIAL

> **NOTE**
>
> For more information about templates and customizing forms in QuickBooks, see page 103.

Exporting Templates

You can also export your custom templates for Invoices, Credit Memos, Cash Sales, Purchase Orders, and Statements.

1 Select *Lists* and then choose **Templates**.

2 Click on the "Academy Glass Invoice" to select it (see Figure 9-44).

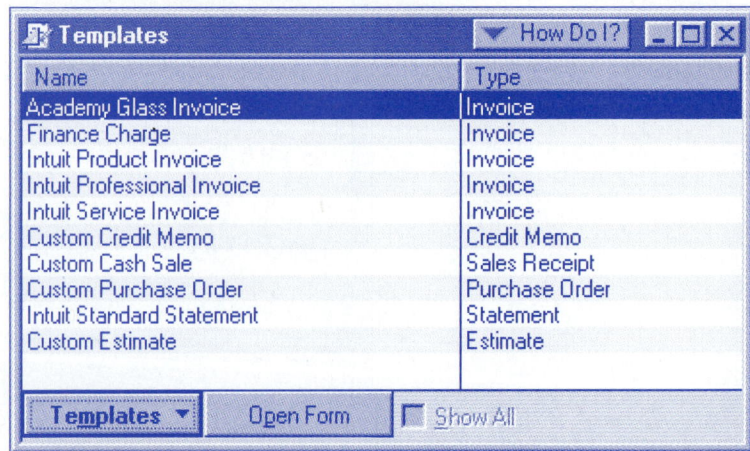

Templates	▼ How Do I? ▢ ▣ ✕
Name	**Type**
Academy Glass Invoice	Invoice
Finance Charge	Invoice
Intuit Product Invoice	Invoice
Intuit Professional Invoice	Invoice
Intuit Service Invoice	Invoice
Custom Credit Memo	Credit Memo
Custom Cash Sale	Sales Receipt
Custom Purchase Order	Purchase Order
Intuit Standard Statement	Statement
Custom Estimate	Estimate

Templates ▼   Open Form   ☐ Show All

Figure 9-44 Select the template to export.

3 Select *Templates* at the bottom of the Templates list, and choose **Export** (see Figure 9-45).

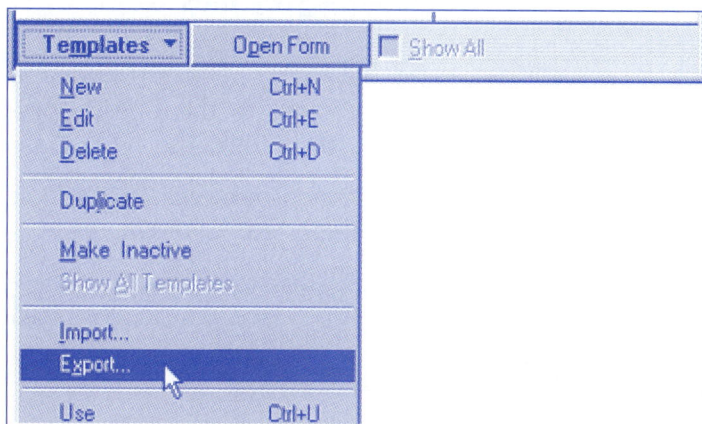

Templates ▼	Open Form	☐ Show All

New   Ctrl+N
Edit   Ctrl+E
Delete   Ctrl+D

Duplicate

Make Inactive
Show All Templates

Import...
Export...
Use   Ctrl+U

Figure 9-45 Select Export from the Templates menu.

4 The file name of "Academy Glass Invoice.DES" is preselected. Browse to the C:\My Documents folder, and click **Save** (see Figure 9-46).

QuickBooks saves exported templates in a special file format with a .DES extension.

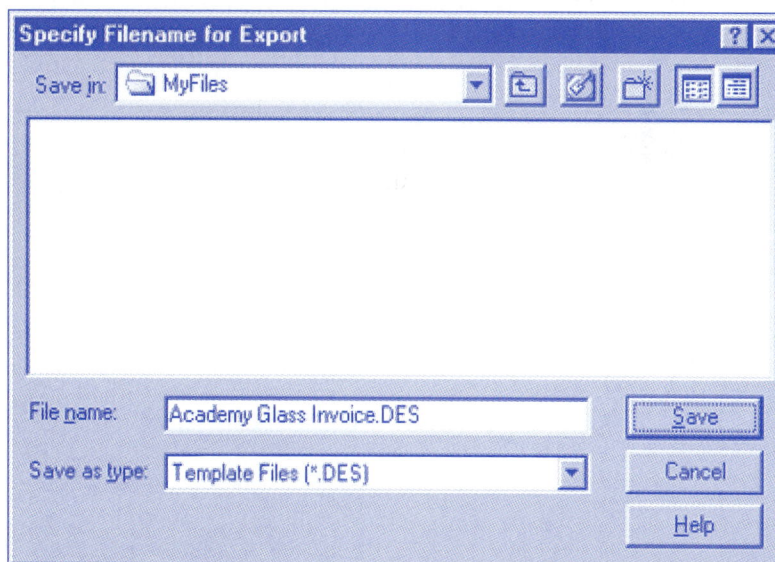

Specify Filename for Export

Save in: MyFiles

File name: Academy Glass Invoice.DES   Save
Save as type: Template Files (*.DES)   Cancel   Help

Figure 9-46 Select the folder in which you will save the exported template.

COMPUTER TUTORIAL

Importing IIF and DES Files

Importing .IIF files

1 Select the *File* menu, choose **Utilities**, and then choose **Import**.

2 Browse to the C:\My Documents folder and click on the "My Lists.IIF" file. Then click **Open** (see Figure 9-47).

3 QuickBooks will display a screen that says "Your data has been imported." Click **OK**.

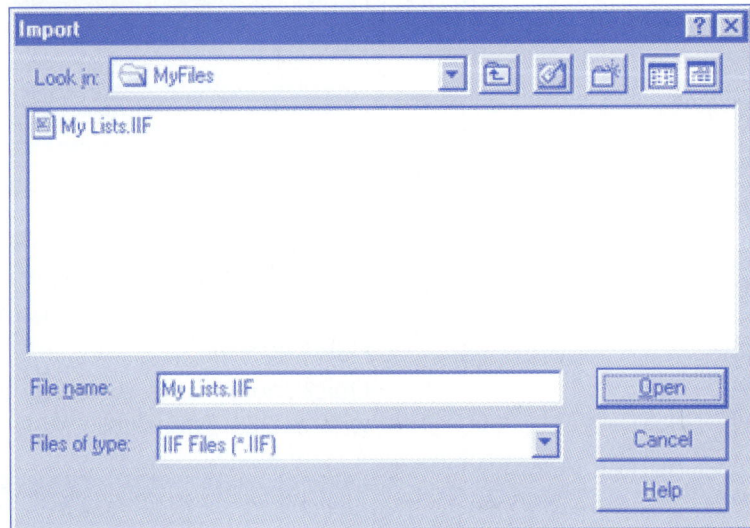

> **NOTE**
>
> It's possible to create your own IIF files, but doing so requires a thorough understanding of the IIF file format. For information on how to create an IIF file, search for "IIF" files in the QuickBooks online Help.

Import

| Look in: | MyFiles |

My Lists.IIF

File name:	My Lists.IIF	Open
Files of type:	IIF Files (*.IIF)	Cancel
		Help

Figure 9-47 Select the file to import.

COMPUTER TUTORIAL

Importing .DES Files

1 Select *Lists* and choose **Templates**.

2 Select *Templates* at the bottom of the Templates List, and choose **Import** (See Figure 9-48).

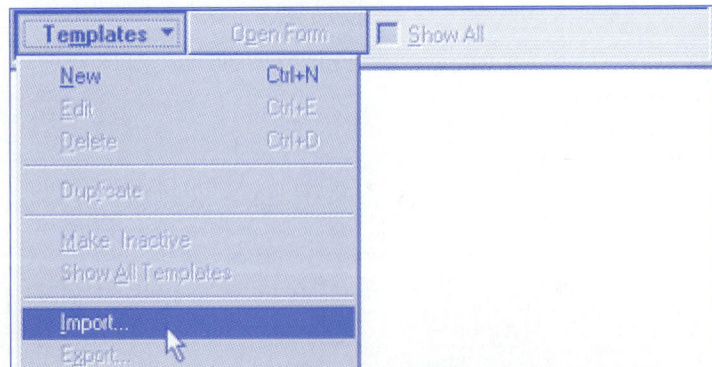

| Templates ▼ | Open Form | ☐ Show All |

New	Ctrl+N
Edit	Ctrl+E
Delete	Ctrl+D
Duplicate	
Make Inactive	
Show All Templates	
Import...	
Export...	

Figure 9-48 Select Import from the Templates menu.

3 Browse to the C:\My Documents folder and click on the "Academy Glass Invoice.DES" file. Then click **Open** (see Figure 9-49).

④ This imports the formatting of the Academy Glass Invoice. If you didn't already have this template in your file, the imported template would show in your templates list.

The Customize Invoice screen may open. Close the screen.

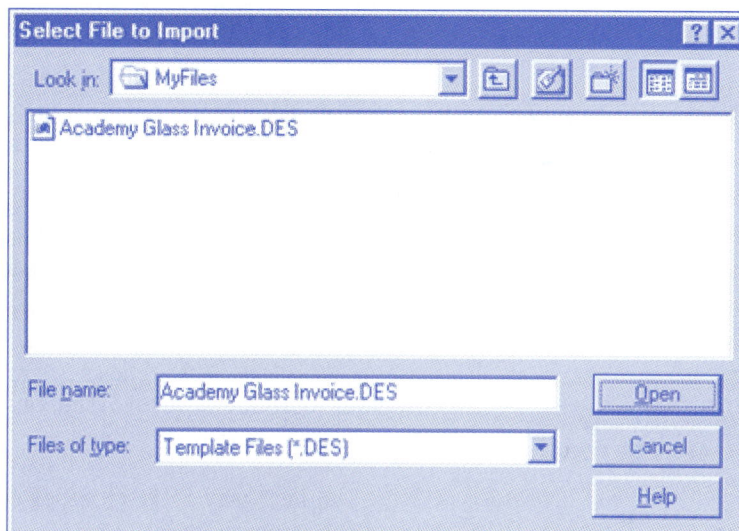

Figure 9-49 Select the file to import.

SUMMARY OF KEY POINTS

In this chapter, you learned how to use QuickBooks to:

◆ Set up and track 1099 vendors (page 451)

◆ Print 1099s (page 454)

◆ Enter adjusting general journal entries (page 458)

◆ Track fixed assets (page 461)

◆ Track loans (page 465)

◆ Memorize and schedule transactions to be automatically entered (page 466)

◆ Close the year and enter special transactions for sole proprietorships and partnerships (page 470)

◆ Set the closing date to lock the company file (page 475)

◆ Import and Export lists and form templates from QuickBooks (page 477)

CHAPTER REVIEW AND APPLICATIONS

Comprehension
QUESTIONS

Done

In your notebook, record answers to the following questions.

1. Discuss the difference between deleting and voiding a transaction in QuickBooks.

2. Why would you not want to make changes to transactions in QuickBooks that are dated in a closed accounting period?

3. How would you set up QuickBooks to automatically enter the depreciation journal entry each month?

4. Explain how QuickBooks automatically closes the year. What effect does it have on your income and expense accounts?

Multiple-Choice
QUESTIONS

Done

In your notebook, record the best answer for each of the following questions.

1. _a_ The best way to track asset cost and depreciation separately on the Balance Sheet is to:
   a. add two subaccounts to each fixed asset. One subaccount tracks the cost of the asset and the other tracks accumulated depreciation.
   b. determine if assets purchased will be expensed immediately or over several years.
   c. associate each asset with an asset number.
   d. recalculate depreciation expense every month.

2. _c_ Which of the following tasks does QuickBooks perform automatically at year-end?
   a. Creates adjusting journal entries to the income and expense accounts which can be viewed in the General Ledger report.
   b. Identifies expenses that are too high in comparison with prior years.
   c. Adjusts the balance in the Retained Earnings account to reflect the net income or loss for the year.
   d. Automatically backs up the data file.

3. _c_ Entering a date in the Closing Date screen accomplishes which of the following:
   a. Determines which date QuickBooks will use to automatically close the year.
   b. Determines which date QuickBooks closes your file.
   c. Locks the data file so that no transactions dated on or before the Closing Date can be added, changed, or deleted.
   d. Prepares a closing entry on that date.

Name _____ **Date** _____

<table>
<tr><td>

Completion

STATEMENTS

Done

</td><td>

In the space provided, write the word(s) that best complete each statement.

1. If you use the *accrual* basis of accounting, the goal is to properly match income and expenses to the period in which the income or expense occur.

2. Use Form 1099-Misc to report payments made to vendors who performed business-related *services* for your company.

3. If your company takes out a loan, set up a *long term liability* account to track it. You will have to split loan payments between interest and principal manually.

4. QuickBooks allows you to set a *Closing date* that effectively locks the file so that no changes can be made to the file on or before a certain date.

5. If a bill payment has not yet been printed and you want to remove it, you should *delete* it. On the other hand, if you have already printed the bill payment, you should _____ *void* _____ it.

</td></tr>
</table>

APPLY YOUR KNOWLEDGE

PROBLEM 9-1

Done

> **Restore the Problem 9-1.QBB file from the CD-ROM and store it on your hard disk according to your instructor's directions.**

Note: This exercise requires that you start with a blank formatted diskette to store your data. If you don't have this, ask your instructor if you can use the hard disk to store these files.

1. Create a General Journal Entry (#2002-2) on 1/31/2002 to recategorize $50.00 from Office Supplies Expense to Postage and Delivery Expense. Use the San Jose class on both sides of the entry. Use the Journal Entries account on the top line of the General Journal Entry as discussed in the chapter. Enter a descriptive memo "Recategorize Postage" on the top line of the entry.

2. Create a General Journal Entry on 1/31/2002 (#2002-3), recording $75.00 in depreciation for Fixed Assets for the San Jose class.

3. Memorize the depreciation journal entry from step 2 and schedule it to be automatically entered every month from February through December.
   Name the transaction "Monthly Depreciation."

4. Enter a Loan Payment check (#334) to Bank of America on 4/19/2002 for $867.88. The Interest portion of the loan payment is $588.00. Class: San Jose.

5. Export your Customer List to a file called "Customers.IIF" on your diskette.

6. Export the Academy Glass Invoice template to a file called "Academy Glass Invoice.DES" on your diskette.

7. Create and print a Balance Sheet as of 1/31/2002.

8. Create and print a Journal report for 1/1/2002 thorough 1/31/2002 (The Journal Report is under **Accountant and Taxes** in the **Reports** menu.) Filter the report to only show Journal transactions.

9. Create and print a Custom Transaction Detail report for 4/1/2002 through 4/30/2002. Filter the report to show only Check transactions.

10. Back up your data to a diskette.

Name _____ Date _____

EXTEND YOUR KNOWLEDGE

PROBLEM 9-2

> **Restore the Problem 9-2.QBB file from the CD-ROM to your hard drive according to your instructor's directions.**

1. Add the following fixed asset accounts and subaccounts to your Chart of Accounts.

   Office Furniture

   Cost (subaccount to Office Furniture)

   Accumulated Depreciation (subaccount to Office Furniture)

   Truck

   Cost (subaccount to Truck)

   Accumulated Depreciation (subaccount to Truck)

2. Record the transactions for April listed below.

April 1	Prepare Check #334 to Sinclair Insurance for $2,400.00. This should be classified as a prepaid expense. The insurance premium of $2,400.00 is for a two-year period, so you'll enter a General Journal Entry later to allocate this expense to the appropriate months. For now, just code the transaction to Prepaid Expense.
April 5	Office furniture purchased from Jones Office Supply, for the San Jose location $2,567.82. Paid with National Bank Visa Gold. Ref. # 72318. Code this purchase to Office Furniture:Cost. (**Note:** QuickFill will automatically enter fill your entry with previously recorded data. Overwrite the QuickFill data with this new information.)
April 9	Prepare Check #335 for $600 to the San Jose Dispatch (Quick Add the vendor) for advertising expenses prepaid for six months. This should be classified as a Prepaid Expense.
April 10	Transfer $12,000 from the Money Market account to the Checking account.
April 11	Prepare Check #336 for $12,500 to Clark Auction, Inc. (Quick Add the vendor) for purchase of used truck. Class: Overhead.

3. Create and print a Balance Sheet (Standard) as of April 30, 2002.

4. Create and print a Profit & Loss (Standard) for January through April 2002.

5. Record the Adjustments listed below. All adjustments should be dated April 30, 2002.

Adjustments

Adj 1.	Ron Berry was incorrectly charged for 6 hours of design service. The actual charge should have been for 5 hours. Mr. Berry has asked for a corrected invoice. Edit Invoice 2002-111 to reflect the correction without changing the original invoice date.
Adj 2.	The freight charges were not added to the Bill (#4431) from Ace Glass. Edit the bill to include freight charges of $47.12 for the 104 Sliders and $53.14 to the 106 Sliders. The new total of the bill should be $2,350.26. (**Hint:** use Quick Math to add the freight amounts to the "amount" column for each item on the bill.)
Adj 3.	Create a General Journal Entry (dated 4/30/02 #2002-2) to allocate the insurance expense for the month (refer to April 1 transaction above). The prepaid amount was $2,400.00 for two years (April 1, 2002 through March 31, 2003), and you need to allocate the expenses for the month of April 2002 (Hint: Debit Liability Insurance Expense, Credit Prepaid Expenses.) Class: Overhead. Memorize the transaction and have it automatically entered into QuickBooks each month as Liability Insurance. (**Hint:** Enter the first General Journal Entry on 4/30/02 and schedule the next General Journal Entry to be entered on 5/31/02 for the next 23 months.)
Adj 4.	Create a General Journal Entry (dated 4/30/02 #2002-3) to allocate the monthly advertising cost (refer to April 9 transaction above). Memorize the transaction and have it automatically entered for the next 5 months beginning on 5/31/02. Class: Overhead.
Adj 5.	Purchase of advertising flyers from Jones Office Supply (Credit Card transaction for $86.48, dated February 15) was incorrectly classified as Office Supplies. Make a correcting General Journal Entry (dated 4/30/02 #2002-4) to reclassify this transaction. The correct account should be Printing and Reproduction (**Hint:** Debit Printing and Reproduction, Credit Office Supplies). Class: San Jose.
Adj 6.	Create a General Journal Entry (dated 4/30/02 #2002-5) to allocate the Depreciation Expense for the Office Furniture for April 2002. The Depreciation Expense is $53.50 (**Hint:** Debit Depreciation Expense, Credit Office Furniture: Accumulated Depreciation.) Class: San Jose. Memorize the transaction but don't have it automatically entered.
Adj 7.	Create a General Journal Entry (dated 4/30/02 #2002-6) to allocate the Depreciation Expense for the Truck for April 2002. The Depreciation Expense is $260.42 (**Hint:** Debit Depreciation Expense, Credit Truck:Accumulated Depreciation.) Class: San Jose. Memorize the transaction but don't have it automatically entered.

6. Print Invoice #2002-111 on blank paper.

7. Print a Journal Report for the month of April 2002, filtered for Journal transaction type (The Journal Report is under **Accountant and Taxes** in the *Reports* menu). Filter the report for Journal transaction type, so that it only displays journal entries for April.

Name _____ Date _____

8. Print a Balance Sheet (Standard) as of April 30, 2002.

9. Print a Statement of Cash Flows for the month of April 2002.

10. Print a Profit and Loss (Standard) for the period of January through April 2002.

DISCUSSION QUESTIONS

These questions are designed to help you apply what you are learning about QuickBooks to your own organization. Use your notebook to record your answers and your thoughts.

1. What circumstances would lead your company to change or delete transactions? What kinds of information does your company require before authorizing these alterations? Why is it important to document these changes?

2. If your company is a for-profit organization, who owns your company? If there is more than one owner, what kind of business relationship do they have?

3. How is capital obtained for the company? How many investors support the company?

4. Does your organization have outstanding loans? If so, how frequently are payments due and how are they handled?

5. Does your organization have a year-end checklist of transactions that must be completed before closing the year? If so, how does it compare to the checklist in this chapter? If not, what transactions on the checklist in this chapter are needed for your organization?

ACTIVITY

1. Research how many people are using QuickBooks in your organization. Determine if all of them should use every function in QuickBooks or whether security levels should be set. Identify the employees that you would group together for various functions.

2. Research whether exporting lists of Customers or Vendors would be helpful to your organization. Evaluate how these lists can be utilized in advertising or newsletter mailing for the sales representatives, secretaries, managers, etc.

Workplace *Applications*

CASE STUDY

2-LEARN.COM

John and Shauna start a new Internet-based company that helps training companies across the nation convert their training materials to a product that can be accessed from any home or office computer with a modem and a microphone. They form the company as a partnership. Both invest $20,000 to get the company running in the first year. However, Shauna works in the company 5 days per week while John just works 3 days per week. Therefore, they have agreed to split profits at year-end with Shauna taking 60% of the profit.

They have decided that Shauna should also be allowed to draw out $500 per month to offset the extra time she works so long as the company's revenue exceeds expenses in that month.

Questions

These questions are designed to help you apply what you are learning about QuickBooks to this case study. Use your notebook to record your answers and your thoughts.

1. Describe if and how you would set up the equity section of the Chart of Accounts.

2. How would you record the monthly draw of $500 for Shauna?

3. At the end of the year, the Net Income for the company was $111,000. The balance in Shauna's Drawing account was $6,000 and the balance in John's Drawing account was $5,000. How would you create the closing entries to close the drawing accounts and allocate the net income to each of the partners?

*inter***NET**
CONNECTION

Are you interested in accounting education and research? Then try
http://www.rutgers.edu/accounting/raw/aaa.

Company File Setup and Maintenance

OBJECTIVES

After completing this chapter, you should be able to:

1. Use the EasyStep Interview to set up your company file.

2. Use the alternative 12-step process of setting up your company file without using the EasyStep Interview.

3. Choose a start date and understand its implications on your setup.

4. Understand what information you need to set up your file.

5. Modify the Chart of Accounts.

6. Set up beginning balances in the General Ledger accounts.

7. Verify your setup balances and compare them with your accountant's reports.

8. Set up users and passwords in your file.

RESTORE THIS FILE

This chapter uses Chapter 10.QBW. To open this file, restore the tutorial template called **Chapter 10.QBB** to your hard disk. (See page 7 for instructions on restoring files).

I n this chapter you will learn how to create a new QuickBooks data file, setup the Chart of Accounts and enter opening balances. You will also learn how to setup user access rights and passwords for each person who will use QuickBooks.

COMPANY FILE SETUP: THE EASYSTEP INTERVIEW

QuickBooks provides an EasyStep Interview that walks you through the setup of a company file. The EasyStep Interview is very simple to use. If you're new to QuickBooks or are unfamiliar with accounting principles, you might find that using the EasyStep Interview is the simplest way to set up your company file. However, if you're familiar with accounting or with QuickBooks, you might find the 12-step process presented on page 504 to be more efficient. You can also use the EasyStep Interview for some of the setup, and the 12-step process for the rest of the setup. It's your choice, so pick the method that is best for you.

Launching the EasyStep Interview

COMPUTER TUTORIAL

❶ Select the *File* menu and choose **New Company**. The EasyStep Interview screen appears (see Figure 10-1).

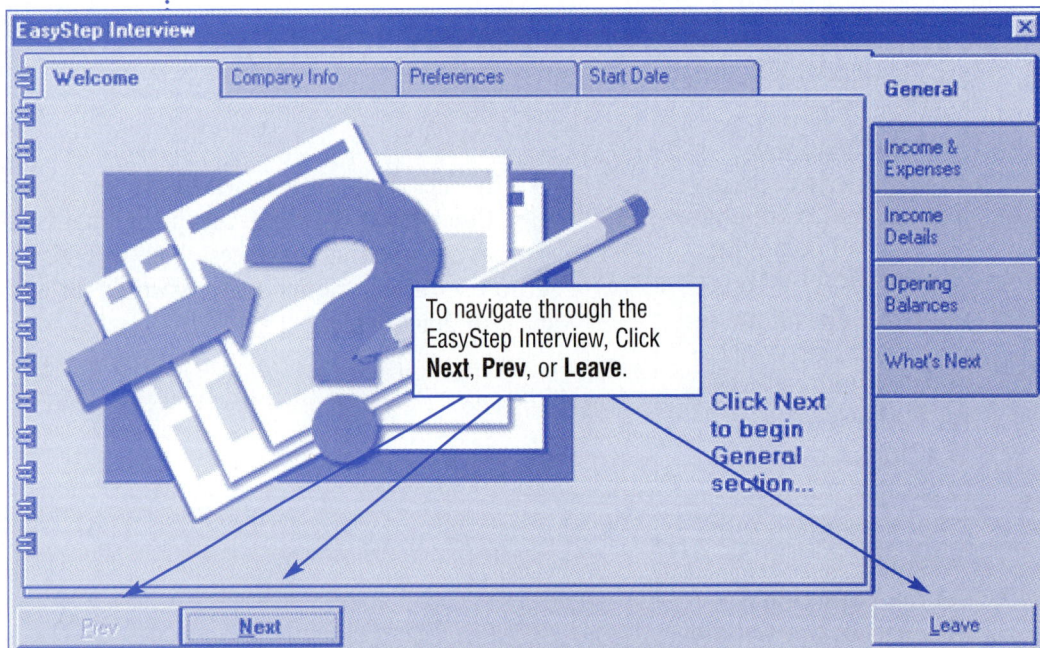

Figure 10-1 The opening screen of the EasyStep Interview

The EasyStep Interview allows you to go step by step through each area of the program that must be set up prior to working with your data. To proceed to the next step in the process click **Next**. To back up in the process, click **Prev**. To cancel the Interview (but retain all changes) click **Leave**.

The Interview asks you a series of questions. As you answer, QuickBooks creates your lists and enters opening balances into your new file.

❷ Click **Next**.

KEY TERM

Professional Advisors are bookkeepers, accountants, software consultants, and CPAs who offer QuickBooks-related consulting services. Some Professional Advisors undergo a testing process to become Certified in QuickBooks. For more information about QuickBooks Professional Advisors, refer to QuickBooks online Help.

③ On the second screen of the Interview (see Figure 10-2), QuickBooks asks if you need any help setting up QuickBooks and provides a link to their website where you can search for a QuickBooks Professional Advisor in your area. Click **Next**.

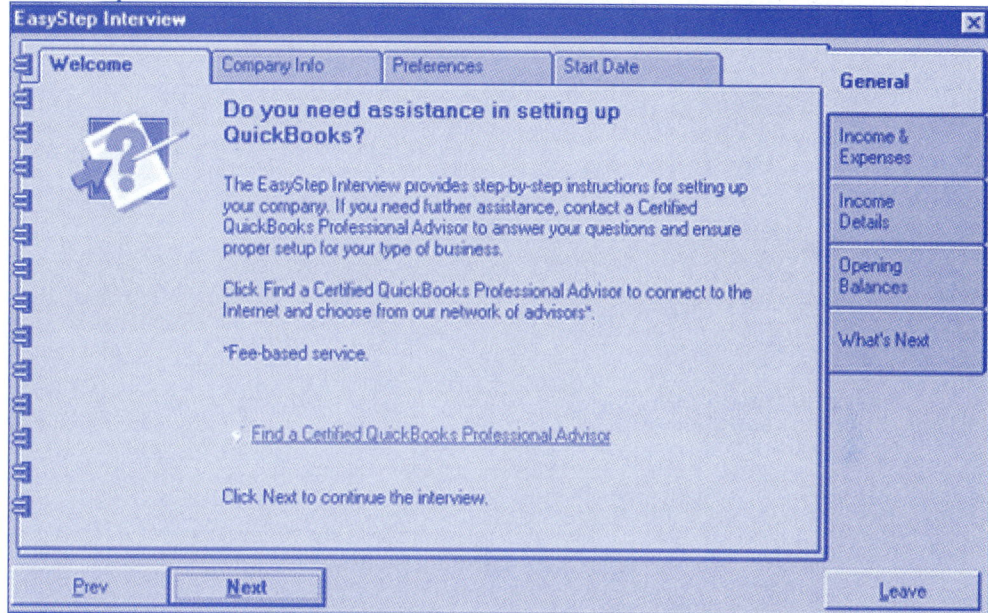

Figure 10-2 The second screen of the EasyStep Interview

On the third screen of the EasyStep Interview (see Figure 10-3), you can either skip the Interview, or continue on to each section, answering questions as you go. If you choose **Skip Interview**, see *Complete Company File Setup* on page 504 for instructions on continuing your company setup.

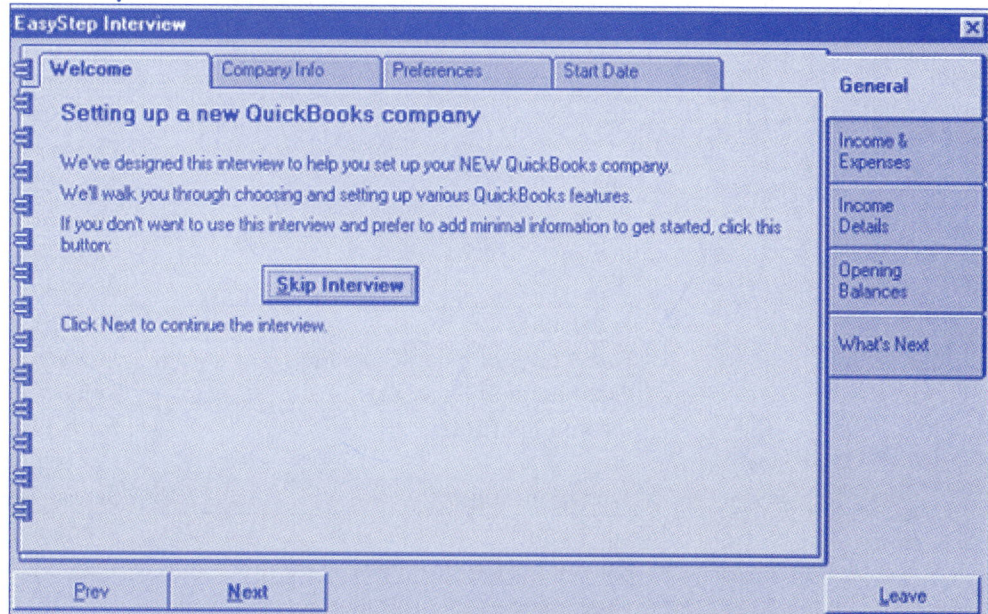

Figure 10-3 The third screen of the EasyStep Interview

④ To continue using the EasyStep Interview, click **Next** (see Figure 10-3).

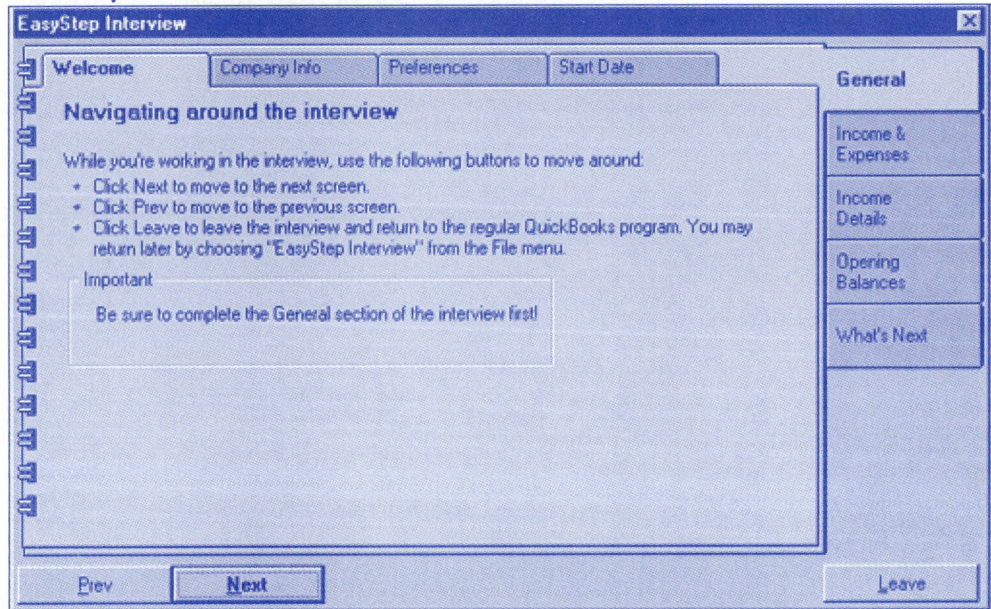

EasyStep Interview

Welcome	Company Info	Preferences	Start Date

General

Income & Expenses

Income Details

Opening Balances

What's Next

Navigating around the interview

While you're working in the interview, use the following buttons to move around:

* Click Next to move to the next screen.
* Click Prev to move to the previous screen.
* Click Leave to leave the interview and return to the regular QuickBooks program. You may return later by choosing "EasyStep Interview" from the File menu.

Important

Be sure to complete the General section of the interview first!

Prev   Next   Leave

Figure 10-4 The instructions for navigating the interview

⑤ Read the Navigating around the interview screen (see Figure 10-4), and continue to click **Next** until you get to the Company Info tab.

⑥ Continue by filling out the Company Info tab of the interview, using the information from Table 10-1.

When you reach a screen where you're unsure about the answer, click the **More** button at the bottom of the interview screen. The on screen Help should answer most of your questions.

Company Info	
Company Name	Academy Glass
Legal Name	Academy Glass, Inc.
Address	123 Main Street Pleasanton, CA 94566
Phone #	925-555-1111
Fax #	925-555-1112
E-mail	info@academyglass.com
Web	www.academyglass.com
Federal ID	11-3456789
First Month of Income Tax Year	January
First Month of Fiscal Year	January
Income Tax Form	Form 1120S (S Corporation)
Type of Business	Service Business
File Name	Academy Glass.QBW
Do you want to use these accounts?	Yes
How many people (besides yourself) will have access to your QuickBooks company	0

Table 10-1 Data for the Company Info tab

7 After you enter your type of business, QuickBooks asks for the file name and the folder in which you want to store the file. Ask your instructor for the folder or disk that you should use to store your file.

The Save As screen (see Figure 10-5) is where you specify the filename and location for your company file. QuickBooks preselects your company name followed by .qbw as your filename. If you want to change the name, type over the preselected name.

In the *Save in* field, select the folder on your hard disk where you want to store the file. You should always keep your data files in a folder separate from your applications, because this keeps your hard disk better organized and it makes it easier to work with backup programs.

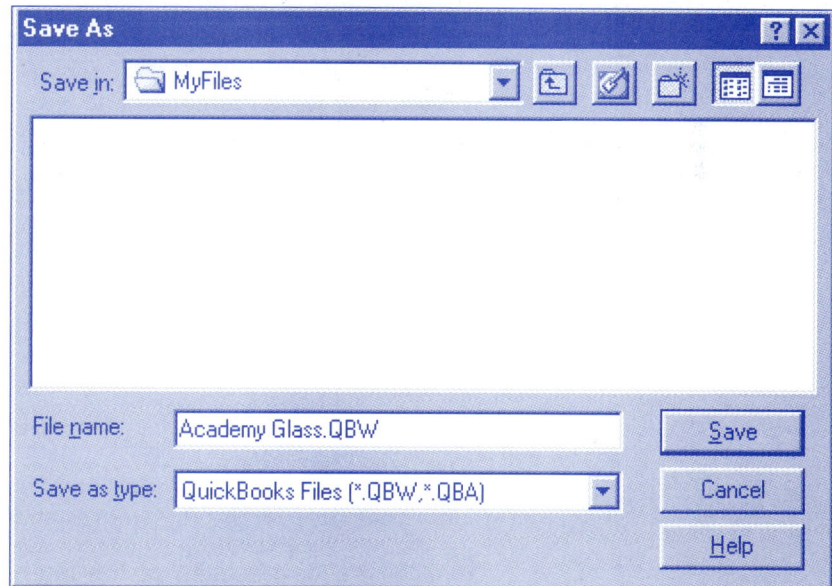

Figure 10-5 The Save As screen

8 Click **Save** and complete the Company Info tab (see Table 10-1).

9 Proceed through the Interview until you reach the Preferences tab, continue filling in the information using Table 10-2.

Preferences	
Does your company maintain inventory?	Yes
Do you want to turn on the inventory feature?	Yes
Do you collect sales tax from your customers?	Yes
Sales Tax	I collect multiple tax rates or have multiple agencies.
Invoice Format	Service
Do you want to use the QuickBooks Payroll feature?	Yes
Do you prepare written or verbal estimates for your customers?	Yes
Do you ever issue more than one Invoice for one estimate?	No
Would you like to track the time that you or your employees spend on each job or project?	No
Do you want to use classes?	Yes
Choose one of the two following ways to track your bill payments.	Enter the bills first and then enter the payments later.
How often would you like to see our Reminders List?	When I ask for it
Start Date	
Company Start Date	12/31/2001

Table 10-2 Data for the Preferences and Start Date tabs

10 In the next section of the interview, QuickBooks allows you to modify the income and expenses section of your Chart of Accounts. We'll modify the Chart of Accounts on page 509. Click **Next** until you reach the screen in Figure 10-6.

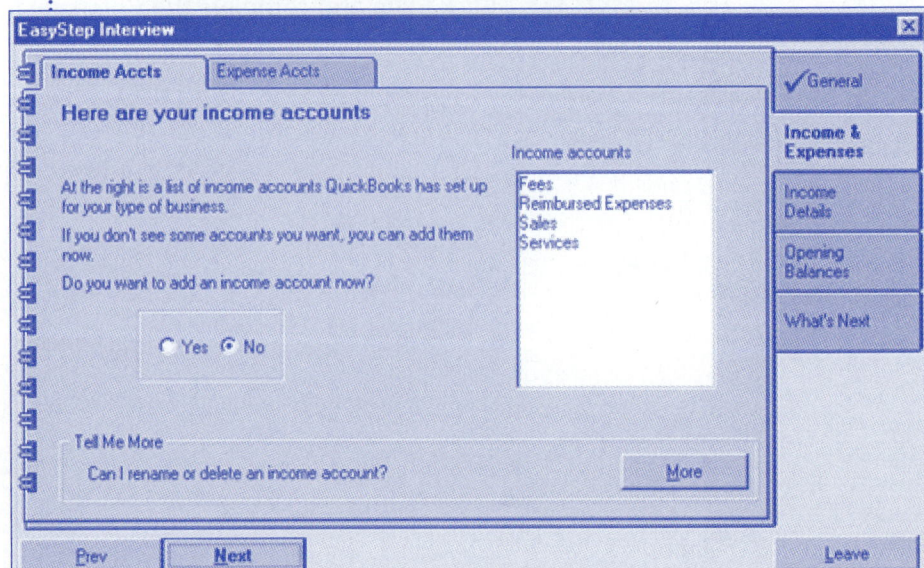

Figure 10-6 The Income Accounts screen

⑪ Select "No" and click **Next**.

⑫ Continue clicking **Next** until you reach the Expense Accounts screen shown in Figure 10-7.

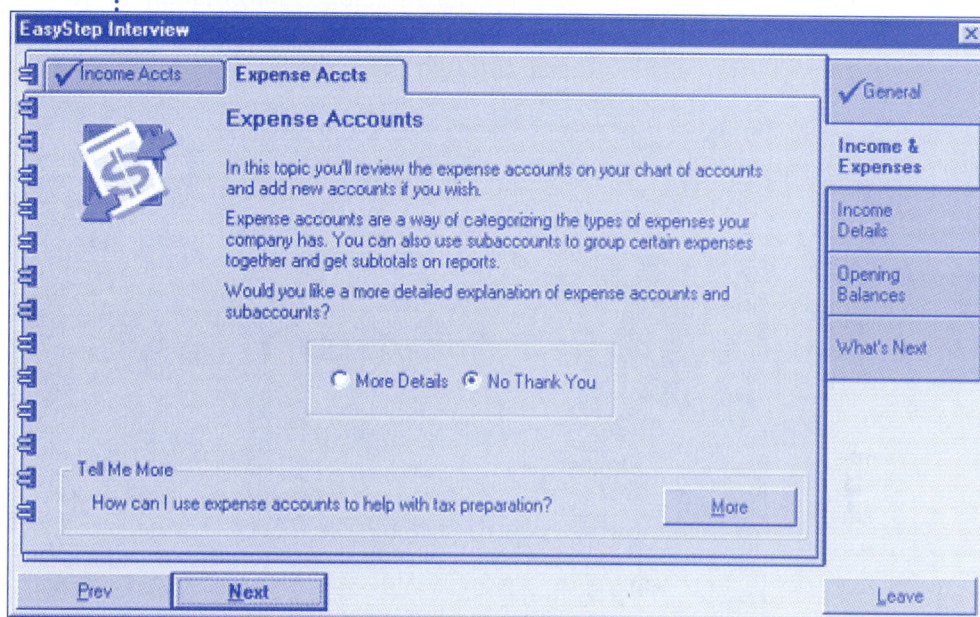

Figure 10-7 The Expense Accounts screen

⑬ Select "No Thank You" on the screen in Figure 10-7, and click **Next**.

⑭ On the screen shown in Figure 10-8, select "No" and click **Next**.

You would use this screen to add expenses to your Chart of Accounts. You can add accounts to the Chart of Accounts at any time, so you don't need to do it in the Interview. See page 512 for detailed instructions for adding accounts.

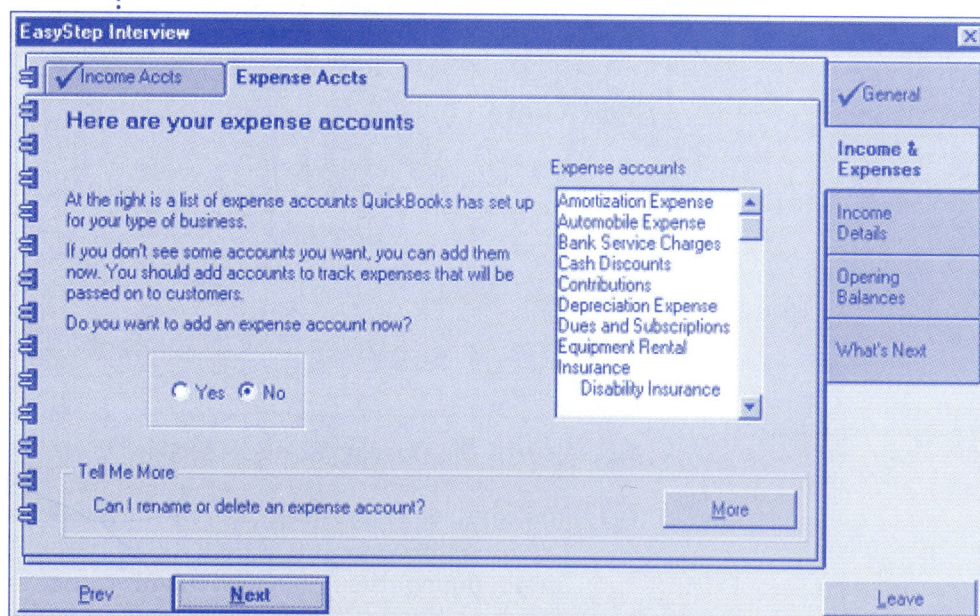

Figure 10-8 Add expense accounts in this screen.

⑮ The Income Details section (see Figure 10-9) is where you define the Items that you buy and sell in your business. To learn more about Items, click the **More** button on each of these screens. This book includes detailed information on Items on page 87. Answer "No" to each of the questions in this section and click **Next** to skip through the screens.

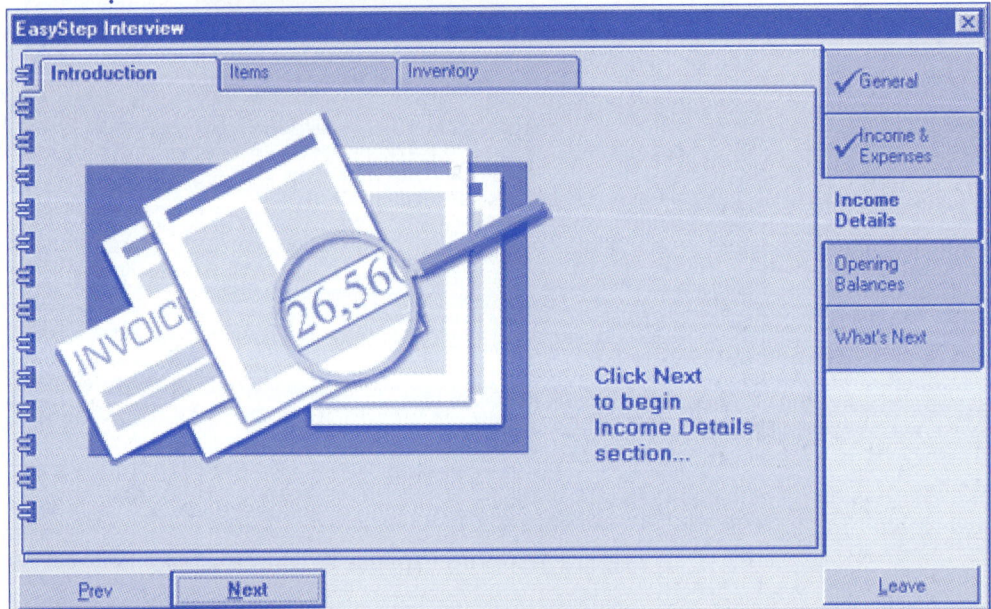

Figure 10-9 Define items in this screen.

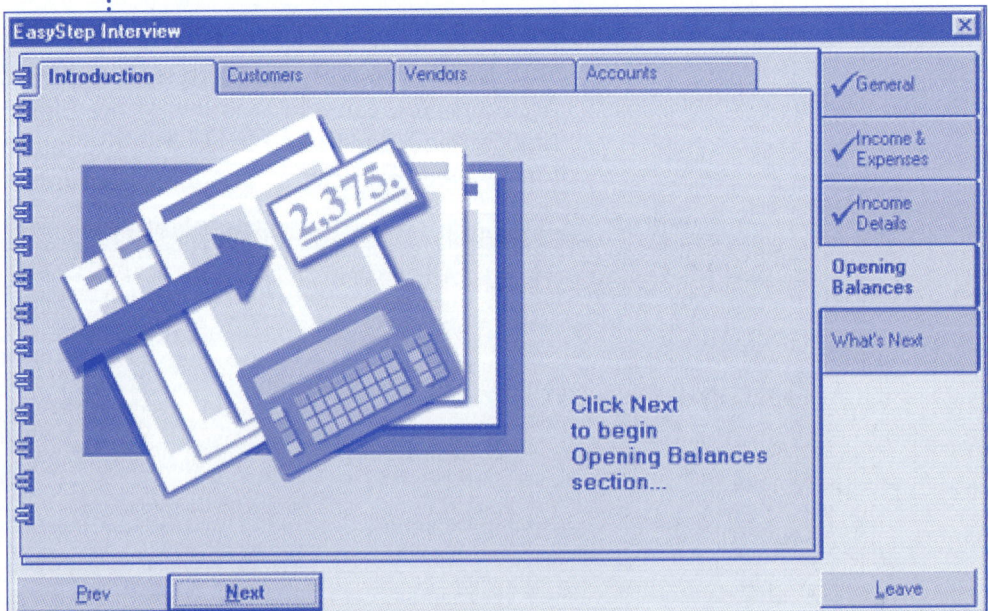

Figure 10-10 The Opening Balances section

⑯ You should always skip the Opening Balances section of the EasyStep Interview (see Figure 10-10) because entering your balances during the Interview might cause problems later. For details on the possible problems caused by entering opening balances during the Interview, see page 500. An alternative method of entering opening balances without using the EasyStep Interview is discussed beginning on page 520.

To skip the Opening Balances section, click the What's Next tab on the right side of the screen. Then click **Next**.

⑰ Read each screen in the What's Next section (see Figure 10-11), clicking **Next** after each screen.

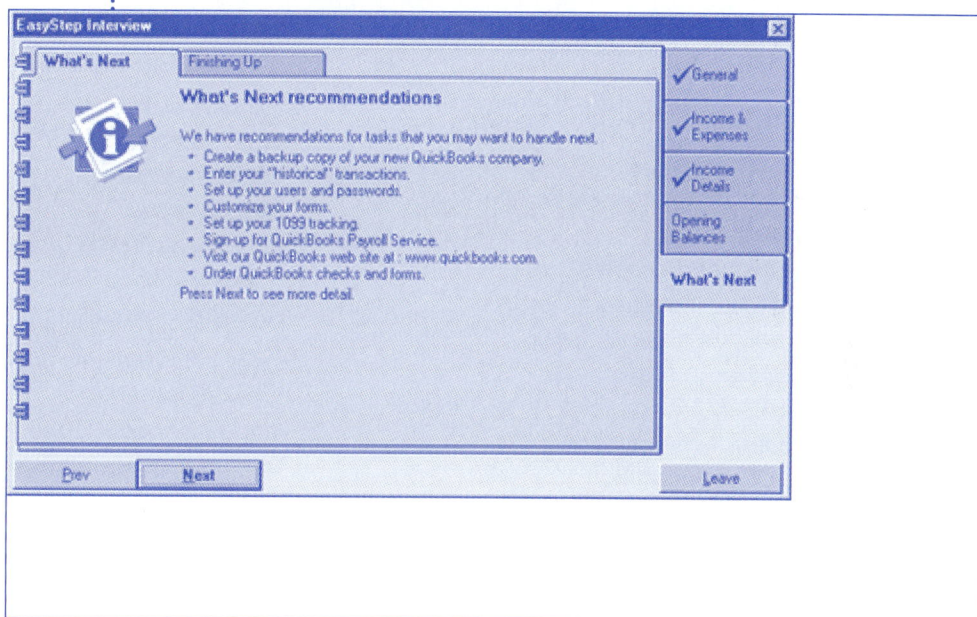

Figure 10-11 The What's Next recommendations screen

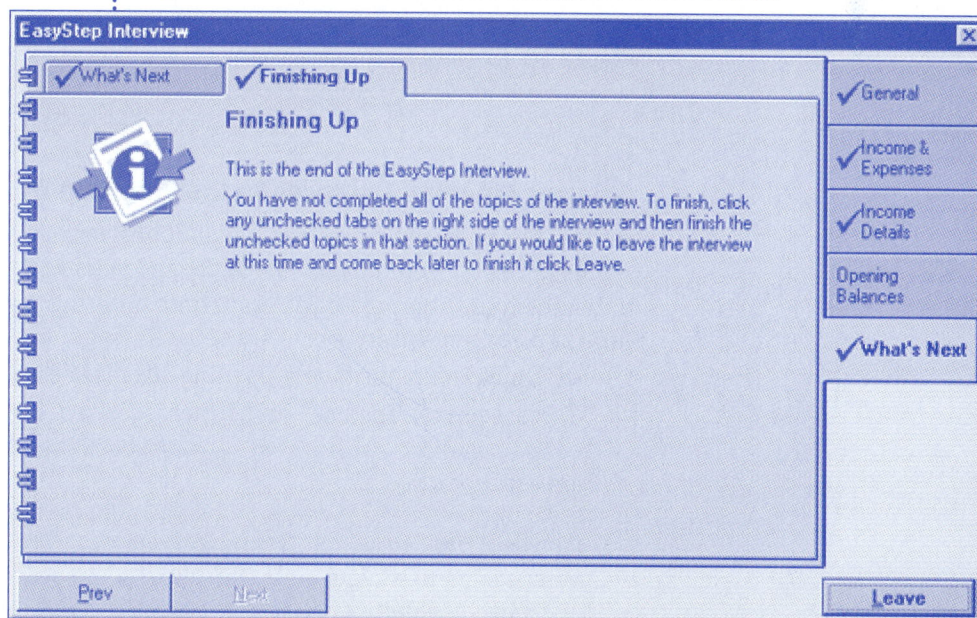

Figure 10-12 The Finishing Up Screen

⑱ When you are finished reading all the screens in the What's Next section, you'll see the screen in Figure 10-12. Click **Leave**. Now you're ready to start using your QuickBooks company file.

⑲ When you leave the EasyStep Interview, you'll see the screen in Figure 10-13. Explore some of the new features in QuickBooks Pro 2001 by clicking on any of the underlined phrases.

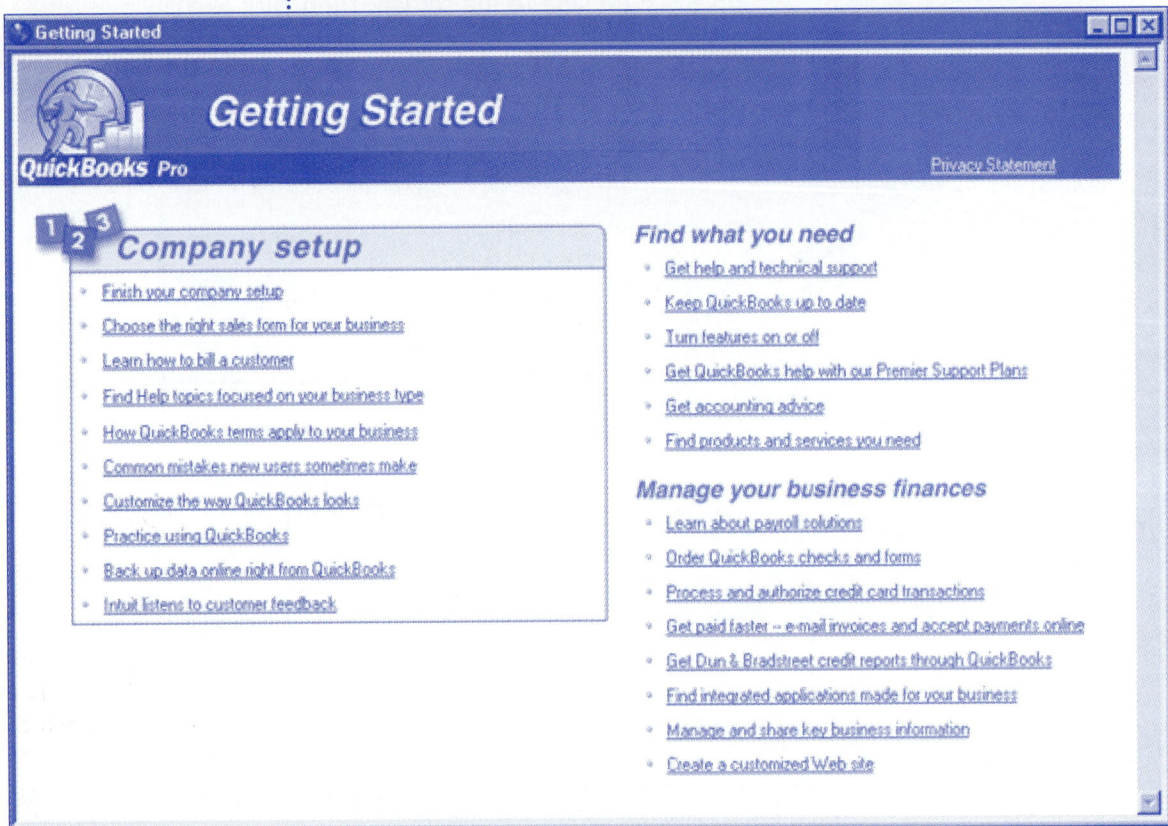

Figure 10-13 New Features screen

Entering Opening Balances in the EasyStep Interview

During the EasyStep Interview, QuickBooks asks you to enter the opening balances for your customers (A/R) and vendors (A/P) as of your start date. The following problems result from entering opening balances during the EasyStep Interview:

◆ QuickBooks posts the opening balances to accounts called "Uncategorized Income" and "Uncategorized Expenses."

IMPORTANT

It is best *not* to enter Opening Balances through the EasyStep Interview. When you do, QuickBooks creates an Invoice that increases (debits) Accounts Receivable, and increases (credits) Uncategorized Income. You or your accountant will then need to adjust the balance in uncategorized income before you can use QuickBooks reports to prepare your tax return. Instead, enter each unpaid Invoice separately after you create the customer record.

◆ If you enter balances for your customers and vendors during the Interview, QuickBooks assigns your start date (12/31/01) to all opening balance transactions. Because of this, your aging reports won't provide the proper aging of these open Invoices and unpaid Bills.

◆ The EasyStep Interview allows you to enter only the total balance due from each customer and the total balance owed to each vendor. Therefore, you won't be able to assign customer Payments to individual Invoices and you won't be able to assign Bill Payments to individual Bills.

◆ Opening balance transactions entered during the Interview do not record class or job-costing information.

◆ After you enter opening balances in the EasyStep Interview, it is not possible to change these balances during the interview. To change any of your setup balances, you'll need to modify the setup transactions directly.

Adjusting Customer and Vendor Opening Balances after the EasyStep Interview

If you choose to set up customer and vendor balances during the EasyStep Interview, many of your reports will be inaccurate for your start date. For example, the A/R and A/P Aging reports will show all amounts as "current" (because of the date on the transactions), even though that may not be the case. Also, if you report on the cash basis, the income and expenses from your customer and vendor open balances will show as "Uncategorized Income" and "Uncategorized Expenses" on your Profit & Loss report for the first year.

To fix these problems, you'll need to fix the opening balance transactions and eliminate the Uncategorized Income and Uncategorized Expenses accounts. Actually, you don't have to eliminate the uncategorized accounts, but your records will be cleaner if you follow this procedure. This process is about the same as entering individual Invoices and Bills for all your opening balances for customers and vendors.

Adjusting Customer Opening Balances

Each customer for whom you entered an open balance will have an Invoice that you must either edit or replace. Similarly, each vendor for whom you entered an open balance will have a Bill that you must either edit or replace.

Don't perform these steps now. They are for reference only.

1. Display the Chart of Accounts.

2. Scroll down to the income accounts and double-click on **Uncategorized Income** (see Figure 10-14).

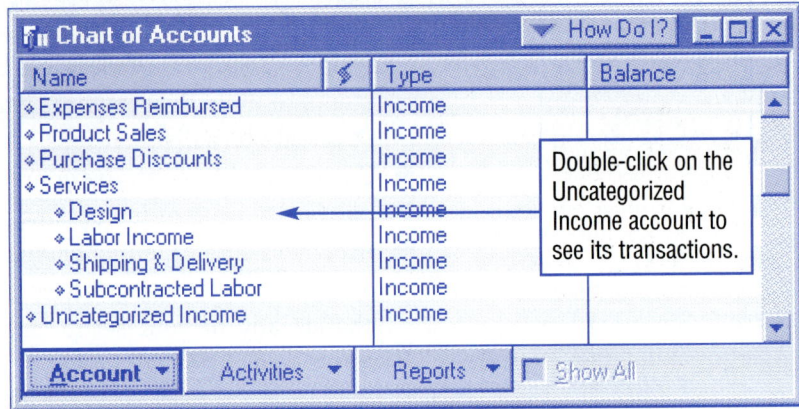

Figure 10-14 Chart of Accounts with Uncategorized Income

QuickBooks would have created this account automatically if you had entered the opening balance for a customer during the EasyStep Interview.

QuickBooks will also create this account automatically if you add an opening balance on the New Customer screen (see Figure 10-15).

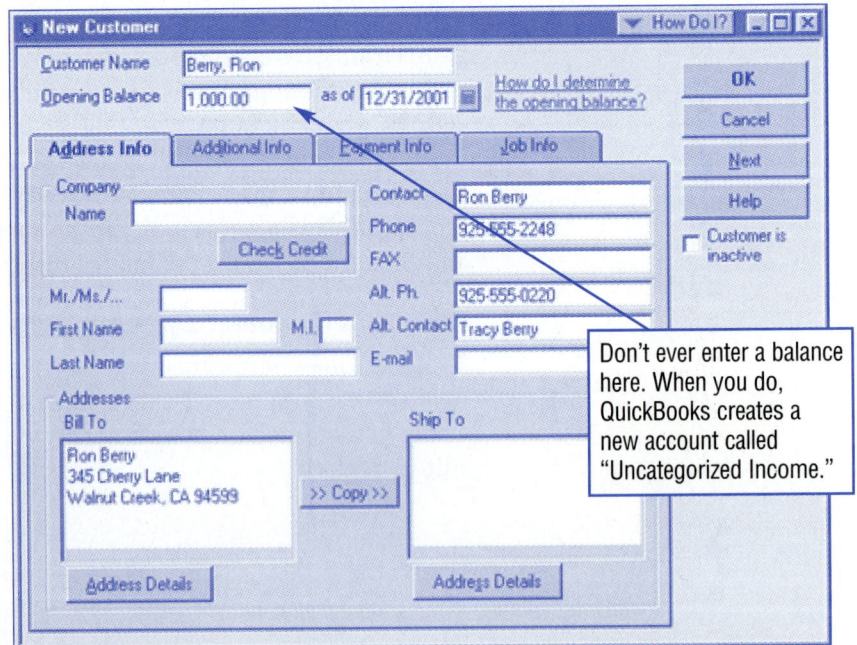

Figure 10-15 Using the *Opening Balance* field when creating a customer record

3. When you double-click on the Uncategorized Income account, QuickBooks creates an Account QuickReport (see Figure 10-16). This report shows each Invoice that QuickBooks created when you entered opening balances for your customers. Set the date range to show all dates by selecting the *Dates* drop-down menu and choosing "All."

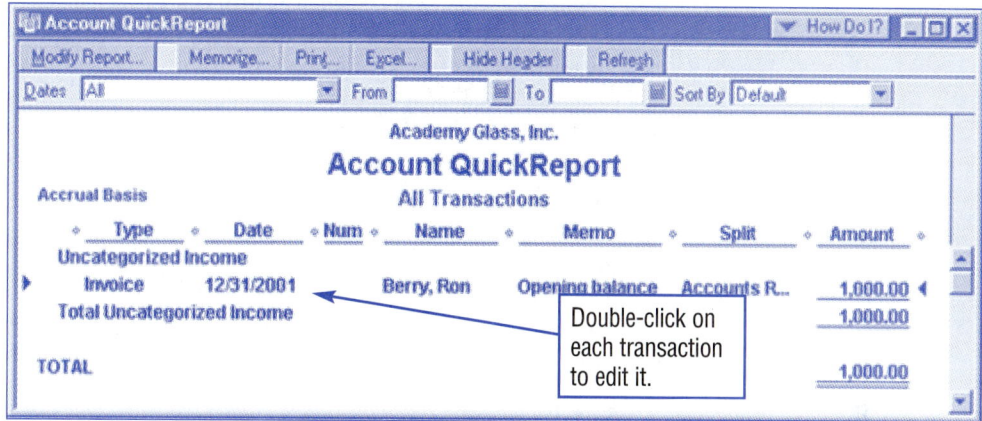

Figure 10-16 The Account QuickReport

4. One at a time, double-click on each transaction in your report. This displays each Invoice that QuickBooks created when you entered the opening balances.

   Notice that on the Invoice in Figure 10-17, the detail lines don't have Items and the Description column shows simply "Opening Balance." This is how QuickBooks created the Invoice when you entered an open balance for a customer during the EasyStep Interview. In order to make this Invoice accurate, edit the Items column to indicate the Items that you sold on the Invoice. Also, change the date to the date of the original Invoice and enter the Invoice number of the original Invoice.

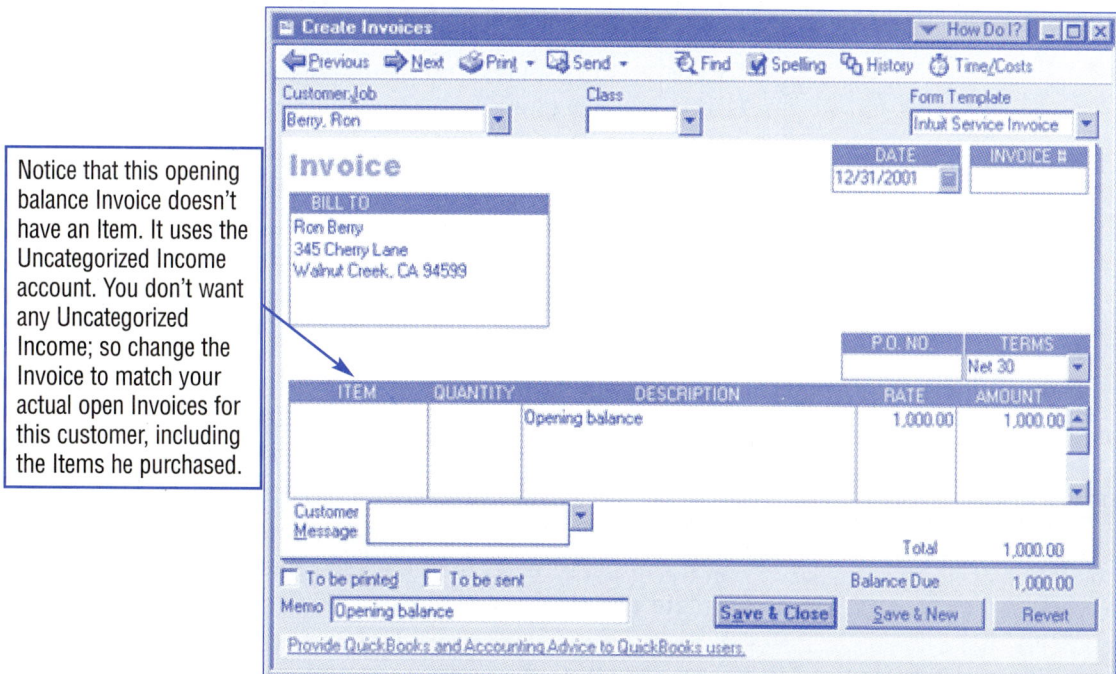

Figure 10-17 The Invoice created by the EasyStep Interview

5. If several open Invoices comprise the opening balance for this customer, delete this Invoice and add separate Invoices for each Invoice that was unpaid as of your start date. Use the dates of the original Invoices and the Items that you actually sold to the customer. You are creating an exact copy of each open Invoice. If the customer has partially paid the Invoice, enter the open balance on the Invoice. See the section entitled *Entering Open Invoices (Accounts Receivable)* on page 530 for more information about entering partially paid Invoices.

6. When you finish editing and/or replacing all of the Invoices that show in the Uncategorized Income account, delete the Uncategorized Income account from the Chart of Accounts. See *Deleting Accounts* on page 515 for more information.

Adjusting Vendor Opening Balances

The procedure for fixing vendor opening balances is very similar to the process above. However, instead of Invoices, edit each of the Bills created by the EasyStep Interview, and replace Uncategorized Expenses with the expense account to which the original Bill was coded.

COMPLETE COMPANY FILE SETUP: A 12-STEP PROCESS

As an alternative to using the EasyStep Interview, you can *manually* set up your company using the process detailed in this section. This process should not take any longer, but it requires that you go into each list and add or edit the information.

The following twelve steps show you how to set up your company file without using the EasyStep Interview.

1. Choose a QuickBooks **start date**.
2. Create a new QuickBooks **company file**.
3. Set up your Chart of Accounts and company **lists**.
4. Enter opening balances for **Balance Sheet** accounts (except A/R, A/P, Inventory, Sales Tax Payable, and Retained Earnings).
5. Enter **Open Items** including **outstanding Checks and Deposits**, **open Invoices**, and **unpaid Bills** as of the start date.
6. If you're setting up mid-year, enter your **year-to-date income and expenses**.
7. Adjust **Sales Tax Payable**.
8. Adjust **Inventory** to match your physical inventory.
9. Set up **payroll lists** and **year-to-date payroll** information.
10. **Close** the **Opening Balance Equity** account into Retained Earnings.
11. **Verify** that your balances match your accountant's Trial Balance on your start date. Create a **Trial Balance** report as of your **start date** and verify the balances.
12. **Back up** your company data and set the **Closing Date** and the **Closing Date Password** to lock the file as of your start date.

Choosing a Start Date – Step 1

Before you create your company file, choose a start date for your company. Your start date is the date you'll use for all your opening balances. Assuming you file taxes on a calendar-year basis, the best start date is December 31. If you file taxes on a fiscal year other than January through December, choose the last day of your fiscal year.

The whole setup process goes faster and easier if you choose the last day of the year. For example, on the last day of the year, after closing the year, only the Balance Sheet accounts have balances. This means you will have fewer account balances to enter during setup. Another reason to choose the end of the year is that it is much easier at tax time if you have all of the information for the whole year in your QuickBooks file.

Don't use January 1 (or the first day of your fiscal year) for your start date, because your opening balances may be included on your first year's Profit & Loss report. This could impact your taxes and distort the picture of the company's financial history.

Keep in mind that you'll need to enter all of the transactions (Checks, Invoices, Deposits, etc.) between your start date and the day you perform the QuickBooks setup. Because of this, your start date has a big impact on how much work you'll do during setup. If you don't want to go back to the end of last year, choose a more recent date, such as the end of last quarter or the end of last month.

If you are starting a **new business**, your start date is the day you formed your company.

NOTE

In order for your records to be complete and accurate, you should also enter every transaction (Check, Invoice, Deposit, etc.) that your company performed between the start date and the day you perform the QuickBooks setup. For example, if you are setting up the file on January 5 with a start date of December 31, you will need to enter all transactions that the company performed on January 1 through January 5 for your records to be complete and accurate.

Creating the Company File – Step 2

If you already created your company file using the EasyStep Interview, you can go directly to *Setting up the Chart of Accounts* on page 509. The following alternative method of creating your company file skips the EasyStep Interview and goes straight into modifying your lists. Note that you can use the EasyStep Interview or this method or a combination of both methods.

COMPUTER TUTORIAL

① Launch QuickBooks.

② Select the *File* menu, and choose **New Company**.

③ Click **Next** on the first screen of the EasyStep Interview (see Figure 10-18).

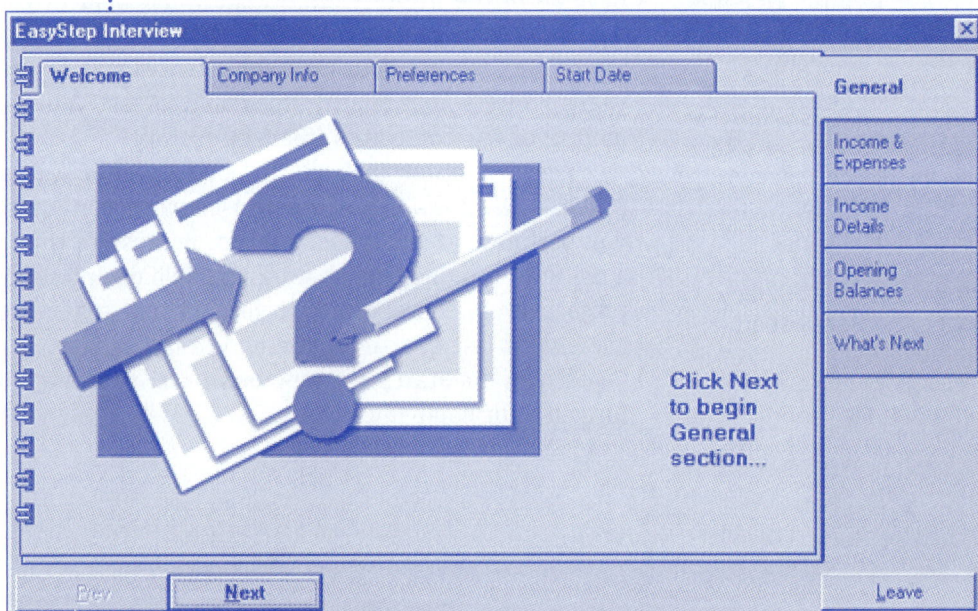

Figure 10-18 The first screen of the EasyStep Interview

④ On the second screen, click **Next**.

5 On the third screen of the EasyStep Interview, click **Skip Interview** (see Figure 10-19).

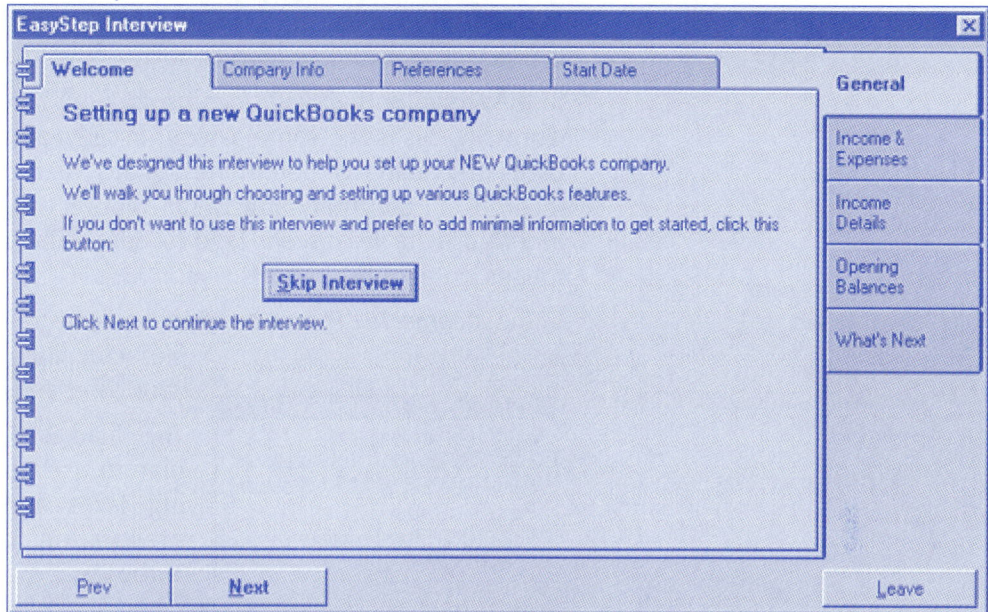

Figure 10-19 The third Screen of the EasyStep Interview

6 Enter your company name and address in the spaces provided, as shown in Figure 10-20.

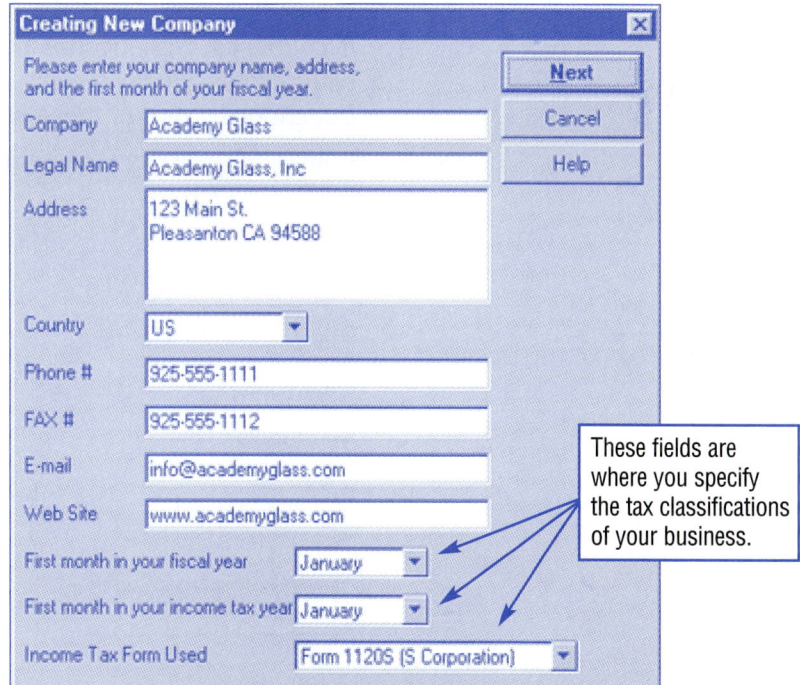

Figure 10-20 Enter your company information.

7 Use the fields at the bottom of the screen to specify the tax classifications of your business (see Figure 10-20).

In the *First month in your fiscal year* field, enter the month. This field is used for year-to-date reports, such as the Profit and Loss report.

In the *First month in your Income tax year* field, enter the month. Normally this is the same as your fiscal year month. QuickBooks uses this field to determine what "year-to-date" means on Income Tax Summary and Detail reports, while it uses the *First month of your fiscal year* field to determine what "year-to-date" means on all other reports.

In the *Income Tax Form Used* field, indicate which form you use to file your income taxes. Choose your company type from this list.

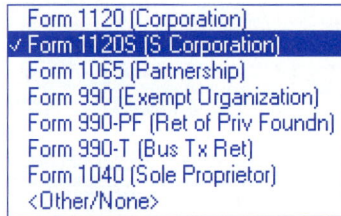

```
Form 1120 (Corporation)
√ Form 1120S (S Corporation)
Form 1065 (Partnership)
Form 990 (Exempt Organization)
Form 990-PF (Ret of Priv Foundn)
Form 990-T (Bus Tx Ret)
Form 1040 (Sole Proprietor)
<Other/None>
```

This field is only relevant if you plan to use QuickBooks for tracking taxes and linking with tax preparation software, such as TurboTax.

Click **Next**.

8 Choose "Service Business" from the Chart of Accounts type list, and click **Next** (see Figure 10-21).

QuickBooks comes with several predefined Charts of Accounts. These lists help you get started by prefilling your Chart of Accounts list with income and expense accounts that companies within your industry typically use. You can always modify the list, but choosing one of these will help you get started.

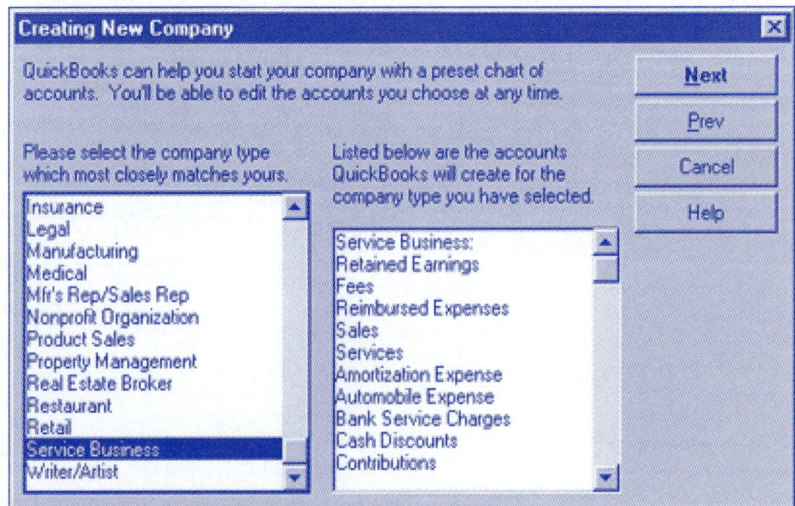

Figure 10-21 Choose the Service Business Chart of Accounts from this list.

⑨ Using the menu in the *Save in* field, browse to the C:\My Documents folder. "Academy Glass.QBW" is preselected in the *File name* field (see Figure 10-22).

The Filename for New Company screen is where you specify the filename and location for your company file. QuickBooks suggests the name by displaying your company name followed by ".QBW." If you want to change the name, type over the suggested name.

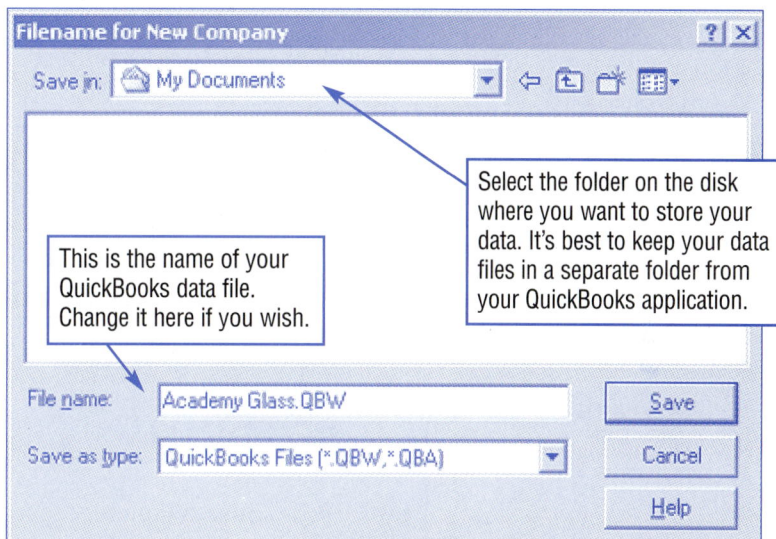

NOTE

You should always keep your data files in a folder separate from your applications, because it keeps your hard disk better organized and it makes it easier to work with backup programs.

Figure 10-22 The Filename for New Company screen

⑩ Click **Cancel** to prevent your new file from being saved. When you create your own file, you will click **Save**.

⑪ Since you cancelled out of the last screen, QuickBooks has no company file open. Use the Chapter 10.QBW file for the rest of this chapter.

Setting Up the Chart of Accounts – Step 3

The Chart of Accounts is one of the most important lists in QuickBooks. It is a list of all the accounts in the General Ledger. If you're not sure how to design your Chart of Accounts, ask your accountant for help.

Account Types

There are five basic account **types** in accounting: assets, liabilities, equity, income and expenses.

QuickBooks breaks these basic account types into subtypes. For example, QuickBooks has five types of assets: **Bank**, **Accounts Receivable**, **Other Current Asset**, **Fixed Asset**, and **Other Asset**. QuickBooks offers four types of liabilities: **Accounts Payable**, **Credit Card**, **Other Current Liability**, and **Long Term Liability**.

Activating Account Numbers

QuickBooks doesn't require account numbers, but it uses the account name to differentiate between accounts. However, if you prefer to have numbers, you can add them to your accounts. If you'd like to include numbers for your accounts, turn on the Account Number feature.

For this section, you will turn on the account numbers, but at the end of *Setting up the Chart of Accounts* section you will turn them off again.

COMPUTER TUTORIAL

1 Select the *Edit* menu, and choose **Preferences** (see Figure 10-23).

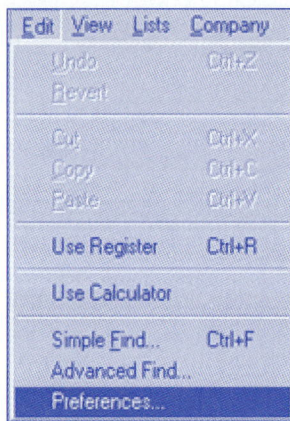

Figure 10-23 Choose Preferences from the Edit menu.

2 In the Preferences screen, click on the **Accounting** icon, and select the Company Preferences tab. Then check the "Use account numbers" box and click **OK**.

The other fields on the screen in Figure 10-24 allow you to control how QuickBooks handles transactions.

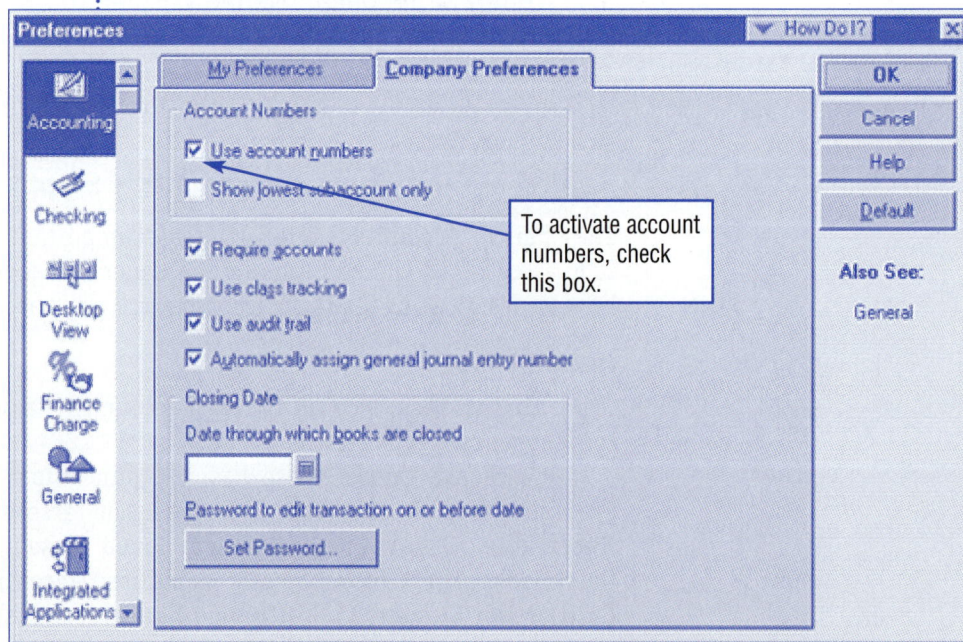

Figure 10-24 The Accounting–Company Preferences screen

DID YOU KNOW The ***Require accounts*** setting forces the user to categorize every transaction to an account in the Chart of Accounts. This setting is essential if you want to avoid uncategorized transactions.

The ***Use class tracking*** setting enables class tracking in the company file.

The ***Use audit trail*** setting is important for providing back-up documentation for transactions. For more information about the Audit Trail function, go to QuickBooks online Help and search the index for Audit Trail.

Now your Chart of Accounts shows numbers as well as account names (see Figure 10-25).

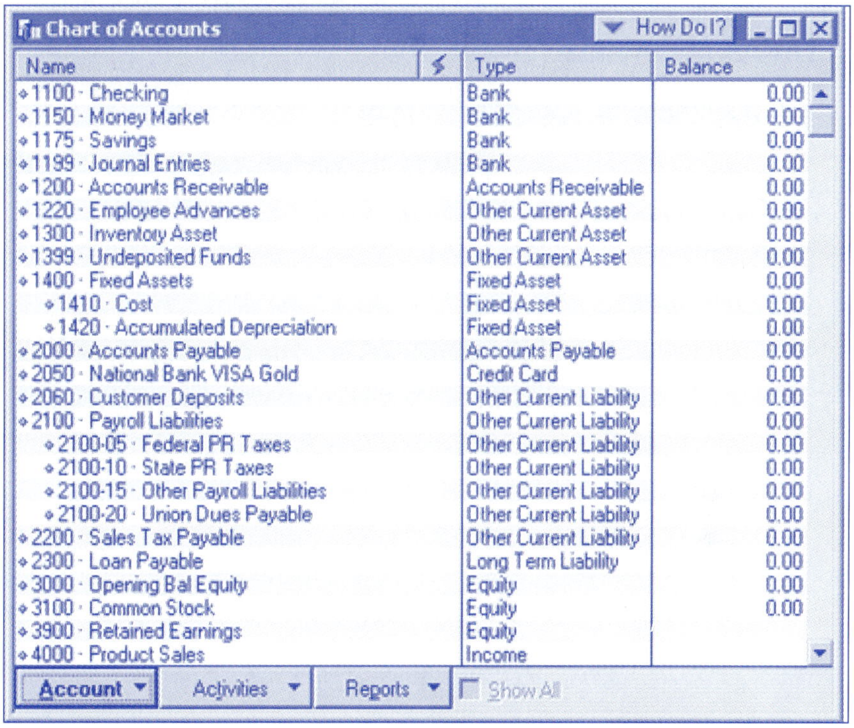

Chart of Accounts
How Do I?
Name
Type
Balance
1100 · Checking | Bank | 0.00
1150 · Money Market | Bank | 0.00
1175 · Savings | Bank | 0.00
1199 · Journal Entries | Bank | 0.00
1200 · Accounts Receivable | Accounts Receivable | 0.00
1220 · Employee Advances | Other Current Asset | 0.00
1300 · Inventory Asset | Other Current Asset | 0.00
1399 · Undeposited Funds | Other Current Asset | 0.00
1400 · Fixed Assets | Fixed Asset | 0.00
1410 · Cost | Fixed Asset | 0.00
1420 · Accumulated Depreciation | Fixed Asset | 0.00
2000 · Accounts Payable | Accounts Payable | 0.00
2050 · National Bank VISA Gold | Credit Card | 0.00
2060 · Customer Deposits | Other Current Liability | 0.00
2100 · Payroll Liabilities | Other Current Liability | 0.00
2100-05 · Federal PR Taxes | Other Current Liability | 0.00
2100-10 · State PR Taxes | Other Current Liability | 0.00
2100-15 · Other Payroll Liabilities | Other Current Liability | 0.00
2100-20 · Union Dues Payable | Other Current Liability | 0.00
2200 · Sales Tax Payable | Other Current Liability | 0.00
2300 · Loan Payable | Long Term Liability | 0.00
3000 · Opening Bal Equity | Equity | 0.00
3100 · Common Stock | Equity | 0.00
3900 · Retained Earnings | Equity
4000 · Product Sales | Income
Account
Activities
Reports
Show All

Figure 10-25 The Chart of Accounts with account numbers

COMPUTER TUTORIAL

━━▶ **ANOTHER** ▶━
━◀ **WAY** ◀━

To open the **Chart of Accounts**, choose Chart of Accounts from the Shortcut List or press <Ctrl+A>.

Adding Accounts

① Select the *Lists* menu, and choose **Chart of Accounts**.

This is the Chart of Accounts list from your sample file (see Figure 10-26).

Name	⚡	Type	Balance
◆1100 · Checking		Bank	0.00
◆1150 · Money Market		Bank	0.00
◆1175 · Savings		Bank	0.00
◆1199 · Journal Entries		Bank	0.00
◆1200 · Accounts Receivable		Accounts Receivable	0.00
◆1220 · Employee Advances		Other Current Asset	0.00
◆1300 · Inventory Asset		Other Current Asset	0.00
◆1399 · Undeposited Funds		Other Current Asset	0.00
◆1400 · Fixed Assets		Fixed Asset	0.00
◆1410 · Cost		Fixed Asset	0.00
◆1420 · Accumulated Depreciation		Fixed Asset	0.00
◆2000 · Accounts Payable		Accounts Payable	0.00
◆2050 · National Bank VISA Gold		Credit Card	0.00
◆2060 · Customer Deposits		Other Current Liability	0.00
◆2100 · Payroll Liabilities		Other Current Liability	0.00
◆2100-05 · Federal PR Taxes		Other Current Liability	0.00
◆2100-10 · State PR Taxes		Other Current Liability	0.00
◆2100-15 · Other Payroll Liabilities		Other Current Liability	0.00
◆2100-20 · Union Dues Payable		Other Current Liability	0.00
◆2200 · Sales Tax Payable		Other Current Liability	0.00
◆2300 · Loan Payable		Long Term Liability	0.00
◆3000 · Opening Bal Equity		Equity	0.00
◆3100 · Common Stock		Equity	0.00
◆3900 · Retained Earnings		Equity	
◆4000 · Product Sales		Income	

Account ▾ | Activities ▾ | Reports ▾ | ☐ Show All

Figure 10-26 The Chart of Accounts list

━━▶ **ANOTHER** ▶━
━◀ **WAY** ◀━

To add a new account, press <Ctrl+N>.

② Click the *Account* menu at the bottom of the Chart of Accounts list and choose **New** (see Figure 10-27).

Account ▾ | Activities ▾

New	Ctrl+N
Edit	Ctrl+E
Delete	Ctrl+D
Make Inactive	
Show All Accounts	
✔ Hierarchical View	
Flat View	
Use	Ctrl+U
Find Transactions in...	
Print List...	Ctrl+P
Re-sort List	

To add a new account, choose New from the Account menu, or press <Ctrl+N>.

Figure 10-27 Adding an account

3 Choose "Expense" from the Type drop-down list (see Figure 10-28).

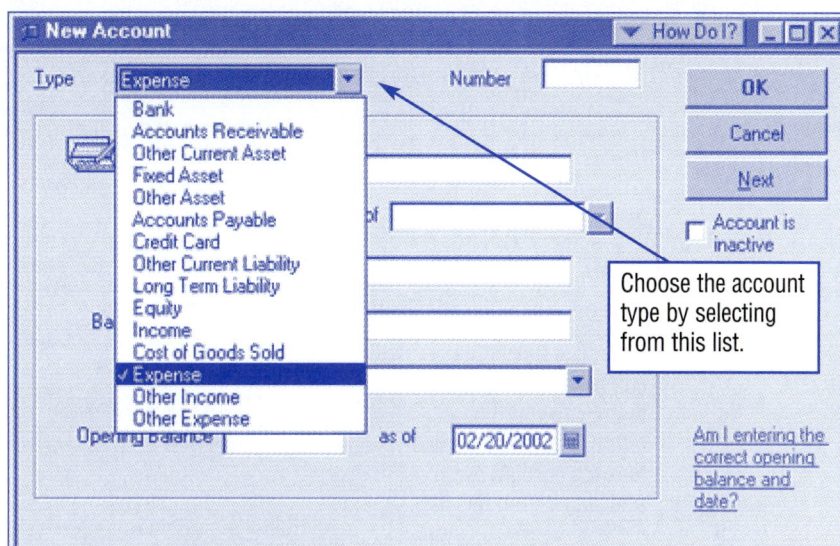

Choose the account type by selecting from this list.

Figure 10-28 Types of accounts

4 Enter "6340" in the *Number* field, and press <TAB>.

5 Enter "Telephone" in the *Name* field, and press <TAB> three times.

6 Enter "Telephone Expense" in the *Description* field, and press <TAB> twice.

The *Description* field is optional. You can show the account descriptions on reports by changing the Reports & Graphs preferences.

7 Select "Deductions: Other deductions" from the Tax Line drop-down list, and press <TAB>.

If you use TurboTax or other QuickBooks-compatible tax software to prepare your tax return, specify the line on your tax return that this account will feed. This allows the tax software to fill out your tax return automatically, based on the data in QuickBooks. If you don't use software to prepare your taxes, leave this field blank.

⑧ Your screen should look like Figure 10-29. Click **OK** to save the account.

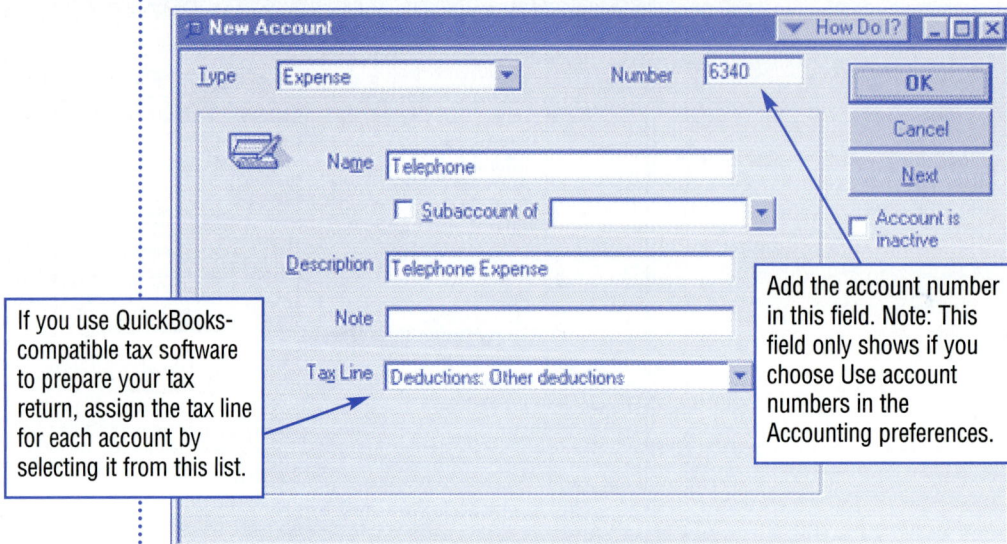

If you use QuickBooks-compatible tax software to prepare your tax return, assign the tax line for each account by selecting it from this list.

Add the account number in this field. Note: This field only shows if you choose Use account numbers in the Accounting preferences.

Figure 10-29 The New Account screen

Adding Subaccounts

If you want more detail in your Chart of Accounts, you can add subaccounts.

COMPUTER TUTORIAL

① Display the Chart of Accounts.

② Select the *Account* menu at the bottom of the list, and choose **New**.

③ Fill out the New Account screen as shown in Figure 10-30. Notice that the *Subaccount of* field is checked and the main account is selected in its field. Click **OK** to save your changes.

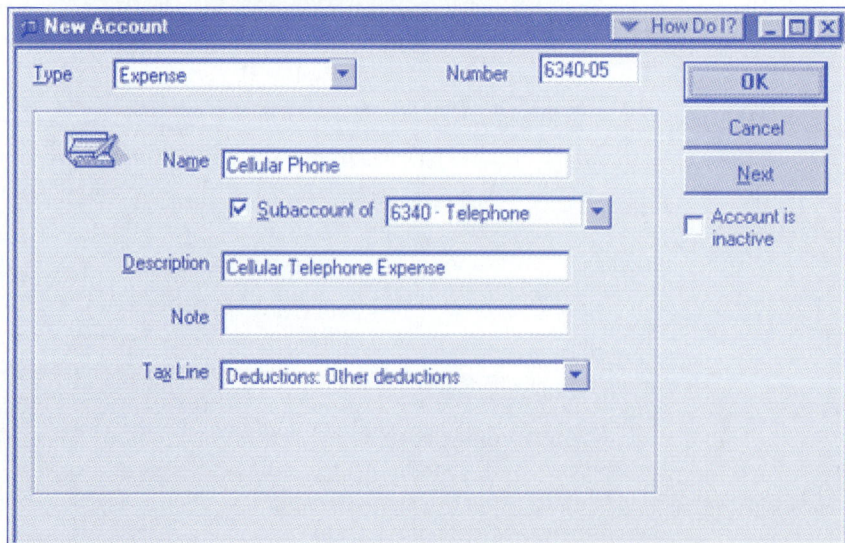

DID YOU KNOW Clicking the Collapse button on reports that include subaccounts (e.g. Balance Sheets and Profit & Loss reports) removes the subaccount detail from the report. The balance of each primary account on the collapsed report is the total of its subaccount balances.

Figure 10-30 Add a subaccount for more detail in the Chart of Accounts.

Removing Accounts from the Chart of Accounts

When you no longer need an account, it is best to remove the account from the Chart of Accounts. Removing unnecessary accounts helps avoid data entry errors by ensuring that no transactions are accidentally posted to the account. There are three ways to remove an account from the Chart of Accounts: deleting the account, deactivate the account or merging the account with another account.

> **IMPORTANT**
>
> If the account you want to delete has transactions dated in a closed accounting period, you should not use Option 1 or Option 3 below. Changing transactions in closed accounting periods could cause discrepancies between QuickBooks reports and the company's financial statements and/or tax returns.

Deleting Accounts – Option 1

To delete an account, follow these steps:

> **Don't perform these steps now. They are for reference only.**

> **NOTE**
>
> QuickBooks won't allow you to delete an account if you have used the account in an Item record or transaction. If this is the case, use either Option 2 or Option 3 below to remove the account from the Chart of Accounts.

1. Select the account in the Chart of Accounts list.
2. Select the *Edit* menu and choose **Delete Account** (see Figure 10-31).

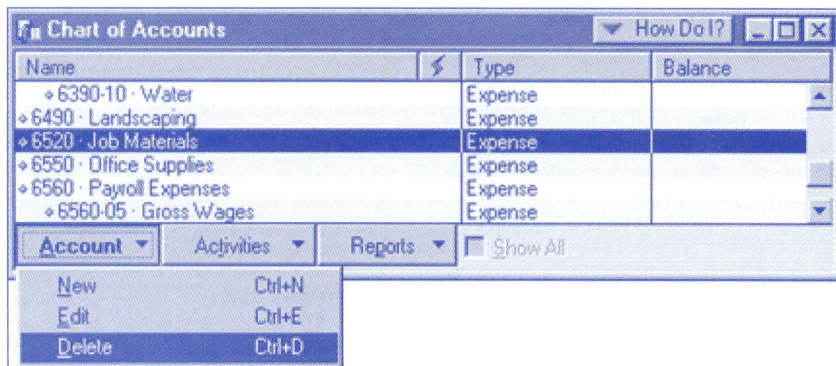

Figure 10-31 Deleting an account from the Chart of Accounts.

Deactivating Accounts – Option 2

If you cannot delete an account, you can deactivate it. Deactivating an account causes it to disappear from the Chart of Accounts. Deactivating an old account reduces the clutter in your lists while preserving your ability to see the account in historical transactions and reports.

When you deactivate a Balance Sheet account (Asset, Liability or Equity Account), create a General Journal Entry to zero the balance in the account you wish to remove from the Chart of Accounts. See Chapter 9 for detailed instructions on the use of General Journal Entries. For example, if Academy Glass opened a line of credit and absorbed one of the existing loans into this new account, they would use a General Journal entry to decrease (debit) the balance in the "Loan Payable" account and to increase (credit) the balance in the new "Line of Credit" account. Once the account balance is zero, they could deactivate the Loan Payable account.

When you deactivate an income or expense account, do not create a General Journal Entry to zero the balance in the account. QuickBooks will automatically zero the balance at the end of your fiscal year.

To make an account inactive, follow these steps:

> **Don't perform these steps now. They are for reference only.**

1. Select the account in the Chart of Accounts.
2. Select the *Account* menu and choose **Make Inactive** (see Figure 10-32).

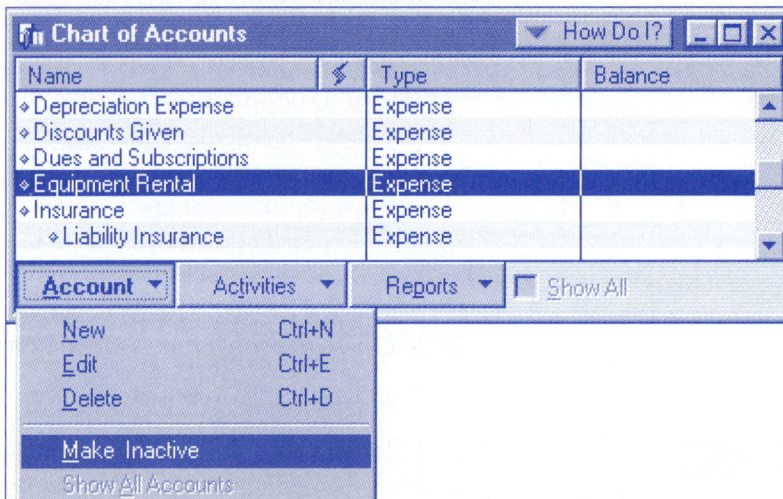

Figure 10-32 Making an account inactive in the Chart of Accounts

To view all accounts, including the inactive accounts, click **Show All** at the bottom of the screen (see Figure 10-33). The icon in the far left column indicates that an account is inactive. To reactivate the account, click on the icon.

NOTE

Even if an account (or item, or name) is inactive, all transactions using that account (or item or name) will show on reports.

DID YOU KNOW You can also deactivate customers, vendors, employees, or Items using this same method.

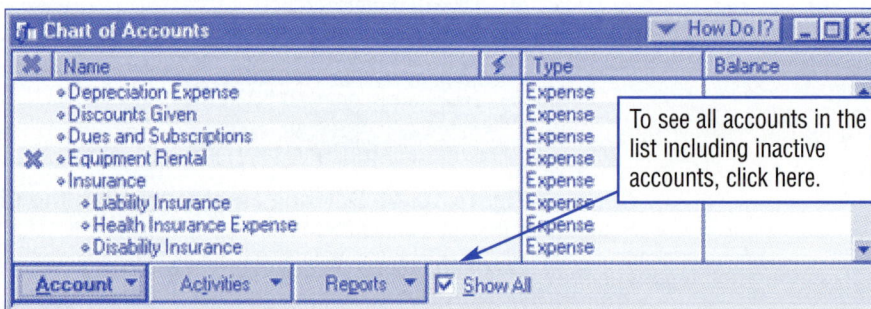

To see all accounts in the list including inactive accounts, click here.

Figure 10-33 When the *Show All* field is checked, all accounts appear in the list.

Merging Accounts – Option 3

When you merge two accounts, QuickBooks edits each transaction so that it posts to the merged (combined) account. For example, if you merge the Entertainment account into the Meals account, QuickBooks will edit each transaction that posts to Entertainment, making it post to Meals instead. Then QuickBooks will remove the Entertainment account from the Chart of Accounts list.

COMPUTER TUTORIAL

1 Display the Chart of Accounts.

2 Select "6350-02 Entertainment."

When merging accounts, select the account whose name you don't want to keep.

3 Select the *Account* menu and choose **Edit**.

4 Enter "Meals" in the *Name* field (see Figure 10-34), and click **OK**.

Enter the name of the account with which you want to merge Entertainment. You must enter the account name exactly as it appears in the Chart of Accounts.

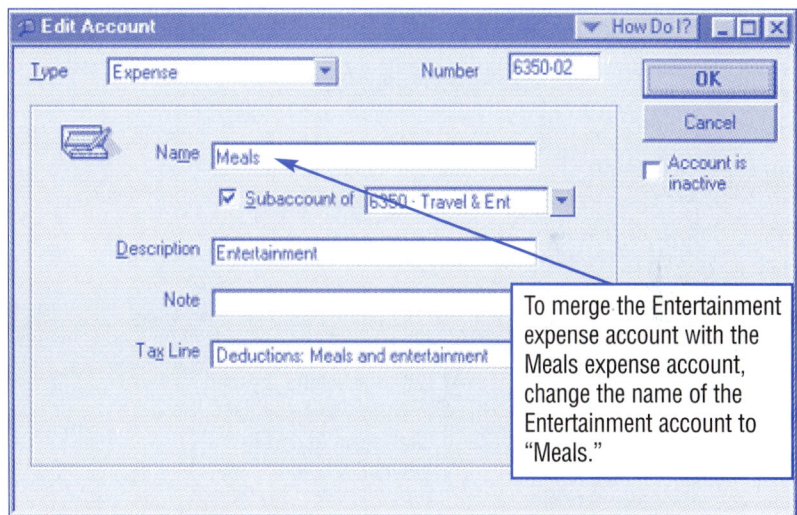

Figure 10-34 Change the name of the account to exactly match the name of another account.

5 Now that the account has the same name as the other account, QuickBooks asks if you want to merge the two accounts (see Figure 10-35). Click **Yes**.

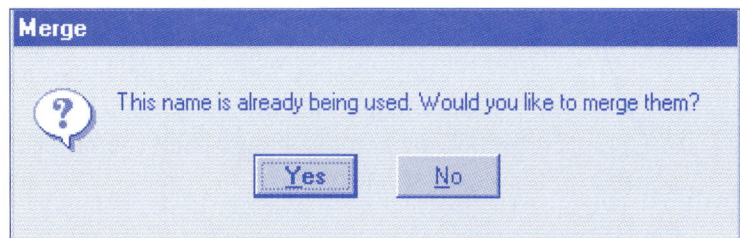

Figure 10-35 Click **Yes** to merge the accounts.

> **IMPORTANT**
>
> Once you merge accounts together, there is no way to find out which account the old transactions were coded to. In this example, all transactions that were coded to Entertainment Expense now show as being coded to Meals. Also, merged accounts cannot be separated except by restoring from a backup.

Reordering the Account List

There are several ways to reorder the Chart of Accounts list. By default, the Chart of Accounts sorts primarily by account type. Notice that all of the bank accounts come first, followed by Accounts Receivable, Other Current Assets, and so on.

You can also re-sort the Chart of Accounts by the account name, account number, online status, or balance. The order of the accounts in the Chart of Accounts determines the order of the accounts in reports.

COMPUTER TUTORIAL

1. Display the Chart of Accounts (see Figure 10-36).

2. Click the Name column heading to sort the list.

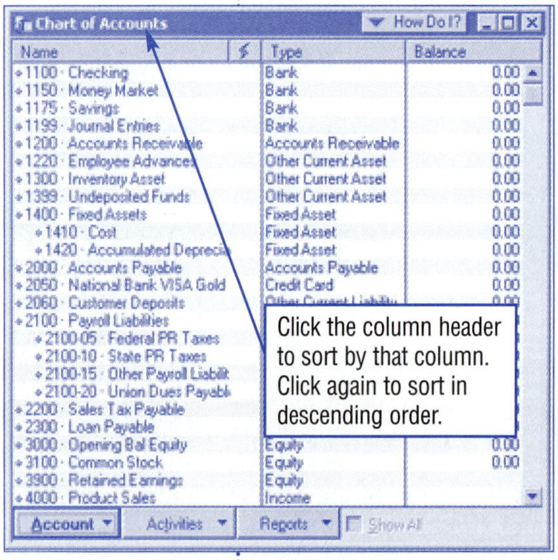

Figure 10-36 Unsorted Chart of Accounts List

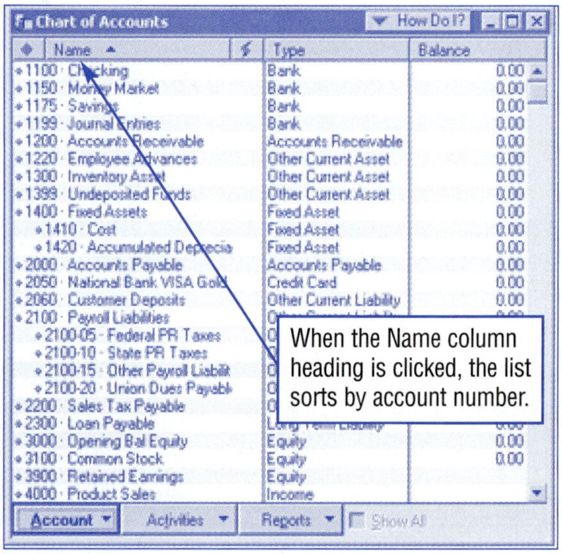

Figure 10-37 Chart of Accounts sorted by name

When account numbers are on and you click the Name header, QuickBooks sorts the list by account number. However, when account numbers are off and you click the Name header, QuickBooks sorts the list by account name. Click the other headers to sort by online status, Type or Balance.

You can also use the mouse to drag the accounts up or down within the same account type. To reorder the Chart of Accounts using the mouse, follow these steps:

Don't perform these steps now. They are for reference only.

1. If you have sorted the list by Name, Online Status, Type or Balance by clicking on the column headers, click on the diamond to the left of the Name column header. This will remove the sorting (see Figure 10-38).

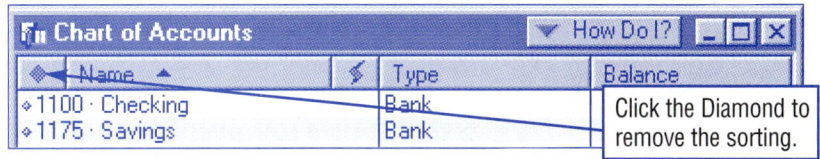

Figure 10-38 Chart of Accounts, sorted by name

2. While holding down the mouse button, drag the account up or down (see Figure 10-39).

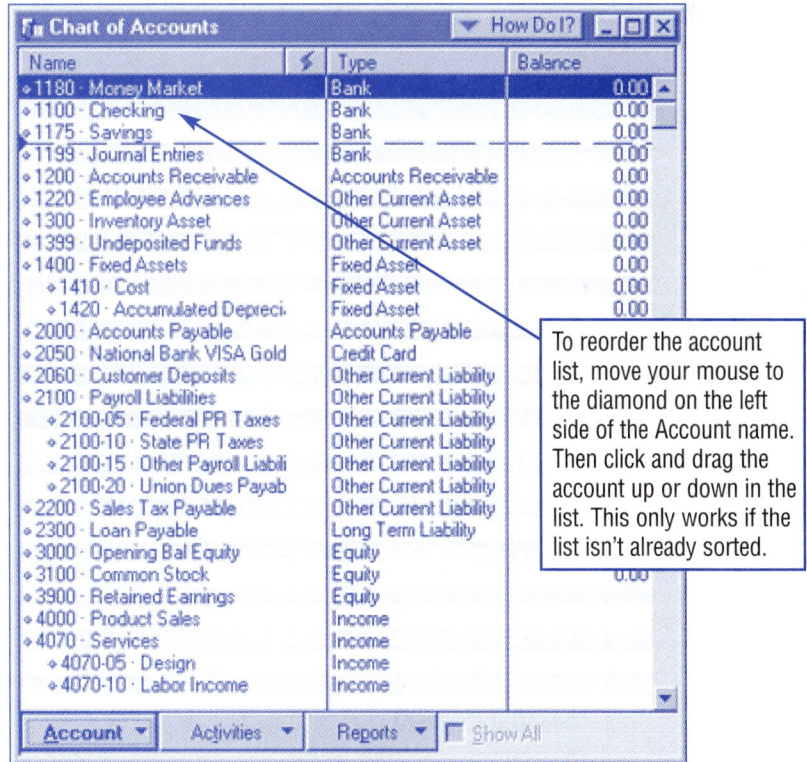

Figure 10-39 Reorder the list by moving an account with the mouse.

COMPUTER TUTORIAL

Deactivating Account Numbers

For the rest of this chapter, we'll turn off the display of account numbers in the Chart of Accounts.

1 Select the *Edit* menu, and choose **Preferences**.

2 In the Preferences screen, click on the Accounting icon and select the Company Preferences tab.

3 Deselect the "Use account numbers" box and then click **OK**.

Setting Up Opening Balances – Step 4

Gathering Your Information

After you've set up your Chart of Accounts, you're ready to enter your opening balances. To set up your opening balances, you'll need to gather several documents, prepared as of your start date. Following is a list of items needed for your setup.

Trial Balance. Ask your accountant to provide you with a Trial Balance for your start date. If your start date is the end of your fiscal year, ask your accountant for an "after-closing" Trial Balance. The term "after-closing" means "after all the income and expenses have been closed into Retained Earnings."

If a Trial Balance is not available, use an after closing Balance Sheet and a year-to-date income statement as of your start date. Figure 10-40 shows a sample Trial Balance for Academy Glass on the start date of 12/31/2001.

Academy Glass
Trial Balance
December 31, 2001

	Debit	Credit
Checking	$17,959.60	
Money Market	$12,100.00	
Accounts Receivable	$ 575.68	
Inventory	$ 1,800.00	
Fixed Assets: Cost	$13,250.00	
Fixed Assets: Accumulated Depreciation		$ 2,300.00
Accounts Payable		$ 142.00
National Bank VISA Gold		$ 2,152.00
Payroll Liabilities: Federal PR Taxes		$ 83.00
Payroll Liabilities: State PR Taxes		$ 285.00
Sales Tax Payable		$ 136.98
Loan Payable		$ 6,700.00
Common Stock		$10,000.00
Retained Earnings		$23,886.30
TOTAL	$45,685.28	$45,685.28

Figure 10-40 The Trial Balance on Academy's start date

Bank Statement (for all bank accounts). You'll need the most recent bank statement prior to your start date. For example, if your start date is 12/31/2001 you'll need the 12/31/2001 bank statements for all of your accounts. Figure 10-41 shows a sample bank statement for Academy Glass on the start date of 12/31/2001.

Account:		Academy Glass–Main Checking		
Last Statement Date	11/30/01	Beginning Balance		$12,155.10
This Statement Date	12/31/01	Less: Checks & Debits		($7,037.40)
		Plus: Deposits & Credits		$10,165.90
		Ending Balance		**$15,283.60**

Checks	Date	Amount	Deposits	Date	Amount
316	2-Dec	$324.00	Customer Deposit	8-Dec	$6,150.00
317	3-Dec	$128.60	Customer Deposit	20-Dec	$4,007.28
318	5-Dec	$83.00	Interest Earned	31-Dec	$8.62
319	8-Dec	$285.00	Total Deposits:		**$10,165.90**
320	10-Dec	$1,528.00			
321	12-Dec	$3,000.00			
322	13-Dec	$276.52			
323	15-Dec	$142.00			
324	28-Dec	$1,260.28			
Total Checks:		**$7,027.40**			

Other Debits		
Service Charge	31-Dec	$10.00
Total Other Debits		**$10.00**

Figure 10-41 The bank statement on Academy's start date

TIP

If your bank statements are not dated at the end of each month, ask your bank to change your statement date to the end of the month.

Outstanding Checks and Deposits. You'll need a list of all your checks and deposits that have not cleared the bank as of the bank statement on or prior to your start date. Table 10-3 shows a list of outstanding deposits and checks for Academy Glass on the start date of 12/31/2001.

Outstanding Deposits at 12/31/01			Outstanding Checks at 12/31/01		
Date	Amount		Date	Check #	Amount
12/30/01	$3000.00		12/26/01	325	$324.00

Table 10-3 Outstanding deposits and checks on Academy's start date

Open Invoices. List each customer invoice including the date of the invoice, amount due, and the Items sold on the invoice (see Table 10-4).

Invoice Number	Invoice Date	Customer:Job	Class	Terms	Rep.	City	Item	Qty.	Amt. Due
3947	12/18/01	Mason, Bob	San Jose	Net 30	JM	Morgan Hill	Skylight Santa Clara tax Total of Invoice	1 unit	$384.00 8.00% $414.72
4003	12/21/01	Anderson Floors:2nd St. Store	San Jose	Net 30	JM	San Jose	Labor 4 Hrs. $40/hr. Total of Invoice		 $160.00 $160.00

Table 10-4 Open Invoices on Academy's start date.

Unpaid Bills. List each vendor bill by date of the bill, amount due, and what items or expenses you purchased on the bill (see Table 10-5).

Bill Number	Bill Date	Vendor	Due	Account/Item	Amt. Job	Class	Billable
2342	12/21/01	Wagner & Son Painting	$142.00	Subcontractors Expense	Mason, Bob	San Jose	Yes

Table 10-5 Unpaid bills on Academy's start date

NOTE

The next three payroll-related lists are necessary only if your start date is in the middle of a calendar year and you want to track payroll details with QuickBooks. If your start date is 12/31, skip these lists and enter the opening balances for payroll liabilities in the liability accounts as shown later in this section.

Employee List and W-4 information for each employee. Gather complete name, address, social security number, and withholding information for each employee.

If your start date is 12/31, you need to enter the detail from these lists only if you want to use QuickBooks to create payroll reports, Form 940, Form 941, or W-2s for the previous year.

Payroll Liabilities by Item. List the amount due for each of your payroll liabilities as of your start date. For example, list the amounts due for federal withholding tax, Social Security (employer), Social Security (employee), and the rest of the payroll liabilities.

Year-to-Date Payroll Detail by Employee. If your start date is not 12/31 and you want QuickBooks to track your payroll, you'll need gross earnings, withholdings, employer taxes, and any other deductions for each employee so far this year. For the most detail, this list should include each employee's earnings for each month this year. For more detail on setting up payroll, see Chapter 7.

Year-to-Date Payroll Tax Deposits. If your start date is not 12/31, list each payroll tax deposit during the year by Payroll Item.

Physical Inventory by Inventory Part. List the quantity and cost for each product in inventory (see Table 10-6).

Physical Inventory at 12/31/00		
Item	Quantity on Hand	Value
104-Slider	6	$1800.00
106-Slider	0	$0

Table 10-6 Physical inventory on Academy's start date

Entering the Opening Balances

To enter your opening balances you'll use one of three methods discussed below. The method you use will depend on three factors:

- ◆ How familiar you are with accounting
- ◆ Whether the account you're editing has transactions or not
- ◆ Whether you intend to use the Bank Reconciliation feature to reconcile your accounts

Of course, when you're starting from scratch, you won't have transactions in any of the accounts, so the second bullet above will not apply during the initial setup process. However, in case you ever have to add opening balances after a file has transactions, you should review and understand all three methods and how they might be appropriate in different situations. Method 1, *directly editing the account*, is appropriate when there are no transactions in the account, when you will reconcile the account using the Bank Reconciliation feature, and when you are unfamiliar with accounting. Use Method 2, *adding a transaction directly in registers*, when accounts already have transactions and you want to add an opening balance for the account. If you intend to reconcile this account with the Bank Reconciliation feature, you will need to perform additional steps after entering the opening balance in the register. See Chapter 4 for more information. You can use Method 3, *using a General Journal Entry to record your opening balances*, if you're familiar with using General Journal Entries and adjusting account balances with debits and credits.

Method 1 – Directly Editing The Account

Use this method if you're less familiar with accounting and if you are just setting up the account. Editing each account from the Chart of Accounts is the simplest way to enter opening balances for your Balance Sheet accounts. This method is simple because it requires no knowledge of accounting, and it automatically posts transactions both to the account you choose and to the Opening Balance Equity account. This method also posts the opening balance in the account to the *Beginning Balance* field of the Bank Reconciliation feature. Because of this, you should always enter your bank balance in the *Opening Balance* field of the New Account screen if you intend to reconcile the account. If you already have transactions in an account, you won't be able to use Method 1; you must use Method 2 or 3 instead.

TIP

If you don't have actual counts and costs for your inventory, you'll need to estimate. However, the accuracy of your reports will be compromised if you don't have accurate setup numbers.

NOTE

When entering opening balances for bank accounts and credit cards, it is very important that you use the ending balance from the bank statement dated on (or just prior to) your start date.

COMPUTER TUTORIAL

To enter the opening balances using Method 1, repeat the following steps for each of your Balance Sheet accounts:

1. Display the Chart of Accounts.

2. Select the "Checking" Bank account.

3. Select the *Account* menu at the bottom of the list, and choose **Edit**.

4. Enter "15,283.60" in the *Opening Balance* field, and press <TAB> (see Figure 10-42).

   The *Opening Balance* and the *as of* fields appear only if the account you're editing does not have transactions.

5. Enter "12/31/2001" in the *as of* field, and click **OK**. Your screen should look like Figure 10-42.

   In the *as of* field, the date that you enter is your start date or the bank statement date, if your bank statement is dated prior to the start date.

Figure 10-42 Enter an opening balance in the Edit Account screen.

6. Repeat the steps above for the Money Market account.

NOTE

QuickBooks does not allow you to use Method 1 to enter the opening balance for Accounts Receivable, Undeposited Funds, Accounts Payable, Sales Tax Payable or Opening Balance Equity. To enter opening balances for these accounts, see Using Journal Entries for Opening Balances and Entering Opening Balances for Accounts Receivable and Accounts Payable.

IMPORTANT

When entering the opening balance for your checking account (and any other account for which you receive statements), enter the ending balance from the bank statement for your start date.

Method 2 – Adding a Transaction Directly in Registers

Use this method if the account already has transactions. If you already have transactions in an account, you can't enter the opening balance by editing the account in the Chart of Accounts. Instead, you'll need to enter a transaction directly in the register for the account.

To enter the opening balance using Method 2, follow these steps:

> **Don't perform these steps now. They are for reference only.**

1. Display the Chart of Accounts.

2. Double-click the account in which you want to enter an opening balance.

If there is already an opening balance transaction in the register, modify it if necessary. If there is no opening balance in the account, enter a new transaction at the bottom of the register to record the opening balance. Use the start date (12/31/01) and code the entry to Opening Balance Equity.

Click **Record** to save the entry.

Because the start date is prior to the other entries in the register, the opening balance entry will sort to the top of the register when you save it.

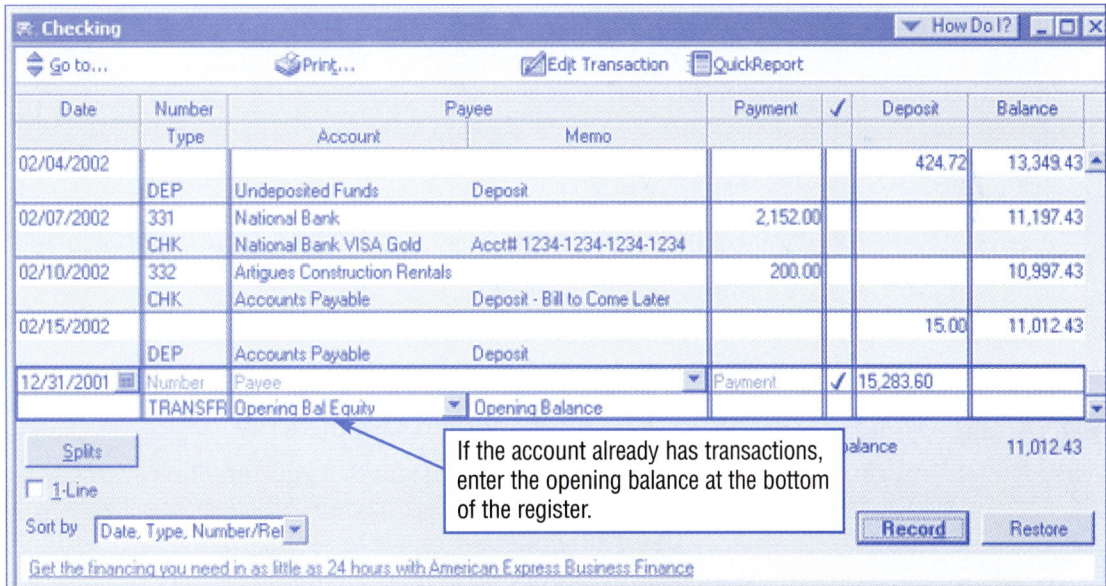

Figure 10-43 Enter an opening balance in the register.

Method 3 – Using a General Journal Entry to Record Opening Balances

Use this method if you're familiar with using Journal Entries. If you feel more comfortable creating General Journal Entries and if you understand debits and credits, you can use a General Journal Entry to record some, but not all, of your opening balances. Do not include the following accounts in the General Journal Entry: Accounts Receivable, Accounts Payable, Inventory, Sales Tax Payable, and Retained Earnings. You will enter the opening balance for these accounts later in the 12-Step setup.

Use the information from the Trial Balance on page 520 to complete the Tutorial.

COMPUTER TUTORIAL

1 Select the *Banking* menu and choose **Make Journal Entry**.

2 Fill in the General Journal Entry as shown on the screen in Figure 10-44.

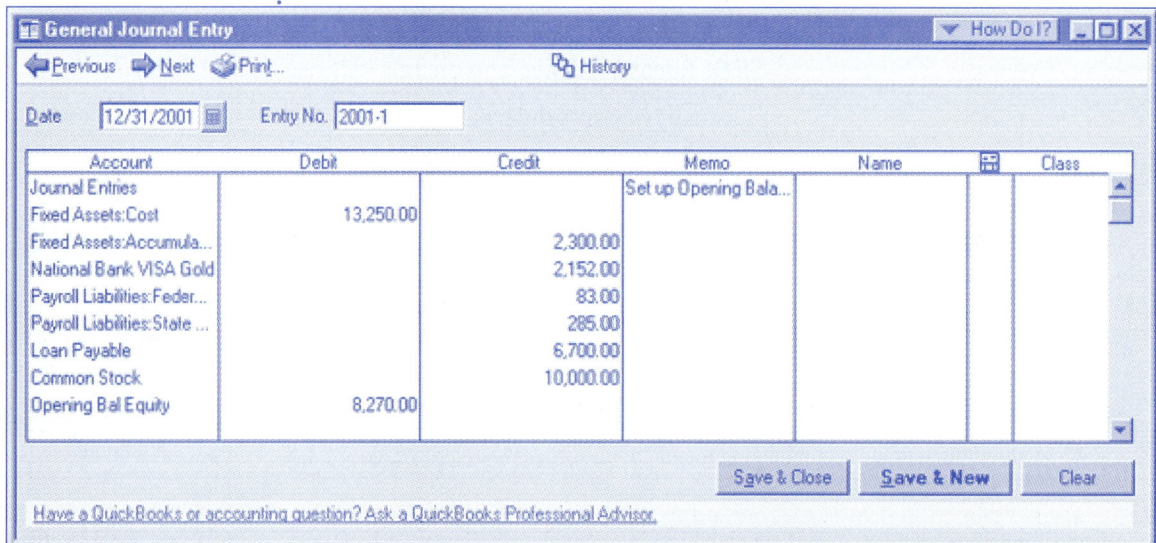

Figure 10-44 Enter an opening balance using a General Journal Entry.

NOTE

On the top line of each General Journal Entry, use an account called "Journal Entries", as shown in Figure 10-44. Use the "Bank" account type when setting up this account in your Chart of Accounts. It will never have a balance, so it will never show on reports, but it will have a register where you'll be able to look at all of your General Journal Entries.

3 Click **Save & Close** to save the entry.

QuickBooks will warn you that you shouldn't normally use General Journal Entries to affect payroll liabilities (see Figure 10-45). While this is true after setup, we're setting up the file, so click **Yes**.

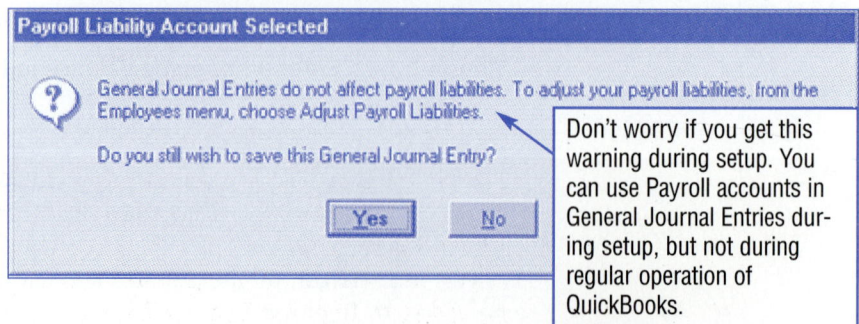

Don't worry if you get this warning during setup. You can use Payroll accounts in General Journal Entries during setup, but not during regular operation of QuickBooks.

Figure 10-45 The Payroll Liability Account Selected warning screen

The General Journal Entry in Figure 10-44 will set up the opening balances in most of the asset, liability, and equity accounts. You will not include some of the asset and liability accounts in this General Journal Entry because you will enter their balances later in the 12 Step setup. For example, you'll exclude Accounts Receivable and Accounts Payable because you will create Invoices and Bills to enter these accounts, respectively. See *Entering Open Bills (Accounts Payable)* on page 529. You will also exclude bank accounts from the General Journal Entry. You must use Method 1 to enter all bank account balances if you want the opening balance to appear on your first Bank Reconciliation in QuickBooks. See *Method 1 – directly editing the account* on page 523.

In the *Accounting 101* section in Chapter 1 you learned that you debit an asset account to increase its balance and you credit a liability or equity account to increase its balance. That is why the General Journal Entry in Figure 10-44 shows a debit of $13,250 for the Fixed Assets:Cost (asset) account and a credit of $6,700 for the Loan Payable (liability) account.

When recording a Journal Entry, remember that total debits must always equal total credits. QuickBooks automatically calculates the amount required to make this entry balance as you create each new line in the General Journal Entry. On the last line of the General Journal Entry, code the amount QuickBooks calculates to the Opening Balance Equity account. This amount may be a debit or a credit, depending on the other figures in the entry.

Although the trial balance doesn't show any balance in Opening Balance Equity, you use this account during setup to keep everything in balance. At the end of the setup process, you'll transfer the balance from this account into Retained Earnings as shown later in the setup steps.

Understanding Opening Balance Equity

As you enter the opening balances for your assets and liabilities, QuickBooks automatically adds offsetting amounts in the Opening Balance Equity account. This account, which is automatically created by QuickBooks, is very useful if used properly. As you'll see later in this section, each of the opening balance transactions you enter into QuickBooks will affect this account. Then, after you have entered all of the opening balances, you'll "close" Opening Balance Equity into Retained Earnings (or Owner's Equity).

Entering Open Items – Step 5

Entering Outstanding Checks and Deposits

For each of your bank accounts and credit cards, enter each outstanding check and deposit as additional transactions in the account register. Each outstanding check and deposit should be entered with the date the check was written or the deposit was made, and the transaction should be coded to Opening Balance Equity.

TIP

Opening Balance Equity is a very useful account. QuickBooks uses this account to offset each of the opening balances in your other accounts. By using the Opening Balance Equity account during setup, you'll be able to quickly access the detail of your setup transactions by looking at the Opening Balance Equity register.

QuickBooks also uses Opening Balance Equity to record errors when the bank reconciliation doesn't match the bank statement. For a discussion of this, see Chapter 4.

This is important to do so that your first bank reconciliation goes smoothly. In order for the reconciliation to go smoothly, you want all of the checks and deposits to show in QuickBooks, so that you can match them with your first bank statement after the start date. If you don't enter the individual transactions, you won't see them in the QuickBooks reconciliation screen. Also, if a transaction never clears the bank, you won't know which transaction it was without going back to your old records.

COMPUTER TUTORIAL

1 With the Chart of Accounts open, double-click on the "Checking" account to display its register.

2 Enter the outstanding checks and deposits in Table 10-3 on page 521 directly in the register (see Figure 10-46).

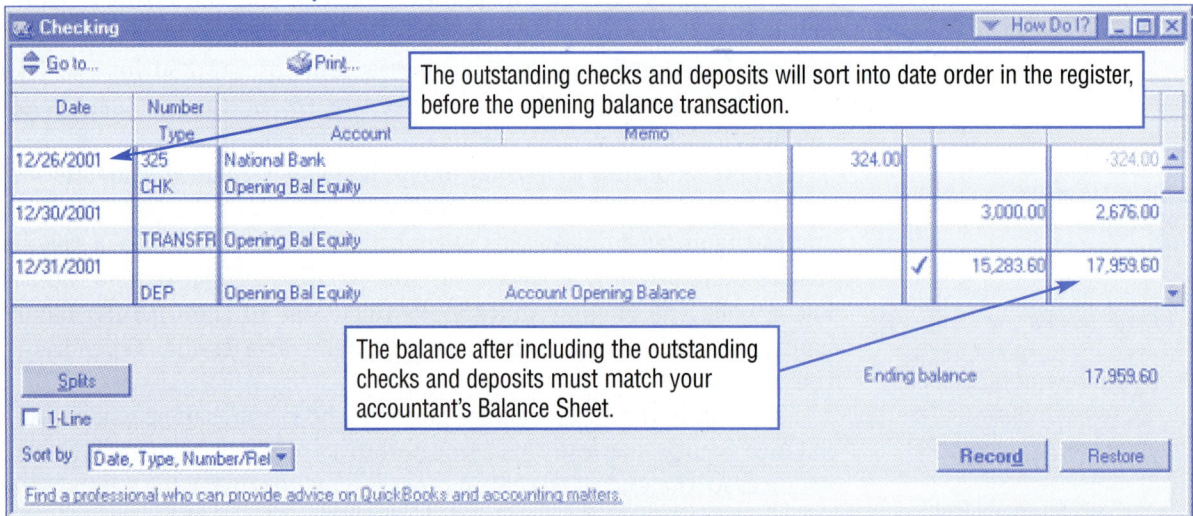

Figure 10-46 The Checking account register with outstanding checks and deposits

Entering Open Bills (Accounts Payable)

Enter the balance of your unpaid bills (the unpaid balance only) and vendor credits as of the start date. Enter each bill (or credit) with the original date of the bill along with all of the details (terms, vendor, etc.) of the bill.

COMPUTER TUTORIAL

1 Choose **Enter Bills** from the Shortcut list.

2 Enter the bill as shown in Figure 10-47.

3 Click **Save & Close** to save the transaction.

Figure 10-47 Enter the open Bill with actual Bill date and the Bill due date.

COMPUTER TUTORIAL

Entering Open Invoices (Accounts Receivable)

Enter the balance of each Invoice (its open balance only) or Credit Memo as of the Start Date. Enter each Invoice with its original date along with all of the details (terms, customer, etc.) of the Invoice.

① Choose **Create Invoices** from the Shortcut list.

② Enter the Invoice as shown in Figure 10-48.

③ Click **Save & New** to save the transaction and display a new Invoice.

Figure 10-48 Enter the open Invoice with the original Invoice date.

NOTE

When you set up your company file, it is important that you enter all Invoices, Credit Memos, Bills, and Bill Credits separately. This is because QuickBooks needs the details of the transactions, such as the date, the terms, and the customer or vendor, in order to correctly prepare aging reports (e.g., Unpaid Bills Detail and A/R Aging Summary).

In addition, when you receive money against one of your prior-year Invoices or pay a prior-year Bill, you'll need individual Invoices and Bills against which to match the receipts and payments.

④ Enter the Invoice as shown in Figure 10-49.

⑤ Click **Save & Close** to save the Invoice.

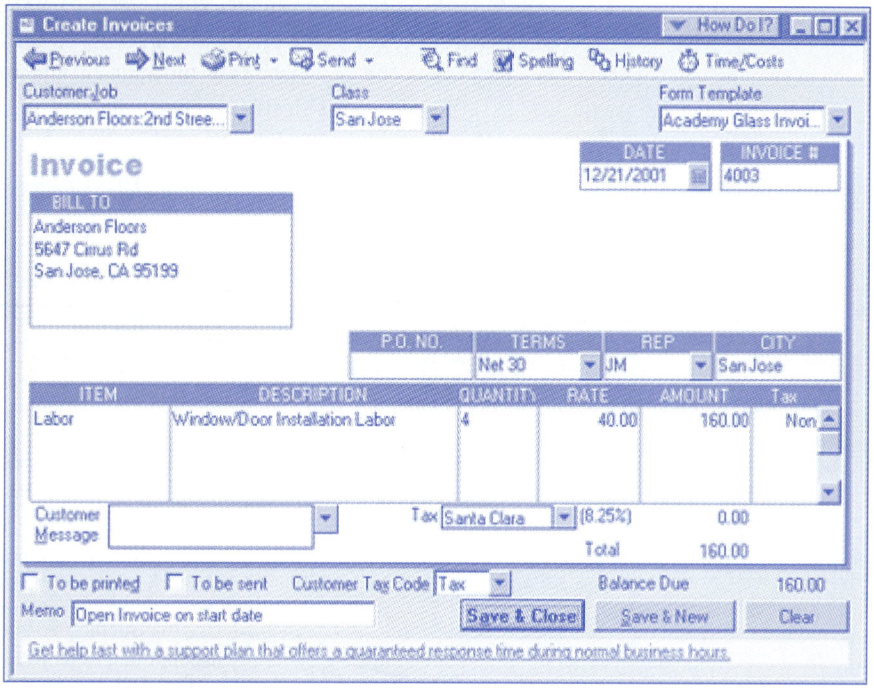

Figure 10-49 Enter this open Invoice.

Entering Open Purchase Orders

If you have open Purchase Orders, enter them individually, just as you did with Bills, Bill Credits, Invoices, and Credit Memos. Enter each Purchase Order with its original date and all of its details. If you have partially received items on the Purchase Order, enter only the quantities yet to be received from the vendor.

Entering Year-to-Date Income and Expenses – Step 6

If your start date is not at the beginning of the fiscal year, use a General Journal Entry to enter your year-to-date income and expenses (see Figure 10-50). The entry allows you to summarize the total income and expenses for the first few months of the year.

The General Journal Entry shown in Figure 10-49 is for reference only. Do not enter it now.

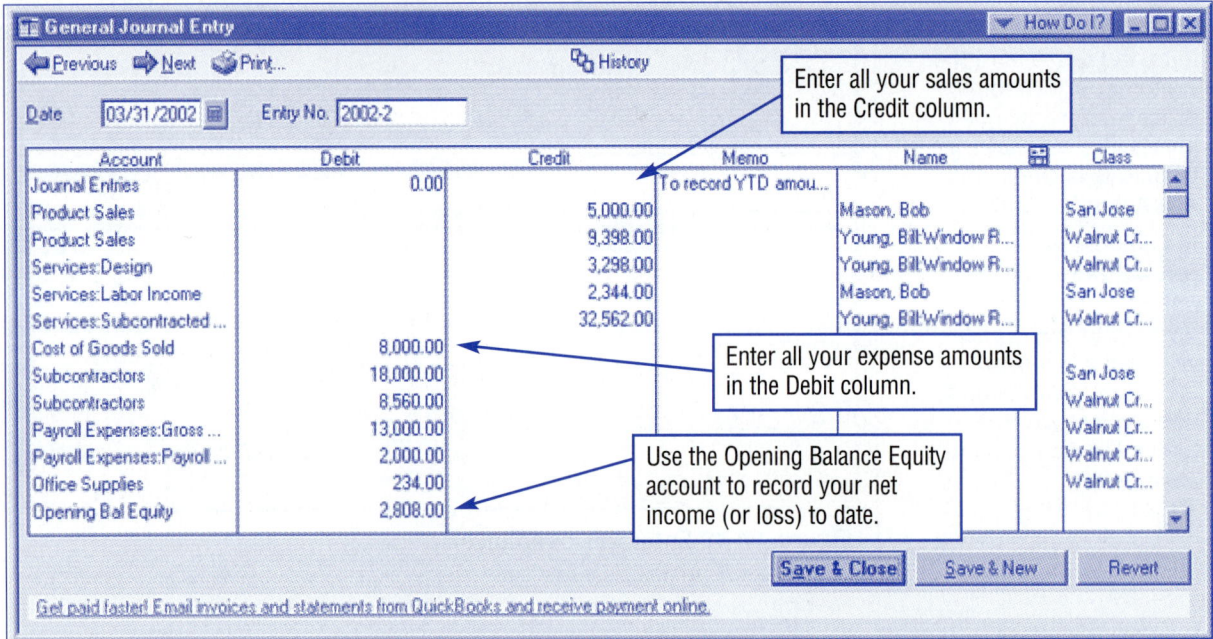

Figure 10-50 The General Journal Entry for a start date after the beginning of the year

Adjusting Opening Balance for Sales Tax Payable – Step 7

To enter the opening balance for Sales Tax Payable, begin by opening the Sales Tax Payable register to view the activity in the account. Notice that there are entries for each of the Invoices you just entered. Since these transactions add to the balance in Sales Tax Payable, you'll need to subtract the current balance in the account from the amount shown on Trial Balance from your accountant (or your 12/31/01 sales tax return). Then create a Sales Tax Adjustment for this difference. This is necessary because the sales tax portion of your open Invoices represents only a portion of the total sales tax liability.

1 Select the *Vendors* menu, choose **Sales Tax**, and then choose **Adjust Sales Tax Due**.

2 Complete the Sales Tax Adjustment screen as shown in Figure 10-51, and click **OK**.

If you pay sales tax to more than one vendor (sales tax agency), you will need to enter a separate adjustment for each vendor.

COMPUTER TUTORIAL

DID YOU KNOW The Sales Tax Adjustment screen creates a General Journal Entry transaction in QuickBooks. Therefore, the Entry No. screen will automatically preselect the next Journal Entry number in sequence. If you prefer, you could enter this adjustment using a General Journal Entry.

Sales Tax Adjustment

Adjustment Date | 12/31/2001 |

Entry No. | 2001-2 | Class |

Sales Tax Vendor | State Board of Equalization |

Adjustment Account | Opening Bal Equity |

Adjustment
- ○ Increase Sales Tax By
- ○ Reduce Sales Tax By
- Amount | 105.30 |

Memo | Adjust Sales Tax Opening Balance |

[OK] [Cancel] [Help]

Figure 10-51 The Sales Tax Adjustment screen

Adjusting Inventory for Actual Counts – Step 8

If you have inventory, you'll need to create an inventory adjustment to adjust the actual quantity and value on hand as of your start date. This is done *after* you enter your outstanding Bills and Invoices, so that the actual inventory counts and costs will be accurate even if some of the Bills and/or Invoices include Inventory Items.

As with the adjustment to Sales Tax Payable, begin by opening the Inventory register to view the activity and the current balance. Also, open the Item List to view the current stock status of each Inventory Item. Then adjust the quantity on hand and value of each item so that inventory will agree with the physical inventory counts and the company's Trial Balance as of your start date.

COMPUTER TUTORIAL

① Select the *Vendors* menu, choose **Inventory Activities**, and then choose **Adjust Quantity/Value on Hand**.

② Enter the actual counts and values according the to physical inventory listed in Table 10-6 on page 523. Use "Opening Balance Equity" as the adjustment account (see Figure 10-52).

③ Click **OK** on the Income or Expense Expected warning screen.

④ Check "Value Adjustment" to see the New Value.

⑤ Click **Save & Close** to record the transaction.

Figure 10-52 Adjust inventory as of the start date.

Setup Payroll Lists and Year-to-Date Payroll Information – Step 9

Setting up payroll in QuickBooks is a lengthy and involved process. See Chapter 7 for more information about setting up the payroll feature.

Closing Opening Balance Equity into Retained Earnings – Step 10

Before you transfer the balance of Opening Balance Equity into Retained Earnings, make sure the account balances in QuickBooks match your accountant's Trial Balance.

COMPUTER TUTORIAL

Proofing Your Trial Balance

1. Select the *Reports* menu, choose **Accountant & Taxes**, and then choose **Trial Balance**.

2. Set the dates for your start date as shown in Figure 10-53.

3. After reviewing the Trial Balance, write down the balance of the Opening Balance Equity account, and close the screen.

Once you've verified that all of the other opening balances are correct, close the Opening Balance Equity account into Retained Earnings.

The balances in income and expense accounts are from outstanding Invoices and Bills. QuickBooks automatically closes these balances into Retained Earnings at the end of the year.

Trial Balance		
Modify Report... Memorize... Print... Excel... Hide Header Collapse Re		
Dates Custom From 12/31/2001 To 12/31/2001 Sor		

Academy Glass, Inc.

Trial Balance

Accrual Basis   As of December 31, 2001

	Dec 31, 01	
	Debit	Credit
Checking	17,959.60	
Money Market	12,100.00	
Journal Entries	0.00	
Accounts Receivable	575.68	
Inventory Asset	1,800.00	
Fixed Assets:Cost	13,250.00	
Fixed Assets:Accumulated Deprecia...		2,300.00
Accounts Payable		142.00
National Bank VISA Gold		2,152.00
Payroll Liabilities:Federal PR Taxes		83.00
Payroll Liabilities:State PR Taxes		285.00
Sales Tax Payable		136.98
Loan Payable		6,700.00
Opening Bal Equity		23,484.30
Common Stock		10,000.00
Product Sales		384.00
Services:Labor Income		160.00
Subcontractors	142.00	
TOTAL	45,827.28	45,827.28

Figure 10-53 The Trial Balance for Academy as of the start date

COMPUTER TUTORIAL

Notice that the Trial Balance looks slightly different than your accountant's report (in Figure 10-40). For example, there are balances in several income and expense accounts, as well as in Opening Balance Equity. Don't worry about this difference; you're not finished with the setup yet.

Your Trial Balance could also differ from your accountant's report if the reporting bases on the two reports are not the same. For example, if you create an accrual basis Trial Balance and your accountant's Trial Balance is cash basis, the balances in the income and expense accounts may be different. Regardless of which method of accounting you use, QuickBooks will close the balances in the income and expense accounts automatically at the appropriate time. Therefore, at this point in your setup, you should create an accrual basis Trial Balance, regardless of which basis you'll ultimately use on reports. Just verify that all of the Balance Sheet account balances are accurate.

The income and expense accounts have balances because you just entered Invoices and Bills for the open Invoices and unpaid Bills. Those Invoices and Bills were dated during the prior year, so those transactions add to income and expenses for that year.

Closing Opening Balance Equity to Retained Earnings

Once you have compared your Trial Balance report to your accountant's report, use a General Journal Entry to transfer (close) the balance in Opening Balance Equity into Retained Earnings.

① Select the *Banking* menu and choose **Make Journal Entry**.

② Set the *Date* field to your start date.

③ Enter the General Journal Entry as shown in Figure 10-54, and click **Save & Close**.

Figure 10-54 The General Journal Entry to close Opening Balance Equity into Retained Earnings

Verifying your Opening Balances– Step 11

When you're finished entering all of the opening balances and you've closed the Opening Balance Equity account into Retained Earnings, verify your Balance Sheet. Create a Balance Sheet for the day after your start date and verify that the numbers match your accountant's Trial Balance.

COMPUTER TUTORIAL

① Select the *Reports* menu, choose **Company & Financial**, and then choose **Balance Sheet Standard**.

② Set the *As of* field to "01/01/2002," the day after your start date (see Figure 10-55).

③ Print the report and close the screen.

Figure 10-55 The Academy Glass Balance Sheet

Setting the Closing Date and Backing up the File – Step 12

Now that you have entered all of your opening balances in the file, create a backup of the file. After you begin entering transactions you should back up your file on a regular basis, but keep the backup you perform in Step 12 of the setup on a separate disk or in a separate folder on your computer's hard drive, so that you always have a clean record of your setup transactions.

Backing up the Data File

For details on backing up your file, see *Backing Up Your Data* beginning on page 567.

Setting the Closing Date to Protect your Setup Balances

For details on setting the Closing Date and Closing Date password, see Chapter 9.

Congratulations! You've finished the setup of your company file. You are now ready to setup users of the file, modify your sales forms, and begin entering transactions.

USERS AND PASSWORDS

Setting Up Users in the Company File

QuickBooks provides a feature for defining "users" of the file. This feature allows the "administrator" (the owner of the file) to set privileges for each user of the file. This provides security and user tracking when several people have access to the same data file.

Each user can have a password, if desired. When a user opens the company file, QuickBooks requires a user name and password. The privileges granted to that user by the administrator determine what functions of QuickBooks they can access. For example, a user might have access to Accounts Receivable, Accounts Payable, and Banking functions, but not payroll or "sensitive activities" like on-line banking. For a complete description of each privilege, click the Help button on the User Setup screens.

COMPUTER TUTORIAL

NOTE

Setting up users and modifying form templates are optional steps you could complete now. If you are the only user of the QuickBooks file and you are content with the default design and format of the QuickBooks sales forms, you do not need to perform the steps in these next two sections when working with your own company file.

① Select the *Company* menu, and choose **Set up Users**.

② Enter "Doug" in the *Administrator's Name* field, and press <TAB> (see Figure 10-56).

③ Enter "1234" in the *Administrator's Password* and *Confirm Password* fields, and click **OK**.

Several privileges are reserved for the Administrator of the file. For example, the Administrator is the only one who can view or change the company information (name, address, etc.) for the file. Also, the Administrator is the only one who can make any changes to Company Preferences. For more information about the file administrator, see QuickBooks online Help.

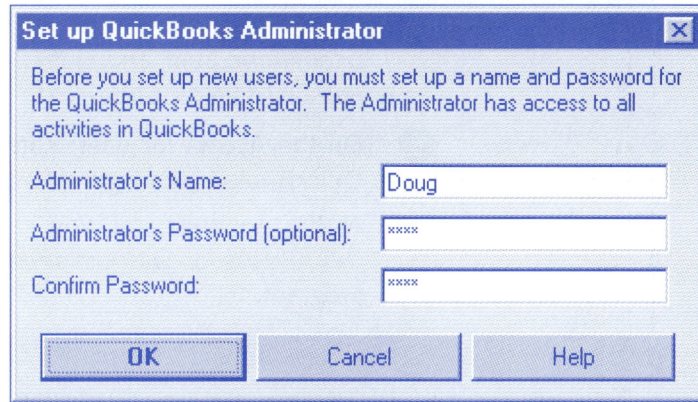

Figure 10-56 Enter the Administrator's name and password.

④ The screen in Figure 10-57 shows the User list for this company file. To create an additional user, click **Add User**.

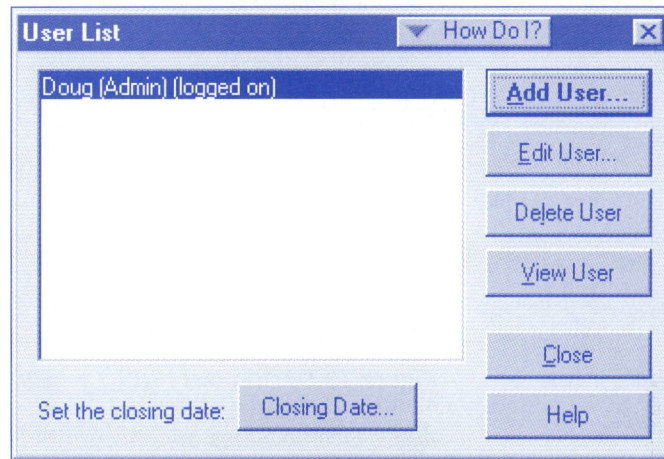

Figure 10-57 The User list for a company file

When you click **Add User**, QuickBooks walks you through a series of screens (a Wizard) where you set privileges for each user (see Figure 10-58). Make your selections as appropriate.

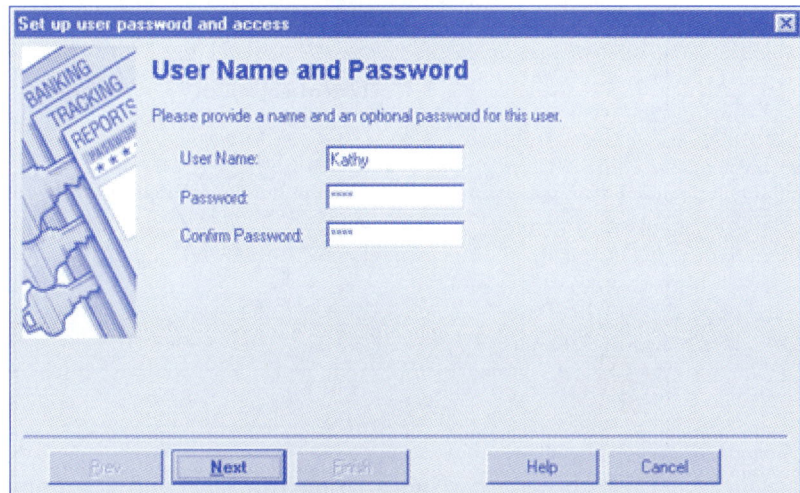

Figure 10-58 The User Name and Password screen

⑤ On the User Name and Password screen, enter "Kathy" in the *User Name* field, and enter "4321" in the *Password* and *Confirm Password* fields. Click **Next**.

⑥ On the Access for user: Kathy screen, select "Selected areas of QuickBooks" (see Figure 10-59). Click **Next**.

As the Administrator, you can give users access to all areas of QuickBooks or you can restrict access to selected areas of the program.

Figure 10-59 You can restrict a user's access.

⑦ On the Sales and Accounts Receivable screen, select **Full Access** and click **Next** (see Figure 10-60).

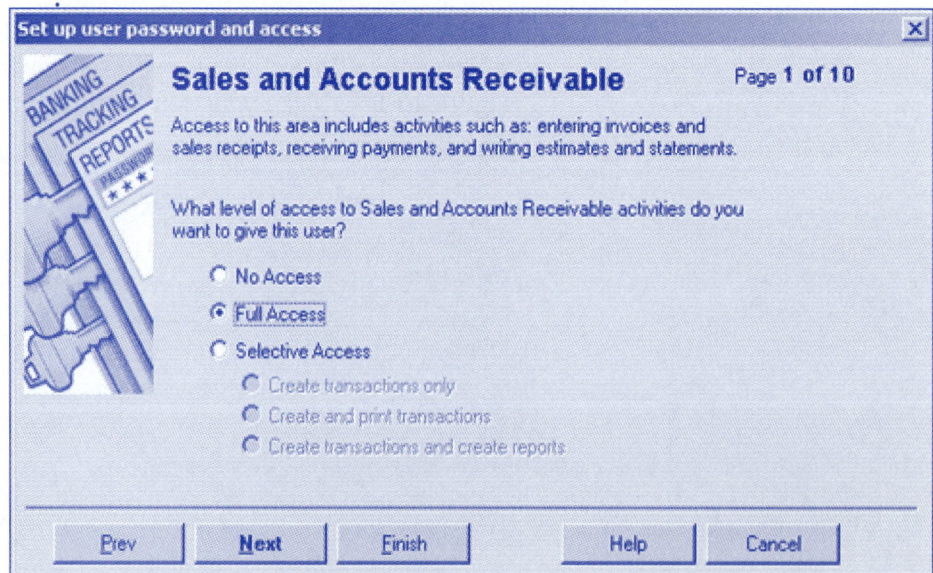

Figure 10-60 The Sales and Accounts Receivable screen

8 Click **Next** on each following screen to view and modify the default settings (see Figure 10-60).

When setting up your own file, set access rights for each new user as appropriate. If you're not sure what to choose, click **Help**. Online Help will fully explain each privilege.

9 On the final screen, review the privileges that you've set for this user (see Figure 10-61). If you want to make any changes, click **Prev** until you see the screen you want to change. To save your new user settings, click **Finish**.

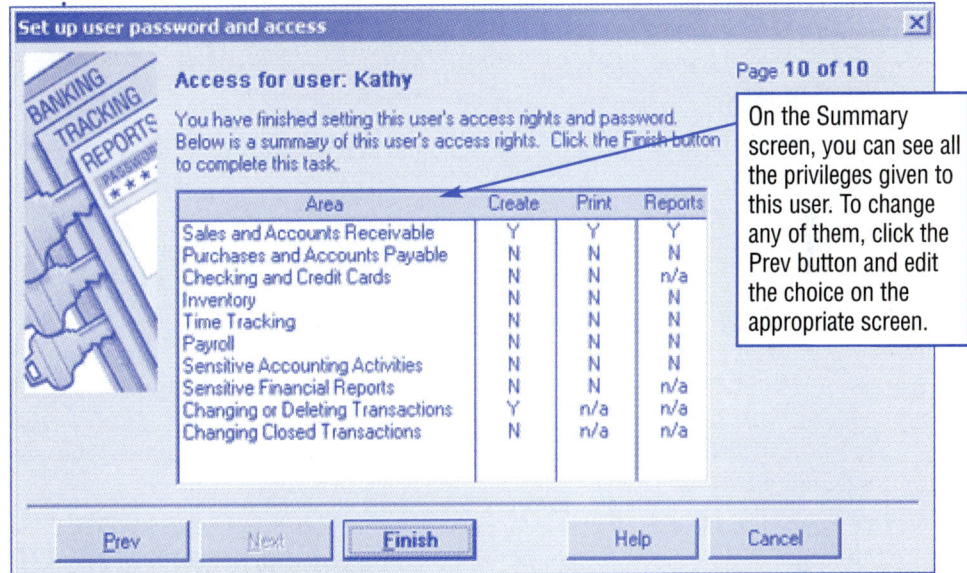

Set up user password and access

Access for user: Kathy   Page **10 of 10**

You have finished setting this user's access rights and password. Below is a summary of this user's access rights. Click the Finish button to complete this task.

Area	Create	Print	Reports
Sales and Accounts Receivable	Y	Y	Y
Purchases and Accounts Payable	N	N	N
Checking and Credit Cards	N	N	n/a
Inventory	N	N	N
Time Tracking	N	N	N
Payroll	N	N	N
Sensitive Accounting Activities	N	N	N
Sensitive Financial Reports	N	N	n/a
Changing or Deleting Transactions	Y	n/a	n/a
Changing Closed Transactions	N	n/a	n/a

On the Summary screen, you can see all the privileges given to this user. To change any of them, click the Prev button and edit the choice on the appropriate screen.

Prev   Next   **Finish**   Help   Cancel

Figure 10-61 The Summary screen

10 Click **Close** on the User List screen.

SUMMARY OF KEY POINTS

In this chapter, you learned how to set up a company file in QuickBooks. Setting up the file is the most important part of making QuickBooks work well for you. Don't forget to verify that the all your balances are correct before using your data file.

Topics covered in this chapter include:

◆ The EasyStep Interview (Page 492)

◆ Adjusting Customer and Vendor Balances after using the EasyStep Interview (Page 501)

◆ Complete Company File Setup – The 12-step process (Page 504)

◆ Choosing a Start Date (Page 505)

◆ Creating the QuickBooks Company File (Page 506)

◆ Setting Up the Chart of Accounts (Page 509)

◆ Gathering your Information for Setting Up Opening Balances (Page 520)

◆ Entering Opening Balances (Page 523)

◆ Entering Year-to-Date Income and Expenses (Page 532)

◆ Adjusting the Opening Balance for Sales Tax Payable (Page 533)

◆ Closing Opening Balance Equity into Retained Earnings (Page 535)

◆ Verifying your Opening Balances (Page 537)

◆ Setting the Closing Date and Backing up the File (Page 537)

◆ Setting up Users and Passwords (Page 538)

Name _____ **Date** _____

CHAPTER REVIEW AND APPLICATIONS

Comprehension
QUESTIONS

Done

In your notebook, record answers to the following questions.

1. If you enter opening balances during the EasyStep Interview in QuickBooks, explain how you would adjust to properly redefine the uncategorized income and expenses generated.

2. Explain how you would set up your Chart of Accounts to separately track state, county, and city taxes and provide a summary total of all taxes paid at the same time.

3. If you have been separately tracking your entertainment and meal expenses, what action would you take if you wanted to track them as one account?

4. Explain the importance of entering your outstanding checks as of the Start Date into the Checking account.

Multiple-Choice
QUESTIONS

In your notebook, record the best answer for each of the following questions.

1. C The best start date for a QuickBooks company file setup is
    a. the first day of the fiscal year (01/01/xx).
    b. the last day of the month before the first month it is used.
    c. the last day of the fiscal year (12/31/xx).
    d. the first day of the quarter chosen for conversion.

2. d The best way to set up A/R and A/P balances in QuickBooks is to
    a. enter the total amount of A/R and A/P on a journal entry for your start date.
    b. enter the balance of each account by editing the accounts in the chart of accounts.
    c. use a special account called A/R Setup (or A/P Setup) to record the opening balances.
    d. enter a separate Invoice for each open invoice and enter a separate Bill for each unpaid bill.

3. a Setting up a company file does not include:
    a. obtaining a business license.
    b. selecting the appropriate chart of accounts for your type of business.
    c. adding accounts to the chart of accounts.
    d. entering Invoices.

4. d A good example of a liability account is
    a. inventory.
    b. accounts receivable.
    c. advertising.
    d. accounts payable.

Multiple-Choice
QUESTIONS
(Continued)

5. _b_ To ensure the accuracy of the information entered during setup, it is important to
   a. know your Retained Earnings
   b. verify that your Trial Balance matches the one provided by your accountant.
   c. start at the beginning of the fiscal period
   d. know everything there is to know about accounting

6. _b_ Close Opening Balance Equity to Retained Earnings by
   a. starting to enter new daily transactions
   b. creating a General Journal Entry
   c. setting the Closing Date, QuickBooks will then make the entry for you
   d. selecting Close Opening Balance on the Activities menu

Completion
STATEMENTS

Done

In the space provided, write the word(s) that best complete each statement.

1. There are five basic account types in accounting: _____ and _____.

2. It is impossible to delete a QuickBooks account if _____.

3. If your start date is not 12/31 and you want QuickBooks to track your payroll, you will need _____, and any other deductions for each employee so far in the year.

4. If you feel comfortable creating General Journal Entries and if you understand debits and credits, you can use a _____ to record some, but not all, of your_____ balances.

Name _____ Date _____

APPLY YOUR KNOWLEDGE

PROBLEM 10-1

Create a new QuickBooks company file for Academy Glass. Use the information from the following tables and figures to completely set up the file using 12/31/2002 as your start date. Use the 12-step setup process discussed in this chapter.

Company Info	
Company Name	Academy Glass
Legal Name	Academy Glass, Inc.
Address	123 Main Street Pleasanton, CA 94588
Country	US
Phone	925-555-1111
Fax	925-555-1112
Email	info@academyglass.com
Website	http://www.academyglass.com
First Month of Income Tax Year	January
First Month of Fiscal Year	January
Income Tax Form	Form 1120S (S Corporation)
Federal ID	11-1234567 **Note:** to enter this number, select Company Information from the Company menu.

Table 10-7 Company Information

Company Preference	
Accounting	Check the "Use Account Numbers" box Check the "Use Class Tracking" box
Payroll & Employees	Select "Full payroll features" Accept the default setting for the remaining preferences
Purchases & Vendors	Select "Inventory and purchase orders are active"
Sales Tax	Click "Yes" on "Do You Charge Sales Tax?" Leave Default Sales Tax settings for: Taxable Sales Tax Code: **Tax** Nontaxable Sales Tax Code: **Non** Owe Sales Tax **as of invoice date (accrual)** Pay Sales Tax **Monthly** Check the "Mark taxable amounts with "T" when printing" box In the *Most common sales tax* field, select **Add New** and add the Santa Clara sales tax item as specified in Table 10-11.

Table 10-8 Company Preferences

Chart of Accounts

Note: It is not necessary to enter descriptions, bank account numbers, or assign tax line items to any of these accounts for this problem. When you create the new data file, QuickBooks will create some accounts on the Chart of Accounts for you. Your goal in this practice is to add, delete or modify the existing Charts of Accounts as necessary so it agrees with the list below.

Account Number	Account Name	Account Type
1100	Checking	Bank
1150	Money Market	Bank
1175	Savings	Bank
1199	Journal Entries	Bank
1200	Accounts Receivable	Accounts Receivable
1220	Employee Advances	Other Current Asset
1300	Inventory Asset	Other Current Asset
1399	Undeposited Funds	Other Current Asset
1400	Fixed Assets	Fixed Asset
1410	Fixed Assets:Cost	Fixed Asset
1420	Fixed Assets:Accumulated Depreciation	Fixed Asset
2000	Accounts Payable	Accounts Payable
2050	National Bank VISA Gold	Credit Card
2060	Customer Deposits	Other Current Liability
2100	Payroll Liabilities	Other Current Liability
2100-05	Payroll Liabilities:Federal PR Taxes	Other Current Liability
2100-10	Payroll Liabilities:State PR Taxes	Other Current Liability
2100-15	Payroll Liabilities:Other Payroll Liabilities	Other Current Liability
2100-20	Payroll Liabilities:Union Dues Payable	Other Current Liability
2200	Sales Tax Payable	Other Current Liability
2300	Loan Payable	Long Term Liability
3000	Opening Bal Equity	Equity
3100	Common Stock	Equity
3900	Retained Earnings	Equity
4000	Product Sales	Income
4070	Services	Income
4070-05	Services:Design	Income
4070-10	Services:Labor Income	Income
4070-15	Services:Subcontracted Labor	Income
4070-20	Services:Shipping & Delivery	Income
4100	Expenses Reimbursed	Income
4200	Discounts Taken	Income
5000	Cost of Goods Sold	Cost of Goods Sold
6000	Reimbursable Expenses	Expense
6020	Advertising	Expense
6050	Automobile Expense	Expense
6055	Bad Debts	Expense
6060	Bank Service Charges	Expense
6070	Bankcard Fees	Expense
6150	Depreciation Expense	Expense
6155	Discounts Given	Expense
6160	Dues and Subscriptions	Expense
6170	Equipment Rental	Expense

(Table continues on next page)

Name _____ Date _____

6180	Insurance	Expense
6180-05	Insurance:Liability Insurance	Expense
6180-10	Insurance:Health Insurance Expense	Expense
6180-15	Insurance:Disability Insurance	Expense
6180-20	Insurance:Work Comp	Expense
6200	Interest Expense	Expense
6220	Inventory Variance	Expense
6230	Licenses and Permits	Expense
6240	Miscellaneous	Expense
6250	Postage and Delivery	Expense
6260	Printing and Reproduction	Expense
6270	Professional Fees	Expense
6270-05	Professional Fees:Accounting	Expense
6270-10	Professional Fees:Legal Fees	Expense
6290	Rent	Expense
6300	Repairs	Expense
6300-05	Repairs:Building Repairs	Expense
6300-10	Repairs:Computer Repairs	Expense
6300-15	Repairs:Equipment Repairs	Expense
6340	Telephone	Expense
6340-05	Telephone:Cellular Phone	Expense
6345	Freight & Delivery	Expense
6350	Travel & Ent	Expense
6350-05	Travel & Ent:Meals	Expense
6350-10	Travel & Ent:Travel	Expense
6390	Utilities	Expense
6390-05	Utilities:Gas and Electric	Expense
6390-10	Utilities:Water	Expense
6490	Landscaping	Expense
6520	Job Materials	Expense
6550	Office Supplies	Expense
6560	Payroll Expenses	Expense
6560-05	Payroll Expenses:Gross Wages	Expense
6560-10	Payroll Expenses:Officer's Compensation	Expense
6560-15	Payroll Expenses:Payroll Taxes	Expense
6560-20	Payroll Expenses:Benefits	Expense
6750	Subcontractors	Expense
6820	Taxes	Expense
6820-05	Taxes:Federal	Expense
6820-10	Taxes:State	Expense
7010	Interest Income	Other Income
7030	Other Income	Other Income
8010	Other Expenses	Other Expense

Table 10-9 The Chart of Accounts

Classes – Academy Glass uses classes to separately track revenues and expenses from each of their locations.

Class Names	San Jose	Walnut Creek	Overhead

Table 10-10 Class Tracking

Items – Below is the Item list that will be used to track products and services sold by Academy Glass.

Type	Item	Description	Tax Code	Account	Price
Service	Design	Window Design Services	Non	Services:Design	$75.00
Service	Labor	Window/Door Installation Labor	Non	Services: Labor Income	$40.00
Inventory Part	104-Slider	10 ft. Slider – Wood Frame Asset Account: Inventory Asset COGS Account: Cost of Goods Sold Cost: $300.00 Preferred Vendor: Ace Glass Reorder Point: 5	Tax	Product Sales	$360.00
Inventory Part	106-Slider	12 ft. Slider – Wood Frame Asset Account: Inventory Asset COGS Account: Cost of Goods Sold Cost: $350.00 Preferred Vendor: Ace Glass Reorder Point: 5	Tax	Product Sales	$420.00
Non-inventory Part	Skylight	Skylight	Tax	Product Sales	$0.00
Non-inventory Part	Window	Window	Tax	Product Sales	$0.00
Other Charge	Bad Debt	Bad Debt – Write off	Non	Bad Debts	$0.00
Other Charge	BounceChg	Return Check Fee	Non	Other Income	$10.00
Other Charge	Deposit	Customer Prepayments & Deposits	Non	Customer Deposits	$0.00
Other Charge	Fin Chg	Finance Charges on Overdue Balance	Non	Interest Income	18.0%
Other Charge	Restocking	Restocking Fee	Non	Product Sales	10.0%
Sales Tax Item	Contra Costa	Contra Costa County Sales Tax Tax Agency: State Board of Equalization	Non	Sales Tax Payable	8.25%
Sales Tax Item	Santa Clara	Santa Clara County Sales Tax Tax Agency: State Board of Equalization	Non	Sales Tax Payable	8.25%
Sales Tax Item	Out of State		Non	Sales Tax Payable	0.00

Table 10-11 The Item List

Terms – Set up the following terms in the Terms list.

Net 30	Net 15	2% 10, Net 30	Due on Receipt

Table 10-12 Terms List

Templates – Duplicate the Standard Product Invoice template and rename it as "Academy Glass Invoice."

Employees – Set up Jim Moen as an employee in the employee list. For now, don't worry about entering his address information or his payroll information.

Sales Reps – Set up Jim Moen as a sales rep in the Sales Rep list.

Name _____ Date _____

Opening Trial Balance – Figure 10-62 shows the ending Trial Balance for Academy Glass on 12/31/2002.

Academy Glass Trial Balance December 31, 2002	Debit	Credit
Checking	$35,290.17	
Money Market	$68,100.00	
Accounts Receivable	$ 2,382.73	
Inventory	$ 1,600.00	
Fixed Assets: Cost	$85,365.00	
Fixed Assets: Accumulated Depreciation		$ 43,550.00
Accounts Payable		$ 338.00
National Bank VISA Gold		$ 2,152.00
Payroll Liabilities: Federal PR Taxes		$ 83.00
Payroll Liabilities: State PR Taxes		$ 285.00
Sales Tax Payable		$ 227.03
Loan Payable		$ 28,625.00
Common Stock		$ 10,000.00
Retained Earnings		$ 107,377.87
TOTAL	**$192,737.90**	**$192,737.90**

Figure 10-62 The trial balance on 12/31/2002

Bank Statements – Figure 10-63 shows the Checking account bank statement for Academy Glass on their Start Date of 12/31/2002. There is no bank statement available for the money market account, but you've been told that there are no outstanding deposits or checks in that account.

Account:			Academy Glass–Main Checking			
Last Statement Date	11/30/2002		Beginning Balance			$32,624.52
This Statement Date	12/31/2002		Less: Checks & Debits			($7,037.40)
			Plus: Deposits & Credits			$10,165.90
			Ending Balance			**$35,753.02**

Checks		Date	Amount	Deposits	Date	Amount
	3466	2-Dec	$324.00	Customer Deposit	8-Dec	$6,150.00
	3467	3-Dec	$128.60	Customer Deposit	20-Dec	$4,007.28
	3468	5-Dec	$83.00	Interest Earned	31-Dec	$8.62
	3469	8-Dec	$285.00	Total Deposits:		**$10,165.90**
	3470	10-Dec	$1,528.00			
	3471	12-Dec	$3,000.00			
	3472	13-Dec	$276.52			
	3473	15-Dec	$142.00			
	3474	28-Dec	$1,260.28			
Total Checks:			**$7,027.40**			

Other Debits			
Service Charge	31-Dec	$10.00	
Total Other Debits		**$10.00**	

Figure 10-63 The bank statement for checking account on 12/31/2002.

Outstanding Checks and Deposits – Table 10-13 shows a list of outstanding checks and deposits in the Checking account on 12/31/2002. "QuickAdd" each of the customer names when prompted.

Outstanding Deposits at 12/31/02			Outstanding Checks at 12/31/02		
Date	**Amount**		**Date**	**Check #**	**Amount**
12/30/02	$3000.00		12/26/02	3475	$3462.85

Table 10-13 Outstanding checks and deposits.

Open Invoices – Table 10-14 shows a list of all open Invoices for Academy Glass on 12/31/2002. "QuickAdd" each of the vendor names when prompted.

Inv #	Invoice Date	Customer:Job	Class	Terms	Rep	Item	Qty	Amt Due
2002-955	12/18/2002	Doughboy Donuts	San Jose	Net 30	JM	Window Skylight Santa Clara Tax Total of Invoice	1 unit 2 units 8.25%	$1,234.00 $345.00ea. $2,082.73
2002-968	12/21/2002	Scotts Shoes	San Jose	Net 30	JM	Design 4 Hrs @ 75/hr Total of Invoice		$300.00 $300.00

Table 10-14 Open Invoices

Unpaid Bills – Academy Glass had one unpaid Bill at 12/31/2002.

Bill #	Bill Date	Terms	Vendor	Amt Due	Account/Item	Job	Class	Billable
52773	12/21/2002	Net 15	Boswell Insulation	338.00	Subcontractors Expense	Scotts Shoes	San Jose	Tax

Table 10-15 Unpaid bills

Physical Inventory by Inventory Part – Below is the physical Inventory counts and values at 12/31/2002.

Physical Inventory at 12/31/2002		
Item	Quantity on Hand	Value
104-Slider	3	$900
106-Slider	2	$700

Table 10-16 Physical Inventory by Inventory Part

Name _____   **Date** _____

After completing the setup, print the following reports:

1. Account Listing

2. Item listing

3. Trial Balance at 12/31/2002

   Notice that the Trial Balance does not match the one in Figure 10-62 exactly. The income and expenses from the open Invoices and unpaid Bills shows in the income and expense accounts. This is CORRECT! When QuickBooks "closes" the year, those numbers will be posted into Retained Earnings. To see it work, change the date on the Trial Balance to 1/1/2003.

4. Open Invoices at 12/31/2002

5. Unpaid Bills at 12/31/2002

6. Inventory Valuation Summary at 12/31/2002

7. Balance Sheet on 1/1/2003

   Notice that Retained Earnings has been adjusted for the income and expenses from last year. This shows how QuickBooks automatically calculates Retained Earnings. If you change the date on the balance sheet to 12/31/2002, you'll see Net Income on the Balance Sheet and the Retained Earnings number will change back to the "before closing" amounts. Try it.

Workplace *Applications*

DISCUSSION QUESTIONS

These questions are designed to help you apply what you are learning about QuickBooks to your own organization. Use your notebook to record your answers and your thoughts.

1. What would be the best start date for using Quick Books in your organization? Why?

2. How many accounts are in your organization's Chart of Accounts? How many subaccounts are there? What is the value of a subaccount to your organization? Or, if you do not have any, could there be a value and what would it be?

3. Consider the accounts that have outlived their usefulness to your company. Is the best approach to merge them, delete them, or deactivate them? Explain your answer.

4. Consider the Items that are no longer relevant to your company. Is it because they are obsolete or no longer sold? Is the best approach to merge them, delete them, or deactivate them? Explain your answer.

5. As your company sets up QuickBooks, what do you think the approach should be to enter opening balances for customers and vendors? Why?

ACTIVITY

Evaluate your company's Chart of Accounts and how well it fits your company's needs. Identify accounts that could be setup as subaccounts or merged into others to better track company income or expenses. Design a Chart of Accounts based on your findings that would best fit your company's needs.

Name _____ Date _____

CASE STUDY

MUSIC CENTRAL

Music Central sells and services musical instruments and offers music lessons. They track several of each type of instrument in inventory but they do not track replacement parts in inventory. All of the piano and guitar lessons are subcontracted to Thomas Teaches Tunes; and all piano maintenance is subcontracted to Key Tuning Company. However, all wind instruments are taught by Music Central employees. The company is located in downtown Boston and is required to charge state, county, and local sales tax. They have just hired you to convert their manual accounting system to QuickBooks.

The company inventories the following types of instruments, and they stock several different brands of each:

Trumpets (2 brands)   Saxophones (3 brands)
Flutes (1 brand)   Clarinets (3 brands)
Guitars (6 brands)   Pianos (3 brands)

The company stocks (but does not track in inventory), the following replacement parts:

Key Pads – Various sizes
Strings – Various sizes
Valves – Various types and sizes
Reeds – Various types and sizes

The company performs the following services:

Trumpet Lesson
Flute Lesson
Saxophone Lesson
Clarinet Lesson
Guitar Lesson (subcontracted)
Piano Tuning/Maint (subcontracted)
Piano Lesson (subcontracted)

Questions

1. Describe how you would approach the setup of the item list for this company. Discuss the trade-offs of tracking each brand of instrument as a separate inventory part, and the impact it will have on the amount of data entry for the bookkeeper. Make recommendations on how you would set up the item list for the company.

2. How would you set up the system to separately track the income and expenses for the subcontracted services?

3. What information would you need from the owner of the company to set up the opening balances for the company, assuming they are a calendar year company and you chose to set them up on 12/31/2002?

4. The owner wants only two people in the company to be able to use Payroll in QuickBooks. How would you set up their access differently from others who are not allowed to use Payroll?

*inter***NET**
CONNECTION

The Small Business Administration (SBA) offers many resources to the entrepreneur. Go to http://www.sba.gov and identify a few of these resource services.

Millennium Financial Planning Business Scenario

After 13 years with his company, Herb Faucett was caught in a corporate downsizing effort. Having spent the last five years as a corporate business manager, it struck him that he should launch his next career phase as an entrepreneur. Taking his severance pay package and the accumulated savings and convincing another displaced employee to join him, he developed a well-thought-out business plan and started Millennium Financial Planning (MFP).

Herb saw great opportunities. He lived in a large Texas city in close proximity to several regional colleges and large universities, as well as hundreds of very large and medium-sized corporations. He planned to offer financial planning, investment, and estate planning seminars plus related consulting services to individual, corporate, and institutional clients. Furthermore, his business plan included the purchase and promotion of planning kits, along with several popular books and instructional videos related to achieving financial success, this he would sell at corporate and collegiate brown-bag lunch seminars. Several times a year he would conduct large seminars on investing strategies and building wealth, as well as offer companion seminars on estate planning and minimizing taxes. To control his new

start-up, he selected QuickBooks software to help manage the business operations while fulfilling fiduciary responsibilities from an accounting, tax, and record-keeping perspective. Along with his colleague, Chester Rankin, the only full-time employee, Herb hired another employee, Christopher R. Porter, on a part-time basis to help launch the company. He leased 1,200 square feet of prime downtown office space.

Using the Chart of Accounts for MFP, you will record the start-up costs, including the purchase of three types of products for resale at the seminars and via direct mail or the Internet. You will use inventory tracking for the books and videos; the planning kits are noninventory products. Sales of all products will be handled as cash sales, whereas the consulting and seminar services will be billed to customers via Invoices. You will record all revenue and expense transactions into one of the three classes that MFP uses to track performance. The classes that have been set up are Consulting/Seminars, Product Sales, and Admin/Other. At the end of each period, you will reconcile the bank statement and then produce financial statements and sales analysis reports, including a report of business performance by class.

PAYROLL PREMISES AND SETUP FOR MFP SIMULATION

Initially, there are three employees set up on the MFP Employee list. Herb Faucett is set up as an owner in the employee list and is therefore not paid regular wages through payroll. Christopher R. Porter is a part-time hourly employee with an hourly regular rate of $12.50, overtime hourly rate of $18.75, and holiday hourly rate of $25.00. He is single, has no dependents, and claims one federal allowance. Payroll costs are allocated to the Admin/Other class. Chester P. Rankin is a salaried employee with an annual salary of $52,000. He is married

and claims two federal allowances. Payroll costs are allocated to the Consulting/Seminars class.

All employees are paid on a biweekly basis. The payroll period begins on Mondays. All employees are domiciled and work in the state of Texas.

Texas SUI (state unemployment) rate for MFP is 0.24% paid by the employer quarterly. A maximum earnings subject to tax is $9,000 annually.

All full- and part-time employees are covered under the company-sponsored medical insurance plan underwritten by Longhorn American Insurance Company. MFP remits the premium monthly to Longhorn American. The company and the employees share the cost of monthly premiums equally. Deductions are made from net pay for the employee portion of the premium in accordance with the following premium schedule.

Total monthly premium for employees with *no dependents* is $100.00. The employee share is $50.00. A payroll deduction from net pay in the amount of $25.00 is automatically made each pay period. Total monthly premium for employees *with dependents* is $200.00. The employee share is $100.00. A payroll deduction from net pay in the amount of $50.00 is automatically made each pay period.

Books, videos, and planning kits are classified as Product Sales and are set up in the Item list. Sales are normally booked at organizational and institutional seminars to individual attendees. All Product Sales are handled as cash sales and are entered using the customer name "Individual Seminar Participants," which has been set up in the Customer list. These prepaid orders are then shipped directly to purchasers from the MFP headquarters location.

Sales tax is charged on all products sold. The Item named TX Sales Tax has been set up to apply the tax of 7.25%, which applies in the county where MFP is located and from which products are shipped.

All bills from vendors are held until the last working day of each month, sorted by due date, and paid in a batch. All cash sales and invoice payments are directed to the Undeposited Funds (Asset) account to await batch deposit with other funds.

CUSTOMERS

The Customer list consists of the following clients, billed with invoices: Central Texas University, Computer Manufacturers USA, Energy Corporation of Texas, Houston Community Campus, and Texas State University and Petroleum Operators, Inc. Individual seminar participants are John R. Clark and M. L. Kountz. One customer record called "Individual Seminar Participants is used to record one summary Cash Sale of all products sold at each seminar.

VENDORS

Braten Investments (Landlord); Education & Medical Fund (Charitable organization); Hotel Legacy (Seminar host); Image Contacts, Inc. (Printing and mailouts); IRS (Payroll liabilities);Lone Star Office Supply (Office supplies); Longhorn American Insurance (Insurance underwriter); Office Supply Depot (Office supplies and equipment); Provident Texas Investors (Investment consultant); Rash Productions (Seminar consultant); South Texas Bell (Telephone and communications provider); Texas Light & Power (Electrical power provider); Texas Media & Publications (Distributor of books, videos, and planning kits); Texas State Comptroller (Texas Sales Tax).

INSTRUCTIONS

1. Restore the Millennium.QBB file to your hard disk (or as your instructor directs).

2. Print a Chart of Accounts.

3. Enter the transactions for May 2002.

4. Reconcile the bank statement for May using the bank statement shown on page 561.

5. Prepare the following reports and graphs: Balance Sheet (Standard) as of 5/31/2002; Profit and Loss (Standard) for May; Profit and Loss (by Class); Statement of Cash Flows for May; Sales by Item Summary for May 1–May 31; Graph—Sales by Month (by Customer) for May 1–May 31.

6. Enter the transactions for June using the bank statement shown on page 562.

7. Reconcile the bank statement for June.

8. Prepare the following reports: Balance Sheet (Standard) as of 6/30/2002; Profit and Loss (Standard) for June; Profit and Loss (by Class) for June; Statement of Cash Flows for June; Sales by Item Summary for June 1–June 30; Graph—Sales by Month (by Customer) for June 1–June 30.

9. Print the General Ledger Report with dates 05/01/2002–06/30/2002 customized to show Debit and Credit columns. Also customize the report to include only accounts In Use.

10. Complete the analysis questions.

TRANSACTIONS

May 2002

1 Deposited $50,000 owner investment check 401 from Herb Faucett to Texas National Bank account to provide cash for operations. Code this deposit to the Investments Equity account. Allocated to Admin/Other Class.

1 Issued Purchase Order 2002–1 to Texas Media and Publications for stocking 50 books and 50 videos. Total purchase order was $2,000.00. Allocated to Product Sales Class.

1 Issued check 1001 to Braten Investments in the amount of $1,800.00 to pay May leasehold rent of $1,500.00 and the required refundable deposit of $300.00. Allocated to Admin/Other Class.

1 Issued Purchase Order 2002–2 to Office Supply Depot for a laptop PC ($2,500.00), copier ($1,100.00), Fax machine ($750.00), and projector with PC interface ($2,500.00) for a total of $6,850.00. These Items are set up and may be selected from the Items list. Allocated to Admin/Other Class.

1 Issued Purchase Order 2002–3 to Lone Star Office Supply for supplies in the amount of $350.00. Allocated to Admin/Other Class.

3 Received office equipment items and bill for $6,850.00 for Purchase Order 2002–2 from Office Supply Depot. Payment is due 06/02/2002. The bill reference number is 68-20.

3 Received supply items and bill for $350.00 for Purchase Order 2002–3 from Lone Star Office Supply. Payment is due 06/02/2002. The bill reference number is 6433.

3 Issued Check 1002 to Office Furniture Rentals, Inc. in the amount of $360.00 for office furniture rental for the month of May. This will be a recurring expense that can be memorized for future use. Allocated to Admin/Other Class.

4 Received 50 books and 50 videos, along with bill for $2,000.00 for Purchase Order 2002–1 from Texas Media and Publications. Payment is due 06/03/2002. Allocated to Product Sales Class. The bill reference number is 8736.

4 Issued Check 1003 in the amount of $300.00 to Longhorn American Insurance for employee health insurance policy premium for the month of May. Allocated $100.00 to Admin/Other Class for Christopher Porter's premium and $200.00 to Consulting/Seminars Class for Chester Rankin's premium. This will be a recurring expense that could be memorized for future use.

14 Paid hourly and salaried employees for time worked during payroll period 05/01/2002 through 05/14/2002. Payroll check 1004 issued to Chester Rankin and check 1005 to Christopher Porter for 64 hours at hourly regular rate.

15 Received 50 planning kits and bill (#8100) for $1,250.00 from Texas Media & Publications. These non- inventory products for resale were ordered by telephone May 1. Allocated to Product Sales Class.

19 Received bill (#2856) for $4,000.00 from Image Contacts, Inc. for printing and mailing of flyers. Allocated to Product Sales Class. Terms were Net 30.

20 Received bill (#8248) for $6,000.00 from Rash Productions for consulting services (outside services) for upcoming seminar to be conducted. Allocated to Consulting/Seminars Class. Terms were Net 30.

24 Conducted on-site brown-bag lunch seminar at Computer Manufacturers USA. Entered one summary cash sale (2002–101) to customer name Individual Seminar Participants recording the sale of 26 books, 13 videos, and 14 planning kits. All participants paid for orders by personal check; payment type is Check, TX sales tax applies; total sales including tax was $3,453.45. These funds were directed to the Undeposited Funds account to await batch deposit with other funds. Allocated to Product Sales Class.

24 Prepared and presented Invoice 2002–101 in the amount of $5,000.00 to Computer Manufacturers USA for on-site seminar conducted on this date. Sales tax does not apply. Allocated to Consulting/Seminars Class.

26 Received $5,000.00 (Check 1069) customer payment from Computer Manufacturers USA for Invoice 2002–101 representing fee for on-site seminar conducted on 05/24/2002. Payment was made by company check 1069. This payment was grouped with other funds in the Undeposited Funds account to await deposit.

27 Issued check 1006 for charitable donation to Education & Medical Fund in the amount of $250.00. Allocated to Consulting/Seminars Class.

28 Paid hourly and salaried employees for time worked during payroll period 05/15/2002– 05/28/2002. Payroll Check 1007 issued to Chester Rankin and Payroll Check 1008 to Christopher Porter for 72 hours at hourly regular rate.

28 Entered one summary cash sale (2002–102) to customer name Individual Seminar Participants recording the sale of 20 books, 10 videos, and 9 planning kits. All participants paid by personal check; payment type is Check. TX sales tax applies; total sales including tax was $2,466.75. These funds were grouped with other funds in the Undeposited Funds account to await batch deposit. Allocated to Product Sales Class.

28 Prepared Invoice 2002-102 for $5,000.00 and presented to Energy Corporation of Texas for on-site seminar conducted on this date. Sales tax does not apply. Allocated to Consulting/Seminars Class.

28 Received bill for $725.00 from Texas Light & Power for May electric power. Bill is net 30, due 06/27/2002. Allocated to Admin/Other Class.

28 Received bill for $390.00 from South Texas Bell for May telephone service. Bill is net 30, due 06/27/2002. Allocated to Admin/Other Class.

31 Received $5,000.00 customer payment from Energy Corporation of Texas for Invoice 2002-102 representing fee for on-site seminar conducted 05/28/2002. Payment was made by company check 2021. This payment was grouped with other funds in the Undeposited Funds account to await deposit.

31 Deposited funds held in Undeposited Funds account to Texas State Bank. Total deposited was $15,920.20, consisting of $3,453.45 from Cash Sale 2002–101, product sales at 05/24/2002 seminar; $2,466.75 from Cash Sale 2002–102, product sales at 05/28/2002 seminar; $5,000.00 from Invoice 2002–101, customer payment (Computer Manufacturers USA); $5,000.00 from Invoice 2002–102, customer payment (Energy Corporation of Texas).

31 Paid all bills on hand in a batch sorted by Due Date. Total paid was $21,565.00 with individual checks issued as follows: 1009 to Image Contacts, Inc., for $4,000 for printing and mailing flyers; 1010 to Lone Star Office Supply for $350.00 for bill received for Purchase Order 2002-103; 1011 to Office Supply Depot for $6,850.00 for bill received for Purchase Order 2002-102; 1012 to Rash Productions, Inc. for $6,000.00 for consulting services; 1013 for $390.00 to South Texas Bell for May telephone service; 1014 for $725.00 to Texas Light & Power for May electric bill; 1015 to Texas Media & Publications for $3,250.00 for bill received for Purchase Order 2002-101 ($2,000.00) and bill payment for 50 planning kits received 05/05/2002.

31 Issued Check 1016 to Clover Computing for $150.00 for computer repairs. The check was voided after a phone call about the repairs.

June 2002

1 Checked inventory quantity on hand from Items List and found only four books available for resale. Issued Purchase Order 2002-104 for 46 books from Texas Media & Publications. Total was $1,150.00. Allocated to Product Sales Class.

1 Issued Check 1017 to Braten Investments for $1,500.00 to pay June leasehold rent. Allocated to Admin/Other Class.

2 Paid $400.20 Texas state sales tax to Texas State Comptroller for the period through 05/31/2002 with check 1018.

3 Received 46 books and bill (5989) for $1,150.00 for Purchase Order 2002–104 from Texas Media and Publications. Payment is due 07/03/2002. Allocated to Product Sales Class.

4 Issued check 1019 in the amount of $300.00 to Longhorn American Insurance for employee health insurance policy premium for the month of June. Allocated $100.00 to Admin/Other Class for Porter's premium and $200.00 to Consulting/Seminars Class for Rankin's premium.

11 Paid hourly and salaried employees for time worked during payroll period 05/29/2002 through 06/11/2002; Chester Rankin Check 1020 and Christopher Porter Check 1021 for 62 hours at Hourly Regular Rate and 8 hours at Hourly Holiday Rate for work on the Memorial Day holiday. Rankin's pay is allocated to Consulting/Seminars Class and Porter's pay is allocated to Admin/Other Class.

11 Entered one summary cash sale (2002–103) to customer name Individual Seminar Participants recording the sale of 30 books, 20 videos, and 15 planning kits. All participants paid for orders by personal check; payment type is Check. TX sales tax applies; total sales including tax was $4,075.50. These funds were directed to the Undeposited Funds account to await batch deposit with other funds. Allocated to Product Sales Class.

11 Prepared Invoice 2002–103 in the amount of $5,000.00 and presented to Texas State University for on-site seminar conducted on this date. Sales tax does not apply. Allocated to Consulting/Seminars Class.

14 Received $5,000.00 customer payment from Texas State University for Invoice 2002–103 representing fee for on-site seminar conducted on 06/11/2002. Payment was made with University check 5091 and was grouped with other funds in the Undeposited Funds account to await deposit.

15 Issued check 1022 in the amount of $1,449.10 to IRS for Federal tax liabilities (Federal withholding, Medicare, and Social Security only) for May 2002.

15 Prepared Invoice 2002–104 billing Petroleum Operators, Inc. for 20 hours of consultation at $250.00 per hour for an invoice total of $5,000.00. Sales tax does not apply. Allocated to Consulting/Seminars Class.

16 Checked books and videos items from Items list and found videos had fallen below order point to only 7 units. Books were down to 20 units. Based on projections, issued Purchase Order 2002–105 for 30 books and 43 videos to Texas Media & Publications. Purchase order total was $1,395.00. These items may be selected from the Items list. Allocated to Product Sales Class.

17 Received payment (check #4015) of $5,000.00 for consultation from Petroleum Operators, Inc. billed on Invoice 2002–104. Payment was grouped with other funds in the Undeposited Funds account to await deposit.

18 Received 30 books and 43 videos and bill (5990) for $1,395.00 from Texas Media & Publications for Purchase Order 2002–105. Payment is due 07/18/2002. Allocated to Product Sales Class.

18 Deposited funds being held in Undeposited Funds account to Texas State Bank. Total deposited was $14,075.50, consisting of $4,075.50 from Cash Sale 2002–103 (sales at 06/11/2002 seminar); $5,000.00 from Invoice 2002–103 (customer payment, Texas State University); $5,000.00 from Invoice 2002–104 (customer payment, Petroleum Operators, Inc.).

21 Conducted on-site brown-bag lunch seminar for Central Texas University. Entered one summary cash sale (2002–104) to customer name Individual Seminar Participants recording the sale of 22 books, 20 videos, and 9 planning kits. All participants paid by personal check; payment type is Check. TX sales tax applies and total sales including tax was $3,003.00. These funds were directed to the Undeposited Funds account to await batch deposit with other funds. Allocated to Product Sales Class.

21 Prepared Invoice 2002–105 in the amount of $5,000.00 and presented to Central Texas University for the on-site seminar conducted on this date. Sales tax does not apply. Allocated to Consulting/Seminars Class.

23 Received $5,000.00 customer payment from Central Texas University for Invoice 2002–105 representing fee for on-site seminar conducted on 06/21/2002. Payment was made by company check 9018. Payment was grouped with other funds in the Undeposited Funds account to await deposit.

24 Entered Bill–Credit (#5990-C) from Texas Media & Publications for $30.00 for two videos returned due to damage in shipment. Allocated to Products Sales Class.

✓ **24** Issued Credit Memo 2002–106 to customer John R. Clark, who returned a book purchased for $50.00 at seminar at Texas Central University 06/21/2002. Credit Memo total was $53.63, which also included sales tax of $3.63 that he had paid. Allocated to Product Sales Class.

✓ **25** Paid hourly and salaried employees for time worked during Payroll Period 06/12/2002–06/25/2002: Chester Rankin Check 1023, Christopher Porter Check 1024 for 60 hours at Regular Hourly Rate. Rankin's pay is allocated to Consulting/Seminars Class and Porter's pay is allocated to Admin/Other Class.

✓ **28** Received bill (#8310) for $920.00 from Texas Light & Power for June electric power. Bill is net 30, due 07/28/2002. Allocated to Admin/Other Class.

✓ **28** Received bill (#6058) for $422.00 from South Texas Bell for June telephone service. Bill is net 30, due 07/28/2002. Allocated to Admin/Other Class.

✓ **29** Item list reports for the two inventory items revealed number on hand of books (29) and videos (27). A physical count verified books on hand but showed a loss of 3 videos. Therefore, the Quantity On Hand for Videos was adjusted down to 25 to match the physical count. The loss was charged to Products for Resale: Adjustments to Inventory account.

✓ **29** Customer M.L. Kountz purchased a planning kit at the seminar at Texas Central University on 6/21/2002, but his check was returned unpaid by the bank. Record two transactions in the checking account register, one for the bounced check (#35466 for $107.25) and the other for the NSF fee charged by the bank ($10.00 coded to bank service charges). Code the bounced check to Accounts Receivable.

✓ **30** Paid Federal payroll tax liabilities (Federal withholding, Medicare and Social Security only) for the month of June. Check #1025 for $1,456.92.

✓ **30** Paid Texas state sales tax of $474.87 to Texas State Comptroller for month ending June 30, 2002, with check 1026.

✓ **30** Using the Payroll Activity—Process Form 941, create the Payroll 941 Report for calendar quarter ending June 30, 2002. State Code is TX and Number of Employees is 2. Deposits were made in a timely manner, so no balance is due. It was necessary to adjust line 9 on Form 941 for fractions of cents by -0.01.

✓ **30** Made deposits of funds being held in Undeposited Funds account to Texas State Bank. Total amount deposited was $8,003.00, which consisted of $3,003.00 from Cash Sale 2002–104 (06/21/2002 seminar); and $5,000.00 from Invoice 2002–104 customer payment (Petroleum Operators, Inc.).

✓ **30** Paid all bills on hand in a batch sorted by due date. Total amount paid was $3,887.00 with individual checks issued as follows: Check 1027 for $422.00 to South Texas Bell for June telephone service; Check 1028 for $920.00 to Texas Light & Power for June electric power; Check 1029 to Texas Media & Publications for $2,545.00 in payment of bills 5989 and 5990.

✓ **30** Using the Pay Payroll Liabilities function, paid Texas Unemployment Tax due for the period 05/01/2002 through 06/30/2002. Paid by check #1030.

✓ **30** Using Credit Memo 2002–106 created on 06/24/2002, issued Refund Check 1031 for $53.63 to customer John R. Clark for the book he returned on that date.

✓ **30** Prepared Credit Memo 2002–107 for $250.00 to Petroleum Operators, Inc. to refund one hour of consultation charged on Invoice 2002–4 on 06/16/2002. Allocated to Consultation/Seminars Class. Issued Refund Check 1032 for $250.00 to the customer.

Analysis Questions

Use the completed reports and template file to answer the following questions. Write your answer in the space to the left of each question.

7,168.44 **1.** What is the net income or net loss for May?

2,745.00 **2.** What is the total Cost of Goods Sold for May?

6,208.44 **3.** What is the total amount of payroll expenses (gross wages and payroll taxes) for May?

12,775.00 **4.** What is the gross profit for May?

_5,520.00_ **5.** What is the Total Product Sales Revenue for June?

_1,500.00_ **6.** What is the amount of rent paid for June?

_6,215.50_ **7.** What is the total cost of payroll for June?

_4,341.08_ **8.** What is the amount of the payroll expenses for consulting/seminars for June?

_5,122.50_ **9.** What is the net income or net loss for June?

_2,039.24_ **10.** What is the net income or net loss for May through June?

_37,098.25_ **11.** What is the net cash increase for May?

_44,705.74_ **12.** What is the cash balance at the end of June?

_10,000.00_ **13.** What is the percentage of total sales provided by seminars for May?

_32.22%_ **14.** What is the percentage of net sales provided by Energy Corporation of Texas for May?

_44,753.25_ **15.** How much does Millennium Financial Planning have in total assets on May 31?

_6,850.00_ **16.** What are the total fixed assets as of June 30?

_51_ **17.** How many books does Millennium Financial Planning have on hand as of June 30?

_40_ **18.** How many videos does Millennium Financial Planning have on hand as of June 30?

Account: Millennium Financial Planning: Main Checking
May 2002 Statement

Last Statement Date:
This Statement Date: 5/31/2002

Beginning Balance	$0.00
Less: checks/debits	($28,749.95)
Plus: deposits/credits	$65,920.20
Ending Balance	$37,098.25

Checks	Date	Amount		Deposits	Date	Amount
1001	1-May	$1,800.00		Customer deposit	1-May	$50,000.00
1002	3-May	$360.00		Customer deposit	31-May	$15,920.00
1003	4-May	$300.00		**Total deposits:**		**$65,920.20**
1004	14-May	$1,592.00 ✓				
1005	14-May	$637.80				
1006	27-May	$250.00				
1007	28-May	$1,592.00				
1008	28-May	$715.15 ✓				
1009	31-May	$4,000.00				
1010	31-May	$350.00				
1011	31-May	$6,850.00				
1012	31-May	$6,000.00				
1013	31-May	$390.00				
1014	31-May	$725.00				
1015	31-May	$3,250.00				
Total checks:		**$28,821.95**				

Other Debits

Service charge	31-May	$10.00
Total other debits:		**$10.00**

Account: Millennium Financial Planning: Main Checking
June 2002 Statement

Last Statement Date: 5/31/2002
This Statement Date: 6/30/2002

Beginning Balance	$37,170.25
Less: checks/debits	($10,363.81)
Plus: deposits/credits	$22,078.50
Ending Balance	$48,896.37

Checks	Date	Amount
1017	1-June	$1,500.00
1018	2-Jun	$400.20
1019	4-Jun	$300.00
1020	11-Jun	$1,592.00
1021	11-Jun	$773.41
1022	15-Jun	$1,449.10
1023	25-Jun	$1,592.00
1024	25-Jun	$598.63
1025	30-Jun	$1,456.92
1026	30-Jun	$474.87
1030	30-Jun	$16.00
Total checks:		**$10,153.13**

Deposits	Date	Amount
Customer deposit	18-Jun	$14,075.50
Customer deposit	30-Jun	$8,003.00
Total deposits:		**$22,078.50**

Other Debits

Returned check	29-Jun	$107.25
Returned check charge	29-Jun	$10.00
Service charge	30-Jun	$10.00
Total other debits:		**$127.25**

Appendix

QUICKBOOKS ACCOUNTS

The Chart of Accounts has several different types of accounts. As you recall from the *Accounting 101* section, some accounts are increased with debits and other accounts are increased with credits. For example, all assets are increased with debits. This means deposits to bank accounts are **debits,** while sales are **credits** to income accounts.

Table A–1, on the next page, shows how each different account type is **increased** with either a debit or a credit. The first column is the *accounting* or *General Ledger* account type. The second column is the QuickBooks account type. Notice that QuickBooks breaks down the assets into several subtypes (Bank, Accounts Receivable, and so on). The third column shows whether a debit or a credit increases the balance in the account. The column on the right shows the financial statement report on which these accounts appear.

General Ledger Account Type	QuickBooks Account Type	Increases with (Debit or Credit)	Reports That Show These Accounts
Asset	Bank	Debit	*Balance Sheet Accounts*
	Accounts Receivable	Debit	
	Other Current Asset	Debit	
	Fixed Asset	Debit	
Liability	Accounts Payable	Credit	
	Credit Card	Credit	
	Other Current Liability	Credit	
	Long Term Liability	Credit	
Equity	Equity	Credit	
Income	Income	Credit	*Income Statement (Profit and Loss) Accounts*
COGS	Cost of Goods Sold	Debit	
Expense	Expense	Debit	
Other Income	Other Income	Credit	
Other Expense	Other Expense	Debit	

Table A–1 QuickBooks reports summary.

KEYBOARD SHORTCUTS

When cursor is in a Date field, this key	Causes the date to become
y	First day of displayed calendar **y**ear.
r	Last day of displayed calendar yea**r**.
m	First day of displayed **m**onth.
h	Last day of displayed mont**h**.
t	**T**oday.
w	First day of displayed **w**eek.
k	Last day of displayed wee**k**.
+	**Next** day.
–	**Previous** day.

Table A–2 Date shortcuts.

When text is selected in any field	Causes this action
Ctrl + x	**Cut** the text to the Clipboard.
Ctrl + c	**Copy** the text to the Clipboard.
Ctrl + v	**Paste** the text to the Clipboard.
Ctrl + z	**Undo** the last change.
Ctrl + d	**Delete** selected transaction or List item.

Table A–3 Cut, Copy, and Paste Command.

When editing a transaction, this key	Causes this action
Tab	**Move** the cursor to the next field.
Shift + Tab	**Move** the cursor to the previous editable field.
Return (or Enter)	**Record** the transaction (when black border is highlighting OK, Next, or Prev button).
Esc	**Cancel** editing and close the current window.
Ctrl + h	Get the **hi**story (A/R or A/P) for the currently selected transaction.
Ctrl + g	**G**o to the other account register affected by this transaction.
Ctrl + y	Display transaction journal.
Ctrl + n	**N**ew transaction (Bill, Check, Deposit, List Item, Invoice).
Ctrl + r	Go to the **register** associated with the current transaction.
Page Up	Scroll register view or reports 1 page up.
Page Down	Scroll register view or reports 1 page down.
Home, Home, Home	Go to the top of a register (first transaction).
End, End, End	Go to the bottom of a register (last transaction).
Ctrl + 1 (or F2)	Display information about QuickBooks and your company file details.
Ctrl + e	**Edit** transaction or List item.

Table A–4 Moving around in QuickBooks.

For more keyboard shortcuts, see the QuickBooks User's Guide.

QUICKBOOKS MENUS

File Menu

New Company...
Open Company...
Open Previous Company   ▶
EasyStep Interview
Close Company
Switch to Multi-user Mode

Back Up...
Restore...
Archive & Condense Data...
Utilities   ▶
Timer   ▶
Accountant's Review   ▶

Print ...   Ctrl+P
Print Forms   ▶
Printer Setup...
Send Forms   ▶

Update QuickBooks...
Exit   Alt+F4

Edit Menu

Undo Typing   Ctrl+Z
Revert

Cut   Ctrl+X
Copy   Ctrl+C
Paste   Ctrl+V

Use Register   Ctrl+R

Use Calculator

Simple Find...   Ctrl+F
Advanced Find...
Preferences...

View Menu

✔ Open Window List

✔ Icon Bar
Customize Icon Bar...
Add "Select Employees To Pay" to Icon Bar...

Shortcut List
Customize Shortcut List...
Add Window to Shortcut List...

One Window
● Multiple Windows

Customize Desktop...

Lists Menu

Chart of Accounts   Ctrl+A
Item List
Price Level List
Sales Tax Code List
Payroll Item List
Class List

Customer:Job List   Ctrl+J
Vendor List
Employee List
Other Names List
Customer & Vendor Profile Lists ▶
Templates

Memorized Transaction List Ctrl+T

Company Menu

Company Navigator
Business Services Navigator
Company Center

Company Information...
Set Up Users...
Change Your Password...
Modify Service Access...
Advanced Service Administration...
Set Up Budgets
To Do List
Reminders
Alerts Manager

Chart of Accounts   Ctrl+A
Make Journal Entry

Write Letters...
Print Mailing Labels...
Synchronize Contacts

Decision Tools   ▶

Company Web Site

Company Services   ▶

Customers Menu

Customer Navigator
Customer Center
Customer Detail Center

Create Invoices   Ctrl+I
Enter Sales Receipts
Create Estimates
Create Credit Memos/Refunds
Enter Statement Charges
Create Statements...
Assess Finance Charges
Receive Payments
Accept Credit Card Payments   ▶
Time Tracking   ▶

Customer:Job List   Ctrl+J
Item List
Change Item Prices

Online Billing   ▶

Check Credit   ▶

Customer Services   ▶

QUICKBOOKS MENUS

Vendors Menu

Vendor Navigator
Vendor Detail Center

Enter Bills
Pay Bills

Sales Tax ▶

Create Purchase Orders
Receive Items and Enter Bill
Receive Items
Enter Bill for Received Items
Inventory Activities ▶

Print 1099s...

Vendor List
Item List
Purchase Orders List

Vendor Services ▶

Employees Menu

Employee Navigator

Pay Employees...
Edit/Void Paychecks...
Pay Payroll Liabilities...
Adjust Payroll Liabilities...
Deposit Refund of Liabilities...
Process Payroll Forms...
Summarize Payroll Data in Excel
Time Tracking ▶
Run Payroll Checkup

Set Up Payroll
Add/Change Payroll Service
Learn About Payroll Options...
Get Payroll Updates
View Payroll Messages
Payroll Service Account Info

Employee List
Payroll Item List

Employees Services ▶

Help Menu

Help & Support
Help Index...
Help on This Window   F1

New Features
Internet Connection Setup
Using QuickBooks for Your Type of Business

Year End Guide
About Automatic Update
QuickBooks Privacy Statement

About QuickBooks Pro 2002...

Banking Menu

Banking Navigator

Write Checks   Ctrl+W
Order Checks Online
Use Register   Ctrl+R
Make Deposits
Transfer Funds
Enter Credit Card Charges
Reconcile
Make Journal Entry

Set Up Online Financial Services ▶
Create Online Banking Message
Inquire About Online Banking Payment
Online Banking Center

Chart of Accounts   Ctrl+A
Other Names List
Memorized Transaction List   Ctrl+T

Banking Services ▶

Window Menu

Cascade
Tile Vertically
Tile Horizontally
Arrange Icons
Close All

Reports Menu

Report Finder
Memorized Reports ▶
Process Multiple Reports

Company & Financial ▶
Customers & Receivables ▶
Sales ▶
Jobs & Time ▶
Vendors & Payables ▶
Purchases ▶
Inventory ▶
Employees & Payroll ▶
Banking ▶
Accountant & Taxes ▶
Budget ▶
List ▶

Custom Summary Report
Custom Transaction Detail Report

QuickReport   Ctrl+Q
Transaction History
Transaction Journal

BACKING UP YOUR DATA

Backing up your data is a very important part of ensuring the safety of your data. If your computer stops working, your hard disk crashes, or you find a corruption in your data file, you'll be glad you have a backup of your data.

You can use any of the media in Table A-5 to store your backed up data.

Media	Data Integrity	Size of Storage	Comments
Diskettes	Fair	1.4MB	Usually too small to fit your whole file, but QuickBooks prompts you for multiple disks if necessary.
Zip Disks	Good	100 or 250MB	Zip disks provide fast, efficient back up with more than enough capacity for most QuickBooks data files.
CD-R Drive	Excellent	600MB	CD-R drives allow you to create CD disks. The data integrity of CD-Rs is excellent, meaning your data is safest on this medium.
Tape Backup	Excellent	>500MB	Tape back up is old technology. It's not recommended for daily file back ups, but it's good to use this for backing up your whole system all at once.
Internet	Good	Unlimited	You can use the Internet to back up your data off site. Talk to your Internet service provider to see what services are available.

Table A–5   Media to store data back-ups

To back up your data, follow these steps:

1. Insert a blank, formatted diskette, or Zip disk into your disk drive.
2. Select the *File* menu and then select **Backup**.
   Notice that the name and location of your current company is displayed on the Back Up Company File screen (Figure A-1).
3. In the Back Up Current Company As section of the Back Up Company File screen, QuickBooks suggests a name and location for your backup file. To change the name of your backup file, select and change the text in the *Filename* field. To change the location (disk and directory) where your backup file will be stored, select and change the text in the *Location* field. Alternatively, click the Change button and select the disk drive and directory where you want your backup file stored.
4. Click **Backup**.
5. QuickBooks will back up your file to the disk drive. If necessary, QuickBooks will prompt you to insert additional diskettes.
6. When the backup process is finished, make sure to remove your backup disk and store it in a safe place.

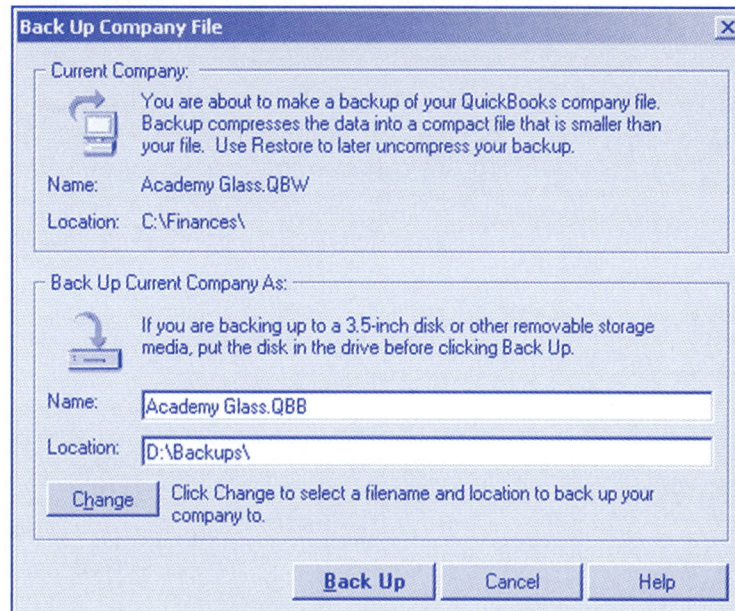

Figure A–1 The Back Up Company File screen

In addition to creating a file with your data (the .QBB file), Quick-Books tags each backup by creating two other files on your disk. These files encode the backup date and time in the file name. They don't contain any of your QuickBooks data. They are placed on the disk to indicate the time and date of each backup. The example below (see Figure A-2) shows the contents of a backup diskette. On this diskette, the same company file was backed up on two consecutive days.

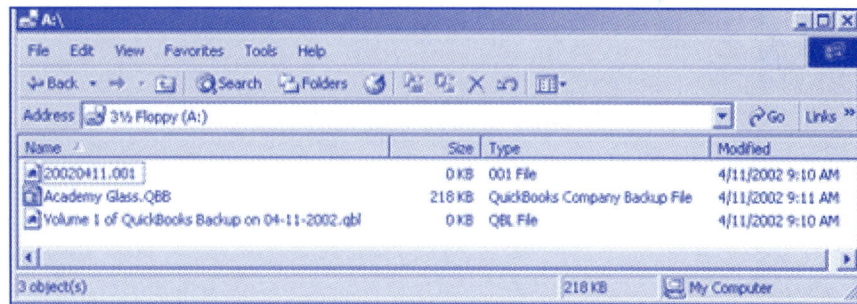

Figure A–2 Windows Explorer view of a QuickBooks backup diskette

The first file is a .001 type file. This designates the first disk of the backup. The file name is eight characters, which allows it to be read in DOS mode if necessary. The eight characters represent the date of the backup. The file name is generated by the system date in your computer. If a second diskette was needed for the backup, the file extension of the first file would change to .002, and the file type would become 002.

The other type of file is a .QBL file. The file name tells you the volume number of the diskette, as well as the date of the backup. This file name can be viewed in Windows.

These two types of files will continue to be recorded if you use the same diskette for the same company. The files do not take up any space on the diskette. The QBB file contains all of the backed up data from your last backup.

Glossary

–A–

Account Numbers In some accounting systems, General Ledger accounts are assigned a specific number which is used when making computer entries. In QuickBooks account numbers are optional.

Accounting Equation Assets = Liabilities + Equity, or Equity = Assets – Liabilities

Accounts In QuickBooks, an account refers to a General Ledger account. You create and modify accounts in the Chart of Accounts. Every transaction (bill, check, invoice, etc.) affects two or more accounts.

Accounts Payable Bills and obligations your company must pay in the future.

Accounts Payable Aging Summary A report that shows how much you owe each vendor over a given date range and the liability age.

Accounts Receivable Claims for future collection from customers.

Accrual Method (Accrual Accounting or Accrual Basis of Accounting) Revenues and expenses are recognized when they occur regardless of when the cash is received or paid.

Addition Item This payroll Item is used to track additional amounts added to paychecks beyond gross wages, such as bonuses and tips.

Adjusting Inventory QuickBooks automatically adjusts inventory each time you purchase or sell inventory Items. However, you can make manual adjustments to inventory. You may need to do this if a physical count indicates a difference, or if the value of your inventory on hand increases or decreases.

Administrator of a company file The person who "owns" the company file. The Administrator can add other users to the file and give them separate passwords and privileges, sets the closing date or any other company preferences.

Aging How many days past due the invoice is. An A/R Aging Summary or Aging Detail lists the customer and amounts due in columns of 30, 60, or 90 days.

Analysis Reports Built-in QuickBooks reports that help you analyze the performance of your business. Includes Profit and Loss report (Income Statement), Profit and Loss by Class report, Profit and Loss by Job report, Balance Sheet, Statement of Cash Flows, Accounts Receivable reports, and Accounts Payable reports.

Assets   Money or items of value owned by the company, to meet financial obligations and continue operations.

Average Cost Method   See *Weighted-Average Cost Method*.

–B–

Back Orders   QuickBooks tracks the status of your back-ordered purchases, but it does not have any features to help you track back orders for your customers. That is, there is no support for taking an "order" in QuickBooks, shipping part of it, and having QuickBooks track the unshipped portion.

Backup Files   QuickBooks backup file names end with ".QBB." In order to use a backup file, you must first "restore" the backup file, and convert it into a data file.

Bad Debt   If an invoice becomes uncollectible you'll need to write off the debt using a Credit Memo.

Balance Sheet   A report listing a company's total assets and total liabilities and equity on a specific date.

Bank Account   A special asset account used to record and track transactions in a bank account.

Bank Deposits   A QuickBooks transaction recording a deposit into a bank account.

Bank Reconciliation   Balancing your QuickBooks bank register with the statement from the bank.

Based on Quantity   This option on the payroll Item/deduction Item, addition Item, or company contribution Item, is used when you wish to calculate a percentage of some other number.

Beginning Balance   Amount shown on a bank statement reflecting the balance at the beginning of the statement period. It should match with the ending balance from the previous bank statement.

Bill   The form used to record a purchase from a vendor to whom you track your liability.

Bounced Checks   Checks returned by a bank due to nonsufficient funds (NSF).

Budgets and **Budget Reports**   You can track your budget by entering budget amounts for each account, job, and class for each month of the year. Then, at any time, you can create a report of your actual income and expenses compared to your budget.

–C–

Calculating items   Calculating items use the amount of the preceding line to calculate their amount. For example, if you enter 10% in the discount item setup screen and then enter the discount item on an invoice, QuickBooks will multiply the line just above the discount item by 10% and enter that number as a negative, in the amount column for the discount line.

Cash Back Goes To   This field is used when making bank deposits, to account for and track which account the cash will be placed in.

Cash Basis of Accounting (Cash Method)   Expenses and revenues are recognized when the cash transaction occurs. This method provides a less accurate picture of your company than the accrual method.

Cash Sales Form   Records the details of what you've sold and to whom you sold it. The entry increases (with a debit) Undeposited Funds, and increases (with a credit) the appropriate sales account.

Chart of Accounts   A list of every account in the General Ledger sorted by account type. Account types are: Bank, Accounts Receivable, Other Current Asset, Fixed Asset, Accounts Payable, Credit Card, Other Current Liability, Long Term Liability, Equity, Income, Cost of Goods Sold, Expense, Other Income, and Other Expense.

Check Numbers   QuickBooks keeps track of check numbers and assigns them as it prints. You have the opportunity to set the check number before it begins printing, which allows you to account for handwritten checks.

Check Refund   The QuickBooks button used to automatically create a refund check.

Classes   A way to separately track income and expenses, defined by the QuickBooks user. For example, a chain of bookstores might assign a different class to each branch store. This would allow the company to track the sales of a particular book at each separate branch store. When you use classes on each transaction (checks, bills, invoices, etc.), the Profit and Loss by Class report shows the profitability of each class.

Closed Accounting Period   Period for which financial statements have been issued and/or tax returns have been filed.

Closing Date   To prevent anyone from voiding or deleting any transactions, you can set the closing date on your file.

COGS   Cost of Goods Sold.

Commission Item   A payroll Item used to track payments of commissions.

Company Contribution Item   A payroll Item used to track additional money that the company contributes as a result of a paycheck. This can be used to match employee contributions to the 401k plan.

Company File   Where you enter and store information unique to your company.

Context Sensitive Help   Depending on your activity at the moment, clicking on Help will give you advice relevant to what you're currently doing.

Cost of Goods Sold   The cost of merchandise sold to customers. It is subtracted from total sales on the income statement to show gross profit.

Credit   A transaction used in a General Journal Entry. A credit is always offset by a debit.

Credit Card Discount Fees   A fee charged by the credit card processing company.

Credit Memo   A document notifying a customer that you have reduced the customer's balance.

Current Accounting Period The accounting period for which financial statements have not been issued and/or taxes have not been filed.

Custom Fields You can add fields to your default settings to track additional information about your customers, vendors, or employees.

Custom Template You can create templates that define layouts and customer forms unique to your business.

Customer A person or business to whom merchandise or services are sold. In order to use sales forms to track customers, you must create a Customer record for each of your customers. The Customer field must be unique among all of the name lists.

Customer Message Printed on the invoice, this is typically a thank-you message, but it can be whatever you choose.

Customer Returns or Credits Recorded using the Credit Memo/Refund window to record returned items already recorded on an invoice as a cash sale.

Customer Statement A QuickBooks form you can generate to show your customer's invoice and payment history, for a time period you specify. May be used to remind a customer there is a balance due on an account.

–D–

Data Files When stored on your hard disk, a QuickBooks data file name always ends with a ".QBW." This is your working file, with which you can enter data or create reports.

Debit A transaction used in a General Journal Entry. A debit is always offset by a credit.

Deduction Item This payroll Item is used to track deductions from paychecks.

Depreciation The periodic write-off of the cost of an asset that will have a useful life of several years.

Discount Date A vendor's terms may include a discount, if the payment is received within a certain number of days. This early-payment incentive deadline is called the discount date.

Discount Information A Receive Payments or Pay Bills option that records a discount.

Discount Item An amount to be subtracted from a sales item.

Double-Entry Accounting A technique that looks at each account as having two sides. Each transaction will affect at least two accounts and will have both a debit and a credit entry. QuickBooks is a double-entry accounting system.

Drop-Down List or Menu A feature for choosing items from a list of choices available for many input areas.

Due Date Calculated by adding the terms to the transaction date.

–E–

EasyStep Interview A feature that walks you through the setup of a company file.

EFTPS   Electronic Federal Tax Payment System.

Employee Defaults   The employee template helps the user reduce the repetitive data entry on each new employee by storing the most common items that affect a typical employee of the company.

Employee Template   The template allows you to enter payroll information that most employees have in common.

Employer ID   QuickBooks prints your Federal Employer Identification Number on tax returns and W-2s.

Enter Bill for Received Item   This QuickBooks function records transactions that are connected to purchase orders.

Enter Bills   When a vendor sends you a bill, you use the Enter Bills function to record the bill and track it through your A/P register.

Equity   The ownership interest in the company. The owners or shareholders of the company have an "Equity Interest" in the company. When a company is sold, all of the assets are sold, all of the liabilities are paid, and the remaining amount is paid out to the owners.

Existing Credits   In the Receive Payments screen, this shows any unapplied payments or Credit Memos from earlier transactions, or an overpayment from a previous invoice.

Expense   An outflow of cash, use of other assets, or incurring of a liability.

Exporting Data   QuickBooks provides the option to export data from lists and reports. Report data can be exported to spreadsheet files.

–F–

401(k) Employee Deduction Item   A payroll Item/deduction Item you can set up to track employee contributions (salary deferral) to the 401(k) plan.

Federal Tax Item   This payroll Item is used to track federal taxes that are withheld from paychecks or paid by the employer.

Federal Unemployment Item   This Payroll Item/Federal Tax Item is an employer-paid tax.

Federal Withholding Item   This Payroll Item/Federal Tax Item is an employee tax and is withheld from paychecks.

FIFO   First-in, first-out. A means of calculating the cost of inventory.

Filter   A way to include or exclude whatever data you want on the Find screen and on reports.

Find Command   You can use the Find command if you're looking for a transaction and you don't know which register to look in, or if you want to find more than just a single transaction.

Fiscal Year   The period in which a company tracks its financial performance, which may or may not coincide with the calendar year.

Form 941   Federal quarterly payroll tax return.

Forms   QuickBooks has electronic forms such as invoices, bills, Credit Memos, and checks. Most data is entered using forms.

Form Template   See *Templates*.

–G–

General Journal Entry   Window used for special transactions or for transactions instead of using a form.

General Ledger   The General Ledger is all accounts in the Chart of Accounts. A General Ledger *report* is a listing of all transactions in every account in the General Ledger. It represents a complete listing of the transactions in the company file.

Group Items   This item allows you to bundle several individual items together. For example, three separate items sold together as a kit or assembly could be tracked as a group item, and the three separate items can also be tracked individually.

–H–

Hourly Item   You can add this payroll Item to meet your needs.

Hourly Wage   This payroll Item/earnings Item is used to track payments to hourly employees.

–I–

Icon Bar   A way of accessing tools and features within QuickBooks. If the Icon Bar is not displayed, you may activate it in the Preference menu.

Income   Inflow of money or assets that results from the sale of goods or services or from the use of money or property.

Income Statement (Profit/Loss Report)   A report listing revenues and expenses during a user-defined time period so you can tell whether you are operating at a profit or loss.

Inventory Asset   A special asset account that tracks the cost of each inventory Item purchased.

Inventory Items/Parts   Inventory you purchase, keep in stock as inventory, and then resell.

Inventory Stock Status by Item Report   See *Stock Status by Item Report*.

Inventory Stock Status by Vendor Report   See *Stock Status by Vendor Report*.

Inventory Valuation Detail Report   See *Valuation Detail Report*.

Inventory Valuation Summary Report   See *Valuation Summary Report*.

Invoice   A form QuickBooks generates to record sales to credit customers. When an invoice is generated for your company, it increases your Accounts Receivable (with a debit) and it increases the appropriate Sales account (with a credit).

Items   Items track details of what is purchased and sold for detailed reports. Example item names are Windows, Doors, Labor.

–J–

Job Costing   A way to track the revenue and expenses specifically related to a job so that the company can see how profitable the job was.

Journal Entry (General Journal Entry)   Window used to record transactions that directly affect the General Ledger without involving QuickBooks forms.

–L–

Layout Designer   A QuickBooks feature that allows you flexibility in form design.

Liabilities   Your company's debts. Includes creditors and sales tax and employee withholdings owed to the government.

LIFO   Last-in, first-out. A means of calculating the cost of inventory.

List Reports   Can be used to print a Customer list, a price list, or mailing labels for one or more of your lists (Customers, Items, Vendors, Employees, Accounts, etc.).

Lists   QuickBooks is based on lists — lists of customers, vendors, employees, invoice templates, payment terms, shipping methods, and so on.

Logo   QuickBooks can automatically add a company logo to your printed forms. However, this slows the printing process.

–M–

Make Deposit   When you deposit money in your bank, you enter the transaction into QuickBooks using the Make Deposit function. If your deposit includes several checks or a mixture of checks and cash, QuickBooks groups the whole deposit onto one transaction so that it matches with your bank statement at the end of the month. Usually your deposit is made up of several items that are stored in your Undeposited Funds account. This transaction decreases (with a credit) Undeposited Funds, and increases (with a debit) Bank Account.

Medical Insurance Deduction   This payroll Item is used when the employee pays part or all of the medical insurance.

Medicare Payroll Item   This payroll Item is both an employer-paid and an employee-paid tax.

Memorizing Reports   After customizing a report, you can memorize the format and filters to avoid repeating the process later.

Memorizing Transactions   QuickBooks can memorize many of your standard transactions. This can be used to automatically adjust accounts on a regular basis. Any transaction in QuickBooks can be memorized except Bill Payments, and payments from customers.

Menus   A way of accessing tools and features within QuickBooks. The Main Menu bar runs along the top of the screen. Choosing one menu creates a submenu with additional choices.

Merchant Account Service   A subscription service provided by QuickBooks for the processing of credit card payments made by your customers.

Mid-Year Payroll Setup If your payroll start date is not December 31, you'll need to enter the year-to-date payroll information for each of your employees before entering your first paychecks.

Modifying Reports You can customize and filter reports to show exactly the information you want.

–N–

Navigator A QuickBooks window with several icons allowing you to select activities and lists with a single click. It also shows reminders, company solutions, related activities and provides access to several reports.

Net Income Amount by which income exceeds expenses.

Net Worth The amount of money a business is worth. Theoretically, the amount that would be left if all assets were sold and all liabilities were paid. Calculated by taking the difference between total assets and total liabilities.

Noninventory Items/Parts Products you buy and sell, but don't keep in inventory. Use this if you don't think you'll need to have detailed reports and inventory status information about some of your products.

NSF A check returned by the bank for insufficient funds in the account is referred to as *NSF*.

Officers' Compensation Salary Item A payroll Item you can create to track officers' compensation separate from the rest of your employees.

–O–

Open Balance The amount owed on an invoice or bill.

Open Invoices List of the outstanding invoice and statement charges for customers.

Opening Balance The amount of money in, or the value of, an account as of the start date.

Opening Balance Equity An automatically created temporary account that is used when entering opening balances for balance sheet accounts.

Other Charge Items These items are used to track charges such as shipping and handling charges.

Other Names A list of names that don't fit into the vendors or customers categories.

Other Tax Item This payroll Item is used to track other state or local taxes that are withheld from paychecks or paid by the employer.

Owner's Drawing Account This account is used to account for a sole proprietor taking money out of the business.

–P–

Partial Payment If you choose to pay only a portion of a bill, QuickBooks tracks the remaining amount due in Accounts Payable.

Pay Bills When you pay your Accounts Payable (bills), use the Pay Bills function. This creates a check in your checking account (or any other account you choose).

Payment Items Used to show payments collected on the face of an invoice.

Payment Method For sales, record payments as Check, Cash, or Credit Card.

Payroll Items A list of everything that affects the amount on a payroll check.

Payroll Liabilities Use the Pay Liabilities function to pay payroll deductions, company contributions, and company taxes.

Payroll Reports Used to report various details about payroll. Payroll reports include the Payroll Summary by Employee report and Payroll Liabilities report.

Payroll Summary Report A report that shows the total amount for each payroll item for every employee during the time period you specify.

Payroll tax tables include the tax rates necessary to calculate an employee's paycheck. This calculation affects the amounts of taxes that are withheld from an employee's check (e.g., Federal and State income tax), as well as the amounts of taxes the company must pay for the employee (e.g., Federal unemployment).

Paystub A summary of information on a paycheck. You can print paystubs for your employees on blank paper, even if you don't use voucher checks, or if you don't print checks from QuickBooks.

Perpetual Inventory Continuous record of increases, decreases, and balance on hand of inventory items.

Petty Cash An amount of cash kept on hand and used to make small payments for business items. A QuickBooks account used to track cash expenditures.

Pop-Up Calendar Instead of entering a date from the keyboard, clicking the Pop-Up Calendar button allows you to click on a particular date.

Preferences QuickBooks allows businesses to custom tailor software features by setting preferences.

Prepaid Expenses Expenses that are paid in advance of when they are used. This requires making a periodic adjustment to match the expense with the time period it occurred.

Print Checks When you have several checks marked "To Print" in the Check Number field, Print Checks will "batch print" the checks.

Professional advisors are bookkeepers, accountants, software consultants, and CPA's who offer QuickBooks – related consulting services. Some professional advisors undergo a testing process to become certified in QuickBooks. For more information about QuickBooks Professional Advisors, refer to QuickBooks online help.

Profit/Loss Report (Income Statement) A report, based on a particular time period, that lists all income and expenses for that period, and shows a net profit or net loss.

Purchase Order A sequentially numbered form used when ordering items that you will receive later. If you use purchase orders, QuickBooks tracks the status of your orders and matches them with the bill from your vendor.

–Q–

Qcards Small windows that pop up to provide context-sensitive help and tips.

Quick Add An option that displays when you enter information on a form for which QuickBooks has no record. The item is automatically added to the correct list with the information entered on the form.

QuickBooks Graphs A visual display of information to match most reports.

QuickBooks Navigator A way of accessing tools and features within QuickBooks. Choices are made by picking icons on a flowchart.

QuickFill A QuickBooks feature that completes the field data based on the first few characters that you type in that field. If QuickFill guesses wrong based on the first few characters that you type, just keep typing until QuickFill guesses the correct data.

QuickMath A feature that allows calculations on specific items.

QuickReports Reports that give information you are most likely to want at a certain place in QuickBooks.

QuickZoom A QuickBooks feature that allows you to see the detail behind numbers on reports.

–R–

Receive Items This QuickBooks function is used to record receipt of inventory items without a bill. This connects to purchase orders to track complete or partial receipt of items.

Receive Payment When you receive payments from your credit customers, this function allows you to match payment with a specific invoice. This transaction decreases (with a credit) Accounts Receivable, and increases (with a debit) Undeposited Funds.

Ref. No. A field that may be used to track information such as the shipper number or vendor's bill number.

Refund After entering a credit memo/refund, clicking the Refund button automatically creates a check to your customer.

Register A register shows all of the activity in an account. It looks similar to your paper checking account register. Each asset, liability, and equity account (except Retained Earnings) has a register showing all of the transactions affecting the account.

Register Reports Shows the transactions in any of your account registers.

Reminders This QuickBooks feature is available from the Lists menu, and reminds you of activities that are scheduled to happen. This includes due bills, which invoices are overdue, transactions that need to be printed, and inventory to reorder.

Rep This field can contain the initials of one of your employees who is the sales representative at the time of sale. There can only be one rep per customer record.

Retained Earnings   An account that QuickBooks automatically creates to track profits from earlier accounting periods that have not been distributed to the company's owners.

Revenue   Inflows of cash or other assets as a result of the operation of a business.

Reversing Entry   An entry made to void an entry.

–S–

Sales Receipt   Record of payment in a cash transaction.

Sales Tax Group Items   If you pay taxes to multiple agencies, you will want to set up a tax group.

Sales Tax Items   Tracks sales taxes in each location you sell taxable goods and services.

Sales Tax Liability Report   Shows you how your sales break down by locality, and how much sales tax has been collected for the period you specify.

Service Items   Can include professional fees or labor that you charge for or pay for.

Shortcut Keys   A way of accessing tools and features within QuickBooks. This method utilizes the keyboard, especially the Alt key and the Ctrl key.

Shortcut List   The on-screen bar that allows you to access tools and features within QuickBooks.

Sick/Vacation Template   This template allows you to define your company policy defaults for sick and vacation time, so you don't have to reenter the same information on each employee record.

Social Security Payroll Item   This payroll Item is both an employer-paid and an employee-paid tax item.

Splitting Transactions   A single payment may need to be applied to more than one account. In order to track these expenses separately, you split this transaction and assign each expense to the appropriate account.

Standard Checks   These checks come three to a page. There is no voucher for your records.

Start Date   The date you choose for entering your opening balances when you set up your company.

State Disability Item   This payroll Item usually is an employee tax, but varies by state.

State Unemployment Item   This payroll Item is usually a company-paid tax, but this varies by state.

State Withholding Item   This payroll Item is an employee tax and is withheld from paychecks.

Stock Status by Item Report   This report is useful for getting a quick snapshot of each inventory part and the number of units on-hand and on-order.

Stock Status by Vendor Report   This report gives you information about your inventory parts, sorted by the Preferred Vendor field in the item.

Subitems They help you to organize the item list. Use subitems to group and subtotal information about similar products or services in sales reports and graphs.

Subtotal Item Displays subtotal on sales forms. Used to group amounts before applying discounts.

Summary Reports Reports that summarize a group of transactions.

–T–

1099 Form 1099-MISC is used to report payments to a vendor in the course of business for services, that when totaled, equal or exceed $600. QuickBooks does not print any other type of 1099 form.

Tax ID A field in the Vendor record for the vendor's tax identification number or social security number. Use this for your 1099 subcontractors. QuickBooks prints this number on the 1099 at the end of the year.

Tax Table Tax information QuickBooks uses to calculate payroll taxes.

Tax Year A field in the company information screen used to calculate year-to-date amounts on tax reports.

Taxes Template This template allows you to define defaults for your employee taxes so that you don't have to enter the same information each time.

Templates QuickBooks provides template forms that you can use as is, or customize.

Terms A field in the Customer and Vendor record that allows you to specify credit terms.

Transaction A business activity that requires an entry in the general ledger. Every transaction creates a debit in one or more accounts and a credit in one or more accounts.

Transaction History A listing that shows which transactions are related or "linked" to a transaction you have selected.

Transaction Reports A display of transactions by customer, vendor, date, and so on.

Transfer Money A choice in the Activities menu that allows you to transfer money between accounts.

Type A field on the list items that can be used to categorize transactions.

–U–

Uncategorized Expenses Expenses not matched to a specific account.

Uncategorized Income Income not matched to a specific account.

Undeposited Funds An account that is used to simulate the cash drawer. This is the account that accumulates money before it is deposited into a bank account.

Use time data to create paychecks Notice that the time sheet information automatically entered the job and class information on the paycheck. This is automatic with QuickBooks when you set an employee's record to use time data to create paychecks.

However, if you didn't use the timesheets, you can manually allocate job and class information directly on the paycheck.

User QuickBooks provides a User feature, which allows the "administrator" to set privileges for each user of the file. This provides security and tracking when several people have access to the same data file.

–V–

Valuation Detail Report This report gives you information about the value of your inventory Items over a date range.

Valuation Summary Report This report gives you information about the value of your inventory Items on a certain date.

Vendor A person or business from which services or merchandise is purchased. In order to enter bills for someone, you must create a Vendor record for them. For credit vendors, you use Accounts Payable to track bills and payments. Cash vendors are those you pay directly with a check, and skip Accounts Payable.

Vendor Balance Detail This report shows the detail of each Bill and payment to each Vendor. Only transactions that go through Accounts Payable show on this report.

Vendor Credits When a vendor credits your account, you record a Bill Credit transaction and apply it to one of your unpaid bills.

Voiding a Check Changes the amount of the transaction to zero but keeps a record of it.

Voucher Check This style of check gives you a record of the check to keep, as well as a voucher that details the bills that are paid on the check. The voucher check gives you one check per page.

–W–

W-2 Employer-generated employee payroll information form used for tax reporting purposes.

W-4 Form W-4 is the IRS form that must be filled out by each of your employees when they join your company. This information form requires employees to provide you with their name, address, social security number, and withholding information.

Wallet Check This style of QuickBooks checks comes three to a page, with small vouchers on the left that you tear off.

Weighted-Average Cost Method Inventory cost method that divides the cost of inventory by the number of units in stock. It is most appropriate when prices paid for inventory do not vary significantly over time, and when inventory turnover is high. QuickBooks calculates the cost of inventory using this method.

–Y–

Yearly Salary   This payroll Item is used to track payments of gross wages to salaried employees.

YTD   Year-to-date.

Index

–Q–